HOKKAIDO

HEILONGJIANG

Harbin

Changchun

JILIN

Vladivostok

Sea of Japan

Shenyang

LIAONING

Sendai

NEI MENGGU

NORTH KOREA

Hohhot

Yellow

Datong

BEIJING

Beijing

Bay of Bohai

Pyeongyang

HONSHU

Tokyo

Tianjin

TIANJIN

HEBEI

Nagoya

Taiyuan

Shijiazhuang

Seoul

Kyoto

SHANXI

Fen

SHANDONG

SOUTH KOREA

Osaka

Jinan

Pusan

SHIKOKU

Luoyang

Zhengzhou

Qufu

Xi'an

HENAN

JIANGSU

JAPAN

SHAANXI

Huai

KYUSHU

Nagasaki

ONGQING

Han

Suizhou

Hefei

ANHUI

Nanjing

Suzhou

Shanghai

Lake Tai

SHANGHAI

Yangzi

HUBEI

Hankou

Hangzhou

Fuchun

Ningbo

Yellow Sea

East China Sea

Yuan

Dongting Lake

Nanchang

Poyang Lake

ZHEJIANG

RYUKYU ISLANDS

qing

Changsha

HUNAN

JIANGXI

PACIFIC

ZHOU

Xiao

Xiang

Gan

Fuzhou

OCEAN

ang

FUJIAN

Taipei

GUANGXI

Xiamen

TAIWAN

Nanning

GUANGDONG

Xi

Guangzhou

Xianggang

HONG KONG

Haikou

HAINAN

South China Sea

PHILIPPINES

⊥⊥⊥ Modern Grand Canal

〰〰 Great Wall

—— Province boundaries in China

▤ North China Plain

▨ Area of major loess deposits

baatar

Modern East Asia

Modern East Asia: From 1600

A Cultural, Social, and Political History
Third Edition

PATRICIA EBREY

University of Washington—Seattle

ANNE WALTHALL

University of California—Irvine

WADSWORTH
CENGAGE Learning·

Australia • Brazil • Japan • Korea • Mexico • Singapore • Spain • United Kingdom • United States

Modern East Asia: A Cultural, Social, and Political History From 1600, Third Edition
Ebrey/Walthall

Editor-in-Chief: Lynn Uhl

Senior Publisher: Suzanne Jeans

Acquiring Sponsoring Editor: Brooke Barbier

Development Editor: Elisa Adams

Assistant Editor: Jamie Bushell

Editorial Assistant: Katie Coaster

Brand Manager: Melissa Larmon

Marketing Development Manager:
Kyle Zimmermann

Senior Content Project Manager:
Carol Newman

Senior Art Director: Cate Rickard Barr

Manufacturing Buyer: Sandee Milewski

Senior Rights Acquisition Specialist:
Jennifer Meyer Dare

Text Designer: Theurer/Briggs Associates

Cover Designer: Sarah Bishins

Cover Image: Detail from *Two Young Women in the 1920s*. Takabatake Kashō (1888–1966)/ Copyright © 2003 Yayoi Museum & Takehisa Yumeji Museum. All rights reserved.

Production Service/Compositor:
Cenveo Publisher Services

For product information and technology assistance, contact us at
Cengage Learning Customer & Sales Support, 1-800-354-9706

For permission to use material from this text or product, submit all requests online at **www.cengage.com/permissions.**
Further permissions questions can be emailed to
permissionrequest@cengage.com.

Library of Congress Control Number: 2012941790

ISBN-13: 978-1-133-60649-9

ISBN-10: 1-133-60649-0

Wadsworth
20 Channel Center Street
Boston, MA 02210
USA

Cengage Learning is a leading provider of customized learning solutions with office locations around the globe, including Singapore, the United Kingdom, Australia, Mexico, Brazil and Japan. Locate your local office at **international.cengage.com/region**

Cengage Learning products are represented in Canada by Nelson Education, Ltd.

For your course and learning solutions, visit **www.cengage.com.**

Purchase any of our products at your local college store or at our preferred online store **www.cengagebrain.com.**

Instructors: Please visit **login.cengage.com** and log in to access instructor-specific resources.

Printed in the United States of America
3 4 5 6 7 18 17 16

BRIEF CONTENTS

CONTENTS

MAPS AND FIGURES

PREFACE

There are many reasons to learn about East Asia. A fifth of the world's population lives there. Every day newspapers carry articles on the rapid transformations of the world economy that make China, Japan, and Korea a growing presence in our lives. Globalization means not only that people are crossing the Pacific in ever-increasing numbers but also that U.S. popular culture is drawing from many sources in East Asia, from Korean martial arts to Japanese anime and Chinese films.

But why approach East Asia through its history rather than, say, its economy or contemporary culture? Many reasons suggest themselves. We cannot gain an adequate understanding of modern phenomena without knowing the stages and processes that led up to them. Moreover, the peoples of East Asia are strongly historically minded. To a much greater extent than in the United States, they know and identify with people and events of a thousand or more years ago. In all three countries, readers still enjoy *The Three Kingdoms,* a novel written in fourteenth-century China about the leaders of three contending states in third-century China. Historical consciousness also underlies the strong sense of separate identities among the people of China, Korea, and Japan. The fact that time and again Korea was able to protect its independence despite the attempts of both China and Japan to conquer it is a central part of Korean identity today. Yet another reason to learn about East Asia's past is its comparative value. As a region that developed nearly independently of the West, East Asia sheds light on the variety of ways human beings have found meaning, formed communities, and governed themselves, expanding our understanding of the human condition.

What makes this East Asian history book distinctive? In it we cover all three countries from a broad range of perspectives, from the earliest signs of human civilization to the present, and we balance the big picture with specific cases. While availing ourselves of the framework provided by politics, we also focus on culture, social issues, and economic change.

WHAT IS NEW IN THE THIRD EDITION

Our first goal in revising this book has been to bring it up to date—to cover the last few years and take account of new scholarship. But we have also put a lot of thought into how we can best serve our audience. Teachers and students who used the first and second editions of this book have told us how much they liked our coverage of social and cultural history, our mini-chapter "Connections," and our boxed features—the Documents, Biographies, Material Culture, and Making Comparisons features. With their encouragement, we continue to scrutinize our choices and in this edition offer several new ones, including new Material Culture features on Japanese portrait statues and matchlocks and China's recent high-speed trains; new biographies of a Korean interpreter, a Japanese radical samurai, and a Chinese geomancer; and new documents from the *Book of Songs* for the Zhou period and "Wild Lilies," for the twentieth century. We also have added an additional Making Comparisons feature on languages.

Two more pervasive changes also deserve mention. On the advice of instructors who have used this book in class, we have added two pedagogical aids. The first is pronunciation glosses aimed to give students the courage to pronounce foreign words in their heads while reading, and out loud in class. These glosses do not aim for linguistic precision; their sole purpose is to help U.S. students approximate the sounds of Chinese, Japanese, and Korean words.

The second addition we have made is to add critical thinking questions at the end of all the documents and biographies. It is our hope that these questions will encourage students to pause and think about what they are reading. Teachers might also consider asking students to prepare answers to them.

The overall conception of this book remains the same as it was from the first edition. The following distinctive characteristics are worth underlining.

COMPARABLE COVERAGE OF KOREA

Part of our original plan for this book was to cover Korea in comparable depth as China and Japan (we ended up giving China about 50 percent of the space, Japan 30 percent, and Korea 20 percent). We know that many teachers have been frustrated in their attempts to cover Korea in their East Asia courses for lack of suitable materials and hope that our efforts prove useful to both them and their students.

A BROAD FOCUS: *CONNECTIONS* CHAPTERS

It is often difficult to keep the larger whole in mind as we tell the separate stories of China, Korea, and Japan. Our solution has been to periodically zoom out to look at the wider region from a global or world-historical perspective. Thus, after every few chapters we have inserted a mini-chapter on developments that link the societies of East Asia both to each other and to the larger global context. We have labeled these mini-chapters "Connections" because they emphasize the many ways each society was connected to outside events and people. For instance, the origins and spread of Buddhism are of great importance to all the societies of East Asia, but much of the story can be told as a common narrative that connects East Asia with the rest of Asia. Similarly, many books write about World War II in East Asia in entirely different ways in their China and Japan chapters. By stepping back and writing about the war from a more global perspective, we help students see the larger picture.

BALANCED CULTURAL, SOCIAL, AND POLITICAL HISTORY

This book strives for balanced coverage of the different strands of history. A basic political narrative is essential to give students a firm sense of chronology and to let them think about issues of change. Moreover, there is no denying that the creation of state structures has much to do with how people lived their lives. Even the fact that people think of themselves as "Chinese," "Korean," or "Japanese" is largely a by-product of political history.

We also believe students should gain an understanding of the philosophies and religions of East Asia. Confucianism and Buddhism have both been of great importance throughout the region, but in very diverse ways, as the historical context has continually changed. Other elements of high culture also deserve coverage, such as the arts of poetry and calligraphy.

Yet we did not want to neglect topics in social, cultural, and economic history, where much of our own work has been concentrated. Even if the state is important to understanding how people lived, so were families, villages, and religious sects. We also wanted to bring in the results of scholarship on those who had been marginalized in the traditional histories, from laborers and minorities to women at all social levels.

MAKING COMPARISONS

There are many similarities among the cultures of East Asia, often because of their direct influence on each other and the wide circulation of some core philosophical, religious, and literary texts. Yet differences are at least as significant and interesting. To help students take stock of what they have learned, from time to time we provide a brief, one-page discussion placed between chapters that compares features of the three countries. The topics in the third edition are languages, food cultures, monarchical institutions, women's situations, neo-Confucianism, slavery, and popular religion.

A SPECIFIC FOCUS: BIOGRAPHIES, DOCUMENTS, AND MATERIAL CULTURE

The potential danger of trying to cover so much is a high level of generalization. To keep our readers engaged and bring our story down to earth, we devote three or four pages per chapter to closer looks at specific people, documents, and material objects.

Biographies

Most chapters have a one-page biography, often about someone who would not normally be mentioned in a history book. We thus highlight a diverse set of individuals, from the most accomplished (such as the eminent Chinese poet Du Fu) to those who are remarkably ordinary people (such as a woman whose job was to mind the neighborhood telephone). Three military men are portrayed; others were physicians, interpreters, entrepreneurs, and founders of religious sects. We also have included some agitators and revolutionaries, and even a winning volleyball coach.

Documents

In our chapters we frequently cite short passages from primary sources, but we believe students also benefit from texts long enough to give them a sense of the genre, the author's point of view, and the circumstances described. A few of those we have included are by famous writers, such as Fukuzawa Yūkichi and Lu Xun. Some are excerpted from well-known pieces of literature, such as the play *The Peony Pavilion* and ancient Japanese poetry collections. Others will be less familiar to teachers and students alike. We selected legal documents, for what they reveal of ordinary people's lives, and religious texts of several sorts to help students see religion and popular beliefs in action. Many authors are utterly serious, complaining bitterly of war or corruption, for instance; others have well-developed senses of humor. All the documents prompt active involvement and critical interpretation because through them students hear the concerns of people of the past.

Material Culture

Texts are not our only sources for reconstructing the past; there is much to be discovered from material remains of many sorts. To give focus to this dimension of history, for each chapter we have selected one element of material culture to describe in some detail. These range from the most mundane—food, drink, clothing, houses, and means of transportation—to objects of art including specific paintings, sculptures, and performing arts. Many of the objects discussed have economic significance—for example, fertilizers and the Grand Canal. Most of the features for the late nineteenth and twentieth centuries bring out ways material culture has changed, along with so much

else in modern times—from the food people eat to their ways of amusing themselves to technological advances such as the transistor that continue to have an impact not only in Asia but across the world.

THINKING LIKE A HISTORIAN

The "Documents" and "Material Culture" features challenge students to draw inferences from primary materials much as historians do. Another way we have tried to help students learn to think like historians is to present history as a set of questions more than a set of answers. What historians are able to say about a period or topic depends not only on the sources available but also on the questions asked. To help students see this, we begin each chapter with a brief discussion of some of the questions that motivate contemporary historians to do research on the time period. Few have easy answers; they are not questions students will be able to resolve simply by reading the chapter. Rather they are real questions, interesting enough to motivate historians to sift through recalcitrant evidence in their efforts to find answers. The earliest chapter on Korea, for instance, poses the question of how the three states on the Korean peninsula were able to survive in the face of Chinese power. The chapter on early nineteenth-century Japan points out that historians have studied the period for clues to the causes of the Meiji Restoration, wanting to know the relative weight to assign to foreign pressure and domestic unrest. For the chapter dealing with China under the Nationalists, we point out that the desire to explain the Communist victory in 1949 has motivated historians to ponder why May Fourth Liberalism lost its appeal and whether the economic politics of the Nationalists could have brought prosperity to China if Japan had not invaded. We hope that posing these questions will help readers see the significance of the topics and issues presented in each chapter.

USING THIS TEXT IN CLASS

East Asian history is commonly taught either as a one-term or one-year course. To fit both schedules, this text is available as a single volume and as two divided chronologically. Since those who divide chronologically might prefer to break at either 1600 or 1800, the period 1600–1800 appears in both the chronologically divided volumes.

INSTRUCTOR SUPPLEMENT

eInstructor's Resource Manual   Prepared by Ethan Segal, Michigan State University. This manual has many features, including learning objectives, chapter outlines, discussion/essay questions, key terms, and activities for the classroom. Available on the instructor's companion website.

ACKNOWLEDGMENTS

For the first edition of this book, the three authors divided the work primarily by country of specialization, with Patricia Ebrey writing the parts on China, Anne Walthall those on Japan, and James Palais those on Korea. The Connections chapters we divided among ourselves chronologically, with Patricia Ebrey taking the early ones (on Prehistory, Buddhism, Cultural Contact Across Eurasia, and the Mongols), Anne Walthall taking the early modern and modern ones (on Europe Enters the Scene, Western Imperialism, and World War II), and James Palais doing the final one on East Asia in the Twenty-First Century. Our original co-author, James Palais, passed away shortly after the first edition was printed in summer 2006. For the second and third editions, Patricia Ebrey revised James Palais's chapters covering up to 1800 and Anne Walthall the remainder.

Many people have contributed to the shaping of this book. The authors have been teaching about the societies of East Asia for three decades, and the ways they approach their subjects owe much to questions from their students, conversations with their colleagues, and the outpouring of scholarship in their fields. As we worked on this text, we received much advice from others, from early suggestions of possible collaborators to critiques of our original proposal and reviews of the drafts of our chapters. The reviewers' reports prompted us to rethink some

generalizations, urged us not to weigh the book down with too much detail, and saved us from a number of embarrassing errors. We appreciate the time and attention the following reviewers gave to helping us produce a better book:

James Anderson, University of North Carolina at Greensboro; R. David Arkush, University of Iowa; Charles Armstrong, Columbia University; Richard Bohr, College of Saint Benedict & Saint John; Craig N. Canning, College of William and Mary; Henry Chan, Minnesota State University; Alan Christy, University of California, SC; Sue Fawn Chung, University of Nevada, Las Vegas; Parks Coble, University of Nebraska; Anthony DeBlasi, University of Albany; Ronald G. Dimberg, University of Virginia; Franklin M. Doeringer, Lawrence University; Alexis Dudden, Connecticut College; Gordon Dutter, Monroe Community College; Susan Fernsebner, Mary Washington College; Karl Friday, University of Georgia; James Gao, University of Maryland; Karl Gerth, University of South Carolina; Andrew Goble, University of Oregon; John B. Henderson, Louisiana State University; Robert Henry, Grossmont College; Jennifer Holt-Dilley, University of Texas at San Antonio; Jeff Hornibrook, SUNY Plattsburgh; William Johnston, Wesleyan University; Fujiya Kawashima, Bowling Green State University; Sun Joo Kim, Harvard University; Ari Daniel Levine, University of Georgia; Huaiyin Li, University of Missouri-Columbia; Jeff Long, Bloomsburg University of Pennsylvania; Andrew McGreevy, Ohio University-Lancaster; Angelene Naw, Judson College; Steve Phillips, Towson University; Jonathan Porter, University of New Mexico; Wesley Sasaki-Uemura, University of Utah; Edward Slack, Eastern Washington University; S. A. Thornton, Arizona State University; Constantine Vaporis, University of Maryland, BC; Lu Yan, University of New Hampshire; Ka-che Yip, University of Maryland, Baltimore County; Theodore Jun Yoo, University of Hawaii at Manoa.

We also are grateful for all the work put into this book by the editorial staff at Wadsworth, Cengage Learning: Brooke Barbier, Elisa Adams, Jamie Bushell, and Katie Coaster.

CONVENTIONS

Throughout this book names are given in East Asian order, with family name preceding personal name. Thus Mao Zedong was from the Mao family, Ashikaga Takauji from the Ashikaga family, and Yi Sŏnggye from the Yi family.

Both Japanese and Korean have phonetic scripts (Japanese a syllabary, Korean an alphabet), though Japanese additionally makes extensive use of Chinese characters. There are standard ways to transcribe these scripts into our alphabet. Here we have used the Hepburn system for transcribing Japanese. For Korean, we have used the revised romanization system of the Ministry of Culture in South Korea.

Chinese does not have a phonetic script. In this book the pinyin system of romanization has been adopted.

The basic vowels, *a, e, i, o,* and *u* in all three languages are pronounced as in Italian, German, and Spanish.

a as in f*a*ther
e as in *e*nd
i as the first *e* in *e*ve (although in Chinese if it comes after an s, ch, or z, it is pronounced as the *e* in *the*)
o as in *o*ld (shorter in length and with less of the *ou* sound of English)
u as in r*u*de (shorter in length than English)

The macron over the *ō* or *ū* in Japanese indicates that the vowel is "long," taking twice as long to say, as though it were doubled. Macrons have been omitted from common place names well known without them, such as Tokyo and Kyoto.

ü in Chinese (used only after *l* or *n*) is like the German *ü*.

The three languages are not so similar when one vowel follows another. In the case of Japanese, each vowel is pronounced as a separate syllable (shōen, is two syllables, shō-en). In Chinese, they create a (one-syllable) diphthong (e.g., *mei*, which is pronounced like may, and *xia*, which sounds like shya). In Korean, two vowels in a row are used to convey a distinct vowel sound; *ae* is like the *a* in *at*; *eo* is like the *u* in *but*; *eu* is like the *oo* in *foot*.

Consonants for Japanese and Korean romanization are close enough to English to give readers little difficulty. In the Chinese case, divergence between how an English speaker would guess a pronunciation and how the word is actually pronounced is greater. The most confusing consonants are listed below:

c *ts* in *ts*ar
z *dz* in a*dz*e
zh *j* in *j*ack
q *ch* in *ch*in
x *sh*

In the case of Chinese, the romanization system does not convey tones, which are also an important element in pronunciation.

We have offered simple pronunciation guides after many words that might give readers trouble. These do not aim at linguistic accuracy; they are at best approximations, based on common American pronunciations, and are provided so that students will feel more comfortable using the words in class. They can be ignored once the reader has gotten the hang of the romanization system.

For both Chinese and Korean, other ways of romanizing the language are also widely used. Through the last edition of this book we used the McCune-Reischauer system for Korean, which uses apostrophes and diacritical marks. Thus, the dynasty that was romanized as Chosŏn in the last edition is now romanized as Joseon. Comparisons of the two systems of romanization can be found at **http://www .eki.ee/wgrs/rom2_ko.pdf**.

In the case of Chinese, pinyin only became the standard system of romanization in recent decades. Some earlier spellings were based on dialects other than Mandarin (Peking, Canton, Sun Yat-sen). More often the Wade-Giles system of romanization was employed. From context, if nothing else, most readers have inferred that Mao Zedong is the same person whose name used to be spelled Mao Tse-tung, or that Wang Anshi is the pinyin form of Wang An-shih. Two older spellings have been retained in this book because they are so widely known (Sun Yatsen and Chiang Kaishek). Charts for converting pinyin to Wade-Giles and vice versa are widely available on the Internet, should anyone want verification of their guesses (see, for instance, **http://www.loc.gov/ catdir/pinyin/romcover.html**).

Modern East Asia

Joseon Korea
(1392–1800)

The Joseon Dynasty was founded in 1392 by Yi Seonggye (E SUNG-geh). The next four centuries were marked by extensive Confucianization. Chinese statecraft and the examination system were copied more closely. The hereditary *yangban* (YANG-bahn), who now had to devote themselves to education in order to gain office, could provide a powerful check on the power of kings, but factionalism divided them. Confucianization reached the level of the family; the family head became recognized as the owner of family property, and women's rights to inherit were largely lost. The dynasty survived serious crises, including invasions by the Japanese and the Manchus. Yet, by the eighteenth century, there were increasing signs of economic growth, social change, and new cultural openness.

Historians of the Joseon (JOE-son) period have looked closely at its elite and government. Did the founding of the dynasty bring social change? Why was factionalism so bitter and so bloody? Did the emphasis on Confucian orthodoxy make factionalism worse? Would Joseon have been stronger if its kings had been able to control their *yangban* officials more effectively? Or did the power of the officials—imbued with Confucian ideas—save the country from tyranny? Given the flaws in the government system and the many crises, why did the dynasty last so long? Joseon's international situation has also been a subject of close scrutiny. Did Joseon benefit from the tributary relationship with Ming China? Why was Joseon unable to repel Hideyoshi's invasion? How did Korea respond to its first encounter with Christianity? Scholars today are also asking basic questions about social and economic change. How large was the population? Why did commercialization lag behind China and Japan? Why was so much labor unfree?

YI SEONGGYE'S RISE TO POWER

In the mid-fourteenth century, the Goryeo (GO-riyo) dynasty was revived after the period of Mongol domination. As discussed in Chapter 10, King Gongmin took steps to strengthen royal power; he strengthened the military,

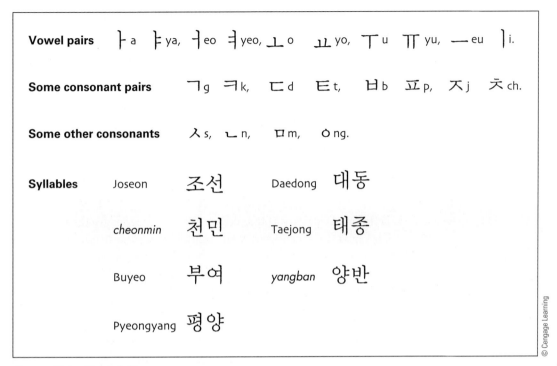

Figure 15.1   Hangul Chart

© Cengage Learning

expanded tax revenue, and promoted Confucianism. After he was assassinated, Confucian reformers allied themselves with a powerful general, Yi Seonggye, who became the force behind the throne. Steps were taken to reclaim authority over prebendal grants, cancel tax-free exemptions to favored *yangban*, and carry out a national land survey. In 1389, Yi eliminated his principal rival, paving the way to declare a new dynasty in 1392. For the name of the dynasty, he chose the phrase used in Chinese sources for the ancient Korean state—Joseon. As its first emperor, he is known as Taejo (TAY-joe, r. 1392–1398). In essence a coup from within, this was a relatively bloodless dynastic transition. Most of the great families of Koryeo survived to play leading roles during Joseon.

Among Taejo's successors were three of the most successful kings in Korean history—Taejong (TAY-jong), Sejong (SAY-jong), and Sejo (SAY-joe)—noted for their achievements in culture, science, and military theory. King Taejong twice called up one hundred thousand corvée laborers to build a new capital at Hanyang (HAN-yang) (Seoul), not far from the Koryeo capital. He strengthened the armed forces, confiscated Buddhist temple and monastery property, and created a sound fiscal base for the state. His son, King Sejong (r. 1418–1450), established a record of accomplishment that

far outshone any of his successors. He improved both the army and navy, defeated the Wakō pirates on Tsushima Island, and extended Joseon's territory north to the Yalu and Tumen rivers. To secure control of those areas, until then settled by Jurchens and other Manchurian groups, he dispatched thousands of Koreans from the south as colonists. He revised the land registration system to make it more equitable. To encourage adoption of more productive agricultural techniques, he published books on agriculture and sericulture. He reinstituted state-sponsored grain loans to peasants to tide them over the spring planting season and famine periods. His legal reforms prohibited cruel punishments, allowed appeals in death penalty cases, and added penalties for masters who beat their slaves without first obtaining official permission. He tried (unsuccessfully) to introduce coins and paper currency.

One of Sejong's most important achievements was founding the Hall of Worthies (*Jiphyeonjeon* [JIP-hyon-jeon]) in 1420, where scholars collected documents and published books. Sejong put this agency in charge of inventing an alphabet in 1443—the first and only one of its kind in East Asia. Sejong's goal was to spread learning beyond the elite *yangban*, who recognized that its use would break their stranglehold on knowledge and therefore opposed it (see Figure 15.1).

Courtyard of a Sixteenth-Century Confucian Academy. A half century after the death of the teacher Yi Eon-jeok (E UN-juck, 1491–1553) the academy where he had taught was dedicated as a shrine to his memory.

Among the books Sejong sponsoredwere *Episodes from the Life of the Buddha*, eulogies of his ancestors, *The Songs of the Flying Dragons*, and *Illustrated Guide to the Three Moral Relationships*, as well as works on science, medicine, and astronomy. Scientific accomplishments of his reign included sundials, an astronomical chart, a new type of water clock, and a rain gauge invented in 1442 (two centuries before Europe's first). The arts and crafts also flourished during this period (see Color Plate 23).

Despite the great accomplishments of King Sejong, he was unable to bequeath political stability to his heirs. His successor died early, and his twelve-year-old grandson was robbed of his throne by his uncle, King Sejo (r. 1455–1468), an act that sowed the seeds of political discord for the rest of the century.

Sejo was devoted to military strategy and published three treatises on it. He authorized attacks against the Jurchens in 1460 and 1467, established military colonies to support troop units, and established the Five Guards Command in 1466 to function as a supreme national defense council. He adopted the famous Chinese ever-normal granaries to stabilize the price of grain by buying or selling grain on the market and he tried, but

failed, to put iron cash into circulation to promote commerce. He also ordered the compilation of a major law code, the *Grand Institutes for Governing the State*.

Sejo antagonized the Confucian officials by patronizing Buddhism and finding ways to circumvent Confucian critics. He neglected the state council, ordered the six ministries to send all their communications directly to him, and abolished the Hall of Worthies. Thus, despite Sejo's accomplishments, his reputation was tarnished, making it easier for Confucian officials to regain their power under subsequent kings.

KINGS AND *YANGBAN* CONFUCIAN OFFICIALS

The early Joseon period saw the culmination of what might have seemed contradictory trends. Kings consolidated their authority through extension of central control. Committed neo-Confucians, as critics of power, circumscribed both the authority of the king and the authority of military men and aristocrats. And *yangban* aristocrats maintained their political and social predominance.

Although for centuries Korean kings had been adopting elements of Chinese statecraft, it was not until the early Joseon period that centralization reached the point where magistrates in all of the three-hundred-odd local districts were appointed by the central government. It was also during this period that the civil service examinations became the main route to high office. As in China, government service became the goal of the elite. The exams were used to select men with literary educations and inclinations to be put in charge of the government apparatus. Birth alone was no longer enough. To advance to high office, passing the examinations became necessary.

Nevertheless, the vast majority of officials in the Joseon Dynasty came from long-established *yangban* families. They were the ones who could best afford education. There was no attempt by any of the early Joseon kings to manumit slaves and challenge the property rights of the *yangban* aristocrats. As competition for government posts increased, the *yangban* found ways to give themselves advantages. They banned the Goryeo practice of allowing *hyangni* (HYANG-ni) (local clerks) to be promoted to the central bureaucracy. They further narrowed the pool of candidates by barring sons of concubines from taking the examinations.

Neo-Confucian scholars inherited Chinese scholars' arguments against Buddhism, such as the claim that the Buddhist emphasis on the individual attainment of enlightenment interfered with the Confucian obligation of filial piety. As a result of their campaigns, many Buddhist monasteries were disbanded and stripped of their land, and eighty thousand of their slaves were converted to government slaves.

Joseon Confucians recognized Ming China as a mature example of a Confucian society, but they did not see Confucian civilization as uniquely Chinese or the Chinese manifestation of it as intrinsically superior. Zealous Korean Confucians aspired to create a more perfect Confucian society, one that adhered more closely to the classics than Ming China did.

Confucian emphasis on filial piety and loyalty to the ruler was useful to the Joseon kings in gaining conformity to their authority. On the other hand, as in China, Confucian scholars viewed themselves as responsible for guiding the ruler toward moral perfection, and they insisted that the ruler should listen to their counsel, even if it tended to hamstring the king's authority and protect their *yangban* class interests.

Did the moral authority of the *yangban* Confucian scholars keep Joseon Korea from becoming a despotism like Ming China? Joseon kings found it

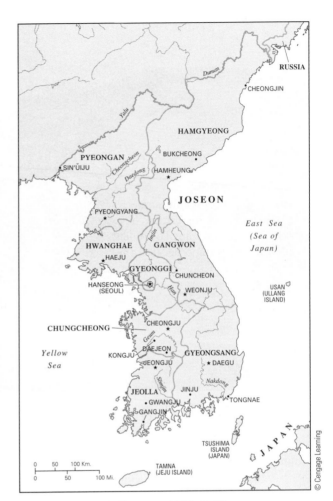

Map 15.1   Joseon Dynasty, 1392–1910

difficult to exercise their theoretically absolute power because of the obstruction and remonstrance of the civil officials, almost all of whom came from *yangban* families with longer histories and more prestige than the Yi royal family. One of Sejo's successors, Yeonsangun (YON-san-goon), took a strong stand against the Confucian establishment. He acted in ever more arbitrary fashion against real and supposed threats to his authority, ordering the execution of people for minor offenses. His critics saw themselves as waging a moral crusade against a usurper and his political appointees, but he thought he was defending his rights as an absolute monarch. He carried out a purge of the literati in 1504, canceled the royal lectures because the lecturers were aggressive in criticizing his actions, and neglected the National Academy. He became so paranoid that a cabal of high officials deposed him in 1506.

Under Yeonsangun's successor, King Jungjong (JOONG-jong), the political tide turned in the opposite direction. The *yangban* Confucians serving as censors, led by Jo Gwangjo (JOE GWANG-joe), disdained those the king had appointed to high offices. Jo persuaded King Jungjong to expand opportunities for neglected but outstanding scholars. When the new "recommendation" examination was held in 1515, however, it turned out that Jo's friends and supporters passed the examinations and immediately joined in his efforts to topple those they labeled unworthy political appointees. By 1519, the king had lost patience with his critics; he purged the young censors and executed Jo. To students of the National Academy, Jo Gwangjo became a martyr to the cause of ethically pure Confucian government. Jo and his associates can also be viewed, however, as politicians playing the moral card to gain political advantage.

By the late sixteenth century, many scholars with high reputations for virtue were holding high office, and they debated the ethical and metaphysical arguments of Zhu Xi. A debate began over which of the two elements, principle (*i, li* in Chinese) or psychophysical force (*ki, qi* in Chinese), was primary. Yi Toegye (E TWAE-geh) held that the nonphysical principle took priority because it contained all the elements of pure virtue, while the younger Yi Yulgok (E YULE-gok) took the view that psychophysical force took priority because without it, the mind would not exist at all.

In China at that time, the main challenge to Zhu Xi's orthodoxy came from Wang Yangming and his followers. Wang challenged Zhu Xi's stress on the need for textual study and emphasized the capacity of everyone to decide what is morally right by looking within himself. Yi Toegye defended Zhu Xi's formula and condemned Wang as a heterodox thinker who relegated the judgment of Confucian virtue to the whims of the imperfect vagaries of the emotions beclouded by *ki*. Yi Toegye's rejection of Wang Yangming set the tone for Korean Confucianism for the rest of the Joseon Dynasty. Yi Toegye's reputation was so powerful at the time that those attracted to Wang Yangming's ideas had to keep their views secret.

The *yangban* preserved their elite position throughout the Joseon period and kept a near monopoly on access to high office (see **Material Culture: Yangban Children's Board Games**). At the same time, the *yangban* stratum grew in size and began to separate into two levels. The percentage of successful examination-passers from the top two dozen

yangban families gradually increased as they became the elite among the *yangban*. Because an average of only thirty men per year passed the examinations, many *yangban* who studied for the examinations had no chance for office and were left in the countryside to make their way there. Some were able to form single-family villages and further strengthen their local power. In other villages, *yangban* power declined because of reforms in tax collection. In order to alleviate the tax burden, village associations were formed of all households regardless of status to divide the tax burden equitably among all families. Thus many *yangban* in the countryside became indistinguishable from ordinary farmers in the ways they lived (though legally they were still distinct).

During the Joseon period, *jungin* (JOONG-in), or middle people, formed a new hereditary class. The *jungin* were clerks, legal specialists, accountants, interpreters, and the like who had lost any hope of rising to regular office but at the same time wanted to save these positions for themselves.

DYNASTIC DECLINE AND THE JAPANESE INVASION

By the sixteenth century, signs of dynastic decline were apparent. Rich landlords expanded their holdings by legal and illegal means at the expense of small-holding commoner peasants. *Yangban* landlords lent money to small holders, then foreclosed when they could not repay. Indebted poor peasants often commended their land to *yangban* and became their slaves to escape both the tax collector and military service. The state failed to remedy this situation by updating tax registers.

Military preparedness also suffered. *Yangban* without office and even rich commoners often could escape military service by bribing clerks to register them falsely as exempt students. Local commanders conspired with them by letting them off actual duty in return for bribes or military cloth tax payments. As a result, there was a serious decline in the number of troops on duty in the army and the local garrisons. Although a new national security agency, the Border Defense Command, had been created in 1522 to deal specifically with defense against Japanese pirate raids, the government failed to stem the hollowing out of the military.

In 1582, Yi Yulgok recommended the creation of an armed force of one hundred thousand men to be

MATERIAL CULTURE

Yangban *Children's Board Games*

Boys in *yangban* families were under a lot of pressure to gain facility in classical Chinese—a written language unrelated to the language they spoke. To be able to recognize people's names and place names, they had to know hundreds of Chinese characters, and if they hoped to take the civil service examinations, they not only had to know several thousand characters but also be able to recognize passages from the Confucian classics and terms used for government offices and policies. Games could make this learning more fun. Shown here are two board games. In both, the goal is to be the first to complete the route, moves determined by the roll of the dice. On the circular board, each circle names a scenic place in Korea. Landing on certain spots can bring favorable winds that speed the journey or obstacles like battlefields that slow it. On the rectangular board, the boxes are the names of government posts, arranged to show career paths. When the player lands on certain spaces, he can be cashiered or even poisoned. Promotion games had been popular in China since the Tang dynasty and helped teach not only the names of offices but also the role of chance in advancement in office.

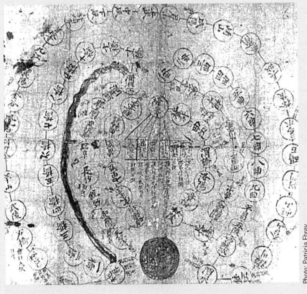

Geography Game

Promotion Game

Photo: Patricia Ebrey

assigned around the country in anticipation of military threats. Other officials called for the establishment of naval bases on strategic islands off the coast and a major army base at Busan to block any attack from Japan. The court, however, failed to act on any of those suggestions, leaving three walled towns—Busan (BOO-sahn), Tongnae (DONG-nae), and Kimhae (KIM-hay)—as the only defense against invasion.

The exacerbation of factionalism also weakened defense. In 1575 competition between two men for appointment to a key post in the ministry of personnel led to a split between what came to be known as Easterners and Westerners, terms related to the location of their homes in the capital, not to different parts of the country. To be sure, personal relations based on blood ties, marriage alliances, schoolboy friendships, and master–disciple relations had shaped political group formation for centuries, but no permanent factional groups were created until 1575. After 1575, factions became hereditary, and frequent purges prevented unity even in times of crisis.

BIOGRAPHY   Interpreter Jeong Myeongsu

Communication between countries that speak different languages depends on interpreters who can convey messages accurately in both directions. In the seventeenth century, with the rise of the Manchus, the need for men who could translate between Manchu and Korean offered those who knew Manchu new chances to rise to wealth and prominence. One of the most successful of these interpreters, Jeong Myeongsu (JUNG MYUNG-sue), started as a lowly soldier who had been captured by the Manchus in 1619 after the defeat of a Korean army sent to aid the Ming. During the next decade, Jeong not only managed to learn to speak the Manchu language, but also gained the trust of the Manchu leaders. By the time of the Manchu invasion of Korea in 1636, both the Manchus and the Joseon court turned to him for advice on how to handle the other. The Joseon court offered him thousands of ounces of silver to help them in the peace negotiation.

One consequence of the resulting treaty was that the Joseon government had to keep a mission headed by the crown prince in the Manchu capital of Shenyang—in a sense, the Manchus were demanding a royal hostage. During the eight years that the Shenyang Residence functioned, Jeong Myeongsu served as a liaison between the Qing ruler and the Korean crown prince. Jeong accompanied Qing envoys to the Joseon court on several diplomatic missions. The Joseon court granted him the rank of minister-without-portfolio in an attempt to curry favor with him and get him working secretly on their behalf. As a middleman, Jeong had information and access that both sides wanted and he was able to play one side off against the other to his advantage. There was also money to be made, both from trade

and from helping Koreans who were trying to ransom their captured relatives.

Despite the base social origins of Jeong's family, with his rise several of his relatives were given government jobs. At first, the *yangban* looked down on him, but as Jeong's power rose, some *yangban* sought connections with him. In 1639 two Koreans serving in the Shenyang Residence brought charges of corruption against Jeong to the Manchu government. They claimed that Jeong Myeongsu had received 2,600 ounces of silver and seven horse-loads of miscellaneous goods as a bribe. The accusers told other Koreans that Jeong should be punished for betraying Joseon by serving the Manchus, but another motivation may well have been their resentment of him as a parvenue. The Manchu authorities sided with Jeong and found the two accusers guilty of making a false accusation and sentenced them to death. The Joseon crown prince tried to get their sentence reduced, but only succeeded in having them hanged rather than beheaded.

Even after the Shenyang Residence was abolished, Jeong Myeongsu continued to have influence at the Joseon court. He advised kings Injo (IN-joe) and Hyojong (HYO-jung) on the appointment of high officials, as well as magistrates and military officials, in the northern provinces. In 1650, however, with the death of the Manchu Dorgon and the succession of a new king in Korea, Jeong Myeongsu fell from power. Still, for more than twenty years he had been able to turn his linguistic and administrative skills into economic and political power.

Questions for Analysis
1. Why did the Joseon court try to get Jeong Myeongsu to work on their behalf?
2. Why didn't *yangban* learn Manchu so that they could exert the sorts of power that Jeong gained?

Although factionalism was looked on negatively because it kept the king from getting impartial advice, Korean officials justified their factions in the same way Chinese officials had in the Song period: moral men had to join forces against the immoral. King Seonjo (SON-joe, r. 1567–1608) disliked the factions but failed to eliminate them. Instead, he made the situation worse by shifting his favor from one faction to another repeatedly.

When a rebellion broke out in the southwest in 1589, King Seonjo accepted the unreasonable charge of the Westerners that the rebellion was an Easterner plot, and he executed more than seventy Easterner officials. He then sent a delegation to Japan in 1591 to assess the intentions of the Japanese leader Hideyoshi. On the delegation's return, Seonjo rejected the warning of the Westerner ambassador that Hideyoshi was preparing an invasion of Korea and took no action to prepare the country for war.

Japan, by contrast, had been engaged in almost constant internal warfare among powerful warlords (daimyo) since the outbreak of the Ōnin War in 1467. The victor in that long struggle was Toyotomi Hideyoshi, an uneducated peasant who had risen from the ranks and now could mobilize the mounted samurai warriors and archers and commoner foot soldiers from all domains of Japan (see Chapter 13). In addition, his armies were equipped with muskets and cannon, which had been introduced into Japan earlier in the century by the Portuguese. In 1592 Hideyoshi asked King Seonjo for free passage through Korea so that he could attack Ming China. When Seonjo refused, Hideyoshi sent his army and quickly overwhelmed the Korean defenders. Hideyoshi's forces occupied Seoul in three weeks and Pyeongyang in two months, then settled in for the winter.

Under the tributary system, the Ming had a moral obligation to send forces to defend Joseon, but the Ming government was at that time plagued by the raids of Manchu tribesmen, internal conflict between powerful eunuchs and Confucian reformers, fiscal shortages, and a decline in the number and quality of soldiers. Still, it mobilized its forces, and seven months after the Japanese invasion, Ming forces began to arrive. Although they succeeded in defeating Japanese forces at Pyeongyang in February 1593, they suffered a stunning defeat just north of Seoul later that month. Ming generals became much more cautious after that and later that year negotiated a truce with the Japanese commander.

The one bright spot in these wars was the repeated victories of Admiral Yi Sunsin's (E SOON-shin) naval forces. His command ship, in the shape of a turtle with a dragon's head at the bow, was unprecedented in its use of iron cladding. Ten oars on each side of the ship allowed it to escape enemy pursuit. Its sides had long iron spikes camouflaged with straw mats to prevent enemy sailors from boarding. The ship had a lower deck with six gun ports and an upper deck with twenty-two gun ports on each side. The cannons fired shells filled with gunpowder and iron splinters. In the undoubtedly exaggerated record, Yi's twelve ships destroyed four hundred ships in one month alone.

Hideyoshi renewed the fighting in 1597 because he was angered by the terms that the Chinese offered, but when he died in 1598, Japanese forces withdrew from the peninsula. Ming military intervention had saved Joseon from destruction, but Korea was left

devastated. About 2 million lives had been lost, and agricultural production was so disrupted that it took a century to reach pre-1592 levels.

Korea severed all relations with Japan after the invasion. Hideyoshi's successor, Tokugawa Ieyasu, had no interest in invading Korea, however, and Korea reestablished relations in a 1609 treaty. The treaty restricted trade to Tongnae, in the southeast, where the Japanese were left to administer their enclave behind a palisade fence. Trade with Japan, limited to a specific number of ships a year, was regulated through tallies that were issued to the head of the Japanese Sō family on Tsushima Island and then distributed to various daimyo throughout Japan.

RELATIONS WITH THE MANCHUS

Just as stable relations with Japan were being established, Korea found itself embroiled in a conflict between the declining Ming Dynasty and the rising Jurchen tribes in Manchuria. In the 1590s, the Jurchens, previously divided into a number of independent small units, were united by Nurhaci, who changed their name from Jurchen to Manchu. Korea soon found itself in a difficult spot between the two rivals, both of whom wanted its aid (see **Biography: Interpreter Jeong Myeongsu**). The Joseon king, Gwanghaegun (GWANG-hay-goon), tried to maintain neutrality, but the vast majority of his own officials wanted him to support the Ming, whose armies had saved Joseon from Hideyoshi.

Factional strife complicated foreign relations during this period. Gwanghaegun was the son of one of King Seonjo's concubines and was appointed crown prince by the king during the Japanese invasion. However, once Seonjo's second queen gave birth to a son, called Great Lord Yeongchang (YOUNG-chang), many officials of the Small Northerner, Southerner, and Westerner factions wanted to depose Gwanghaegun on the grounds that the son of a queen took ritual precedence over the son of a concubine. With the support of the Great Northerner faction, Gwanghaegun had Grand Prince Yeongchang and his younger brother assassinated for plotting against him.

In 1623 the Westerner faction led a coup to depose Gwanghaegun. They replaced him with King Seonjo's grandson, known posthumously as King Injo. All the Northerners who had supported Gwanghaegun were executed or banished, and they remained out of high office for the next two centuries. Upon seizing power, the Westerners reversed Gwanghaegun's

Samsung Museum of Art, Leeum/Samsun Foundation

Landscape of the Diamond Mountains. This painting by Jeong Seon (JUNG Sun, 1676–1759) depicts the landscape of the Diamond Mountains (Geumgangsan [GEUM-gang-san]) with a touch of animistic spirits in the swaying mountains. Joseon Dynasty.

controversial foreign policy and supported the Ming against the Manchus.

Injo prepared for war with the Manchus but kept much of his army near the capital to guard against potential rebels. When the Manchus invaded Korea in 1627 with a force of 30,000, they overran Korean resistance and imposed a peace treaty on King Injo. When the king stubbornly refused Manchu demands, they sent an invasion force of 120,000 men. Because the Joseon border commander failed to transmit the war beacon signals to the capital on time, King Injo received word of the invasion only two days before Manchu troops arrived at Hanyang (present-day Seoul). Surrounded, he was forced to submit to the Qing demand that he sever relations with the Ming Dynasty and enroll as a Qing tributary. This was seven years before the Manchus conquered China in 1644.

To help pay for its expansion, the Manchus levied heavy tribute demands on Joseon. Not until the end of the seventeenth century did Joseon kings abandon anti-Qing policies and the Qing court lighten its tribute demands. Most Korean *yangban*, however, still held the Manchus in contempt and remained loyal to the memory of the Ming.

Why did the Manchus leave Korea independent but fully conquer China? Like the Mongols before them, the Manchus apparently did not see Korea as much of a prize. Early on, they were satisfied to extract tribute from Joseon to help them in their campaigns into China. After the conquest of the Ming, they had so much territory to administer that adding to it was not a high priority. The Qing did later add territories when security was at stake, but Joseon proved a nonthreatening vassal that could safely be allowed to remain autonomous.

INTERNAL POLITICS IN THE SEVENTEENTH AND EIGHTEENTH CENTURIES

The poor showing of the Joseon army during the Japanese and Manchu invasions made reorganization of the armed forces necessary. Everyone recognized that evasion of military service had been a major problem, and so attention was turned to requiring military duty from slaves. Nevertheless, evasion by the *yangban* persisted.

Factionalism reemerged when what seemed a minor ritual issue led to a series of major purges and executions. It began in 1659 when Song Siyeol (SONG SHE-yeol) of the Westerner faction insisted that a member of the royal family should perform a lesser degree of mourning for the deceased King Hyojong because he was the second son of King Injo. The Southerner faction, led by Yun Hyu (YOON Hugh), accused Song and the Westerners of impugning the legitimacy of King Hyojong and his heirs. The Southerners eventually persuaded King Hyojong to adopt their position and dismiss Song. Westerners who disliked Song's uncompromising and arrogant leadership of the Westerner faction split to form their own Disciples faction, leaving Song and his supporters to form their own Patriarchs faction. King Sukjong (SOOK-jong, r. 1674–1720) contributed to the conflict by switching his support almost whimsically. He replaced Patriarchs and Disciples with Southerners in 1689 because they opposed his decision to replace his first queen with a palace concubine and then turned around and purged the Southerners in 1694 after he lost interest in her. When the Patriarchs regained power, they excluded the descendants of Southerners from office until the late eighteenth century.

The Patriarchs and Disciples factions then turned against each other during a succession dispute. In 1727 King Yeongjo (YOUNG-joe) decided that the time had come to put an end to factional strife. He appointed moderate members of both the Disciples' and Patriarchs' factions and excluded not only vengeful members of those two factions but Northerners and Southerners as well. The radical Disciples, however, rose up in rebellion in 1728. King Yeongjo put the rebellion down and maintained his coalition cabinet, but the rebellion alerted him to serious danger in the future if he endangered *yangban* interests.

Worse was to come. In 1749, the king had given the fifteen-year-old Crown Prince Sado (SAW-doe) responsibility as prince regent to take over many of his responsibilities, but Sado's fear of his father's ridicule pushed him over the edge of sanity. He released his pent-up frustrations in paroxysms of rage in which he murdered palace ladies who offended him. (See **Documents: Lady Hyegyeong's Memoirs.**) In 1762 the king decided to lock the prince in a small rice chest in the palace courtyard and left him to starve to death, which he did eight days later. This action immediately split the government into those (mostly Patriarchs) who agreed with the king's decision and those (mostly Southerners) who sympathized with the deceased crown prince, laying the groundwork for another round of purges. Years later in 1776 when the son of the deceased Crown Prince Sado came to the throne as Jeongjo (JUNG-joe), he ardently desired a way to honor his father and take revenge on the factions against him. In 1795 he led a procession of six thousand men to his father's burial site, saying his goal was to celebrate his mother's seventieth birthday.

Jeongjo wanted to be a model king like the ancient Chinese sage kings but was hampered by the factionalism of his officials. Jeongjo chastised his officials for their devotion to their own private interests and their failure to master the moral teachings of the Chinese classics. To rectify this problem, he ordered the importation of Chinese classical texts for the new Royal Library and turned the library staff into his own private cabinet for advising him on state affairs. Nevertheless, he banned the free importation of books from China because he saw many as subversive, including works by Wang Yangming, popular novels, and treatises on Christian theology. Jeongjo's efforts to be a model king did not bring about the moral transformation of society that Confucian theory predicted; to the contrary, plotters tried to have him assassinated seven times.

Procession for Crown Prince Sado. Procession returning from a visit to Hwaseong (HWA-sung) (modern Suwon) to Seoul in 1795 led by King Jeongjo with his mother, Lady Hyegyeong, to honor his father, Crown Prince Sado, who had been murdered by his own father, King Yeongjo, in 1762.

ECONOMIC GROWTH AND THE DECLINE OF SLAVERY

During the Joseon period, the Korean economy was not as advanced as that of China or Japan, but it was gradually commercializing. During the early Joseon period, the economy was predominantly agrarian with limited commercial activity. All taxes were paid in kind or by physical labor. Most artisans were slaves who served the needs of the *yangban* and the royal house. Commerce in the capital was restricted to monopoly merchants and in the countryside to itinerant peddlers and fifth-day markets. Commercial towns and permanent shops were rare. National defense was based on military service for all adult males except for merchants, slaves, and men in official schools; sons of *yangban* with official rank (not necessarily office) were allowed to serve in special guard units set aside for them.

Many government fiscal policies were in need of reform, especially the tribute tax on local products, the maldistribution of the land tax burden, and the military conscription system. The local products tribute tax originated as a fixed and unchanging assessment on local villages that specialized in the production of certain goods, but when many villages ceased producing those products, they had to pay fees to so-called tribute merchants to procure those products elsewhere. This practice of tribute contracting was regarded by the authorities as illegal, and those caught doing it were subject to punishment and fines, but there was no other way for villagers to meet their tribute tax quotas. Yet although tribute contracting was illegal, it contributed to the expansion of commercial activities by private merchants in the countryside.

After the invasions, the Joseon government extended military service to private slaves for the first time. It also replaced local product payments in kind by imposing an extra land tax in grain, which it used to purchase the special goods it needed. The new tax was adopted gradually, but by 1708 the new system covered the entire country and more than doubled the tax burden on landowners. The law stimulated increased commercial activity, particularly among private, unlicensed merchants.

In 1650, the official Kim Yuk (KIM-yook) returned from a trip to China with large quantities of currency he had purchased with funds saved from his expenses. He received King Hyojong's approval to put the coins into circulation, and in 1654 he persuaded the king to order that the cash be accepted in payment of the tax. This marked the first use of money in about one hundred years.

The Joseon population grew to 14 million by 1810, a 40 percent increase from 1650. Connected to this growth were increases in agricultural productivity, allowing farmers to abandon the fallow system under which land was periodically left fallow for a year or two to recover fertility. The conversion of dry fields to wet, irrigated ones also increased productivity, as did the adoption of transplanting rice seedlings (in place of sowing seeds directly in the field). Yet, even as late as 1900, average production per acre in Korea was about 15 bushels, about the same as in China in 1400 and about one-third less than production in Japan and China around 1880.

The eighteenth century witnessed expanded commercial activity. Although the number of commercial towns remained small, the number of periodic fifth-day markets increased. Seoul was the largest city, with about two hundred thousand people. Market growth was slowed when the government decided to stop minting coins in 1697 because of inflation from excessive minting. That policy continued for thirty-three years and produced deflation. The court reluctantly agreed to mint more cash in 1731, and minting continued for the rest of the dynasty.

Private, unlicensed merchants began to compete with the licensed merchants in the capital. In the 1740s the government capitulated and stopped prosecuting merchants who traded in monopoly goods without licenses. In 1791 the court adopted a compromise solution, the joint-sales policy, which protected monopoly privileges for only six shops in Seoul and allowed private merchants to manufacture or sell all other products.

In the early Joseon period, both private and government slavery were pervasive. State slaves alone in the late fifteenth century numbered about 350,000, and government efforts to limit private slaveholding never got far. Yet, as the economy became more commercialized in the eighteenth century, slavery declined. Between 1750 and 1790, there was a sharp reduction in the slave population from about 30 percent to less than 10 percent of the population. King Yeongjo contributed a little to this reduction when in 1730 he approved readopting the matrilineal rule governing the inheritance of

DOCUMENTS   Lady Hyegyeong's Memoirs

One of the most outstanding literary works of the Joseon period is Memoirs of Lady Hyegyeong *(HAY-gyon) (*Hanjungnok *[HAN-joong-nok], or Records Written in Silence), written in* hangul *by the wife of Crown Prince Sado, who was starved to death by his father, King Yeongjo, in 1762. The book consists of four accounts written in 1795, 1801, 1802, and 1805. No other source provides a better introduction to the vicissitudes of palace life, particularly at a time when the slightest slip could mean death. In fact, Lady Hyegyeong's uncle and younger brother were executed in 1776 and 1801, respectively. In her Memoir of 1805, excerpted here, she tries to explain why Crown Prince Sado became mentally ill.*

His Majesty's [King Yeongjo] sagacious heart became irritated with small things at the Prince's quarters, mostly imperceptible and of an unspecified nature. Consequently, without really knowing why, he visited his son less frequently. This happened just as the Prince began to grow; that is just when a child, suffering some inattention or relaxation of control, might easily fall under other influences. As the Prince was often left to himself at this stage, he began to get into trouble....

In his study sessions with tutors, however, Prince Sado was a serious and attentive student.... Thus it is all the more sad that, in his father's presence, the prince grew inarticulate and hesitant out of fear and nervousness. His Majesty became more and more exasperated with him during these encounters in which the Prince was hopelessly tongue-tied. He was alternately angry and concerned about his son. Nonetheless, he never sought a closer relationship with his son, never sought to spend more time with him or to teach him himself. He continued to keep the Prince at a distance, hoping that his son would become on his own the heir he dreamed of. How could this not lead to trouble?...

[When he was ten], the Prince's behavior became strange indeed. It was not just the behavior of a child playing excitedly or loudly. Something was definitely wrong with him. The ladies-in-waiting became quite concerned, whispering to each other of their fears. In the ninth month of that year, the Prince fell gravely ill, often losing consciousness....

[In 1749, when Sado was fifteen, King Yeongjo appointed him Prince-Regent to sit in court and conduct business.] There was

slave status by offspring of mixed slave–commoner marriages. The main cause of the decline, however, was the increase in the number of runaway slaves. Instead of paying the cost of chasing after them, *yangban* and rich landlords took advantage of the recent increase in landless peasants to whom they could rent their land. Escaped slaves did not necessarily see a rise in income and standard of living because now they had to pay rents to landlords, interest on grain loans from the state or private lenders, and the commoner military cloth tax. Another factor in the decline in the slave population was that the government had begun to replace official slaves with hired commoner labor. The number of official slaves dropped from 350,000 in 1590 to 60,000 by 1801.

CULTURAL DEVELOPMENTS

The social and economic changes of the seventeenth and eighteenth centuries were accompanied by a new openness to cultural variety and innovative thinking.

Literature

Literary activity burgeoned in the seventeenth and eighteenth centuries. Poetry remained a favorite pastime of both men (in Chinese) and women (in Korean, using the *hangul* [HAN-gul] alphabet). The favorite forms during this period were the short *sijo* (SHE-joe) poems, their longer versions (*saseol sijo* [SAH-sul SHE-joe]), and the still longer

nothing that the Prince-Regent did that His Majesty found satisfactory. He was constantly discontented and angry with his son. It reached a point where the occurrence of cold spells, droughts, poor harvests, strange natural omens, or calamities caused His Majesty to denounce "the Prince-Regent's insufficient virtue" and to reproach the Prince most severely....

[In 1757]...Prince Sado began to kill. The first person he killed was Kim Hanchae (KIM HAN-chae), the eunuch who happened to be on duty that day. The Prince came in with the severed head and displayed it to the ladies-in-waiting. The bloody head, the first I ever saw, was simply a horrifying sight. As if he had to kill to release his rage, the Prince harmed many ladies-in-waiting....

In the ninth month of that year, Prince Sado took in Bingae, a lady-in-waiting....Before this, he had been intimate with many ladies-in-waiting. Whoever resisted him in any way he beat until he rent her flesh and consummated the act afterwards. Needless to say, no one welcomed his advances. Despite the many women he had been intimate with, he neither cared for anyone for long nor showed any particular fondness while it lasted. This was true even of the secondary consort who had borne him children. It was different with Bingae (BING-ae) [Prince Sado's concubine who bore him two children]. He was mad about her....His Majesty learned of Bingae. He was highly provoked. He summoned the Prince to question him, "How dare you do that?"

By this time [1761], whenever he was seized by his illness the Prince invariably hurt people. For some time now, Bingae had been the only one to attend the prince when he dressed. Hopelessly in the grip of the disease, he grew oblivious even of his beloved. One day, for one of his outings incognito, he was suddenly overwhelmed by a fit of rage and beat her senseless. No sooner had he left than Bingae drew her last breath there where he left her. How pitiful her end was!...Upon his return, Prince Sado heard of what had happened, but he said nothing. He was not in his senses.

Questions for Analysis

1. How does Lady Hyegyeong understand her husband's illness?
2. What made it possible for the prince to keep killing people?

Source: From JaHyon Kim Haboush, transl., *The Memoirs of Lady Hyegyóng* (University of California Press, 1996). Copyright © 1996. Reprinted by permission of The University of California Press.

---

lyrical *gasa* (GA-sa). Poems in Korean (unlike those in Chinese) did not use rhymes; poetic language instead depended on alliteration and cadence.

Hundreds of short tales and long novels were also written during this period, either by men in classical Chinese or by women in Korean. Many of the stories deal with women. Some portray women defending their womanly virtues, but suffering is another common theme. In some tales, lowly courtesans steal their lovers' money or humiliate them in public. The most popular of all tales concerned a woman named Chunhyang (CHOON-hyang). It was both a didactic tale of the triumph of womanly virtue over evil and a romantic tale about the son of a *yangban* official who fell in love with the daughter of a courtesan who did not want to become one herself. In defiance of convention, the two wed secretly at the age of fifteen. The husband then left for Seoul to prepare for the civil service examinations, which he passed in first place. Meanwhile, a cruel governor arrived in Chunhyang's town and demanded that the young woman become his concubine. When she refused, he ordered her beaten unmercifully and threw her in jail to die. The husband then returned as a secret inspector to cashier the governor, and the two lived happily ever after. The story contains many dream sequences, Buddhist awareness of karma, life after death, and resignation to fate. The erotic description of the two lovers affirms the superiority of love over stifling convention, undoubtedly one reason that the story has remained so popular.

One of the great classic novels, *Nine Cloud Dream*, was written by Kim Manjung (KIM MAHN-joong,

1637–1692), a high official and member of the Patriarch faction who was twice dismissed in purges. Set in Tang China, the novel's main message is Buddhist. A monk dreams that he is reborn and sees his life unfold—the glories of a Confucian education, promotion to high office, and unrestricted access to sex with two wives and seven concubines. But then he wakes up and sees the emptiness of it all. In this story, the wives and concubines are all independent, resourceful women who stand out as more vivid characters than the male protagonist.

Two other famous literary works of the period are more political in nature. *The True History of Queen Inhyeon* (IN-hyun), written by an unknown member of the Patriarch faction, was a partisan account aimed at defending Queen Inhyeon of the Min family, who was deposed by the king in 1689 and then later reinstated. The other was Lady Hyegyeong's brilliant memoirs of her life in the palace married to the mad Prince Sado (see **Documents: Lady Hyegyeong's Memoirs**).

Popular oral literature also flourished. Rural dances and local masked plays were often biting in their satire. *Pansori* (PAN-sori) was an oral song tradition that became popular in the countryside in the eighteenth century. It was performed by the singer as a chant, usually accompanied by a drummer who varied the tempo according to the mood of each segment. Famous singers could improvise. Many of the songs mocked the *yangban*, but as time passed, classical Chinese phrases were inserted into the songs to appeal to *yangban* as well as commoners.

Northern Learning

For much of the Joseon period, Confucianism was intellectually rigid. This too changed in the eighteenth century as scholarly circles became more open to new ideas. One important group, dubbed the Northern Learning group, challenged the conventional prejudice against the Manchus. They urged that Korea learn from the Qing Dynasty to improve the economy and the material aspects of life. Most came from the minority Southerner or Northerner factions.

When Hong Daeyong (HONG DAY-young) accompanied his uncle on a mission to the Qing capital in 1765, he became interested in Western astronomy and mathematics. He rejected the idea that China was either at the center of the earth or the only enlightened country on earth, and he criticized his fellow *yangban* for focusing only on China and neglecting the history and culture of their own country. He also criticized *yangban* disdain for manual labor and the backwardness and poverty of the Joseon economy.

Pak Jiwon (PARK GEE-one), one of Hong's disciples, left a detailed record of his travels as a member of a tribute mission to China in 1780. He attacked the *yangban* monopoly of the examination system and satirized them in stories like *Master Heo* (HUH) and *The Yangban*. He demanded an end to discrimination against sons of concubines, the manumission of official slaves, and adoption of a land-limitation scheme. He encouraged everyone to engage in commerce and industry and recommended improving transportation by copying the superior carts and boats used in Qing China.

Pak Jega (PARK JAY-gah) was a Southerner who studied with Pak Jiwon. In 1786 he proposed that the king invite Christian missionaries in China to come to Korea to teach Western astronomy and mathematics. In his 1788 book titled *Northern Learning*, he expanded on themes introduced by Hong Daeyong and Bak Jiwon and urged the king to appoint the best merchants to office and expand trade with Qing China. Northern Learning represented a liberalization of intellectual thought, but it had a very limited effect on government policy because anti-Manchu prejudice and the Confucian bias against merchants were too deeply entrenched.

Christianity and Western Learning

After the Jesuit Francis Xavier arrived in Japan in 1549, many Japanese were converted to Christianity (see **Connections: Europe Enters the Scene**). Some Korean captives who were taken to Japan during Hideyoshi's invasions converted, but they had a negligible effect on Korea. Many of Matteo Ricci's works in Chinese on Catholic theology and Western mathematics, astronomy, and geography were brought into Korea from China in the early seventeenth century, and they had more impact. The Koreans lumped Christian theology and Western science together in a single term, *Western Learning*. Koreans were won over to Western astronomical ideas and adopted the Western calendar in 1653, nine years after the Qing Dynasty did.

Scholars who looked into Christianity in the 1720s often rejected its basic premises. Yi Imyeong (E E-myoung) in 1720 rejected the Catholic notion of heaven and hell, and Yi Ik's (E IK) disciple, Sin Hudam

(SHIN WHO-dahm), in 1724 condemned Christianity for its resemblance to Buddhism in its selfish emphasis on individual salvation and its concern with life after death. Much Jesuit philosophical argument passed over the heads of Confucian scholars, who were interested primarily in whether Catholic doctrines would aid or hinder adherence to Confucian social morality. What did attract Korean attention was the pope's 1715 condemnation of Chinese ancestral rites as idolatry and the Yongzheng emperor's subsequent ban against Christian proselytization.

In 1784 the student Yi Seunghun (E SOONG-hoon) traveled to China to be baptized, only to be refused by the Catholic missionaries because of his inadequate knowledge of Catholic doctrine. Still, he brought back Christian texts to proselytize among acquaintances. Several dozen men formed the first Christian congregation and worshipped at the home of the *jungin* Kim Beomu (KIM BUM-woo), who became Korea's first Christian martyr.

In 1788 two high officials asked the king to ban European books. The Southerner Councilor of the Right, who had many Catholic relatives, pleaded with King Jeongjo not to punish the Christians for their ignorance. The king agreed, but he also ordered the destruction of all Christian books. In 1791, after being reminded of the pope's ruling on ancestral rites, two Catholics who were also Southerners burned the ancestral tablets for the mother of one of them. When they refused to recant, King Jeongjo ordered their decapitation and forced their associates to commit apostasy.

The first Christian missionary to Korea, the Chinese Zhou Wenmo, was discovered in 1794. King Jeongjo executed him and demoted or exiled Southerners suspected of being sympathetic. King Jeongjo's attempt at toleration had backfired, and he adopted a hard line against both Southerners and Christians.

THE FAMILY AND WOMEN IN THE CONFUCIAN AGE

Joseon Confucianists were zealous in their efforts to reshape Korea into a model Confucian society. Korea's original family system was quite different from China's, so making Koreans conform to the strictures in the Chinese classics required much more radical change in Korea than it ever had in China.

In Goryeo times, the Korean family was neither patriarchal nor patrilineal. Sons-in-law usually lived with their wives' families for several years before setting up their own homes. Oldest daughters often stayed permanently in their parents' home, and continuing a family through a daughter was an accepted practice. Women inherited equal shares of their parents' property and could take their property into marriage and maintain control of it; if they had no children to inherit the property, it was returned to their natal family. Both men and women remarried if widowed. Men could have several wives who were treated equally. Ancestor worship was not common, and funerals were largely Buddhist affairs. Rather than bury the dead in coffins, families followed the Buddhist practice of cremation. Mourning, too, followed Buddhist customs and was generally limited to one hundred days.

To the early Joseon Confucian scholars, all these practices needed to be reformed, and *yangban* should set the example for the rest of society. Some reforms were accepted relatively quickly. By the end of the fifteenth century, *yangban* were observing Confucian mourning prescriptions. This is seen in Choe Bu's accounts of his travels in China after he was shipwrecked there in 1488. At the time, he was in mourning for his father and made every effort to follow all the rules. By the late fifteenth century, *yangban* were also more often adopting nephews and other close patrilineal relatives when they had no sons, rather than letting a daughter inherit the family property. Remarriage of widows also declined markedly, perhaps in part due to a law issued in 1474 that barred sons of remarried widows from taking the civil service examinations. By the eighteenth century, Confucian ancestor worship had completely replaced Buddhist ceremonies for the deceased, and the Confucian pattern of patriarchal domination of the family reached its zenith. It took about three hundred years before Buddhist burial practices and beliefs were replaced at the lowest level of society.

Confucian promotion of patrilineal kinship led to the compilation of genealogies. At the beginning of the dynasty, women were listed in the family genealogy along with their brothers in the order of birth. By the eighteenth century, however, women were all listed after their brothers, and when they married, their names were expunged and listed instead in their husband's genealogy as the daughter of their father. Their personal names were not even recorded.

One reason practices of this sort spread is that the lower levels of *yangban* society, whose members had no hopes of official careers, saw meticulous observance of Confucian family practices as a way to show their *yangban* credentials. But Confucians thought that these practices should be observed by all, and they encouraged moral tracts written in *hangul* to spread them to those with less education.

Because Korean reformers were copying the system described in the Chinese classics, not the family system of China in their day, many differences between the two family systems persisted. Perhaps most significant, whereas in China distinctions in status between brothers had been greatly reduced from Han times on and by law all brothers were to receive equal shares of property, Korea adhered to the classical rules that discriminated against younger sons and, even more so, sons of concubines.

How were women' lives affected by these changes in law and ideology? Women in *yangban* families were affected most because their behavior impinged on the social standing of the family, putting them under more pressure to conform to such ideals as avoiding contact with men who were not relatives. Certainly women could still have considerable power within the family, especially older women who chose spouses for their children and had daughters-in-law subordinate to them.

Moreover, we should not assume that women always bought into the dominant ideology. Even in families where the men were Confucians, the women continued to engage in religious practices usually frowned on by men. They prayed to mountains, trees, and household gods. They regarded their dreams as predictive of the sex and capacity of a new child, and they had to take care to defend the family against bad omens around the home. A special ceremony might be held for cutting the umbilical cord, and precautions were taken so that the spirits of women who died in labor or committed suicide would not harm surviving members of the family. Women also attended religious festivals, such as the Tano Festival (see Color Plate 24).

In popular religion, women were active agents. They hired shamans, usually female ones (*mudang* [MOO-dang]), to go into a trance and communicate with the angry spirits of a woman's own dead parents and grandparents, who were believed to cause sickness and other problems among family members. Women, as well as many men, continued to believe in Buddhist ideas despite Confucian condemnation, particularly transmigration, karma, and punishment in Buddhist hell, especially when facing illness or impending death. Literature of the Joseon period, as just discussed, often depicts women as independent-minded and articulate.

SUMMARY

After the end of Mongol domination, a general founded the Joseon Dynasty, which lasted almost as long as the Chinese Ming and Qing Dynasties together. The first four kings were notable for political and cultural accomplishments. Of them, King Sejong is especially notable for his strengthening of the armed forces, settlement of the northern frontier area, legal reforms, book projects, scientific interests, and sponsorship of a new phonetic writing system (*hangul*). Hangul made possible the development of literature in the vernacular language, which could be written and read by those who knew no Chinese, including women.

Neo-Confucianism became firmly established as the ideology of the *yangban* class in the Joseon period. Confucian scholars did not see Confucian civilization as specifically Chinese; the more zealous aspired to make Korea a more perfect Confucian society. This can be seen in the efforts to get Korean *yangban* to adhere to the more strictly patrilineal form of the family celebrated in Confucian texts.

The greatest crisis of the Joseon period was the Japanese invasions under Hideyoshi, which cost about two million Korean lives. Joseon military readiness had declined during the long period of peace, and factionalism at court made it difficult to get the government united in its response. Japan, by contrast, had been engaged in civil war for a century and had mastered the use of firearms, giving it the advantage. Although Korea had impressive victories at sea, Hideyoshi was able to land his armies and advanced as far as Pyeongyang within two months. A few months later, Ming forces arrived to help Korea and push back the Japanese army. Hideyoshi did not accept a peace settlement and renewed the fighting in 1597, and it was only after Hideyoshi died in 1598 that the Japanese troops were fully withdrawn.

The next major challenge was the Manchus, who were gaining strength on Joseon's northern border. Again, factional strife made a united response difficult. The Manchus invaded and forced the Joseon government to accept unfavorable terms. Many *yangban* maintained their loyalty to the Ming Dynasty even after the Qing had succeeded it in China.

The eighteenth century was a period of economic growth in Korea, as it was in China and Japan. Currency came back into use, trade grew, and agricultural technology was improved. The population grew to about 14 million by the end of the century. Slavery declined from about 30 percent of the population to less than 10 percent. There was at the same time a new openness to cultural innovation. Fiction flourished, both short tales and long novels. Some scholars took an interest in the Western learning and Christianity that missionaries and traders were bringing to China, mostly learning about it from books in Chinese or trips to China, as in this period no Westerners were allowed into Korea.

How different was Korea in 1800 than in 1392? Much, of course, had not changed. Korea was still unified under kings of the same dynasty who competed for power with the entrenched *yangban* elite. But in other regards, life in Korea had changed dramatically. Buddhism had been pushed to the sidelines as aggressive Confucianization prevailed. Although Korean food, houses, and clothing remained distinct, many other features of Korean life were strongly affected by the Confucianization campaigns, which changed such basic social practices as where people lived after marriage and how family property was transmitted. The economy had evolved from one rooted in control over land and people with very little use of money to one where coins circulated, trade was more prevalent, and slavery had declined substantially. The *yangban* stratum had steadily expanded and gradually divided into a national elite who held office and local *yangban* with much less power. The national *yangban* elite in turn were divided into largely hereditary factions who competed for control of the court. Intellectually, while the most learned continued to follow trends in China, it had become more common for intellectual leaders to develop ideas in original ways.

How similar were the situations of women in premodern China, Korea, and Japan? In broad terms, if we compare East Asia and Europe in 1700 or 1800, women in each of the three countries of East Asia were probably more like each other than like women in England or France. In China, Korea, and Japan, men could take concubines and could divorce their wives relatively easily, but women could not divorce their husbands, and wives were expected to act deferentially in the presence of men. Girls did not go to schools with boys, and male literacy was substantially higher than female literacy. In all three countries, female entertainers were also a prominent part of social life; they associated with men of high rank but did not have high social standing themselves. In all three countries, too, historians have tended to see women's situations as declining over time, with the high point in the period between 650 and 1050.

Despite these broad similarities, the history of women's positions and gender ideology in China, Korea, and Japan differs in many significant ways. The Chinese family was patrilineal and patriarchal from as far back as historians can trace, but in Korea during the Silla and Goryeo periods and in Japan during the Nara and Heian periods, people traced kinship through both men and women, and it was more common for a newly married couple to live with the wife's family than with the husband's. Over time, however, the family systems of both Korea and Japan grew more patrilineal and patriarchal. One reason for these shifts might be the influence of Chinese law codes, which were used as models in both Korea and Japan. Beyond that, in the case of medieval Japan, scholars have pointed to the shift in the structure of elite. In samurai families, property came to be transmitted to a single heir, marriages became more durable, and wives moved in with their husbands' families. In the case of Korea, scholars have given more weight to the commitment of *yangban* to Confucianism and the conscious efforts made to instill such Confucian virtues as filial piety and wifely deference. Still, neither Korea nor Japan went as far as China in the patrilineal direction. In Korea, maternal kinship mattered, and the son of a *yangban* father and a lowborn mother could not take the civil service examinations.

The issue of women's literacy and writing is tied less to Confucianism and more to writing systems. With the development of the *kana* syllabary in the ninth century, it became much easier to write in Japanese. Japanese women were quick to make use of the new way to write, and Heian women wrote an astonishing number of books. The script is not the full story, however, because although it continued to be available in later centuries, women writers attracted less attention after the Heian period. In Korea, the invention of *hangul* in the fifteenth century similarly made it possible to write in Korean. As in Japan, women predominated among earlier users of the script, and many more writings by women survived after the development of *hangul* than before. In the Chinese case, by contrast, women stuck with the more literary way to write after writing in the vernacular became established. By Qing times, there were more women who published poetry than in any earlier period. By this time, ways to write that reflected speech more closely had been developed and were used to write fiction and drama, but women rarely wrote in these vernacular forms. Instead, they chose to use the more elegant classical language.

In the case of China, the impression that women's situations deteriorated is based above all on the spread of footbinding and growing pressure on widows not to remarry. Both these customs can be traced back to the Song period, but they penetrated more deeply through society in later centuries. Footbinding was not copied by Korea or Japan, or even by most non-Han ethnic groups within China. Widow chastity, however, did become the ideal in Korea as Confucianism gained strength in the Joseon period. The government went so far as to ban the sons of remarried widows from taking the civil service examinations.

For all three countries, there is a large discrepancy between what didactic texts say women should do, the way they are portrayed in fiction and anecdotes, and what women's writings suggest. Before concluding that women were submissive in late traditional East Asia, we should recall the highly varied women portrayed in literature, such as resourceful servants and overbearing mothers-in-law, not to mention malicious schemers, and the opportunities they seized to shape their own lives.

Europe Enters the Scene

TRADE ROUTES FLOURISHED BETWEEN NORTHEAST and Southeast Asia long before European adventurers, merchants, and Catholic missionaries entered the South China Sea. Lured by Asian silks, porcelain, and spices, ships under the Portuguese flag were the first to risk the voyage in the early sixteenth century. The Spanish, British, and Dutch followed. In early seventeenth-century Japan, early eighteenth-century China, and early nineteenth-century Korea, rulers put a stop to missionary activities, although for different reasons. Trade between Europe and East Asia continued, but it was confined to specific ports in China and Japan.

Hemmed in by Spain, Portugal relied on trade to fill the royal treasury. At the beginning of the fifteenth century, Portuguese ships started exploring the west coast of Africa in search of gold. African gold then financed a voyage around the Cape of Good Hope in 1488. From there, the Portuguese established a colony at Goa on the west coast of India and followed Muslim and Indian trade routes to the Spice Islands of Indonesia. Once Queen Isabella and her husband, Ferdinand, captured Grenada, the last Muslim emirate in Spain, in 1492, they funded Christopher Columbus's voyage across the Atlantic in hopes of finding an alternative route to China. Two years later, the pope divided the world beyond Europe between Spain and Portugal. Spain's sphere included most of the so-called New World except Brazil; Portugal went east.

China's contact with Portugal began in 1511 when Admiral Alfonso de Albuquerque captured the Chinese trading center of Malacca near the tip of the Malay Peninsula. With this as a base, the first official Portuguese embassy followed traders to China in 1517. The embassy behaved badly by refusing to conform to Chinese customs, while ship captains acted more like pirates than traders. Few Portuguese were willing to risk the long voyage in tiny ships around the Horn of Africa, across the wide expanse of the Indian Ocean, and through the Strait of Malacca to the South China Sea. Most were neither officials dispatched from the Portuguese court nor explorers seeking glory and territory. What they had in limited resources and manpower had to go toward making a living in competition with local traders. (See Map C5.1.)

Although Ming emperors at Beijing tried repeatedly to prohibit maritime travel, they could not stop the Portuguese or seafaring people on the south China coast who made little distinction between trade, smuggling, and piracy. In 1521, the Ming tried to ban the Portuguese from China. Two years later, an expedition authorized by the Portuguese king and charged with negotiating a friendship treaty defeated its mission by firing on Chinese warships near Guangzhou. In 1557, without informing Beijing, local Chinese officials decided that the way to regulate trade was to allow the Portuguese to build a trading post on vacant land near the mouth of the Pearl River, called Macao by the Portuguese. It became the first destination for all Europeans going to China until the nineteenth century, and it remained a Portuguese settlement until 1999.

The only significant products Portuguese traders brought to networks that had already developed in East Asia were New World crops such as corn, sweet potatoes, chili peppers, and tobacco. They are said to have reached Japan by accident in 1543 when a typhoon blew a ship with a mixed crew of Southeast Asians to a small island called Tanegashima. Japanese historians long credited the Portuguese for bringing both the gun and syphilis to Japan, but it is now thought that syphilis arrived earlier and that guns from Southeast Asia landed at various places around the same time, both carried by pre-existing trade routes. In later decades of the sixteenth century, Portuguese traders profited from the Ming ban on Japanese ships because they had raided the coast. The Portuguese carried 20 metric tons of Japanese

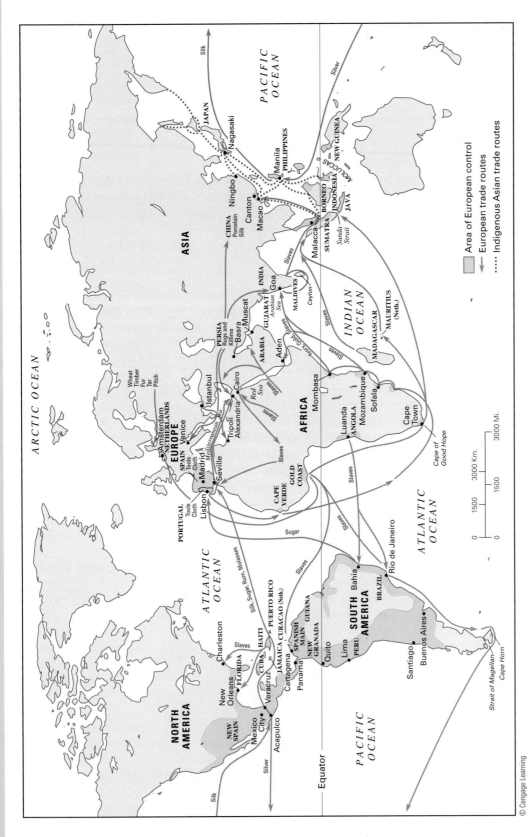

© Cengage Learning

Map C5.1   Seaborne Trading Empires in the Sixteenth and Seventeenth Centuries

silver a year to China in exchange for silk, sugar, medicine, and dye.

Trade between China and Europe increased in the late sixteenth century through an economic connection that included the Americas following the discovery by Andrés de Urdaneta of a return route for sailing ships across the Pacific to Mexico. China needed foreign silver because its monetary system depended on it and domestic production had declined after 1430. China bought Japanese silver carried on Portuguese ships as well as 50 percent of all silver mined in Mexico and Bolivia. Carried in Spanish ships, New World silver came through Manila, founded in 1571 when Spain made the Philippines a colony. Later disruptions in the flow of silver from Japan and the New World in 1639 contributed to the fall of the Ming. Spanish silver bought manufactured goods—Chinese silk, porcelain, and lacquer—that dominated the luxury trade in Europe and funded Spain's wars against multiple enemies for generations.

Portuguese merchants seeking profits in East Asia faced competition from their government when the Portuguese viceroy at Goa made the Japan trade a royal monopoly in 1550. The Ming approved because their officials also wanted to see trade regularized. Each year, a captain major appointed by the crown sent ships to Japan, where warlords competed to attract the ships to their ports. (See Color Plate 20.) The governor of Macao forbade the sending of goods to Japan on private ships via third-party countries, especially the Philippines. His directives were futile; Portuguese and Spanish traders with crews drawn from all over East and Southeast Asia found Manila too convenient to abandon.

Catholic missionaries seeking converts who followed the traders hoped to keep the European religious wars that undermined the pope's spiritual authority secret from Asia. The first were Jesuits, from the order founded by Ignatius Loyola in 1534 to promote Catholic scholarship and combat the Protestant Reformation initiated by Martin Luther. Jesuits insisted that Christianizing China and Japan was not to be done with the intent to conquer, as had been the case in the New World. As individuals, they displayed a rare sensitivity to other cultures. They were willing to find universal principles of belief outside a European context, but they served an institution that refused to compromise with local beliefs and practices. Despite the efforts of charismatic missionaries, the Catholic Church never gained the influence in East Asia enjoyed by that other foreign religion, Buddhism.

The Jesuit priest Francis Xavier had worked in India and the Indies before China and Japan attracted his attention. After many misadventures, he landed on Satsuma in 1549 where the Satsuma lord treated him well in hopes that he would attract the official Portuguese trading ships the next year. When the ships went instead to the island of Hirado (**He-rah-doe**), Satsuma expelled Xavier's party. Xavier traveled throughout western Japan as far as Kyoto, preaching wherever warlords gave permission. Asked why the Chinese knew nothing of Christianity if it was indeed an ancient and true religion, Xavier decided that Japan would become Christian only if China led the way. His efforts to enter China ended when he died on an island off the China coast in December 1552.

Jesuits and Dominicans soon joined the missionaries and converts Xavier left behind in Japan. In 1565, Louis Frois met Oda Nobunaga, who befriended the Jesuits to annoy his Buddhist enemies. In 1580, Jesuits acquired Nagasaki from a warlord interested in promoting trade with Portuguese ships. Two years later, four young Kyushu samurai left Nagasaki for Lisbon and Rome, where they helped Jesuits get a papal bull that put Japan off limits to other orders. Because it could not be enforced, quarrels between the Catholic orders over how best to present Christianity to East Asia damaged the missionaries' credibility in the eyes of Asian rulers.

Warlords trying to unite Japan under secular authority became increasingly suspicious of Christianity. If an absolute god demanded absolute loyalty, where did that leave the bonds between lord and retainer? Suppression began in 1587 and intensified nine years later when the pilot of a ship wrecked on the Japanese coast allegedly pointed out that soldiers had followed Spanish missionaries to the Philippines. In 1614, Tokugawa Ieyasu decided that missionaries undermined the social order and were not essential to foreign trade. He ordered them expelled under threat of execution. He also tortured and killed Christian converts who refused to renounce their faith. Among the martyrs were Koreans who had been brought to Japan as slaves during Toyotomi Hideyoshi's invasions in the 1590s. The shogunate broke off relations with Catholic countries in 1624. The remaining Christians practiced their religion in secret by crafting statues of the Virgin Mary in the guise of Kannon, the Buddhist goddess of mercy.

Christianity arrived later in China. Not until 1583 did the Jesuit Matteo Ricci receive permission to move farther inland than Macao. Once he had educated himself in the style of Chinese literati, he set himself up in Nanjing. In 1601 he received tacit permission from the emperor to live in Beijing. From him the Chinese learned Western-style geography, astronomy, and Euclidean mathematics. In the years after Ricci's death in 1611, Jesuits regulated the Chinese lunar calendar. Anti-foreign officials sometimes harassed them, but the Jesuits retained their standing with Chinese literati through the collapse of the Ming Dynasty and the founding of the Qing in 1644. Allowed into China after 1633, Catholic monks who lived on alms criticized Jesuits for aiming their efforts at the ruling class and trying to fit Christian ideas into the Chinese worldview rather than remaining European in approach and appealing to the masses.

Ricci and his Jesuit successors believed that Confucianism as a philosophy could be brought into line with Christian beliefs. Not only did Confucianists and Christians share similar concerns for morality and virtue, but Confucian rites of filial piety performed for the ancestors did not constitute a form of worship, which made Confucianism compatible with Christianity. Monks who lived by begging disagreed. In 1715, religious and political quarrels in Europe, worsened by long-standing hostility to the Jesuits, resulted in Ricci's accommodation with Chinese practices being deemed heretical. Angry at this insult, the Kangxi emperor forbade all Christian missionary work in China, although he allowed Jesuits to remain in Beijing to assist with the calendar. A Jesuit portrait painter later proved popular at the courts of his son and grandson. The negative outcome to the "rites controversy" over whether Christian converts should be allowed to maintain ancestral altars, plus accusations that missionaries had meddled in the imperial succession, led the Qing to view all Europeans with suspicion.

China's rulers also limited trade for strategic reasons. Between 1655 and 1675, the Qing banned maritime trade to isolate Ming loyalists on Taiwan. In addition to official trade at the state level, the Qing permitted merchants to trade with foreigners, but only under tight control. After 1759, all maritime trade, whether with Southeast Asia or Europe, was confined to Canton (Guangzhou). Merchants put up with these restrictions because, in exchange for silver, China provided luxury items and tea, a bulk ware introduced to Europe in 1607.

Lunds Universitetsbibliotek, Rarsamlingen, nr. 50

Trade Practices in East Asia. When European ships visited Chinese or Japanese ports, they were supposed to unload their guns before trade could begin. This painting shows the guns under a roof next to the sheds where trade was conducted.

Following the European religious wars of the latter half of the sixteenth century, the profits to be made in East and Southeast Asia lured traders from Protestant countries. Determined not to allow their Catholic rivals to dominate the world, Protestant nations sent explorers across the oceans; at the same time, Britain's defeat of the Spanish Armada in 1588 began Spain's long decline. Early in the seventeenth century, the Dutch gained a competitive advantage in the world spice trade by opening a faster sailing route across the southern Indian Ocean before turning northward to Java. Both nations established East India companies in 1600 whose ability to capitalize trade far exceeded that of the merchants of Spain and Portugal.

Like Qing emperors, seventeenth-century Japanese shoguns tried to regulate foreign trade by confining it to specific harbors. In contrast to the sixteenth century, they also tried to prevent the increasingly short supply of precious metals from leaving the country by practicing import substitution for silk and sugar. A Dutch ship carrying a mixed crew of men from Europe and the New World arrived in 1600. (Of the original five ships with a crew of 461 men, only one ship and 25 men survived to reach Japan.) The British arrived in 1613. Both Dutch and British came as representatives of trading companies, not of their governments. Disappointed with scant profits, the British shut down their quarters. Unhappy with what it deemed smuggling, in 1635 the shogunate issued a maritime ban that forbade all Japanese from sailing overseas and ordered those who had migrated to Southeast Asia to return home or face permanent exile. The thriving Japanese community at Hoi An in Vietnam disappeared. In a further attempt to control unregulated trade and piracy, the shogunate later banned the building of oceangoing ships. In 1641, it ordered the Dutch to move to the artificial island called Dejima in Nagasaki bay originally constructed for the Portuguese. The annual visits by Dutch ships allowed an exchange of information, maintained Japan's connections with trade routes to Southeast Asia, and opened the door to Western science and medicine.

Korea proved unfriendly to merchants and missionaries alike. In the seventeenth century, British and Dutch traders made several attempts to insert their goods into the trade route between Korea and Japan that later developed into a triangular trade carrying Japanese copper, Korean ginseng, and Chinese silver. Memories of piracy, fear of unregulated trade that smacked of smuggling, and suspicion of European motives led the government to reject them. Korean scholars in residence at the Chinese court read the Jesuits' religious, scientific, and mathematical texts and took them back to Korea, where they attracted a small following for Catholic Christianity. The converts soon became embroiled in the factional infighting that characterized politics in eighteenth-century Korea and suffered severe persecution starting in 1791. No European missionary or merchant tried to visit Korea until three French priests landed illegally in 1836–1837. The Korean court had them and their converts executed in 1839 for spreading the "evil teaching" that ran counter to the dictates of filial piety.

Europeans had only minimal impact on East Asia before the nineteenth century. Except for a few outposts, they seized no territory, and what they tried to take, they could not always hold. In the Indian Ocean, the Portuguese found themselves on the defensive when Arabs expelled them from the Red Sea, Aden, Muscat, and Mombasa over the course of the sixteenth and seventeenth centuries. Between the Mughal conquest of the 1520s and the Afghan attacks in the 1750s, the most serious threats suffered by the South Asian subcontinent were from non-Europeans. In the seventeenth century the Chinese navy expelled the Dutch from the Pescadores Islands and from outposts on Taiwan. Although trade increased between the sixteenth and eighteenth centuries, with the exception of the Philippines, it did not yet lead to colonization as it had in the New World.

The Creation of the Manchu Empire (1600–1800)

The seventeenth and eighteenth centuries were the age of the Manchus (man-choo). As the Ming Dynasty fell into disorder, the Jurchens put together an efficient state beyond Ming's northeastern border and adopted the name *Manchu* for themselves. After they were called in to help suppress peasant rebellions, the Manchus took the throne themselves, founding the Qing Dynasty (1644–1911). Many Chinese did all they could to resist the Manchus out of loyalty to the Ming, but by the eighteenth century, Chinese and Manchus had learned to accommodate each other. In many ways, the eighteenth century was the high point of traditional Chinese civilization. The Manchus created a multiethnic empire, adding Taiwan, Mongolia, Tibet, and Xinjiang to their realm, making the Qing Empire comparable to the other multinational empires of the early modern world, such as the Ottoman, Russian, and Habsburg empires.

Many historians have been attracted to research on the seventeenth and eighteenth centuries because it provides a baseline of traditional China before the rapid changes of the modern era. In addition to the usual questions of why the Ming fell and the Qing succeeded, scholars have recently been asking questions about the Manchus themselves. Who were they, and how did their history shape the way they ruled China? How did they compel the allegiance of peoples of different backgrounds? How did they manage to give traditional Chinese political forms a new lease on life? Other historians have focused more on what was going on among the Chinese during these two crucial centuries. Was population growth a sign of prosperity? Or was it beginning to cause problems? How did scholars respond to Manchu rule?

THE MANCHUS

The Manchus were descended from the Jurchens, who had ruled north China during the Jin Dynasty (1127–1234). Although they had not maintained the written language that the Jin had created, they had maintained their hairstyle. A Manchu man shaved the front of his head and wore the rest of his hair in a long braid (called a queue). The language the Manchus spoke belongs to the Tungus family, making it close to some of the languages spoken in nearby Siberia and distantly related to Korean and Japanese.

During the Ming Dynasty, the Manchus had lived in dispersed communities in what is loosely called Manchuria (the modern provinces of Liaoning [leeow-ning], Jilin [jee-lin], and Heilongjiang [hay-lung-jyang]). In the more densely populated southern part of Manchuria, Manchus lived in close contact with Mongols, Koreans, and Chinese, the latter especially in the Ming prefecture of Liaodong. (See Map 16.1.) The Manchus were not nomads but rather hunters, fishers, and farmers. Like the Mongols, they had a tribal social structure and were excellent horsemen and archers. Also like the Mongols, their society was strongly hierarchical, with elites and slaves. Slaves, often Korean or Chinese, were generally acquired through capture. From the Mongols, the Manchus had adopted Lamaist Buddhism, originally from Tibet, and it coexisted with their native shamanistic religion. Manchu shamans were men or women who had experienced a spiritual death and rebirth and, as a consequence, could travel to and influence the world of the spirits.

Both the Joseon Dynasty in Korea and the Ming Dynasty in China welcomed diplomatic missions from Manchu chieftains, seeing them as a counterbalance to the Mongols. Written communication was frequently in Mongolian, the lingua franca of the region. Along the border with the Ming were officially approved markets where Manchus brought horses, furs, honey, and ginseng to exchange for Chinese tea, cotton, silk, rice, salt, and tools. By the 1580s, there were five such markets that convened monthly, and unofficial trade occurred as well.

The Manchus credited their own rise to Nurhaci (1559–1626), who in 1583 at age twenty-four became the leader of one group of Manchus. Over the next few decades, he was able to expand his territories, in the process not only uniting the Manchus but also creating a social–political–military organization that brought together Manchus, Mongols, and Chinese. A Korean who traveled to Nurhaci's headquarters in 1595–1596 encountered many small Jurchen settlements, most no larger than twenty households, supported by fishing, hunting for pelts, collecting pine nuts or ginseng, or growing crops such as wheat, millet, and barley. Villages were often at odds with each other over resources, and men did not leave their villages without arming themselves with bows and arrows or swords. Interspersed among these Manchu settlements were groups of nomadic Mongols who lived in yurts in open areas. The Korean visitor observed that Nurhaci had in his employ men from the Ming territory of Liaodong who could speak both Chinese and Manchu and could write in Chinese. Nurhaci's knowledge of China and Chinese ways was not entirely secondhand, however. In 1590, he had led an embassy to Beijing, and the next year he offered to join the Ming effort to repel the Japanese invasion of Korea. Nurhaci and his children married Mongols as well as Manchus, and these marriages cemented alliances.

Like Chinggis, who had reorganized his armies to reduce the importance of tribal affiliations, Nurhaci created a new social basis for his armies in units called *banners*, identified by their colors. Each banner was made up of a set of military companies but included the families and slaves of the soldiers as well. Each company had a captain whose position was hereditary. Many of the commanding officers were drawn from Nurhaci's own lineage. Over time new companies and new banners were formed, and by 1644 there were twenty-four banners (eight each Manchu, Mongol, and Chinese banners). When new groups of Manchus were defeated, they were distributed among several banners to lessen their potential for subversion.

In 1616, Nurhaci declared war on the Ming Empire by calling himself khan of the revived Jin Dynasty and listing his grievances against the Ming. In 1621 his forces overran Liaodong and incorporated it into his state. After Nurhaci died in 1626, his son Hong Taiji succeeded him. In consolidating the Jin state, then centered on Mukden, Hong Taiji grudgingly made use of Chinese bureaucrats, but his goal was to replace them with a multiethnic elite equally competent in warfare and documents. In 1636, Hong Taiji renamed his state Qing ("pure"). When he died in 1643 at age forty-six, his brother Dorgon was made regent for his five-year-old son, Fulin, the Shunzhi emperor (r. 1643–1661).

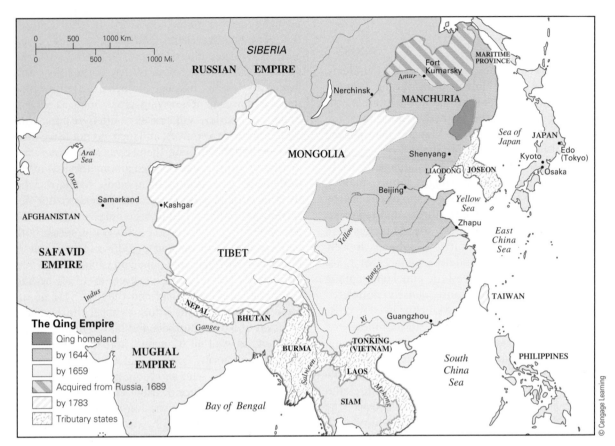

Map 16.1 **The Manchu Empire at Its Height**

The distinguished Ming general Wu Sangui (woo sahn-gway) (1612–1678), a native of Liaodong, was near the eastern end of the Great Wall when he heard that the rebel Li Zicheng (lee dzih-chuhng) had captured Beijing. Dorgon proposed to Wu that they join forces and liberate Beijing. Wu opened the gates of the Great Wall to let the Manchus in, and within a couple of weeks they had occupied Beijing. When the Manchus made clear that they intended to conquer the rest of the country and take the throne themselves, Wu joined forces with them, as did many other Chinese generals.

MING LOYALISM

When word of the fall of Beijing to the Manchus reached the Yangzi valley, Ming officials selected a Ming prince to succeed to the throne and shifted the capital to Nanjing, the Ming secondary capital. They

were thus following the strategy that had allowed the Song Dynasty to continue to flourish after it had lost the north in 1126. The Ming court offered to buy off the Manchus, just as the Song had bought off the Jurchens. Dorgon, however, saw no need to check his ambitions. He sent Wu Sangui and several Manchu generals to pursue the rebel forces across north China. Li Zicheng was eliminated in 1645, Zhang Xianzhong (jahng shyen-juhng) in 1647.

At the same time, Qing forces set about trying to defeat the Ming forces in the south. Quite a few able officials joined the Ming cause, but leadership was not well coordinated. Shi Kefa (shih kuh-fah), a scholar-official who had risen to minister of war in Nanjing, took charge of defense and stationed his army at Yangzhou. Many other generals, however, defected to the Manchu side, and their soldiers were incorporated into the Qing armies. As the Qing forces moved south, many local officials opened the gates of their cities and surrendered. Shi Kefa refused to surrender Yangzhou, and a five-day battle ensued. The Manchu general was so angered at Shi's resistance that he unleashed his army to take revenge on the city, slaughtering hundreds of thousands. As cities in the south fell, large numbers of Ming loyalists committed suicide, their wives, mothers, and daughters frequently joining them.

In the summer of 1645, the Manchu command ordered all Chinese serving in its armies to shave the front of their heads in the Manchu fashion, presumably to make it easier to recognize which side they were on. Soon this order was extended to all Chinese men, a measure that aroused deep resentment and made it easier for the Ming loyalists to organize resistance. When those newly conquered by the Qing refused to shave their hair, Manchu commanders felt justified in ordering the slaughter of defiant cities such as Jiading, Changshu, and Jiangyin. Still, Ming loyalist resistance continued long after little hope remained. The Manchus did not defeat the two main camps until 1661–1662, and even then Zheng Cheng-gong (juhng chuhng-gung, Koxinga) was able to hold out in Taiwan until 1683.

Ming loyalism also took less militant forms. Several leading thinkers of this period had time to think and write because they refused to serve the Qing. Their critiques of the Ming and its failings led to searching inquiries into China's heritage of dynastic rule. Huang Zongxi (hwang dzung-shyee) (1610–1695) served the Ming resistance court at Nanjing and followed it when it had to retreat, but after 1649 he lived in retirement at his home in Zhejiang province. The Manchu conquest was so traumatic an event that he reconsidered many of the basic tenets of Chinese political order. He came to the conclusion that the Ming's problems were not minor ones like inadequate supervision of eunuchs but much more major ones, such as the imperial institution itself.

Gu Yanwu (goo yen-woo) (1613–1682) participated in the defense of his native city, then watched his mother starve herself rather than live under Manchu rule. He traveled across north China in search of a better understanding of Ming weaknesses, looking into economic topics Confucian scholars had rarely studied in depth, such as banking, mining, and farming. He had only disdain for scholars who wasted their time on empty speculation or literary elegance when there were so many practical problems awaiting solution. He thought that the Ming had suffered from overcentralization and advocated greater local autonomy.

A third example is Wang Fuzhi (wahng foo-jih) (1619–1692). He had passed the provincial exams under the Ming, but marauding rebels made it impossible for him to get to Beijing to take the *jinshi* exams in 1642. After Beijing fell to the Manchus two years later, Wang joined the resistance. He raised troops in his native Hunan province and held a minor post at the court of the Ming pretender for a while, but he fell victim to factional strife and in 1650 withdrew to live as a retired scholar. Wang saw an urgent need not only to return Confucianism to its roots but also to protect Chinese civilization from the "barbarians." He insisted that it was as important to distinguish Chinese from barbarians as it was to distinguish superior men from petty men. It is natural for rulers to protect their followers from intruders: "Now even the ants have rulers who preside over the territory of their nests, and when red ants or flying white ants penetrate their gates, the ruler organizes all his own kind into troops to bite and kill the intruders, drive them far away from the anthill, and prevent foreign interference."[*] The Ming rulers had failed in this basic responsibility.

THE QING AT ITS HEIGHT

For more than a century, China was ruled by just three rulers, each of whom was hard working, talented, and committed to making the Qing Dynasty a success. The policies and institutions they put in place gave China a respite from war and disorder, and the Chinese population seems to have nearly doubled during this period, from between 150 and 175 million to between 300 and 325 million. Population growth during the course of the eighteenth century has been attributed to many factors: global warming that extended the growing season; expanded use of New World crops; slowing of the spread of new diseases that had accompanied the sixteenth-century expansion of global traffic; and the efficiency of the Qing government in providing relief in times of famine. Some scholars have recently argued that China's overall standard of living in the mid-eighteenth century was comparable to Europe's and that the standards of China's most developed regions, such as the Jiangnan region, compared favorably to the most developed regions of

---

[*]W. Theodore de Bary and Richard Lufrano, *Sources of Chinese Tradition from 1600 Through the Twentieth Century* (New York: Columbia University Press, 2000), p. 35.

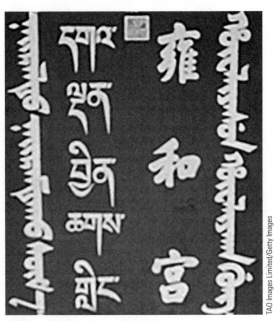

Official Languages. The Qing government issued documents in the four main languages of its realm. On this name plaque at a government-sponsored temple in Beijing, the name is given first in Manchu, then Chinese, then Tibetan, and finally Mongolian (reading from right to left).

Europe at the time, such as England and the Netherlands. Life expectancy, food consumption, and even facilities for transportation were at similar levels (see **Biography: Jiang Chun, Salt Merchant**).

Kangxi

After the Shunzhi emperor died of smallpox (which struck many Manchus after they settled in Beijing), one of his sons who had already survived the disease was selected to succeed him. Known as the Kangxi (kahng-shyee) emperor (r. 1661–1722), he lived to see the Qing Empire firmly established.

The Kangxi emperor proved adept at meeting the expectations of both the Chinese and Manchu elites. At age fourteen, he announced that he would begin ruling on his own and had his regent imprisoned. He could speak, read, and write Chinese and appreciated the value of persuading educated Chinese that the Manchus had a legitimate claim to the Mandate of Heaven. Most of the political institutions of the Ming Dynasty had been taken over relatively unchanged, including the examination system, and the Kangxi emperor worked to attract Ming loyalists

who had been unwilling to serve the Qing. He undertook a series of tours of the south, where resistance had been strongest, and held a special exam to select men to compile the official history of the Ming Dynasty.

The main military challenge the Kangxi emperor faced was the revolt of Wu Sangui and two other Chinese generals who in the early years of the conquest had been given vast tracts of land in the south as rewards for joining the Qing. Wu was made, in effect, satrap of Yunnan and Guizhou, and it was his armies that had pursued the last Ming pretender into Burma. When the Qing began to curb the power of these generals in 1673, Wu declared himself the ruler of an independent state, and the other two "feudatories" joined him. The south was not yet fully reconciled to Qing rule, but Wu, as a turncoat himself, did not attract a large following. Although it took eight years, the military structure that the Qing had put together proved strong enough to defeat this challenge. At the conclusion of these campaigns, Taiwan, where the last of the Ming loyalists had held out, was made part of Fujian province, fully incorporating it into China proper.

By annexing Mongolia, the Kangxi emperor made sure the Qing Dynasty would not have the northern border problems the Ming had faced. (See Map 16.1.) In 1696 he led an army of eighty thousand men into Mongolia, and within a few years Manchu supremacy was accepted there. Qing forces were equipped with cannons and muskets, giving them military superiority over the Mongols, who were armed with bows and arrows only. They thus could dominate the steppe cheaply, effectively ending two thousand years of northern border defense problems.

The Qing also asserted its presence in Tibet. This came about after a group of Western Mongols tried to find a new place for themselves in Tibet. The army the Qing sent after them occupied Lhasa in 1718. In the 1720s, the Qing presence in Tibet was made firm with the establishment of a permanent garrison of banner soldiers. By this time, the Qing Empire was coming into proximity of the expanding Russian Empire. In 1689 the Manchu and the Russian rulers approved a treaty—written in Russian, Manchu, Chinese, and Latin—defining their borders in Manchuria and regulating trade. Another treaty in 1727 allowed a Russian ecclesiastical mission to reside in Beijing and a caravan to make a trip from Russia to Beijing once every three years. The Russians were especially interested in securing a steady supply of tea.

BIOGRAPHY   Jiang Chun, Salt Merchant

Jiang Chun's (jyahng chun) (1725–1793) great-great-grandfather moved to Yangzhou to enter the salt trade centered there. Salt was a special commodity because the government claimed a monopoly over it and licensed merchants to transport and sell it. Salt merchants could grow exceptionally rich; it has been estimated that the twenty to thirty head merchants could pocket 50,000 to 100,000 taels of silver a year from the salt business alone. Government connections made possible the great wealth of the salt merchants, and the government regularly called on them to contribute huge sums for disaster relief, repair of the waterworks, or visits of the emperor.

As the Jiang family grew rich, many of its men pursued scholarly or official careers (often gaining positions through purchase, a legal but less prestigious route). But in each generation one man, like Jiang Chun, served as one of the head salt merchants. Although there are several biographical sketches of Jiang Chun, they say little about him as a merchant.

A description of the great sites of Yangzhou written in 1795 provides an elaborate description of Jiang Chun's garden, naming its halls, ponds, towers, terraces, and so on. In addition to discussing Jiang and his talented kinsmen, the author added notes on thirty-nine men of talent in his entourage, including scholars, painters, poets, calligraphers, physicians, musicians, connoisseurs able to authenticate antiquities, craftsmen-painters good at portraits, gardeners expert in pruning plum trees, and the architects who had designed the buildings in his garden. Some had lived in different buildings of his estate for years, sometimes decades. Jiang also kept two opera troupes, one that specialized in Kunqu (kun-chyew), the other in Huapu (hwa-poo), which was performed in the local Yangzhou accent. Jiang once organized an archery contest in his Garden of Pure Fragrance. A prominent courtesan was among the guests and scored three bull's-eyes in a row, an event other guests celebrated in poems.

The Qianlong emperor made six visits to Yangzhou on his "southern tours of inspection" (in 1751, 1757, 1762, 1765, 1780, and 1784). Jiang met him every time, and during the last four visits, Jiang hosted the imperial party at one or both of his famous gardens. In fact, the name "Garden of Pure Fragrance" was chosen by Qianlong. The emperor wrote out the three characters of the name, which Jiang then had carved in stone and placed in a special pavilion. On one of his visits, Qianlong put Jiang's seven-year-old son on his lap, patted his head, and took off an ornamental purse and gave it to the boy, which Jiang's biographer Yuan Mei (ywan may) considered an exceptional honor. In 1765, Qianlong gave Jiang Chun four sable skin pelts and two ornamental silk pouches. Jiang Chun's thank-you note has been preserved in the archives. Qianlong must have had some discussions of practical matters with Jiang Chun, because he once told the new director-general handling transport of tax grain to consult the experienced and knowledgeable Jiang Chun if he needed any advice.

In 1768 the top salt administration officials were accused of gross embezzlement and cashiered. Jiang Chun, like the other salt merchants, had to go to the capital to testify during the investigation. Qianlong, Yuan Mei tells us, was impressed by Jiang Chun's demeanor and made sure that the charges against him were dismissed. Nevertheless, by 1771, Jiang was out of money. Qianlong, we are told, personally lent him 500,000 taels as working capital (to be repaid with 10 percent annual interest).

None of Jiang Chun's children lived to adulthood. He adopted his brother's son, but that boy also died young. When Chun was on his deathbed at age sixty-nine, he selected another nephew to succeed him. After Jiang Chun died, on Qianlong's suggestion, the Yangzhou salt merchants purchased his famous garden to use as a clubhouse. The 50,000 taels they paid for the garden became his adopted son's main source of income.

Questions for Analysis
1. Why did the biographers of a merchant concentrate more on how he spent money than on how he earned it?
2. Why was meeting the emperor such an honor?

The Kangxi emperor took a personal interest in the European Jesuit priests who served at court as astronomers and cartographers and translated many European works into Chinese. However, when the pope sided with the Dominican and Franciscan orders in China who opposed allowing converts to maintain ancestral altars (known as the "rites controversy"), he objected strongly to the pope's issuing directives about how Chinese should behave. He outlawed Christian missionaries, though he did allow Jesuit scientists and painters to remain in Beijing.

The Kangxi emperor's heir ruled for twelve years as the Yongzheng (yung-juhng) emperor (r. 1723–1735), taking the throne when he was forty-five years old. A hard-working ruler, he tightened central control over the government. He oversaw a rationalization of the tax structure, substituting new levies for a patchwork of taxes and fees.

Qianlong

The Yongzheng emperor's heir, known as the Qianlong (chyen-lung) emperor (r. 1736–1795), benefited from his father's fiscal reforms, and during his reign, the Qing government regularly ran surpluses. It was during the Qianlong reign that the Qing Empire was expanded to its maximum extent, with the addition of Chinese Turkestan (the modern province of Xinjiang [shin-jyahng]). Both the Han and Tang Dynasties had stationed troops in the region, exercising a loose suzerainty, but neither Song nor Ming had tried to control the area. The Qing won the region in the 1750s through a series of campaigns against Uighur and Dzungar Mongol forces. Like Tibet, loosely annexed a few decades earlier, this region was ruled lightly. The local population kept their own religious leaders and did not have to wear the queue.

The Qianlong emperor put much of his energy into impressing his subjects with his magnificence. He understood that the Qing capacity to hold the empire together rested on their ability to speak in the political and religious idioms of those they ruled. In addition to Manchu and Chinese, he learned to converse in Mongolian, Uighur, Tibetan, and Tangut and addressed envoys in their own languages. He was as much a patron of Lamaist Buddhism as of Chinese Confucianism. He initiated a massive project to translate the Tibetan Buddhist canon into Mongolian and Manchu. He also had huge multilingual dictionaries compiled.

He had the child Dalai Lamas raised and educated in Beijing. He made much of the Buddhist notion of the "wheel-turning king" (cakravartin), the ruler who through his conquests moves the world toward the next stage in universal salvation (see Color Plate 21).

To demonstrate to the Chinese scholar-official elite that he was a sage emperor, Qianlong worked on affairs of state from dawn until early afternoon, when he turned to reading, painting, and calligraphy. He took credit for writing more than forty-two thousand poems and ninety-two books of prose. He inscribed his own poetry on hundreds of masterpieces of Chinese painting and calligraphy that he had gathered into the palace collections. He especially liked works of fine craftsmanship, and his taste influenced artistic styles of the day. The Qianlong emperor was ostentatiously devoted to his mother, visiting her daily and tending to her comfort with all the devotion of the most filial Chinese son. He took several tours down the Grand Canal to the Jiangnan (jyahng-nahn) area, in part to emulate his grandfather and in part to entertain his mother. Many of his gestures were costly. His southern tours cost ten times what the Kangxi emperor's had cost and included the construction of temporary palaces and triumphal arches.

For all these displays of Chinese virtues, the Qianlong emperor still was not fully confident that the Chinese supported his rule, and he was quick to act on any suspicion of anti-Manchu thoughts or actions (see **Documents: Fang Bao's "Random Notes from Prison"**). After more than thirty years on the throne, when rumors reached the Qianlong emperor that sorcerers were "stealing souls" by clipping the ends of men's queues, he suspected a seditious plot and had his officials interrogate men under torture until they found more and more evidence of a nonexistent plot. A few years after that episode, the Qianlong emperor carried out a huge literary inquisition. During the compilation of the *Complete Books of the Four Treasuries*, an effort to catalogue nearly all books in China, he began to suspect that some governors were holding back books with seditious content. He ordered full searches for books with disparaging references to the Manchus or previous alien conquerors. Sometimes passages were omitted or rewritten, but when the entire book was offensive, it was destroyed. So thorough was the proscription that no copies survive of more than two thousand titles.

The Qianlong emperor lived into his eighties, but his political judgment began to decline in his sixties when he began to favor a handsome and intelligent young imperial bodyguard named Heshen (huh shuhn). Heshen was rapidly promoted to posts normally held by experienced civil officials, including posts with power over revenue and civil service appointments. When the emperor did nothing to stop Heshen's blatant corruption, officials began to worry that he was becoming senile. By this time, uprisings in several parts of the country were proving difficult to suppress. Heshen supplied the Qianlong emperor with rosy reports of the progress in suppressing the rebellions, all the while pocketing much of the military appropriations himself.

The Qianlong emperor abdicated in 1795 in order not to rule longer than his grandfather, the Kangxi emperor, but he continued to dominate court until he died in 1799 at age eighty-nine.

The Banner System

The Kangxi, Yongzheng, and Qianlong emperors used the banner system to maintain military control and preserve the Manchus' privileges. In the first few decades of the Qing, as the country was pacified, banner forces were settled across China in more than ninety garrisons, usually within the walls of a city. All the Chinese who lived in the northern half of Beijing were forced out to clear the area for bannermen, and Beijing became very much a Manchu city. In other major cities, such as Hangzhou, Nanjing, Xi'an, and Taiyuan (ty-ywan), large sections were cleared for the banners' use. The bannermen became in a sense a hereditary occupational caste, ranked above others in society, whose members were expected to devote themselves to service to the state. They were also expected to live apart from nonbanner Chinese and were not allowed to intermarry with them.

Outside the cities, lands were expropriated to provide support for the garrisons, some 2 million acres altogether, with the densest area in the region around Beijing. In China proper, bannermen did not cultivate the fields (as they had in Manchuria) but rather lived off stipends from the rents, paid part in silver and part in grain. The dynasty supported banner soldiers and their families from cradle to grave, with special allocations for travel, weddings, and funerals. Once the conquest was complete, the banner population grew faster than the need for soldiers, so within a couple of generations, there were not

Image copyright © The Metropolitan Museum of Art. Image source: Art Resource, NY

Imperial Bodyguard Zhanyinbao. Dated 1760, this life-size portrait was done by a court artist in the European-influenced style favored by the Qianlong emperor.

enough positions in the banner armies for all adult males in the banners. Yet bannermen were not allowed to pursue occupations other than soldier or official. As a consequence, many led lives of forced idleness, surviving on stipends paid to relatives. By the time of the Qianlong emperor, this had become enough of a problem that he had most of the Chinese bannermen removed from the banner system and reclassified as commoners, increasing the Manchu dominance of the banner population.

Bannermen had facilitated entry into government service. Special quotas for Manchus allowed them to gain more than 5 percent of the *jinshi* degrees, even though they never exceeded 1 percent of the population. Advancement was also easier for bannermen because many posts, especially in Beijing, were reserved for them, including half of all the top posts. In the middle and lower ranks of the Beijing bureaucracy, Manchus greatly outnumbered Chinese. One

DOCUMENTS   Fang Bao's "Random Notes from Prison"

As more and more varied types of sources survive, it becomes possible to get better glimpses of the less pleasant sides of life. The ordeal of judicial confinement was hardly new to the eighteenth century, but it was not until then that we have a depiction as vivid as that provided by Fang Bao (fahng bow) (1668–1749). In 1711 he and his family members were arrested because he had written a preface for the collected works of one of his friends, and the friend's writings had just been condemned for language implying support for revival of the Ming Dynasty. After Fang spent two years in prison, he was pardoned and went on to hold a series of literary posts. Despite this brush with imperial censorship, Fang was willing in his account of his time in prison to point to the inhumane way people not yet found guilty of a crime were treated and the corruption of prison personnel, who demanded cash in exchange for better treatment.

In the prison there were four old cells. Each cell had five rooms. The jail guards lived in the center with a window in the front of their quarters for light. At the end of this room there was another opening for ventilation. There were no such windows for the other four rooms and yet more than two hundred prisoners were always confined there. Each day toward dusk, the cells were locked and the odor of the urine and excrement would mingle with that of the food and drink. Moreover, in the coldest months of the winter, the poor prisoners had to sleep on the ground and when the spring breezes came everyone got sick. The established rule in the prison was that the door would be unlocked only at dawn. During the night, the living and the dead slept side by side with no room to turn their bodies and this is why so many people became infected. Even more terrible was that robbers, veteran criminals, and murderers who were imprisoned for serious offenses had strong constitutions and only one or two out of ten would be infected and even so they would recover immediately. Those who died from the malady were all light offenders or sequestered witnesses who would not normally be subjected to legal penalties.

I said: "In the capital there are the metropolitan prefectural prison and the censorial prisons of the five wards. How is it then that the Board of Punishment's prison has so many prisoners?" [My fellow prisoner, the magistrate] Mr. Du answered: "...The chiefs and deputy heads of the Fourteen Bureaus like to get new prisoners;

study suggests that about 70 percent of the metropolitan agencies' positions were reserved for bannermen and less then 20 percent for Chinese (the rest were unspecified). In the provinces, Manchus did not dominate in the same way, except at the top level of governors and governors-general, where they held about half the posts.

Bannermen had legal privileges as well. They fell under the jurisdiction of imperial commissioners, not the local magistrate or prefect. If both a Chinese and a Manchu were brought into court to testify, the Chinese was required to kneel before the magistrate, but the Manchu could stand. If each were found guilty of the same crime, the Manchu would receive a lighter punishment—for instance, wearing the cangue (a large wooden collar) for sixty days instead of being exiled for life.

Despite the many privileges given to Manchu bannermen, impoverishment of the banner population quickly became a problem. Although the government from time to time forgave all bannermen's debts, many went bankrupt. Company commanders sometimes sold off banner land to provide stipends, which made it more difficult to provide support thereafter. The Qianlong emperor also tried resettling Manchus back in Manchuria, but those used to urban life in China rarely were willing to return to farming, and most sneaked back as soon as possible.

Within a generation of settling in China proper, bannermen were using the Chinese dialect of the Beijing

the clerks, prison officials, and guards all benefit from having so many prisoners. If there is the slightest pretext or connection they use every method to trap new prisoners. Once someone is put into the prison his guilt or innocence does not matter. The prisoner's hands and feet are shackled and he is put in one of the old cells until he can bear the suffering no more. Then he is led to obtain bail and permitted to live outside the jail. His family's property is assessed to decide the payment and the officials and clerks all split it. Middling households and those just above exhaust their wealth to get bail. Those families somewhat less wealthy seek to have the shackles removed and to obtain lodging [for the prisoner relative] in the custody sheds outside the jail. This also costs tens of silver taels. As for the poorest prisoners or those with no one to rely on, their shackles are not loosened at all and they are used as examples to warn others. Sometimes cellmates guilty of serious crimes are bailed out but those guilty of small crimes and the innocent suffer the most poisonous abuse. They store up their anger and indignation, fail to eat or sleep normally, are not treated with medicine, and when they get sick they often die.

"I have humbly witnessed our Emperor's virtuous love for all beings which is as great as that of the sages of the past ages. Whenever he examines the documents related to a case, he tries to find life for those who should die. But now it has come to this [state of affairs] for the innocent. A virtuous gentleman might save many lives if he were to speak to the Emperor saying: 'Leaving aside those prisoners sentenced to death or exiled to border regions for great crimes, should not small offenders and those involved in a case but not convicted be placed in a separate place without chaining their hands and feet?'"...

My cellmate Old Zhu, Young Yu, and a certain government official named Seng who all died of illness in prison should not have been heavily punished. There was also a certain person who accused his own son of unfiliality. The [father's] neighbors [involved in the case only as witnesses] were all chained and imprisoned in the old cells. They cried all night long. I was moved by this and so I made inquiries. Everyone corroborated this account and so I am writing this document.

Questions for Analysis

1. What gave Fang Bao the courage to report on prison conditions?
2. Does Fang suggest any solution to the prison problem? What made reform difficult?

Source: "Fang Bao's Random Notes from Prison", from *The Search for Modern China, A Documentary Collection* by Pei Kai Cheng, Michael Lestz and Jonathan Spence. Copyright © 1999 by W.W. Norton & Company, Inc. Used by permission of by W.W. Norton & Company, Inc.

area as their common language. The Qing emperors repeatedly called on the Manchus to study both spoken and written Manchu, but it became a second language learned at school rather than a primary language. Other features of Manchu culture were more easily preserved, such as the use of personal names alone to refer to people. (Manchus had names for families and clans but did not use them as part of their personal names.)

The elements of Manchu culture most important to the state were their martial traditions and their skill as horsemen and archers. Life in the cities and long stretches of peace took a toll on these skills, despite the best efforts of the emperors to inspire martial spirit. The Qianlong emperor himself was fully literate in Chinese, but he discouraged the Manchu bannermen from developing interests in Chinese culture. He knew the history of the Jin Dynasty and the problems the Jurchens had faced with soldiers living in China taking up Chinese ways, and he did everything he could think of to prevent this. Although the Qing court was as opulent as any other in Chinese history, the emperor tried to convince the bannermen that frugality was a Manchu characteristic, to be maintained if they were not to lose their ethnic identity.

Perhaps because they were favored in so many ways, the bannermen proved a very loyal service elite. Unlike their counterparts in other large empires, the banner armies never turned on the ruling house or used the resources that had been assigned to them to challenge central authority.

CONTACTS WITH EUROPE

The Qing regulated its relations with countries beyond its borders through a diplomatic system modeled on the Ming one. Countries like Korea, Ryukyu, Japan, Vietnam, and many of the other states of Southeast Asia sent envoys to the court at Beijing. Europeans were not full players in this system, but they had a marginal presence.

Trading contacts with Europe were concentrated at Guangzhou in the far south (see **Connection: Europe Enters the Scene**). Soon after 1600, the Dutch East India Company had largely dislodged the Spanish and Portuguese from the trade with China, Japan, and the East Indies. Before long, the British East India Company began to compete with the Dutch for the spice trade. In the seventeenth century, the British and Dutch sought primarily porcelains and silk, but in the eighteenth century, tea became the commodity in most demand. By the end of the century, tea made up 80 percent of Chinese exports to Europe.

In the early eighteenth century, China enjoyed a positive reputation among the educated in Europe. China was the source of prized luxuries: tea, silk, porcelain, cloisonné, wallpaper, and folding fans. The Manchu emperors were seen as wise and benevolent rulers. Voltaire wrote of the rationalism of Confucianism and saw advantages to the Chinese political system as rulers did not put up with parasitical aristocrats or hypocritical priests.

By the end of the eighteenth century, British merchants were dissatisfied with the restrictions imposed on trade by the Qing government. The Qing, like the Ming before it, specified where merchants of particular countries could trade, and the Europeans were to trade only in Guangzhou, even though tea was grown mostly in the Yangzi valley, adding the cost of transporting it south to the price the foreign merchants had to pay. The merchants in Guangzhou who dealt with Western merchants formed their own guild, and the Qing government made them guarantee that the European merchants obeyed Qing rules. As the system evolved, the Europeans had to pay cash for goods purchased and were forbidden to enter the walled city of Guangzhou, ride in sedan chairs, bring women or weapons into their quarters, and learn Chinese.

As British purchases of tea escalated, the balance of trade became more lopsided, but British merchants could not find goods that Chinese merchants would buy from them. The British government also was dissatisfied. It was becoming suspicious of the British East India Company, which had made great fortunes from its trade with China, and wanted to open direct diplomatic relations with China in part as a way to curb the company. To accomplish all this, King George III sent Lord George Macartney, the former ambassador to Russia and former governor of Madras, to China. Macartney was instructed to secure a place for British traders near the tea-producing areas, negotiate a commercial treaty, create a desire for British products, arrange for diplomatic representation in Beijing, and open Japan and Southeast Asia to British commerce as well. He traveled with an entourage of eighty-four and six hundred cases packed with British goods that he hoped would impress the Chinese court and attract trade: clocks, telescopes, knives, globes, plate glass, Wedgwood pottery, landscape paintings, woolen cloth, and carpets. The only member of the British party able to speak Chinese, however, was a twelve-year-old boy who had learned some Chinese by talking with Chinese on the long voyage.

After Lord Macartney arrived in Guangzhou in 1793, he requested permission to see the emperor in order to present a letter to him from George III. Although the letter had been written in Chinese, its language was not appropriate for addressing an emperor. Still, the British party was eventually allowed to proceed to Beijing. Once there, another obstacle emerged: when instructed on how to behave on seeing the emperor, Macartney objected to having to perform the kowtow (kneeling on both knees and bowing his head to the ground).

Finally Macartney was permitted to meet more informally with the Qianlong emperor at his summer retreat. No negotiations followed this meeting, however, because the Qing court saw no merit in Macartney's requests. It was as interested in maintaining its existing system of regulated trade as Britain was interested in doing away with it.

Several members of the Macartney mission wrote books about China on their return. These books, often illustrated, contained descriptions of many elements of Chinese culture and social customs, less rosy than the reports of the Jesuits a century or two earlier. The official account of the embassy, prepared by George Staunton, depicted Chinese women as subjugated: "Women, especially in the lower walks of life, are bred with little other principle than that of implicit obedience to their fathers or their husbands." Although the wives of the peasantry worked very hard at domestic tasks and did all the weaving in the country, they were treated badly: "Not withstanding all the merit of these helpmates to their husbands, the latter arrogate an extraordinary dominion over them, and hold them at such distance, as not always to allow them to sit at table, behind which, in such case, they attend as handmaids."[*] From books like these, Europeans began to see more of the complexity of China. The Chinese, by contrast, did not learn much about Europe or Britain from this encounter.

SOCIAL AND CULTURAL CROSSCURRENTS

During the late Ming, Chinese culture had been remarkably open and fluid. Especially in the cities of Jiangnan, new books of all sorts were being published; the theater flourished; and intellectuals took an interest in ideas of Buddhist, Daoist, or even European origin and, encouraged by Wang Yangming's teachings, pursued truth in individualistic ways.

The Conservative Turn

With the collapse of the social order in the early seventeenth century and the conquest by the Manchus, many Confucian scholars concluded that the Ming fell as a result of moral laxity. Wang Yangming and his followers, by validating emotion and spontaneity, had undermined commitment to duty and respect for authority. The solution, many thought, was to return to Zhu Xi's teachings, with their emphasis on objective standards outside the individual.

This conservative turn was manifested in several ways. Laws against homosexuality were made harsher. Because literati argued that drama and fiction were socially subversive, theaters were closed and novels banned. Qian Daxian (chyen dah-shyen), a highly learned scholar, went so far as to argue that the vernacular novel was the main threat to Confucian orthodoxy. The cult of widow chastity reached new heights, with local histories recording more and more widows who refused to remarry, including those who lived their entire lives as the celibate "widows" of men to whom they had been engaged but who had died before they had even met.

The conservative turn in scholarship fostered a new interest in rigorous textual analysis. Some Confucian scholars turned back to the Han commentaries on the classics, hoping that they could free their understandings of the texts from the contamination of Buddhist and Daoist ideas that had infiltrated Tang and Song commentaries. Others wanted to rely solely on the classics themselves and to concentrate on verifiable facts. Yan Ruoju (yen rwaw-jyu) compiled a guide to the place names in the Four Books and proved that the "old text" version of the *Book of Documents* could not be genuine. Research of this sort required access to large libraries, and it thrived primarily in Jiangnan, with its high densities of both books and scholars.

There are always those who resist calls for decorum and strenuous moral effort, and in the eighteenth century, both the Manchu rulers and the Chinese intellectual elite provided room for the less conventional to contribute in creative ways. Exploration of the potential of ink painting for self-expression reached a high point in the eighteenth century with a closely affiliated group of painters known as the Eight Eccentrics of Yangzhou (see **Material Culture: Jin Nong's Inscribed Portrait of a Buddhist Monk**). These painters had no difficulty finding patrons, even among social and cultural conservatives. Similarly, Yuan Mei, on familiar terms with the great classicists and philologists of his day, was willing to risk their censure by taking on women as poetry students. One of his female poetry students, Luo Qilan (law chee-lahn), wrote in 1797 to defend him from charges of impropriety, arguing that if Confucius had believed in the principle that women's words spoken inside a chamber must stay indoors, he would have removed poems by women from the *Book of Poetry*.

The Dream of Red Mansions

Women with poetic talents figure prominently in an eighteenth-century novel, *The Dream of Red Mansions* (also called *Story of the Stone*), considered by many the most successful of all works of Chinese fiction. Concerned with the grand themes of love and desire, money and power, life and death, and truth and illusion, it is at the same time a psychologically sensitive novel of manners. The author of the first eighty chapters was Cao Xueqin (tsow shwe-chin) (1715–1764). He died before the novel was completed, but another writer added forty chapters to complete it before it was published in 1791. Cao Xueqin came from a

---

[*]George Staunton, *An Authentic Account of an Embassy from the King of Great Britain to the Emperor of China* (London: W. Bulmer, 1798), 2:109.

MATERIAL CULTURE

Jin Nong's Inscribed Portrait of a Buddhist Monk

Chinese painters often combined words and images, sometimes inscribing poems or explanations of the occasions that gave rise to the paintings on the paintings themselves. The highly individualistic painters of the eighteenth century, known as the Eight Eccentrics of Yangzhou, sometimes carried this practice to the extreme, filling all the space on a painting with their writing. The painting shown here, by Jin Nong (jin nung) (1687–1764), is dated 1760. Writing in his highly distinctive calligraphy, Jin Nong fills the space around the Buddha with a history of the painting of images of Buddhas followed by personal remarks:

> I am now a man beyond seventy years of age who has no false ideas and desires. Though physically I am in the dusty world, I earnestly try to live cleanly. I wash my ten fingers, burn incense, and hold the brush to record the dignity and seriousness of humanity. What I do is not far from the ancient tradition. I offer good wishes to all men on earth.
>
> In the second lunar month, 1760, on the date when Buddha achieved enlightenment, I painted several Buddha images, four Bodhisattvas, sixteen Lohans, and distributed these sacred materials. These works are the product of my deep conviction, not in the style of famous masters of the Jin and Tang. My inspiration came from the Longmen caves that were carved a thousand years ago. When my priest friend, Defeng commented, "These paintings found [a new school] and will be followed by the coming generations," I roared with laughter.*

---

*Tseng Yuho, trans., *A History of Chinese Calligraphy* (Hong Kong: University of Hong Kong Press, 1993), p. 94, slightly modified.

Portrait of a Monk. This hanging scroll, painted by Jin Nong in 1760 in ink and colors on paper, measures 133 by 62.5 cm.

Tianjing Museum/Cultural Relics Press

Chinese family that had risen with the Manchus. As bondservants of the ruling house, his family was in a position to gain great wealth and power managing enterprises for the rulers. In the eighteenth century, however, the family lost favor and went bankrupt.

The *Dream* portrays in magnificent detail the affairs of the comparably wealthy Jia family. The central characters of the novel are three adolescents: Jia Baoyu (jya bow-yew) and his two female cousins of other surnames who come to live with his family. One of the cousins, Lin Daiyu (lin dy-yew), is sickly and difficult; the other, Xue Baochai (shwe bow-chy), is capable and cheerful. A magnificent garden is built in the family compound in order to receive a visit from Baoyu's sister, who had become an imperial consort. After the visit, Baoyu, his cousins, and their personal servants move into the garden, an idyllic world of youth and beauty. This magical period comes to an end when Baoyu is tricked into marrying Baochai (thinking he is marrying Daiyu). While the wedding is taking place, Daiyu is on her sickbed, dying of consumption. The novel ends with Baoyu passing the *jinshi* examinations, only to leave his wife and family to pursue religious goals.

Much of the power of *Dream* comes from the many subplots and the host of minor characters from all walks of life—officials, aristocrats, monks and nuns, pageboys, gardeners, country relatives, princes, gamblers, prostitutes, actors, and innkeepers. The seamier side of political life is portrayed through memorable cases of abuse of power. The machinations of family politics are just as vividly captured through numerous incidents in which family members compete for advantage. The maids in the family are often unable to keep the lustful men away, in the process attracting the anger of the men's wives. A concubine of Baoyu's father plots demon possession against both Baoyu and his sister-in-law, the household manager Xifeng (shee-fung). One of Baoyu's mother's maids commits suicide after Baoyu flirts with her. This incident, coupled with Baoyu's dalliance with an actor, provokes his father into administering a severe beating.

At one point Baochai notices that Daiyu has unconsciously quoted a line from a play. She then confesses that since she was seven or eight, she and the other children in her family had read plays:

> All of us younger people hated serious books but liked reading poetry and plays. The boys had got lots and lots of plays: The Western Chamber, The Lute-Player, A Hundred Yuan Plays—*just about everything you could think of. They used to read them behind our backs, and we girls used to read them behind theirs. Eventually the grown-ups got to know about it and then there were beatings and lectures and burnings of books—and that was the end of that.*[*]

---

[*]Cao Xueqin, *The Story of the Stone*, vol. 2, trans. David Hawkes (New York: Penguin Books, 1977), p. 333.

THE LESS ADVANTAGED AND THE DISAFFECTED

The eighteenth century is considered one of the most prosperous periods in Chinese history, when the government frequently ran a surplus and the population grew rapidly. General prosperity, however, did not mean that everyone benefited equally or that conflict and strife disappeared.

Qing China was both huge and economically diverse. Regions varied in density of population, types of crops grown, extent of trade, and so on. The most advanced area, with the highest level of wealth and commercial development, is generally referred to as the Jiangnan ("south of the Yangzi River") region or sometimes just as "the south." In that region, cultivation was intensive and farmers often sold much of what they grew. It was common for cultivators to rent land from absentee landlords for fixed cash amounts, agreed to in written contracts. In most places in north China, a majority of the farmers owned their own land, but their farms were often tiny, and they might well be no richer than tenant farmers in the south. There were also differences within regions between core areas centered on major cities and more peripheral areas, where population density was much lower because the land was harder to farm. During the course of the eighteenth century, as the population grew, people pushed into these peripheral areas, clearing upland areas and moving to the frontiers, in the process often pushing out aboriginal peoples who had lived in the area for centuries. New World crops, such as sweet potatoes, white potatoes, peanuts, and tobacco, made possible exploitation of land previously rejected as too hilly or infertile.

Villages all across China were "open," not closed corporate villages as in Japan (see Chapter 17). That is, villages held no land in common and had little say in who could buy or sell land or houses there. Because small farmers could easily fall into debt and sell or mortgage all or part of their land, the wealth of village families could vary markedly. Families whose land was not adequate for their support often put effort into sideline work—their women and children weaving mats and baskets, for instance. During the winter, when there was little work to be done in the fields, the men might go into nearby towns to look for temporary jobs.

In some parts of the country, single-surname villages were common, with all males descended from a common patrilineal ancestor who had set-tled in the area centuries earlier. In those cases, vil-lage organization and lineage organization would overlap, with the lineage ancestral hall serving as the center of village life. In villages or clusters of villages where families with several surnames lived, the temple to a local god often served as the focus for communal activities.

Villages were connected to each other through marriages and marketing. Villagers normally mar-ried people from another village, so their mother's brothers and sisters and their father's sisters would reside in other local villages. Men and boys made regular trips to market towns, sometimes several hours away by foot, in order to sell agricultural sur-plus and buy needed tools or foodstuffs such as salt and oil. Farmers also needed to cooperate across village lines in order to maintain water-control sys-tems, whether the diking of rivers prone to flood-ing or the diverting of water into irrigation canals or reservoirs. For projects of this sort, the local village heads might get together, or each village might be represented by several of its larger landowners. Written agreements would be drawn up recording what the different parties had pledged to do. When one party thought another was diverting more water than agreed upon, a complaint could be taken to the county magistrate to adjudicate.

By Qing times, there was relatively little in the way of legal status distinctions among the rural pop-ulation. Slavery was insignificant (a contrast with Korea), and there were no nationwide outcast groups (a contrast with Japan). But that does not mean that there was no discrimination. In certain localities, particular groups might be treated as lower than commoners—such as the so-called Boat People in Guangdong and the Duomin (daw-min) in Zhejiang who worked as musicians, funeral managers, and yamen runners. In addition, ethnic differences were a common basis for discrimination. Throughout the south, local indigenous peoples—called Miao, Yao, Zhuang, and many other names—were often exploited and treated with contempt.

The routine of village life was from time to time disrupted by calamity, most often in the form of too little or too much water—flooding or drought. North China was particularly subject to drought, though occasionally heavy rains led to breaks in the dikes along the Yellow River, leading to devastat-ing floods. In the drainage area of the Yangzi River, floods were more common than droughts.

When lack of rain ruined a harvest, better-off farmers might be able to hold out till the next har-vest, but those without much in the way of reserves would have to try other strategies—ranging from pawning their clothes, tools, and land, to foraging for edible plants in forests, to sending out able-bodied men to look for work in nearby towns, to the entire family's taking to the roads in search of food. When a drought lasted through two harvests or covered a large geographical area, the numbers of refugees on the road would swell. Bands of hungry men might well seize the grain stores of the rich or crops in the field. Starving peasants would also de-scend on cities, expecting local officials to open soup kitchens and refugee camps. The lack of sanitation in these camps, coupled with the weakened condi-tion of the refugees, made it all too easy for epidem-ics to spread, adding to the famine's death toll.

Bad harvests hurt townsfolk as well because they led to rapid escalation in the price of food. Understanding the law of supply and demand, towns-people would gather to prevent merchants from send-ing their grain to areas with severe shortages, fearing price rises. They would also protest officials who did not keep government granaries open long enough to bring down prices. Sometimes officials called on troops to quell these sorts of food riots.

The Qing government was remarkably successful in curbing the death toll of major famines by care-ful administration of granaries and provision of di-rect relief. Its success contributed to the rapid rise in population in the eighteenth century.

This population growth, coupled with the prac-tice of partible inheritance, led to the proliferation of farms too small to support a family. In addition, many men could not marry because of a shortage of marriageable women—caused not only by the rich taking extra women as concubines but also by sex-selective infanticide practiced by poor families unwilling to rear another daughter. Men with little or no land and unable to marry commonly would leave their villages in search of work. Some would travel with their tools to do carpentry or farm work. Others found jobs pulling the boats that carried grain up the Grand Canal or working in cities as dock-hands, sedan chair carriers, or night-soil collectors. When copper mines were opened in the southwest, unemployed men traveled long distances to get work as miners. Both the government and settled villagers were wary of these rootless men. They were quick to suspect strangers when crimes occurred.

Single men often found support in groups called brotherhoods or secret societies. The best known of these brotherhoods was called the Heaven and Earth Society, but other names were also used, such as the Three Harmonies Society or the Three Dots Society. (In English they are often called the Triads.) To marginalized men, the attraction was security, mutual aid, and empowerment. Drawing on ideas from Daoism and popular religion, the groups promised access to supernatural powers through rituals and cultivation. Appearing first in the 1760s, the Heaven and Earth Society spread quickly through Taiwan, Fujian, Jiangxi, Guangdong, and Guangxi (gwahng-shee). Government functionaries and urban workers were among their members. The societies were explicitly anti-establishment in that they espoused a rhetoric of "overthrow the Qing and restore the Ming." Members away from home could get in touch with members elsewhere through secret signals or passwords. Lodge brothers helped each other with loans, funeral costs, and lawsuits. Lodges would arbitrate disputes between members and mete out punishments for cheating at gambling and other offenses. But their morality was not Confucian. Many lodges controlled gambling, narcotics, prostitution, and smuggling in their region. The first uprising led by the Heaven and Earth Society occurred in the 1780s in Taiwan, after which the Qing government tried without much success to suppress the society.

The Qing government was also wary of the White Lotus Society, which drew on folk Buddhist teachings that dated back to the Song period. This society had been an important element in the rebellions at the end of the Yuan Dynasty. It was not approved by regular Buddhist clergy because of its syncretic teachings, married clergy, and noncanonical scriptures. It incorporated millenarian doctrines derived from both Manichaeism and the Buddhist idea of the future Maitreya Buddha who would usher in an era of peace. Its central deity was the Eternal Mother, the original progenitor of all humankind. Grieving that her earthly children had lost their way, she wanted to bring them back to the Original Home, identified with nirvana. She sent Buddhas to earth to teach people the true way to salvation. When the end was near, floods, fires, and winds would destroy everyone who lacked faith in the Eternal Mother. Adherents were taught that repeating the mantra "Eternal Progenitor in Our Original Home in the World of True Emptiness" would bring blessings and protection from calamities. Martial arts

exercises and breathing techniques that circulated *qi* were also taught as other ways to cure illnesses and promote health.

White Lotus teachings had particular appeal to women, who were welcomed as members on the same terms as men. When leaders were arrested or executed, often their wives took over. A Qing official whose city was seized by White Lotus forces described the woman who led the local group:

> When she emerges in a home, five or six young women will hold tobacco bags and towels for her, and she will be seated at the center of the hall. Both men and women make obeisance: the man puts the palm of his right hand on the back of his left hand and the woman, the palm of her left hand on the back of her right hand. They kowtow in reverence.*

The White Lotus sect survived repeated attempts by the government to suppress it, probably because local congregations did not depend on a central establishment. The sect was especially strong in the central provinces, from Sichuan and Shaanxi to Shandong. Itinerant prophets and teachers carried the message to new places. Leaders of these sects often combined talk of salvation with martial arts and herbal healing. In 1774 a White Lotus leader in Shandong convinced his followers that he was the Future Buddha and that his techniques would make them invulnerable, even though they were armed only with spears. They were able to capture several small towns before the Qing sent in massive armies to quell them.

Many White Lotus adherents were pious vegetarians who tried to live good lives. An offshoot of the White Lotus called the Luo sect established a mission to help canal boatmen far from their homes who normally had no means of support for several months in the winter. The sect set up hostels in Suzhou and Hangzhou where the boatmen could stay for free and could get meals on credit, to be repaid when they were paid in advance for the next year's work. Because many of these men were never able to marry, the hostels also served as retirement homes for elderly boatmen. The Qing government, however, was deeply suspicious and had all the hostels destroyed.

---

*Cited in Kwang-ching Liu, "Religion and Politics in the White Lotus Rebellion of 1796 in Hubei," in *Heterodoxy in Late Imperial China*, ed. K. Liu and R. Shek (Honolulu: University of Hawaii Press, 2004), pp. 295–296.

In 1793 the Qing government initiated a major investigation of White Lotus congregations, which soon had to take up arms to protect themselves from predatory elements in the local government. In 1796 open revolt began in Hubei and soon spread to Sichuan and Shaanxi. White Lotus forces held fortified villages and towns, and they used those bases to raid larger cities. Armed bands often joined them—martial arts groups and bandits alike. It took the government more than eight years to fully annihilate White Lotus forces.

Non-Han ethnic groups constituted another segment of society that often felt aggrieved. As the Han Chinese population swelled, more and more settlers moved into Miao (myow) territories, often expropriating Miao land. The Miao aborigines put up fierce resistance beginning in the 1720s, and officials repeatedly tried to find ways to separate the Miao and the Han settlers, but with little success. In 1795 there was a great revolt of Miao along the Hunan-Guizhou border, where a Han ethnic group called the Hakka had recently been moving in. The Qing government found the Miao uprisings to be as difficult to suppress as the concurrent White Lotus ones.

SUMMARY

The Qing Dynasty was founded by the Manchus, the new name given to the descendants of the Jurchens of the Jin Dynasty, which had held north China before the rise of the Mongols. In the late sixteenth and early seventeenth centuries, the Manchus organized a strong state outside the Ming borders. They organized their armies into divisions called "banners" as a way to limit the importance of tribal affiliations; in addition to Manchu banners, there were also Mongol and Chinese banners. After a Ming general asked the Manchus to help suppress the rebels who had captured Beijing, the Manchus not only took the capital but went on to conquer the rest of the country.

Many of the Chinese educated elite alive during the conquest did everything in their power to resist the Manchus in deep dread of another "barbarian" dynasty. Yet the Manchus proved to be very different sorts of rulers than the Mongols had been. For more than a century, from 1662 to 1795, three very competent emperors reigned, the Kangxi, Yongzheng, and Qianlong emperors. They presided over a huge expansion of the empire with victories over the Mongols and Tibetans. They depended on Chinese officials and soldiers to help administer their empire, but they perfected ways to ensure that the Manchus would maintain their dominance. These included special quotas and legal privileges for bannermen and the requirement that they live separately from the Chinese. Mastery of reading and writing in Manchu was strongly encouraged, but in time most Manchus living in China came to use Chinese more than Manchu.

In an effort to win over the Chinese elite, the Manchu rulers made a point to patronize Chinese culture, and many facets of Chinese culture thrived during this period, ranging from historical research to manufacturing technology. However, the Manchu rulers were highly sensitive to ethnic slights, which may have made Chinese in high office especially cautious. In intellectual circles, the spontaneity and openness of the late Ming gave way to a more conservative turn. The cult of widow chastity reached such extremes that girls whose fiancés had died would commit themselves to stay chaste their entire lives as "widows" of men they had not yet married. Some scholars even argued that fiction was a threat to the Confucian social order. Fortunately, they did not succeed in suppressing fiction; to the contrary, perhaps the greatest Chinese novel was written in the eighteenth century, *The Dream of Red Mansions*.

In the early eighteenth century, interest in China was widespread in Europe. Not only was the taste for tea growing steadily, but taste for things Chinese extended to silk, porcelain, and even wallpaper. China's political system was viewed positively because it seemed to be a land where government was in the hands of the educated, rather than an aristocracy or a church hierarchy.

The standard of living in the eighteenth century was high, and the population was growing. The Qing government contributed to population growth through its efforts to deal with famines caused by droughts and floods. As the number of people who wanted to farm increased, more and more people moved into peripheral areas, both upland and along the frontiers, often displacing the original inhabitants, such as the Miao or Yao. New World crops such as potatoes and peanuts made possible exploitation of land previously considered unsuited to agriculture. Those who could not support themselves by farming found jobs pulling boats on the Grand Canal, working in mines, or sought work in cities as dockworkers.

Benefits were not spread evenly, of course, and as in prior periods, many people struggled. The marginalized and disaffected were particularly likely to join secret societies such as the Heaven and Earth Society (Triads) or religious sects such as the White Lotus Society. The Qing government from time to time tried to suppress these societies, which were often anti-establishment.

How different was China in 1800 than in 1600? By 1800, China had been under alien rule for a century and a half. Most Chinese of all social levels had gotten used to the Manchus, who administered the country through institutions much like those earlier Chinese dynasties had employed. The geographic scope of the empire was much bigger: for the first time, China was administered as part of the same polity as Tibet and Xinjiang. The population was significantly larger, probably reaching at least 300,000 by 1800. Culture was more conservative than it had been in the last decades of the Ming Dynasty, with standards of proper behavior more rigid. Contact with Europe was increasing, to a large extent because Europeans wanted to buy China's tea, silk, and porcelains, but few people in China were aware of these trade relations.

Edo Japan
(1603–1800)

The social and political order imposed by the Tokugawa shoguns consolidated trends long in the making. The creation of villages as corporate communities and the warlord domains, the separation of samurai from commoners, and the growth of and restrictions on commerce all began in the late sixteenth century. The structure of family life, in particular, eldest sons taking all and the custom of brides serving their husbands' families, continued practices already apparent in the fourteenth century. Yet peace also made possible cottage industries that some historians deem proto-industrialization, unprecedented urbanization, and a flourishing of theater, fiction, poetry, and intellectual life.

What distinguished the Tokugawa shogunate from previous military regimes? What were the consequences of the political settlement for economic and demographic growth? To what extent did the shoguns' efforts to restrict foreign contact isolate Japan? What did samurai do without battles to fight? How did urban and rural commoners make their presence felt?

TOKUGAWA SETTLEMENT (SEVENTEENTH CENTURY)

Land surveys and separation of warriors from the land were aimed at ordering society. The Tokugawa brought an end to the conflicts caused by rivalry between brothers by insisting on primogeniture (eldest son inheritance) for the military ruling class and confiscating domains torn apart by succession disputes. As a result, a daimyo's personality and competence mattered less than his office, and the retainers' loyalty focused on the position, not the individual. The monarch and his court lived, according to the popular saying, "above the clouds" in Kyoto. Samurai stood at the top of the official status order, followed by commoners in order of their contributions to society. In principle no one was to change residence or status, nor was marriage permitted across status lines. In reality, status boundaries were fluid. Because changing names changed identity, a commoner woman took an aristocratic name when serving a military household.

Actors and prostitutes became celebrities, and the exclusive right to work with animal skins made some outcasts wealthy.

Tokugawa Social Hierarchy

Core Social Statuses	Other Social Groups (Between Statuses)	Outcasts
Samurai	Priests	Blind Female
Farmers	Doctors	Entertainers
Artisans	Monks	Beggars
Merchants		Prostitutes
		Actors
		Non-Humans *(Hinin)*
		Polluted Ones
		(Kawata)

This status order restricted rural communities to farmers. In the seventeenth century, most villages had at least one dominant family, often descended from a warrior who had returned to the land, which monopolized the position of headman. A council of elders of landholding farmers provided a sounding board for matters related to village affairs. Their households included family members, house servants, and field workers. In central and eastern Japan, complex lineage systems with multiple branches complicated relations within villages. Across Japan, social, economic, and political inequality structured village life. The men who claimed descent from village founders expected to be treated with deference; they claimed the largest and best fields and they dominated village politics. Their wives shared their prestige; a male of lesser standing had to treat such women with respect.

Villages divided up the countryside. A village contained residential plots, rice paddies, and dry fields, each assigned to households. In some regions agricultural lands periodically rotated from family to family. These families cooperated in doing the heavy work of leveling rice paddies and building dikes, managing irrigation networks, and transplanting rice seedlings into the paddies. Women performed this last backbreaking task in a carryover of medieval religious beliefs that sanctified it as a fertility ritual (see Color Plate 18). Beyond this basic level, each household was on its own. Village boundaries also enclosed wastelands and forests, with access to their products regulated by the village council. As a corporation led by the headman, the village was collectively responsible for paying taxes, both the yearly tribute measured in units of rice (*koku*—1 *koku* equals 5.1 bushels of rice, the amount needed to feed one man for a year) and various additional taxes—for example, fees for the privilege of exploiting forest resources.

Villages constituted the building blocks of domains ruled by daimyo. The shogun had the largest domain concentrated chiefly in eastern and central Japan, totaling approximately one-fourth of the total agricultural base. Vassal daimyo (*fudai*) were hereditary retainers who governed domains and also served as the shogun's chief advisers and his first line of defense against potential foes. According to a decree of 1634, only vassals whose domains contained more than 10,000 *koku* enjoyed the status of daimyo. The shogun's retainers with smaller fiefs, often made up of parcels in several villages, were called *hatamoto* (HAH-tah-moe-toe) ("beneath the banner"). In addition, the shogun commanded the services of thousands of housemen who received stipends from the shogun's warehouses. Daimyo who had been shogun Tokugawa Ieyasu's rivals or peers were deemed outside lords (*tozama*, TOE-zah-mah). Fewer in number than the vassal daimyo, the mightiest controlled large domains that functioned almost as nations. Some of Ieyasu's descendants also numbered among the daimyo. They were neither wealthy nor politically powerful, but they enjoyed great prestige. All daimyo, who numbered between 250 and 280, had retainer bands to be supported and employed.

Government

The government pieced together by the Tokugawa shoguns developed an elaborate bureaucracy (later called a *bakufu*—tent government). The senior councilors—four to five men who rotated on a monthly basis, each of them a vassal daimyo worth at least 30,000 *koku*—took responsibility for policy decisions, personnel matters, and supervising the daimyo. Their assistants, also vassal daimyo, handled matters relating to the shogun's retainers. The *hatamoto* staffed the administration, beginning with the magistrates in charge of finances, cities, and temples and shrines. Finance magistrates supervised the district administrators responsible for seeing that the villagers paid their taxes and keeping peace in the countryside. They also managed the increasingly futile task of balancing expenditures with income. Their staff, and those of the other magistrates, included an array of functionaries, guards, and servants. Although the shogun had reduced the size of his army in the seventeenth century, he was never able to provide more than part-time employment to his retainers; 42 percent of *hatamoto* (1,676 in 1829) served in the fatigue regiment, the default category for men without office. Each daimyo likewise had more advisers, accountants, liaison officers, attendants, tax collectors, doctors, teachers, guards, servants, and placeholders than he needed.

The shogunal and domainal governments developed the most complex, sophisticated, and coherent bureaucracies Japan had ever seen. Retainers learned to wield a brush as well as a sword, understand high finance, and accustom themselves to routinized office jobs, but administrative systems also retained non-modern elements. The shogun bestowed his former family name of Matsudaira on important *fudai* and *tozama* daimyo, both as an honor and as a reminder that rulers were kin. Opportunities for promotion depended on hereditary rank; men born of guards stayed guards. The senior councilors may have been policy experts, but they were also the shogun's vassals. Their duties included watching him perform rites to his ancestors, lecture on the Chinese classics, and dance in Nō. When he left the castle to go hawking or to visit one of them, they and their retainers had to attend him. The shogun maintained a large staff of palace women ordered in a female bureaucracy to serve him, his wife, and his mother in the great interior (*ōoku*, OH-oh-ku). Their responsibilities included a yearly round of ceremonies and managing gift exchanges with the Kyoto court and daimyo families.

Although the daimyo ran their domains as they saw fit, the shogunate started to issue decrees to regulate their behavior in 1615. It limited the number of guns allowed per castle and restricted castle repairs. The daimyo were not to harbor criminals, collude against the shogun, or marry without the shogun's permission. They all had to contribute men and money to the shogun's building projects, and they could be relocated from one domain to another at the shogun's pleasure. Most important, the shogunate

issued increasingly strict guidelines governing the daimyo's attendance on the shogun. Known as *sankin kōtai* (SAHN-keen CO-tah-e) and formalized in 1635, this system required that each daimyo spend half of his time in his domain and half in the shogun's capital at Edo. Each daimyo's wife and heir had to live in Edo as hostages. Designed to keep the daimyo both loyal to the shogun and effective in local administration, the system counteracted the dispersal of retainers that had weakened the Kamakura regime and the competition among men at the center of power that had destroyed the Ashikaga. *Sankin kōtai* also had the unintended consequence of stimulating trade, encouraging travel, and promoting cultural exchange.

The shogunate took certain national responsibilities for itself. It refurbished the highway system with post stations and checkpoints to keep guns out of Edo and female hostages in. For its own defense, it forbade the building of bridges over major rivers. It oversaw the development of coastal shipping routes, took over the mines for precious metals, and minted copper, silver, and gold coins. In a boon for historians, it established an official handwriting style for documents. It forbade the practice of Christianity and set up a nationwide system of temple registration to ensure compliance. In 1635 it forbade Japanese to travel overseas and banned foreign books. Four years later it regulated relations with the West by allowing only the Dutch to trade at Nagasaki while oversight of trade and diplomacy with neighboring countries was delegated to three domains: Satsuma for the Ryukyus, Tsushima (TUZ-she-mah) for Korea, and Matsumae (MAH-tzu-mah-eh) for the Ainu and the north. The shogunate supervised trade with China that took place at Nagasaki; it had less control over Chinese goods that arrived indirectly through the Ryukyus and Hokkaido.

Under the Tokugawa regime, people from the Ryukyu Islands found themselves forced into much closer proximity to Japan. An independent kingdom with tributary ties to China as well as to Japan in the sixteenth century, the Ryukyus suffered invasion by Satsuma in 1609. Although the king survived and trade with China continued, he had to surrender control over his islands' diplomatic and economic affairs, and that harmed the islanders' well-being. Intellectuals in the Ryukyus tried to craft a new identity by claiming that although they were politically subordinate to Japan, they achieved moral parity

Ainu Feeding a Hawk. This mid-nineteenth-century drawing of an Ainu feeding a hawk depicts the bird as being almost as large as its captor. The Ainu is stereotypically hairy with full beard and heavy eyebrows.

with both Japan and China by cultivating the way of the Confucian sage.

Relations with the Ainu in Hokkaido evolved differently. There the shogunate had the Matsumae family with long-standing ties to the region establish a domain on the island's southern tip in return for the privilege of monopolizing trade with the Ainu. In 1669 conflict between Ainu tribes over access to game and fish escalated into a war to rid Hokkaido of the Japanese. Following its vicious suppression, the Ainu and the Japanese solidified distinct ethnic identities that incorporated elements of the other— eagle feathers and otter pelts for the Japanese ruling class and ironware, rice, and saké for the Ainu. Between 1590 and 1800, the Ainu became increasingly dependent on trade with Japan for their survival, while occasional epidemics brought by traders ravaged their population. Many ended up working as contract laborers in fisheries that shipped food and fertilizer to Japan.

The Tokugawa shogunate survived for more than 250 years not simply because it dominated Japan militarily but because, like sixteenth-century conquerors, Ieyasu and his heirs recognized the importance of ideology in transforming power into authority. Oda Nobunaga had claimed that he acted on behalf of the realm, not his private, selfish interests.

Running his domain became public administration (*kōgi*). He also built a shrine to himself. Hideyoshi actively promoted a cult to his own divinity.

The title given Ieyasu after his death transformed him into the "Buddha incarnate as the sun god of the east." Enshrined at Nikkō, he protected the shogunate from evil spirits and worked for the good of all people. (See Map 17.1.) The third shogun Iemitsu (E-eh-me-tzu) claimed that the just social order ruled by shogunate followed the way of heaven (*tendō*, TEHN-doe). This way is natural, unchanging, eternal, and hierarchical. The ruler displays the benevolence of the Buddha, the warrior preserves the peace, and the commoners are obedient. The fifth shogun, Tsunayoshi (TZU-nah-yo-she), tried to domesticate the warriors by codifying mourning rituals, lecturing on Confucian classics, and forbidding the killing of animals, especially dogs (used for target practice). His successor reversed this last item, and the eighth shogun, Yoshimune (YO-she-mu-neh), sought to revive the martial arts. One aim of later reforms between 1787 and 1793 was to recalibrate the balance between brush and sword, suggesting that, for samurai, how to follow the way of heaven was not self-evident.

Agricultural Transformations and the Commercial Revolution

Farmers, merchants, artisans, and rulers quickly exploited the peace dividend. Large- and small-scale land reclamation projects, often funded by merchants at a daimyo's urging, opened new rice paddies and expanded arable land by 45 percent. Rivers were diked and new channels dug to bring irrigation water to fields. Countless building projects, partly to repair the ravages of war in Kyoto but mainly to build the daimyo mansions, shogunal palaces, and merchant quarters in the new capital at Edo and the castle towns, seriously depleted forests. By the end of the seventeenth century, floods sweeping down denuded mountains threatened hard-won fields. The shogunate tried to regulate the use of forestry products, but the agricultural base continued to press against ecological limits. (See **Material Culture: Night Soil.**)

The introduction of better seeds and new crops intensified the use of land and labor. Detailed observations of soil types and climatic conditions led to the development of rice varieties suited for specific local conditions. Fast-ripening rice spread

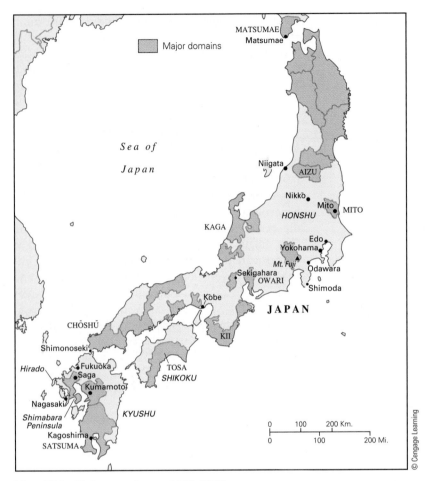

Map 17.1   Tokugawa Japan, 1600–1868

cultivation into the marginal lands of the northeast. Farther south, it allowed the sowing of a second crop, often wheat, although some paddies in Kyushu supported two rice crops a year. As in China and Korea, corn, tobacco, and sweet potatoes, products of the New World, became dry field staples along with barley and millet. In a trend that continued throughout the Tokugawa period, seventeenth-century agricultural experts traveled Japan building social networks of like-minded experimenters, seeking the most advanced methods for increasing crop yields, and spreading their findings through books.

Farmers also grew cash crops and developed products based on Chinese technology. The spread of cotton growing in western Japan beginning in the sixteenth century reduced the hours women had to spend preparing cloth for their families while revolutionizing clothing and bedding. During the seventeenth century, Japan imported Chinese silk and sugar. By the 1730s for silk and the 1830s for sugar, domestic production provided substitutes. The daimyo competed in developing products for export by hiring teachers to show farmers how to harvest lacquer, make paper, and raise silkworms and promoting distinctive styles of wooden combs, paper hair ties, and pottery. Merchants supplied the capital to farmers who provided the labor, although a few rural entrepreneurs profited from distributing raw materials and transporting goods. Lights fueled by rapeseed oil enabled work to continue after dark. Increases in agricultural productivity spurred demand for nonagricultural goods. The growth of cottage industries diversified income sources and led

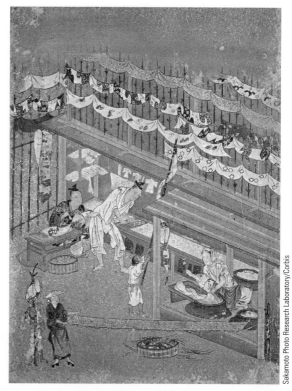

Artisans. Cottage industries relied on families. Both the pattern dyers depicted on the screen to the right and the weavers shown on the screen to the left employed men and women, children and grandparents.

to a virtuous cycle of interaction between agriculture and manufacturing. Neither entrepreneurs nor domains tried to set up large-scale production units. Instead they emphasized quality and variety, trying to beat the competition by producing regional specialties found nowhere else.

The agricultural and commercial revolutions meant higher per capita productivity and a trend toward smaller families. After almost a threefold increase in the seventeenth century, Japan's population remained surprisingly stagnant in contrast to the populations of China and Korea at the same time. In villages the extended families characteristic of earlier times broke down into main families and branches or landlords and tenants. Most households cultivated parcels just big enough to support a stem family of grandparents, parents, and children without enough to bestow on more than one heir. Historians have supposed that farmers practiced abortion and infanticide lest they have more children than they could afford. Even if the sole son died, the ease of adoption

meant that a family could usually find someone to carry on the family line. Other factors were also at work. Men often left their homes for months at a time to work in towns and cities, especially during the winter. The female age at marriage went up in central Japan because women increasingly worked to gain experience before settling down. Disease mattered: Smallpox can reduce male fertility by 50 percent. Syphilis struck urban populations. Periodic famines hit some regions harder than others. In the early nineteenth century, population decline in the impoverished northeast offset growth in the more commercially developed and prosperous west.

One characteristic of Japan's early modern growth was that while labor remained in the countryside, capital largely concentrated in cities. Not until the late eighteenth century did rural entrepreneurs acquire significant amounts of capital, and they often depended on urban merchants for financial backing. Daimyo traveling on *sankin kōtai* marketed rice they collected in taxes to merchants

MATERIAL CULTURE

Night Soil

A large city produces huge quantities of human waste, but the Edo city government left the disposal of this waste in the hands of individual landlords. Members of the ruling class contracted with nearby villages to bring vegetables to their compounds and remove garbage. Communal toilet facilities in each commoner ward also had to be cleaned.

In the eighteenth century, farmers began to plant crops where once they had foraged for green fertilizer, forcing them to look outside their communities for ways to improve the soil. Vegetable farmers near Edo carted away night soil and other organic wastes to supplement the manure they produced themselves. Separated into solids and liquid and cooked in its own heat to kill harmful bacteria, night soil became a valuable commodity.

Starting in the late eighteenth century, townspeople expected farmers to pay for the privilege of collecting night soil. Landlords insisted that tenants use their toilets and tried to sell their product to the highest bidder. Transactions between subcontractors, wholesalers, and middlemen so raised costs that farmers formed regional alliances to petition the shogunate to keep prices down.

The price placed on night soil reflected status inequality. Landlords segregated toilets by sex because men's excrement was valued more highly than women's. Samurai received more for theirs than did commoners. An eighteenth-century farmhouse had a toilet for samurai made of polished wood. The tenant farmers and family members used an open pit.

Photos: Patricia Ebrey

Toilets. The photo on the left depicts a toilet for the use of samurai officials next to the formal reception room at a village headman's house. On the opposite side behind the stable is the pit for family and servants (right).

---

in Osaka who advanced them money and letters of credit. Redeemable at the merchant's branch in Edo, these letters served as Japan's first paper money. Domains later printed their own currency, modeled on religious talismans to gain users' trust. Merchants either advanced the money to make specialty products or bought them at a discount to sell to urban consumers. Some merchants acted as suppliers to daimyo and their women, stimulating the desire for high-quality labor-intensive goods. Others catered to the broader market by selling cotton cloth, lamp oil, and soy sauce. At the end of the seventeenth

century, a few Osaka and Edo merchants had become extremely wealthy, and a number of daimyo found themselves deeply in debt.

Urban Life and Culture

Edo's layout mirrored the shogun's strategic concerns. Taking advantage of advances in fortification technology, the shogun's castle was enclosed behind multiple stone walls surrounded by moats. The shogunate drained the swamp on which the city was built through canals that provided

Color Plate 17
Noh Robe. Fabric and design signaled age, status, and gender. Designed to reflect torch light, the silver triangles on this eighteenth-century robe signified that the actor played the role of a demon serpent.

Color Plate 18
Rice Planting. This sixteenth-century painting of Rice Planting depicts it as a fertility festival with men providing the music while women work.

Color Plate 19
The Garden of the Master of Nets. A large pond is the central feature of the Garden of the Master of Nets in Suzhou. Notice the use of plants, rocks, and walkways.

Color Plate 20
Arrival of the Portuguese. This six-panel folding screen depicts the Arrival of the Portuguese—soldiers in short pants, merchants in balloon pants, and priests in black robes accompanied by African servants.

Color Plate 21
The Qianlong Emperor Receiving Tribute Horses. This detail from a 1757 painting by the Italian court painter Giuseppe Castiglione (1688–1768) shows the reception of envoys from the Kazakhs. Note how the envoy, presenting a pure white horse, is kneeling to the ground (performing the kowtow).

Color Plate 22
Dry Goods Store in Surugacho. In this painting entitled Dry Goods Store in Surugacho, Edo, customers take off their shoes to enter the shop. Male clerks serve female customers while others gather around the manager. The owner is at the back of the store.

Color Plate 23
Inlaid Stationary Box.
This fifteenth-century
box is an example of the
very fine lacquerware
produced in Joseon
Korea inlaid with
mother-of-pearl in a
floral design.

Color Plate 24
Women at the Tano
Festival, by Sin
Yunbok (1758–?),
Joseon Dynasty. This
painting captures
the eroticism that is
frequently associated
with Sin Yunbok's
depiction of women.
Notice the two boy
monks stealing a glance
at the women from
behind the rocks.

transportation for goods and people. Bridges over moats were faced with guardhouses, forcing the traveler to make a sharp turn, and no roads led directly to the castle. Vassal daimyo and the shogun's retainers lived nearby, providing another ring of protection. The wealthy *tozama* daimyo had large compounds containing barracks for their retainers, storehouses, mansions, and gardens. None was allowed moats and stone walls, and compounds for the vassal daimyo surrounded them. Each daimyo maintained multiple compounds; the total number was more than one thousand. The ruling class took the healthful high ground for itself, leaving the lowlands directly east and south of the castle for commoners. Scattered throughout the city were shrines and temples. Daimyo castle towns followed a similar pattern of segregating people according to status and occupation.

The seventeenth century saw an unprecedented jump in urban growth, from little more than 1 percent of Japan's population to almost 15 percent after 1700. In addition to the castle towns were three metropolises: Kyoto became a manufacturing center for luxury goods, Osaka served as Japan's chief market, and Edo's swollen population of daimyo and bureaucrats made it a consumption center. Urbanization stimulated the growth of commercial publishing that created and fed a reading public hungry for knowledge and amusement. It provided space for exhibitions from religious icons to plants and flowers and for private salons where scholars, artists, and writers met patrons. Urban residents paid for services—hairdressing, entertainment—that had once been provided by servants. They bought processed food and cloth that their ancestors had made themselves. Labor and leisure were oriented toward the market, and buying finished products saved time. This transformation stimulated a consumption revolution—the increased demand for a greater variety of goods, from durable luxury items such as carved wooden transoms placed above doors to drug foods such as saké and tobacco.

Unprecedented urban prosperity culminated in the Genroku (GEHN-row-ku) era (1688–1704), the heyday of townsman culture, justly celebrated in art and literature. Ihara Saikaku wrote stories about the samurai passion for boys, but most of his works focused on the townspeople in books such as *Five Women Who Loved Love* and *The Life of an Amorous Man*. He also wrote books on how to make and keep money.

(See **Documents: Ihara Saikaku's "Sensible Advice on Domestic Economy."**) Matsuo Bashō (MAH-tzu-oh BAH-show) raised the seventeen-syllable verse form known as haiku (HAH-e-ku) to a fine art, in the process making poetry accessible to commoners in town and country. Passing by a battlefield, he wrote: "A thicket of summer grass, all that remains of warriors' dreams."[*] Chikamatsu Monzaemon (CHE-kah-mah-tzu MOAN-zah-eh-moan) wrote scripts for the puppet theater that explored the interplay between social obligations and human feeling, as when a young man in love with a prostitute wants to buy her out of her contract with a brothel owner but lacks the money to do so without ruining his family's business. Caught between love and duty, the couple resolves the dilemma by committing double suicide. Although Chikamatsu wrote for puppets, the literary artistry of his scripts endeared them to amateur performers and raised the quality of theatrical performances.

Two pleasure zones are associated with the Genroku era: the brothel district and the theaters, often located near each other on the margins of respectable society. These constituted the "floating world" (*ukiyo*, U-key-yo) celebrated in woodblock prints of prostitutes, actors, and pornography. In the early seventeenth century, entrepreneurs in the three metropolises petitioned the shogunate to establish districts for prostitution where it could be regulated and controlled. A moat and walls surrounded Edo's Yoshiwara (YO-she-wah-rah) with a main gate where guards noted the men who entered and prevented women from leaving. The earliest customers were daimyo and samurai. Merchants whose lavish spending brought them fame soon eclipsed them. In this status-conscious society, prostitutes too were ranked.

Kabuki (KAH-bu-key) began in the early seventeenth century on a riverbank in Kyoto where a prostitute erected a stage on which to sing and dance to attract customers. Fights over her charms led the shogunate to forbid women from appearing on stage in 1629. Boys then replaced them as actors and prostitutes. Again the shogunate stepped in to quell disorder, banning all but mature men from performing in public. To make up for a lack of sex appeal, actors developed the techniques of acting, singing, and dancing and performed on elaborate and frequently changing sets that made kabuki into a spectacle. It became enormously

---

[*]Translated by Anne Walthall from Matsuo Mashō, *Oku no hosomichi* (*The Narrow Road to the Deep North*), Tanabe Seiko, ed. (Tokyo: Kōdansha, 1989).

DOCUMENTS   Ihara Saikaku's "Sensible Advice on Domestic Economy"

Ihara Saikaku (E-hah-rah SAH-e-kah-ku) (1642–1693) is often considered Japan's first professional author because he lived by his pen, writing haiku, short stories, novels, and essays that described life in Osaka during the townspeople's heyday. Here he feeds the merchants' obsession with money by focusing on the details of daily life.

"The immutable rule in regard to the division of family property at the time of marriage," said the experienced go-between from Kyoto, "is as follows: Let us suppose that a certain man is worth a thousand *kan*. To the eldest son at his marriage will go four hundred *kan*, together with the family residence. The second son's share will be three hundred *kan*, and he too is entitled to a house of his own. The third son will be adopted into another family, requiring a portion of one hundred *kan*. If there is a daughter, her dowry will be thirty *kan*, in addition to a bridal trousseau worth twenty *kan*. It is advisable to marry her off to the son of a family of lower financial status. Formerly it was not unusual to spend forty *kan* on the trousseau and allot ten *kan* for the dowry, but because people today are more interested in cash, it is now customary to give the daughter silver in the lacquered chest and copper in the extra one. Even if the girl is so ugly that she can't afford to sit near the candle at night, that dowry of thirty *kan* will make her bloom into a very flowery bride!

"In matchmaking, money is a very important consideration. If thirty *kan* of silver is deposited with a trustworthy merchant at six-tenths percent interest per month, the income will total one hundred and eighty *momme* monthly, which will more than suffice to support four women: the bride, her personal maid, a second maid, and a seamstress. How unselfish must be the disposition of a bride who will not only look after the household faithfully, meantime taking care never to displease her husband's family, but also at the same time will actually pay for the food she eats! If you are looking merely for beauty, then go where women are made up solely to that end, to the licensed quarters. You are free to visit them any time of night you may wish, and thoroughly enjoy it, but next morning you will have to pay out seventy-one *momme*—which is not in the least enjoyable!

"It is better on the whole to give up dissipation in good time, for a roué is seldom happy in later life. So even if life at home seems dry and tasteless, you'd better have patience with a supper of cold rice, potluck bean curd, and dried fish. You may lie down whenever you like, at perfect ease, and have a maid massage you down to the very tips of your toes. If you want tea, you may sip it while your wife holds the cup for you. A man in his own household

popular, with the highest acclaim reserved for the men who specialized in playing women. It put the scandals arising in townspeople's society on stage, but it became best known for swashbuckling melodramas set in the past, for the shogunate forbade any discussion of its own affairs or those of contemporary samurai society.

Intellectual Trends

The Edo period saw an explosion in intellectual pursuits. Deprived of the opportunity to gain fame in battle, some samurai turned to scholarship and made serious efforts to understand their society. In the seventeenth century, Hayashi Razan (HAH-yah-she RAH-zahn) formulated the Tokugawa ideology in neo-Confucian terms that saw the social order as a reflection of the visible natural order in that both relied on the same underlying principle. Among his students was Yamaga Sokō (YAH-mah-gah SO-co), famous for defining a way for samurai to survive during a time of peace: "The business of the samurai consists in reflecting on his own station in life, in discharging loyal service to his master,…in deepening his fidelity in associations

is the commander supreme, whose authority none will dare to question, and there is none to condemn you. There's no need to seek further for genuine pleasure.

"Then, too, there are certain business advantages to staying home. Your clerks will stop their imprudent visits to the Yasaka quarters and their clandestine meetings at that rendezvous in Oike. And when in the shop, since they can't appear to be completely idle, maybe they'll look over those reports from the Edo branch office, or do some other work that they have been putting off doing—all to the profit of you, the master! The apprentice boys will diligently twist wastepaper into string, and in order to impress you, the master, sitting in the inner room, they will practice penmanship to their profit. Kyushichi, whose habit it is to retire early, will take the straw packing from around the yellowtail and make rope on which to string coins; while Take, in order to make things go more smoothly tomorrow, will prepare the vegetables for breakfast. The seamstress during the time you're at home will take off as many knots of Hino silk as she ordinarily does in a whole day. Even the cat keeps a wary watch in the kitchen and when she hears the least sound in the vicinity of the fish hanger she will mew to scare away the rats. If such unmeasured profit as this results from the master's remaining at home just one night, think how vast will be the benefits that will accrue within the space of a whole year! So even if you are not entirely satisfied with your wife, you have to exercise discretion and realize that in the gay quarters all is but vanity. For a young master to be well aware of this is the secret of the successful running of his household."

Such was the counsel offered by the veteran go-between.

Be that as it may, let me say that the women of today, under the influence of the styles of the gay quarters, dress exactly like professional entertainers. Prominent drapers' wives, who in public are addressed as mesdames, are dressed so as to be mistaken for high-class courtesans; the wives of small shopkeepers, who once served as clerks of the drapers, look exactly like courtesans one grade lower. Again, the kimono worn by wives of tailors and embroiderers who live on the side streets bear a startling resemblance to those of the women employed in teahouses. It is fun to spot them in a crowd dressed in conformity with their respective degrees of fortune.

Questions for Analysis
1. What should merchants do if they want to prosper?
2. What should merchants look for in a wife?
3. Compare how merchants divide up their property with the rules for inheritance in samurai households.

Source: Used with permission of Charles E. Tuttle Company from *The Scheming World*, translated by Masanori Takatsuka and David C. Stubbs, 1965; permission conveyed through Copyright Clearance Center, Inc.

with friends, and…in devoting himself to duty above all."* Kyoto scholar Itō Jinsai (E-toe GENE-sah-e) likewise began as a neo-Confucianist, only to reject the notion of an underlying principle in favor of studying Confucius himself. (For a comparative discussion of neo-Confucianism, see **Making Comparisons** following this chapter.) For him, the purpose of scholarship was to show how to put morality based on benevolence and love into practice, a goal that commoners as well as samurai could achieve. Such was the prestige of Chinese philosophy that any man who wanted to become learned had to employ Chinese categories of thought. Women were not subject to this restriction, but for that reason, they had little access to scholarship beyond the study of Japanese poetry. (See **Biography: Tadano Makuzu.**)

Ogyū Sorai (OH-geyu SOH-rah-e) gained influence by attacking the neo-Confucian Hayashi school and Itō Jinsai. He argued that only the most ancient Chinese texts, those that came before Confucius, were worthy of study because they contained the

*Ryusaku Tsunoda et al., eds., *Sources of the Japanese Tradition* (New York: Columbia University Press, 1959), 1:390.

teachings of the sage kings, the creators of civilization. The social order did not reflect the natural order of beasts; instead it was an artificial construct, made in history, and that was good. Men needed rules lest their passions run away with them. Japan was fortunate that its own sage king Ieyasu had created the shogunate, and his deeds were not for mere mortals to challenge. Sorai's rational bureaucratic view of government called on samurai to devote themselves to public duty. In 1703 forty-seven retainers from the Akō (AH-co) domain assassinated their dead lord's enemy (an incident dramatized as "The Treasury of Loyal Retainers," *Chūshingura*, CHEW-sheen-gu-rah) because, they claimed, their honor as samurai left them no choice. Sorai applauded the deed but agreed with the shogunate that because they had broken the law against private vendettas, they had to atone by committing suicide. As long as people obeyed the law, government had no business interfering in their lives.

The eighteenth century saw an increase in schools and thinkers. Dazai Shundai (DAH-zah-e SHOE-n-dah-e) explored political economy. He urged daimyo to supplement flat revenues coming from an agrarian tax base by promoting the production of goods for export to other domains. Kaiho Seiryō (KAH-i-hoh SEH-e-reyo) took Shundai's ideas a step farther by arguing that all social relationships are predicated on the measured exchange of goods and services, a principle understood by merchants but not, unfortunately, by samurai. Andō Shōeki (AHN-doe SHOW-eh-key) claimed that Sorai's sage kings were thieves and liars who created governments to deceive and cheat the farmers. In his eyes, the samurai were no better than parasites.

Merchants pondered business ethics. Troubled by the excesses of the Genroku period when some merchants had gone bankrupt through lavish spending and making bad loans to daimyo, Ishida Baigan (E-she-dah BAH-e-gahn) founded the Shingaku (SHEEN-gah-ku) school (literally, study of the heart). He argued that merchants deserved to make a just profit because profit for them was like the samurai's stipend. They should devote themselves to their businesses with the same devotion a samurai owed his lord and, like the samurai, they should strive for moral perfection. Texts and teachers could guide this quest, but it could be completed only through meditation and the practice of diligence, thrift, and fortitude. Baigan and his followers had no political agenda; the idea that merchants might have something to

say to samurai was left to the merchant academy in Osaka, the Kaitokudō (KAH-e-toe-ku-doe), founded in 1724. Its teachers denied that merchants caused hardships through their pursuit of profit. Merchants, they argued, played a crucial role in society by helping goods circulate based on objective and accurate calculations. When they applied this principle to domain finances, their advice ought to be followed. A number of them gained coveted positions as advisers to daimyo and shogun.

Other thinkers found inspiration in Japan's past. The greatest was Motoori Norinaga (MOE-toe-o-re NO-re-nah-gah), whose computer-like memory enabled him to decipher the patterns of Chinese characters used to write *Kojiki* (CO-g-key), Japan's most ancient history. Through the study of history and literary classics, he affirmed Japan's unique position in the world as the sole country ruled by descendants of the sun goddess, and he celebrated the private world of the individual. Based as they were on the spontaneity of human feeling, Japanese values were superior to those of other peoples. "In foreign countries, they place logic first, even when it comes to revering the gods…all this is but shallow human reasoning." The Chinese had introduced rules that, although they might be necessary in China where people were naturally inclined toward error, were entirely unsuited to Japan, where people were naturally perfect in their possession of the "true heart" (*magokoro*, MAH-go-co-row).[*] Even when he was asked by a daimyo to comment on the conditions of his day, Norinaga remained apolitical, claiming only that rulers should live in accordance with the way of the gods found in the study of history and poetry.

Official interest in Western studies began in 1720 when Shogun Yoshimune lifted the ban on Western books so long as they did not promote Christianity. Japanese doctors and scientists, attracted to what was called "Dutch studies," paid little attention to Western philosophy; their enthusiasm was for practical matters, in particular the study of human anatomy, astronomy, geography, and military science. Sugita Genpaku (SUE-ge-tah GEHN-pah-ku) discovered that a Dutch human anatomy book provided names for body parts not found in Chinese medical texts. In 1771 he watched the dissection of a criminal's corpse, a fifty-year-old woman, performed by an outcast. Although this was not the first dissection

---

[*]Sey Nakamura, "The Way of the Gods: Motoori Norinaga's Naobi no Mitama," *Monumenta Nipponica* 46 (Spring 1991): 39.

BIOGRAPHY

Male intellectuals focused on morality, politics, and economics. Tadano Makuzu (TAH-dah-no MAH-ku-zu) (1763–1825) drew on her observations and experience to analyze human relations.

Born Kudō Ayako (KU-doe AH-ya-co), she grew up in a lively family of parents, grandmother, and seven siblings. At age nine she insisted that her mother teach her classical Japanese poetry. Ayako enjoyed her grandmother's company because she was a cheerful and attractive woman who loved kabuki. To complete her education, at fifteen Ayako became an attendant to the lord of Sendai's daughter, a position she held for ten years.

Ayako's father, Heisuke (HEH-e-su-keh), had many friends who shared his interests in medicine, botany, foreign trade, and Western countries. He hoped to arrange a good marriage for Ayako should his proposal for the colonization of Hokkaido and trade with Russia lead to a position with the shogunate. The fall of his patron in 1786 thwarted his career and his plans for his daughter.

When Ayako left service, she was too old to make a good match. In 1789 she was married to a man so decrepit that she cried until she was returned to her parents. Eight years later her father found her a husband in a widower with three sons, Tadano Iga Tsurayoshi (E-gah TZU-rah-yo-she), a high-ranking Sendai retainer with an income four times that of the Kudō family. Marrying Iga meant that Ayako had to leave the city of her birth for Sendai, a move she likened to "the journey to hell." There she spent

Tadano Makuzu, Daughter of the Samurai

the remainder of her life, visited only occasionally by her husband, who remained on duty in Edo.

Signed with the pen name Makuzu, "Solitary Thoughts" sums up Ayako's views on her society distilled during her years of isolation in Sendai. She bemoans her ignorance of Confucianism because her father thought it inappropriate knowledge for a woman. It was of little use even for men, she believed, because it was too clumsy to regulate the niceties of Japanese behavior. Like other intellectuals of her day, she pitied the samurai for not understanding the principle of money. Instead of a well-ordered harmonious society, she saw competition, hatred, and strife: "Each person in our country strives to enrich him or herself alone without thinking of the foreign threat or begrudging the cost to the country." Townspeople despised warriors: "They take secret delight in the warriors' descent into poverty, hating them like sworn enemies." Competition governed even relations between the sexes: "When men and women make love, they battle for superiority by rubbing their genitals together."

Questions for Analysis
1. What kinds of opportunities did Makuzu have as a daughter of the samurai?
2. What kind of constraints did Makuzu face?
3. What did Makuzu think of her society?

Source: Bettina Gramlich-Oka, *Thinking Like a Man: Tadano Makuzu (1763–1825)* (Leiden: Brill Academic Publishers, 2006).

---

performed in Japan, the evidence of his own eyes plus the Dutch text led him to invent Japanese terms for pancreas, nerve, and other body parts; these terms were later exported to China. The faith in reason based on experience and the benefits of experiments promoted by the Chinese "practical learning" school already constituted one strand of Japanese intellectual life; the opportunity to engage with Western scientific texts developed it further. Sugita spread his ideas through his writing and salons, whose members ranged from merchants to daimyo. Western instruments such as the telescope and microscope fascinated intellectuals. The insights they gained into

the natural world percolated into popular culture when Utagawa Kunisada (U-tah-gah-wah KU-knee-sah-dah) drew pictures of greatly magnified insects to illustrate a story about monsters.

MATURATION AND DECAY (EIGHTEENTH CENTURY)

Following the excesses of the Genroku period, the shogun's and the daimyo's officials fretted over the state of government finances and their retainers' morale. The miserly Ieyasu had left stores of gold bullion, but his heirs spent them so freely that by the 1690s, the shogunate had to devalue the currency. Creeping inflation eroded the value of tax revenues and samurai stipends, while the growing availability of consumer products stimulated demand. Shogun Yoshimune responded by instituting reforms in the 1720s. To aid the samurai who received their stipends in rice, he supported rice prices even though urban consumers complained. He assessed a "voluntary contribution" of a rice donation in proportion to their domain's size from all daimyo in return for spending less time in Edo on *sankin kōtai*. Instead of basing taxes on each year's harvest, he tried to get rid of changes in revenues by establishing a fixed tax rate. He allowed villages to open new fields in regions previously set aside to provide forage and fertilizer and encouraged the cultivation of cash crops. To reduce expenses, he issued regulations governing the quality of clothing people of different statuses could wear and cut the staff of palace women. He set up a petition box, already tried in some domains, to allow commoners' suggestions to reach his ear. A famine caused by a plague of locusts in western Japan in 1732 brought the reform period to an end.

Popular Culture

In contrast to the ruling class, urban commoners generally enjoyed the benefits of the consumption revolution. By 1750, Edo's population reached well over 1 million inhabitants, making it perhaps the largest city in the world at the time. A fish market filled the hub of the city at Nihonbashi (KNEE-hohn-bah-she); the surrounding streets were lined with shops selling goods of every sort. Restaurants catered to people for whom dining out had become a pleasure while innkeepers who specialized in lodging for plaintiffs became proto-lawyers in an increasingly lawsuit-driven society. The draper Echigoya (EH-che-go-yah) innovated a fixed price system for cash (see Color Plate 22). The world's first commodity futures market opened in Osaka. Kabuki actors advertised stores and products during their routines starting in 1715. In 1774 a popular actor put his name on cosmetics sold in his store, mentioned his products on stage, and placed them in woodblock prints. Best-selling authors accepted money to praise products such as toothpaste and pipes.

The spread of commerce made education both possible and necessary. In thousands of villages across Japan, priests, village officials, and rural entrepreneurs opened schools to provide the basics in reading and math. Coupled with private academies in castle towns and cities for samurai and merchants, their efforts led to impressive rates of literacy by the mid-nineteenth century: approximately 40 percent for men and between 10 and 15 percent for women. Students studied texts that delivered a moral lesson; those for women emphasized docility, modesty, and self-restraint lest the young working woman slip from seamstress to prostitute. Publishers printed one-page almanacs and Buddhist mandalas (pictures of the cosmos) as well as pamphlets giving advice on agriculture and etiquette. Some students read well enough to enjoy multivolume works of historical fiction, but for many, the aim was more practical: to learn when to plant crops and how to calculate profit and loss.

In the eighteenth century the national road system designed to bring daimyo to Edo started to attract commoners. Although the shogunate prohibited travel in the interests of preserving order, it allowed pilgrimages, visits to relatives, and trips to medicinal hot springs. With a passport issued by a local official giving name, physical description, and destination, travelers set off, usually on foot, always in groups, accompanied by neighbors to see them to the community border. Many traveled in confraternities (societies created for a specific purpose) that raised money to send a few members on pilgrimage each year. The most popular destination was Ise, with its outer shrine to the god of agriculture. Because few travelers were likely to repeat the pilgrimage experience, they were determined to see as much as possible. They took enormous detours through temple circuits and stopped in Edo and Osaka for sightseeing and theater. Men traveled in the prime of life; women traveled either before they were married or after they had a daughter-in-law to raise the children and run the household. Rather than suffer the invasive inspection procedures required at checkpoints, women hired guides to show them byways. Men and women bought souvenirs to ship back home and distribute to those who had given them money before they left. They kept diaries of their trips; some were little more than expense accounts while others were lengthy descriptions of things seen and heard.

Not every pilgrim was literate or had the permission of a local official. Driven, they said, by the need

時
美
競 女 立

泉
女
房

Woman Reading. Created by Kikugawa Eisen in the early nineteenth century, this portrait of an ordinary woman depicts her engrossed in reading a selection of poems. The woodblock print is from a series titled "Mirror of contemporary beautiful women."

to make a pilgrimage to Ise or some other sacred spot, they escaped from parents or employers with nothing but the clothes on their backs. They depended on the charity of strangers who hoped to earn some of the merit of making the pilgrimage by giving alms. They also fell prey to bandits and pimps. At approximately sixty-year intervals, thousands of people left towns and villages to make a thanksgiving pilgrimage (*okage mairi,* oh-KAH-geh MAH-e-re) to the inner shrine of the sun goddess at Ise. Many never returned home. Instead they found their way to cities, where they joined a floating population of day laborers and prostitutes.

Hard Times and Rural Uprisings

The underside to prosperity, resentment at status distinctions, and injustice gave rise to thousands of incidents of rural protest. The corporate structure of the village meant that protest was organized collectively. When farmers lodged complaints against unjust officials or pleas that the tax burden be reduced following a crop failure, they petitioned the lord to show compassion to the honorable farmers because their hardships threatened their survival. As the village's representative, the headman was supposed to take the responsibility for seeking help from samurai officials dealing with rural affairs. If officials deemed the matter worthy of consideration, they passed it up the chain of command. If at any point an official decided not to trouble his superiors, those below had no legal recourse. According to rural legend, in the seventeenth century a few brave headmen, typified by Sakura Sōgorō (SAH-ku-rah SOW-go-row), made a direct appeal to the daimyo or, in Sōgorō's case, to the shogun. Sōgorō paid for his audacity by suffering crucifixion along with his wife and saw his sons executed before his eyes. Although historians doubt that he ever existed, he became Japan's most famous peasant martyr.

Few headmen in the eighteenth century were willing to risk their families to help their neighbors. Instead of an individual groveling before his superiors, farmers marched together to state their grievances en masse. They called their deeds *ikki*, harking back to the leagues that had bedeviled political authorities in the sixteenth century. In 1764, approximately two hundred thousand farmers marched toward Edo to protest new demands for forced labor to transport officials and their goods on the national roads. Smaller outbursts disrupted domains, peaking at times of economic hardship. Seldom did any district erupt more than once, and protestors wanted help, not revolution. Yet fear that rural protest would expose such weaknesses in domainal administration that the shogun would transfer the daimyo or simply dispossess him limited efforts to tax the products of farmers' labor.

The 1780s brought hard times to Japan. Mount Asama erupted in 1783, spewing ash that blocked sunlight all summer. Crop failures made worse by misguided policies led to famine, a catastrophe repeated in 1787. It is said that the population declined by 920,000. In the eyes of many sufferers, the cause of their distress was not so much natural disaster as human wrongdoing. Unlike earlier rural protests that had demanded tax relief and government aid, the majority of incidents in the 1780s focused on commercial issues and evil merchants accused of hoarding grain while people starved. Commoners rioted for five days in Edo, punishing merchants by smashing their stores, trampling rice in the mud, and pouring saké in the street.

The famine exposed problems at all levels of society. The shogunate had struggled for years with an inadequate tax base and the increasing competition among daimyo, merchants, and farmers for access to commercial income. Under the direction of senior councilor Tanuma Okitsugu (TAH-new-mah OH-key-tzu-gu), it had proposed schemes to force merchants to buy shares in organizations (guilds) granted a monopoly over trade in a specified item. The guild then paid regular fees in "thank you" money to the shogun. These monopolies angered those excluded—producers forced to accept lower prices for their goods and daimyo who had their own schemes for profiting from trade. Following the Edo riot, the shogunate launched a second reform led by essayist, novelist, and staunch neo-Confucian Matsudaira Sadanobu (MAH-tzu-dah-e-rah SAH-dah-no-bu) to rectify finances and morals. He established new standards for bureaucratic conduct that endured to modern times. His "Edo first" policy ensured that the city remained quiet for almost eighty years.

Sadanobu's reforms also had a darker side. A floating population of men without families or property worked as day laborers in fields and cities. Sadanobu had those in Edo rounded up and confined to an island in the bay. From there they were transported to the gold mine on Sado in the Japan Sea, where most of them died within two or three years. Other officials condemned the harshness of this measure, and it was not repeated. Instead governments encouraged commoners to police themselves.

SUMMARY

The military regime established by the Tokugawa shoguns was designed to preserve order and enhance stability. Everyone was expected to stay put, working at the same occupation as his ancestors for generation after generation. The shoguns balanced the need for effective local administration with their fear of treachery by forcing the daimyo to divide their time between their domains and the shogun's capital at Edo where they had to leave hostages as a pledge of good behavior. To regulate foreign trade, the shogunate limited where it could take place.

Starting in the seventeenth century, rising agricultural yields led to a boom in cottage industries and a commercial revolution. Labor stayed in the countryside while capital came from cities. Japan's urban population swelled with samurai and the merchants, artisans, and entertainers who supplied them with goods and services, from food to prostitutes. Faced with underemployment, some samurai turned to intellectual pursuits, debating Japan's place in the world, the nature of society, and the best way for governments to stay solvent.

By the end of the eighteenth century, the regime's scorecard was decidedly mixed. Governments and the military ruling class were chronically in debt while attempts to place new burdens on farmers, famines, and the perception that evil merchants profited from high prices sparked uprisings and riots. At the same time, men and women, townspeople and farmers sought education, supported a thriving publishing industry, and enjoyed the delights of travel.

What difference did two hundred years of peace make to Japan? Because the shogunate restricted foreign trade, historians once assumed that Japan stagnated. Such was not the case. New bureaucratic procedures taught military men how to handle routine paperwork. Ideologues preached the virtue of the public performance of duty. To a certain extent, loyalty to lord became loyalty to the domain and was no longer tied to reward. To keep up with economic development, people had to work harder. Commerce boomed, and people let their pocketbooks regulate their behavior.

To be sure, farmers suffered under heavy taxes. Merchants had to accept arbitrary restrictions on commerce and pay forced loans whenever governments faced financial crisis. Many samurai could not afford the pleasure districts, nor did their offices keep them occupied. They retreated to the private world of intellectual stimulation and the pursuit of pleasure, where they joined townspeople and rural entrepreneurs in creating a vibrant popular culture.

As a philosophical system and set of practices, what historians today call neo-Confucianism had a lasting impact on China, Korea, and Japan. It was distinguished by a search for a unifying explanation for the universe, the physical world, and human nature. Philosophers found this explanation in *li* (principle or pattern), an invisible underlying principle that informs everything. Plants, mountains, and people are what they are because of *li*, and *li* provides the link between them. Thus all things are fundamentally one, a view of the world with strong Buddhist overtones. At the same time, *li* is different in different objects—the principle in men is different from the principle in women. What makes things different and gives them their physicality is *qi*—often translated as "ether," "physical force," or "matter." According to the great Song philosopher Zhu Xi (1130–1200), neither *li* nor *qi* could exist without the other.

Some philosophers believed that because human beings had both *li* and *qi*, knowledge should be sought through meditation; others believed that it should be sought by studying books and examining the external world. What mediates between *li* and *qi* in human beings is *xin*—mind or heart. In its underlying form, *xin* is pure and flawless; in its physical form, it is clouded by desires (*yu*) and feelings (*qing*). Because desires and feelings can lead to evil, they have to be regulated.

Zhu Xi used rules and rites centered on the virtues promoted in the Chinese classics to regulate individual behavior and family life in accordance with *li*. He warned that although food and sex are necessary to sustain life, tasty food and too much contact with women stimulate desire. Men and women should lead separate lives, and the wife's position should be superior to that of concubines. To train people in the key virtue of filial piety (reverence for parents), Zhu Xi detailed the appropriate rites for paying homage to ancestors. The household head and his wife played the central role, and the wife knew that she, unlike concubines, would join the ancestors on the family altar.

In Yuan, Ming, and Qing China, Zhu Xi's commentaries on the Confucian classics became required reading for all who hoped to pass the civil service examinations. The effects of this government-imposed orthodoxy were not as stagnating as one might expect, and in both Ming and Qing times some neo-Confucian thinkers rejected Zhu Xi's understandings and proposed radically different ideas.

In Korea, Joseon-period *yangban* opposed to Buddhism seized on neo-Confucianism so as to order social relations and explore the nature of the universe. In the sixteenth century, scholars delved deeply into the relationship between *li* and *qi*, disputing which came first and trying to quantify their relative importance. In the eighteenth century, the positions staked out in this debate became aligned with different factions and justified purges.

Yangban incorporated separation of the sexes and filial piety into their daily lives. They reformed gender relations in the fifteenth century by reducing women's status and property rights. As in China, they emphasized integrity, which for a widow meant that she must never remarry. Their houses had walls and courtyards to separate male quarters at the front from female quarters at the back. Only sons by the primary wife could participate fully in *yangban* society, especially in taking civil service exams. The king had to venerate his father's wife in public rituals; if his mother had been a concubine, she received nothing but private rites. When a man died, his eldest son moved to a grass hut beside the tomb where he performed elaborate rituals to feed and honor the departed.

In Tokugawa Japan, neo-Confucianism served the ideology of rule. The social hierarchy was deemed to reflect the natural order; by a sleight of hand, warriors turned into gentlemen. Even shoguns lectured on the classics praised by Zhu Xi and hired scholars to lecture on similarly suitable topics. While recognizing the centrality of filial piety and compiling records of filial children, samurai turned loyalty into an abstract, all-encompassing standard for behavior. While some scholars investigated the external world, others lauded desire and human feeling. A merchant philosopher taught meditation to clear the cloudy heart.

Living the neo-Confucian way was more problematic. Only wealthy members of the warrior class had the resources to segregate their living space. They distinguished between wife and concubines as much for political reasons as for moral reasons, although birth mothers received greater public respect than in Korea. Rather than waste a political asset, they had their sisters and daughters marry repeatedly. At the turn of the eighteenth century, the shogun codified mourning rituals that took into consideration the complex family relationships created by adoption, but Buddhist ritual specialists continued to mediate between the dead and the living. Even the most devoted follower of Zhu Xi's teachings could not bring himself to wail at his father's grave.

PART FOUR

The Age of Western Imperialism (1800–1900)

Western Imperialism (1800–1900)

IN CONTRAST TO THE FRAIL WOODEN-hulled sailing ships that carried Europeans to the Pacific Ocean in the sixteenth century, nineteenth-century vessels might be powered by coal-fueled steam engines. The industrial revolution that rescued Europe from the ecological trap of reliance on agricultural products propelled technological innovations in weaponry and an expansion of the state's ability to command men and resources. Following in the wake of trading companies, government officials regulated and taxed commerce, then administered territories, and finally recruited natives into disciplined, drilled uniformed battalions capable of projecting their force thousands of miles from European homelands. No longer latecomers in previously existing maritime trade, Europeans transformed their trading posts from India to Indonesia into colonies.

During the eighteenth century, European states had relied on trading posts scattered across the Indian Ocean and the Pacific, the only colony there being Spain's in the Philippines. Under Catherine the Great, Russia extended its reach across Siberia to Alaska and sent explorers down the Kamchatka peninsula, along the coast of Sakhalin, and into Hokkaido. Confrontations with Japanese officials led to sporadic efforts to open diplomatic relations. Having defeated the French in India in the middle of the eighteenth century, the British East India Company spearheaded the battle for markets, which brought administrators and troops to protect mercantile interests and made Britain the greatest of the European powers. While France was embroiled in revolution, Britain sent an official mission to China in 1793. Headed by Lord George Macartney, its aim was to get rid of what the British saw as unnecessary restrictions on trade that limited the number, destination, and schedules of their ships. Because control over trade helped stabilize the social order, reduced smuggling, and reaffirmed the Qing emperor's superiority over all other monarchs, the mission failed.

The wars fought by Napoleon Bonaparte in the name of France following the French Revolution remade the map of Europe and contributed to a new sense of nationalism. In Asia, Britain took over the Dutch colony at Batavia in Indonesia because Napoleon had made his brother King of the Netherlands. The Dutch never told Japan that the only place flying the Dutch flag was Dejima in Nagasaki harbor. The Napoleonic Wars spilled over into European colonial possessions in Latin America where wars of liberation that started in 1809 resulted in the creation of independent nations in the 1820s. The heightened focus on nationhood required a clear setting of boundaries and sovereignty. No longer would small states such as Vietnam, the Ryukyus, and Korea be permitted to claim quasi-autonomy under China's mantle, and every inch of land had to belong somewhere. Rulers and the educated classes imagined communities in which everyone spoke the same language, professed similar beliefs, and despised foreigners. The eighteenth-century cosmopolitan Enlightenment admiration for Chinese civilization and Confucian rationality gave way to disdain for godless heathens who failed to appreciate the superiority of Western technology. In contrast to older empires that allowed natives to participate in running their affairs, new empires discriminated between the white man and everyone else.

By bringing decades of peace to Europe, Napoleon's defeat at Waterloo in 1815 freed nations to compete for Great Power status. Great Power status required colonies, and competition with other nations spurred imperialism. France reestablished its dominance in much of North Africa, contended with Britain for ports in Burma, and tried to force a commercial treaty on Vietnam. In 1816, Britain was at war with Nepal

Timeline: Western Advances in Asia

1793: Earl of Macartney travels to Beijing seeking diplomatic recognition; Russians seek same in Japan.

1797: Broughton, a British captain, surveys east coast of Korea.

1804: Russian advances in Siberia and Sea of Okhotsk culminate in emissary to Japan.

1805–1812: Russia builds forts in Alaska and northern California.

1808: British warship enters Nagasaki harbor.

1811: Britain captures Java from the Dutch; returned in 1816.

1816: Anglo-Nepalese War.

1819: Raffles, a British official, occupies Singapore for Britain.

1820: Vietnam bans Christianity and expels missionaries.

1824–1826: First Anglo-Burmese War.

1837: U.S. ship *Morrison* tries and fails to establish relations with Japan.

1839–1840: Opium War and First Anglo-Afghan War.

1842: Treaty of Nanjing.

1846: U.S. Commodore Biddle seeks trade with Japan; refused.

1852: Second Anglo-Burmese War.

1853–1854: U.S. Commodore Perry forces unequal treaty on Japan.

1856–1857: Arrow War between Britain, France, and China.

1857–1858: Indian Rebellion; British East India Company abolished.

1858: Treaties of Tianjin; Japan signs commercial treaty with United States.

1860: British and French troops occupy Beijing.

1862: Treaty of Saigon: France occupies three provinces in south Vietnam.

1863: France gains protectorate over Cambodia.

1866: France sends punitive expedition to Korea.

1871: United States sends ships to open Korea to foreign trade by force; repulsed.

1874: France acquires control over all of south Vietnam; Japan sends an armed expedition to Taiwan.

1876: Japan signs unequal treaty with Korea.

1877: Queen Victoria proclaimed empress of India.

1882: Korea signs unequal treaties with United States and other Great Powers.

1884–1885: France makes Vietnam a colony.

1885–1886: Third Anglo-Burmese War.

1893: France gains protectorate over Laos.

1894–1895: Sino-Japanese War.

1898: European powers scramble for territory and concessions in China.

1898: United States seizes the Philippines from Spain; annexes Hawai'i.

1900: Boxer Rebellion in China against foreigners.

---

when it dispatched a second mission to the Qing court. Because the envoy refused to participate in the customary rituals that regulated relations between tribute nations and the Son of Heaven, including the kowtow, the emperor refused to see him. Britain had already established ports on the Malay Peninsula; adding Singapore gave it a harbor to protect and supply British ships sailing between India and China. British ships started appearing off the coast of Japan, sometimes threatening the natives in their search for food and fuel. After Burmese troops, encouraged by the French, threatened Bengal, the first Anglo-Burmese War ended in victory for Britain, a large indemnity (compensation for Britain's losses) extracted from the Burmese, a British diplomat stationed at the Burmese court, and British control over the Bay of Bengal.

Bengal supplied the opium that Britain used to buy tea. By 1750, Britain was importing well over 2 million pounds of tea from China a year, and demand was rising. Having little that China found of value, the British at first had to pay for tea with silver, thus leading to a negative trade balance. After 1761 the balance began to shift in Britain's favor. The East India Company allowed the illegal export of Bengali opium into China, bought tea for homeland consumption, and used the silver left over as a result of the trade surplus to finance its operation and the British administration of Bengal. From the British point of view, that drug addicts multiplied as the price of opium dropped and the supply increased and that bribes to allow drug trafficking corrupted local officials simply demonstrated Chinese racial inferiority.

British merchants remained unhappy with trading conditions in China. Textile manufacturers wanted to sell machine-made cloth, and private traders resented the East India Company monopoly. When the monopoly was abolished in 1834, the government named Lord Napier to supervise trade in Guangzhou. He tried to bypass the Cohong, the merchant guild responsible to the Qing court for managing foreign trade, and to negotiate directly with the provincial governor-general, who saw no reason to sully his dignity by dealing with barbarians. Diplomatic quarrels led to a confrontation between British warships and Chinese defenses before Napier was forced to withdraw. Trade continued, although with British merchants calling for warships to enforce their demands to eliminate the Cohong monopoly over foreign trade and to open ports farther north.

The Opium War tested Chinese morality against British technology and opened a new chapter in international relations. In 1839, Imperial Commissioner Lin Zexu arrived in Guangzhou with orders to suppress the drug trade. He moved swiftly against dealers and users and demanded that opium under foreign control be turned over to him. When the British merchants refused, he stopped trade altogether. He appealed to Queen Victoria to allow him the same right to regulate trade and suppress drugs that her officials enjoyed in Britain. When the traders reluctantly turned over their stocks, he allowed them to flee to the Portuguese city of Macao and then to Hong Kong while he washed twenty thousand chests of opium out to sea. Indignant at the loss of their property without compensation, the traders appealed to Parliament. A fleet that included four armed steamships carrying Indian troops under British officers refused to contest the defenses Lin had built to protect Guangzhou. Four ships blockaded the river mouth downstream while the rest of the fleet sailed north to harass Chinese shipping along the coast. By the time the fleet reached Tianjin, the closest port to Beijing, the Qing court realized that it had to negotiate. In the first round of negotiations, China agreed to pay an indemnity to compensate British merchants for their destroyed property and to allow expanded trade in Guangzhou, direct access to Qing officials, and British possession of Hong Kong. When these terms proved unsatisfactory to the British home government, another round of fighting forced China to make additional concessions.

China's defeat in the Opium War forced it to open to the West and opened a new era in Western imperialism. (See Color Plate 25.) It marked the first time a Western power claimed victory in battle in East Asia, a disaster that sent shock waves through Japan, though not through Korea, which received its information only through official channels in Beijing. The Treaty of Nanjing opened five ports to British residency and trade, abolished the Cohong, and ceded Hong Kong to Britain. A supplementary treaty signed a year later fixed low tariffs on British imports and included the most favored nation clause whereby Britain automatically received any privilege China granted any other Western power. In 1844, Americans signed a treaty with China that gave the United States the right to build churches and hospitals and to protect American nationals from the Chinese judicial system. "Extraterritoriality" meant that with the exception of opium traders, Americans in China were subject to American laws, judges, courts, and prisons. The British automatically participated in this infringement on Chinese sovereignty, as did other Western powers that signed treaties with China. Historian Akira Iriye has termed this "multilateral imperialism."[*] Because China and its subjects did not enjoy the same privileges abroad, most favored nation status and extraterritoriality became the hallmarks of the unequal treaty system.

Following in the British wake, American traders, whalers, and missionaries lured their government into conflicts across the Pacific. During the 1840s, swift clipper ships with clouds of sail dominated

---

[*]A. Iriye, "Imperialism in East Asia," in *Modern East Asia: Essays in Interpretation*, ed. J. B. Crowley (New York: Harcourt, Brace & World, 1970), p. 129.

trade routes. In 1846 an American ship shelled what is now Danang in central Vietnam to win the release of an American missionary who had ignored prohibitions on preaching while Commodore James Biddle tried to open negotiations with Japan, only to suffer a humiliating rejection. The United States completed its westward continental expansion in 1848 when it wrested California from Mexico during the California gold rush. (It acquired Alaska by purchase from Russia in 1867.) In developing steamer routes across the Pacific to Shanghai, it saw potential in Japan's coalfields. Whalers, too, needed access to fuel and fresh water. In 1853, Commodore Matthew Perry sailed into Uraga Bay near Edo. He forced the shogun's officials to accept a letter proposing a friendship treaty and promised to return the next year for their response. Despite Japanese efforts to fend him off, Perry obtained the Kanagawa treaty of friendship that opened two small ports to American ships, allowed an American consul to live on Japanese soil, and provided for most favored nation treatment.

The Americans took the lead in imposing modern diplomatic relations on Japan because Britain was busy elsewhere. Angered by what it considered unreasonable objections to trade and to the exploitation of Burma's magnificent teak forests, Britain launched two more wars against Burma that resulted in Burma becoming a British colony. Allied with France, Austria, Prussia, and the Ottoman Empire, Britain also fought the Crimean War of 1853–1856 against Russia for control over the mouth of the Danube and the Black Sea. Britain's rule in India suffered a temporary setback with the 1857 rebellion, but the result was to strengthen Britain's hand in dealing with the remaining principalities, many of which had to accept British advisers and the protection of British troops.

Determined to open new markets, Western powers continued to make demands on East Asia. After suppressing the 1857 Indian rebellion, Britain joined with France to attack Guangzhou and capture its governor-general, who had refused to pass their demands on to Beijing. Again the menace of foreign ships at Tianjin compelled the emperor to sign new treaties. Britain, France, the United States, and Russia gained eleven new treaty ports, foreign vessels on the Yangzi, freedom of travel for foreigners in the interior, tolerance for missionaries and their converts, low tariffs, foreign ambassadors resident in Beijing, and the legalization of opium imports. When the Qing court tried to postpone the ambassadors' arrival and had the audacity to fire on British ships from new fortifications at Tianjin, the British and French retaliated by marching twenty thousand troops, many from India, to Beijing, where they destroyed the summer palace outside the city. In 1858, Townsend Harris, the American consul resident in Japan, pointed to what the European powers had achieved with their gunboats in China to convince the shogun's government to sign a commercial treaty with the United States. In addition to setting low tariffs on American goods, it extended the principle of extraterritoriality to Westerners in Japan. Angry at the murder of missionaries, a combined French and Spanish fleet attacked Vietnam in 1858. France went on to get most of southern Vietnam, a large indemnity, and a commercial treaty.

Western inroads in East Asia waxed and waned in consort with conflicts elsewhere. In 1861, Russian sailors occupied Tsushima, an island in the strait between Japan and Korea, in part to prevent a similar action by the British and in part to gain a warm-water port. Unable to win official backing for this maneuver, they withdrew. During the American Civil War, 1861–1865, the United States managed only one military initiative: support for reopening the straits of Shimonoseki after Japan tried to close them. France, by contrast, made considerable gains. In 1863 it forced the Cambodian king to accept its protection. Two years later, it annexed two more provinces in south Vietnam and attacked Korea to retaliate for the execution of Catholic priests who had entered the country illegally. France's defeat in the Franco-Prussian War in 1871 put a temporary halt to its ambitions in Asia. In the meantime, a small American squadron tried to duplicate Perry's success in Korea. When Korea refused to negotiate, the squadron raided Korean forts guarding the entrance to Seoul and withdrew.

In contrast to priests who first spread Catholicism around the globe, nineteenth-century missionaries who likewise took the world as their stage often did not belong to a religious group and were as likely to be female as male. Unlike the Jesuits, who had tried to get along with rulers and adjust to local practices, missionaries from Britain and the United States had a vision of Christianity that admitted no compromise with what they deemed heathen practices and beliefs. Impatient at treaties that restricted their God-given mission, they caused more than one international incident. Yet they also built hospitals, schools, and orphanages where none had existed before. They

Peabody Essex Museum, Salem, MA/The Bridgeman Art Library

A Factory at Guangzhou. Supervised by a merchant, Chinese workers prepare tea and porcelain for export.

educated women and promoted some degree of gender equality. In Japan they opposed the practice of taking concubines, and in China, foot-binding. They taught Western science and political philosophy, opening a window on new ideas used to advantage by East Asian reformers and revolutionaries.

Western imperialism demanded new countermeasures from China and Japan. Both nations started sending diplomatic missions abroad in the 1860s, in part to try to revise the unequal treaties or at least lessen their effects and in part to study their opponents. Korea too sent study missions to China, Japan, and the United States in the early 1880s. To the north, China resolved its boundary disputes with Russia. Trade increased, especially after the completion of the Suez Canal in 1869 halved travel time between Europe and East Asia and stimulated the development of more efficient, faster steamships. The laying of telegraphic cables made communication between East and West practically instantaneous.

Western imperialism led directly and indirectly to increased migration within Asia and between Asia and the rest of the world. British plantation owners on the Malay Peninsula imported Indian workers. Disruptions in the local economy sent Indian merchants into Central Asia, Burma, and the South Pacific. Chinese seafarers, merchants, and laborers established overseas communities across Southeast Asia, notably in Java and Singapore. They also migrated to the United States, Hawai'i, Cuba, and Peru, where they were brutally exploited because their government was perceived as too weak to protect them. The nineteenth century thus witnessed an Asian diaspora, led primarily by Indians and Chinese, which followed trade networks and filtered into colonies established by the Great Powers.

Japan soon began to mimic the Western claim that imperialism was necessary to civilize the savages by acquainting them with the material and spiritual benefits of modern technology and mechanisms of social control. In 1871 it proposed an unequal treaty with China, only to be rejected. Three years later, it sent a military expedition to Taiwan to retaliate for the murder of Ryukyuan fishermen. After the Qing court agreed to pay an indemnity, Japan withdrew.

A similar plan to invade Korea did not materialize only because Japan's leaders did not think they were ready. Instead, Japan imposed a treaty on Korea that gave it the same privileges of most favored nation status and extraterritoriality that Westerners enjoyed in Japan. It also solidified its northern boundary by agreeing with Russia that while Sakhalin would become part of Russia, the Kuril Islands belonged to Japan.

Rivalries between the Great Powers soon brought fresh waves of Western imperialism across Asia. In 1882 the United States became the first Western power to sign a commercial treaty with Korea. Thanks to the most favored nation clause, the European powers and Japan immediately gained the same privileges. After Vietnam appealed for help from China, its nominal overlord, the French attacked a new naval base in China, forcing China to grant that Vietnam existed as a separate country and watch it disappear with Cambodia and, later, Laos into a French colony. Sandwiched between British Burma and French Indochina, Thailand remained independent by agreeing to a series of unequal treaties. Russia and Britain tried to outbid each other for influence in Korea, while one faction at the Korean court sought American intervention to preserve Korean independence.

In contrast to East Asia where the European drive to establish colonies confronted countries with highly developed systems of rule, the prevalence of malaria staved off Africa's colonization until quinine (an ingredient in tonic water) became widely available. Following decades of European explorers in Africa, King Leopold II of Belgium in 1876 fostered the founding of the International Association for the Exploration and Civilization of Africa, while the British and French took over Egyptian finances to manage that country's debt to its European creditors. (Britain performed a similar role in China when it undertook to collect customs duties for the Qing court.) Belgium, Germany, Italy, Portugal, and Spain joined Britain and France in carving Africa into protectorates and colonies that varied somewhat in their exploitation of natural resources and the brutal treatment of natives. (See Map C6.1.)

Imperialism in Asia entered a new phase when China and Japan fought over Korea in 1894–1895. When the Korean king requested help from China in suppressing rebellion, Japan responded first, lest China gain what it saw as unacceptable influence over the Korean court. Japan's victories on land and sea enabled it to claim Taiwan, the Pescadores

islands, the Liaodong peninsula in Manchuria, forts on the Shandong peninsula, commercial favors, and the usual bank-breaking indemnity. Russia opposed the Japanese land grab owing to its own designs on Manchuria and Korea; Germany had growing commercial interests in China and wanted to divert Russia away from central Europe; and France had an alliance with Russia. The three nations launched the Triple Intervention to make Japan restore the Liaodong and Shandong peninsulas to China. In a move that the Japanese public saw as blatant hypocrisy, the French then gained concessions in southern China for railroads and mines, and Russia got an eighty-year lease over the Liaodong peninsula from China that was later expanded to include Port Arthur. When the Germans built forts on portions of the Shandong peninsula, Britain took a naval base across from Port Arthur. Competition between the European powers prevented any of them from making China its colony. Instead they scrambled for concessions by carving out spheres of influence dominated by officials and traders, primarily along the coast and up the Yangzi River. Uneasy at the prospect of being shut out of the market for Chinese goods and souls, American merchants and missionaries called on their government to act. Secretary of State John Hay urged the European powers and Japan to adopt an "open door" policy that would stop the spheres of influence from excluding Americans. The other powers agreed, although with reservations that protected their interests.

Even beyond the spheres of influence, missionaries brought change to northern and eastern China. Their letters to parishes back home heightened awareness of and interest in Chinese affairs. Missionaries also proved disruptive. When they forbade the rituals associated with ancestor worship, they seemingly threatened the fabric of family life. Because converts often came from the lower rungs of society, missionary efforts to protect them against the gentry or to rescue them from the courts of district magistrates provoked outrage by local elites. When the missionary presence provoked violence, the Western powers dispatched gunboats and troops to intimidate officials.

Although attacks on missionaries often complicated relations between the Western powers and China, none matched the consequences of the so-called Boxer Rebellion. It began in Shandong in 1898 as an anti-foreign movement that combined martial arts with rituals promising protection against weapons,

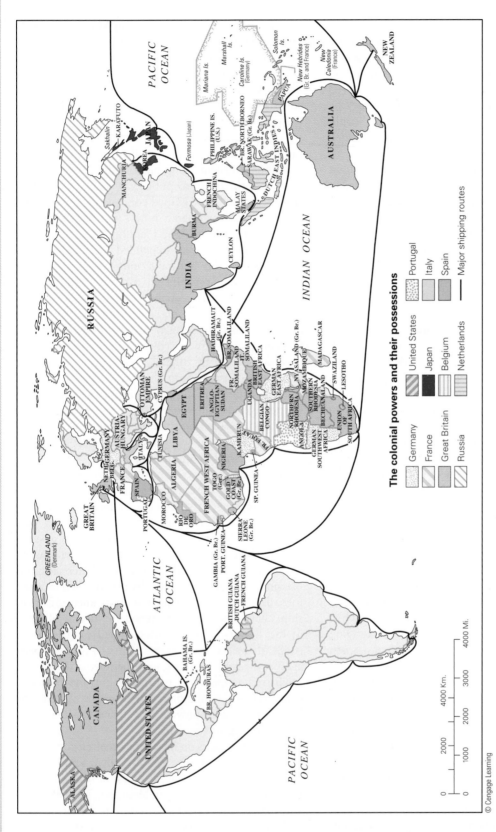

© Cengage Learning

Map C6.1   Western Imperialism in the Late Nineteenth Century

somewhat similar to the Ghost Dance that rallied the Sioux against American encroachment in the Dakotas in the late 1880s. Boxers attacked converts and missionaries, sometimes with the quiet approval of Qing officials. They routed Western troops sent to reinforce the defenses for the diplomatic community in Beijing and tore up railroad tracks between Tianjin and the capital. The Qing court ordered the massacre of all foreigners on Chinese soil and declared war on the foreign powers.

Faced with a common threat, the Western powers and Japan united against China. Efforts by Chinese generals in central and south China to suppress anti-foreign activity in their areas helped Americans convince the other powers not to expand the scale of conflict beyond an expeditionary force sent to liberate the diplomatic community under siege in Beijing. When the expeditionary force reached the city in August 1900, the Qing court fled to Xi'an. Japanese soldiers watched with amazement as Western troops ran amok for three days in an orgy of looting, rape, and murder. Negotiations over the size of the indemnity to be extracted from China and its distribution among the powers dragged on for a year. The indemnity imposed a crushing financial burden on the Chinese government and absorbed funds needed for economic development. Only rivalry among the powers, and particularly distrust of Russia, stopped proposals for China's dismemberment.

The nineteenth century marked the heyday of Western imperialism as practice and ideology. Following the spread of Darwin's ideas on evolution and the survival of the fittest, Herbert Spencer and others developed the notion of Social Darwinism. They thought that not just species but also nations stood in danger of extinction unless they emerged victorious in the ceaseless competition between them. States that did not understand this principle or found themselves too weak to resist modern military technology naturally fell prey to conquerors from afar. Social Darwinism provided new justification for the Westerners' sense of racial superiority. Some used this notion to justify cruel exploitation of native populations. Others felt it their duty to bring civilization to the heathens. After the American

colonization of the Philippines and annexation of Hawai`i, Rudyard Kipling wrote:

> Take up the White Man's burden—
> Send forth the best ye breed—
> Go bind your sons to exile
> To serve your captives' need;
> To wait in heavy harness,
> On fluttered folk and wild—
> Your new-caught, sullen peoples,
> Half-devil and half-child."
>
> . . . .
>
> Take up the White Man's burden—
> The savage wars of peace
> Fill full the mouth of Famine
> And bid the sickness cease;
> And when your goal is nearest
> The end for others sought,
> Watch sloth and heathen Folly
> Bring all your hopes to nought.*

Western imperialism in East Asia took a different form than in the rest of the world. Rather than establish colonies (Hong Kong and Macao being the exception), the Western powers imposed unequal treaties. Although they used Asian labor for difficult, dangerous jobs such as building the transcontinental railroad in the United States, they issued discriminatory exclusion laws to prevent first Chinese and then Japanese from living permanently in their countries or becoming citizens. By dint of a Westernization project that involved writing Western-style commercial, civil, and criminal legal codes plus the creation of a modern army, Japan gained abolition of most favored nation treatment and extraterritoriality in 1899. Its victory in war with Russia to win control of the Liaodong peninsula in 1904–1905 gave hope to people all over Asia that Western dominance might pass.

---

*R. Kipling, "The White Man's Burden," *McChary's Magazine* 12:4 (February 1899): 0-004.

China in Decline (1800–1900)

During the early nineteenth century, the Qing Dynasty seemed to be slipping into dynastic decline. Revenues were no longer adequate to cover the costs of administration. Rural poverty was worsening. Then in midcentury, some of the bloodiest rebellions in Chinese history broke out. On top of this, a new enemy had appeared on China's shores, one able to land its ships where it liked and destroy Chinese defenses with its cannons.

Yet the Qing Dynasty did not fall. The generals who suppressed the rebellions did not take to fighting among themselves to see which of them could found the next dynasty, as had happened so many times before in Chinese history. Some credit should go to the Qing elite, who in the 1860s and 1870s took on the task of self-strengthening. Yet progress, though real, was never rapid enough, and late in the century China suffered further blows to its pride: first its defeat by Japan in 1894–1895 and then the allied occupation of Beijing in 1900.

These internal and external threats and the way the Qing responded to them have preoccupied most historians who study nineteenth-century China. What made China's encounter with the West so different in the nineteenth century than in the eighteenth? How many of China's problems came from within and how many from outside forces? Does putting stress on the new challenges of Western imperialism distort understanding of this period, making the West into the actor and China merely a reactor? Did it matter that China's rulers during this period were Manchu? Were the forces of global capitalism and imperialism so skewed against China that different policies would have made little difference?

ECONOMIC AND FISCAL PROBLEMS

The peace that the Qing Dynasty brought to China allowed the population to grow rapidly. Although scholars have not come to a consensus on the details of China's population growth, there is wide agreement that by the beginning of the nineteenth century, China had a population of about 300 million and was continuing to grow, reaching about 400 million by 1850. The traditional Chinese view of population increase was positive: growth was a sign of peace and prosperity. Through the eighteenth century, most still accepted that view. As developed areas became more crowded, farmers tried cultivating more intensively, making more use of irrigation and fertilizer and weeding more regularly, techniques that made denser populations possible in the richest areas. Others moved to less crowded regions, both at the peripheries of the long-settled areas and the thinly populated southwest, previously occupied largely by minority peoples. The only lands suited to agriculture that were out of bounds were those in Manchuria, which the Qing maintained as a preserve for the Manchus.

In the early nineteenth century, China's standard of living fell behind Europe's. As farms grew smaller and surplus labor depressed wages, the average standard of living suffered. When all the best lands were occupied, conflicts over rights to water or tenancy increased. Hard times also led to increased female infanticide because families felt they could not afford to raise more than two or three children and saw sons as necessities. A shortage of marriageable women resulted, reducing the incentive for young men to stay near home and do as their elders told them. Many young men who took to the road in hope of finding better opportunities never found permanent homes; instead they became part of a floating population of unemployed, moving around in search of work. They would take seasonal farm work or work as boatmen, charcoal burners, night soil collectors, and the like. In cities they might become sedan chair carriers, beggars, or thieves. Women, even poor ones, had an easier time finding a place in a home because of the demand for maids and concubines. But poverty fed the traffic in women; poor families sold their daughters for cash, perhaps expecting them to become rich men's concubines, though many ended up as prostitutes. Population growth also added to the burdens placed on local governments. Although the population doubled and tripled, the number of counties and county officials stayed the same. Magistrates often found that they had to turn to the local elite for help, even turning tax collection over to them.

During the Qianlong reign, the government had resources to try to improve the lot of the poor. But in the nineteenth century, even determined emperors like the Daoguang (dow-gwang) emperor (r. 1821–1850)

were chronically short of revenue for crucial public works and relief measures. The Daoguang emperor set an example of frugality at court and encouraged his officials to cut every possible cost, but the fiscal situation steadily worsened. He ordered repairs to the Grand Canal (see **Material Culture: The Grand Canal**), yet the years of neglect meant that more and more tax grain had to be sent by sea, exacerbating unemployment in north China.

Another problem the emperor faced was supporting the hereditary military force, the banners, which in a manner reminiscent of the decline of the Ming hereditary soldiers was no longer effective in war. To suppress the rebellions of the late eighteenth century, the government was forced to turn to local militias and the professional (as opposed to hereditary) army of Chinese recruits called the Army of the Green Standard. Because the banners were so tied to Manchu identity and privileges, the emperor could not simply disband them, as the Ming had its hereditary military households. The best the Daoguang emperor could hope for was to keep bannermen from becoming beggars, bandits, opium smugglers, or opium addicts.

MIDCENTURY CRISES

The decline of the Qing military forces was made evident to all in the 1840s and 1850s when the dynasty had to cope with military crises along its coastlines and throughout its interior.

The Opium War

As discussed in Chapter 16, the Qing Dynasty dealt with foreign countries according to a set of rules it had largely taken over from the Ming Dynasty. Europeans were permitted to trade only at the port of Guangzhou and only through licensed Chinese merchants. In the eighteenth century, the balance of trade was in China's favor because Great Britain and other Western nations used silver to pay for steadily increasing purchases of tea. British traders found few buyers when they brought British and Indian goods to Guangzhou to sell. When Macartney asked the Qianlong emperor to alter the way trade was conducted, the emperor saw no reason to approve his request.

As discussed in **Connections: The Age of Western Imperialism (1800–1900)**, all this soon changed. By the late eighteenth century, the British had found

MATERIAL CULTURE

The Grand Canal

Transport canals were dug in China from ancient times. The first Grand Canal connecting Luoyang to the Yangzi River was completed during the Sui Dynasty. During Song times the canal extended south to Hangzhou, and in Yuan times it reached north to Beijing. During the Ming period the government invested a lot of effort in maintaining the Grand Canal because it carried a large share of the tax grain.

The canal that the Qing inherited was 1,747 kilometers long and crossed five major rivers. It had to rise to 138 feet above sea level to get over the mountains of western Shandong. This necessitated an elaborate system of locks, dams, sluice gates, and slipways. Pulleys driven by animal or human labor pulled boats through sluice gates and skips. Because the canal crossed the Yellow River, maintaining the dikes on the river was crucial to keep floods with their heavy deposits of silt from clogging the canal.

By the early nineteenth century, more than fifty thousand hereditary boatmen and migrant laborers worked moving the tax grain up the canal from the southeast to the capital. In 1824 the grain ships en route to Beijing became mired in silt because the canal had not been properly maintained. Boatmen were put to work making repairs, but more and more grain tax had to be sent by the sea route. By 1850 the canal was largely abandoned. Unemployed boatmen were prominent among those who joined the Nian (nyan) rebellion in the 1850s.

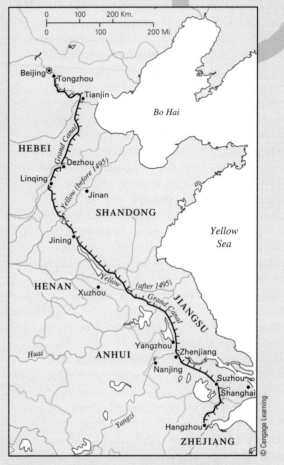

Map 18.1   Grand Canal During the Ming and Qing Dynasties

something the Chinese would buy: opium. Made from poppy plants, opium had been used in China for medicinal purposes for several centuries. Once a way was found to smoke pure opium sap in pipes, opium became a recreational drug that people took to relieve pain and boredom and to make tedious or taxing work more bearable. The drawback was that it was addictive; those who stopped taking it suffered chills, nausea, and muscle cramps. The Daoguang emperor was outraged when an 1831 investigation showed that members of the imperial clan, high officials, and bannermen were among those addicted

to opium. Once addicted, people would do almost anything to keep up their supply of the drug, even pawning their clothing and selling their children. To fight addiction, the Chinese government banned both the production and the importation of opium in 1800. In 1813 it went further and outlawed the smoking of opium, punishing it with a beating of a hundred blows.

The opium that the British brought to China was grown in India. Following the British acquisition of large parts of India, the East India Company invested heavily in planting and processing opium, over which it had a profitable monopoly. Once China made trade in opium illegal, the company did not distribute opium itself; rather, licensed private traders, Americans as well as British, carried the drug to China. Chinese smugglers bought opium from British and American traders anchored off the coast, then distributed it through a series of middlemen, making it difficult for the Qing government to catch the major dealers.

By 1831 there were between one hundred and two hundred Chinese smugglers' boats plying the Guangdong coastal waters. The competition among private traders led to a price war in China that drove the price of opium down and thus spread addiction. Imports increased rapidly, from forty-five hundred chests smuggled into China in 1810 to forty thousand chests in 1838, enough to supply 2 million addicts. By this point, it was China that suffered a drain of silver. The outflow increased from about 2 million ounces of silver per year in the 1820s to about 9 million in the 1830s. This silver drain hurt farmers because their taxes were assessed in silver. A tax obligation of 1 ounce of silver took about 1,500 cash to pay in 1800, but 2,700 cash in 1830.

The Daoguang emperor called for debate on how to deal with this crisis. Some court officials advocated legalizing the sale of opium and taxing it, which would help alleviate the government revenue shortfalls and perhaps make the drug expensive enough to deter some people from trying it. Other officials strongly disagreed, believing that an evil like opium had to be stopped. The governor-general, Lin Zexu (lin dzuh-shyew), argued that rather than concentrate on the users, the government should go after those who imported or sold the drug. Unless trade in the drug was suppressed, he argued, the Qing would have no soldiers to fight the enemy and no funds to support an army. Lin's impassioned stand and his reputation as incorruptible led the Daoguang emperor in late 1838 to assign him the task of suppressing the opium trade. Once Lin arrived at Guangzhou, he made rapid progress, arresting some seventeen hundred Chinese dealers and seizing seventy thousand opium pipes. He demanded that foreign firms turn over their opium stores as well, offering tea in exchange. When his appeals failed, Lin stopped all trade and placed a siege on the Western merchants' enclave. After six weeks, the merchants relented and turned over their opium, some 2.6 million pounds. Lin set five hundred laborers to work for twenty-two days to destroy the opium by mixing it with salt and lime and washing it into the sea. He pressured the Portuguese to expel the uncooperative British from Macao, as a consequence of which they settled on the barren island of Hong Kong.

To the British superintendent of trade, Lin's act was an affront to British dignity and cause enough for war. The British saw China as out of step with the modern world in which all "civilized" nations practiced free trade and maintained "normal" international relations through envoys and treaties. With the encouragement of their merchants in China, the British sent from India a small, mobile expeditionary force of forty-two ships, many of them leased from the major opium trader Jardine, Matheson, and Company. Because Lin had strengthened defenses at Guangzhou, the British sailed north and shut down the major ports of Ningbo and Tianjin (tyan-jin), forcing the Qing to negotiate. (See Map 18.1.) A preliminary agreement called for ceding Hong Kong, repaying the British the cost of their expedition, and allowing direct diplomatic intercourse between the new countries.

In both countries, the response was outrage. The Daoguang emperor had withdrawn his support for Lin as soon as the war broke out and had sent him into exile in the far northwest; now the official who negotiated the treaty was also treated like a criminal. The English sent a second, larger force, which attacked Guangzhou, occupied other ports, including Shanghai (shahng-hy), as it proceeded up the coast, and finally sailed up the Yangzi River to Nanjing. Dozens of Qing officers, both Manchu and Chinese, committed suicide when they saw that they could not repel the British (see **Biography: Manchu Bannerman Guancheng**).

At this point, the Qing government had no choice but to capitulate. Concluded at gunpoint, the 1842 Treaty of Nanjing provided benefits for Britain but not for China, making it "unequal." It was soon followed by an amended agreement and treaties with the United States and France. This set of treaties mandated ambassadors in Beijing, opened five ports to international trade, fixed the tariff on imported goods at 5 percent, imposed an indemnity of 21 million silver dollars on China to cover Britain's war costs, and ceded the island of Hong Kong to Britain. Through the clause on extraterritoriality, British subjects in China were answerable only to British law, even in disputes with Chinese. The most favored nation clause meant that whenever one nation extracted a new privilege from China, it was extended automatically to Britain. Western imperialism had its first victory in China.

At the Daoguang court, the aftermath of this de-bacle was a bitter struggle between war and peace factions reminiscent of the similar disputes during the Song Dynasty. Those who had favored compromising with the "sea barbarians" to avoid further hostilities included the Manchu chancellor Mujangga; those op-posed were mostly Chinese degree holders who had supported Lin Zexu and believed the Qing should have put up stronger resistance. After the Daoguang emperor died in 1850, his successor announced his determination to make no more concessions by dis-missing Mujangga and bringing back Lin Zexu. The court kept finding excuses not to accept foreign dip-lomats in Beijing, and its compliance with the com-mercial clauses fell far short of Western expectations.

The Opium War exposed the fact that Qing military technology was hopelessly obsolete. The Qing had no navy. Britain had not only large men-of-war but also new shallow-draft steamships that could sail up rivers. Thus, the British could land troops wherever they liked. Troops would pillage, then return to their ships to attack a new target. On a single day in 1841, a British steam-powered warship with long-distance artillery destroyed nine war junks, five forts, two mili-tary stations, and a shore battery. Even when Qing forces fought on land, they were no match for the British troops. To fight British soldiers armed with rifles, the Chinese and Manchu soldiers used swords, spears, clubs, and arrows. The minority with firearms had only matchlock muskets that required soldiers to ignite each load of gunpowder by hand.

Taiping Rebellion

Beginning less than a decade after the Opium War, the Qing Dynasty faced some of the most destructive rebellions in world history. The bloodiest was the Taiping Rebellion (1851–1864), which cost some 20 to 30 million lives.

Like many of China's earlier insurrections, this one had its organizational base in an unorthodox religious sect. The founder of this sect was Hong Xiuquan (hung shyou-chwan) (1814–1864). Hong was a Hakka (the Hakkas were a large Han Chinese ethnic group that spoke a distinct dialect and lived predominantly in the far south). Although from a humble background, Hong had spent years attempting the civil service ex-aminations. His career as a religious leader began with visions of a golden-bearded old man and a middle-aged man who addressed him as younger brother and told him to annihilate devils. After reading a Christian tract that a missionary in Guangzhou had given to

him, Hong interpreted his visions to mean that he was Jesus's younger brother. He began preaching, calling on people to destroy idols and ancestral temples, give up opium and alcohol, and renounce foot bind-ing and prostitution. Hong spent two months study-ing with a Christian preacher and adopted the Ten Commandments, monotheism, and the practice of communal prayer and hymns. He called his group the God Worshipping Society and soon attracted many followers, especially among the Hakkas.

Hong was a visionary, not an organizer, and other leaders emerged who learned how to manipulate him. In 1848, while Hong and his closest associ-ate were away from their headquarters, an illiterate charcoal maker and local bully named Yang Xiuqing (yahng shyou-ching) elevated himself and three oth-ers to top posts within the God Worshippers. To claim superiority over Hong, Yang announced that when he spoke, it was the voice of God the Father, putting him above Hong, the mere younger brother.

In 1850 the Taiping leaders told all God Worshippers to leave their homes, pool their money into a common treasury, and move to Thistle Mountain in Guangxi province, a site that soon became a huge military camp. In 1851, Hong declared himself king of the Heavenly Kingdom of Great Peace (Taiping, ty-ping), an act of open insurrection. Men were to abandon the Manchu queue and let their hair grow long. Hong's true believ-ers were brave in battle, maintained strict discipline, and seized large stores of government weapons as they campaigned. Their religious zeal propelled them to de-stroy local temples, even though this alienated many commoners. They regularly forced those whose villages they captured to join their movement, enrolling men and women into separate work and military teams. Some brigades of women soldiers fought Qing forces.

Once news of the progress of the rebellion reached the court, Qing troops were dispatched to disperse the Taipings and arrest their leaders. (See Map 18.2.) To the shock of the court, the Qing troops were soundly defeated. The rebels tried to stoke anti-Manchu feel-ings, saying that they had "stolen" China. Manchu bannermen and their families were often slaughtered after Taiping forces took a city.

After making Nanjing their capital, the Taipings announced plans for a utopian society based on the equalization of landholdings and the equality of men and women. Women could take the civil service examinations, which were based on Hong Xiuquan's teachings and translations of the Bible. Christian missionaries at first were excited about the prospect of revolutionaries spreading Christianity but quickly

BIOGRAPHY

Manchu Bannerman Guancheng

Guancheng (gwan-chuhng) (ca. 1790–1843) was born the son of a Manchu bannerman of the Hangzhou garrisons, stationed at the nearby port of Zhapu (jah-poo). Although he would be considered Manchu through descent on the male line, both his mother and his father's mother were daughters of Chinese bannermen in the same garrisons. His father died when he was an infant, and he was raised by his mother and his deceased elder brother's widow. In his youth the banner garrisons were chronically short of funds for bannerman stipends and payments for widows and orphans; therefore, he most likely grew up in straitened circumstances. Still, he attended banner schools, where he studied both Chinese and Manchu. By the age of twenty he was working as a tutor himself, and at age twenty-seven he attained the *juren* degree, availing himself of the special quota for Manchu bannermen. By then he also had a Chinese name, Guan Weitong, which used part of his personal name as a Chinese family name. (In Manchu, his clan name was Gūwalgiya, but Manchu clan names were not used as terms of address.) To supplement his family's income, Guancheng took on some publishing jobs during this period.

In the late 1820s, Guancheng traveled to Beijing to take the *jinshi* examinations. Beijing was the great center of Manchu life, home to perhaps 150,000 Manchus. Opium addiction had already become a major problem among the underemployed bannermen, something Guancheng would undoubtedly have noticed. But it was also home to Manchu nobles who lived a highly cultivated life. The highest-ranking member of his clan had a mansion in the city and welcomed Guancheng to his social circle. There he met descendants of Qing emperors and heard much lore about Manchu court life. The language in which they discussed these subjects was, however, Chinese.

Although Guancheng did not pass the *jinshi* exam, he was given an honorary degree and in 1833 was appointed a probationary magistrate of a county in Sichuan. He took two of his sons, ages nine and eleven, with him to Sichuan but sent his wife and two youngest sons back to Zhapu. At first he was rapidly transferred from one county to another, then from 1834 to 1842 had a long stint as magistrate of Nanchuan county, a tea-producing region 39 miles south of the Yangzi River. Local non-Chinese rebelled during his tenure, adding to hardships caused by locusts. Still, his son remembered the time in Sichuan as very enjoyable.

When Guancheng returned to Zhapu in 1842 at age fifty-three, he was something of a celebrity—a local bannerman who had succeeded in the outside world. His home community, meanwhile, had suffered a devastating blow. In 1840, at the start of the Opium War, British ships had shelled the Zhapu ports. Despite attempts to reinforce the garrisons for a possible return of the British, when they did in fact return in the spring of 1842, Zhapu's defenses proved sorely lacking. Many of those who did not die defending Zhapu took their own lives afterward, often first killing their wives and children. On his return, Guancheng, though ill himself, took on the task of writing and printing an account of the heroism of the bannermen in the defense of Zhapu. He wanted help for those who had survived and honor for those who had died. "The officers, soldiers, men and women of our garrison were ill-prepared for this, the corpses having been found piled against buildings and even suspended from the battlements. In mourning our nation's dead, how could we bear to allow these loyal clansmen to be buried without benefit of ceremony?"* After Guancheng died in early 1843, his son issued a revised "Record of Martyrs."

Questions for Analysis

1. What difference did it make that Guancheng was a Manchu?
2. Why would Guancheng have wanted to record the stories of those who failed to defend their garrison?

---

*Translated in Pamela Kyle Crossley, *Orphan Warriors: Three Manchu Generations and the End of the Qing World* (Princeton, N.J.: Princeton University Press, 1990), p. 115.

---

concluded that the Christian elements in Taiping doctrines were heretical. When the Taipings tried to take Shanghai in 1860 and 1862, the Western residents organized counterattacks.

In time the Taipings were weakened by internal dissension. After Yang claimed that God the Father insisted that Hong should be beaten for kicking one of Yang's concubines, Hong arranged to have Yang executed. The king entrusted with this task killed not only Yang and his family but also twenty thousand followers, leading to another round of revenge killings.

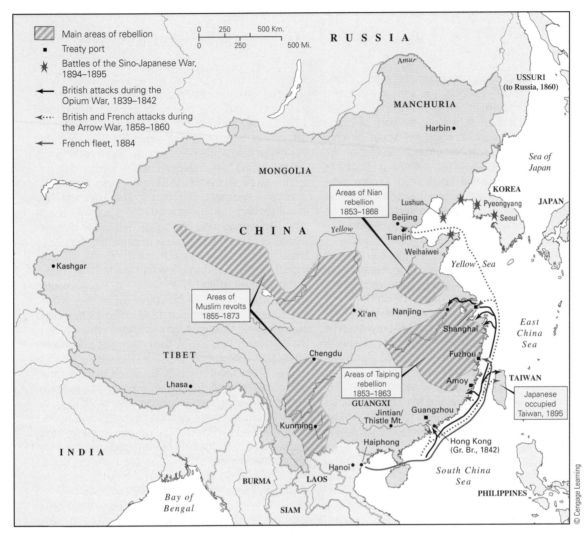

Map 18.2   Internal and External Conflicts During the Nineteenth Century

The Chinese elite were horrified by the Taiping movement with its bizarre foreign gods and women soldiers. In many places, local officials and landlords organized their own defense, repairing city walls, gathering food to withstand a siege, and arming and drilling recruits. The Qing government soon realized that it would have to turn to such locally raised armies if it wished to make progress against the Taipings.

The man they turned to, Zeng Guofan (dzuhng gaw-fahn) (1811–1872), was at home in Hunan province to mourn his mother when the rebels drew near. Knowing the failings of the Qing armies, he organized a local defense force in a new way. He recruited officers from among the Confucian-educated elite and had them recruit their own soldiers from among farmers in their region. Zeng was given permission to draw on local tax receipts and so could pay the soldiers and officers well. Soldiers were loyal to their officers and the officers to Zeng, creating an essentially private army. After Zeng constructed 240 war junks so that he could attack by river and gathered some modern Western weapons such as artillery, he set about recovering Hunan province bit by bit. The Taipings, however, also made advances, and Zeng needed twelve years and 120,000 troops before he fully defeated the Taipings. Generals under him, including close relatives and his protégés Li Hongzhang (lee hung-jahng) and Zuo Zongtang (dzaw dzung-tahng), played major roles in the slow stranglehold placed over the

Taiping capital at Nanjing. When Nanjing fell, none of the Taipings survived. Elsewhere in south China, the Taipings held out longer, with some armies relocating to Taiwan and Vietnam. In Vietnam, where they were known as the Black Flags, they took an active part in resistance to French colonial expansion.

The devastation wreaked both by the Taipings' campaigns and the Qing campaigns to suppress them was horrendous. One Western observer wrote in 1865 that China's plains were "strewn with human skeletons," its rivers "polluted with floating carcasses."[*] Much of the productive power of the lower Yangzi region was ruined for a generation.

Other Rebellions

The Taipings were turned back when they took their campaign into north China, but that region soon found itself torn apart by homegrown insurrections. Along the route of the Grand Canal, poverty and unemployment had driven many villagers into banditry. These groups of the disaffected, called Nian (nyen) gangs, engaged in a variety of predatory practices. Riding horseback, they would seize villagers' crops, rob traveling merchants, and kidnap the wealthy to hold them for ransom. Severe flooding in 1851 weakened the dikes of the Yellow River, which gave way in 1855, leading to a devastating shift in the Yellow River from south of the Shandong peninsula to north of it. Those made homeless by the floods joined the Nian bands simply to survive. Many joined on a seasonal basis, staying home in the summer and winter but raiding and plundering in the autumn and spring. After the Taipings fell in 1864, some of their soldiers joined the Nian rebellion. In 1865, when it was clear that the Qing regular armies had failed to suppress the Nian, Zeng Guofan and Li Hongzhang were assigned the long and difficult task.

With the transfer of armies to the interior to fight the Taipings and Nian rebels, uprisings also got out of hand in the northwest and southwest. These rebellions drew from and also exacerbated ethnic tensions and hatreds. In Yunnan, the large Muslim population had grievances based on Han Chinese settlers' moving into their territory and seizing resources such as copper, gold, and silver mines. As tensions escalated, so did feuds and violence. Han Chinese formed militias to kill

---

*Cited in R. Keith Schoppa, *Revolution and Its Past: Identities and Change in Modern Chinese History* (Upper Saddle River, N.J.: Prentice Hall, 2002), p. 64.

Muslims, who in retaliation assassinated Chinese officials. Rebels captured the city of Dali and announced the sultanate of Panthay. The remote location of Yunnan and its mountainous topography made it difficult for the Qing to send troops there. The Qing was able to regain control in 1873 only because it learned to play opposing factions of Muslims against each other.

The Muslim rebellion in the northwest (Gansu) was rooted in the spread of a mystical school of Islam known as Sufism, but much of the violence came from long-standing antagonism between the Han Chinese and the Muslims. By 1867 all of Gansu was in Muslim hands, and the Qing dispatched Zuo Zongtang (1812–1885) to retake the region. Zuo classed Sufis as heterodox, like White Lotus or Taiping sectarians, and ordered their slaughter. The campaign took five years and consisted largely of sieges during which the population slowly starved. Zuo Zongtang marched his troops into Xinjiang, which might well have broken away from Qing control otherwise.

The Second Opium War

While the Qing court was struggling to suppress the Taiping, Nian, and Muslim rebellions, it had to face demands from foreign powers as well. Russia, seeing China's weakness, penetrated the Amur River valley, violating the borders agreed to in 1689. In new treaties of 1858–1860, Russia gained the maritime provinces of eastern Manchuria down to Vladivostok. A large part of the reason the Qing decided to march an army into Xinjiang was fear of Russian expansion there.

Britain and France were pressing China as well. Both sides wanted the trade agreement reached after the Opium War renegotiated, though for different reasons. On the grounds that China had failed to implement all the provisions agreed to a decade earlier, the British and French decided to make swift, brutal coastal attacks, a repeat of the Opium War. (They called it the Arrow War, from the name of a ship that gave the British a pretext for war.) Guangzhou was easily captured at the end of 1857 and held for three years. By mid-1858, the French and British ships were in the north and took the forts at Tianjin. At this point, the Qing court in Beijing sent senior officials to negotiate. When the British threatened to march on Beijing unless they were allowed permanent diplomatic representation in Beijing, the hard-pressed Manchu negotiator conceded. Also secured in these treaties were the opening of ten new ports; permission for Westerners, including missionaries, to travel through China; a fixed transit

Library of Congress, LC-USZ62-13819

Li Hongzhang. The eminent statesman let a photographer take a picture of him seated in a sedan chair in the courtyard of his office in Tianjin.

tariff for foreign goods within China of no more than 2.5 percent; and an indemnity of 4 million ounces of silver for the British and 2 million for the French. Each side was to have its rulers ratify the treaties and return in a year for the signing.

The Qing emperor was strongly opposed to allowing ambassadors to reside in Beijing, viewing them as little better than spies. When the British returned and insisted on taking their ships up the Beihe (bay-huh) River toward Beijing instead of going overland, as the Qing wanted them to, Qing forces withstood them. A new expedition was then dispatched with eleven thousand British soldiers and sixty-seven hundred French ones. When Qing authorities did not let them have their way on all matters, they charged into Beijing. The Russian ambassador, already in residence in Beijing, talked the British out of burning the palace in retaliation. The British and French then marched to the summer palace located northwest of the city, a complex of two hundred or so buildings. They looted the buildings of furniture, porcelains, robes, and whatever else attracted them and then torched the entire 10-square-mile complex. The Russian ambassador this time approached the Qing court and talked them into accepting the offered terms, which included having to pay a larger indemnity of 16 million ounces

of silver and transfer of the Kowloon peninsula opposite Hong Kong island to Britain.

Because the Western powers gained many advantages through these unequal treaties, after 1860 they increasingly saw propping up the faltering Qing Dynasty as in their interest.

SELF-STRENGTHENING

In 1861 the Xianfeng (shyen-fung) emperor died and was succeeded by a young son. The child's uncle, Prince Gong (gung), and his mother, Empress Dowager Cixi (tsih-shee), served as regents. A change in emperor normally meant a change in chancellors and other high officials, making it easier for the court to take new directions. Certainly, new policies were needed; much of the most productive parts of the country had been laid waste by the rebellions, none of which was yet suppressed, and the British and French had only recently left Beijing after extracting new concessions.

In that same year, a scholar named Feng Guifen (fung gway-fuhn) (1809–1874) wrote a set of essays presenting the case for wide-ranging reforms. He had taken refuge in Shanghai during the Taiping War and there had seen how the Westerners defended the city. In his essays he pointed out that China was a hundred times bigger than France and two hundred times bigger than Great Britain. "Why are Western nations small and yet strong? Why are we large and yet weak?" He called for hiring a few "barbarians" to help set up shipyards and arsenals in each major port. To get ambitious men to take on the task of managing these enterprises, he proposed rewarding them with examination degrees if the ships and weapons produced were as good as those of the foreigners. He also proposed setting up translation bureaus to translate Western books on mathematics and the sciences. Westerners should be hired to teach groups of boys Western languages. "China has many brilliant people. There must be some who can learn from the barbarians and surpass them."[*] He pointed out that many Westerners had learned the Chinese language and much about the country; surely there should be Chinese people just as capable. To improve the morale of officials, he proposed subjecting high officials to election by lower-ranking officials. Local elites would be given the power to nominate

---

[*]W. Theodore de Bary and Richard Lufrano, *Sources of Chinese Tradition: From 1600 Through the Twentieth Century* (New York: Columbia University Press, 2000), pp. 236, 237.

local officials, thus broadening political participation considerably. Undoubtedly influenced by what he had learned of foreign election practices, he specified that the votes were to be counted.

An important minority of officials, including Zeng Guofan and Li Hongzhang, were more and more persuaded by these sorts of arguments. Prince Gong sided with them, and changes were made not only in how soldiers were trained and weapons produced but also in the conduct of foreign affairs. Arsenals and dockyards were established, schools opened to teach European languages and international law, and a foreign office established to manage diplomatic affairs, with Prince Gong in charge. By 1880, China had embassies in London, Paris, Berlin, Madrid, Washington, Tokyo, and St. Petersburg.

Li Hongzhang's Self-Strengthening Projects, 1862–1893

1862 Created gun factories at Shanghai with British and German instructors

1863 Established a foreign language school in Shanghai

1864 Created a gun factory at Suzhou

1865 Established Jiangnan Arsenal at Shanghai with a translation bureau attached, jointly with Zeng Guofan

1867 Established Nanjing Arsenal

1870 Expanded machine factory in Tianjin

1872 Sent officers to study in Germany. Made request to open coal and iron mines. Jointly with Zeng recommended sending teenagers to study in the U.S. Supported China Merchants' Steam Navigation Company as a "government-supervised merchant enterprise."

1876 Sent seven officers to Germany

1877 Created the Bureau for the Kaiping Coal Mines in Tianjin

1878 Established the Shanghai Cotton Mill

1880 Established a naval academy in Tianjin. Requested permission to build a railroad.

1882 Began construction of a harbor and shipyard at Port Arthur

1884 Sent naval students and apprentices to Europe to learn shipbuilding and navigation

1885 Established a military academy in Tianjin with German teachers

1887 Established a mint at Tianjin. Began gold mining operation in Heilongjiang.

1888 Established the Beiyang fleet

1891 Established a paper mill in Shanghai

1893 Set up a general office for mechanized textile manufacturing

---

After Zeng Guofan's death in 1872, Li Hongzhang emerged as the leading Chinese political figure. From 1872 to 1901 he served as the governor-general of Zhili (jih-lee) province (modern Hebei) and headed one of the most important of the new armies. As the Chinese learned more about Western ways, Li and other modernizers came to recognize that guns and ships were merely the surface manifestation of the Western powers' economic strength. To catch up with the West, they argued, China would have to initiate new industries, which in the 1870s and 1880s included railway lines, steam navigation companies, coal mines, telegraph lines, and cotton-spinning and weaving factories. By the 1890s knowledge of the West had improved considerably. Newspapers covering world affairs had begun publication in Shanghai and Hong Kong, and more and more Western works were being translated.

For a while, China seemed to be taking the same direction as Meiji Japan (see Chapter 20), but resistance in China proved much stronger. Conservatives thought that copying Western practices compounded defeat. The high official Woren (waw-run) objected to the establishment of an interpreters' college on the grounds that "from ancient down to modern times" there had never been "anyone who could use mathematics to raise a nation from a state of decline or to strengthen it in times of weakness."[*] Even men like Zeng Guofan, who saw the need to modernize the military, had little respect for merchants and profit seeking.

Although to the Qing court new policies were being introduced at a rapid rate, the court never became enthusiastic about the prospect of fundamental change. Most of those in power were apprehensive about the ways changes in education or military organization would undermine inherited values and the existing power structure. Repeated humiliations by foreigners from the 1840s on fostered political rancor and denunciations of men in power. Both the court and much of the population remained opposed to doing anything that smacked of giving in to the arrogant and uncouth foreigners. As a consequence, the reforms were never fundamental enough to solve China's problems. Guo Songtao (gwo sung-tau), China's first ambassador to Britain (1877–1879), sent letters from London to Li Hongzhang praising

---

[*]Ssu-yü Teng and John K. Fairbank, *China's Response to the West* (Cambridge: Harvard University Press, 1979), p. 76, modified.

both the British parliamentary government and its industries. On his return he became a persona non grata, and the court ordered that the printing blocks carved to publish his diary be destroyed.

Empress Dowager Cixi

During the self-strengthening period, the most powerful person at court was Empress Dowager Cixi. In 1875, when her son, the Tongzhi (tung-jih) emperor, was nineteen, he died of smallpox, barely having had a chance to rule on his own. Cixi chose his cousin to succeed him, who is known as the Guangxu (gwahng-shyew) emperor (r. 1875–1908). By selecting a boy of four, Cixi could continue in power as regent for many years to come.

Cixi was a skillful political operator. She recognized the Manchu establishment's fears that they were being sidelined and presented herself to them as a staunch defender of Manchu privileges. She needed modernizers like Li Hongzhang and cajoled them with titles and honors, but she kept them in check by also encouraging their conservative critics.

It was under Cixi's watch that the old tribute system was finally dismantled. Three neighboring countries—Korea, the Ryukyu Islands, and Vietnam—had been regular, loyal tributaries, making them seem to Westerners not fully independent countries. Japan forced the Ryukyus away from China in the 1870s. In the 1880s, France forced Vietnam away.

Although no part of Vietnam had been under direct Chinese rule since Tang times, Chinese influence there had remained strong. The Vietnamese government was closely modeled on the Chinese, supported Zhu Xi's Confucian teachings, and used examinations to recruit officials. Official documents and histories were written in Chinese. By the mid-nineteenth century, France was eyeing "Indochina" as the best target for imperialist expansion, given Britain's strength in India. This brought France into conflict with the Qing, which viewed Vietnam as one of its most loyal vassal states, next only to Korea. In 1874, France gained privileges in Vietnam through treaties and in 1882 seized Hanoi. When the Vietnamese ruler requested Chinese help, realists like Prince Gong and Li Hongzhang urged avoiding war, but a shrill group of conservative critics insisted that China had to stop giving in because appeasement only encouraged the bullying of the powers. Cixi hesitated, called on Li Hongzhang

Empress Dowager Cixi. Cixi spent more than half a century in the palace. She entered in 1852, became Empress Dowager in 1861, and had her nephew, the Guangxu emperor, put under house arrest in 1898.

Free Gallery of Art and Arthur M. Sackler Gallery Archives, Smithsonian Institution, SC-GR-252 Photographer: Xunling

to negotiate, and then scuttled the draft treaty when she was flooded with protests about its terms. When the French issued an ultimatum that China withdraw its forces from Vietnam or they would attack China, Cixi sided with the conservative critics. Skirmishes between the Qing and the French quickly escalated into war. The French sailed their fleet 20 miles up the Min River to Fuzhou, home port of a quarter of the new Chinese navy and the site of the main shipyard. In just fifteen minutes on August 23, 1884, the French fleet destroyed the shipyard and all but two of the twenty-three Chinese warships. About three thousand Chinese were killed in the action. Cixi had adopted the conservative position and stood firm; the result was not only humiliating but also a fiscal disaster. The only consolation, a bittersweet one, was that Li Hongzhang had disobeyed her order to send his northern fleet to Fuzhou to help.

Reparations Imposed on China
(or, the Loser Pays)

1842	21 million ounces of silver to Great Britain at conclusion of the Opium War
1858	4 million ounces of silver to Britain and 2 million to France at conclusion of the Second Opium War
1860	16 million ounces of silver, divided evenly between Britain and France after attack on Beijing
1862–1869	400,000 ounces of silver to compensate for violence against missionaries
1870	490,000 ounces of silver to France after the Tianjin massacre
1873	500,000 ounces of silver to Japan after the Japanese incursion into Taiwan
1881	5 million ounces of silver to Russia for Qing reoccupation of the Ili valley in Xinjiang
1895	200 million ounces of silver to Japan after the Sino-Japanese War
1897	30 million ounces of silver to Japan for its withdrawal of troops from Liaodong
1901	450 million silver dollars to the countries that invaded to relieve the legation quarters

Cixi officially retired in 1889 when the Guangxu emperor was nineteen *sui* and she was fifty-five. She insisted, however, on reading all memorials and approving key appointments. Because the court was filled with her supporters, the emperor had little room to go his own way, even after he began to form his own views about reform.

FOREIGNERS IN CHINA

After 1860 the number of Westerners in China grew steadily, and a distinct treaty port culture evolved. The foreign concessions at treaty ports were areas carved out of existing Chinese cities. They had foreign police and foreign law courts and collected their own taxes, a situation the Qing accepted with little protest, even though most of the population within the concessions continued to be Chinese. At the treaty ports, the presence of the British and Indians was especially strong, and the habits of the British Empire tended to spill over into these cities. Foreign warships anchored at the docks of the treaty ports, ready to make a show of force. Although missionaries and merchants often had little love for each other, they had similar tendencies to turn to their consuls for support when they got into conflicts with Chinese. When missionaries or their converts were attacked or killed, gunboats were often sent to the nearest port to threaten retaliation, a practice termed *gunboat diplomacy.*

When the disorder of the Taiping Rebellion disrupted tariff collection in Shanghai and Amoy, the British and American consuls there collected the tariffs themselves, a practice later regularized into a permanent Imperial Maritime Customs staffed at its higher level by Westerners. In addition to recording and collecting tariffs, the customs published annual reports on the outlook for trade at each port and undertook projects to improve communications, such as telegraph and postal systems.

By 1900 there were one hundred treaty ports, but only Shanghai, Tianjin, Hankou, Guangzhou, and Dalian (at the southern tip of Manchuria) became major centers of foreign residence. (Hong Kong was counted not as a treaty port but as a colony.) The streetlights and tall buildings in the Western-dominated parts of these cities showed Chinese what Western "progress" was all about. The Chinese in these cities also felt the disdain of the Westerners toward China and the Chinese. To Westerners, the Chinese educated class seemed too obtuse to understand progress. Couldn't they see that the world outside China had changed drastically in the last century and that China's response to it was disastrously out of date?

Away from the treaty ports, missionaries were the Westerners the Chinese were most likely to encounter. Once China agreed in the treaty of 1860 to allow missionaries to travel through China, they came in large numbers. Unlike merchants in the treaty ports, missionaries had no choice but to mix with the local population, and they spent much of their time with ordinary, poor Chinese, finding the best opportunities for conversion among them.

Missionaries often ran orphanages, a "good work" that also helped produce converts, but the Chinese suspected that they were buying babies for nefarious purposes. Widely circulated antimissionary tracts were often filled with inflammatory charges of this sort. The volatility of relations between Chinese and foreign missionaries led to tragedy in Tianjin on a June day in 1870. French troops had been based there from 1860 to 1863; the French had taken over a former palace for their consulate; and they had built a cathedral at the site of a former Chinese temple—all reasons for the local population to resent them. At the cathedral, nuns ran an orphanage. They welcomed (and even paid small sums to receive) sick and dying children, wanting to baptize them before they died. When an epidemic swept through the orphanage in June 1870, so many orphans died that rumors spread that they were being killed for their body parts. Scandalous purposes seemed confirmed when the nuns would not let parents retrieve their children. When a local official came to search the premises, a fight broke out between converts and onlookers. The official ordered soldiers to put a stop to the disturbance. Meanwhile, the French consul, carrying two pistols, charged into the official's office and shot at him. After the consul was restrained, the official, unhurt, advised him not to go back on the street, where an angry crowd had formed. Claiming he was afraid of no Chinese, the consul went out anyway. On the street, he recognized the city magistrate, whom he shot at, again missing. The crowd then killed the consul and the officer with him, as well as twelve priests and nuns, seven other foreigners, and several dozen Chinese converts. The French victims were mutilated and the cathedral and four American and British churches burned. Although the French consul had incited the violence, it was the Chinese who had to pay reparations as well as punish members of the mob and send a mission of apology to France.

By 1900 there were 886 Catholic and about 3,000 Protestant missionaries in China, more than half of them women. Over the course of the nineteenth century, more and more missionaries concentrated on medicine or education, which were better received by the Chinese than preaching. By 1905 there were about three hundred fully qualified physicians doing medical missionary work, and the 250 mission hospitals and dispensaries treated about 2 million patients. Missionary hospitals in Hong Kong also ran a medical school that trained hundreds of Chinese as physicians. At their schools, missionaries helped spread Western learning. For their elementary schools, missionaries produced textbooks in Chinese on a full range of subjects. They translated dozens of standard works into Chinese, especially in the natural sciences, mathematics, history, and international law. By 1906 there were nearly sixty thousand students attending twenty-four hundred Christian schools. Most of this activity was supported by contributions sent from the United States and Britain. Missionaries in China had more success in spreading Western learning than in gaining converts: by 1900 fewer than 1 million Chinese were Christians.

THE FAILURES OF REFORM

Despite the enormous efforts it put into trying to catch up, the end of the nineteenth century brought China more humiliation. First came the discovery that Japan had so successfully modernized that it posed a threat to China. Japan had not been much of a concern to China since Hideoyoshi's invasion of Korea in the late Ming period. In the 1870s, Japan began making demands on China and in the 1890s seemed to be looking for a pretext for war.

As discussed in Chapter 20, Korea provided the pretext. When an insurrection broke out in Korea in 1894, both China and Japan rushed to send troops. After Japan sank a steamship carrying Chinese troops, both countries declared war. The results proved that the past decade of accelerated efforts to upgrade the military were still not enough. In the climactic naval battle off the Yalu River, four of the twelve Chinese ships involved were sunk, four were seriously damaged, and the others fled. By contrast, none of the twelve Japanese ships was seriously damaged. An even worse loss came when the Japanese went overland to take the Chinese port city of Weihaiwei (way-hy-way) in Shandong province, then turned the Chinese guns on the Chinese fleet in the bay. This was a defeat not of Chinese weapons but of Chinese organization and strategy.

China sued for peace and sent Li Hongzhang to Japan to negotiate a settlement. In addition to a huge indemnity, China agreed to cede Taiwan and Liaodong (the southern tip of Manchuria) to Japan and to allow Japan to open factories in China. (Liaodong was returned to the Qing for an additional indemnity after pressure from the European powers.) China had to borrow from consortiums of banks in Russia, France, Britain, and Germany to pay the indemnity, securing the loans with future customs revenue. From this point until 1949, China was continually in debt to foreign banks, which made reform all the more difficult.

European imperialism was at a high point in the 1890s, with countries scrambling to get territories in Africa and Southeast Asia. China's helplessness in the face of aggression led to a scramble among the European powers for concessions and protectorates in China. At the high point of this rush in 1898, it appeared that the European powers might divide China among themselves the way they had recently divided Africa. Russia obtained permission to extend the Trans-Siberian railway across Manchuria to Vladivostok and secured a leasehold over the Liaodong Peninsula. Germany seized the port of Qingdao in Shandong province, and the British stepped in to keep Russia and Germany in check by taking a port (Weihaiwei) that lay between their concessions. France concentrated on concessions in the south and southwest, near its colonies in Southeast Asia.

The mixture of fear and outrage that many of the educated class felt as China suffered blow after blow began to give rise to attitudes that can be labeled nationalism. The two most important intellectual leaders to give shape to these feelings were Kang Youwei (kahng yoe-way) (1858–1927) and Liang Qichao (lyang chee-chow) (1873–1929), both from Guangdong province. Kang was a committed Confucian, dedicated to the ideals of personal virtue and service to society. He reinterpreted the classics to justify reform, arguing that Confucius had been a reformer, not a mere transmitter as he had portrayed himself in the *Analects*. Liang, fifteen years younger, was Kang's most brilliant follower and went even further than Kang in advocating political change. Liang contended that self-strengthening efforts had focused too narrowly on technology and ignored the need for cultural and political change. The examination system should be scrapped and a national school system instituted. China needed a stronger sense of national solidarity and a new type of state in which the people participated in rule. In 1895 Kang, Liang, and like-minded men began setting up study societies in several large cities. In Hunan province, for instance, fourteen study societies were founded in 1897 and 1898, the largest with more than twelve hundred members. Some of these societies started publishing newspapers (see **Documents: Comparing the Power of China and Western Nations**). Worrisome to the court was the fact that some of these societies expressed anti-Manchu sentiments, seeming to imply that many of China's problems could be solved if only the Chinese were ruling China.

The bannermen had been a hereditary military caste, in some ways comparable to the samurai in Edo Japan. In Japan, when the special status of the samurai was abolished, samurai had not only joined the new armies in large numbers as officers, but many had successfully switched to other occupations requiring skill or learning. The hereditary military caste of the Qing did not fare as well. Many bannermen became alarmed, not seeing how the banner population could survive without government handouts. Although banner garrisons had schools for banner children, many were illiterate and unprepared to step forward as the country modernized.

In the spring of 1895, provincial graduates in Beijing for the triennial *jinshi* examinations submitted petitions on how to respond to the crisis caused by the war with Japan. Some twelve hundred signed the "ten-thousand word petition" written by Kang Youwei. Kang called for an assembly elected by the general populace. Such an assembly would solve China's most pressing problems:

> *Above, they are to broaden His Majesty's sagelike understanding, so that he can sit in one hall and know the four seas. Below, they are to bring together the minds and wills of the empire, so that all can share cares and pleasures, forgetting the distinction between public and private.... Sovereign and people will be of one body, and China will be as one family.... So when funds are to be raised, what sums cannot be raised? When soldiers are to be trained, what numbers cannot be trained? With 400 million minds as one mind: how could the empire be stronger?*[*]

In January 1898 the emperor invited Kang Youwei to discuss his ideas with the high officials at court. Afterward Kang sent the emperor three memorials on constitutions, national assemblies, and political reform. Kang even implied that the Qing rulers should abandon the queue, noting that Western dress had been adopted in Japan and that the Japanese emperor had cut his hair short. In June the emperor gave Kang a five-hour audience. Over the next hundred days, the emperor issued more than one hundred decrees on everything from revamping the examination system to setting up national school, banking, postal, and patent systems. He was redesigning the Qing as a constitutional monarchy with modern financial and educational infrastructures.

After three months, Empress Dowager Cixi had had enough and staged a coup with the help of Yuan Shikai's army. She had the Guangxu emperor locked up and executed those reformers she could capture. All the reform edicts were revoked. Kang and Liang,

---

*Translated in Philip A. Kuhn, *Origins of the Modern Chinese State* (Stanford, Calif.: Stanford University Press, 2002), p. 123.

DOCUMENTS

Comparing the Power of China and Western Nations

This essay was written in 1898 by Mai Menghua (my mung-hwa) (1874–1915), a twenty-four-year-old follower of Kang Youwei. It responds to conservative critics who saw Kang's program as weakening the ruler's hand. Mai argues that modern Western governments are in fact much stronger than the Chinese government.

Nowadays, men of broad learning all say China is weak because the power of the ruler is mighty while the power of the people is slight. Those who like to map out plans for the nation say that the Western nations are strong because their way is exactly the opposite of this. Mai Menghua says: This is not so. China's misfortunes arise not because the people have no power but because the ruler has no power. Hence, over all five continents and throughout all past ages, no ruler has had less power than in present-day China, and no rulers have had more power than in present-day European nations. There are far too many points for me to compare them all here, but permit me to say something about a few.

In Western countries, the age, birth, and death of every person in every household is reported to the officials, who record and investigate it. An omission in a report is punished as a criminal offense. In China, birth, death, and taking care of oneself are all personal matters, beyond state intervention. In Western countries, when property is inherited by descendants, the amount of the property and its location must be reported and registered with the authorities. An inheritance tax must be paid before the property is transmitted to the inheritors. In China, people give and take as they please, and the state is unable to investigate. In Western countries, when children reach the age of eight [*sui*], they all go to elementary school. Doting parents who neglect their children's studies are punished. In China, 70 to 80 percent of the population is indolent, worthless, uncouth and illiterate, and the state can do nothing to encourage them to improve themselves. In Western countries, one must go through school to become an official, and unless one does adequately, one cannot make his own way. In China, one can be a slave in the marketplace in the morning, and bedecked in the robes of high office by evening, and this is beyond the capacity of the state to control. In Western countries, the currency system is fixed by the court; one country has the pound, another the ruble, and another the franc, but each currency is uniform throughout the entire

safely out of Beijing at the time, fled to Japan, where each lived for years.

THE BOXER REBELLION

In the summer of 1898, while the Guangxu emperor was issuing reform edicts, Shandong province was suffering from a break in the dikes on the Yellow River, which flooded some two thousand villages and made millions of people refugees. Not only was that year's crop ruined, but also in many places the land could not be planted even the next spring. When the government failed to provide effective relief, antigovernment resentment began to stir. Another local grievance concerned the high-handed behavior of Christian missionaries, especially a group of German missionaries who actively interfered in their converts' lawsuits, claiming the privileges of extraterritoriality for the converts. They also irritated people by forbidding their converts to contribute to traditional village festivals that involved parading statues of the local gods.

Not surprisingly, this region soon exploded into violence. Small groups began pillaging the property of missionaries and their converts. They were dubbed "Boxers" by foreigners because of their martial arts practices. The Boxers also practiced spirit possession, which allowed individuals to achieve direct

country, and no one dares to differ. In China, each of the 80 provinces has a different currency, and the shape of the money is different. The people are satisfied with what they are accustomed to, and the state is unable to enforce uniformity.

In Western countries, only the government may print and distribute paper money within its borders. In China, banks in every province and money changers in every port make and circulate their own money, and the state is unable to audit and prohibit them. In Western countries, all new buildings are inspected by officials, who examine the quality of the construction materials as a precaution against collapse causing injuries. Older houses are periodically inspected, and ordered demolished or repaired. In China, one can construct as one pleases. Even if there are cracks and flaws, the state cannot supervise and reprove the builder. In Western countries, roads and highways must be broad and spacious, neat and clean. There are legal penalties for discarding trash [on the roads]. Broad roads in Chinese cities are swamped in urine and litter, filled with beggars and corpses, and the state is unable to clean them up. In Western countries, all doctors must be graduates of medical schools and be certified before they can practice medicine. In China, those who fail to do well academically switch to the medical profession; quack doctors, who casually kill patients, are

everywhere, and the state is unable to punish them. In Western countries, the postal service is controlled by the government. In China, post offices run by private persons are everywhere, and the government is unable to unify them.

In Western countries, there is an official for commerce. Inferior goods cannot be sold in the market. New inventions are patented, and other merchants are forbidden to manufacture imitations. In China, dishonest merchants are everywhere, devising illicit means to make imitation products, and everything is of inferior quality, and yet the state has no control. In Western countries, wherever railroads pass, homes, temples, huts, or gravestones must be demolished. No one dares obstruct the opening up of new mineral resources in mountains. In China, conservatives raise an outcry and block every major project, and the state is unable to punish them.

Questions for Analysis

1. What does Mai see as attractive in a state that can control society at a deep level?
2. Does it make sense that the Chinese government was despotic and at the same time unable to control society?

Source: Republished with permission of ABC-CLIO Inc., from *Changing China: Readings in the History of China from the Opium War to the Present* by J. Mason Gentzler, 1977; permission conveyed through Copyright Clearance Center, Inc.

communication with their gods and gain a sense of personal power. After the governor of Shandong suppressed them in 1899, they began drifting into other provinces, even into the capital, where they recruited new members with placards urging the Chinese to kill all foreigners as well as Chinese contaminated by their influence. They blamed the drought on the anger of the gods at the foreign intrusion. (See Color Plater 26.)

The foreign powers demanded that the Qing government suppress the attacks on foreigners. Cixi, apparently hoping that the Chinese people, if aroused, could solve her foreign problem for her, did little to stop the Boxers. Eight foreign powers announced

that they would send troops to protect missionaries. Then, on June 20, 1900, the German minister was shot dead in the street. Cixi, having been told by pro-Boxer Manchus that the European powers wanted her to retire and restore the emperor to the throne, declared war on the eight powers. Although she had repeatedly seen China defeated when it was fighting only one of these powers, she deluded herself into thinking that if the people became sufficiently enraged, they could drive all eight out and solve the foreign problem once and for all.

Foreigners in the capital, including missionaries who had recently moved there for safety, barricaded themselves in the Northern Cathedral and two miles away

Bettmann/Corbis

Captured Boxers. Most of the men who joined the Boxers had previously worked as laborers, porters, field hands, or the like and suffered from the deteriorating economic situation.

in the legation quarter. After the Boxers laid siege to the legation quarter, an eight-nation force (including Japan) sent twenty thousand troops to lift the siege. Cixi and the emperor fled by cart to Xi'an hundreds of miles away. By the end of the year, there were forty-five thousand foreign troops in north China. Most of the Boxers tried to disappear into the north China countryside, but the foreign troops spent six months hunting them down, making raids on Chinese towns and villages.

Antiforeign violence also occurred elsewhere in the country, especially in Shanxi, where the governor sided with the Boxers and had missionaries and their converts executed. Most of the governors-general, however, including Li Hongzhang and Yuan Shikai (ywan shih-ky), simply ignored the empress dowager's declaration of war.

In the negotiations that led to the Boxer Protocol, China had to accept a long list of penalties, including cancellation of the examinations for five years (punishment for gentry collaboration), execution of the officials involved, destruction of forts and railway posts, and payment of a staggering indemnity of 450 million silver dollars.

THE DECLINE OF THE QING EMPIRE IN COMPARATIVE PERSPECTIVE

Late Qing reformers often urged the court to follow in the footsteps of Japan, which had adopted not merely Western technology but also Western ideas about political organization and even Western dress.

Ever since, it has been common to compare the fates of Qing China and Edo Japan and ask why Japan was so much more successful at modernizing its government and economy.

The main arguments for lumping China and Japan together are that they were geographically close (both were "the Far East" to Europeans), and some significant features of Japanese culture had been derived from China, such as Confucianism and the use of Chinese characters in writing. The differences, however, should not be minimized. China in the nineteenth century was not an independent country but rather part of the multiethnic empire of the Manchus, making it more similar to other large multiethnic empires, like the Mughals in India, the Ottomans in the Middle East, the Romanovs in Russia, and even the Hapsburgs in eastern Europe. Even if only the China proper part of the Qing is considered, it was a much larger country than Japan in both territory and population, with all that that implied in terms of political structure.

Another common way to frame the experiences of China during this period is to compare it to other countries where Western imperialism was felt. Those Chinese who urged the court to follow Japan's example also warned of being carved up like Africa or taken over like India. But only small pieces of the Qing Empire were directly ruled by foreign powers in China, giving its history a different trajectory.

Better comparisons for the Qing Dynasty during this period are probably the Ottoman and Russian empires. All three were multiethnic, land-based Eurasian empires, with long experience with mounted horsemen of the steppe—and in the case of both the Ottomans and the Qing, currently ruled by groups that claimed this tradition themselves. All three knew how to deal with problems of defending long land borders but were not naval powers. During the eighteenth century, all had experienced rapid population growth that had reduced the standard of living for much of the population by the mid-nineteenth century. By then the military pressure put on each of them both by internal unrest and foreign pressure forced them to spend more on military preparedness at the cost of deficit financing. As the importance of cavalry declined in warfare, each lost its military advantages. During this period Western sea powers sought to profit from trade with them, forcing all three empires to accept their terms, but not trying to take over management of the empires. The sea powers gained more by making loans to them, which kept them in a type of debt bondage, thus securing their advantage through treaties without any of the responsibilities of direct rule.

In each of these empires during the mid- and late nineteenth centuries, the elites were divided between Westernizers and traditionalists, each looking for ways to strengthen the government. Urban merchants were usually more willing to see changes made than were the imperial elite, who had the biggest stake in the existing power structure. Even when modernizers won out, improvements were generally too little or too late to make much difference when the next confrontation with Western powers came. Reform programs could not outpace the destructive effect of economic decline, social turmoil, and the intrusion of the West. Foreign powers did not encourage domestic challenges to the dynastic rulers, perhaps fearing that they would lose the privileges they had gained through treaties. Thus, many of those who sought radical change came to oppose both the foreign powers and the ruling dynasty, giving rise to modern nationalism.

SUMMARY

In the nineteenth century China's world standing declined as a result of both foreign intervention and internal unrest. The Qing government's efforts to suppress opium imports led to a brief Opium War against the British. Decisively defeated, the Qing had to make numerous concessions that opened China to trade on Britain's terms.

Within its borders, China faced unprecedented population pressure and worsening economic conditions. The conditions were ripe for uprisings to spread. The most devastating of these was the Taiping Rebellion, which swept across much of southern and central China. The leader of this rebellion, Hong Xiuquan, was a religious visionary who called on people to destroy idols and renounce alcohol, opium, footbinding, and prostitution. After he declared a new dynasty, he reminded people that the Manchus were alien conquerors, using anti-Manchu sentiment to rally his troops. He had his followers let their hair grow and abandon the queue. His followers were organized into armies that did remarkably well against the Manchu bannermen. These rebellions proved very difficult for the Qing armies to suppress.

During this crisis, the Chinese elite rallied around the dynasty and in many places organized local defense. The most important of these literati-turned-generals was Zeng Guofan, who raised an army in his home province of Hunan. Zeng Guofan and his protégé Li Hongzhang came to realize how far China had fallen behind Europe in military force and advocated concerted efforts to modernize the military and learn other secrets of Western success. The "self-strengthening" movement that they led involved everything from translating Western books and bringing over Western teachers, to building gun factories and teaching foreign languages, sending students abroad to study, and setting up textile and paper factories and building railroads. Conservatives were against many of these measures, seeing nothing desirable in Western culture. For a quarter century the most powerful person at court was the Empress Dowager Cixi, who tried to protect Manchu interests while also encouraging modernizers. The measures were also expensive, at a time when the government's resources were thin. Defeats by the French in 1884 and the Japanese in 1895 gave ample evidence that China had not caught up.

China's seeming helplessness in the face of aggression set off a scramble among the European colonial powers for concessions and protectorates, thinking China might end up divided among them as Africa had recently been. Some Chinese intellectuals, most notably Kang Youwei and Liang Qichao, began advocating major political change, with more participation by the people. The young Guangxu, newly ruling on his own, announced a series of reforms, but these frightened Cixi, and she was quickly removed from power.

The nineteenth century ended with more problems. An anti-foreign uprising broke out not far from the capital (the Boxer Rebellion), and the rebels began converging on Beijing. The Manchu court, perhaps hopeful that the rebels could drive out the foreigners, withdrew from the capital, and the foreigners barricaded themselves against the rebels' onslaught. The outcome was a disaster for China. Eight foreign countries joined forces to relieve the siege, after which they demanded an enormous indemnity from China.

How different was China in 1900 compared to 1800? At the beginning of the nineteenth century, most Chinese had no reason to question the long-held belief that China was the central kingdom: no other country had so many people, Chinese products were in great demand in foreign countries, and the borders had recently been expanded. Chinese civilization thus seemed in no danger. By 1900 this confidence was gone. In addition to traditional evidence of dynastic decline—peasant poverty, social unrest, government bankruptcy—new foreign adversaries had emerged. China had been humiliated repeatedly in military encounters with Western nations and more recently with Japan. It was also deeply in debt to these countries because of imposed indemnities. Most of the educated class had come to feel that drastic measures needed to be taken. Chinese civilization—not just the Qing Dynasty—was at stake.

Japan in Turmoil (1800–1867)

Many commoners in Japan's cities and villages prospered during the first three decades of the nineteenth century, but the same could not be said for the laboring poor, the low-status samurai, or the daimyo wrestling with shortfalls in their domain's finances. Despite prosperity in some places, problems such as vagrancy, gambling, and prostitution threatened the social order valued by administrators and wealthy entrepreneurs. Added to domestic distress was an increasing fear of threats from abroad. The shogunate's futile attempts to deal with these problems weakened it in the eyes of the military ruling class. Its decision to seek approval for foreign treaties from the monarch opened the door for wide-ranging debate that brought commoners as well as officials into a new political public realm. Beset on all sides, the shogunate collapsed at the end of 1867, ushering in a regime headed by the newly named emperor.

Historians have long searched the early nineteenth century for clues as to what brought about the restoration of imperial rule under the Meiji emperor. Those who emphasize domestic factors point to the way the social and political order came unglued in the early nineteenth century. But that begs the question of whether the fall of the Tokugawa shogunate should be seen as a coup d'état (in which one set of rulers simply replaces another, similar set) or a revolution. Was it primarily the effect of domestic changes or a reaction to foreign pressure?

DOMESTIC DISCONTENTS (1800–1842)

Early-nineteenth-century villages had to deal with internal conflict. Outcasts deemed polluted because they dealt with dead animals protested discrimination, humiliation, and insults. In dividing the village tax assessment among the farmers, headmen tended to treat expenses for family business and village administration as one and the same. The walls around their houses had gates; the roofs had eaves that marked their superior status. Complaints against headmen perceived to be unjust, efforts to clarify the costs of village administration, and demands that the headman stop lording over his neighbors led to lawsuits that sometimes dragged on for decades. A stubborn headman might be subjected to ostracism, his family cut off from all interactions with other villagers for generations. Sometimes disputes resulted in having a farmer's representative join the village council to verify the tax assessment. In villages where the position of headman had once been hereditary, it might instead rotate among a group of families. Some villages started having heads of household elect the headman. When a woman was the house head, she too voted.

In eastern Japan, village leaders agonized over fields gone to waste because of population decline. Gamblers preyed on unsuspecting youths, and bandits stole crops, goods, and women. In response village officials organized regional leagues, inserting a new level of administration between the village and ruling authority. In the 1780s in the region around Osaka, these leagues launched province-wide appeals to get rid of restrictions on commerce and to regulate the price of herring-based fertilizer from Hokkaido. In 1805 the shogunate started sending security patrols through the Edo hinterland, where villages might be fragmented among several domains. Headmen organized militia; they hired unemployed swordsmen, some running protection rackets, to keep the peace. Longer-term solutions came in the teachings of the peasant sage Ninomiya Sontoku (KNEE-no-me-yah SOWN-toe-ku) who gave new life to villages, increasing their population and bringing fields back into production by preaching an ethic of diligence, fortitude, and frugality to repay the bounty of the gods while starting mutual aid associations to give farmers who had fallen into debt access to low-interest loans. His emphasis on rational planning to squeeze the most from land and labor demanded steady work habits instilled in men and women alike.

Scholars of Japan's ancient past, Hirata Atsutane (HE-rah-tah AH-tzu-tah-neh) and his followers, offered a vision of a just social order that largely ignored existing political structures. Although they accepted the shogun's authority and the Confucian principles of social inequality, they sought the wellspring of human virtue in Japan's ancient past and looked to the monarch as a manifest god who linked the divine and human worlds. Atsutane claimed to be a disciple of Motoori Norinaga, thus putting him in the mainstream of native Japanese thought. Unlike his teacher, he did not see the afterlife as a filthy, polluted realm but rather as an invisible world that parallels the visible world. There the dead watch over and protect their descendants. Although far removed from farm work himself, Atsutane valued agricultural practices, which brought people into communion with the gods and each other. Village officials and rural entrepreneurs were his most numerous disciples because they believed his message to contain the secret for giving new life to the village community without threatening their role either socially or economically.

Domain Reforms

Faced with challenges from below, rural entrepreneurs looked for new ways to bolster their prestige. Rather than marry within the village, they found marriage partners of similar background a day's walk or more away. They educated themselves; they also educated their daughters to a higher standard than an ordinary farmer. They studied Chinese philosophy and classical poetry as well as Western science and geography and took up swordsmanship. In the 1830s and 1840s, their search for ways to enhance their dignity meshed with their rulers' need for funds. In return for loans, wealthy commoners received permission to wear swords and to use surnames, privileges supposedly reserved for the samurai.

The willingness of daimyo to sell privileges to commoners was but one sign that their governments verged on bankruptcy. Owing to farmers' protests, tax revenues had long since ceased to cover the expenses of carrying unneeded retainers on the books, supporting the daimyo's women and children in the style to which life in Edo had accustomed them, and traveling back and forth to Edo by the daimyo and his retinue. Daimyo borrowed money from merchants guaranteed by future tax receipts. In the 1830s, domains across Japan tried to reform administrations and finances. Those that tried to increase exports and restrict imports disrupted markets and created shortages. Some created monopolies by strengthening existing controls: Satsuma doubled its profits in sugar. Most domains tried to reduce expenses by cutting costs. Concerned that luxury-loving commoners both threatened samurai privilege and encouraged samurai extravagance, domains issued laws regulating expenses that forbade socially inferior people from wearing silk clothing, ornamental hairpins, and other products of the commercial revolution.

The samurai, especially those in the lower ranks, grew frustrated at their prospects. Wealthy commoners in crested kimono and carrying swords challenged the markers of their superior status. The system of hereditary ranks relegated educated, capable samurai to dead-end menial tasks. During domain reforms, low-ranking samurai proposed that men of talent and ability be promoted to decision-making positions. Satsuma heeded this call, allowing Saigō Takamori (SAH-e-go TAH-kah-moe-re) to rise from rural administrator to the daimyo's adviser in 1854. Efforts to promote men from below often led to fights between factions when upper-status samurai insisted on preserving their hereditary privileges. "Borrowing" stipends posed the most common threat to samurai welfare. While some domains tried to limit salary cuts to samurai without regular bureaucratic assignments and pretended that the cuts were temporary, others insisted that everyone must make sacrifices. In one case, guards assigned to escort a daimyo to his regular audience with the shogun protested unpaid salaries by going on strike.

Conditions reached a crisis when poor harvests in the 1830s recalled the famines of the 1780s. Commoners assumed that food shortages owed more to greedy merchants than to crop failures. They turned on village leaders for not offering relief, and they called on the gods of world renewal (*yonaoshi*, YO-nah-oh-she) to save them from economic hardship and political indifference. Women played an active role, marching with men to protest arbitrary government policies and complaining to rice merchants that hoarding grain threatened the poor with starvation. A retired shogunal policeman named Ōshio Heihachirō (OH-she-oh HEH-e-hah-che-row) decided that government and merchants had become morally bankrupt. Raised in the Confucian tradition that deemed bureaucratic work a service to the people, Ōshio had also studied Wang Yangming, who argued that at a time of crisis, a man had to use his intuition, not the bureaucratic procedures, to guide his behavior (see Chapter 14). In 1836, Ōshio petitioned the Osaka city magistrate to save the starving. When the magistrate did nothing, Ōshio sold his books to buy food. Finally he issued a manifesto that charged the shogun's officials with corruption and led an army of farmers against the city. A quarter of Osaka burned before government troops caught up with him; he committed suicide.

Religion and Play

One response to economic hardships and political indifference came in the form of new religions. In 1838 a spirit possessed a long-suffering rural woman named Nakayama Miki (NAH-kah-yah-mah ME-key) and deemed her to be the "shogun of heaven" and the mouthpiece for the true and original god of salvation. She insisted that her family sell all their property and use the proceeds to help the poor. According to the god's divine wisdom (*tenri*, TEHN-re), the shogun and daimyo were far too removed from daily life to aid the people; instead, the people should trust in the god of world renewal and work together, helping each other in time of need. Like other new religions of the time, Tenri-kyō taught belief in a world to come that would be unlike the socially stratified vertical system of the past and present. In a renewed world saturated with divine goodness, the poor would receive help, and everyone, men and women, would be equal.

An alternative to the new religions came in the form of play. Dominated by the theater, urban culture celebrated the body and its pleasures. Townspeople employed the possibilities presented by multiple identities—merchant, poet, sword-wearing samurai—to escape from the categories imposed by the status system (see **Documents: Kohei's Lawsuit**). Readers of popular literature in the 1830s had alternatives to instructive tracts that bolstered the official status order. They indulged in novels that depicted the immediate world of human feelings, such as Jippensha Ikku's (G-ppen-shaw E-kku) travelogues featuring an irreverent pair of commoners who poked fun at self-important samurai, stole when they could, seduced serving maids, and laughed at farts. Woodblock prints and kabuki, in particular ghost stories staged by Tsuruya Namboku (TZU-ru-yah NAHN-bow-ku) and his successors, featured gruesome murders. In 1850 the story of the peasant martyr Sakura Sōgorō appeared on stage with scenes of his crucifixion and reincarnation as an angry spirit. Although dramas might be set in the daimyo's domestic quarters, the subjects of action were commoners who acted according to the logic of everyday life.

Japanese commoners played hard. Festivals in town and country became increasingly elaborate, and laborers demanded more of them. Kabuki troupes discovered the money to be made in touring the countryside. In prosperous regions, villages built kabuki stages and competed in presenting plays to their neighbors. Urban entertainment districts, for example, the one surrounding Asakusa (AH-sah-ku-sah) temple in Edo, with theaters, variety shows, and shops featuring female clerks combined appeals to prayer and play. Play constituted one way to appeal to the gods that gave the pursuit of pleasure a spiritual dimension.

DOCUMENTS   Kohei's Lawsuit

Many disputes between commoners ended up in court. The summary of a conflict over inheritance that follows, titled "Action by Kohei of Haruki-chō, Hongō, against Heisuke of Sugamo-chō and Kurōbei of Fujimae-chō, Komagome as to the succession and division of personality of Sawamura Gisaburō, Master Carpenter," exposes a complex set of family relations and the way people crossed supposedly strict occupational and status boundaries. Note that the people involved in the suit, including the deceased, took different names depending on the occupation of the moment.

5th month, 1849, Inquiry by the city magistrate to the engineering magistrates:

Kohei demanded succession and division of personality of Sawamura Gisaburō, master-carpenter, subject to your lordships' authority, producing for evidence Gisaburō's will written by a person other than the testator; the defendants, on the other hand, deny the validity of the will, and the parties are at issue.

Kohei alleges that his sister's husband Sawamura Gisaburō made a will so that his personality may be divided according to the will, and that Gisaburō's adopted son Kosuke may be made to succeed Gisaburō.

Rubric: This Kosuke was one who, calling himself Utazō, tenanted the land of Ichibei in Yanaka, and was engaged in the management of a public bathhouse. Four years ago, in 1845, he was adopted by Gisaburō, and in the 11th month of the same year, his petition to be a master-carpenter on probation was granted. It has been found that he is still living in a separate house on Ichibei's land and is working as a master-carpenter on probation.

What Heisuke alleges is as follows: His adoptive father Sawamura Gisaburō was a master-carpenter in service of the shogunate.

Gisaburō was formerly called Heisuke and was engaged in the management of a tavern at Sugamo-chō. About that time this person [Heisuke] was adopted by Gisaburō and in

1835 he succeeded to Gisaburō's family name. Gisaburō served as a master-carpenter from 1810, and from 1812 to 1834 he was also registered in the census book of Sugamo-chō under the name of Heisuke. Therefore it seems that he was entered in two different census registers.

Gisaburō bought two years ago in 1846 a piece of land at the market in front of Yushima Tenjin Shrine, and on this occasion Heisuke advanced part of the purchase money. On the deed of sale, the land was entered as the property of Sei, daughter of Saku, Gisaburō's concubine. Gisaburō had a house on this land repaired for Saku to occupy. Lately he himself moved into this concubine's house, and because of old age, he called in one Kosuke, who is more in the relation of a servant to him, to wait on him, and had this Kosuke, by nominally adopting him, serve as a master-carpenter on probation. Besides the above piece of land, some other lots in Gisaburō's possession have been nominally the property of Gisaburō's grandson Chōsuke, for whom Heisuke has acted as guardian. The deeds of sale of these lands were kept by Gisaburō, as they were often used, by agreement of Gisaburō and Heisuke, for financing the business when Gisaburō engaged in various contracts, government and otherwise. When in 1847 Gisaburō married Sei, Saku's

Another sign that the practices of everyday life had escaped the shogun's control can be seen in prostitution. Unlicensed prostitutes plied their trade in informal entertainment districts that had sprung up across Edo and in castle towns. Post stations hired maids to lure customers to inns and teahouses, where singers, dancers, and servants often sold themselves.

The development of a commercial economy contributed to the spread of prostitution in two ways: it put more money in the pockets of potential customers and it made female labor into a commodity. When women lacked opportunities to supplement the family income by raising silkworms or working for wages, prostitution became the logical alternative.

daughter [by her former husband] to one Mohachi and had Mohachi inherit the family name of Yoshikawa, palanquin-maker for the Shogunate, Heisuke on Gisaburō's request, advanced 500 *ryō* to Gisaburō to cover the expenses. Since Heisuke had advanced Gisaburō great sums of money for the latter's contract business, government and otherwise, Heisuke should be given the right to decide on the succession and other matters.

Yasuda Chōsuke is son to Hanzaemon and grandson to Gisaburō and was formerly called Toraichirō. He is registered as a houseowner of Fujimae-chō. He has served, under the guardianship of the defendant Heisuke, as purveyor and contractor of commodities and laborers for the Fukiage Garden [in the shogun's palace] and is living with his father.

Nakamura Hanzaemon is adopted husband to Hisa born to Gisaburō by Gin, his former wife, since divorced. He was formerly called Shōgorō, and while tenant of a shop belonging to Kanbei, Fujimae-chō, Komagome, was engaged in dealing in socks. He is said to have become a guard in service of the Banner Magistrates for the Shogunate.

The defendant Kurōbei is nephew to Sawamura Gisaburō and head of Gisaburō's original family. Because of this relationship, Gisaburō, repairing a house on his land, had Kurōbei and his wife Chiyo, whose other name is Shige, live there. Even now Gisaburō's domicile is registered at the office of the Engineering Department as at this house on Kurōbei's land. So it was rumored that the boxes containing Gisaburō's papers and books etc. are kept in the above Kurōbei's go-down [storehouse], including the instruments pertaining to the various money transactions which Gisaburō mentioned in his will.

The plaintiff says that when, during this autumn, he went to negotiate with Heisuke and Kurōbei, Kurōbei together with the ward officers admitted plainly that he had in his care the papers in question. The plaintiff continues that it seems possible, however, that Heisuke, taking advantage of his having access to the household of the Lord of Kaga through his business in contracting for transport horses, may have here done something tricky; that there is no box containing instruments kept now at Kurōbei's house in Fujimae-chō. It is suspected that it has since been taken to Heisuke's house. Heisuke has for several years past been in the habit of advancing loans to the household of the Lord of Kaga out of money belonging to Sawamura Gisaburō.

Instrument of Settlement to be filed: Both parties have agreed that we should petition for Gisaburō's adopted son Sawamura Kosuke to succeed Gisaburō, and should agree that neither party has grounds on which to dispute further about the deposit instruments said to be entrusted by Gisaburō with Heisuke and Kurōbei and about the money which Heisuke claims to have advanced Gisaburō, since the issue utterly lacks proof. Therefore we have come to a compromise, and will never in future resort to action or dispute.

Questions for Analysis

1. What are the issues in this lawsuit?
2. What kinds of people are involved in this lawsuit?
3. Why is the conflict over Gisaburō's personality, not just his possessions?

Source: John Henry Wigmore, ed., *Law and Justice in Tokugawa Japan, Pt. VIII-A: Persons: Legal Precedents* (Tokyo: University of Tokyo Press, 1982). Copyright © 1982 by The Japan Foundation. Reprinted with permission.

As part of a reform effort in 1841, the shogunate tried to reduce what it saw as the excesses of urban culture. It clamped down on unlicensed prostitution by closing teahouses and other sites where women sold their bodies. It forbade women to dress men's hair, teach them music, serve as attendants at archery ranges, or perform onstage in public. In an effort to promote public morality, it even outlawed men and women sharing public baths. Gambling, lotteries, and full-body tattoos were forbidden. The shogunate tightened censorship over the publishing industry, refusing to permit romantic novels such as the serial best-seller, *The False Murasaki and the Rustic Genji* by Ryūtei Tanehiko (REYU-teh-e TAH-neh-he-co).

Theaters and entertainment districts received undesired attention. The shogunate condemned extravagance and ordered commoners not to dress, eat, or house themselves above their station. It tried to enforce these regulations by making examples of outrageous violations, but to little effect.

FOREIGN AFFAIRS (1793–1858)

The Russians were the first foreigners to encroach on Japan. During the eighteenth century, they started to trade with the Ainu in the Kuril Islands and Kamchatka. In 1793, Adam Laxman tried to open relations between Russia and Japan. He got as far as Nagasaki, only to be rebuffed by the shogunate because respect for its ancestors prohibited it from initiating new foreign relations. In 1798 the shogunate sent an expedition to Hokkaido to assess the Russian threat. Based on its report, the shogunate decided to annex Hokkaido and Sakhalin. Its reach exceeded its grasp; it did not have the army to defend either. Russians again asked for permission to trade at Nagasaki in 1804. When that was not forthcoming, officers attacked trading posts on Sakhalin and the Kurils in 1806 and 1807. In 1811, Japan captured Vasilii Golovnin, the captain of a Russian surveying crew, and held him at Hakodate for two years before Russia secured his release. His captivity narrative intrigued readers across Europe.

The Closing of Japan

The British posed a more serious threat. In 1808 their warship *Phaeton* barged into Nagasaki bay in search of Dutch ships. Despite orders from the Nagasaki city magistrate to destroy it, the *Phaeton* left with food and supplies. In two incidents in 1824, British whaling ships raided villages on the coast north of Edo and southern Kyushu. The first village belonged to the Mito (ME-toe) domain, home to one of the shogun's relatives, the anti-foreign Tokugawa Nariaki (NAH-re-ah-key). The second was located in Satsuma, the powerful outside (*tozama*) domain that dominated the Ryukyus. The next year, the shogunate issued new instructions for dealing with Westerners. With the exception of Dutch ships allowed at Nagasaki, all foreign ships, regardless of the circumstances, were to be driven off without hesitation. This order announced that the shogunate was closing the country to the West, its first truly isolationist policy.

The decision to close the country came as a result not only of foreign threats but also of information gathered by scholars and officials. The head of the shogunate's translation bureau, established in 1811, argued that foreigners must be kept away from Japan lest they subvert the gullible masses with Christian teachings. In 1825 an adviser to Tokugawa Nariaki named Aizawa Seishisai (AH-e-zah-wah SEH-e-she-sah-e) wrote his "New Theses" (*Shinron*, SHEEN-rown). Mito scholars believed that loyalty to their lord was based on his loyalty to the monarch. Although they accepted neo-Confucian principles, they also believed that Japan was superior to all other countries, including China, because the monarch was descended from the sun goddess. Aizawa had studied writings about the West, and he questioned the British sailors who had landed on the Mito coast in 1824. *Shinron* argued that Japan had to beware of foreigners, even if they said they came only to trade. Trade would weaken Japan because Japan would lose precious metals and because the pursuit of novelty and luxury items would erode the people's moral fiber. But traders brought something worse than goods: Christianity. They hoped to seduce the foolish commoners with their religion, turn them against their rightful leaders, and "conquer from within by recruiting the local inhabitants into their ranks." To counter the threat of "barbarian teachings," Aizawa urged his lord to convince the shogunate to take educational, religious, and military action that would reform the armed forces by allowing daimyo to recruit farmers as soldiers and educate the masses in Japan's unique spiritual essence (*kokutai*, CO-ku-tah-e).[*] *Shinron* had a lasting impact on nationalist thought.

Despite the domain's poverty, the Mito reform movement of the 1830s largely involved strengthening coastal defenses, a policy followed by a handful of other domains. Some ignored the shogunate's restrictions on the number of guns permitted each castle. Mito and Saga in Kyushu built reverberatory furnaces to cast cannon while *tozama* domains in southwestern Japan bought mortars, howitzers, and field guns from weapons dealers in Nagasaki and also manufactured their own. Fear of foreigners spurred a renewed emphasis on military training. Domains also mobilized militia to man coastal lookout points and serve as a first line of defense. They competed for access to military

---

[*]Bob Tadashi Wakabayashi, *Anti-Foreignism and Western Learning in Early Modern Japan* (Cambridge, Mass.: Harvard University Press, 1986), p. 211.

technology, and they refused to cooperate in developing systems to warn of approaching foreign ships. They saw themselves as defending not an entity known as Japan but rather their own territory. Building coastal fortifications increased their isolation from each other while weakening the shogun's authority.

The shogunate too tried to improve its military, spurred by reports of the British victory over China in the Opium War. (See **Connections: The Age of Western Imperialism [1800–1900]**.) In the 1841–1842 reform, it began to adopt Western military technology and trained a small unit of foot soldiers in the use of modern guns. It also tried to reassert its authority by ordering an end to domain monopolies that interfered in commerce, seeking to transfer daimyo from one domain to another, and threatening to outlaw copper coins and paper money minted in the domains. In 1843 the shogun had the daimyo provide a 150,000-man escort for his pilgrimage to Nikkō where he worshipped at the shrine for his ancestors in a reminder of Tokugawa supremacy. At the same time, the shogunate relaxed its policy toward foreigners: shipwrecked sailors were to be helped, Japanese castaways were to be allowed to return home, and ships in need were to receive supplies before being sent on their way.

Unequal Treaties with the United States

When Commodore Matthew C. Perry sailed four ships into Edo Bay on July 8, 1853, he had been preceded by the unsuccessful 1846 expedition under Commodore James Biddle, and the Dutch had warned of his arrival. Perry treated the shogunate's exclusion order with disdain, and he refused to shift anchorage until he had handed over a letter from President Millard Fillmore addressed to the monarch. He paraded his men on shore, opened his gunports to expose his cannons, and announced that he would return the next year for a reply. This time he had six ships under his command, having commandeered two more in Hong Kong. Intimidated by this display of force, the shogunate signed a friendship treaty with the United States. Japan made all the concessions: American ships were to be allowed to call at Shimoda (SHE-moe-dah) and Hakodate (HAH-co-dah-teh) and to obtain coal and other supplies. Shipwrecked sailors were to be treated fairly, and the United States had the right to station a consul at Shimoda.

Perry brought gifts that displayed the wonders of the Industrial Revolution—a telegraph using Morse

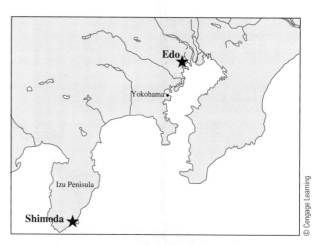

Map 19.1 Location of Shimoda relative to Edo. The shogunate knew it had to acquiesce in demands by the United States to have a consul stationed in Japan, but by choosing the tiny port of Shimoda, it tried to isolate the consul as much as possible.

code and a quarter-size steam locomotive with carriages and track. Sailors in blackface put on a minstrel show. Men and women flocked to see the strange black ships with their steam stacks and guns.

The shogunate soon had to make further concessions. In 1856, Townsend Harris arrived as the first U.S. consul at Shimoda, to the alarm of the shogunate's officials, who had not anticipated that a barbarian would live on Japan's sacred soil. A failed businessman in the China trade, Harris was determined to sign a commercial treaty with Japan. Realizing Shimoda's isolation, he bullied Japanese officials to allow him to negotiate in Edo. Fearing that delay might bring the same gunboats to Japan that had devastated China's coast, officials signed the treaty Harris wanted on July 29, 1858. According to its provisions, the two countries were to exchange diplomatic representatives. Japan was to open six cities to foreign residence and trade just as the Chinese treaty ports had earlier been opened, and it had to accept low tariffs on imported goods, whereas its own exports faced steep tariffs in the United States. Finally, it had to allow foreign residents and visitors the privilege of extraterritoriality. Japan soon signed similar treaties with the Netherlands, Britain, France, and Russia.

Debates on the Foreign Threat

Unnerved by the unprecedented responsibility of signing treaties with Western powers, the shogunate

Portrait of American Official. This image depicts an American official who landed with Perry at Uraga bay. This woodblock print emphasizes facial features most like those of demons—large nose and red mouth with gaping teeth.

ended its 250-year-old monopoly over foreign policy. In 1854 it asked leading daimyo for their opinions; in 1858 it asked the monarch Kōmei (CO-meh-e) to endorse the Harris commercial treaty. In neither case did it achieve a consensus. Worse, Kōmei rejected the treaty, urged the shogun to consult the leading daimyo, and demanded that the foreigners be expelled. When the shogunate signed the treaty against Kōmei's wishes, it was considered treason. People from many walks of life began to collect and debate information on political affairs. By ignoring laws against discussing contemporary events and creating a new public political realm, they helped bring about what hindsight has deemed as the last days of the shogunate.

Some voices supported engagement with the West. Sakuma Shōzan (SAH-ku-mah SHOW-zahn) argued that Japan should strengthen itself by obtaining advanced Western military technology and

fuse Western science to Japan's Confucian ethical base. Only by opening Japan to trade could it gain the knowledge and tools needed to compete in the emerging world order. His ideas found supporters among advisers to important daimyo such as Yokoi Shōnan (YO-co-e SHOW-nahn), who popularized the slogan *fukoku kyōhei* (FU-co-ku KEYO-heh-e) (rich country, strong army), taken from a line in the Chinese classics. Both Sakuma and Yokoi died at the hands of anti-foreign assassins.

The men who opposed signing treaties with the West had a rational basis for their position. Tokugawa Nariaki believed that allowing trade with the West would weaken Japan both materially, in that Japan would lose precious metals in exchange for trifles, and spiritually, because it would be infected by Christianity. The only way to revive Japan's martial spirit was to fight, even though fighting meant certain defeat. Yoshida Shōin (YO-ko-e SHOW-een) had studied military science in Chōshū (CHOE-shoe). In 1854 he opened a small school where he taught public policy under the rubric *sonnō jōi* (SOWN-no JOE-e) (revere the monarch and expel the barbarian). By this he meant that the monarch should participate in policy decisions and the foreigners must be driven off. He was furious that by spinelessly signing the treaties, the shogunate had made Japan look weak in the eyes of the world.

The social networks that had previously transmitted information on agricultural innovation and the rice market now broadcast news of current events. Doctors, merchants, and samurai in Edo told friends and relatives in the countryside about Perry's arrival and the shogun's response. Their letters circulated widely, and the recipients copied their contents into diaries to discuss with like-minded neighbors. Preachers for the Hirata School and experts in swordsmanship linked people across domain boundaries. Broadsheets (*kawaraban*, KAH-wah-rah-bahn) reported gossip on the treaty negotiations. They circulated primarily in urban areas, where they could be easily and anonymously sold, but travelers also took them back to villages. A few commoners presented plans for coastal defense to their daimyo for forwarding to the shogun. They traveled to Edo and Kyoto to see for themselves the changes taking place (see **Material Culture: From Palanquin to Rickshaw**).

MATERIAL CULTURE

From Palanquin to Rickshaw

Before the coming of the railroad, feet provided the means of locomotion for most Japanese travelers. Arising at 4:00 A.M. and moving briskly on straw sandals, they generally covered thirty miles a day before seeking an inn for the night. Occasionally a traveler rented a horse for a day's journey, but most horses were pack animals. Boats plied the Inland Sea and Lake Biwa, carrying travelers as well as goods. Given the boats' reputation for capsizing, many travelers preferred to walk.

The chief alternative to feet was the palanquin. These came in several sizes and styles, depending on their function and the status of the user. Most travelers rode in a wicker basket seated on a cushion, grasping a strap to keep their balance. Rural entrepreneurs transported their brides in enclosed palanquins; in cities these were reserved for the daimyo and high-ranking samurai. Most palanquins were carried by two men, with relays running in front and back.

The rickshaw replaced the palanquin. Invented in 1869 by Izumi Yōsuke (E-zu-me Yo-su-keh), a restaurateur in Tokyo (formerly Edo), it substituted human-powered carriages for horse-drawn coaches. Built in various sizes to carry up to four people and with various designs, depending on whether strength or speed was the object, rickshaws spread from Japan to China and the rest of Asia. They made unmerciful demands on human labor, but they were cheap, simple to make and repair, and nonpolluting. Nothing could beat them for short distances until the taxi arrived in 1912.

Tokyo National Museum/DNPartcom

Fifty-Three Stations on the Tōkaidō. At Kusatsu, one of the fifty-three stations on the Tōkaidō depicted in woodblock prints by Hiroshige, travelers rest their weary feet. Three types of palanquins are featured in this scene.

POLITICAL TURMOIL (1858–1864)

Kōmei's disapproval of the Harris treaty and a dispute over who would be the next shogun paralyzed the shogunate. Prodded by Satsuma, Mito, and other activist daimyo, Kōmei urged officials to appoint Nariaki's son, Hitotsubashi Yoshinobu (HE-toe-tzu-bah-she YO-she-no-bu), seen as more capable than the man who had the stronger claim by blood, Tokugawa Iemochi (E-eh-mo-che). The senior councilors rejected interference in the decision that was theirs alone to make. They appointed a vassal daimyo, Ii Naosuke (EE NAH-oh-su-keh), regent for Iemochi and chief senior councilor. Ii purged his daimyo opponents and arrested, exiled, or executed more than one hundred men employed as agents by daimyo and court nobles. In 1859 the shogunate executed Yoshida Shōin for plotting to assassinate the shogun's messenger to Kyoto. With the daimyo and other opponents silenced, Ii asserted that the shogunate had sole responsibility for foreign affairs.

On a snowy morning in the third month of 1860, young samurai from Mito and Satsuma assassinated Ii outside Edo castle. Angry at his murder of men they revered, they committed their lives to the politics of direct action. Their deed mobilized public opinion against Ii by deeming him a traitor for having executed men of high purpose (*shishi*, SHE-she) whose only aim was to serve the monarch. Equally alarming, the assassins had overcome the distrust that had previously poisoned relations between *tozama* (outside) domains such as Satsuma and Mito, home to the shogun's relative. The shogunate abandoned its authoritarian stance and tried to make amends. It proposed a union of court and military (*kōbu gattai*, CO-bu GAH-ttah-e) that would give important *tozama* and the shogun's relatives advisory positions on foreign affairs and reinstated daimyo purged by Ii. It sealed the deal by having Shogun Iemochi wed Kōmei's younger half-sister, Kazunomiya (KAH-zu-no-me-yah), in return for a promise to expel the barbarians.

Within this framework of cooperation, self-styled "able" daimyo called for national reforms to match the military reforms they had carried out at home. They urged the shogunate to employ men of talent and ability, regardless of where they came from; promote the study of Western technology; and strengthen the nation's defenses. To fund these goals, the shogunate agreed to cut its expenses, reduce the daimyo's stays in Edo to one hundred days every three years, and permit the daimyo to take families held hostage in Edo back to their domains. Women and servants had to abandon the only city they had ever known for life in provincial backwaters.

The *shishi* demanded expulsion of the barbarians as Kōmei had requested. Young and reckless, they ran away from their domains to study swordsmanship in Edo and Kyoto and study the ideas of Aizawa Seishisai and Yoshida Shōin. Filled with the Japanese spirit (*Yamato damashii*, YAH-mah-toe DAH-mah-she-e), they swaggered through the streets, less concerned with personal grooming than with purity of purpose. As soon as Yokohama opened as a treaty port in 1859, they launched a reign of terror against foreign merchants, sailors, and officials. (See Color Plate 27.) Following Kazunomiya's marriage, *shishi* in Kyoto assassinated advisers to the daimyo and nobles they held responsible.

Monarch, shogun, and daimyo feared that the *shishi*'s antics would so weaken the established political order as to invite foreign invasion. Satsuma forced its radicals to return home in disgrace. When *shishi* tried to capture the palace in the eighth month of 1863, planning to place Kōmei at the head of an army to unite western Japan under the slogan of "Restore monarchical rule," Satsuma allied with the shogun's forces to drive them from Kyoto. Many fled to Chōshū. The daimyo of Tosa forced *shishi* in his domain to leave or commit suicide. *Shishi*-led uprisings in the foothills of Yamato and at Ikuno near the Japan Sea were brutally suppressed. Conflict between radical expulsionists and conservatives in Mito erupted in civil war. In the seventh month of 1864, Chōshū *shishi* returned to Kyoto supported by samurai from other domains and rural militia. Once again, the shogunate routed them (see **Biography: Kusaka Genzui, Radical Samurai**).

The exploits performed by *shishi* had less impact on policy than on public opinion. They increased the monarchy's visibility and ruptured the alliance between shogun and court. But how significant was the expansion of a public political sphere based on the discussion and exchange of information given that 60 percent of the population was illiterate? Most commoners remained bystanders. Historians who emphasize that commoners remained on the sidelines during the years leading to the Meiji Restoration and that therefore it cannot be deemed a revolution from below overlook a similar inertia

BIOGRAPHY   Kusaka Genzui, Radical Samurai

Born the year of the Opium War in China (1840), Kusaka Genzui's (KU-sah-kah GEHN-su-e) short career as a radical who acted in the emperor's name shows how one low-ranking samurai sought a cause worthy of his talent and ambition.

Trained to become a doctor like his fathers before him in Chōshū, Kusaka's attention turned to national and international affairs when at age seventeen he entered the private academy founded by Yoshida Shōin, influential critic of the shogunate for having caved in to the foreigners. Within a year, Kusaka's scholastic aptitude got him sent to Edo for advanced study. There the domain kept him so short of funds that he complained, "I never visit courtesans or spend a cent on women." Nervous at the political connections he was developing with men from other domains, Chōshū soon summoned him home. Following Yoshida's execution by the shogunate in 1859, Kusaka took over the academy's leadership while traveling back and forth to Kyoto, not always with official permission, and meeting activists from other domains who snuck into Chōshū. He urged the *shishi* to band together, writing to a like-minded man in Tosa, "If both your domain and mine were destroyed achieving justice, it would be of no consequence."

Kusaka penned his most important writings while confined to his home and cut off from outside contact in 1862. He urged restricting foreigners to only three treaty ports lest they "usurp the nation and beguile the people," he criticized restrictions that prevented Japanese from traveling abroad, he proposed a reform of government that would replace the shogun with the emperor while leaving the domains intact, and he urged what all men of talent but low birth wanted—government positions to be filled by capable men regardless of their family background.

Once released from house confinement, Kusaka divided his time between Kyoto where he spied for his domain and Chōshū where he organized military units to protect the emperor. Caught in the shifting political currents of the time, Chōshū went from being the imperial court's darling to being an outlaw. In summer 1864, units of Chōshū's army advanced on the capital despite orders to withdraw. Although Kusaka counseled patience, other commanders demanded bold action. Unwilling to stand aside while his friends charged into battle, Kusaka joined them. Wounded by rifle fire during a fight under the monarch's walls, he committed suicide.

Kusaka became a hero to young men like himself both at the time of the Meiji Restoration in 1868 and later because he had shown himself willing to fight a battle he knew he could not win and to sacrifice his life for a principle.

Questions for Analysis
1. How did Kusaka explain and justify his attacks on established institutions?
2. Did Kusaka die a meaningful death?

Source: Based on Thomas M. Huber, *The Revolutionary Origins of Modern Japan* (Stanford: Stanford University Press, 1981).

in the ruling class. Most daimyo did nothing, either because they sided with the shogun out of loyalty and self-interest, he being the ultimate guarantor of their office, or because opposing factions had gridlocked their administration. Most samurai remained chained to their lord through the twin virtues of loyalty and obedience. They had less to do with the eventual outcome than did rural entrepreneurs who provided supplies to traveling *shishi*, enlisted their tenants in rural militia, and supported the monarchy or the shogunate with their pocketbooks.

THE FALL OF THE SHOGUNATE (1864–1867)

The *shishi*'s attacks on foreigners and the shogun's forces had unforeseen consequences. The British demanded that Satsuma men who had killed a British merchant be handed over to them and an indemnity paid. When Satsuma refused, British ships bombarded Kagoshima in the seventh month of 1863. Despite its military reforms, Satsuma was

National Diet Library, Tokyo, Japan

Ee ja nai ka. As amulets fall from the sky, men, women, and children, some in costume, dance in thanksgiving, shouting, "Ain't it great?" *(Ee ja nai ka?).*

still no match for foreign gunboats. In the eleventh month, it signed a peace treaty accepting British demands. In compliance with Kōmei's decree that the barbarians be expelled in the fifth month of 1863, Chōshū gunners started firing on foreign ships in the straits of Shimonoseki. More than a year later, the foreigners retaliated. Just days before they attacked Chōshū, the shogunate had it branded an enemy of the court for harboring *shishi* and sent a coalition of daimyo troops to its borders. Chōshū backed down. It apologized for its misdeeds, expelled radical court nobles who had sought refuge there in 1863, and executed three high-ranking officials. The shogunate declared victory and withdrew its forces.

The shogunate had less success controlling the consequences of foreign trade. Beginning in 1859, foreign merchants in the treaty ports at Nagasaki and Yokohama discovered that the silver-to-gold ratio in Japan was one-third what it was in the West, meaning that any man with silver in his pockets could buy gold at ludicrously low prices. The gold rush ended only when the shogunate re-coined and devalued gold, silver, and copper. When it granted daimyo

permission to mint money, counterfeiters flooded the market, and inflation soared. Foreign merchants bought tea and silk in exchange for weapons, making money out of gunrunning but also leading to a sudden expansion in cash crops on rice paddies. Weavers lost work because they could not compete with foreigners for silk thread. In the summer of 1866, rising unemployment, crop failures, inflation, and the shogunate's efforts to tax trade created the conditions for the most widespread riots in Edo history, particularly in the shogun's stronghold of eastern Japan.

The shogunate hoped to use new taxes levied on foreign trade to fund its military modernization program. It imported thousands of weapons through Yokohama and drilled its retainer band and farmer recruits in rifle companies. It sent missions abroad— in 1860 to sign a friendship treaty with the United States; later to study foreign technology. In 1861 it opened a naval training school at Hyōgo followed four years later by an ironworks at Yokohama and a shipyard at Yokosuka. It also received Kōmei's approval for signing foreign treaties, and it marginalized the *tozama* daimyo by excluding them from policymaking circles.

By reasserting its authority and building up its military, the shogunate upset its previous balance of power with the daimyo. When it announced a second campaign to punish Chōshū because *shishi* had returned to positions of power, it pushed former enemies together. Chōshū and Satsuma formed an alliance in the first month of 1866. Both had launched self-strengthening programs, using emergency funds to buy arms through Nagasaki, sending retainers on fact-finding missions abroad, and organizing Western-style armies. Now they argued that the shogunate ought not move against Chōshū when pressing domestic and foreign problems remained to be solved. Few domains responded to the shogun's call; riots in Edo and Osaka tied down garrisons; and the attack on Chōshū ended in humiliating defeat. Iemochi's death at just that juncture provided the shogunate with a face-saving out. But when Kōmei died unexpectedly just five months later, the shogunate lost its strongest supporter at court. Unlike the shogun's opponents, who now believed that Japan should have but a single ruler, Kōmei had supported the division of power that left administrative and foreign affairs in the shogun's hands.

Hitotsubashi Yoshinobu reigned as shogun for less than a year. At first he tried to reassert the shogun's authority and continue military reforms. His efforts stirred up turmoil and strengthened the alliance against him. In the eighth month of 1867, a new popular movement swept the Pacific coast from the inland sea to Edo. Claiming that amulets inscribed with the name of the sun goddess that promised a prosperous future had fallen from heaven, men and women danced in the streets chanting, "Ain't it great?" (*Ee ja nai ka?*, EEH jah nah-i kah). When the movement reached eastern Japan, dancers threw stones at foreigners to drive out barbarian demons and rehearsed a mock funeral for the shogunate. In the tenth month, the court issued a secret decree to Satsuma and Chōshū to overthrow the Tokugawa. Realizing he could no longer function as shogun, Yoshinobu returned his patent of office to the monarch, bringing nearly eight hundred years of military regimes to an end.

In the name of the Meiji emperor, Kōmei's fifteen-year-old son, leaders of the Sat-chō (Satsuma and Chōshū) forces abolished the offices of shogun and regent and replaced them with new advisory positions open to daimyo, court nobles, and "men of talent." They declared Yoshinobu a traitor to the emperor, revoked his court rank, and confiscated his family lands. When the shogunate fought back, it was defeated after four days of fighting outside Kyoto in the first days of 1868. The imperial armies moved slowly north, hamstrung for lack of cash, which forced them to demand loans from wealthy commoners. The long-standing hostility between eastern and western Japan prolonged the fighting until Aizu fell in the ninth month after suffering heavy casualties of men and women. The last stronghold of the shogun's support at Hakodate did not surrender until the middle of 1869, supported to the end by the American envoy. Both official and popular opinion feared that prolonged civil war might give foreign troops an excuse to invade Japan, making the better alternative to unite around the new emperor. Although retainers died, Yoshinobu and the daimyo of Aizu survived to take their places in the new imperial peerage and join their efforts to the task of strengthening state and economy to compete in the new world order. Hirata disciples and other imperial loyalists rushed to offer their services to the new government; people in Edo watched warily as their old masters were replaced with new.

SUMMARY

By the early nineteenth century, the social and political order crafted in the seventeenth century had ceased to fit everyday practice. Farmers charged hereditary village officials with corruption and arrogance while they struggled to deal with the threats posed by gamblers, bandits, and population decline. Some commoners turned to the promise of paradise offered by new religions; others sought release in play. Despite efforts to promote and tax commercial products or promote frugality, daimyo discovered that the gap between income from flat or declining revenues and expenses continued to grow, forcing many of them to cut their retainers' stipends. Capable and ambitious samurai chafed at status restrictions that prevented them from exercising their talents.

While intellectuals and officials worried that society was falling apart, Western powers started making new demands on Japan for friendship treaties and trade agreements. They succeeded in imposing unequal treaties that forced Japan to open treaty ports to foreign residence and give foreigners rights unavailable to Japanese in their countries. Faced with this unprecedented threat, the shogunate blinked. Rather than make a unilateral decision, it opened foreign policy to public discussion by asking monarch and daimyo for input, only to discover that few agreed on what to do.

Debates over how to deal with the foreign threat led to repression, reform, and resistance. In 1858–1859 the shogunate tried to silence its critics, only to have the tables turned with the assassination of its chief minister. It then tried to conciliate daimyo and court by giving them more autonomy while radical samurai assassinated individuals who, they thought, had shown disrespect to the monarch. Commoners too expressed their outrage at political paralysis and foreign trade that disrupted existing markets in a variety of popular movements from dances to riots. Fear of foreign intervention may have kept Japan from exploding into civil war, but when the shogunate tried to rebuild its military along modern lines and reassert its authority, powerful daimyo from the southwestern domain forced the shogun to step down. A brief war in 1868 resulted in a clear-cut victory for the forces fighting under the banner of the Meiji emperor.

What changed between 1800 and 1868? Long before the Meiji Restoration, the commercial economy, opportunities for travel, and information networks eroded the status and geographical divisions that kept people in their place. Reforms by shogun and daimyo to shore up their authority and fill government coffers could not conceal the gap between reality and their ideal of the proper relations between rulers and commoners. Debates over how to deal with the foreign threat added further strain to the system by drawing more people into the public political sphere. When the shogunate collapsed in 1867, it left behind a dynamic economy, a pool of able administrators, and a population well educated for its time. Also passed on to the new government was a set of treaties with Western powers that recast Japan's relations with the outside world and opened the country to foreign trade, though not on terms favorable to Japan.

Meiji Transformation (1868–1900)

Making the Meiji (MEH-e-g) emperor the head of state (called a restoration because the new regime claimed to restore the emperor to the power his ancestors had exercised in the eighth century) marked the beginning of profound changes in Japanese politics, culture, and society. A small group of self-selected men (called oligarchs because they monopolized power), who had led the drive to overthrow the shogun, abolished status distinctions that had put social groups into separate compartments and centralized government. Fearful of the West, they understood the need to import Western military technology, industry, legal norms, constitutional thought, science, dress, and food. (See **Material Culture: New Food for a New Nation.**) They built railroads, shipyards, and schools; created a new ideology to rally the citizens; colonized the Ryukyu Islands and Hokkaido; projected Japan's power abroad in Taiwan and Korea; and renegotiated treaties. They faced much opposition, often from within their own ranks. Farmers rioted against new state policies that threatened their livelihood; samurai rebelled at the loss of their traditional identity; local notables promoted democracy. Intellectuals, novelists, and essayists hammered out new identities that refused to fit a single pattern. By the end of the century, modernity had arrived.

To what extent did changes in the latter half of the nineteenth century build on what had gone before? Did the Meiji Restoration herald a revolution in politics and society, or simply a transition? Did modernization mean westernization?

THE MEIJI STATE (1868–1900)

Oligarchs who created the new centralized government had little idea of what they hoped to accomplish and disagreed on what to do. A loose group of samurai from Satsuma and Chōshū, plus a few activist Kyoto aristocrats and imperial loyalists from other domains, they had varied interests and

MATERIAL CULTURE

New Food for a New Nation

Although rice had been grown in Japan since the eighth century B.C.E., it did not become a staple of the average Japanese diet until imported from Korea and China starting in 1873. Before that, most people ate wheat, barley, and millet. Between 1869 and 1900, the per capita consumption of rice went from 3.5 bushels a year to 5 bushels a year. Rice balls became common in lunch boxes, and except for the poor, steamed rice replaced rice gruel for breakfast.

The Meiji government officially promoted the eating of meat because it was thought to produce stronger workers and soldiers. In 1869 it established the Tsukiji beef company. In 1871 a butcher shop in Tokyo's Asakusa district became popular by selling beef for sukiyaki, a Meiji period invention, as well as milk, cheese, and butter. In the 1880s butcher shops started selling horse meat. It was cheaper than beef or pork and redder than chicken.

Vegetables, fruits, and breads had a harder sell. Asparagus, cabbage, cauliflower, and tomatoes did not blend easily into Japanese cuisine. Importing apples and grapes stimulated the cultivation and spread of native fruits such as persimmon, Satsuma tangerine, and Asian pear. Bread and cakes became popular only after they were modified to suit Japanese taste.

By selectively adapting Western foods, Japanese people developed a much more varied diet than they had in the past. They ate more, and what they ate was generally more nutritious, although overly refined rice caused beriberi in soldiers. An improved diet made most people stronger and healthier while increasing life expectancy and childbearing rates. A population of approximately 33 million at midcentury had grown to 45 million by the end of the nineteenth century.

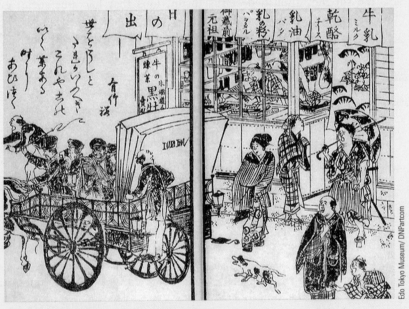

Aguranabe. This flyer advertising Aguranabe, a butcher shop, linked eating beef to "civilization and enlightenment."

goals. Their first pronouncement came in the Oath of 1868, offered by the emperor in the company of court nobles and daimyo to the gods of heaven and earth. In it he promised that everyone was to unite in promoting the nation's well-being, government policy was to be decided through public discussion, all would be allowed to fulfill their just ambitions, "the uncivilized customs of former times shall be broken through," and "intellect and learning shall be sought throughout the world in order to establish the foundations of the

Empire."[*] The Five Injunctions issued to commoners the next day had a different message. They were to practice the Confucian virtues of loyalty, filial piety, chastity, obedience, and harmony; stop demonstrations and protests; shun Christianity; conform to international public law; and stay in Japan. Emigration to Hawaii began almost immediately.

Ambiguities in the oath speak to the oligarchs' lack of agreement on national goals. The nation's well-being could justify both a national land tax and universal military conscription as well as private entrepreneurs and compulsory education. None of the men present expected public discussion of national affairs to include anyone but themselves. In contrast to the past, when each daimyo had set policy for his domain, it meant that decisions and power were to be centralized. It did not mean parliamentary democracy, although it was later interpreted that way. By implying that hereditary status distinctions would be abolished, the third clause held out the promise of social mobility. Abolishing old customs acknowledged the reality of cultural imperialism inherent in international law and unequal treaties. The purpose of gaining knowledge was to serve the state.

At first, oligarchs looked to eighth-century models for a new government. The Council of State became the highest deliberative body, assisted by a board of 106 advisers, the activists in the Meiji Restoration, who made the real decisions. The Council of Shinto Affairs enjoyed a brief existence equal to the Council of State. This structure was reorganized four times in the next four months. Most daimyo remained in control of their domains, leaving the oligarchs who spoke in the emperor's name only the former shogun's lands. Money offered to the emperor from daimyo, the shogun's former retainers, merchants, and rural entrepreneurs staved off fiscal crisis in the short run, while the need to find tax revenues to fund the government forced the oligarchs to take hesitant steps toward centralization.

Centralization required convincing the daimyo to give up their domains. Some daimyo hoped to play a larger role in national affairs; some concentrated their efforts on strengthening their domains. Most stayed aloof from government and isolated from each other. In 1869, the daimyo of Satsuma and Chōshū agreed to make a formal declaration of returning their land and population registers to the emperor, with the understanding that he would

then confirm their holdings as governors. The government put all the retainers above the level of foot soldiers into a single category called former samurai (*shizoku*, SHE-zo-ku). To streamline local administration and centralize tax collection, in 1871 the oligarchs abolished some 270 domains and established prefectures. (See Map 20.1.) They started the process of consolidating 170,000 towns and villages into larger administrative units with new local officials and created a household registration system whereby each household head had to establish a place of legal residence and inform the government of births, deaths, marriages, and divorces in his family.

Daimyo readily accepted the loss of their hereditary lands. The most important became prefectural governors controlling a larger territory than they had before because the number of prefectures was a mere seventy-two, later reduced to fifty. All daimyo benefited by no longer having responsibility for their domains' debts and being guaranteed a substantial income for their personal use without having to support standing armies of retainers. In place of their former titles, they received court rank. In return for giving up their already limited autonomy, they received wealth and prestige.

Abolishing domains disinherited roughly 2 million *shizoku*. All they received were small stipends later changed to government bonds. Oligarchs urged them to find another line of work, in agriculture, forestry, business, and the colonization of Hokkaido. Some succeeded; many did not. The shogun's former bureaucrats staffed the new government, but most domain samurai remained in castle towns. Political power had become sufficiently bureaucratized over the course of the Edo period that neither samurai nor daimyo became landed gentry.

Having taken the first steps toward a more centralized state, in 1871, one faction of oligarchs left for the United States and Europe in a delegation of forty-nine officials and fifty-eight students plus five girls. Headed by Iwakura Tomomi (E-wah-ku-rah TOE-moe-me), a former court noble, their goal was to convince the Western powers to revise the unequal treaties that infringed on Japanese sovereignty. Informed by President Ulysses S. Grant that Western powers would never consent to treaty revision unless Japan reformed its laws and institutions along Western lines, the diplomatic mission became a study mission. Officials inspected prisons, schools, factories, and government agencies, trying to learn the secret of wealth and power that the West had created through industrialization and centralized government. They

---

[*]Donald L. Keene, *Emperor of Japan: Meiji and His World, 1852–1912* (New York: Columbia University Press, 2002), p. 139.

Map 20.1   Modern Japan

expected their absence to prevent any initiatives by the leaders left behind. In 1873, when Saigō Takamori (SAH-e-go TAH-kah-moe-re) proposed to invade Korea for having insulted the emperor in the first diplomatic exchange following the restoration, they rushed home to stop him. They opposed not the use of force but its timing. Domestic reform had to precede the use of military force abroad.

Reforms and Opposition

The abolition of domains took place during social reforms that did not suit everyone. For many farmers, the emperor's progress from Kyoto to Edo (renamed Tokyo in 1869) in 1868 symbolized the Meiji

Restoration. This, they felt, would usher in new prosperity and social justice. Instead, village officials continued to collect taxes, rents remained the same, and moneylenders charged high interest. Disappointment fueled the rage with which people punished what they saw as wrongdoing. When the new government replaced familiar faces in domain administrations with men from foreign parts, this too led to protest, as did the official end to discrimination against outcasts when status distinctions were erased and the outcasts became "new commoners." The first ten years of the Meiji period saw more protest and more violence than at any time during the Edo period.

Bureaucrats initiated reforms and technological innovations to strengthen the state against its domestic and foreign enemies. They hired Western experts to transform government, economy, infrastructure, and education. Drawing on Western models, they issued civil and criminal codes that replaced different regulations for samurai and commoners with rule by law that considered only the nature of the crime. They built telegraph lines and railroads to improve communications and foster unity. On January 1, 1873, they replaced the lunar calendar that farmers had used as a guide to planting and harvesting with the Western calendar. They outlawed traditional hairstyles for men and suppressed village festivals. Having received these directives without warning or explanation, farmers rioted in defense of time-honored custom.

Religious practices also provoked strife. In the third month of 1868, the oligarchs ordered the separation of Shinto and Buddhism and the changing of what had been shrine-temple complexes into shrines by getting rid of Buddhist statues, rituals, and priests. In some regions, officials infected with Hirata Atsutane's doctrines destroyed Buddhist temples where the farmers' ancestral tablets were kept. Building Yasukuni (YAH-su-ku-knee) shrine to house the war dead in 1869 used Shinto to promote national goals while the creation of State Shinto in the 1870s consolidated local shrines and placed them under the Ise shrine to the sun goddess. Rather than shrines containing only gods particular to their region, people also had to accept gods of national significance. New religions founded in the Edo period received official recognition as Sect Shinto, but Meiji-period new religions were viewed with suspicion and often persecuted. (See **Biography: Deguchi Nao, Founder of a New Religion.**) Farmers protested the destruction of their familiar temples, and Buddhist priests fought back by using Buddhism as a weapon against Christianity, recalling ties to the imperial house and helping immigrants in Hokkaido.

Directives that had immediate effects and aroused the strongest opposition dealt with education, the military, and taxes. In 1872, the government decreed eight years of compulsory education for all children (shortened to four in 1879 and then increased to six in 1907) to fit them for their responsibilities as productive citizens in a modern nation, but communities had to pay for schools themselves. Outraged at the cost, farmers destroyed or damaged nearly two hundred schools between 1873 and 1877. Pre-Meiji teachers continued their unlicensed schools and talked parents out of sending their children to new ones. Needing their children's labor or unable to afford tuition, many parents never enrolled daughters or even sons or allowed them

to attend school for only a few months. Over time, the number of children in school increased, reaching 90 percent in the twentieth century.

The slogan of the day was "Rich Country, Strong Army." In January 1873, the government issued a conscription ordinance crafted by Yamagata Aritomo (YAH-mah-gah-tah Ah-re-toe-moe) based on German and French models that summoned all males over the age of twenty to serve on active duty in the armed forces for three years, followed by four years in the reserves. Heads and heirs of family farms and businesses received exemptions, and exemptions could be purchased. This ordinance put Japan's defense on the shoulders of the masses and provided a way to educate conscripts and their families in the goals of government leaders. By revoking the samurai's monopoly of force, it did more than any other reform to eliminate status distinctions and create equality of opportunity.

Both farmers and *shizoku* opposed conscription. The ordinance used the term "blood tax," meaning that all citizens should willingly sacrifice themselves for their country. Farmers who took it literally assumed that the government wanted their blood. Even those who understood the message believed that they could best contribute to the nation by growing crops. Commoners opposed to conscription led demonstrations in sixteen localities in the months after the ordinance's announcement. Samurai opposition took longer to develop but cost more lives. Conservative oligarchs such as Saigō Takamori had already insisted that the national army be composed of the men bred to military service. When Iwakura and his faction outvoted Saigō on whether to invade Korea, he left the government. In 1876, the government ordered *shizoku* to stop wearing the two swords that distinguished them from the rest of the population. Between 1874 and 1877, more than thirty rebellions erupted in defense of samurai privilege. The largest and last, in Satsuma and led by Saigō, required the mobilization of sixty-five thousand troops and took eight months to suppress. Saigō committed suicide. In 1878, samurai counterrevolution ended with the assassination of the oligarch Ōkubo Toshimichi (OH-ku-bow TOE-she-me-che), also from Satsuma, because he had opposed invading Korea and arbitrarily initiated reforms.

Satsuma rebels also had reason to oppose the 1873 tax law. Applied nationwide to agricultural land, its aim was to provide a steady flow of income for the government by replacing the old hodgepodge of domain taxes on fluctuating harvests with a single,

BIOGRAPHY   Deguchi Nao, Founder of a New Religion

As one of the women who played a major role in creating Japan's new religions, Deguchi Nao (DEH-gu-che NAH-oh) (1836–1918), an illiterate commoner, became a prophet.

Nao was born in a castle town near Kyoto to a family on its way down. Her grandfather had the privilege of wearing a sword and using a surname as an official carpenter. Her father squandered his life on drink and died when Nao was nine. Nao went to work for a merchant who provided her with room and board; her earnings went to her mother. Nao helped with the cooking and cleaning; she spun thread and strung coins, thereby gaining a reputation for diligence and hard work. In her third year of service, the domain awarded her a prize for being a filial daughter.

Nao hoped to marry the man she loved, but her widowed aunt Yuri insisted that she accept an arranged marriage and be adopted into the Deguchi family as Yuri herself had done. Yuri drowned herself after Nao repeatedly rejected her offer. A few days later, Nao developed a high fever and lost consciousness. Upon her recovery, she attributed her illness to Yuri's vengeful spirit. To placate it and care for the Deguchi ancestral tablets, Nao agreed to marry the man Yuri had selected for her and continue the Deguchi house.

Nao's husband was no better than her father. By 1872 she had borne five children and was living in a rented house in Ayabe. She opened a small restaurant, and when it failed, she sold sweet-bean buns. She continued to have children—eleven in all, three of whom died in infancy. When her husband became paralyzed from a fall off a roof in 1885, Nao collected rags to support her family. His death in 1887 freed her to work in a silk-spinning factory as well.

One winter morning in 1892 while she was out collecting rags, Nao became possessed by a god. The experience transformed her personality and her outlook on the world. Instead of being gentle and humble, she became dignified, filled with divinely inspired authority. She rejected the social order because it rewarded vice and valued money, and she claimed that because the oligarchs and the emperor were responsible for these conditions, they exemplified absolute evil. They would soon be destroyed and replaced by a divine order of harmony and equality. Under the spell of her god, this formerly illiterate woman wrote hundreds of texts that spelled out what was wrong with the world and what was to come. She also became a faith healer. In 1899, her adopted son Deguchi Onisaburō (OH-knee-sah-bu-row) organized a sect called Ōmoto-kyō (OH-moe-toe-keyo) based on her revelations. Under his leadership, the group grew rapidly and suffered repeated government persecutions. Nao quarreled with him over his interpretation of her writings and his refusal to reject all that was modern. She died frustrated that she had not been able to reconstruct the world in accordance with her beliefs.

Questions for Analysis
1. How did Nao become a prophet?
2. What was Nao's message?
3. How does Nao fit within the context of Japanese religious beliefs?

Source: Emily Groszos Ooms, *Women and Millenarian Protest in Meiji Japan: Deguchi Nao and Ōmoto-kyō* (Ithaca, N.Y.: East Asia Program, Cornell University, 1993).

---

uniform property tax. In most regions of Japan, land surveys that accompanied the new tax simply confirmed the property rights farmers already enjoyed. Satsuma domain had allowed *gōshi* (GO-she) (rustic warriors) to assign land to cultivators and treat them like tenant farmers. Faced with loss of income as well as hereditary status and privilege, *gōshi* became the shock troops for the Satsuma rebellion.

Even though Meiji oligarchs tried to promote industry and demanded loans from merchants, they had an agrarian mindset. Nearly 80 percent of the government's revenues came from tax on agricultural land through the 1880s. Farmers with market access for their products benefited; those who misjudged the market or suffered a crop failure had to sell their land to pay taxes. In some areas, officials imposed the new tax while requiring farmers to continue to pay the additional taxes it was supposed to replace. Farmers petitioned for help; they killed officials suspected of being corrupt. In 1876, widespread, if uncoordinated, opposition to the tax forced the government to reduce it from 3 percent of assessed value to 2.5 percent.

Fiscal Year	Land Tax	Liquor Tax	Customs Duties	Income Tax	Corporation Tax	Business Tax	Sugar Excise	Inheritance Tax	Other
1872	90.1	1.5	3.3	—	—	—	—	—	5.1
1880	72.3	14.9	4.4	—	—	—	—	—	8.4
1890	58.1	22.9	6.9	1.6	—	—	—	—	10.5
1900	34.6	38.0	10.9	4.3	1.2	3.9	1.3	—	5.8
1910	23.8	26.2	15.3	10.0	2.9	7.0	5.1	0.9	8.8
1920	10.2	22.6	11.1	23.5	11.8	6.6	6.8	1.1	6.3
1930	7.9	26.4	15.1	22.1	6.6	6.2	9.6	3.5	2.6
1940	0.9	8.9	2.9	34.0	11.7	2.6	3.2	1.6	33.9

Composition of Tax Revenues, 1872–1940 (%)

Source: Based on Minami Ryōshin, *The Economic Development of Japan: A Quantitative Study,* trans. Ralph Thompson and Minami with assistance from David Merriman (New York: St. Martin's Press, 1986), p. 340.

While dealing with opposition from outside the government, oligarchs also quarreled among themselves. They created and abolished ministries to consolidate their power or deny rivals and argued over what kind of government Japan was to have. In the early 1870s, Kido Takayoshi (KEY-doh TAH-kah-yo-she) and Ōkubo advocated some popular representation in government lest arbitrary rule generate unrest. Their proposal contained a veiled attack on Itō Hirobumi (E-toe HE-row-bu-me) and Yamagata. Angry at having been shut out of power, Itagaki Taisuke (E-tah-gah-key Tah-e-su-keh) left the government in 1874, joined with disaffected *shizoku* from his home domain of Tosa to form the Patriotic Party, and petitioned the government to establish an elected national assembly. He disbanded the party when he was invited back into the government in 1875 at the Osaka Conference where the oligarchs agreed to establish prefectural assemblies (done in 1878) and plan for a national assembly. Four months later, the emperor announced that he would promulgate a constitution after due deliberation.

Constitution and National Assembly

Publicity generated by the promise of a national assembly and constitution helped create the Popular Rights Movement. *Shizoku,* village officials, rural entrepreneurs, journalists, intellectuals, and prefectural assemblymen held meetings and circulated petitions for an immediate national assembly signed by hundreds of thousands of people. Radicals and poverty-stricken farmers rioted and planned attacks

on the government in the name of human rights. A woman who held property demanded to be allowed to vote in prefectural elections (she was denied). Kishida Toshiko (KEY-she-dah Toe-she-co) and Fukuda Hideko (Fu-ku-dah HE-deh-co), both women, gave public lectures at which they demanded rights, liberty, education, and equality for women. Baba Tatsui (BAH-bah TAH-tzu-e) drew on Social Darwinism to argue that because democracy based on an egalitarian society was the most advanced form of government, it should come immediately. Local notables drafted model constitutions. Activists who criticized the oligarchs for blocking channels between emperor and people argued that a representative government would harmonize imperial and popular will by providing a forum for the free expression of popular opinion, thereby strengthening the nation. Drawing on French and British natural rights theories, Ueki Emori (U-eh-key EH-moe-re) crafted a theory of popular sovereignty and right of revolution.

Oligarchs responded to the Popular Rights Movement by issuing increasingly severe peace preservation laws. Press censorship began in 1875; the 1880 Ordinance on Public Meetings stationed policemen at assemblies to ensure that the speakers did not depart from texts that had been approved beforehand. Excluded from audiences were soldiers, off-duty police, teachers, and students. Demonstrations in Fukushima opposed to a particularly arbitrary governor in 1882, the Chichibu uprising of 1884 that mobilized tenant farmers in demanding debt relief, and other violent incidents met with mass arrests and executions. Having learned the cost of direct action, local notables organized political parties to get ready for the first election for the national assembly promised in 1890.

The Meiji Constitution defined institutions created before it was issued. In 1878 the military General Staff was made directly responsible to the emperor, by-passing the War Ministry run by bureaucrats. A new peerage destined to fill the upper house of the two-chamber national assembly, known as the Diet, was announced in 1884. First made up of oligarchs, former daimyo, and Kyoto nobility, over time it expanded to include entrepreneurs and academics. The lower house was to be elected by commoners. The cabinet, which made policy, replaced the Council of State in 1885. It was filled with ministers in charge of education, finance, foreign affairs, and other bureaucracies under the prime minister appointed by the emperor.

Itō Hirobumi drafted the constitution in great secrecy. He traveled to Europe in 1882 where for nine months he studied in Berlin under the most respected constitutional theorists of his day. Itō and his brain trust then created a document that defined the emperor in terms of his descent from the gods and employed Western notions of the rights and obligations of citizens. Once the constitution was finished, the Privy Council, a new institution headed by Itō, met to discuss it. On February 11, 1889, the date chosen to be the anniversary of Jimmu's enthronement 2,349 years earlier, the Meiji emperor bestowed the constitution on the prime minister. Three days of festivities announced to people across the nation that they were now citizens of a state founded on principles enshrined in a constitution.

Oligarchs wanted a constitution that secured the governing bodies and protected the imperial house through which they exercised power, and they distrusted "ignorant" masses. After its promulgation, they designated themselves *genrō* (GEHN-row), elder statesmen, charged with picking cabinet ministers for the emperor. The constitution defined the emperor as sovereign and sacred. The emperor:

- exercises executive power through the cabinet
- exercises legislative power with the consent of the Imperial Diet
- has supreme command of the army and navy
- declares war, makes peace, and concludes treaties
- determines the government's organization
- convokes the Diet and dissolves the lower house

Subjects had rights and duties to:

- present petitions, provided that they observe the proper form of respect
- enjoy freedom of religious belief within limits not prejudicial to peace and order and not antagonistic to their duties as subjects
- enjoy freedom of speech, within the limits set by law*

Subjects had to serve in the military, a clause that excluded women from the category of "subject."

Japan's first experiment with parliamentary democracy nearly did not work. Although Itō and Yamagata had assumed that party politics had no place in an institution directly responsible to the emperor, they had to deal with opposition parties headed by Itagaki and other men who had been ejected from the oligarch's inner circle. Suffrage (the right to vote) was limited to men paying at least fifteen yen a year in property taxes, a qualification met by only 1.1 percent of the population, most of them in rural areas. Once elected, members discovered that the Diet had more power than the oligarchs had intended. Diet members could criticize the cabinet in memorials to the emperor; they could make speeches, published in newspapers, that outside the Diet might have landed them in jail. They had the power to approve the budget. If they refused, the previous year's budget remained in effect, but it seldom covered the government's needs. When the Diet opposed the cabinet, the prime minister dissolved it, forcing members into a costly reelection campaign. Campaign finance scandals and vote buying tarnished the reputations of politicians and oligarchs alike. Twenty-five men died during the 1892 election, most at the hands of the police.

Divided by personality and self-interest, oligarchs had to seek political support outside their narrow circle. In so doing, they enlarged the realm of political action to include bureaucrats, military officers, and politicians. In 1898, Itō had the sometime oligarchs Ōkuma Shigenobu (OH-ku-mah SHE-geh-no-bu), head of the Progressive Party, and Itagaki Taisuke, leader of the Liberal Party, participate in a coalition cabinet as prime minister and home minister, respectively. Horrified that Itō had caved in to politicians, Yamagata Aritomo sabotaged their cabinet by having the army minister refuse to accept cuts

---

*Hugh Borton, *Japan's Modern Century* (New York: Ronald Press Co., 1955), pp. 490–507.

Triptych Showing Inauguration of the First Diet. Members of the upper house dressed in uniform are in the foreground; lower house members sit farther back. The emperor is in the box at upper left. *[Gotō Yoshikage, Japanese, 1858–1922 Publisher: Yoshida Ichimatsu, Japanese The Imperial Diet of Japan (Dai Nihon teikoku gikai no zu) Japanese, Meiji era, 1890 (Meiji 23), printed November 13, published November 14 Woodblock print (nishiki-e); ink and color on paper. Vertical ban triptych; 35.8 × 73.1 cm (14 1/8 × 28 3/4 in.) Museum of Fine Arts, Boston Jean S. and Frederic A. Sharf Collection, 2000. 535a-c. Photograph © 2012 Museum of Fine Arts, Boston]*

in the military budget. A few months later, Yamagata became prime minister for the second time. To increase military autonomy, he made it a requirement that all army and navy ministers be active-duty officers. To weaken the power of political parties and their resistance to higher taxes, he expanded the suffrage to 2.2 percent of the population and gave more representation to urban districts. In 1900, Itō responded by forming and becoming president of a new political party, the Friends of Government. His compromise with politicians dramatized the oligarchs' difficulty in controlling the institutions they had created.

Industrialization

Oligarchs promoted economic reform and industrialization. They took over the arms-related industries already established by the domains and the shogunate, placing some under state control to supply the military; others were sold to cronies at favorable terms. Iwasaki Yatarō (E-wah-sah-key YAH-tah-ro) founded Mitsubishi (ME-tzu-be-she) enterprises on the maritime shipping line he acquired from Tosa and expanded it with low-interest government loans. The oligarchs had foreign experts write banking laws; they set up banks and issued paper currency. They made their first investments in advanced and expensive technologies, the kind needed to build railroads and shipyards. Although building support industries for the military constituted their main priority, they also worried about the effects of unequal treaties on the balance of payments and unemployment. To maintain social stability and to compete with foreign products, they built cotton-spinning and weaving factories to make cloth for the domestic market and imported French silk-spinning technology to produce thread for export. They founded a sugar refinery to help growers market their crop and compete with Chinese sugar. By bringing the state's resources to bear on industry, oligarchs squeezed out private capital.

Agriculture supported industrial growth. Agricultural development groups, seed exchange societies, journals, and lecture circuits taught farmers about new seed varieties, commercial fertilizers, and equipment, leading to growth rates in annual agricultural productivity of between 1.5 and 1.7 percent in the late nineteenth century. Because the land tax remained fixed, the increase put more income in the hands of rural entrepreneurs for use in promoting small-scale industry. Farmers were already accustomed to producing handicrafts; eliminating internal restrictions on trade made it easier for them to market their goods.

Entrepreneurs and artisans developed intermediate technologies that adapted Western machines to Japanese circumstances. They modified the manufacture of new daily necessities such as matches to suit the domestic and Asian markets and undersold Western brands. The metric system, the new calendar, and Western timepieces brought the standardization and regularization modeled by military organization to ordinary work practices. Local clubs tried to preserve handicrafts in the face of foreign imports and sought national and international markets for specialty products. They pooled capital to upgrade local skills, brought in foreign technology when it fit their needs, and hosted industrial exhibitions to spread technological knowledge and stimulate competition. In the mid-1870s, small waterpowered silk-spinning factories spread throughout the mountain valleys of central Japan, close to the silk-producing regions and a work force of young women. By 1900, silk thread accounted for one-third of the value of Japan's commodity exports, and textiles totaled more than half.

Another model for private enterprise was Shibusawa Eiichi (SHE-bu-sah-wah EH-e-e-che). Son of a rural entrepreneur, he used his connections with oligarchs to become president of First National Bank and provided capital for the construction of a privately owned shipyard at the mouth of Tokyo Bay. In 1880 he started the Osaka Spinning Mill, the first of more than one hundred companies. Thanks to investments like his, by the beginning of the twentieth century Japan's imports were of raw materials; it exported manufactured goods. Other entrepreneurs built equipment for railroads, mines, and factories. Many thrived with the government as their biggest customer, justifying their immense wealth by insisting that they worked for the good of the nation.

In 1880 the government faced financial disaster. It had printed money recklessly during the 1870s to finance its projects, and private banks issued their own notes. It spent heavily suppressing *shizoku* rebellions and other police actions; most of the industries it built operated at a loss. Inflation that doubled the price of rice in Tokyo between 1877 and 1880 reduced the value of property tax revenues, taxes did not cover spending, and the negative balance of payments sucked gold and silver out of the country.

Snark/Art Resource, NY

Spinning Mill. Established by the government in 1873, this spinning mill in Tomioka relies on the latest technology imported from France housed in a modern brick building with glazed windows where rows of young women happily work away, overseen by a French supervisor who guides visitors through the plant.

From an economic point of view, Japan faced the most serious crisis of the Meiji period.

After bitter debate, the oligarchs decided on a deflationary policy of retrenchment. Finance Minister Matsukata Masayoshi (MAH-tzu-kah-tah MAH-sah-yo-she) balanced the budget, reduced government spending until it fell within revenues, and established a sound currency backed by gold and silver. Except for railroad, telegraph, and military-related industries, he sold at a loss all industries that the government had tried to develop. He recalled students sent abroad on government scholarships, fired foreign experts, enacted sin taxes on tobacco and sake, and increased old taxes. Between 1881 and 1885, he reduced the quantity of currency by 20 percent and stifled commerce. Farmers who saw the price of rice fall 50 percent while taxes remained the same worked longer hours to increase production. Bad loans bankrupted banks started with samurai capital while small businesses collapsed. The ranks of tenant farmers and factory workers swelled. By 1886 key industries had become concentrated in the hands of a few wealthy capitalists with excellent government connections. The government had rid itself of drains on its income, the budget was balanced, and prices were stable.

By the 1890s Japan had a substantial work force in light and heavy industry. Silk-spinning factories employed single farmwomen who worked eighteen-hour days when demand was high. When they contracted tuberculosis, as many did, they were returned to their families. The spread of the disease made it modern Japan's most severe epidemic. The women who worked twelve-hour shifts in cotton mills were often married. Factory owners assumed that because women did not maintain households independent of fathers or husbands, they could keep wages low. The first strike in Japan's industrial history occurred at a silk-spinning factory in Kōfu in 1885 where women protested a proposed increase in hours and decrease in pay. Women unable to find factory work turned to prostitution. Poor women from Kyushu lured to brothels in Southeast Asia remitted money to their families that helped Japan's balance of payments.

Male factory workers in heavy industry earned up to five times the wages of women. They worked under bosses called *oyakata* (OH-yah-kah-tah) who contracted for specific jobs. Because workers ran the factory floor, they were able to retain a measure of autonomy that gave them pride in their work. Those who possessed skills in high demand moved at will from one factory to another. Despite these advantages, wages barely covered the rent for a shack in the slums and a dismal diet of rice and vegetables. In 1898 railroad workers launched the largest strike of the nineteenth century with demands for respect, higher status, and an increase in overtime pay.

Conditions for miners were worse. The low wages, dangerous work, and prison-like barracks made it so difficult to attract workers that the owner of the Ashio copper mine contracted for convict labor. By the end of the nineteenth century, the mine's demand for timber had stripped surrounding hills, leading to deadly floods. Toxic wastes from the mine had killed marine life in the Watarase River, devastated farmland, and caused premature deaths. Dealing with environmental damage pitted proponents of "Rich Country, Strong Army" against the well-being of ordinary citizens in a conflict that was to play out repeatedly in Japan's modern history.

Civilization and Enlightenment

Local notables who had responded enthusiastically to the Popular Rights Movement wanted to bring a cultural revolution to their villages. In place of hidebound customs, they wanted "Civilization and Enlightenment," a slogan promoted by urban intellectuals and by oligarchs bent on modernizing communications, hairstyles, and education. The Meiji 6 Society founded in Tokyo in 1873 published a journal in which the members debated representative government, foreign affairs, modernizing the Japanese language, ethics, religion, and roles for women. That same year, local notable Ida Bunzō (E-dah BOON-zo) bought a copy of Samuel Smiles's *Self Help*. In a local magazine, he explained the virtues of sticking to a task and frugality, competition and progress, moral responsibility and the national interest. Other local notables used informal discussion groups to promote better hygiene and social improvement through hospitals, new foods, better roads, and technological innovation based on Western models. They tried to overcome their neighbors' opposition to the government-mandated schools that they saw as the best way to improve conditions for rural people and raise Japan's standing in the world.

The man who coined the phrase "Civilization and Enlightenment" was Fukuzawa Yukichi (FU-ku-zah-wah YU-key-che), a leading member of the Meiji 6 Society. In 1868 he founded Keiō (KEH-e-oh) University for the study of Western science and business. His multivolume *Western Matters* described modern institutions—schools, hospitals, newspapers, libraries, and museums—and Western ideas regarding the importance of entrepreneurship and achievement. In the bestseller *Encouragement of Learning*, he criticized Japan for its backwardness and urged citizens to seek learning for its practical value in the modern world. He also served as adviser to Mitsubishi and Mitsui, destined to become the largest conglomerates in Japan. Although he advocated equality, freedom, and education for women, he kept his daughters ignorant and arranged their marriages.

Civilization and enlightenment also pertained to personal appearance. To use Western technology, it was more efficient to wear Western-style clothes. Replacing distinctive styles of samurai armor with standardized military uniforms submerged the individual in the ranks. Uniforms also distinguished policemen from civilians. Changing appearances might help Japan gain the respect of foreigners who flaunted their cultural superiority. The government issued directives to men to stop shaving the tops of their heads and to women to stop blackening their teeth and shaving their eyebrows, with the emperor and empress leading the way. At his first public performance, the Meiji emperor had dressed in the court robes of his ancestors while wearing cosmetics and powder with false eyebrows smudged on his forehead. Within two years he had changed to Western-style uniforms, cut his hair, and grown a beard. The empress too appeared in Western-style clothing and hairstyles.

The new nobility and educated elite followed the imperial family's example. In 1883 the foreign minister built a modern two-story brick building called Deer-Cry Pavilion that contained a restaurant, billiard room, and ballroom. Invitations to garden parties, charity balls, and receptions went to Japanese and foreigners, husbands and wives, a startling innovation because samurai women had not previously socialized with their husbands. Western-style dancing by couples was customary, even at parties far from Tokyo sponsored by prefectural governments. The late 1880s government became known as the "dancing cabinet."

Newspapers, journals, and other mass media exemplified and promoted civilization and enlightenment. Woodblock prints used chemical dyes to depict the marvels of westernization. Prints of horse-drawn carriages, steam engines, new schools, and red brick buildings illuminated by gaslight in Tokyo's downtown Ginza district inspired progressive youths to seek modernity. (See Color Plate 28.) Magazines for women urged them to become educated in modern modes of thought to help them fulfill their roles as "good wives and wise mothers."

The professional journalist Fukuchi Gen'ichirō (FU-ku-che GEHN-e-che-ro) covered Saigō's rebellion in 1877 and later became chief editor of the influential *Tokyo Daily Newspaper*. It was a so-called big paper written in a style only the highly educated could read, with a focus on politics and serious editorials. Founded in 1874, the *Yomiuri Newspaper* aimed at the barely literate. Like other "small papers," it covered scandals and titillating stories of sex and murder. Hawked on street corners, it exploited the growing market for information and entertainment.

Modern newspapers serialized modern novels. In 1885 the fan of kabuki and student of English literature Tsubouchi Shōyō (TZU-boh-u-che SHOW-yo)

wrote *Essence of the Novel*, which tried to define a new realistic literature. *Floating Clouds* (1887–1889) by Futabatei Shimei (FOO-tah-ba-teh-e SHE-meh-e) is deemed Japan's first modern novel because it tried to get inside the leading character's head and used language close to everyday speech. Perhaps the most subtle and gifted writer was Higuchi Ichiyō (HE-gu-che E-che-yo), who gained fame in the male world of letters only at the end of her short life. Dominated at the end of the century by the medical doctor Mori Ōgai (MOE-re OH-gah-e), who had studied in Germany, and Natsume Sōseki (NAH-tzu-meh SO-seh-key), who had studied in Britain, this world embraced modernity while questioning the superiority of Western civilization.

CONSERVATIVE RESURGENCE (1880s–1900)

By the middle of the 1880s, many people thought that aping Western customs had gone too far. They tried to hold onto traditional values while accepting the need for Western rationalism in scientific inquiry and Western technology. In 1882 Kanō Jigorō (KAH-no G-go-row) began the transformation of martial arts into judo through the scientific selection of techniques from earlier schools specializing in unarmed combat. He emphasized that judo built character in a way that complemented developments in the study of ethics by religious figures and Western-trained philosophers. By establishing an absolute standard for "the good," they sought to use community values to suppress socially disruptive thought. The head of the Hygiene Bureau, Gotō Shimpei (GO-toe SHEEN-peh-e), claimed that the only way to get people to respond to public health initiatives was to work through established community structures and appeal to community values. Bureaucrats tried to promote social welfare and a collectivist ethic through factory laws, tenancy laws, and agricultural cooperatives for fear that a social revolution might undo their efforts to build a strong state. In 1890 the revised Police Security Regulations forbade women to participate in politics. The intent was to eliminate the need for selfish and unpatriotic competition and conflict.

The educational system bore the brunt of the conservative resurgence. In the 1870s it provided strictly utilitarian knowledge; in the mid-1880s it added Confucian ethics, Shinto mythology, and civic rituals. For the few who could afford to go beyond compulsory schooling, the Educational Code of 1872 had specified that a rigorous examination system would qualify students for middle schools, and the best would then take examinations for university. Founded in 1877, Tokyo University remained the only public institution at that level until 1897. Private universities such as Keiō and missionary schools provided lesser avenues for educational advancement. In 1886 the Ministry of Education established specialized higher schools above the middle schools. The First Higher School funneled students into Tokyo University for positions in the most prestigious ministries. Some higher schools offered degrees in liberal arts for students going on to universities and then to careers in the bureaucracy or business world. Others were vocational schools, military schools, teacher's colleges, and women's colleges. Each socialized the students by crafting character suitable to their station in life.

Education prepared citizens to serve the nation; it also provided a stepping stone for personal advancement. Oligarchs opened the ranks of government service to men who had demonstrated talent and ability measured through academic achievement, but only men from families wealthy enough to support them through years of schooling had any chance of success. Women were to serve the state as wives and mothers. Class and gender thus placed limits on equality, and the promise of social mobility concealed an economically stratified society.

Education trained citizens in civic virtues personified by the emperor. In the 1870s and 1880s he toured Japan to unite the people under his gaze. Newspaper reports of his diligent work habits and concern for his subjects' welfare made him into a symbol of national unity and progress. He moved his headquarters to Hiroshima during the Sino-Japanese War (1894–1895); celebrated war victories; and appeared at imperial funerals, weddings, and wedding anniversaries. Given pride of place in every school and public building, his portrait had to be treated with utmost respect. In 1890 he issued the Imperial Rescript on Education. It urged students to practice filial piety, harmony, sincerity, and benevolence; to respect the constitution; to obey the laws; and to be loyal to the *kokutai* (CO-ku-tah-e) (national polity).

The 1898 Civil Code adjusted the norms of Western legal systems to the conservative concern for civic morality. Unless the primacy of the house and the male authority of the household head were maintained in law, the legal scholar Hozumi Yatsuka (HOH-zu-me YAH-tzu-kah) warned, reverence for the ancestors, loyalty, and filial piety would perish. The Civil Code upheld legal equality, individual choice, and personal ownership of property for all men and single women, regardless of their former social status. Succession was to follow the male line, with all assets to go to the eldest son. A husband had authority to dispose of his wife's lands and buildings, though not her personal property (her trousseau); he decided when and whether to register a marriage and their children. As in the Edo period, divorce by mutual consent freed both partners for remarriage. The Civil Code thus balanced a concern for social stability and modern Western norms with an understanding of customary practice.

IMPERIALISM AND MODERNITY (1870s–1895)

When Japan appropriated and adapted Western industrial technology, legal institutions, constitutional theory, and culture, it also studied Western imperialism. Social Darwinism taught that nations had to conquer or be conquered. Seeing what had happened to China and India, Fukuzawa Yukichi urged Japan to "leave Asia" for fear that it too might be conquered. (See **Documents: Fukuzawa Yukichi's "Leaving Asia."**)

The connection between modernity and imperialism appeared early in the Meiji period. As part of Japan's overtures to China in 1870 it tried to impose an unequal treaty because having taken steps toward a modern centralized state made it the more civilized. A treaty negotiated in 1871 granted mutual extraterritoriality. In 1874 Japan used the murder of Ryukyuan fishermen by Taiwanese three years earlier as an excuse to send an expeditionary force to Taiwan. The pretext was to punish the Taiwanese; a covert aim was to bring civilization to the natives by establishing a colony. The war dragged on for five months before a settlement reached in Beijing acknowledged China's claims to Taiwan and Japan's claims to the Ryukyus. The expeditionary force withdrew, though not before Japanese newspapers had celebrated its victory over barbarism.

The Ryukyus and Hokkaido became internal colonies. In 1871 the Ryukyus were made part of Kagoshima prefecture. In 1879 the king was invited to reside in Tokyo and become a member of the

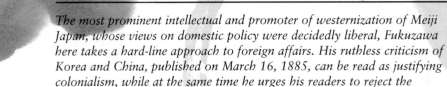

DOCUMENTS   Fukuzawa Yukichi's "Leaving Asia"

The most prominent intellectual and promoter of westernization of Meiji Japan, whose views on domestic policy were decidedly liberal, Fukuzawa here takes a hard-line approach to foreign affairs. His ruthless criticism of Korea and China, published on March 16, 1885, can be read as justifying colonialism, while at the same time he urges his readers to reject the civilization they had to offer. In 1895, ten years after writing this call to action, he rejoiced at Japan's victory over China.

Japan is located in the eastern extremities of Asia, but the spirit of its people has already moved away from the old conventions of Asia to Western civilization. Unfortunately for Japan, there are two neighboring countries. One is called China and another Korea. These two peoples, like the Japanese people, have been nurtured by Asiatic political thoughts and mores. It may be that we are different races of people, or it may be due to the differences in our hereditary or education: significant differences mark the three peoples. The Chinese and Koreans are more like each other and together they do not show as much similarity to the Japanese. These two peoples do not know how to progress either personally or as a nation. In this day and age with transportation becoming so convenient, they cannot be blind to the manifestations of Western civilization. But they say that what is seen or heard cannot influence the disposition of their minds. Their love affairs with ancient ways and old customs remain as strong as they were centuries ago. In this new and vibrant theater of civilization when we speak of education, they only refer back to Confucianism. As for school education, they can only cite precepts of humanity, righteousness, decorum, and knowledge. While professing their abhorrence to ostentation, in reality they show their ignorance of truth and principles. As for their morality, one only has to observe their unspeakable acts of cruelty and shamelessness. Yet they remain arrogant and show no sign of self-examination.

In my view, these two countries cannot survive as independent nations with the onslaught of Western civilization to the East. Their concerned citizens might yet find a way to engage in a massive reform, on the scale of our Meiji Restoration, and they could change their governments and bring about a renewal of spirit

new Japanese nobility while a Japanese governor took his place. Japanese fishermen and settlers had already spread as far north as Sakhalin and the Kuril Islands, territory that Russia claimed. In 1874 Japan evacuated Sakhalin and negotiated a treaty ceding it to Russia in exchange for Japanese control of the Kurils. Hokkaido became a Japanese prefecture, and a modern definition of property ownership resulted in land the Ainu had customarily used for hunting and fishing being sold to Japanese developers. Without material support, Ainu culture lost its meaning.

Japan's relations with Korea also illustrate the relationship between modernity and imperialism. The diplomatic mission sent to "open" Korea in 1875–1876 imitated Perry's tactics in 1853–1854 and imposed a treaty that replicated the unequal treaties Japan had signed in the 1850s. The following years saw successive incidents as factions at the Korean court supported by Japan and China collided over the country's future course. In Japanese eyes, Korea was a weak, backward nation, easy prey for aggressive Western powers. A German military adviser warned that were Korea to be controlled by any other power, it would become a dagger pointing at the heart of Japan. In 1890 Yamagata Aritomo linked parliamentary politics with a militant international stance by telling the first Diet that for Japan to maintain its independence, it had to protect its territorial boundary, the line of sovereignty, and an outer perimeter of neighboring territory, a line of interest. Korea fell within Japan's line of interest.

among their peoples. If that could happen they would indeed be fortunate. However, it is more likely that would never happen, and within a few short years they will be wiped off the world with their lands divided among the civilized nations.

From the perspectives of civilized Westerners, they may see what is happening in China and Korea and judge Japan accordingly, because of the three countries' geographical proximity. The governments of China and Korea still retain their autocratic manners and do not abide by the rule of law. Westerners may consider Japan likewise a lawless society. Natives of China and Korea are deep in their hocus pocus of nonscientific behavior. Western scholars may think that Japan still remains a country dedicated to Yin-Yang and the five elements. Chinese are mean-spirited and shameless, and the chivalry of the Japanese people is lost on Westerners. Koreans punish their convicts in an atrocious manner, and that is imputed to the Japanese as a heartless people. There are many more examples I can cite. It is no different from the case of a righteous man living in a neighborhood of a town known for foolishness, lawlessness, atrocity, and heartlessness. His action is so rare that it is always buried under the ugliness of his neighbors' activities. When these incidents are multiplied, that can affect our normal conduct of diplomatic relations. How unfortunate it is for Japan.

What must we do today? We do not have time to wait for the enlightenment of our neighbors so that we can work together toward the development of Asia. It is better for us to leave the ranks of Asian nations and cast our lot with civilized nations of the West. As for the way of dealing with China and Korea, no special treatment is necessary just because they happen to be our neighbors. Any person who cherishes a bad friend cannot escape his notoriety. We simply erase from our minds our bad friends in Asia.

Questions for Analysis

1. In Fukuzawa's eyes, what was wrong with Korea and China?
2. Why did Fukuzawa think it important for Japan to turn its back to these countries?
3. What did Fukuzawa mean by "leaving Asia"?

Source: David J. Lu, *Japan a Documentary History: the late Tokugawa period to the present.* Armonk, New York: M.E. Sharpe, 1997, pp. 351–353, modified.

Pressure brought by domestic public opinion to revise the unequal treaties affected Japan's diplomatic relations with its Asian neighbors. When negotiations for revision stalled in the face of Western opposition, clamor intensified for an aggressive stance toward China and Korea on the part of patriotic Popular Rights advocates as much as conservatives. In 1886 Britain and Germany proposed the partial abolition of extraterritoriality in exchange for allowing unrestricted travel by foreigners. The strength of domestic opposition to this compromise was so strong that the foreign minister had to resign. Finally, in 1894 Western powers promised to abolish extraterritoriality and to give Japan tariff autonomy in 1899.

Treaty negotiations took place in the context of the first Sino-Japanese War of 1894–1895. (See Chapter 18.) Fought over Korea, it lasted only nine months; Japanese troops expelled the Chinese army from Korea, defeated the north Chinese navy, captured Port Arthur and the Liaodong peninsula in south Manchuria, and seized a port on the Shandong peninsula. The Treaty of Shimonoseki in April 1895 gave Japan Taiwan and the Pescadores, Port Arthur and the Liaodong peninsula, an indemnity, and a promise by China to respect Korea's autonomy. Japan's victory took Western powers by surprise. In their eyes, it threatened peace and stability in East Asia. A week after the treaty was signed, Russia (with its own designs on Manchuria), France (Russia's ally), and Germany (hoping to steer Russian expansion toward what was now referred to as the Far East) collectively advised Japan to surrender its claim to territories in China. Despite popular outcry at the "Triple Intervention," the government had no choice but to obey. Russia then grabbed control of Port Arthur and the Liaodong peninsula.

SUMMARY

Building a state capable of confronting domestic and foreign challenges proved difficult for the oligarchs—the men who had appointed themselves to be its leaders. They had to buy off the former ruling class of daimyo and samurai, centralize administration, develop a tax base, create a national education system, and reform the military, all the while facing criticism from within their own ranks and opposition from outside. The Constitution of 1889 and the Diet (national assembly) tried to balance the oligarch's desire for stability and control with the promise of parliamentary democracy.

Industrialization too got off to a rocky start. Although a few entrepreneurs used connections to government to their profit, others found that state-operated enterprises were squeezing them out before the oligarchs divested the government of everything but control over transportation, communications, and industries related to the military. Businessmen grew wealthy; the ranks of male and female workers swelled. To protest inhumane working conditions and demand better wages, they went on strike.

To counter the destabilizing effects of increased social mobility, new ideas, and changing industrial relations, the oligarchs and other conservatives promoted unity and harmony. They had the emperor model the man of character; they used education to promote civic virtues; they reinforced the authority exercised by the male head of household through legal codes. Even foreign adventures made a contribution: a sense of national identity that could unite factory owners with factory workers demanded imperialist enterprises to divert attention from their differences.

Japan did to its Asian neighbors what the Western powers had done to it by imposing unequal treaties. In the process of demarcating its boundaries, it turned the Ryukyu Islands and Hokkaido into internal colonies. Having negotiated an end to the unequal treaties, it fought a war with China that would have given it significant territory on the Asian mainland had Western powers not pressured it to back down.

How should we assess the changes that Japan experienced in the latter part of the nineteenth century? Historians who note that ordinary people's lives changed only gradually if at all prefer to speak of a Meiji "transition." Others who point to the official abolition of status distinctions and restrictions on mobility as well as new opportunities for political action talk about revolution. Comparing 1868 with the end of the nineteenth century makes it hard to deny that Japan had been transformed from a decentralized, largely agrarian regime into a centralized industrializing nation. Molded by schools and the military, informed by newspapers and journals, the peoples of Japan had become citizens. They had learned to ride on trains, wear Western-style clothes, and be self-reliant in striving for success. In dealing with the outside world, they had discovered that economic development and national defense required expansion abroad. Adaptation of Western models to local circumstances meant that Japan did not simply undergo a process of westernization. After all, the effects of modernity on community life, family relations, and definitions of individual identity required wrenching changes in Western nations as well.

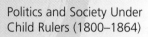

CHAPTER TWENTY-ONE

Korea in the Turbulent Nineteenth Century (1800–1895)

Nineteenth century Korea faced many challenges: three rebellions caused largely by the state's failure to solve long-standing institutional and economic problems, intermittent persecution of Catholics, a series of young kings whose wives' relatives dominated the government, and the threat to national survival by foreign imperialism. The last half of the century saw the birth of Korea's first new religion, failed attempts at reform followed by conservative Confucian anti-foreignism, and unprecedented Chinese interference in Korean affairs. Domestic rebellion and a strengthened Japan brought Chinese influence to an end in the Sino-Japanese War of 1894–1895 and seemingly opened a path for serious reform.

What were the reasons behind the rebellions and the state's lack of response to them and foreign aggression? What changed in the lives of people outside of government? What was Korea's role in the Sino-Japanese War and how does that war speak to Korea's relations with its neighbors?

POLITICS AND SOCIETY UNDER CHILD RULERS (1800–1864)

King Jeongjo's (JUNG-joe) death in 1800, leaving an heir of only eleven years old, marked the beginning of politics dominated by relatives of the king's wife, a situation that lasted to the end of the century. One reason was that all four nineteenth-century kings came to the throne as children under regencies established by the eldest living dowager (widowed) queen or were selected by such dowager regents when there was no crown prince. The dowager regent retained power until she resigned voluntarily or the king decided that it was time for him to rule on his own. Male relatives of dowager regents and queens benefited from this system in that they received appointment to high office.

Conflict between clans for control of the king turned on which had ties to the eldest living dowager and which supplied the king's wife. When King Cheoljong (CHEOL-jong) died without an heir in 1863, Queen Sinjeong (SHIN-jung) of the Pungyang Jo (POONG-yang JOE) clan, whose husband had died in 1830 before he could ascend the throne, was the eldest living queen. She selected the twelve-year-old second son of King Cheoljong's second cousin to be the new king, King Gojong (GO-jong). His father received the title of Daewongun (DAY-won-goon), or grand prince, a title reserved for the father of a king who had never been king himself. The dowager became regent and held the position for only two years, to 1866, but the young King Gojong was kept unaware of his right to rule. Instead, the Daewongun continued as de facto regent from 1863 to 1874 even though he had no formal title or position. He and his supporters clashed repeatedly with his son's wife, Queen Min (MIN), and her clan, causing his political fortunes to rise and fall with startling frequency until his death in 1898.

Social Change and New Social Policies

The early nineteenth century found the government grappling with the consequences of social change. New diseases such as cholera, deforestation that led to flooding, and drought brought an end to the eighteenth-century rise in population. Instead the population dropped to 12.4 million by 1816 and then fluctuated between 12.2 and 12.7 million until 1876, in contrast to the population increases seen during the same period in China and Japan.

As the *yangban* (YANG-bahn) became more entrenched in central government, intermediate groups between them and the commoners also came to be defined by hereditary status. Like the *yangban*, they married within their own groups, and they often monopolized specialized occupations. Historians today call them secondary status groups, although they disagree over whether the last two listed below belong there or whether they should be seen instead as a marginalized regional elite and a military aristocracy.

- *Jungin* (JOONG-in)—technical specialists in foreign languages, law, medicine, and finance
- *Hyangni* (HYANG-ni)—clerks in local administration
- *Seoeol* (SUH-ul)—children and descendants of concubines
- Elites from the northern provinces formally classified as *yangban* but kept out of central administration because of where they were from
- *Muhan* (MOO-han)—military officials also classified as *yangban* but discriminated against because they were eligible to take only the military, not the civil service, examinations

Members of these groups appear with increasing frequency in nineteenth-century records of art, literature, and reform and in twentieth-century politics. In 1801, the dowager regent freed most of the sixty-seven thousand official slaves, except for slaves working in local offices. This measure recognized what had already happened; many government slaves had gained their freedom either through military service or purchase, and the remainder no longer worked for the government. Some slaves owned slaves; some slaves owned land. The 1801 decree liberalized the slave system, but hereditary slavery for several million private slaves continued to 1886. Although slavery itself was abolished in 1894, the mostly *yangban* slave masters retained their power until the dynasty was near its end. (See **Making Comparisons: Slavery.**)

The factional strife that had dominated Korean politics in the eighteenth century had consequences for religious policy. While freeing official slaves, the dowager regent authorized renewed persecution of Catholics and other minority factions. Supported by the Patriarch faction and the Party of Principle, she ordered the institution of a five-family mutual surveillance system to ferret out Christians in the Southerner faction. Sent into exile for his beliefs, Jeong Dasan wrote several treatises proposing reforms in local administration and the penal system. Also banished were a Chinese missionary and the previous king's half-brother, wife, and daughter-in-law. The situation for Christians worsened when officials intercepted a letter from the Christian Hwang Sayeong (HWANG SA-young) to the papal court in Rome requesting a military expedition from France to protect Korean Christians from persecution. Outraged by this act of treason, the dowager regent executed more than three hundred Christians that year alone and persecuted members of the Southerner faction and Party of Expediency. These factions were kept out of office for another half-century.

The Christian issue emerged once again in 1839 when the government executed three French missionaries and scores of converts. Six years later it martyred Korea's first priest, Kim Daegeon (KIM DAY-gun), trained in Macao, who had preached in secret. Between waves of persecution, the number of converts continued to grow. Instead of being primarily *yangban*, they now tended to be people in intermediate status groups and commoners, including a remarkable number of women.

National Museum of Korea, Seoul, Korea

"Wrestling" by Kim Hongdo (KIM HONG-doe). The first painter to depict daily life in Korea, Kim Hongdo here illustrates an informal match before an audience of men and women. Note the peddler waiting for a sale.

Social Ferment and Popular Culture

The nineteenth century saw important developments in intellectual life and popular culture. Men of *yangban* origin played less of a role than men from secondary social statuses who spread new ideas in an effort to make sense of society and promote reform. Many elements associated with Korea's traditional culture today either arose during this period or took on the form by which they are now known.

The practical learning school blossomed in the early nineteenth century. Based on empirical observation and the careful comparison of texts, it produced scholars who challenged the Confucian orthodoxy promoted at court. Seo Yugu's (SUH YOU-gooh) *Sixteen Treatises Written in Retirement* contained his thoughts on agricultural practices, economic developments, and *yangban* leisure pursuits. *Observations on Examining Two Stone Inscriptions* by Kim Jeonghui (KIM JUNG-hwi), also a famous poet and calligrapher, recorded his detailed comparisons of sixth-century stone monuments.

Men whose social backgrounds blocked them from bureaucratic office compiled biographies of superior men who had likewise suffered from discrimination. Written by a man from a fallen *yangban* family, Choe Hangi's (CHAE HAN-gi) *Personnel Administration* (1860) proposed that the government select its officials from men of talent and ability regardless of their status background while urging openness to foreigners. The specialist Seong Haeeung (SUNG HAE-ung) took a similar stance in advocating reform of the tax and forced labor systems, arguing that taxes should be collected in cash and that the government should pay workers rather than expect them to work for free. The wife of a practical learning scholar, Bingheogak Yi (BING HUH-gak YI), compiled an encyclopedia of women's work, some of it commercial enterprises, as a guide for her daughters and to make the point that women should be respected for their achievements, literary and economic.

Men from the secondary status groups composed works across a range of genres. They wrote poetry, compiled in 1857 into *Third Selection of Poems of the People*; they wrote historical novels that celebrated the glories of Korea's martial past. Sin Jaehyo (SHIN JAE-hyo) composed lyrics for *pansori* (PAWN-so-ri, stories sung to drum accompaniment). Music, painting, and dance crossed the social divide, with anonymous artists imitating subjects admired by *yangban* and producing paintings to brighten the walls of temples. Combining dance, song, and narrative, masked drama flourished. One famous passage from *Festival at Naval Headquarters* mocked the *yangban* by using a food image that must have been highly satisfying for a commoner audience:

> I'll eat them raw at low tide, cram my maw at
>   high tide,
>
> Devour my *yangban* masters nine and ninety.
>
> Then I'll eat one more and lo!
>
> A dragon now become, mount the throne of
>   Heaven.*

---

*Reprinted by permission of the publisher from *A New History of Korea* by Ki-baik Lee, translated by Edward W. Wagner with Edward J. Shultz, p. 260, Cambridge, Mass.: Harvard University Press, Copyright © 1984 by Edward W. Wagner.

Men practiced a range of martial arts, some derived from Chinese traditions. Kim Hongdo sketched wrestlers performing as they had since the Goguryeo (GO-goo-ryeo) era in a style akin to Japanese sumo.

Economic Developments and Rebellion

Historians disagree over the extent of economic development in the decades before foreigners made their presence felt. Many of the positive indications seen in the eighteenth century—the spread of markets and signs of commercialization—did not lead to greater output.

Farmers adopted a number of strategies for survival, one of the most prevalent being the *gye* (GYEH), a voluntary organization that promoted mutual assistance. Like similar credit associations that arose in Japan, the *gye* provided a mechanism for people to pool funds and then take turns using the capital. Early *gye* had specific functions: to give members access to support groups and the large sums needed to pay for funerals and weddings. Even *yangban* and wealthy households joined them. Later *gye* pooled resources to overcome hardship. Some had specific community-wide goals, such as repairing an irrigation system, whereas others allowed individual members to use the money for diverse purposes. The *gye* still function in modern Korea, where they provide a means for women to gain access to credit, and in overseas communities where immigrants lack access to banks.

Other survival strategies included planting New World crops and opening marginal fields. The sweet potato arrived via Japan in 1763; the white potato arrived via China around 1840. Both were cultivated as insurance against famine. Another nineteenth-century addition to the diet was cabbage (see **Material Culture: Gimchi**). Despite these dietary supplements, tenant farmers and farmers of small plots led a precarious existence. After a year or two of poor harvests, they abandoned their fields, wandered the country, and died of starvation by the thousands. In desperation they practiced slash-and-burn agriculture on hillsides that stripped the uplands of trees and increased the frequency of floods. Some peasants joined bands of brigands that coalesced into small armies and ravaged the countryside. When all else failed, they migrated into Manchuria and the Russian Maritime Province.

Rebellions constitute the chief indicators of social unrest in the nineteenth century. A major rebellion

MATERIAL CULTURE

Gimchi

The food most associated with Korean cuisine is gimchi (GIM-chi), but it developed into its current form only in the nineteenth century.

Koreans began pickling vegetables, especially long radishes, in salt to preserve them through long winter months around the seventh century. In the twelfth century, spices and seasonings such as soy sauce came to be added, and people started eating gimchi year-round. Although hot red peppers originating in the Americas arrived in Korea from Japan following Hideyoshi's invasion of 1592, it took two hundred years for them to be used to flavor gimchi. The peppers give gimchi its distinctive red color. The final, essential ingredient is Chinese cabbage (*baechu* [BEH-chu]), introduced in the nineteenth century. Although other vegetables continue to be pickled, cabbage became the favorite. A Joseon cookbook explains how to make gimchi for the royal court:

> First, cut well-washed cabbages and radishes into small chunks and salt them. Second, mix them with chopped hot red pepper, garlic, dropwort (minari [MI-na-ri]), leaf mustards (gat [GAHT]), and seaweed. Third, boil fermented fish in water and cool it. Fourth, add the fish sauce to the blended vegetables. Fifth, store the mixture in a pot and wait till it is fermented.*

Today pickled cabbage is eaten across northern Eurasia, but the spiciest is gimchi, prepared not only in Korea but also in eastern Siberia.

---

*http://www.koreanrestaurantguide.com/kimch/kimch_0.htm

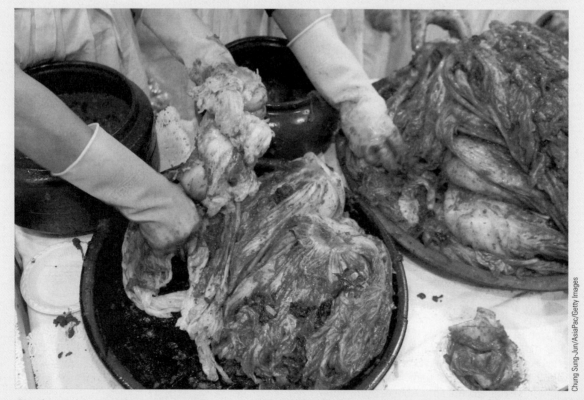

Gimchi. Making gimchi requires cabbage, spices, salt, and other seasonings that can stain and damage the skin—hence the gloves.

Chung Sung-Jun/AsiaPac/Getty Images

DOCUMENTS

Donghak Beliefs

*Here Choe Jeu (CHAE JEH-ooh), founder of the Donghak (DONG-hak)
religion, describes how external pressure and domestic turmoil so afflicted his
mind that he became ill. In that state, he had conversations with the Supreme
Being, who offered him solutions to the issues facing him and Korea as a whole.
This conversion narrative, a testimony to faith, illustrates the path to belief.*

CHOE JEU ON PROPAGATING VIRTUE

From the distant past up to the present day,
every year without fail spring has eventually
turned into autumn, and all four seasons have
come and gone in the proper sequence. This
is a display for the entire world to see of how
the Lord of Heaven regulates the changes
and transformations in the universe. Yet ignorant folk know only that rain and dew are
natural phenomena and do not know how
it is that they are able to benefit from them.

Recently people have tended to do whatever they feel like doing instead of acting in
accordance with heavenly principles. They no
longer pay any attention to the decrees of
heaven. I have worried about this night and
day, but did not know what to do about it.

It got worse in 1860. That is when I learned
that Westerners, claiming that they were only
doing what the Lord of Heaven wanted them
to do and were not trying to be rich or to lord
it over others, began using military force to
seize territory all over the world. Everywhere
they went they set up churches and promoted
their way of doing things. I asked myself if this
really could be happening, and if so, how
could such things happen?

Then a totally unexpected event occurred
one day in the fourth month of that year. All
of a sudden a chill came over my heart and my
whole body shivered. It was as if I had abrupt-
ly fallen ill, but I couldn't tell what sort of illness had attacked me. Then my ears seemed
to pick up a strange voice. It is difficult to
describe. The closest I can come to describ-
ing it is to say that it sounded like the voice
of one of those immortals who lives deep in
the mountains. I was frightened and asked,
"Who are you?" An answer came back, "You
don't have to be afraid. I am the one whom
human beings call the Lord Above. Don't you
know who the Lord Above is?" Startled, I
asked why he was talking to me. He replied,
"So far I haven't been able to accomplish all

that I have wanted to accomplish. Therefore
I have sent you into this world so that you
can teach human beings the right way to do
things. So cast all fear and doubt aside and
listen to me."

I then asked, "Do you want me to teach
people the Western way of doing things?" He
replied, "No, not at all. I have a talisman that
is called the 'medicine of the mountain immortals.' It resembles the Great Ultimate [the
name neo-Confucians give to the wellspring of
all existence]. Take this talisman and use it to
heal people of the various diseases that afflict
them. Also, I am giving you an incantation that
I want you to use to teach human beings on
my behalf. If you do this, you will live a long life
and will propagate virtue all over the world."

This all happened at a time when terrible
diseases were sweeping across our country.
Everyone was worried day and night that they
or someone dear to them might be the next
victim. It was our bad luck that this was happening at the same time that Westerners were
on a rampage. I wondered if there wasn't
some way to help our country and put the
minds of the people at ease.

Unfortunately people these days don't understand what a precarious situation we are
in. If they happen to hear what I have to say, it
goes in one ear and out the other. Even worse,
some of them criticize me publicly. They are
ignorant of the way and don't follow it. This is
really a pitiful situation.

Questions for Analysis

1. What are the circumstances that led Choe Jeu to
   his beliefs?
2. What does Choe Jeu see as the answers to his
   problems and those of Korea?
3. Where do these answers come from?

Robert E. Buswell, Jr., ed., *Religions of Korea in
Practice*, Princeton University Press. Reprinted by
permission of Princeton University Press.

led by fallen *yangban* and professional geomancer Hong Gyeongrae (HONG GYONG-nae) broke out in the northwest Pyeongan province in 1811. One cause was perceived injustice in the taxation and service systems, but general discontent with the discrimination against northerners practiced by central administration officials and resentment at being blocked from promotion to high office led men of secondary status groups to organize an army of rebels. Although it was quickly suppressed, small-scale outbreaks continued.

In 1862 the government's failure to solve the problems of injustices in the collection of the land tax and military cloth tax and in the distribution of grain relief and loans provided the main cause for a series of rebellions throughout the country, primarily in the three southern provinces. Although taxes had earlier been combined into a single land tax, corruption by clerks and magistrates more than offset the reductions gained from distributing taxes equally among all residents. More massive and widespread than earlier outbreaks of social unrest, the rebellion of 1862 lacked central organization. Despite a few attacks against *yangban* landlords, it was aimed mainly at government officials. Although *yangban* participated in the planning of some protests, they usually withdrew when the uprising became violent. Armed with bamboo spears, commoners provided the leadership in dozens of spontaneous uprisings that killed government functionaries and burned official buildings. Rather than trying to suppress the protests by force, the government sent officials to punish corrupt magistrates, investigate abuses of the tax system, and pacify the people.

Choe Jeu and the Donghak Religion

A more lasting response to social dislocation came in the form of a new religion. Discontented with his life as a déclassé *yangban* (his mother had remarried, thus barring him from the civil service examination) and appalled at the sorry situation of his country, Choe Jeu experienced a vision in which he believed Hanulnim (HA-neul-lim, the Lord of Heaven) entrusted him with the task of spreading a new faith to the Korean people and saving mankind on earth. Choe also created a potion for curing illness and attaining immortality by burning special amulets and mixing the ash with water. He called the faith Donghak (Eastern Learning, or "Korean National Teaching"). It combined Confucian ethics with Buddhist faith, the Daoist search for

longevity, geomancy, and the use of talismans, curses, and shamanistic appeals to spirits in a mixture that was supposed to counteract Western learning and Christianity (see **Documents: Donghak Beliefs**).

Jeu's followers were mostly commoners and slaves because the *yangban* regarded his departure from Confucian orthodoxy as unacceptable. They also rejected his teaching that all men were equal in their duty to serve the Lord of Heaven with whom they were united by their very nature. His ideas thus constituted a threat to both the stability of the dynasty and the purity of Confucian belief. Although he was not involved in the many local rebellions that began in the south in 1862, the government arrested him the next year for fomenting dissent with his heterodox teaching. In 1864, the government had his head cut off. The movement went underground and did not reemerge (except for one minor rising in 1879) until 1893. Even in 1864 it signaled that popular discontent was calling into question the ability of Confucian orthodoxy to solve the problems Korea faced.

ATTEMPTS AT REFORM AND EXTERNAL PRESSURE (1864–1894)

The year 1864 marks a divide in Korea's nineteenth century. Although Korean diplomats at the Qing court received news of China's defeat in the Opium War, its magnitude remained concealed from them. (See **Connections: The Age of Western Imperialism**.) Wei Yuan's *An Illustrated Essay of the Maritime Nations* had reached Korea in 1845, but its recommendations for improving defenses against Westerners had been ignored. Later foreign encroachments on China and Japan also had little effect on policy until China gave Russia a lease on the Liaodong peninsula next to Korea in 1860. Official responses to the foreign threat had to wait until King Gojong took the throne at the age of twelve with his father, the Daewongun, behind him.

The Daewongun tried to revive dynastic power and the Korean state by pursuing a course of domestic reform and foreign isolationism. To elevate the prestige and power of the king, he rebuilt the Gyeongbok (GYONG-bok) Palace left in ruins after Hideyoshi's invasion of 1592. He addressed the causes of the 1862 rebellions; abolished the majority of private academies in the provinces (they had become centers of *yangban* factional interest); persecuted Korean Catholics for suspected treasonous collaboration with foreigners; minted the first multiple-denomination coin in Korean history, the 100-cash, to pay for expenses; and resisted Western and foreign demands for treaties and trade. The reform program resulted in a land survey to register land hidden from tax collectors, forcing *yangban* households to pay the military cloth tax for the first time (but in the names of their slaves to save them embarrassment) and cancelling past-due loans in the official grain loan program administered by district magistrates. Farmers escaped from permanent indebtedness, and the Daewongun shifted the administration of grain loans from corrupt district magistrates and their clerks to local elders.

These reforms were less radical than they seemed because the land survey did not cover the whole country, and *yangban* living in villages had already been included with their neighbors in paying the combined tax. Nonetheless, *yangban* found the obligation to pay the military cloth tax particularly galling because it was a direct affront to their status. The abolition of all but forty-seven private academies dedicated to Confucian worthies from the dominant factions was an insult to both hereditary factions and past titans of Confucian scholarship. Government spending and the inflation that resulted from the 100-cash were a violation of conservative Confucian attitudes toward extravagance.

Reaction to Reforms

The Daewongun received more criticism for his domestic reforms than for his fear of foreigners. Conservative Confucians opposed institutional tinkering and believed that good government required only frugality, the reduction of taxes, and the cultivation of Confucian virtue. Almost all Confucian scholars supported his foreign policy, their favorite slogan being "Defend Confucian correctness against foreign perversity." With their support, the Daewongun rejected all requests from foreigners for treaties because he was determined to avoid the unequal treaty system imposed on China and Japan.

In 1866, when Korean Catholics offered to mediate with the Russians in their demands for trade, the Daewongun suspected a plot to undermine Korean security. He ordered a nationwide persecution of Korean Catholics that lasted to 1871 and reduced their ranks from twenty thousand to eight thousand. In 1866, the French landed troops on Ganghwa Island to punish the Koreans for their refusal to tolerate Christianity, but Korean troops were able to force the small French force to withdraw.

Military Pressure from the West

Western powers tried repeatedly to change the Daewongun's isolationist stance. In 1866, a ship under the U.S. flag, the *General Sherman*, with an English captain and a crew of Malays and Chinese, rampaged up the Daedong River near Pyeongyang and demanded trade. Irate local residents attacked the ship, burned it to ashes, and killed its crew. The governor of Pyeongan (PYONG-ahn) Province quickly received approval from the Daewongun for his plan to strengthen coastal defenses by building new forts along the coast, particularly one at the mouth of the Daedong River; recruit more soldiers skilled in the use of firearms; and institute a special examination for them.

Another memorial aimed at self-strengthening was based on Wei Yuan's *Illustrated Essay of the Maritime Nations*. Wei had written that the secret of Western strength was the domination of the seas by a small number of skilled troops with superior cannon, not superior numbers, thus, the memorial recommended that Korea concentrate on building advanced cannon and sea mines and distribute them to coastal garrisons. The Daewongun ordered the construction of three new warships and a cannon for laying mines. He even ordered construction of Korea's first steamboat in 1867, although it failed its trial on water and had to be broken up for scrap metal.

In the bizarre foreign incident of 1868, the German adventurer Ernst Oppert tried to dig up the bones of the Daewongun's father to hold them as ransom before Korean troops forced his withdrawal. In 1871, the United States landed marines on Ganghwa Island to teach the Koreans a lesson for the *General Sherman* incident and to demand a treaty of trade and amity by killing dozens of Korean defenders. There is no evidence that new warships, cannon, and mine-laying cannon played any role in either of these two incidents. The Daewongun declared victories for Korean arms when the foreigners withdrew. He issued a

Map 21.1   Military Pressure from the West, 1866 and 1871

manifesto that anyone who advocated peace with the foreigner was a traitor to the state.

Frustration caused by ambiguity over who was responsible for the conduct of Korean foreign relations under the Chinese tributary system provides one explanation for the foreigners' use of violence. They wanted to know whether Korea was a sovereign nation with a king who had the authority to sign treaties. If not, they would negotiate with China as Korea's overlord. Not only did the Daewongun

BIOGRAPHY   Queen Min

Like other women from *yangban* families who married royalty, Queen Min used her connection to the King to gain positions for her relatives and influence for herself.

Born in 1851, Queen Min maneuvered to preserve Korea's independence at a desperate time in its history. Selected for King Gojong by his father, the Daewongun, because her branch of the Yeohung Min (YUH-heung MIN) had little power, Min entered the palace when Gojong was thirteen and she was fourteen. The marriage took place a year later. On seeing this teenage bride, the Daewongun is said to have commented, "She is a woman of great determination and much poise of manner." After their differences became apparent, he remarked sarcastically, "She evidently aspires to be a doctor of letters; look out for her."

Animosity between the wife and the father of King Gojong had political consequences. Queen Min had only one son, born five years after her marriage, who died within three days. She found it all too easy to believe rumors that the Daewongun had poisoned the boy. After the king's father was forced into retirement in 1874, she moved her relatives into positions of power. Her first brush with death came in 1882 when members of the old capital guard units, angry about arrears in salary, invaded the palace to murder her and her relatives. For the next thirteen years, her faction maneuvered between China and Japan, favoring whichever side promised the least interference in Korea's affairs but always opposed to the Daewongun. In 1895, she chose Russia. The Japanese minister in Seoul decided that to eliminate the Min family from politics, it was essential to assassinate her. In October he sent Japanese police disguised as Korean guards into the palace, where they killed Queen Min and burned her body on the spot. Once again the Daewongun took charge of government.

Queen Min. Queen Min of the Yeohung Min family, 1851–1895, was assassinated by Japanese thugs and soldiers in the palace in 1895. This picture commemorates her posthumous title of Empress Myeongseong.

Dr. Yushin Yoo/Visual Connection Archive

When King Gojong was declared emperor of the great Han Dynasty in 1897, Queen Min received the posthumous title of Empress Myeongseong (MYUNG-sung).

Questions for Analysis
1. What kind of woman was Queen Min?
2. What were Queen Min's politics?
3. What roles did Queen Min play in Korean history?

refuse to negotiate with them, but the Qing government also evaded responsibility because it knew that if Koreans violated any provision in a treaty with a foreign power, that power would demand compensation from China.

In 1868, Japan added to the pressure on Korea from abroad. When the new government sent a note in the Meiji emperor's name to the king of Korea asking for a treaty of trade and amity, the Daewongun refused even to accept the note on the grounds that there was only one legitimate emperor, the emperor of the Qing Dynasty in China. Japanese resentment over what radical samurai perceived as an insult to the Meiji emperor almost resulted in Japan's invasion of Korea in 1873 before cooler heads prevailed. (See Chapter 20.)

The Ganghwa Treaty of 1876

Korea's isolationist stance began to change once Queen Min and her faction convinced King Gojong that he, not his father, should rule (see **Biography: Queen Min**). She had considerable influence over her husband, and her male relatives remained in power to 1894. Their faction advocated accepting communications from the Meiji emperor on the grounds that his title was a domestic issue irrelevant to Korea and that eliminating animosity and restoring amity with Japan would result in a continuation of the trade relations and friendship that had prevailed from 1609 to 1868. Learning of this new attitude, Japan created an excuse for hostile action by sending a survey ship up the Korean coast in 1875 in the expectation that Korean shore batteries would fire on it. When the Koreans obliged by doing so, Japan landed a battalion of troops on Ganghwa Island and threatened military action unless King Gojong signed the Ganghwa Treaty with Japan in 1876.

As Korea's first modern treaty, the Ganghwa Treaty had most of the provisions of the unequal treaty system. King Gojong agreed to open three ports to trade with Japan—Busan and two more to be selected in the future—and limited Japanese merchants under the treaty to a small radius around them. Imposing extraterritoriality on Korea gave Japanese in the treaty ports the right to run their own affairs. King Gojong assumed that Japan would be content to trade without invading Korean space elsewhere or making further demands. In fact, he had opened the door not only to trade but also to foreign interference.

First Attempts at Modern Diplomacy

King Gojong accepted the Ganghwa Treaty's provisions on China's recommendation. At first he had opposed the opening of two new ports and the demands for a Japanese delegation to be resident in Seoul until a recommendation titled "Strategy for Korea" sent to him in 1880 by Huang Zunxian, a Chinese official resident in Tokyo, persuaded him to reconsider his position. Huang argued that Korea should negotiate treaties with all the Western powers as a means of self-protection.

Huang Zunxian's recommendation was in line with Li Hongzhang's policy for Korea. Advocate of self-strengthening and chief of Qing Dynasty relations with Joseon (JOE-sun), Li sought to capitalize on the rivalries among the imperialist powers to check any attempt by Russia and Japan to strip China of its dominance over Korea. He realized that China was militarily too weak to maintain its tributary control over Korea by force, and his policy depended on the willingness of foreign powers with little interest in trade with Korea to check their imperialist rivals. It allowed China to maintain control until the Sino-Japanese War of 1894, but only by changing the nature of the tributary system itself.

During the next five years, King Gojong took a number of steps to promote reform and self-strengthening, always shadowed by conservative opposition. He dispatched a secret investigative mission to Japan to report on developments there, followed by a second study mission in 1881. Another training mission went to China to study military science. King Gojong agreed to open two additional ports to Japan at Incheon (IN-chon) and Wonsan (WON-san) and to allow the first Japanese minister to Korea to establish a legation in Seoul. In 1881, he set up the Office for Management of State Affairs to handle diplomacy, trade with foreign states, and reform, and he welcomed the first Japanese ambassador. He also hired a Japanese officer to train a small unit of troops in the capital in Western military tactics and weapons. These initiatives aroused a conservative protest movement. In the fall of 1881, when a plot by the Daewongun to overthrow the king and abolish the new Office was uncovered, the Daewongun's subordinates were arrested and executed.

In charting the treacherous territory of modern diplomacy, Korea relied heavily on China. King Gojong consulted with China on how to make modern weapons and conduct negotiations with the United States and other Western powers. In 1881, Li Hongzhang negotiated with Commodore Robert W. Shufeldt of the U.S. Navy to conclude a treaty of amity and trade between the United States and Korea. It contained several elements of the unequal treaty system such as extraterritoriality and the most favored nation clause, which guaranteed the United States any advantages obtained by other foreign powers in future treaties with Korea. During negotiations, Li Hongzhang tried to insert a clause indicating that Korea was a tributary of China. Shufeldt refused to accept it because the United States would never agree to sign a treaty with a dependency. He compromised by allowing King Gojong to send a letter to President Chester A. Arthur declaring that Korea was both "self-governing" and a Chinese tributary, a description that fit the reality because the Qing regime had never interfered with either Korea's domestic problems or its relations with Japan. The United States ignored the contradiction and acted as if Korea was a sovereign state. Signed by King Gojong and Shufeldt in May 1882 and soon followed by similar arrangements with other nations, the treaty did not change the fact that both Korea and China regarded the tributary relationship as undamaged.

China's policy of noninterference in Korea's domestic affairs soon changed. Incensed at favorable treatment afforded the new Japanese-trained unit in the capital and delay in the payment of their salaries, members of the old capital guard units killed a Japanese training official, burned the Japanese legation, and drove the ambassador and his party from Korea. They even invaded the palace seeking the queen and her relatives, but the Queen was able to escape. The rebels forced King Gojong to recall his father, the Daewongun, to the capital and appoint him chief of administration. Fearing that the Daewongun's hostility to Japan might provoke a Japanese invasion of Korea, China dispatched forty-five hundred troops to Seoul. Invited to what was supposed to be a friendly meeting, the Daewongun found himself hustled onto a Chinese ship, transported to China, and kept under close watch for three years. After his departure, Chinese troops wiped out the rebels.

Kidnapping the de facto head of state and the king's father was unprecedented. It marked a departure from the tradition of noninterference in Korean affairs and transformed China's relations with Korea to that enjoyed by Western imperialists. For the first time, China negotiated a commercial treaty with Korea that provided privileges for Chinese merchants trading in Korea that were denied other states. China also instructed King Gojong to pay compensation to Japan to prevent any hostilities. The Chinese restored the king, queen, and her relatives to power and allowed them to punish the Daewongun's supporters.

Late in 1882, King Gojong called on Koreans to submit memorials recommending policy to fit the times. He received one hundred private memorials, of which one-fifth advocated reform. Many cited *Iyan* (*Simple Talk*) by Zheng Guanying, a Chinese merchant associated with a Western company. Zheng had written the book in 1862 to alert China to the need to manufacture Western-style weapons by hiring Western experts. Many Korean reformers traveled to China to meet Zheng, and his book exerted greater influence in Korea than in China. His main theme was the need to adopt Western technology while maintaining fundamental Confucian values. Gojong republished the book in *hangul* in 1883 and urged everyone to read it. This formula was to prove as inadequate for meaningful reform in Korea as it had in China because Western culture included more than machines and tools.

Abortive Reform and the 1884 *Gapsin* Coup

In contrast to anti-foreign conservatives associated with the Daewongun and gradualists around Queen Min who took a pro-China stance, a more radical faction, several of whom belonged to the secondary status groups, believed that Korea had to follow Japan's lead. Calling for social equality, the appointment of men with talent and ability, centralized administration, and enlightenment, it convinced King Gojong to institute a number of reforms in 1883: a modern post office, the Ministry of Culture and Information, and publication of the first newspaper, the *Seoul Weekly*. The government also sponsored some forty students to study military and technical subjects in Japan. Fearing that if they did not act first they would be killed and hoping that conflict with France over Vietnam would keep China too busy to interfere, members of the radical faction under the leadership of Kim

Okgyun organized a coup to seize power. Because the conspirators had no support inside Korea, Kim Okgyun (KIM OHK-gyun) convinced the head of the Japanese legation to let him use legation guards. The coup leaders seized the palace, held King Gojong captive as their symbol of legitimacy, summoned high officials to court, and decapitated them on the spot.

Before the coup leaders had time to issue any orders, China acted. Led by Yuan Shikai, Chinese legation guards and regular Korean troops attacked the palace, killed a half-dozen leaders, and drove the rest of the plotters, along with the Japanese ambassador and his entourage, out of the country. Once again, China's intervention turned the political situation in its favor and blocked the opportunity for significant reform. Following negotiations with Japan, China forced Korea to pay Japan reparations for the murder of Japanese victims and property damage. Because the Japanese ambassador had authorized the use of Japanese troops to aid the plotters without prior authorization from Tokyo, he was tried in Japanese courts but let off for lack of evidence.

Qing Control

For the years between 1884 and 1894, Japan accepted China's domination of Korea's affairs. To avert conflict between the two nations, it negotiated the Convention of Tianjin with Li Hongzhang in 1885 by which both sides withdrew their troops and agreed that neither would supply officers to train Korean soldiers. If either Japan or China should feel it necessary to send an army, it would inform the other in advance. Later that year, Li Hongzhang appointed Yuan Shikai resident commissioner for Korea, the first instance of a Chinese overseer on Korean territory since the departure of the Mongols in the mid-fourteenth century. For the next decade, Yuan sat at King Gojong's side, preventing him from doing anything that might interfere with China's control over Korea and lead to national independence. King Gojong was not even allowed to dispatch ambassadors to foreign countries. When the British navy temporarily seized Geomun (GUH-moon) Island off the southern coast of Korea in 1885 as a feint to block the Russians from obtaining a leasehold at Wonsan and expanding their influence into Korea, China took no action

to force the British to retreat. Russia, which both China and Japan perceived as a threat to their interests, also accepted the continuation of China's traditional relationship with Korea.

Yuan Shikai also interfered in Korea's domestic affairs. When a provincial Korean official blocked the export of rice and beans to Japan in 1888 to preserve food stocks during a famine after Japanese merchants had purchased them, Yuan insisted that Korea pay the penalty demanded by Japan. He obstructed Japanese efforts to build a telegraph line from Busan (BOO-san) to Seoul and to reform Korean coinage at the Korean court's request while blocking Korean attempts to obtain foreign loans and foreign military advisers. Yuan's actions demonstrated that China's direct intervention in Korea's foreign and domestic affairs had become part of the new relationship.

Introducing Modern Institutions and Modern Technology

By the 1880s some reformers realized that Korea needed to modernize its institutions. In 1883 a government official in the treaty port of Wonsan opened the first modern private school to teach foreign languages, history, geography, and the natural sciences to people who came in daily contact with foreigners. The following year saw a reorganization of the bureaucracy and the establishment of a Western-style post office, followed by a customs agency overseen by the German P. G. von Moellendorff. While under house arrest in 1887, Yu Giljun (YU GIL-joon), who had studied in Japan while living with Fukuzawa Yukichi and then in the United States, wrote his famous account of conditions in Western nations, *Gyeonmun (GYON-moon, What I Saw and Heard in the West)*, that advocated adopting Western institutions.

In the 1890s, Japanese and other businessmen fostered interest in trade, modern transportation projects, and the exploitation of natural resources. Electricity announced its presence by lighting up the king's palace in 1887 while loans from China and Germany allowed Korea to build telegraph lines linking the treaty ports with the capital. Trains started running between Incheon and Seoul, and a railroad bridge connected Seoul and Noryangjin (NO-ryang-jin) over the Han River in 1900. The first streetcar arrived in 1898, demonstrating to the populace its advantage over palanquins for female *yangban*, donkeys and horses for male *yangban*, and ox-drawn carts for commoners. The laying of tracks for streetcars and trains was followed by streets paved in cobblestones or crushed stone, overcoming one of the most important obstacles to rapid transportation of goods and people: dirt roads that turned to impassable mud in the rainy season.

Protestant Christianity

Just as Korean Catholics had found their faith in the late eighteenth century before the arrival of missionaries, so too did Koreans start practicing Protestant Christianity before guidance came from the West. During the 1880s, Protestant missionaries from the United States brought education and medicine to China, Japan, and Korea. The first sweetened their message with the demonstration of good works, such as the construction of hospitals and schools. Having gained acceptance by King Gojong and Queen Min for saving the life of her relative during the *Gapsin* (GAHP-shin) coup of December 4, 1884, the Presbyterian and doctor Horace Allen became physician to the royal court and established the first Western hospital the next year. With this as a starting point, the government launched a smallpox eradication program across the country. Allen later gave up his status as missionary, became a secretary to the Korean legation in Washington, D.C., and then served as the U.S. ambassador to Korea. As a businessman, he arranged opportunities for Americans to exploit Korea's best gold mine and to build rail and trolley lines, Seoul's waterworks, and a telephone service.

In 1885 the Methodists Henry G. Appenzeller, Dr. William B. Scranton, and Scranton's wife, Mary Fitch Scranton, arrived in Korea. William Scranton founded the first Methodist hospital and taught Western medical techniques. Appenzeller started the *Baejae hakdang* (BEH-jae HAK-dang, School for Training Men of Talent), and Mary Scranton opened the first school for women, which Queen Min dubbed *Ehwa hakdang* (E-hwa HAK-dang, Pear Blossom School). Ewha University is still Korea's premier institution of higher learning for women. Little attached to Confucian norms that discriminated against them, men from secondary status groups and businessmen supported the missionaries

even though preaching heterodox beliefs was still punishable by death.

Over the next fifteen years, Protestant missionaries and Japanese businessmen introduced hospitals, schools, banks, currency, telegraph lines, electric power lines, and brick buildings for public offices. Most of these developments occurred in Seoul, Pyeongyang, and a few border towns. Only a small segment of the urban population had the opportunity to gain a modern education or to read newspapers published by men trying to promote new ideas.

THE DONGHAK REBELLION AND THE SINO-JAPANESE WAR (1894–1895)

Both economic hardship and religious persecution played roles in the Donghak Rebellion, the largest uprising in Korean history. The treaties signed with foreign powers worsened conditions for ordinary people. Japan bought Korean rice, but the profits from the increase in prices went to middlemen, not producers. Japanese fishery companies invaded Korean coastal waters, and Japanese ships took over Korea's carrying trade. Droughts in 1876–1877 and 1880–1889 reduced tax revenues, but state expenditures had risen with the payment of indemnities to foreigners and the need to finance modern institutions such as the army. Desperate for income, the government allowed tax collectors ever more leeway in oppressing the farmers. Under its second patriarch, Choe Sihyeong (CHAE SHI-hyung), the Donghak had petitioned the government repeatedly for an end to persecution and for religious toleration. Furious at corrupt officials, determined to drive the Min faction from court, opposed to the presence of Japanese and other foreigners on Korean soil, and antagonistic to Christianity, the Donghak launched an insurrection in 1894.

Having lost confidence in his army's ability to repress the Donghak rebels, King Gojong asked China for help. Before it arrived, he reached an agreement with the Donghak military leader, Jeon Bongjun (JEON BOHNG-joon], to call off the rebellion in return for religious toleration and a promise to allow the Donghak to administer their captured territory. Nonetheless, Japan took this opportunity to force a war on China by sending more troops to

Jeon Bongjun (1854–1895). The leader of the Donghak rebel army after his capture in 1895.

Korea than had China and by making unacceptable demands. Japan attacked China without bothering to declare war, surrounded the Korean palace, and kept the king and queen under detention while the war continued. (For information on the course of this war, see Chapter 18.)

Gabo Cabinet Reforms

Shortly before attacking China, Japan put a pro-Japanese cabinet in the royal palace to foster reforms under its guidance that eventually came to be led by Pak Yeonghyo (PARK YOUNG-hyo) and Seo Gwangbeom (SUH GWANG-bum), former participants in the 1884 coup exiled to Japan. Alarmed by Japan's takeover of the Korean government and

the return of men they regarded as the traitors of 1884, the Donghak under Jeon Bongjun rose again to drive Japan out of the country. This time, they had to fight against superior Japanese forces with advanced weapons and units of the Korean army. While this struggle was underway, King Gojong also proved obstructive. He finally agreed to exclude the queen and her relatives from decisions and to consult with ministers before making them. He then declared the end of Korea's tributary relationship with the Qing Dynasty.

Launched by men who had studied abroad and hoped to emulate Meiji Japan, the reform program aimed at remaking government and society. It called for rationalizing the bureaucracy, abolishing sinecures (offices with salaries attached that require little to no work), establishing a regular budget and a uniform currency, ending the king's control over the treasury, creating a new judicial structure with professional judges and a modern police and military, initiating a modern educational system through high school for both sexes (compulsory through primary school), and expanding railroads and telegraph lines. It allowed widows to remarry and abolished slavery. It promised universal health care. It put an end to civil service examinations based on Confucian classics, status distinctions between *yangban* and commoners, economic controls, and the mistreatment of wives. It promoted national identity through the use of *hangul* on government documents and the teaching of Korean history, not Chinese, in the new schools.

The reform measures had mixed results. Not all slaves were freed immediately, and members of the educated *yangban* elite continued to monopolize admission to government office under the new system of examinations run by individual ministries. On the other hand, opening the door to upward mobility to non-*yangban* allowed the educated members of the secondary status groups to begin their trek up the bureaucratic ladder, a trend that continued into the colonial period.

The reform cabinet lasted sixteen months. The Triple Intervention in April 1895 by Russia, France, and Germany to force Japan to give up its territorial gains following the Sino-Japanese War meant that Japan had to retreat from Korea as well. Pak Yeonghyo's ambition to become prime minister was foiled when a Japanese legation official leaked his proposal to assassinate the queen. He barely escaped to Japan. One faction at court centered on Queen Min favored turning to Russia as a counterbalance to Japan. When the Japanese minister to Seoul orchestrated her assassination, it roused the ire of the Korean people and caused deep embarrassment to the Japanese government. A few hundred armed Koreans loyal to the queen attacked the palace to murder members of the cabinet but were driven off by Japanese guards. The cabinet then had King Gojong issue a decree for all adult men to cut off their topknots, a traditional Korean marker of adulthood. Short hair had been adopted in Meiji Japan to signal a rejection of old customs and a commitment to modernity, but Korean men stood by the old ways, attacking authorities all over the country. After King Gojong escaped to the Russian legation, he fired the Gabo (GA-bo) cabinet.

SUMMARY

By 1800, the Yi Dynasty, which had ruled Korea for more than 400 years, had made so many compromises with powerful factions of *yangban* officials that the rulers had little leeway in which to confront social change and international pressure. The government took positive measures to improve the lot of slaves; it persecuted Christian converts. At the same time, it had to deal with a series of rebellions caused in part by maladministration.

Korea experienced considerable cultural and social ferment during this period, from advances in scholarship to art celebrating commoner life to criticisms of the ruling class. The spread of revolving credit associations gave commoners access to capital. Businessmen from the secondary status groups discovered ways to become wealthy outside of the traditional government official path to riches. A notable response to social dislocation came in the Donghak new religion that claimed a decidedly Korean worldview.

In 1864, the Korean government launched a series of reforms to deal with social dislocation while becoming increasingly isolationist. The reforms ran into opposition by the *yangban* who resisted the assault on their hereditary privileges. The isolationist policy foundered in the face of military pressure from the West and Japan. Disputes over how to deal with foreigners that pitted the king's father against his wife provided openings for China and then Japan to become increasingly influential in Korea's affairs. Conflict between these two nations, which led to the Sino-Japanese War of 1894-1895, resulted in Japan's ascendency.

While foreigners fought over who was to control Korea, Koreans tried to deal with the confluence of domestic problems and foreign threats. Should Korea try to hang on to the old ways or should it follow Japan in pursuing Western technology? Building modern schools, often started by Protestant missionaries, and modern infrastructure mainly benefited people in cities. In the countryside, economic hardship and religious persecution led to the Donghak rebellion, intervention by China and Japan, and the short-lived Gabo cabinet reforms under Japanese auspices.

How did Korea change during the nineteenth century? Population decline, rebellions, and reports of famines indicate that life got harder for commoners. In contrast, popular entertainments and tales of martial valor suggest that society was opening up to groups that fit poorly within the old social hierarchy. Korea's most successful reforms were those that meshed with the desires of men from secondary status groups long suppressed by *yangban* to achieve upward mobility through education and government service. In terms of international relations, wrangling by *yangban* factions and the king's relatives slowed Korea's response to foreign pressure, but by 1895 it had ended its tributary relationship with China, its diplomacy rested on treaties, and it had started to build a modern state. As we will see in Chapter 23, these attempts at reform came too late to prevent Korea from becoming a Japanese colony.

The tale of *Sanshō the Bailiff*, set in Japan's Heian period, tells of a mother and two children kidnapped and sold into slavery. The mother was forced to become a prostitute, and the children found work as field hands. In an era of labor shortages, their fate was not uncommon. People also became slaves in China and Korea, though not necessarily in the same way. Human capital now determines a nation's ability to compete in the modern world; in the days when land meant nothing without the labor to work it, slaves were human capital.

In Japan, documents regarding slavery point to its connection with war. Third-century Chinese sources mention that warriors enslaved the vanquished; sixteenth-century European accounts tell how warriors kidnapped commoners and sold them, sometimes overseas to Southeast Asia. During the late twelfth and early thirteenth centuries, famine forced the starving to sell themselves or family members for food. Debt was the third reason people became slaves. Some became personal slaves; others became field hands. A person might become a slave for a specified time period or a lifetime. The thirteenth-century law code tried to specify whether a slave's children were also slaves, suggesting that slavery could become hereditary. In transfer documents, slaves were listed alongside livestock as possessions. As the population and hence the labor supply rose after 1280, slavery apparently became less common even though traffic in children continued. After the last upswing in the 1500s, when some villages may have been as much as 20 percent slave, slavery largely disappeared.

In China, the incidence of slavery varied by region as well as era. Slaves, many captured in war, provided a substantial portion of the labor force during Shang. Slaves also figured in human sacrifices, either to appease the gods or to follow the king in death. Slavery declined thereafter in core regions, though the government might enslave the relatives of those who committed the most serious crimes. Han Dynasty eunuchs who served the emperor were slaves, many captured from "southern barbarians," a practice that continued into late imperial times. As in Japan, debt forced men to sell family members into slavery.

Slavery was a common practice among the tribal societies along China's borders, which often waged war to get slaves—both from other nomadic groups and from settled Chinese. Following the fall of the Han and depopulation of the north, nomads launched slave raids to acquire labor, and the southern Chinese dynasties had such a difficult time keeping men under arms that they reached farther south in search of slaves to be made into soldiers. The Mongols used captives to perform heavy labor; once they had conquered China, they sold off parts of the population. Down to the nineteenth century, families in distress had the option of selling off their women as bondservants or prostitutes. This happened in Japan as well, but whether this system of poor relief should be seen as slavery or as indentured servitude is still debated.

In the period after 1000, slave labor played a larger role in the economy of Korea than in that of China or Japan. Slavery first appears in Korean records during the Three Kingdoms era, when the rise of aristocracy brought about a lowering in the status of many farm laborers. Generals and aristocratic officials received land grants and war captives to work them. Silla kings set up separate villages for slaves. Some had been acquired through conquest; others had become slaves as punishment for crimes. Aristocrats continued to own slaves, whom they armed for conflicts with each other. They held onto their position and their slaves through the founding of the Goryeo Dynasty. A decree from 1037 codified what had been customary: slavery was a hereditary status. The government owned public slaves; aristocrats and temples bought and sold private slaves. Within a century, slaves constituted a good 30 percent of the population, a situation that continued into Joseon. If either parent of a child was a slave, the child too became a slave. In some cases, slaves paid their owners fixed fees in the form of goods and services; anything else they produced they could keep for themselves. Some were slaves in name only. When king and officials fled Japan's invasion of 1592, slaves burned slave rosters and Ministry of Punishments offices. Slavery started to decline in the eighteenth century when the government offered freedom in return for military service. In 1801, it took the first steps in freeing government slaves, but slaves remained in private hands until 1894 and beyond.

East Asia in the Modern World

Rise of Modern Japan (1900–1931)

The early 1900s found Japan deeply entangled in world affairs. Although wars abroad brought it colonies and strengthened its national identity, on the home front Japan faced the competing pulls of democracy and totalitarianism, of modernity and conservatism. The institutions that gave the state power over citizens' everyday lives—conscription, education, and mass media—also opened the way for people to oppose state policies, create new community-based organizations to promote local welfare, and define their individual goals. A new middle class provided a ready market for popular culture, while the expansion of the industrial labor force led some to fear social unrest. Modern life seemed concentrated in the cities, to the disgust of those who wanted to uphold pristine Japanese values found, they believed, in the countryside.

Historians often analyze the first decades of the twentieth century to explain what came after. To what extent was Japan's descent into fascism preordained? Why did countervailing forces fail? What was this period's legacy for postwar Japan?

JAPAN'S DRIVE FOR GREAT POWER STATUS

Japan began its drive for great power status by signing an alliance with Britain in 1902 that, for the first time, treated an Asian nation as an equal partner and committed each country to come to the defense of the other should a third party join the enemy in time of war. When Japan went to war against Russia in 1904–1905, it functioned as planned by limiting the scope of the conflict. Russia's leasehold on the Liaodong peninsula and fortification of Port Arthur threatened Japan's interests in Korea. When Russia refused to make concessions, Japan's military launched a surprise attack on Port Arthur. It hoped to win a short war before Russia could mobilize its larger army and bring it to the scene of battle, but the siege dragged on longer than expected. By the time Port Arthur fell, Japan's army was exhausted.

U.S. President Theodore Roosevelt offered to negotiate a peace settlement. The Treaty of Portsmouth gave Japan the southern half of Sakhalin (called Karafuto in Japanese), Russia's leasehold on the Liaodong peninsula, the South Manchurian Railway built by the Russians between Port Arthur and Mukden and its associated mining concessions, and Russian acknowledgment of Japan's dominance in Korea. In demonstrating that a "yellow race" could beat the "white," Japan inspired Asians with hopes that they could throw off the colonial yoke.

Japan and Korea

Two days before Japan declared war on Russia, it had landed troops in Korea. During the siege of Port Arthur, it forced the Korean king to accept a limited protectorate that made Korea Japan's ally and subject to Japan's lead in administrative matters. The Japanese army then occupied the country. Six months later while the siege was still going on, Korea had to accept Japanese financial and diplomatic advisers. They reformed the currency and drew up a government budget, taking over the communications system for reasons of national security while the army imposed martial law to prevent sabotage. The Taft-Katsura Agreement of 1905, signed two months before the Treaty of Portsmouth, acknowledged Japan's control of Korea in return for Japan's acquiescence in U.S. colonization of the Philippines.

In 1906, Korea became a Japanese protectorate, with Itō Hirobumi, author of Japan's constitution, as resident general. Government offices had to obey Japanese advisers, courts came under the jurisdiction of Japanese judges, the Korean army was disbanded, a Japanese police force maintained order, and Japan took over Korea's diplomatic relations. When the Korean king complained to the Hague Peace Conference of 1907, Itō forced him to abdicate. In 1909, a Korean nationalist assassinated Itō. Japan annexed Korea the following year and formalized control over Taiwan to join the ranks of imperial powers. Both Korea and Taiwan remained in the Japanese empire for the next thirty-five years. (See Map 22.1.)

Japan envisioned that its empire would bring not only prestige but also coal and iron for its factories, food for its people, a market for the export of finished products, and space for its expanding population. Taiwan supplied sugar financed by Japanese capital and, after 1920, rice produced on family farms that also promoted the island's economic development. The Oriental Development Company bought land in Korea to sell to Japanese settlers, channeled capital to Japanese-owned businesses, and participated in

Courtesy, The Saitama Municipal Cartoon Art Museum

Cartoon of Empress Jingū and Britannia. This cartoon of legendary Empress Jingū, invader of Korea, and Britannia celebrates the 1902 signing of the Anglo-Japanese alliance. These symbols representing Japan and Great Britain cast a benevolent, protective gaze over Korea.

the development of Manchurian mines. The military government improved the infrastructure by building roads and railways and opening schools while ruthlessly suppressing all dissent. Japanese who migrated to Korea had a higher standard of living than did Koreans and enjoyed special privileges in education and employment.

Japan and China

The First World War that started in Europe in 1914 and spread to East Asia thanks to Japan's 1902 Alliance with Britain proved advantageous for Japan both economically and diplomatically. Because Germany was Britain's enemy, Japan was justified in absorbing Germany's leasehold on China's Shandong province and acquiring a mandate over German-held islands in the Pacific. In 1918, Allied forces joined Japan in

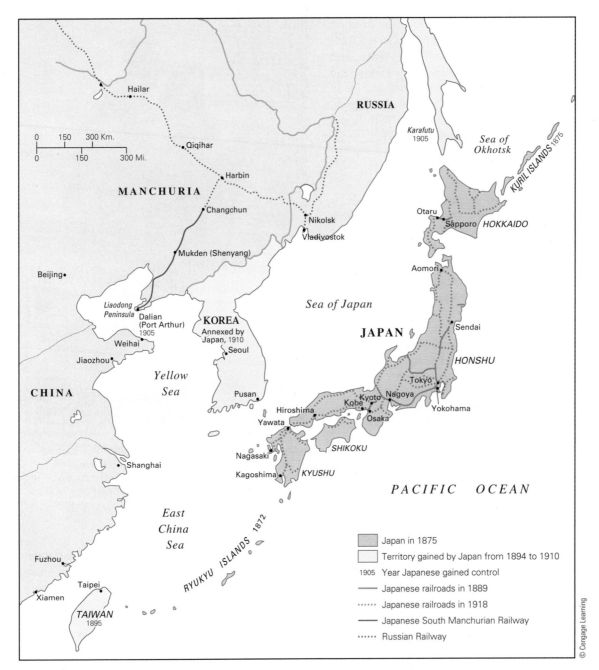

Map 22.1   Japanese Imperial Expansion, 1868–1910

invading Siberia following the Russian Revolution that brought the Communists to power.

Japan also tried to impose on China its infamous Twenty-One Demands. Most of these ratified and prolonged Japan's existing privileges in Manchuria and along the China coast. China complained bitterly about the Twenty-One Demands at the Versailles Peace Conference that brought World War I to a close, but to no avail. Despite the open door policy promoted by the United States, no Western power was willing to challenge Japan's interests in China. The last set of Japan's "requests" would have turned China into a Japanese protectorate, but public outcry in China and abroad forced Japan to back down.

Japan and the West

Following World War I, Japan collaborated with Western powers. It joined the League of Nations and in 1921 participated in the multilateral Washington Conference, designed to preserve the status quo in the Pacific and China and prevent a new naval arms race. A delegation of Japanese businessmen sent abroad in 1921–1922 to negotiate trade deals demonstrated Japan's commitment to participation in the developed world's economy. Japan had been unable to get a clause on racial equality in the Versailles Peace Treaty, and in 1924 the United States offended Japan by passing the Oriental Exclusion Act. Despite this insult, Japan signed the Kellogg-Briand Pact of 1928 outlawing war in the settlement of international disputes. In 1930 Japan's civilian diplomats agreed to additional limitations on the size of its navy in the London Naval Treaty despite the navy's objections and without addressing the army's concerns regarding China. When the army acted on its own to take over Manchuria, it ended the era of cooperation with the West.

ECONOMIC DEVELOPMENT

In the early twentieth century, Japanese corporations took advantage of technological and managerial innovations during the "second industrial revolution." The nation's electrical technology became second to none. Electric streetcars appeared in Kyoto in 1895, and 85 percent of Japanese households had electricity in 1935, compared with 68 percent in the United States. Techniques of mass production required both standardized equipment and scientific management, or Taylorism, a U.S. theory of rational labor practice that Japan adapted to make its work force more efficient. Localities hoping to attract businesses developed research centers to find foreign technology, channel it to the factory floor, and modify foreign products for domestic consumption. Larger enterprises developed new metallurgical and chemical technologies, often at the prompting of the Japanese military, which promoted the automobile and airplane.

A dual structure characterized Japan's modern economy. Conglomerates called *zaibatsu* (ZAH-e-bah-tzu) (financial cliques) dominated the most modern sectors of the economy—mining, shipbuilding, machinery, steel, and chemicals—and produced standardized, high-volume products. Although each company within the *zaibatsu* pursued a single enterprise and remained legally distinct, access to the *zaibatsu*'s capital through its bank, a central advisory committee that set policy and long-term goals, and interlocking boards of directors tied them together. In some cases, *zaibatsu* cooperated in cartels that divided up raw materials and access to markets, as in the textile industry and maritime shipping. *Zaibatsu* chairmen enjoyed access to bureaucrats and cabinet ministers, who steered public investment their way and smoothed the regulatory road. The other side of Japan's economy consisted of small firms that made specialty and basic consumer goods such as processed food, housing, and clothing. They produced ceramics and toys for export by the *zaibatsu* and functioned as suppliers and subcontractors to the large enterprises.

World War I and the 1920s

Japan's industrial sector was well placed to take advantage of World War I. Coal mined in Japan fueled its locomotives, factories, and generators, and its steel works had capacity to spare. Mitsubishi built ships and operated a worldwide shipping line in competition with another *zaibatsu*-backed shipping company—OSK. These and other enterprises profited from the Allies' demand for munitions and war-related materiel. Japanese textiles and consumer goods filled the vacuum left by the departure of British exports from Asia. Business profits soared, and Japan's gross national product jumped by 40 percent between 1914 and 1918. The percentage of real national income contributed by manufacturing passed that of agriculture.

Unevenness between different sectors of the economy and cycles of contraction and expansion characterized the 1920s. Japanese companies assumed demand would continue after World War I. But when Britain took back markets in China and South Asia and European manufacturing replaced Japanese exports, Japan's companies found themselves overextended financially and forced to lay off workers. They had just pulled out of the postwar recession when the Great Kanto Earthquake of September 1, 1923, leveled factories and workshops between Tokyo and Yokohama; 140,000 people died, and 570,000 structures (70 percent of Tokyo and 60 percent of Yokohama) were destroyed. Aftershocks ruptured gas and water pipes, snapped electrical lines, and

Real National Income Produced in Japan, 1878–1936 (million yen at 1928–1932 prices)

Year	Total	Primary Industry	Secondary Industry	Tertiary Industry
1878	1,117	691	95	331
1890	2,308	1,429	224	655
1900	3,640	1,671	818	1,151
1914	5,665	2,127	1,354	2,184
1920	6,316	2,147	1,686	2,483
1925	9,268	2,779	2,216	4,273
1929	10,962	2,740	2,911	5,311
1930	12,715	2,477	3,550	6,688
1931	13,726	2,372	3,716	7,638
1932	13,843	2,594	3,987	7,262
1936	16,133	3,149	5,096	7,888

Primary industry = agriculture, forestry, fisheries. Secondary industry = mining, manufacturing, construction, transportation, communication, and utilities. Tertiary industry = commerce and services.

Source: G. C. Allen, *A Short Economic History of Modern Japan* (New York: St. Martin's Press, 1981), p. 284.

halted transportation and communications. Most companies rebuilt using generous credit provided through the government to banks, which led to a credit crisis in 1927. Trouble came to the domestic market when silk sales slipped and cotton mills in China cut into Japan's biggest Asian market.

In contrast to stagnation and decline in the textile and agricultural sectors, the old *zaibatsu* grew by absorbing existing enterprises and diversifying into new areas. Founded in 1908, the Chisso (CHE-ssoh) chemical corporation became a new *zaibatsu* through diversification, expanded to become Japan's third largest manufacturer, and industrialized northern Korea. Yet when the Great Depression hit at the end of 1929, Japan's economy was already depressed. Japan joined other industrialized nations in imposing steep tariffs on imports, secure in the knowledge that except for oil and scrap iron used in making steel, its colonies had given it the requirements for a self-sufficient economy.

CONSTITUTIONAL GOVERNMENT

In the public's eyes, oligarchs' efforts to control the selection of cabinet ministers after the inauguration of the Diet in 1890 demonstrated the persistence of a clique government dominated by men from Satsuma and Chōshū. To counter Itō Hirobumi (author of the Constitution) in the lower house, the military's founder Yamagata Aritomo forged a faction of conservative bureaucrats, prefectural governors, and members of the Privy Council and the upper house. In 1907 he made it possible for the military to issue orders in the emperor's name independent of the prime minister. Itō's protégé among elected politicians, Hara Takashi (HAH-rah TAH-kah-she), had experience in the Foreign Ministry and business world that helped him arrange compromises between oligarchs and Diet and showed him the way to manipulate the bureaucracy. During the Russo-Japanese War, Hara promised Seiyūkai (SEH-e-yu-kah-e) (Friends of Government Party) support for the cabinet and convinced Yamagata to trust him with the powerful position of home minister.

Hara used his control over the Home Ministry to make Seiyūkai the dominant party in the Diet. The Home Ministry appointed prefectural governors and district chiefs and ran the police, health bureau, and public works bureau, so Hara worked with bureaucrats in the Tokyo office and built a following for Seiyūkai in prefectural offices. Because prefectural officials supervised elections and influenced the local economy, a prefecture with a bureaucracy that supported Seiyūkai was likely to elect Seiyūkai politicians to the Diet. Hara also perfected pork barrel politics: Unlike early parties that simply opposed government spending and tried to cut taxes, Seiyūkai followed a "positive policy" of government spending for economic development. Railroad lines spidered across the country, linking cities, towns, and centers of Seiyūkai support in remote mountain villages. Roads, schools, bridges, irrigation works, and harbors graced the districts that voted Seiyūkai.

Even before Hara became prime minister in 1918, Diet members had mastered manipulating the electorate. Businessmen provided political funds in return for favors and offered politicians and bureaucrats positions on their companies' boards of directors. In buying votes, some Diet members relied on election brokers. Others used prefectural assembly members, tainting them as well with the stench of corruption. Playing on Yamagata's fears of a socialist revolution following the Bolshevik takeover in Russia and nationwide rice riots in Japan in 1918, Hara convinced him that party control of an expanded electorate was the safest way to channel popular unrest. The 1919 expansion of the electorate from 2.2 to 5 percent of the population benefited conservative small rural landlords, not urban workers. In 1921 an unemployed railroad worker assassinated Hara because of what he saw as Hara's disdain for the military.

Between 1924 and 1932, power to select the cabinet shifted back and forth between the two major parties in the lower house. Former bureaucrats and prefectural governors became politicians and ran for the Diet. Although it was not in Seiyūkai's interest to widen the electorate beyond its conservative base, the pressure of public opinion, maneuvering by other political parties, and the Privy Council's fear of social upheaval led the Diet to pass a bill for universal suffrage for males over age twenty-five in 1925. In the next election three years later, eight proletarian candidates were elected out of 450 contested seats, thus giving workers a voice in politics without endangering the conservative majority.

The politics of compromise developed by Hara continued after party-dominated cabinets became the rule. The Privy Council, House of Peers, much of the bureaucracy, and the military remained beyond the parties' control. Despite the efforts of constitutional scholar Minobe Tatsukichi (ME-no-beh TAH-tzu-key-che) to devise a theoretical legitimization for party cabinets, they rested on neither law nor precedent but on a pragmatic balance of power.

The crises of the late 1920s and early 1930s tested the limits of Japan's constitutionally sanctioned parliamentary democracy. Japan had to deal with the worldwide Great Depression and fears of Russian and Chinese threats to Manchuria. Right-wing ultranationalists inside the military and outside the government accused the parties of treason for having weakened Japan through their corrupt pursuit of self-interest. In 1930 one of their number attacked Prime Minister Hamaguchi Osachi (HAH-mahgu-che OH-sah-che) for having signed the controversial London Naval Treaty. Hamaguchi died of his wounds nine months later. Convinced that the party cabinet was about to sacrifice Japan's interests in Asia, colonels in the army acted unilaterally in taking over Manchuria.

The early months of 1932 saw assassinations of a former finance minister and an industrialist blamed for hardships brought on by the Great Depression. Prime Minister Inukai Tsuyoshi (E-new-kah-e TZU-yo-she) also died at the hands of a group of naval cadets, junior army officers, and civilians. The next prime minister was a military man, as were his successors up to 1945, with two exceptions who both supported the military. The parties still dominated the lower house, but they received only minor cabinet appointments. Even during fifteen years of war from 1931 to 1945, the Diet continued to function. The cabinet continued to decide policy, although the military's right of access to the emperor meant its actions were beyond debate. The constitution remained the law of the land.

Imperial Democracy

According to critics in Japan before World War II, liberalism's focus on the individual contradicted the notion that all Japanese were part of the same body politic, *kokutai*, also translated as "national essence." Democracy was a foreign import, directly opposed to indigenous custom based on harmony, consensus, and service to the emperor. Many Japanese people proved these critics wrong by striving for a more open government and society. In the early twentieth century, the struggle for democracy engaged academic theorists, journalists, feminists, outcasts, and working men and women who expressed themselves in riots and in efforts to organize unions.

For Japanese intellectuals, liberalism meant representative government, constitutionalism, and rule by law along with individual rights and freedom from undue governmental interference in the individual's life. It distinguished between the naturalness of society and the artifice of the state. In contrast, imperial ideology defined the emperor as present from the beginning of time, uniting state and society without the artifice of government institutions. Liberals were patriots. They approved of the government's efforts to promote industrialization and make Japan the equal of the West, and they never questioned the centrality of the emperor even while criticizing the men and institutions in his government.

Intellectuals who professed liberal views jeopardized their careers. Yoshino Sakuzō (YO-she-no SAH-ku-zo) had to resign his position at Tokyo University because he argued that people are the basis of the state and the aim of the state is to promote their well-being. The public interest, that of people as a whole, has to supersede private, partial interests of oligarchs, bureaucrats, politicians, and businessmen. Minobe Tatsukichi argued that according to the constitution, the Diet—in particular the lower house—was the organ that represented the people. Sovereignty lay not in the emperor but in the state, and the emperor was one of its organs. In 1935 Minobe was accused of disrespect for the emperor, his writings were banned, and his membership in the upper house was revoked.

Women and Democracy

Educated women promoted democracy through their organizations and deeds. Teachers, many of them Christian or influenced by missionaries, hoped to improve and reform society. In 1886 the Tokyo Women's Reform Society opposed concubinage and prostitution, both deemed trafficking in women, a cause also taken up by the Woman's Christian Temperance Union. Because oligarchs kept concubines and the Meiji emperor fathered the crown prince on a concubine, the notion that civilized behavior included sexual fidelity was a hard sell. More acceptable was the Reform Society's work in aiding earthquake victims and providing financial support for former prostitutes. In 1901 members of the Reform Society joined the Greater Japan Women's Patriotic Association. Under its sponsorship they could speak in public to women, and they received government support for their activities.

The staging of Henrik Ibsen's *A Doll's House* in 1911 and the inauguration of the journal *Bluestocking* marked the arrival of the "new woman" in Japan. The play offered a scandalous alternative to the government-sponsored ideology of "good wife and wise mother" when its central character, Nora, walked out on husband and children. Matsui Sumako (MAH-tzu-e SU-mah-co), who played Nora,

gained fame as Japan's first Western-style actress. Her tumultuous private life dramatized her rejection of domesticity.

Bluestocking started as a literary magazine, but it soon became a forum for discussing women's roles and expectations. Feminist activist Hiratsuka Raichō (HE-rah-tzu-kah RAH-e-choe) and poet translator and social critic Yosano Akiko (YO-sah-no AH-key-co) debated state support for motherhood, Hiratsuka wanting government protection and Yosano arguing that state support would be degrading and would cost women their independence. They agreed, however, that marriage is not sacrosanct, patriarchy need not go unchallenged, and women ought to have equal legal, educational, and social rights.

In the 1920s, feminists advocated family planning and women's suffrage. Female activist Katō Shidzue brought U.S. sex educator Margaret Sanger to Japan in 1924 to promote birth control as a way of dealing with the threat to family budgets and women's health posed by bearing too many children. The government refused Sanger permission to land until she promised to make no public speeches.

The examples of Britain and the United States that granted women the vote after World War I, and the growing numbers of women who followed politics in mass-circulation newspapers and magazines, convinced some politicians and bureaucrats that political rights for women were a mark of advanced societies. In 1922 the Diet revoked the law that barred women from political meetings. In 1931 a bill for local women's suffrage passed the lower house but foundered on a conservative coalition in the House of Peers. Give women the right to vote and they will stop having children, predicted one baron. The end to party cabinets left no politicians willing to support proposals for women's political rights.

Mass Movements

Modern mass movements emerged in the context of Japanese imperialism. In 1905 newspapers and speechmakers informed the public that the Russo-Japanese War had concluded without the indemnity that a Great Power like Japan deserved from a defeated foe, and with only a small territorial gain to justify the sacrifices made by Japanese troops. Riots began at Tokyo's Hibiya Park outside the palace in response and continued for three days as rioters destroyed fifteen streetcars and more than 70 percent of police

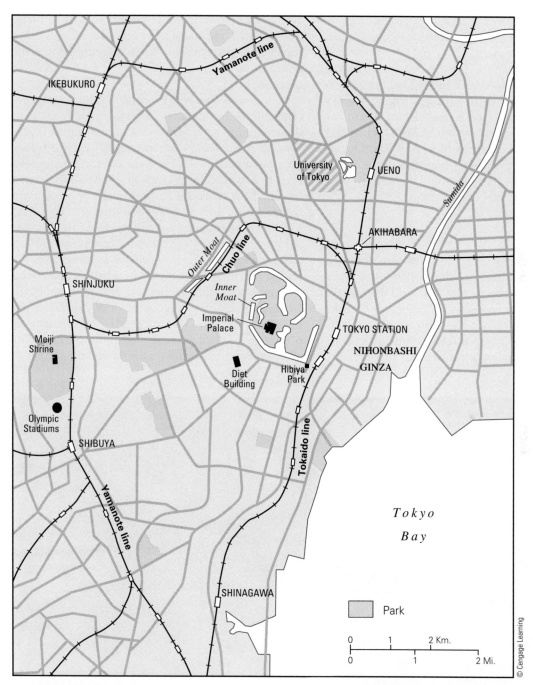

Map 22.2   Modern Tokyo

boxes that provided shelter for policemen stationed across the city. (See Map 22.2.) Smaller riots erupted in Kobe and Yokohama, and all but two of the forty-four prefectures reported rallies in cities, towns, and villages. Between 1905 and the rice riots of 1918, Tokyo experienced nine serious riots, many of them part of larger movements that swept the nation. Although rioters attacked police stations and government offices, they did so in the name of the emperor. By conflating imperial and popular will, they differentiated between evil advisers behind the throne and the throne itself.

Rice riots in 1918 protested high prices, degrading work conditions, and government incompetence. They began with fishermen's wives who organized demonstrations along the Toyama coast and grew to include urban rioters who criticized war profiteers and asserted a right to free speech, tenant farmers who demanded lower rents and decent treatment from landlords, and coal miners who demanded higher wages and respect as human beings. Out of the rice riots grew the mass movements of the 1920s for *burakumin* (BU-rah-ku-meen) (hereditary outcast) liberation and labor organization.

Burakumin Liberation Movements

Outcasts had found that the transformations of the late nineteenth century did not improve their lot. Losing the monopoly they had held over leatherwork and other lucrative, if unpleasant, tasks brought them poverty. The household registration system made it impossible for outcasts to escape their past. Schools refused to admit them, employers to hire them, landlords to rent to them, public baths and barbers to serve them, and other Japanese to marry them. When conscripted into the military, they were assigned menial tasks and never promoted.

In the early twentieth century, the central government set up advisory committees to deal with the issue of poverty lest socialism creep into Japan. Because *burakumin* were among the worst off, they became one focus. In 1908 the cabinet encouraged them to emigrate. In 1911 the Home Ministry started to distribute funds for improvement of *burakumin* communities, and in 1920 it started the Harmony Movement to mobilize *burakumin* to work for gradual reform. Private organizations lent support. Both government and private agencies assumed that the reason for discrimination lay in what was perceived as *burakumin* filth, ignorance, and immorality. In 1922 a group of young *burakumin* organized the Leveller's Society (*Suiheisha*, SU-e-heh-e-shah) to protest discrimination and promote the equality of all Japanese subjects before the emperor.

Woman Farm Worker. Prewar Japanese farms relied on human labor for production, and women worked alongside men in the fields. This woman is carrying the farm implements that she and her husband will need for the day's tasks.

Division of Rare and Manuscript Collections, Cornell University Library

The *burakumin* liberation movement of the 1920s blamed *burakumin* problems on prejudice and discrimination. The goal was to change social attitudes, but Leveller's Society members could not agree on tactics. Some believed in educational programs and nonviolent confrontations that aimed at greater democracy. Others wanted a social revolution to overthrow capitalism by challenging institutions known to oppose fair practices. Denunciation campaigns targeted primary schools that permitted students and staff to insult *burakumin* and public officials and individuals who uttered disparaging remarks. The offenders would have to offer an apology, sometimes publicized in newspapers. In 1926, the first year of the Shōwa (SHOW-wah) emperor's reign, antimilitarism plus anger at the treatment of conscript *burakumin* led to a movement urging *burakumin* not to comply with military organizations. Despite police repression, denunciation campaigns continued into the 1930s. Only after the outbreak of the China war in 1937 did the Leveller's Society agree to support national unity and the war effort.

Tenant Farmer Movements

The 1898 Civil Code gave landlords the right to buy, sell, and lease land without any protection for tenants who might have farmed it for generations. Of Japan's farm families, 28 percent owned no land, while another 41 percent owned some and rented the rest. Tenants and tenant-owners organized unions in the 1910s to demand rent reductions and the right of cultivation, especially in the most economically advanced regions in central and western Japan, where landlords had previously been in the forefront of encouraging agricultural improvements. The tenants established a national federation in 1922 that grew to nearly seven hundred branches. In the 1920s, more than eighteen thousand disputes between tenants and landlords filled police dockets.

Agricultural conditions had worsened even before 1930. The economic downturn in the 1920s, when synthetic fibers replaced silk and the government allowed the import of rice from Asia, reduced the demand for agricultural products and unskilled labor. Real income for farm families declined by 30 percent. Unseasonably cold weather in the agriculturally backward northeast brought crop failures between 1931 and 1933. Landlords tried to take back tenanted land, refused to reduce rents,

or even tried to raise them. Debt-ridden farmers migrated to Japan's overseas colonies for relief or sold their daughters into prostitution. Tenants petitioned the Agriculture Ministry for rural assistance. The ministry responded by organizing cooperatives and providing funds for development. In central and western Japan, where absentee landlords no longer performed ceremonial and support functions, tenants abandoned the deference in which landlords had been held. Their habit of looking on the land they cultivated as theirs led to rent refusals and conflict. With the coming of war in 1937, agricultural conditions improved when the government moved to limit rice imports and tenant unions disbanded in the drive for national unity.

Labor Union Movements

Industrial development led to labor activism, though not labor solidarity. Heavy industry employed highly skilled and relatively well-paid male workers sufficiently educated to read newspapers and understand socialist theory. Textile mills continued to hire cheaper and, it was hoped, docile women and girls. Even in 1930, women constituted more than 50 percent of the factory work force. Urban women found jobs as teachers, journalists, nurses, clerks, ticket sellers, bus conductors, telephone operators, actresses, and café hostesses. Small firms employed male and female workers at low wages to manufacture parts for other sectors of the economy. Below them were rickshaw pullers and delivery boys. At the bottom were the miners.

Worker grievances and the ability to organize varied across industries and within factories. The 1907 riot at the Ashio (AH-she-oh) mine originated with ore diggers, the most highly paid workers, not copper refinery workers, whose wages had recently dropped and who feared being laid off. The expansion in heavy industry and the need to raise productivity prompted factory owners to reduce worker autonomy by eliminating bosses who stood between workers and owners and contracted for specific jobs. Workers countered with demands that they be treated with respect. (See **Documents: Negotiations Between Strike Group Representatives and Company Directors**.) In 1912 they organized the Friendship Society to provide mutual aid, self-improvement classes, and improved relations with employers. If employees worked hard and deferred to foremen, factory owners ought to treat them with benevolence. In response,

DOCUMENTS

Negotiations Between Strike Group Representatives and Company Directors

This confrontation between strike group representatives Itō, Iwasa, and Shiga and company directors for the Yokohama Dock Company Tōjō and Miyanaga on September 28, 1921, exposes conflict between workers and management over work conditions and financial issues such as wages and severance pay.

Itō: Today the three of us have come as worker representatives with this petition.

Miyanaga: Does this demand for a 20 percent daily wage increase mean an average wage increase of 20 percent for all the workers?

Iwasa: Our wages average 1 yen 60 sen. Out of 1,000 people, if there is one getting 3 yen, the rest are getting around 1 yen 40 sen. With days off, one month is 25 days and, with a wife and children, we can't make ends meet. This is why we have asked for a pay raise. With the present severance pay, if one of us is fired, he is reduced to poverty.

Miyanaga: We want you to understand the company's situation. As you are well aware, the economy, especially the shipbuilding industry, is facing a severe depression. The question of how to support the workers in this situation is one that troubles us greatly. Because of the shipbuilding depression there have been many layoffs, and aware of your anxiety about this, the other day we announced that we would not carry out any large-scale layoffs. As for ship repairs, which this company has been engaged in since its founding, in good times we were able to charge the shipowners a good price, but today the situation is so bad that, even if we offer a price below cost, they won't take it. Shipbuilding revived briefly after the war and we were able to make some profit, but now we are making no profit and are taking orders at a loss. In this depression, we are taking on such orders because we do not want to have to lay off you workers. We understand well your plight, but, even at present pay levels, the situation is as I have described, so we would hope to have your understanding regarding the pay raise. You also raised demands regarding severance and retirement pay. As I have already noted, our policy is to avoid layoffs at all costs in the hopes that this will reduce your anxiety, so we would like to gain your understanding on these points also.

Itō: Are you saying you will absolutely not lay off any workers?

Miyanaga: I can't promise "absolutely" but…

Miyanaga and Itō (together): Insofar as possible.

Itō: In that case wouldn't it be better to decide on severance pay and relieve our anxieties in that way?

employers instituted a seniority system of raises and offered fringe benefits to keep their skilled workers.

In many cases, implementation of benefits came only after workers had launched work stoppages and strikes. More than one hundred labor disputes erupted between 1902 and 1917. In 1919 the Hara cabinet interpreted the Public Order and Police Act of 1900 to mean that workers might organize unions and go on strike so long as they remained nonviolent. In 1921 the Friendship Society became the Japan Federation of Labor. Union membership burgeoned in the 1920s, although it never included more than 8 percent of the industrial work force. Hundreds of strikes a year roiled both heavy and textile industries. Although owners resisted unionization, workers bargained collectively for higher wages, severance pay, a minimum

Miyanaga: Our thinking is that it would be even kinder to take the policy of avoiding layoffs rather than getting involved in the severance pay issue.

Itō: So you mean to say that there is no necessity to decide on severance pay? If your policy is not to lay off workers, well, this is a bit of an extreme example, but in that case wouldn't it be just as well to set severance pay at 10 to 20 thousand yen?

Miyanaga: I didn't say that there was no need. We are now considering the issue of severance pay.

Itō: You say "insofar as possible," but does that mean that in the eventuality of a layoff you will handle it as in the past?

Miyanaga: We are now also considering the possibility of increasing the level in the future.

Iwasa: Isn't what you are saying merely that, if you accept our demands, your profit will be narrowed? For us this is a matter of life and death.

Miyanaga: You say "our profits are narrowed," but in fact, not only are we not expecting any profit, but the company is going so far as to operate at a loss.

Itō: We have already heard at length from Mr. Yamaguchi on this point and understand it well. In any case, we regard the fact that the company will not now announce its intention to change the present severance pay as an indication of the company's total lack of sincerity regarding this entire affair. Let's go back and report this to all the others.

Miyanaga: You say that we are insincere, but as I have already explained the company is striving to promote your welfare and guarantee your security, and we'd like you to report this to the others.

Iwasa: The other day a worker named Tsukui, who was working in one of your manufacturing shops, was fired for going to another shop and talking to a worker there. You said that this was a violation of company rules, so he was fired. But this is something which other workers are constantly doing. If you look for such little matters and fire someone every day, pretty soon you'll have fired all the workers. Therefore, all your kind words are just the attitude of a man who stands laughing after having strangled seven people. We'll go and report this situation to all the other workers.

Questions for Analysis

1. What are the differences and similarities in the attitudes of the two sides regarding company goals?
2. What are the differences and similarities in the attitudes of the two sides regarding the value of work?
3. What are the differences and similarities in the attitudes of the two sides regarding how workers should be treated?

Source: Excerpt adapted from Andrew Gordon, *The Evolution of Labor Relations in Japan: Heavy Industry, 1853–1955* (Cambridge, Mass.: Council on East Asian Studies, Harvard University, 1985), pp. 116–119. © 1985 The President and Fellows of Harvard College. By permission of the Harvard University Asia Center.

wage, better working conditions, shorter workdays, an end to child labor, and improved housing.

Minorities

Although nationalist propaganda assured the Japanese people that they were uniquely homogeneous, the collision between colonialism and modernity created groups that society perceived as different. The government defined the Ainu who inhabited Hokkaido as "formerly indigenous people" and demanded that they assimilate into the Japanese mainstream by renouncing their nomadic lifestyle and settling in villages. Officials who supervised their transformation into tenant farmers, laborers, and welfare recipients in the course of selling off their lands and opening

Hokkaido to development saw them as a dying race. Many Ainu accepted the necessity of assimilation despite discrimination at the hands of employers, teachers, and non-Ainu neighbors. Others objected to contradictory policies that made them renounce their own language and forgo their customs of tattooing and earrings while setting them up as tourist attractions and anthropological exhibits. During the 1920s, Ainu scholars recorded Ainu songs, legends, and customs while Ainu activists created self-help programs to cope with alcoholism and violence. Social critics drew on radical thought to counter prejudice and discrimination. Fearful lest Hokkaido become communist with the Soviet Union so close to its border, government officials and assimilationist Ainu founded the Ainu Society in 1930 to improve the individual lot through education and to remind Ainu of the gratitude they owed the emperor.

The government's attitude toward the inhabitants of the Ryukyu Islands was more complicated. Unlike the Ainu, Ryukyuans had a social hierarchy topped by a monarch and aristocracy that made sense in the eyes of Japanese accustomed to inherent social inequality. Ryukyuan nobles used their status to gain favors from the prefectural governor's office and insisted on their right to speak for the commoners. When government officials and individuals placed them on a par with the Ainu, this was, they felt, an insult to their superior culture.

Nearly three hundred thousand Koreans lived in Japan by 1930. The earliest arrivals in the late nineteenth century were students of Japan's resistance to Western imperialism. Next came workers forced from their villages by colonial policies that expropriated land and put Japan's dietary needs first. Enticed by labor contractors who promised employment in factories, mines, and construction, workers ended up in low-paying jobs and substandard housing. Excluded from skilled labor except when they were used to break strikes, they performed dirty and dangerous jobs shunned by Japanese at wages half those of Japanese workers. Although the government made Koreans citizens of Japan and promoted an ideology of racial brotherhood under the emperor, in reality Koreans in Japan were deemed inherently stupid, lazy, fond of fighting, and vicious. Accused of having set fires and poisoned wells following the Great Kanto Earthquake, thousands died at the hands of Japanese vigilantes.

Koreans who showed intellectual promise earned the mistrust of Japanese officials, who feared, with reason, that they harbored anti-Japanese sentiment.

Korean students in Japan suffered arrest, imprisonment, and death for supporting national resistance movements and joining Japanese students who professed universal brotherhood, socialism, and communism. The Osaka Confederation of Korean Laborers earned official hostility when it called for an end to capitalism. Moderate Korean residents feared that opposition to colonialism would only invite repression and organized mutual aid societies to help Koreans find work, adequate housing, and health care. Government officials promoted assimilation policies to bring Koreans gradually and peacefully into Japanese society, while emphasizing that ethnically they could never become Japanese.

Radicals

The Japanese government suppressed ideas it deemed dangerous. In 1901 the Socialist Democratic Party enjoyed mere hours of existence before being outlawed. It advocated public ownership of land, capital, and communications; abolition of the military; education funded by the state; workers' rights to unionize; universal suffrage; and abolition of the House of Peers. It did not reject the emperor system, unlike the socialists Kōtoku Shūsui (CO-toe-ku SHOE-su-e) and Kanno Suga (KAH-no SU-gah). Kōtoku opposed capitalists, militarists, aristocrats, and politicians on behalf of workers and farmers. Kanno advocated overthrow of the government and assassination of the emperor. In what is known as the Great Treason Trial of 1911, they were convicted and sentenced to death, although they were innocent of the specific charges brought against them.

Anarchist ōsugi Sakae (OH-su-ge SAH-kah-eh) believed that society consists of two classes: the conquerors and the suppressed, and that it was up to workers to abolish the state and destroy capitalism. Following the Great Kanto Earthquake, he and his wife, the feminist and anarchist Itō Noe (E-toe No-eh), were strangled by the police. The nihilist Kaneko Fumiko (KAH-neh-co FU-me-co) advocated Korean independence. She died in prison. In 1933, the proletarian writer Kobayashi Takiji (CO-bah-yah-she TAH-key-g), who had graphically depicted the brutal conditions of fishermen in *The Cannery Boat* (1929), died at the hands of the police.

During the 1920s, a few socialists enjoyed a brief opportunity to spread their views. The Red Wave Society, founded in 1921, urged women to join the fight against capitalist society that enslaved them inside and outside the home. Political activist Sakai Toshihiko (SAH-kah-e TOE-she-he-ko) organized a study group to discuss socialist ideas in the late 1890s. In 1922, he participated in the secret founding of the Japanese Communist Party. The left-wing writer Inuta Shigeru (E-new-tah SHE-geh-rue) launched a literary movement that advocated self-rule for farmers through land reform. Professor of economics Kawakami Hajime (KAH-wah-kah-me HAH-g-meh) took a tortuous path from religious movements and nationalism to Marxism, revolutionary communism, and the study of historical materialism.

Between 1927 and 1937, socialists and communists debated the nature of Japanese capitalism, seeking to find a balance between universal Marxist categories and Japanese history that would determine the kinds of political action possible in the present. The Peace Preservation Law of 1925 promised punishment for attacks on the emperor system or capitalism. In the early 1930s, the police arrested more than ten thousand people a year for spreading ideas disloyal to the emperor and dangerous to the *kokutai*. Their intent was to force people to abandon socialist thought and convert to a belief in Japan's sacred unity under the emperor. Men and women who refused to confess and convert remained in prison until after World War II.

MODERN URBAN CULTURE

Industrial growth and expansion of the government bureaucracy created a new middle class of salaried white-collar workers. (See **Material Culture: Houses for the Middle Class**.) In contrast to the old middle class of shopkeepers and landlords, these workers got their jobs through educational achievement and enjoyed the security of lifetime employment with fringe benefits, such as subsidized housing and medical care. Income depended on seniority as much as on skill or achievement. In his novels *Sanshirō* (1908) and *Kokoro* (1914), Natsume Sōseki depicted socially mobile young men from the countryside. The character Sanshirō found himself torn between an academic career, the glittering world of business, and a return to his village. *Kokoro* expressed the sense that the era of great expectations passed with the death of the Meiji emperor in 1912. His son, the Taishō emperor, was universally seen as a lesser figure. In the 1920s, opportunities for becoming

extremely rich declined, but the new middle class continued to grow.

The Great Kanto Earthquake of 1923 brought both brick buildings and wooden houses down in Tokyo and other cities. Rebuilt in steel and concrete, downtown Tokyo provided the urban setting for modern Japanese culture. Even before the earthquake, the new middle class had started moving south and west of Tokyo's city limits, and private railroads and the real estate developers who owned them only intensified this trend. With the exception of publishers, light industry moved east of the city; heavy industry moved south to Kawasaki following the earthquake. The space left behind filled with offices, retail shops, and entertainment arcades.

Modern culture incorporated a second wave of westernization driven not by national goals but by individual inclinations. Dry goods stores had already become department stores at the turn of the century. After the earthquake, department stores added theaters, galleries, exhibition halls, and rooftop arcades. In 1926, vending machines started providing refreshment for travelers at Tokyo and Ueno stations. In 1927, the first subway in Asia connected corporate headquarters in Ginza with movie houses and cafés in Asakusa. Mass transit changed urban patterns of work, family life, leisure, and consumption. Unlike the old middle class whose members lived behind their businesses and shopped in the neighborhood, the white-collar worker commuted from his suburban home to his work downtown. Entertainment districts that grew up around train terminals enticed commuters to spend evenings relaxing away from work.

The new middle class consumed a modern culture removed from politics. Mass literacy spurred the development of mass media. Self-help books and magazines taught the rudiments of popular science, how to be modern, how to succeed in business, and how to create the perfect home environment. (See Color Plate 29.) By 1920, eleven hundred newspapers found 6 to 7 million buyers. Registered magazines were ten times that number. Journals for men appealed to the highbrow, the middlebrow, and the vulgar. Women's journals were targeted according to class, and girls' and boys' journals divided the market into ever more discrete segments.

Retail bookstores jumped from three thousand in 1914 to more than ten thousand in 1927. They sold complete editions of Western authors in translation, serious works of idealist philosophy by the Kyoto

MATERIAL CULTURE

Houses for the Middle Class

Houses built after the Great Kanto Earthquake for the new middle class were derived from Western architectural styles. Rooms had fewer functions but greater privacy than before. They had walls and doors and were further separated from one another by corridors. Guests were received at the front of the house in the parlor, decorated with sofa, chairs, and carpet. In line with the changing social etiquette of the time, guests were discouraged from making unexpected calls, and the telephone gave them little excuse for doing so. The family living room overlooked the garden. Although located on the dark north side of the house, the kitchen had a floor, unlike in older houses. Bedrooms were on the second floor. A modern water supply made it possible for each house to have its own bath.

New middle-class furnishings were designed chiefly for entertainment and convenience, rather than being objects with which to impress guests. The living room ideally contained a phonograph and a radio. Appliances included the gas range for cooking, a gas heater with ceramic grill, an electric fan, and an electric rice cooker. For reasons of etiquette and security, old-style houses had required that someone always be home to greet guests and guard the premises. Western-style front doors made it easy for the housewife to lock the door and go shopping, visit friends, or see a movie.

From Homu raifu (Home Life), published 1935–1940. Publisher: Osaka-shi: Osaka Mainichi Shinbunsha. © Cengage Learning 2014

Modern Living Room. This modern living room was photographed for the journal *Homu raifu (Home Life)*. Chairs, tables, lamp, potted plants, a sofa, and cushions provide a Western-style backdrop for the woman wearing a kimono.

BIOGRAPHY   Kobayashi Ichizō, Entrepreneur

Entrepreneur, politician, and diplomat, Kobayashi Ichizō (CO-bah-yah-she E-che-zo) (1873–1957) fostered consumer culture by founding a railroad, a department store, a baseball team, and the Takarazuka (TAH-kah-rah-zu-kah) Girl's Theater.

Kobayashi had wanted to become a writer, but after graduating from Keiō University, he joined the Mitsui Bank in 1893. In 1906 he left the bank to become executive director for a private electrical railroad near Osaka. Through hard work and creative planning in the building of new lines and improving service, he made his company dominant in train travel between Osaka and Kobe. In 1918 he became president of the newly named Hankyū (HAHN-keyu) electric railroad. To attract riders, he expanded into real estate by building suburban housing developments for the new middle class.

Kobayashi's interests tended toward popular culture. One of his train lines went to Takarazuka, an old hot springs resort. To lure customers, he built a zoo and, in 1913, the Takarazuka Girl's Theater. In 1919 he founded the Takarazuka Music Academy to train young women for his productions. The first revue with chorus line and musical spectaculars was *Mon Paris*, staged in 1927. Having watched commuters surge through the Hankyū terminal in Osaka, Kobayashi opened a market adjacent to the station in 1924. Five years later it became the Hankyū department store with restaurants, an art gallery, and a bookstore.

Kobayashi also founded the Tōhō (TOE-hoh) Cinema Company to make and distribute films. He built his movie empire with a mass audience in mind by scheduling show times and setting ticket prices for the benefit of workers. In 1936 he joined other railroad magnates and real estate developers to establish Japan's first professional baseball league, to give people another reason to ride trains in search of entertainment. Loyal fans still cheer the Hankyū Braves. In 1940, Kobayashi reached the pinnacle of his career by becoming commerce and industry minister and special ambassador in charge of trade to the Netherlands.

Kobayashi insisted that the performers in the Takarazuka Girl's Theater be of unquestionable virtue; his aim was to provide entertainment for respectable women and to mold his actresses' characters so they could later perform as good wives and wise mothers on their most important stage, the home. The Music Academy provided training in etiquette, ethics, and homemaking as well as singing and dancing. On stage, women played male roles; they also played Asians from countries incorporated into the Japanese empire. Lest actresses aspire to make the theater a profession, Kobayashi insisted that they retire at the peak of their popularity while they were still considered young enough to make a good match.

Questions for Analysis
1. Why did Kobayashi take an interest in popular culture?
2. What did Kobayashi contribute to modern Japanese culture?
3. What were Kobayashi's target audiences?

Source: Jennifer E. Robertson, *Takarazuka: Sexual Politics and Popular Culture in Modern Japan* (Berkeley: University of California Press, 1998).

School, novels by such best-selling male authors as Tanizaki Junichirō (TAH-knee-zah-key JUNE-e-che-row) and female authors as Uno Chiyo (U-no CHE-yo), and illustrated books given to escapist sensationalism. Cinemas showed films from abroad alongside domestically produced animated cartoons and historical dramas, and as in the West, movie stars became celebrities. Government-operated radio stations started broadcasting in the mid-1920s while record companies churned out recordings of patriotic songs. Popular music celebrated romantic love and the delights of Tokyo, including hanging out in downtown Ginza. A cheap escape from the workaday world was to watch small balls bounce down a pachinko board, a vertical version of the pinball machine.

Modern mass culture promoted a privatizing world of pleasure and self-expression. Women danced in chorus lines and performed in Takarazuka Girl's Theater. (See **Biography: Kobayashi Ichizō, Entrepreneur.**)

In the novel *Naomi* (1924–1925), Tanizaki depicted the transformation of a café waitress into a *modan gaaru* ("modern girl"; *moga* for short) who bobbed her hair, wore revealing dresses, and danced the Charleston. The *moga*'s less flamboyant companion was the *mobo* ("modern boy"); together they scandalized onlookers by smoking cigarettes and holding hands in public. The late 1920s are often characterized by the words *ero*, *guro*, and *nansensu*—eroticism, grotesquerie, and nonsense, referring to both the new flood of foreign words in urban vocabularies and the perceived decline in public morals. Materialism, individualism, and decadence had apparently replaced the beautiful Japanese virtues of diligence, decorum, and duty.

ALTERNATIVES TO MODERNITY

People repelled by modern culture found solace in folk traditions of rural Japan, high art of ancient Japan, and communities of the devout created by the new religions. Ethnographer Yanagita Kunio (YAH-nah-gy-tah KU-knee-oh) sought a cultural authenticity that had been lost in urban areas. Traveling from Tohoku to the Ryukyus, he collected folk tales and documented what he viewed as pristine customs of the folk. Industrialist and builder of the Mitsui *zaibatsu,* Masuda Takashi (MAH-sue-dah TAH-kah-she) tried to preserve Japan's artistic inheritance and supported the government's system for designating cultural artifacts as national treasures. First established in 1897, the designation "national treasure" applied foremost to religious objects from the region around the ancient capital of Kyoto, declared Japan's sovereignty over its past, magnified differences between Japan and the outside world, and demonstrated that Japan possessed a world-class culture.

New religions provided alternative visions of modernity that did not please the state. Deguchi Onisaburō (DEH-gu-che OH-knee-sah-bu-row), organizer of ōmoto-kyō (OH-moe-toe-keyo), criticized government policies that disadvantaged the poor. In the 1920s, he proclaimed that as the Maitreya—the Buddha of the future—he would establish a new order on earth, a message that found believers even among government officials and army officers. In the early 1930s, Deguchi founded a semimilitaristic youth group to restore the kingdom of God at Ōmoto-kyō headquarters. Ōmoto-kyō was suppressed in 1921 and again in 1935.

New religions founded after 1905 more commonly based their teachings on Nichiren Buddhism and answered the needs of uprooted, underprivileged masses in the cities. Charismatic leaders preached a gospel of social equality and promised either a pure new world or salvation to come. They emphasized faith healing, deliverance from suffering, and a focus on this world's benefits. For recent urban migrants, new religions provided self-help groups, a sense of identity, and a community that was neither self-righteously traditional nor modern enough to be alienating.

Twentieth-century agrarianism was more virulently antimodernist. It identified agriculture as the ethical foundation of the state even though agriculture was no longer the country's main source of wealth. Its supporters professed a farm *bushidō* (way of the warrior) that assimilated the farmers' virtues of diligence, frugality, fortitude, and harmony with loyalty and self-sacrifice on behalf of the state. Agrarianism blamed city life for making people selfish and ambitious; it detested capitalism for increasing the corrupting power of money, destroying the farm family economy, and eroding harmony between city and country. It demanded a spiritual alternative to materialism and a national alternative to universal socialism. Its nostalgic search for a return to a primitive rural society that manifested the *kokutai* frequently turned violent in the 1930s.

SUMMARY

Foreign affairs resonated through Japan's economy, politics, society, and culture. The urge to gain power and status to challenge white supremacy and rise in the hierarchy of nations shaped Japan's national identity. Colonies became an economic necessity, both to supply raw materials for Japan's emerging industries and to provide living space for its teeming population.

The second industrial revolution brought development to Japan's economy, which was characterized by unevenness. Huge conglomerates, modern factories, a modern middle class of salaried workers, and an industrial workforce existed alongside the old middle class of small businesses. A business cycle of expansion during World War I and contraction in the decade of the 1920s meant that Japan's economy was depressed even before the worldwide Great Depression of the 1930s.

Although the oligarchs had planned to control the government and provide guidelines for business through the bureaucracy, they soon discovered that politicians acted more independently than they had anticipated. Outside the Diet, intellectuals debated the meaning of representative government, radicals tried to preach socialism and even communism, educated women brought women's issues before the public, and mass movements of outcasts, tenant farmers, workers, and minorities tried to win state intervention to improve their lives.

By destroying much of old Tokyo, the Great Kanto Earthquake of 1923 accelerated the trend to separate factories from office buildings, work from home. It thus opened a space for modern urban culture that was characterized by a new middle class that valued education, devoured mass media, and apparently placed individual goals above service to the nation. Although proponents of agriculture as the foundation of the state were the most vehement critics of modern life, supporters of new religions and intellectuals who sought a more authentic cultural identity also proposed alternatives to modernity.

How did Japan change during the first third of the twentieth century? On the positive side, it developed a robust parliamentary democracy supported by an electorate that encompassed the entire male population. The industrialized economy and modern bureaucracy fostered the growth of a well-educated middle class. The development of mass media provided opportunities for mass movements that aimed at improving the lot of the downtrodden. Whether they liked it or not, the complexity of modern society gave people the opportunity to make choices rather than simply follow the ways of their forebears and to pursue private, individual goals.

Yet historians also see darker currents. On an institutional level, the military became increasingly independent of civilian control. Although it provided employment, the industrial sector left workers in poverty. Modern Japan contained conflicting visions of what it meant to be Japanese, who should be incorporated into the nation and how, and what Japan's role in the world should be. The relatively peaceful world of the 1920s allowed space for controversy. When the Great Depression struck in 1930, plural and critical voices within Japan appeared as dangerous as threats from abroad to Japan's economic and national security. When we return to Japan in Chapter 26, we will see how these trends played out in the context of war.

CHAPTER TWENTY-THREE

Modernizing Korea and Colonial Rule (1896–1945)

After the Sino-Japanese War ended in 1895, Korea had a brief period to debate its future and launch modernizing projects before losing independence to Japan. The colonial period involved major social, economic, cultural, and ideological transformations that entailed both human suffering and possibilities for development. One legacy was the rise of nationalism and the introduction of communism that created the basis for political division after 1945.

Should attention focus on how people suffered under Japanese oppression or on the progress made in economic development, education, opportunities for women, and introduction of modern mass culture? Who did the right thing: anti-Japanese (often communist) guerrilla fighters who patriotically resisted Japanese imperialism, cultural nationalists who accepted Japanese control and tried to educate the masses in national consciousness over the long term, or expatriate nationalists in the United States who worked to persuade Western nations to liberate Korea? And how should collaborators—Korean landlords and businessmen who not only prospered under Japan but also supported Japan's efforts in the late 1930s to eliminate Korean language and culture—be judged?

ATTEMPTS AT REFORM (1896–1910)

Competition between Japan and Russia gave Koreans the opportunity to promote reforms, nationalism, and modern social and political organizations. Competition also meant constraints when both Russia and Japan demanded concessions. In the end, Korea's efforts to remain independent came to naught when the court of world opinion sided with Japan.

Russia's Interests

Russia's development of Siberia that started in the late nineteenth century gave it a narrow boundary with northeastern Korea south of the trans-Siberian railway. In 1896, Russia began construction of a second railway, the Chinese Eastern Railway, which stretched across Manchuria. The next year, it obtained a twenty-five-year lease on Port Arthur (Dalian) on the Liaodong peninsula, which it had taken away from Japan in 1895, and it obtained railroad rights to connect it with the Chinese Eastern Railway. (Refer back to Map 22.1.) Japan could only watch these events in ever-growing frustration.

In 1896, King Gojong escaped from Japanese control in his palace and fled to the Russian legation. Russia and Japan then signed two agreements that granted Russia equal rights with Japan to station legation guards and grant loans to the Korean government. While Russia's influence spread over north Korea, Japan concentrated on the south. Korea also signed a secret agreement in which Russia promised to protect King Gojong and provide military and financial aid. Strapped for funds to pay off indemnities and finance his government, King Gojong began to lease rights to the exploitation of natural resources—lumber to the Russians, gold mines to the Americans, and railroad construction to the Japanese and others—in return for loans. After he returned to his palace in 1897, he changed the name of his kingdom to The Great Empire of Korea and adopted the title of emperor to put himself on par with Chinese, Russian, and Japanese rulers.

Nationalist Movements

Popular reaction against the king's sacrifice of national resources gave rise to the first explicitly nationalist movements as Koreans struggled to find a national identity fit for the modern age. After King Gojong dismissed the Gabo (GA-bo) reform cabinet upon his arrival at the Russian legation, a street mob killed reform ministers, and the new conservative cabinet reversed the edict to cut topknots. Outside the government, men from the secondary status groups who filled the new Independence Club demanded the dismissal of corrupt officials and strove to educate people on the need to modernize the country. The Club organized street meetings and education sessions and established a newspaper, *The Independent*, written in the vernacular and English. Membership in the group increased as its leaders made public speeches, established branches in small towns, campaigned for the construction of an Independence Gate as a sign of liberation from subservience to China, held mass meetings and demonstrations in Seoul, and demanded and received seats on the king's council. Its leaders included men like Seo Jaepil (SUH JAE-pil), an American citizen who returned to Korea; Rhee Syngman (RI Sing-man), who had attended Baejae (BEH-jae) Christian missionary school; and Yun Chiho (YOON CHI-ho), who visited Japan and was educated in the United States. In the spirit of American progressivism, they denigrated Korea's heritage while proclaiming the need to create a truly independent nation.

Although the Independence Club was banned after two years, it inspired elite women to debate sexual equality and education for women in the context of Korean nationalism. They organized the Chanyang-hoe (CHAHN-yang-hwae) (Promotion Society) in 1898 to form a school for women and the Yeouhoe (YUH-ooh-hwae) (Friends of Women) the next year to demand the abolition of concubinage. Esther Park, the first woman doctor, began practice at the Women's Hospital in 1900 and taught sanitation in addition to clinical work.

For the first time, women started taking public action. On the national front, they established organizations to pay back foreign debts incurred by the regime, protested administrative corruption, called for independence, and organized groups in support of various causes. To deal with domestic issues, they founded societies in 1906 and 1907 to campaign for women's education, oppose separation of the sexes, stop wearing shawls to cover their faces in public, establish a hospital, and publish a new journal, *Women's Times*. One of their number, Louise Yim wrote vividly about her struggles to achieve more independence for women (see **Documents: Louise Yim's Writings on Female Independence**).

One sign of the rise of a modern civil society is the appearance of organizations advocating political goals outside the government. Inaugurated in 1904, the Korea Preservation Society opposed attempts by Japan to turn state land into private land for sale to Japanese developers. As its name suggests, the Society for the Study of Constitutional Government advocated institutional change to deal with the challenges threatening Korea. When it was outlawed, its successor took the name of the Korea Self-Strengthening Society. It tried to promote economic development and the spread of education.

DOCUMENTS

Louise Yim's Writings on Female Independence

Louise Yim (Im Yeongsin [IM YOUNG-shin]) was a patriot who suffered torture for participating in resistance to Japanese rule. She earned a B.A. and an M.A. from the University of Southern California and served in the Republic of Korea National Assembly after the Korean War (1950–1953).

On Grammar School

Often I stood outside the boys' school, which my father had started, and I would listen to the boys repeating the lessons after their teacher. One day after the boys had gone home I went inside the little, square, mud-walled building.

"May I speak?" I asked Cho Tugy, the teacher.

He was so startled that he dropped a pencil. Then he saw me and smiled.

"If I may have the honor to listen," he replied formally.

"Would it be possible for a girl to learn how to read and write?"

He said nothing for a little while. I was afraid he would laugh and send me home. Then he said:

"If the gods have given you the courage to ask, we can hope they have given you the power to learn, little one. Come to school anytime and I will teach you."

By the time I was twelve [1912], there were rumors that Korean girls were going to be forced to marry Japanese. Therefore, all parents were in a hurry to get their daughters married. My sister was to marry soon and my turn was to be next.

One day, two women came to my room. I knew right away who they were. They were matchmakers. I had never hated anybody as much as I did those two women. I felt as though they were trying to imprison me. Instead of answering their questions, I questioned them and I lectured them. They were shocked and sometimes they put their hands to their faces and moaned as I spoke.

I told them it was a crime to force marriage on a girl too young to know what it was all about. This was almost too much for them to bear. A Korean child was not supposed to speak this way to her elders.

When they left, I heard one say to the other, "We will speak to her mother. She will come to no good, that one. Her blood is wild."

On High School, CA. 1916

I knew then that the masculine belief that females did not have a place in the national life of Korea was the belief of men who knew nothing about women and in their ignorance shut them out of the family's life too. It has always been a great mystery to me why men think that women are different from them intellectually. I wish I could go to every man and tell him that besides certain physical differences and the ability of a woman to bear children, a woman thinks of all the things a man does. Just because she allows herself to be exiled in the kitchen a woman does not give up her feelings as an individual.

Questions for Analysis

1. In Yim's recollections of her childhood, what stands out?
2. What kinds of criticisms did Yim level against the society into which she was born?
3. What did Yim think of men?

Source: Louise Yim, *My Forty Year Fight for Korea* (Seoul: Chungang University, 1964), pp. 27, 39, 56.

Other organizations aimed at similar goals, though they often had to organize in secret as Japanese pressure intensified. Newspapers, too, rallied to the cause of Korean independence, particularly after the Russo-Japanese War. They publicized acts of Japanese aggression, at least until forced to close by Japanese censorship. Even the manner of their demise contributed to heightening Korean political consciousness.

Korea's first new religion took on the trappings of a fully organized institution and supported nationalist goals. In 1905, the Donghak movement changed its name to Religion of the Heavenly Way (Cheondogyo [CHEON-doh-gyo]). Having supported an uprising against official corruption, Son Byeonghui (SON BYUNG-hwi), the third patriarch, had gone into exile in Japan before returning to form the Progressive Party, which then linked up with the Unity and Progress Society. Both went farther than the Independence Club in seeking members among rural farmers as well as city dwellers. Under Song Byeongjun (SOHNG BYUNG-joon), the Unity and Progress Society favored Japanese leadership in achieving reform and volunteered to assist Japanese forces during the Russo-Japanese War. Its collaboration led to a split with the Progressive Party. Another new religion with nationalist overtones was the Daejonggyo (DAY-jong-gyo) that worshipped the ancestor of the Korean race.

The development of modern culture was inseparable from the rise in nationalism. The demand for education in Western learning with practical application for protecting Korea from foreign aggression led to the founding of at least 2,250 private academies across the country. Although most trained men, a few, founded by Koreans and missionaries, educated women. Schools also provided venues for debates and campaigns that heightened the students' patriotism. Weaned from their addiction to Chinese culture, scholars studied Korean language, history, and literature. They also published books on nation-building experiences elsewhere in the world. Outside academe, the "new novel," a precursor to modern Korean fiction, emerged. Its protagonists advocated Korean independence and a new Korea founded on principles of social equality, equality of men and women, and replacement of superstition with rationality. Sung to the melodies of Western hymns or popular music, songs glorifying Korea spread nationalist sentiment across the country.

The Russo-Japanese War (1904–1905)

For years before war broke out, Russia and Japan contended for concessions inside Korea. In 1901, Japan made plans to complete the railway between Busan and Seoul and build a connection from Seoul to Uiju (WI-jew) next to the border with Manchuria, while Russia tried to expand its leasehold around the Yalu River. Owing to its growing mistrust of Russia, Japan entered into an alliance with Great Britain in 1902. This measure prevented Germany

and France from supporting Russia and opened the possibility of a war by Japan against Russia alone (see Chapter 22).

Despite a last-ditch appeal by Korea for neutralization of the Korean peninsula, when the Russo-Japanese War began in February 1904, Japan sent an invasion force to occupy Seoul. During the war, Japan appointed advisers to all the Korean ministries. Although Russia withdrew from Korea after its defeat in 1905, in extending its alliance with Japan, Britain allowed Japan to take any action it saw fit in Korea, as did the United States.

Following the war, in November 1905, Japan established a protectorate over Korea. When Emperor Gojong and several of his ministers refused to sign the Eulsa (EUL-sah) protectorate treaty, Itō Hirobumi, who was in charge of the negotiations with the Joseon court, ignored him and declared that a majority of ministers had approved it. Min Yeong-hwan, the dead queen's nephew and military aide to the emperor, committed suicide in protest.

Itō headed the new residency general that Japan created for Korea. His vision was to maintain an "independent" Korean government that would willingly carry out institutional reforms under Japanese guidance. To this end, he used Japanese police and regular army units to maintain order while Emperor Gojong was left on the throne as a figurehead.

Despite Korean attempts to rally foreign opinion to its side, Japan outmaneuvered it. Emperor Gojong secretly sent messages to heads of European states for help in gaining independence. In 1907 the American missionary Homer Hulbert led a mission to the Second International Conference on Peace at The Hague to present Korea's case. The mission was refused admission because Korea had ceased to exist once it became a protectorate. Japan claimed to have become a civilized nation; according to international law, only civilized nations were deemed sovereign, and as a result of Japan's public relations campaign, Korea was seen as uncivilized.

Koreans launched fierce opposition to Itō's initiatives. When he dethroned Gojong in favor of his son, leading government officials committed suicide, riots broke out in the street, and merchants declared a nationwide strike. The Korean army having been dissolved on Itō's orders, the discharged soldiers began a guerrilla war that lasted for four years before it was crushed by superior Japanese forces, resulting in the loss of thousands of lives. At Itō's directive, the Korean Home Ministry took charge of peace preservation, banned freedom of association, and instituted censorship of newspapers and books. Itō's plan to place a nominally independent Korea behind a facade of Japanese paternalism finally failed. When he made a trip to Manchuria to gain Russia's agreement to Japan's annexing of Korea, An Jung-geun, a Korean patriot, assassinated him in Harbin. The new resident general, Terauchi Masatake (TEH-rah-u-che MAH-sah-tah-keh), clamped down on all criticism of Japanese policy. On August 22, 1910, Korea became Japan's colony, as announced to Koreans on August 29.

JAPANESE COLONIAL RULE (1910–1945)

Japan's colonial rule went through three phases. The first was the period of military rule from 1910 to 1919, during which Japan created a police state called the Government-General (GG) of Chōsen (CHO-sehn). It eliminated all Korean political participation, restricted Korean business activity, and invested heavily in the promotion of rice cultivation for export to Japan. It granted authority to the police to levy fines, detain suspects for long periods, and use violence on the spot, torture in interrogations, and flogging as punishment for minor offenses even though these measures had been banned in Japan in 1882.

Despite suppression, Korean nationalist movements continued. At first they worked underground, mainly through religious groups organized by Christians, new religions, and Buddhists because Japan was reluctant to persecute Christianity and offend Western nations. They erupted on March 1, 1919, when thirty-three patriots signed a Declaration of Independence and marched peacefully to the Japanese authorities to petition for liberation. They had been inspired by U.S. President Woodrow Wilson's call for self-determination for people subject to foreign rule following World War I, and they expected support from the United States and other Western powers. In contrast to earlier political clubs, the participants in the March First Movement came from all walks of life and from all over the country, marking a significant spread of national consciousness.

The March First Movement forced Japan to change its policy. At first it responded to nonviolent demonstrations with mass arrests and executions. Then it shifted to a "cultural government" policy, which allowed a certain degree of freedom of speech and association and permitted the establishment of Korean businesses. That policy marked the second phase of colonial rule and lasted until the Manchurian Incident of 1931, when the Japanese army in Manchuria overthrew the Chinese governor and established the puppet state of Manchukuo.

The third phase lasted from the Manchurian Incident to the defeat of Japan by the United States in 1945 (see **Connections: World War II**). During this period, Japan invested huge amounts of capital in heavy industry and infrastructure in Korea in support of Japan's wars while repressing the freedoms that had flourished in the 1920s. After 1937 it instituted military conscription, forced labor, and Korean assimilation to Japan. It forced Koreans to use the Japanese language, worship the Japanese emperor in Shinto shrines, and adopt Japanese names in an effort to eradicate Korean identity.

Scholars' views of Korea's colonial period generally divide into two broad categories. The first takes a negative view of Japan, focusing on its tyranny, its exploitation of the Korean economy, its reduction of the mass of the population to bare subsistence, its prevention of modern industrial development, and its attempt to obliterate Korean culture without granting equal citizenship rights. The second fits the colonial experience into major trends that lasted to the end of the twentieth century. These included abolishing inherited social status that had blocked social mobility; liberating women from male domination; introducing modern mass education for both sexes; fostering the growth of mass media and popular culture; creating a modern economy through investment in railroads, bridges, and harbors; establishing a modern financial sector in the 1920s; and industrializing the peninsula in the 1930s. A small middle class of businessmen and shopkeepers arose, and a half-million farmers were converted to factory workers and miners. In retrospect, the most important economic contribution was Japan's use of state-led industrialization involving planning and controls of all kinds to catch up to the advanced economies of Western imperialists. This process, now known as developmentalism, was a far cry from the free-market capitalism of Britain and the United States, but it opened the eyes of some Koreans to economic development without liberal democracy.

March First Movement. Japan's initial response to the March 1 movement was repression—the mass execution of demonstrators performed in public.

Japan's Impact on Rural Korea

Colonial economic policy aimed at expanding agricultural production by investing in reclamation, irrigation, chemical fertilizer, and the introduction of new seeds to grow rice for export to Japan. To create an efficient land tax for raising revenue, the colonial government adopted a land registration program in 1911 to record the owners of all land. Korean nationalists and scholars have condemned this policy as a sham designed to transfer land from Korean owners to Japanese by force or trickery. Japan justified it on the grounds that Joseon Dynasty law had not clearly defined landownership. Although private landownership had been the economic basis of the Korean aristocracy at least for a thousand years, security of tenure was weak because judges in civil cases were district magistrates from *yangban* families who defended landlord interests. Written evidence of who owned the land existed in the form of deeds, inheritance documents, bills of sale, and state registries, but not every owner possessed them. Because landowners had often not registered their land with the state to avoid taxes, the government had lacked funds to modernize its military and fund development projects.

At first the land registration program did not result in a major transfer of land from Korean to Japanese hands. From 1910 to 1925, Korea experienced an economic boom and a rise in the price of rice. Korean landlords, most of whom were *yangban*, fared far better than sharecroppers—tenants whose income fluctuated with the harvest, at least half of which went to the landlord. Japan succeeded in winning *yangban* landlords' acceptance of colonial rule by granting them noble titles and guaranteeing their private property rights. As a result, landlords took little part in active nationalist resistance to Japanese rule.

Conditions changed following the onset of the world economic depression that started in 1929. Indebted smallholders lost their land to Japanese creditors. By 1940 the price of rice had dropped to

39 percent of the 1925 price. Korean farmers who both owned and rented land earned a reasonable living, but tenant farmers did not. Rice consumption declined because of exports to Japan, and although millet from Manchuria arrived to supplement their diet, Koreans perceived this as a poor substitute for their favorite staple food.

Farmers took political measures to protect their livelihood. Established in 1924, the Joseon Labor-Farmer General Alliance supported the many tenant disputes of the 1920s and tried to wage class struggle against the capitalist class. Farmers later left to form their own General Korean Farmer Alliance. Middling farmers, rather than the poorest sharecroppers, led the tenant disputes and demanded reduction in sharecropping fees from 50 to 40 percent or less of the crop. Most tenant disputes ended favorably before 1925. Many smallholders having gone bankrupt after 1929, the percentage of tenant households increased from 41 to 50 percent of the farm population in the 1930s, and the number of tenant unions increased from about 30 in 1922 to 1,301 in 1933. In the early 1930s sixty-nine radical farmer unions challenged local officials. In 1933 the Japanese government instituted the Tenancy Mediation Law to resolve tenant disputes in the courts, and many were resolved in favor of tenants. After Japan ended its policy of promoting rice production in 1934, agriculture declined steadily until 1945. Farmers took the route of passive resistance—failing to fulfill contracts or hiding crops from the authorities. After Japan attacked Pearl Harbor in 1941, the GG banned all tenant protest, leading to intense sharecropper resentment.

The colonial government encouraged Korean migration to northeastern Manchuria to ease rural distress and expand Japan's influence. Unlike Chinese farmers, Korean settlers had access to loans from Japanese banks that enabled them to invest in better tools and seeds. They obtained favorable rates for buying land and support for forming agrarian cooperatives. In southern Manchuria, by contrast, Koreans lacked rights to own property or even to work. Japanese officials in the northeast protected Koreans in disputes with the local population, so long as Koreans retained passports issued by colonial authority and did not become naturalized Chinese citizens. Koreans accepted this arrangement because it allowed them to retain their Korean identity. By 1942 approximately 1.5 million Koreans had settled in Manchuria, where they provided shelter for anti-Japanese political movements. In Chinese eyes, they were agents of Japan.

The Growth of Korean Industry

In the 1920s, Korean businesses emerged despite limited capital resources. Large landlords launched a number of small-scale enterprises—for example, the Gyeongseong (GYONG-sung) textile corporation founded by Kim Yeonsu (KIM YEON-su) and Kim Seongsu (KIM SUNG-su), members of a landlord family from Jeolla province in the southwest. The Kim brothers used capital accumulated from tenant rents to establish the company; when it was threatened by bankruptcy, they turned to Japanese banks for working capital that saved the company and allowed it to expand. They also received help from Japanese trading companies in marketing products. The GG summoned the Kims to offer their opinions in economic policy councils and provided protection by letting the Kims' company carve out a niche in the cheap textile sector of the Korean economy while Japanese textile companies produced more expensive goods.

Most Korean companies in dyeing, paper, leather, ceramics, and milling were undercapitalized small-scale operations that supplied goods for the domestic market, such as Korean-owned breweries that split their market with Japanese companies. Landlords and rich merchants from south Jeolla (JEOL-lah) province capitalized the Donga (DONG-ah) Rubber Company with three hundred thousand yen, and a Korean merchant raised fifty thousand yen to found the Pando (BAN-doe) Rubber Company. By 1930, Korean rubber factories outnumbered the Japanese thirty to seventeen. The dominant industry in Korean hands other than cheap textiles was food processing while most Korean metal factories were no more than blacksmiths' shops.

Japanese investment in Korea dwarfed the paid-in capital of Korean firms. Japan Steel erected a plant at Songrim (SUNG-rim), and Japan Mining had a smelting plant at Chinnampo (JIN-nam-poe), both in northern Korea. The Japanese conglomerate Mitsui founded the Sansei Mining Company, Mitsubishi the Joseon Coal Company, and Noguchi the Joseon Nitrogen Company to make fertilizer. Japanese firms also established chemical, electrical, textile, mining, and railroad companies. They provided hydroelectric power, railroad lines from Busan to the Manchurian border, and cement, chemicals, and the like for export to China. They purchased large amounts of forestland

and invested in cotton textiles, food processing, brewing, milling, paper, and printing. Although some argue that Japan took an economic interest in Korea to obtain raw materials and markets for its exports, Japan invested more than it ever received in profits because it put strategic and political objectives first.

In the 1930s, Japan built up both infrastructure and industry to support its puppet state of Manchukuo and to supply essential equipment to its military stationed there. By 1941, more than 90 percent of the capital invested in Korean industry came from Japan. A south-to-north railroad trunk line funneled goods from both Japan and Korea into Manchuria and, after the outbreak of the Sino-Japanese War in 1937, to China. Investment in hydroelectric power plants along the Yalu River and elsewhere and power lines throughout the country provided energy for steel, chemical, machinery, metal, and machine factories to support Japan's war effort. Most weapons were manufactured in Japan, leaving repairs, vehicles, and shipbuilding to the Korean machine industry. Japan subsidized the Mitsui, Mitsubishi, and Sumitomo conglomerates' mines for copper, zinc, manganese, tungsten, molybdenum, and other metals for military purposes. The average annual growth in Korea's industrial production in the 1930s was 15 percent, almost double the rate from 1910 to 1928.

During the 1930s and into the 1940s Koreans continued to develop small-scale businesses. They owned about a fifth of metal, machine, tools, and chemical plants as well as ceramics kilns and wood and lumber mills; roughly half of pharmaceutical companies, rice mills, and printing; more than 70 percent of beverages; and more than 90 percent of textile firms. Gyeongseong Textile Corporation took advantage of Japanese expansion to set up textile plants in Manchuria and to buy a textile plant in Nanjing after the Nanjing massacre of 1937. When Gyeongseong had problems over wages and working conditions, it summoned Japanese police to put down strikes. Other businessmen such as Min Gyusik (MIN GYEW-shik) and Pak Heungsik (PARK HEUNG-shik) received financing from the Japanese Development Bank. Pak established a range of enterprises including Korea's first department store, the Hwasin (HWA-shin), and became one of Korea's wealthiest businessmen. Yi Byeongcheol (YI BYUNG-cheol) started with a rice mill and then prospered in the liquor business.

After liberation in 1945, businessmen such as the Kim brothers of the Gyeongseong Corporation garnered a reputation for being "national capitalists." It was said that they placed the welfare of the Korean nation above the profits they made through working with Japan, even though the evidence shows that they became full partners in Japanese imperialism on the continent. Korean businessmen could not have prospered or survived unless they cooperated with Japan, but recently they have been condemned for collaboration.

Although Japan did not aim to improve the welfare of the Korean population, Korea became industrialized. Korean capitalists became the core of a new middle class, and a minuscule working class expanded to about five hundred thousand by the time Japan was defeated in 1945, not counting factory workers, miners, and other forced laborers in Japan and Manchuria. Even before 1910, the royal mint and private textile companies had begun to hire women workers. With farmers abandoning their homes for higher-paying jobs, the expansion of industry stimulated urbanization. Korea was beginning to take on the features of an advanced industrial economy, with most Koreans as the underclass.

Education and Modern Mass Culture

In the 1920s, the liberalization allowed by the colonial government came hedged with restrictions. The GG allowed newspapers, magazines, and books to be published in Korean, but it subjected all publications to the sharp eyes of Japanese censors. It expanded primary education, but it limited the number of Korean private schools while restricting compulsory education to the first few grades. It founded a single university in Seoul as part of the imperial university system, Keijō (Gyeongseong in Korean) Imperial University, with a student population that was one-third Korean. Only a small minority of well-to-do students was allowed to attend it or colleges in Japan. Despite its aim to assimilate Koreans into Japanese culture, the GG established separate (and better) schools for Japanese students in Korea.

Modernity opened opportunities for women. Urban women took the lead in promoting new standards of hygiene and sanitation in rural areas, just as they did in Japan. Women established education centers, including night schools in churches and rural areas, to educate the illiterate. They founded Songjukhoe (SONG-juke-hwae) (Pine and Bamboo Society) in 1910 to foster national consciousness. Buddhist women organized the Buddhist Women's Association in 1920. Helen Kim, a Christian and the first person to receive the doctorate in Korean history (from Columbia University in 1929), and other women from Ewha School took a tour of rural areas to enlighten the public before the police put a stop to their efforts. She and Kim Pilye (KIM PIL-yeh) organized the Korean YWCA in 1922. Many women received training in nursing either in Japan or at the Women's Medical College under the missionary nurse Margaret Edmond. The first women's medical school, the Gyeongseong Medical College, was founded in 1928. The GG hired female clerical workers; private industry put women in factories.

The civil code issued under Japanese auspices in 1912 generally confirmed traditional practices regarding male succession to family headship, ownership of property, and the sole right of men to initiate divorce. In 1918 women were given the right to petition for divorce, provided they had approval from both their husband and parents. A 1922 ordinance elevated the minimal age of marriage for women to fifteen, banned polygamy and concubinage, and allowed a woman to divorce her husband for polygamy or adultery, criminal activity, insult, or abandonment for three years. These provisions did not halt discriminatory practices against women.

Women found a public voice with the advent of two women's journals in the 1920s: Kim Wonju's (KIM WON-jew) *The New Woman* and Na Hyeseok's *Women's World*. Socialist women's groups appeared in 1924. They and non-socialist women demanded abolition of early marriage, female slavery, licensed prostitution, and wage discrimination.

Korean literature in the language of ordinary Koreans flourished with support from the New Culture Movement launched by Korean nationalists. One founder of the Gyeongseong Corporation, Kim Seongsu, established the *East Asia Daily* newspaper and Boseong (BO-sung) Normal School (later Goryeo University). Influenced by Tolstoy, Yi Gwangsu (YI GWANG-su) published the first modern novel, *Heartless,* in 1917, followed by *Rebirth*, *Earth*, and many others. Hyeon Jingeon (HYUN JIN-gun) portrayed the suffering of common men and women under traditional customs and colonial rule. His novel about a Baekje general who resisted Tang armies was banned. Kim Dongin (KIM Dong-in) established *Creation* magazine in 1919 and wrote about the denizens of the slums and the life of a shaman. Yi Hyoseok (YI HYO-suck) joined the KAPF (Korean Art Proletarian Federation) literary movement from 1928 to 1932. Like almost all other members of KAPF, he abandoned socialism to write about itinerant peddlers and the alienation produced by urban life. In 1936, Yi Sang (YI SAHNG) wrote a stream-of-consciousness story, "Wings," about a self-centered husband who dealt with his wife's prostitution by sealing his mind from the shame of external facts.

Korea's modern mass media began during the colonial period even though, for the first decade after annexation, Japan monopolized film production. With the beginning of "cultural government" policy, the first Korean films appeared: *Righteous Revenge* (1919) directed by Kim Dosan (KIM DOE-sahn) and *Plighted Love Under the Moon* (1923) directed by Yun Baeknam (YOON BECK-nam). There were close to 9 million moviegoers by 1935. Despite censorship, the movies *Arirang* (Ah-ri-rang, 1926) and *Searching for Love* (1928), directed by Na Ungyu (NAH UHN-gyu), and *Wandering* (1928), by Kim Yuyeong (KIM YU-young), produced by the KAPF, told stories of oppression of farmers by landlords and the evils of Japanese imperialism. Linked to the movie by the same name, *Arirang* is the best known of Korean songs. It tells of partings—of lovers kept apart by a hill, of workers drafted from their homes to rebuild the Gyeongbok Palace, of Koreans separated from their nation. Before Japan banned Korean films in 1935, the Korean film industry had produced some 160 silent movies.

Radio broadcasting began in 1927 under the Japanese Korean Broadcasting Company. Korean-language programs expanded from one-third to one-half of airtime, and in 1933 the first all-Korean station was allowed. It devoted many programs to Korean history, science, the arts, international affairs, translations of Western plays, popular songs with a distinct Korean flavor, and instruction in the use of *hangul* and the standardization of Korean grammar. Even after the ban on the use of Korean in public in 1938, GG tolerated Korean-language radio programs. In the 1930s newspapers, mass-circulation magazines, films, and radio spread the tastes in fashion and fiction of the admittedly tiny urban middle class to a wider audience and signaled the arrival of a growing consumer culture.

Militant Nationalism

The colonial period spurred Koreans to debate different definitions of national identity. Some intellectuals looked back on Korea's past and saw only a sad history of subservience, both political and cultural, to China. Students radicalized in Japan returned to Korea to organize study groups with socialist agendas. Militant nationalists viewed the colonial period in black-and-white terms: one was either a true patriot willing to die for national liberation and independence or a collaborator who worked with the Japanese and gained riches as a landlord or businessman. They therefore expected the struggle against Japanese rule to kill two birds with one stone by overthrowing the Japanese and Korean capitalists and landlords and achieving Korean independence. In their eyes, Korea needed militancy and struggle as healthy antidotes to its long history of submission to Chinese power and culture. Although the colonial government moderated the harshness of its first decade of rule, it increased the number of police and intensified surveillance. It also hoped to co-opt potential militants and convert them to the harmless pursuit of educational and cultural projects.

The movement to establish a Korean Provisional Government (KPG) in exile with a provisional national assembly began in April 1919 in Shanghai. The assembly drew up a constitution for a Great Korean People's Republic, and in 1922 it chose Rhee Syngman as president. Yi Donghwi (YI DONG-hwi), a guerrilla commander in 1907 who later joined the Communist Party in Vladivostok, became prime minister, thus combining conservative right-wing and radical left-wing elements. Yi Donghwi favored military action against Japan, while Rhee preferred diplomacy to sway the United States and other powers to intervene on behalf of Korean independence. Yi Donghwi soon left Shanghai in disgust and returned to Manchuria to resume armed struggle. Rhee went to work in the United States.

Between 1919 and 1924, about fifty Korean anarchists formed a terrorist group, the Uiyeoldan (WE-yeol-dan) (Righteous Brotherhood), which carried out at least three hundred acts of violence. After some failed assassination attempts, all three hundred members were exterminated by Japanese police. Patriot and anarchist Sin Chaeho (SHIN CHAE-ho) also founded the Anarchist Black Youth League in 1921 that dissolved three years later.

In contrast to the anarchists, Korean nationalists such as authors Yi Gwangsu, Yun Chiho, and others believed that the Korean public lacked national consciousness and needed more education before forming the basis for a viable nationalist movement. Yi's slogan, "Reconstruction!", meant just that. He and others known as "cultural nationalists" postponed national independence into the indefinite future.

The Rise of Communism

Communists and radical noncommunist nationalists claimed that cultural nationalism was nothing better than outright collaboration. Their intense nationalism arose from a new awareness of the long history of Korea's subordination to Chinese dynasties and Chinese culture, particularly to the Confucian ethical justification of tributary relations. Writers such as Sin Chaeho began a new history-writing tradition of extolling examples of militancy and resistance in the Goguryeo Dynasty and the leading military heroes of the Korean past.

Soon after the Russian Revolution of 1917, a number of Koreans living across Russia formed communist parties. Together with Yi Donghwi, Alexandra Kim formed the first Korean People's Socialist Party in Siberia. The early Korean communists were divided geographically between groups in Moscow, Siberia, Manchuria, Shanghai, and Korea proper. Inside Korea, communists supported strikes and succeeded in establishing a Korean Communist Party in 1925 before Japanese police broke it up. By 1928, Korean communists had again been forced to seek shelter outside Korea.

In the eyes of Korean nationalists, Marxist–Leninist theory that justified communism offered a powerful interpretation of their nation's plight. They were attracted to Lenin's economic explanation of the rise of imperialism as the product of monopoly capitalism, capitalism's last stage, in which core capitalist states, having saturated their domestic markets, sought colonies around the globe to provide cheap raw materials and markets for their manufactured products. This theory thus fitted Korea into a universal system of historical development. Korean communists believed that the struggle against Japan would lead simultaneously to the overthrow of capitalism and national liberation. In practical terms, the Soviet Union was the only country offering financial and spiritual support to Korean and other national liberation movements.

Establishing Communist parties meant accepting direction from the Comintern (international headquarters for communist parties) in Moscow. As it had in China, the Comintern decided that Korea was still in a "feudal" stage of development without a proletariat (working class), and it pushed the Korean communists to form a united front with bourgeois (middle class) nationalists to achieve a bourgeois-democratic revolution. Although Korean communists opposed joining class enemies in a united front, they gave in to Comintern pressure and joined the New Root Society in 1927, only a couple of months before Chiang Kaishek, the leader of the Chinese Nationalist Party, attacked his communist allies (see Chapter 24). In 1927, women organized the Friends of the Rose of Sharon, which included some socialists and cooperated with the New Root Society. This Society helped organize strikes and tenancy disputes before planning a nationwide protest demonstration after a massive anti-Japanese student protest movement broke out in Gwangju in Jeolla province in 1929; however, police arrested the leaders before it could take place. Thereafter, the headquarters turned more moderate, even deciding to support the Korean self-government movement and use the legal system to improve conditions. Dissatisfied with this weak posture, communist members called for the Society's dissolution in December 1930. The women's organization also closed down.

Manchuria

During the 1920s, the Government General of Korea encouraged Koreans to set up their own institutions to govern themselves in Manchuria. The Korean Association provided aid for the poor, public facilities such as cemeteries, public hygiene to control contagious diseases, instruction in farming methods, management of irrigation systems, education, and cultural activities. About 84 percent of the Korean population joined. It also oversaw the Financial Association that made loans to rich landlords at reasonable rates and the Mutual Aid Association that made small loans to tenant farmers. Although these organizations functioned for Japan's benefit as a colonial power, they also provided cover for their leaders to support anti-Japanese activities.

Koreans who resisted Japanese imperialism moved back and forth across national boundaries. They began in Manchuria in 1919, only to be chased into the Soviet Union's Maritime Province by Japanese forces where Korean military units joined the Soviet Red Army in battles against the Japanese army dispatched to Siberia in 1918 to attack the new Soviet regime. Confrontation ended when the Soviet Union reached a peace agreement with Japan in 1921.

After the Japanese army in Manchuria had established the puppet regime of Manchukuo, Kim Il Sung, the future leader of the Democratic People's Republic of Korea, organized a small guerrilla unit of eighteen men in northern Manchuria. Jiandao in south Manchuria just north of the Yalu River, where Koreans composed 76 percent of the population, became the center of anti-Japanese activity. In 1934, guerrilla commanders in that area led the nine hundred men of the Second Division of the Northeast People's Revolutionary Army in hundreds of engagements against Japan.

In 1934, Korean communist guerrillas faced a series of crises. Koreans fed up with radical reform created self-defense leagues against "bandits." Chinese communists in Manchuria had incorporated Korean communists in their ranks but insisted that they devote themselves to China's struggle against Japan and not dilute the effort by attacking Japanese in Korea. Accusing their Korean communist allies of being spies for Japan, they began a purge that killed anywhere from five hundred to two thousand Korean communists. The Korean patriot Kim San, sent to Manchuria to help smooth relations between Chinese and Korean communists, found himself arrested (see **Biography: Kim San, Communist Revolutionary**). Persecution continued until March 1935, when the Chinese General Wei Zhengmin called a halt. There is circumstantial evidence that Kim Il Sung (KIM IL-sung), who was fluent in Chinese and close friends with Wei, played a crucial role in persuading him to stop.

Korean exiles in China and Manchuria disagreed on the best course of action to take against Japan. Allied with different factions in China's United Front, they also had to take their hosts' interests into account. In Manchuria, Kim Il Sung had a choice between forming his own unit to operate independently or keeping his unit with Chinese communist forces. Kim chose to keep his men with a Chinese unit because it afforded a better chance of survival, even though he has been criticized for bowing to Chinese interests. On June 4, 1937, he launched the most successful guerrilla raid against the Japanese in the Korean peninsula at Bocheonbo (BO-cheon-bo), just south of the Yalu River. He occupied it for a day, retreated, defeated a pursuing Japanese police force, and a few days later joined another force to attack the Yokoyama timber camp. Although Japan followed the attack with a bloody reprisal against the town, Kim earned a reputation for daring heroism.

BIOGRAPHY   Kim San, Communist Revolutionary

Kim San (KIM SAHN) (a pseudonym for Jang Jirak (JANG GEE-rak), 1905–?) was one of many Korean patriots who became a communist to fight for Korean national liberation against Japanese imperialism. He did it by moving to China and joining the Chinese communist movement because it was easier to fight Japanese imperialism there than in Korea. In 1937 he was in Mao Zedong's base in Yan'an in northwest China when Helen Foster Snow, journalist Edgar Snow's wife, interviewed him and transcribed his life story into English.

Born to a poor farmer family in 1905 just south of Pyeongyang, seven-year-old Kim San was shocked when two Japanese policemen came to his home where they slapped and bloodied his mother's face because she had delayed reporting for a vaccination. His mother brought him up as a Christian and provided personal warmth. His father's detachment and harsh discipline turned him away from Confucianism and caused him to run away to live with a married brother nearby.

In grammar school Kim San admired the anti-Japanese guerrillas. He entered a Christian middle school but left at the age of fourteen to join the March First Movement of 1919. Amazed at the passive reaction of Christians who prayed while Japanese police massacred unarmed civilians, he abandoned Christianity, belief in God, and trust in nonviolence.

Kim San attended school in Tokyo where he met Japanese anarchists and Marxists. He left his studies there and traveled to Manchuria to attend a Korean Nationalist military school for three months. In 1920 he moved to Shanghai and then in 1921 to Beijing, where he was enrolled in the Union Medical College for more than three years. He studied Marxist theory, joined the Korean Communist Youth Organization, and then left school to join the Chinese Nationalists when the Canton uprising against foreign aggression occurred in 1925. Appalled at Chiang Kaishek's massacre of communists in Shanghai in 1927, Kim joined the communists in the Canton commune, only to be forced by the Nationalists to flee to the Hailufeng Soviet nearby in 1928. When the Nationalists surrounded it, he escaped through the mountains, where his health was ruined from exposure, malaria, and tuberculosis.

Kim San returned to Beijing to become secretary of the Beijing Communist Party. When he was sent to Manchuria in 1932 to smooth relations between Chinese and Korean communists, he was arrested and subjected to water torture for forty days. Released because he refused to confess membership in the Communist Party, he returned to Beijing only to suffer repeated impeachment by fellow Communists for leftist deviation in 1931 and rightist deviation the next year. In 1933, Chinese Nationalists held him under arrest for a brief period. After he recovered from a suicidal depression, he moved to Mao's headquarters in Yan'an in 1937. After that date, neither he nor his two wives and child were ever heard of again.

Kim San summarized his career as a revolutionary as follows:

> *My whole life has been a series of failures, and the history of my country has been a history of failure. I have had only one victory—over myself. This one small victory, however, is enough to give me confidence to go on. Fortunately, the tragedy and defeat I have experienced have not broken but strengthened me. I have few illusions left, but I have not lost faith in men and in the ability of men to create history.* [*]

Questions for Analysis

1. What motivated Kim San to devote his life to revolution?
2. What did Kim San have to give up?
3. What did Kim San achieve?

---

[*]Nym Wales, *Song of Ariran* (San Francisco: Rampart Press, 1941), p. 315.

Korea During the Asia-Pacific War

After Japan started war with China in 1937, it looked to Korea for support. The colonial government drafted Koreans for forced labor in Japanese and Manchurian mines and factories (see Material Culture: A Colonial Gold Mine), recruited young men into the Japanese army, and abducted or enticed thousands of Korean women with false promises of jobs and then forced them to become "comfort women" (prostitutes) for Japanese troops in active theaters of operations in China, Manchuria,

Sajinuro ponun Choson sidae: Cho P'ung-yong haesol (The Choson Period in Pictures: Life and Customs), volume 2, p. 120. © Cengage Learning 2014

Comfort Women. Korean comfort women photographed in China at the end of the war. Note that the woman on the right is pregnant.

the South Sea islands, and Southeast Asia. Some young Korean men took to the hills to evade forced labor and military conscription (PARK JUNG-he), but most were trapped. Then there was Park Chunghee, the dictator of South Korea from 1961 to 1979, who graduated from a military academy in Japan and became an officer in the Japanese army in Manchuria to do battle against opponents of Japanese colonialism, including Korean guerrillas. Once Japan's industrial base became the target of bombs toward the end of the war, Japan started building more factories in Manchuria and northern Korea. Korean manufacturers took advantage of Japan's need for supplies to earn handsome profits and the ire of their compatriots.

Koreans who continued the struggle for independence had to move outside of Japanese-controlled territories. Kim Il Sung fought skirmishes in Manchuria against Japan between 1937 and 1940 until Japan eliminated the Chinese communist armies in Manchuria and forced him to cross into Russian territory. Kim's men joined Chinese guerrillas in a Russian training camp near Vladivostok, and Kim was appointed major in the new 88th Division of the Far Eastern Command of the Soviet army. Some Korean communists in China commanded the Korean Volunteer Corps while others enrolled in Chinese units under Mao Zedong in Yan'an. Noncommunist nationalists such as Kim Gu fought with Chinese Nationalist forces. An Changho organized the Corps for Promoting Scholars in Los Angeles in 1911 and joined the Korean Provisional Government in Shanghai where he was arrested in 1932 and sent to jail in Korea. Rhee Syngman spent two decades in the United States trying to gain support for Korean liberation. In the end, neither communists nor non-communists succeeded in obtaining Korea's independence, nor did they agree on how to shape Korea's future.

MATERIAL CULTURE

A Colonial Gold Mine

In the name of industrialization, Japan opened mines in Korea and Manchuria to provide raw materials for factories. Rather than use machinery or develop new, initially more expensive techniques, Japan relied on labor intensification—pickaxes, not bulldozers; manpower, not trucks. This photograph shows the labor hierarchy, with workers scraping at the soil or carrying rocks on their backs, a foreman giving directions, and, standing on the bank above, a manager in a Western-style hat. The only sign of mechanization is the cogwheel behind him. The Korean laborers received lower wages than those paid to Japanese, even when they did the same type of work. Conditions were so harsh that many Koreans went into hiding or took refuge in the hills to avoid being drafted to work in mines.

Courtesy, Somundang Publishing Company, Seoul. © Cengage Learning 2014

Korean Miners. Korean miners mobilized by Japan during the 1930s for mining alluvial gold in South Jeolla province.

SUMMARY

"Korea is like a minnow caught between two whales" is a common way to phrase Korea's options in modern times. Whether the mainland whale was seen as China before 1895 or Russia thereafter, Japan swallowed Korea in 1910. In the meantime, the king and his government tried to placate the whales while urban intellectuals, male and female, many educated abroad, began the creation of a modern civil society characterized by multiple organizations—including new schools that taught Korean instead of Chinese history—and proposals to mold Korea's future into one of equality and rationality.

Historians looking back at Japan's takeover of Korea sometimes see an unstoppable march toward total control that obscures the twists and turns in Japan's actions. The protectorate created after the Russo-Japanese War envisioned an independent Korea guided by Japan. When Koreans demonstrated their dislike of Japan's interference, Japan responded first with harsh measures under a police state, then with "cultural" policy that allowed Koreans a degree of freedom in their personal lives, and then after the Fifteen Year War began in 1931, with brutal exploitation.

Following its suppression of the March 1, 1919, movement, Japan opened the door to economic, social, and cultural liberalization. It rationalized landownership and allowed large Japanese conglomerates to dominate heavy industry. Some Korean businessmen made fortunes in textiles and light industry while owners of small-scale businesses lived a more precarious existence.

Japan claimed to be bringing modern education to the mass of Koreans, but not at the same level that modern education achieved in Japan. Educated women began to work outside the home, publish in magazines, and speak publicly on women's issues. Modern Korean literature and film developed despite colonial censorship; even the radio stations under Japanese control broadcast items of interest to ordinary Koreans and promoted a consumer culture.

Japan's colonization of Korea sparked the rise of militant nationalism. Activists sought answers to the question of how Korea had allowed itself to be colonized that would lead to Korean independence. They disagreed on tactics and policy, some fleeing to the United States to garner support for Korea, others arming themselves first in Manchuria and then in the Soviet Union and China to overthrow both Japanese rule and the capitalist system that supported it.

What were the effects of Japanese colonial rule on Korea? By allowing Korean landlords and businessmen to flourish, it established models for successful enterprises. By breaking down hereditary status barriers, it opened opportunities to people previously blocked from upward mobility. By introducing modern education, it allowed some Koreans to study science, foreign languages, and social science, and it enabled the birth of modern mass culture. It also forced the migration of millions of Koreans to Japanese factories and mines across the Japanese empire. It eliminated meaningful participation in the political process. It encouraged a growing economic gap between capitalist industrialists and wealthy landlords versus a new working class and a mass of sharecropping tenants. In short, Japanese colonialism produced wealth and poverty, acceptance and hatred, revolutionary potential and conservative reaction. As we will see in Chapter 28, these divisions heightened by animosity between the Soviet Union and the United States, would tear Korea apart after the war.

Remaking China (1900–1927)

The first decade of the twentieth century was a period of rapid change in China, especially in cities and among the educated. Chinese cities were being paved, lighted, and policed. The Qing court announced plans for gradual transition to a constitutional monarchy. Voluntary reform societies tackled problems like foot binding and opium smoking. Then, in 1911, the Qing Dynasty was overthrown. Although the dynasty handed over its armies to the republican government under Yuan Shikai (ywan shih-ky), military unity was soon lost, and regional armies and warlords competed to secure bases. In the 1920s, the Nationalist Party under Sun Yatsen built a base in Guangdong, and in 1926 launched the Northern Expedition, which reunified the country.

Nationalism was central to much of the cultural activity of this period. Patriots wanted to reconstitute China as a nation of the Chinese people and make it strong enough to stand up to foreign threats. A new type of intellectual emerged: trained at modern universities or abroad, deeply concerned with China's fate, and attracted to Western ideas ranging from science and democracy to anarchism and communism. Young people attacked old social norms, especially filial piety and arranged marriages. The encounters between new and old and East and West stimulated a literary and scholarly renaissance.

Understanding these changes has been the central goal of most of the research on this period. Who led the way in the changes to the Chinese economy, education, and political organization? How was resistance to change overcome? What role did foreign countries play? Did the militarization of society slow down or speed up other changes? Which changes were felt even by farmers in the countryside?

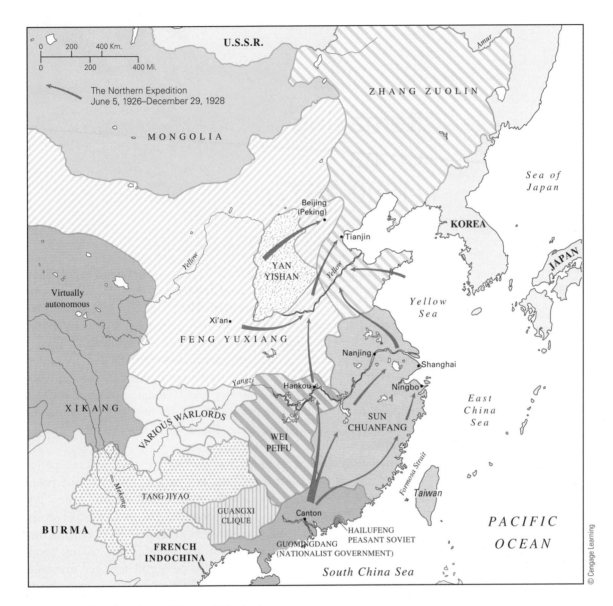

Map 24.1   Northern Expedition and Warlords

THE END OF MONARCHY

As the twentieth century opened, the Qing Dynasty needed to regain the people's confidence after the debacle brought on by its support of the Boxers and the imperialists' subsequent intervention. It faced a fiscal crisis. The Boxer Protocol of 1901 imposed a staggering indemnity of 450 million silver dollars, twice as large as the one exacted by Japan a few years earlier and nearly twice the government's annual revenues. It was to be paid from customs revenue in thirty-nine annual installments, with interest. When interest on existing foreign loans was added, the debts absorbed all of the customs revenue. Little was left for the ordinary operation of the government, much less investment in modernization.

Local Activism

Forced to look after their own interests, local elites increasingly took on modernization projects. They set up new schools and started periodicals, which by one estimate increased tenfold from 1901 to 1910.

Interest in Western forms of government was growing as people asked how the European powers and Japan had gained wealth and power. Yan Fu (yen foo), one of the first to study in England, published translations of books such as J. S. Mill's *On Liberty* (1903) and Montesquieu's *The Spirit of Laws* (1909). Yan Fu argued that the Western form of government freed the energy of the individual, which could then be channeled toward national goals. As he saw it, the West had achieved wealth and power through a complex package, a key part of which was a very differently conceived nation-state. Yan Fu once commented that only 30 percent of China's troubles were caused by foreigners; the rest were its own fault and could be remedied by its own actions.

Interest in Western forms of government did not translate into positive feelings toward the Western powers, which were seen as gaining a stranglehold on the Chinese economy. Activists solicited funds to buy back railroads built by foreign firms. Between 1905 and 1907, there were boycotts of the United States for its immigration restriction law and its mistreatment of Chinese at the 1904 World's Fair in Saint Louis. In treaty ports, protests were staged over Westerners' extraterritoriality. Some protesters even talked of waging their own opium war after the British refused to stop shipping opium to China on the grounds that opium cultivation in China had not been fully eradicated.

During this period, Japan served as an incubator of Chinese nationalism. By 1906, of the thirteen thousand students studying abroad, ten thousand were in Tokyo. The experience of living in a foreign country, where they felt humiliated by China's weakness and backwardness, aroused nationalistic feelings in the students, who often formed groups to discuss how Japan had modernized so rapidly and what could be done in China. One student newspaper reported, "Japanese schools are as numerous as our opium dens, Japanese students as numerous as our opium addicts."[*] The two best-known reformers, Kang Youwei and Liang Qichao, had settled in Japan. In Chinese magazines published in Japan, Liang promoted the idea that China could become strong through "democracy," which to him meant a government that drew its strength from the people, but not necessarily a representative government or one that defended individual rights. Liang had traveled in the United States for five months in 1903 and found the American form of populist democracy unsatisfactory. He preferred the statist ideas and constitutional monarchies of Japan and Germany. When Japan defeated Russia in 1905 (see Chapter 22), some reformers drew the inference that Japan's constitutional form of government had enabled it to best autocratic Russia.

The Anti-Manchu Revolutionary Movement

Ever since the late nineteenth century, some people had argued that the root of China's problems lay in its subjugation by a different "race": the Manchus. In 1903 the nineteen-year-old Zou Rong published an inflammatory tract calling for the creation of a revolutionary army to "wipe out the five million barbarian Manchus, wash away the shame of two hundred and sixty years of cruelty and oppression, and make China clean once again."[†] He described the "sacred Han race, descendants of the Yellow Emperor," as the slaves of the Manchus and in danger of extermination. The language of Social Darwinism, with its talk of countries in desperate competition for survival, seemed to many to describe China's plight accurately.

The anti-Manchu revolutionary who would eventually be mythologized as the founding figure of the Chinese republic was Sun Yatsen (Sun Zhongshan, soon juhng-shahn) (1866–1925). Like Hong Xiuquan, Kang Youwei, and Liang Qichao before him, Sun came from Guangdong province. Unlike them, he was neither from a literati family nor trained in the Confucian classics. Several of his close relatives had emigrated, and in 1879 he was sent to join a brother in Hawaii. Later he went to Hong Kong to study Western medicine, completing his degree in 1892. In Hong Kong, Sun and his friends began discussing the advantages of a republic. The best way to overthrow the Manchus, they concluded, would be to ally with the secret societies so pervasive in south China. Groups like the Triads were anti-Manchu, had large mass followings, and had an organizational base reaching from one province to another, making them an ideal base for an insurrection, they thought.

[*]Cited in Douglas R. Reynolds, *China, 1898–1912: The Xinzheng Revolution and Japan* (Cambridge, Mass.: Harvard University Press, 1993), p. 62.

[†]Cited in Michael Gasster, "The Republican Revolutionary Movement," in *Cambridge History of China*, vol. 11, pt. 2 (Cambridge: Cambridge University Press, 1980), p. 482.

Sun set up the first two chapters of the Revive China Society in Hawaii and Hong Kong. The society's efforts to instigate an uprising with secret society members as the muscle never got very far, however. In 1896, Sun cut off his queue and began wearing Western clothes. He spent time in England, where he discovered that many Westerners saw flaws in their own institutions and were advocating a variety of socialist solutions. Sun began to think that China could skip ahead of the West by going directly to a more progressive form of government. In Japan in 1905 some Japanese helped Sun join forces with the more radical of the student revolutionaries to form the Revolutionary Alliance. Despite the difference in social background, the students from educated families were excited by Sun's promise of quick solutions to China's problems. This alliance sponsored seven or eight attempts at uprisings over the next few years. Sun himself continued to spend most of his time abroad in search of funds and foreign backers, especially overseas Chinese.

In these years Sun worked out his theory of the Three People's Principles: nationalism (which opposed both rule by Manchus and domination by foreign powers), democracy (which to Sun meant elections and a constitution), and the "people's livelihood," a vague sort of socialism with equalization of landholdings and curbs on capital. Sun admitted that the Chinese people were unaccustomed to political participation; nevertheless, he believed that they could be guided toward democracy through a period of political tutelage, during which the revolutionaries would promulgate a provisional constitution and people would begin electing local officials.

The Manchu Reform Movement

Amid all this activism and agitation, the Manchu court began to edge in the direction of parliamentary government. Empress Dowager Cixi in 1901 announced the establishment of a national school system and called for putting questions about foreign government and science on the civil service examinations. In 1905 she took the momentous step of abolishing the civil service examination system altogether, a system that had set the framework for relations between the government and the elite for a millennium. New military academies were set up and new armies formed, trained by German or Japanese instructors. With the death of Li Hongzhang in 1901, Yuan Shikai emerged as the most powerful general, serving as both commander of the Northern Army and head of the Baoding Military Academy.

In 1905, Cixi approved sending a mission abroad to study constitutional forms of government. On its return the next year, the commission recommended the Japanese model, which retained the monarchy and had it bestow the constitution on the country (rather than a constitution that made the people sovereign). In 1907 plans for national and provincial assemblies were announced, with a full constitution to be in place by 1917. The next year, the seventy-three-year-old Cixi died (the thirty-three-year-old Guangxu emperor had died suspiciously the day before). She had arranged for a three-year-old to succeed her. His regents did not prove to be particularly effective leaders and soon dismissed Yuan Shikai. Hope for a Japanese-style constitutional monarchy looked less and less promising.

Still, in 1909 assemblies met in each province and sent representatives to Beijing. Although less than 1 percent of the population had been allowed to vote, the elections generated excitement about participatory government. The provincial assemblies circulated three petitions calling for the immediate convening of the national assembly, the last reportedly signed by 25 million people. In 1910 the provisional national assembly met, with one hundred members elected by the provincial assemblies and one hundred appointed by the court. Anti-Manchu feelings rose, however, when in May 1911 the court announced the formation of a cabinet with eight Manchu, one Mongol, and only four Chinese members.

The 1911 Revolution

The Manchu court's efforts to institute reform from above satisfied very few, and in October 1911 a plot by revolutionaries finally triggered the collapse of the Qing Dynasty. In the city of Wuchang (woo-chahng) on the Yangzi River, a bomb accidentally exploded in the headquarters of a revolutionary group. When the police came to investigate, they found lists of the revolutionaries, including many officers of the new army division located there. Once the police set out to arrest those listed, the army officers, facing certain execution, staged a coup. The local officials fled, and the army took over the city in less than a day. The revolutionaries then telegraphed the other provinces asking them to declare their independence. Within six weeks, fifteen provinces had seceded.

Cutting Off a Queue. After the success of the 1911 revolution, soldiers often forced men to cut off their queues.

Roger-Viollet/Getty Images

THE PRESIDENCY OF YUAN SHIKAI AND THE EMERGENCE OF THE WARLORDS

Yuan Shikai had strong credentials as a reformer of the old, self-strengthening type. While governor, he had initiated reforms in education, commerce, and industry, and his army not only was equipped with modern weapons but also was trained along lines established by German and Japanese advisers. He believed in careful central planning of the sort Germany and Japan had shown could be effective. He was committed to a strong China but not a republican one. If local or provincial assemblies were empowered to act as they liked, how could China move rapidly toward a modern nation-state?

Yuan did not prevent parliamentary elections from being held in 1913. However, when Sun Yat-sen's new Nationalist Party won a plurality of the seats, Yuan was unwilling to accept the outcome. The key Nationalist organizer, Song Jiaoren (sung jyow-run), was soon assassinated, and the shocked public assumed Yuan was responsible. Then Yuan, without consulting the national assembly, negotiated a $100 million loan from a foreign consortium. By summer the Nationalist Party was organizing open revolt against Yuan, and seven provincial governments declared their independence. This second revolution ended in military rout, and Sun Yatsen and other Nationalist leaders once more fled to Japan. Yuan outlawed the Nationalist Party; in 1914 he abolished all assemblies down to the county level, trying to nip participatory democracy in the bud.

Yuan did undertake some progressive projects, extending elementary education, suppressing opium cultivation, and promoting judicial reform. But he was out of touch with the mood of younger people, especially when he announced that Confucianism would be made the state religion. When in August 1915 he announced that he would become emperor, the educated and politically aware elite were outraged, their protests dying down only after Yuan died unexpectedly in June 1916.

During the decade after Yuan Shikai's death, China was politically fragmented. Without a central strongman, commanders in Yuan's old army, governors of provinces, and even gangsters built their own power bases. The outer regions of the Qing Empire, such as Tibet and Mongolia, declared their independence. Tibet soon fell under British sway and Mongolia under Russian. Manchuria was more and more dominated

The Qing court did not immediately capitulate. In desperation it turned to Yuan Shikai, whom the court had dismissed only a few years before, and asked him to mount a military campaign against the revolutionaries. Yuan went back and forth between the court and the revolutionaries, seeing what he could get from each. The biggest fear of the revolutionaries was foreign intervention; to avoid that, they were willing to compromise. In the end, agreement was reached to establish a republic with Yuan as president; the emperor would abdicate, but he and his entourage would be allowed to remain in the Forbidden City, receive generous allowances, and keep much of their property. Thus, unlike the Bourbons in France or the Romanovs in Russia, the Manchu royal family suffered neither executions nor humiliations when it was deposed.

In February 1912, the last Qing emperor abdicated, and in March Yuan Shikai took over as president. As a mark of solidarity with the revolutionaries, men cut off their queues, the symbol of their subordination to the Manchus.

by Japan. In the far south, Sun Yatsen and his allies tried to build a power base for the Nationalist revolutionaries. A government of sorts was maintained in Beijing under the domination of whichever warlord held the region. It was hardly stable, however, with six different presidents and twenty-five successive cabinets. For a while, the key struggle seemed to be for control of the north, as the strongest warlords waged highly destructive wars across north China.

Warlords, not surprisingly, did little to maintain infrastructure or advance modernization. They disrupted rail lines and allowed the dikes on the Yellow River to deteriorate, leading to some catastrophic floods. They caused havoc in the countryside because the armies lived off the land, looting wherever they moved. One warlord reported, "My men would surround a village before dawn and fire several shots to intimidate the people. We told them to come out and give up. This was the classic way of raiding a village. Sometimes we killed and carried away little pigs.... We took corn, rice, potatoes, taro."[*] Because they also needed money to buy weapons, warlords instituted all sorts of new taxes. Foreign countries were more than willing to sell modern arms to the warlords, often backing their own favorite contender. Opium cultivation had been nearly eradicated in many places until the warlords entered the scene and forced peasants to grow it as a revenue source.

TOWARD A MORE MODERN CHINA

Social, cultural, and political change was rapid in the early decades of the twentieth century, some of it flowing directly from the pens of those advocating change of many sorts, some of it the direct or indirect consequence of changes in China's economy and political situation. Even forms of entertainment changed (see **Material Culture: Shanghai's Great World Pleasure Palace**).

The New Culture Movement

Young people who received a modern education felt that they had inherited the obligation of the literati to advise those in power. Their modern education, they believed, uniquely qualified them to "save" China. They had expected much of the 1911 revolution, only to have their hopes dashed.

The newly reorganized Beijing University played a central role in this New Culture movement. Chen Duxiu, the founder of the periodical *New Youth*, was appointed dean of letters. Chen had received a traditional education and had taken the civil service examinations before studying in Japan and France. A participant in the 1911 revolution, he became a zealous advocate of individual freedom. In the first issue of *New Youth* in 1915, Chen challenged the long-standing Confucian value of deference toward elders. Youth, he asserted, was worth celebrating: "Youth is like early spring, like the rising sun, like the trees and grass in bud, like a newly sharpened blade." He urged his readers not to waste their "fleeting time in arguing with the older generation on this and that, hoping for them to be reborn and remodeled." They should think for themselves and not let the old contaminate them. In other articles, he wrote that Confucianism had to be rejected before China could attain equality and human rights: "We must be thoroughly aware of the incompatibility between Confucianism and the new belief, the new society, and the new state."[†] To him, "loyalty, filial piety, chastity, and righteousness" were nothing but "a slavish morality."[‡] Young people responded enthusiastically to his attack on filial piety and began challenging the authority of their parents to make decisions for them about school, work, and marriage. Conflict between parents and their marriage-age children became extremely common as the young insisted on choosing their own spouses.

Soon leaders of the New Culture movement proposed ending use of the classical literary language that had been the mark of the educated person for two thousand years. The leader of the movement to write in the vernacular was Hu Shi (hoo shih), appointed to the faculty of Beijing University by Chen Duxiu (chuhn doo-shyow) after he returned from seven years studying philosophy in the United States. "A dead language," Hu declared, "can never produce a living literature."[§] Because Chinese civilization

---

[*]Cited in James E. Sheridan, *China in Disintegration* (New York: Free Press, 1975), p. 91.

[†]Cited in Chow Tse-tsung, *The May Fourth Movement: Intellectual Revolution in Modern China* (Stanford: Stanford University Press, 1960), p. 482.
[‡]Ssu-yu Teng and John K. Fairbank, *China's Response to the West: A Documentary Survey* (New York: Atheneum, 1971), p. 241.
[§]Cited in Leo Ou-fan Lee, "Literary Trends I: The Quest for Modernity, 1895–1927," in *Cambridge History of China*, vol. 12, ed. John K. Fairbank (Cambridge: Cambridge University Press, 1983), p. 467.

MATERIAL CULTURE

Shanghai's Great World Pleasure Palace

Commonplaces of modern life such as malls and window shopping were once new and controversial. In China, they usually appeared first in Shanghai. In 1917 an entrepreneur who had made his fortune in medicine built the Great World, a six-story amusement park touted as the Crystal Palace and Coney Island rolled into one. At the intersection of two major roads in the International District, from the outside it seemed an agglomeration of European building motifs with columns holding up a decorative tower. Inside, it catered more to Chinese tastes, and its customers were primarily Chinese. On the first floor were gaming tables, slot machines, magicians, acrobats, and sing-song girls, with fans, incense, fireworks, and other miscellaneous things for sale. On the next floor were restaurants as well as acting troupes, midwives, barbers, and earwax extractors. The third floor had photographers, jugglers, ice cream parlors, and girls in high-slit dresses. The fourth floor had masseurs, acupuncturists, and dancers. The fifth floor had storytellers, peep shows, scribes who composed love letters, and a temple. On the top floor were tightrope walkers, places to play mahjong, lottery tickets, and marriage brokers.

Great World Pleasure Palace. The building is seen here in a postcard from the 1920s (*"Great World Entertainment Centre, 1941," postcard, by An Lan. Chromolithograph on paper, Collection of the Shanghai History Museum*)

had been so closely tied to this language, Hu's assertions came dangerously close to declaring Chinese civilization dead. Hu Shi did recognize that the old written language had allowed speakers of mutually unintelligible dialects to communicate with each other and thus had been a source of unity. However, he argued that once a national literature was produced in vernacular Chinese, a standard dialect would establish itself, much as standard vernaculars had gained hold in France and Germany. Chen Duxiu concurred with Hu, and soon *New Youth* was written entirely in vernacular Chinese.

One of the first to write well in the vernacular was Lu Xun (loo shyun) (1881–1936). In 1902, Lu had gone to Japan to study medicine after traditional doctors had failed to cure his father of tuberculosis. He gave up medicine, however, after watching a newsreel of the Russo-Japanese War that showed a group of Chinese watching apathetically as Japanese in Manchuria executed a Chinese accused of spying for the Russians. From this Lu Xun concluded that it was more important to change the spirit of the Chinese than to protect their bodies. He began reading widely in European literature, especially Russian. The May 1918 issue of *New Youth* contained his first vernacular short story, "Diary of a Madman." In it the main character goes mad (or is taken to be mad) after he discovers that what his elders saw as lofty values was nothing more than cannibalism. The protagonist of his longest story, "The True Story of Ah Q," is a man of low social standing. Always on the lookout for a way to get ahead, he is too cowardly and self-deceiving ever to succeed. No matter how he is humiliated, he claims moral superiority. His ears prick up in 1911 when he hears talk of a revolution, but soon he discovers that the old, classically educated elite and the new, foreign-educated elite are collaborating to take over the revolution for themselves and want him to stay away. In the end, he is executed by representatives of the revolution for a robbery he would have liked to have committed but actually had not managed to pull off. In stories like these, Lu Xun gave voice to those troubled by China's prospects and weary of China's old order but wary of promises of easy solutions. Lu Xun put the blame for China's plight on China's own flaws much more than on the flaws of foreigners. (See **Documents: Lu Xun's "Sudden Notions."**)

By 1919 *New Youth* had been joined by many other periodicals aimed at young people aspiring for a New China. Magazines were filled with articles on Western ideas of all sorts, including socialism, anarchism, democracy, liberalism, Darwinism, pragmatism, and science. The key goals were enlightenment and national survival. The movement to write in the vernacular caught on quickly. In 1921 the Ministry of Education decided that henceforth elementary school textbooks would be written in the vernacular.

Industrial Development

Despite the political and cultural turmoil of the first two decades of the twentieth century, a modern economy began to take off in China. China had opened some modern enterprises as early as 1872, when Li Hongzhang had started the China Merchant Steamship Navigation Company; however, those were government-supervised and -supported ventures, not true capitalist ones. In 1895, Japan won the right to open factories in China. Other imperialist powers leaped at the chance to set up factories as well because labor costs in China were very low by international standards. By the eve of World War I, China had an emerging bourgeoisie made up of merchants, bankers, industrialists, compradors working for foreign firms, and overseas Chinese engaged in import–export. Foreign investment grew rapidly, with big increases especially in Japanese investment. In the first decade of the century, more and more chambers of commerce had been established in cities large and small, giving this bourgeoisie more of a voice in politics. With the deterioration of the national government after 1915, often the chambers of commerce took over running cities, seeing to sanitation, education, and police. Many of those who returned from study abroad took jobs in modern enterprises, where their foreign degrees brought prestige and often higher salaries. (See **Biography: Sophia Chen and H. C. Zen, a Modern Couple.**)

Commercial Press Pay Scale by College, 1912–1927 (yuan per month)	
Chinese college	80
Japanese college	100–120
Japanese imperial college	150
Western college	200
Harvard, Yale, Oxford, Cambridge	250

World War I gave China's businesses and industries a chance to flourish. Britain, France, Germany, and Russia were preoccupied with what was happening in Europe and no longer had spare goods to export. Imports from the West thus dropped dramatically, giving Chinese manufacturers a chance to sell more profitably. At the same time, the demand for products from China increased, helping China's export industries. The number of Chinese textile mills increased from 22 in 1911 to 109 in 1921. Tonnage of coal produced grew from 13 million tons to 20 million tons between 1913 and 1919. Modern banking took off: between 1912 and 1923, the number of modern banks soared from 7 to 131. Telephone and electric companies were formed not

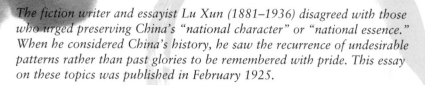

DOCUMENTS
Lu Xun's "Sudden Notions"

The fiction writer and essayist Lu Xun (1881–1936) disagreed with those who urged preserving China's "national character" or "national essence." When he considered China's history, he saw the recurrence of undesirable patterns rather than past glories to be remembered with pride. This essay on these topics was published in February 1925.

I used to believe the statements that the twenty-four dynastic histories were simply "records of mutual slaughter" or "family histories of rulers." Later, when I read them for myself, I realized this was a fallacy.

All these histories portray the soul of China and indicate what the country's future will be, but the truth is buried so deep in flowery phrases and nonsense it is very hard to grasp it; just as, when the moon shines through thick foliage onto moss, only checkered shadows can be seen. If we read unofficial records and anecdotes, though, we can understand more easily, for here at least the writers did not have to put on the airs of official historians.

The Qin and Han Dynasties are too far from us and too different to be worth discussing. Few records were written in the Yuan Dynasty. But most of the annals of the Tang, Song, and Ming Dynasties have come down to us. And if we compare the events recorded during the Five Dynasties period or the Southern Song Dynasty and the end of the Ming Dynasty with modern conditions, it is amazing how alike they are. It seems as if China alone is untouched by the passage of time. The Chinese Republic today is still the China of those earlier ages.

If we compare our era with the end of the Ming Dynasty, our China is not so corrupt, disrupted, cruel or despotic—we have not yet reached the limit.

But neither did the corruption and disruption of the last years of the Ming Dynasty reach the limit, for Li Zicheng and Zhang Xianzhong rebelled. And neither did their cruelty and despotism reach the limit, for the Manchu troops entered China.

Can it be that "national character" is so difficult to change? If so, we can more or less guess what our fate will be. As is so often said, "It will be the same old story."

Luckily no one can say for certain that the national character will never change. And though this uncertainty means that we face the threat of annihilation—something we have never experienced—we can also hope for a national revival, which is equally unprecedented. This may be of some comfort to reformers.

But even this slight comfort may be cancelled by the pens of those who boast of the ancient culture, drowned by the words of those who slander the modern culture, or wiped out by the deeds of those who pose as exponents of the modern culture. For "it will be the same old story."

Actually, all these men belong to one type: they are all clever people, who know that even if China collapses they will not suffer, for they can always adapt themselves to circumstances. If anybody doubts this let him read the essays in praise of the Manchus' military prowess written in the Qing Dynasty by Chinese, and filled with such terms as "our great forces" and "our army." Who could imagine that this was the army that had conquered us? One would be led to suppose that the Chinese had marched to wipe out some corrupt barbarians.

But since such men always come out on top, presumably they will never die out. In China, they are the best fitted to survive; and, so long as they survive, China will never cease having repetitions of her former fate.

"Vast territory, abundant resources, and a great population"—with such excellent material, are we able only to go round and round in circles?

Questions for Analysis
1. Which features of China's past did Lu Xun think persisted to his day?
2. Why does Lu Xun think clever people have a better chance of surviving?

Source: From *Lu Xun: Selected Works* translated by Yang Xianyi and Gladys Yang. Copyright ©1980 by Foreign Languages Press. Reprinted with permission of Cypress Book (US) Co.

BIOGRAPHY

Sophia Chen and H. C. Zen, a Modern Couple

The first generation to return to China from study abroad found many opportunities to put its new skills to work. Although many of its members returned to marry spouses their families had selected for them, others, like Sophia Chen (1890–1976) and H. C. Zen (1886–1961), found their own marriage partners while abroad.

H. C. Zen was the English name taken by Ren Hongjun (run hung-jyun). He was born into an educated family in Sichuan and in 1904 graduated from a modern middle school, then took the first stage of civil service examinations. After the exam system was abolished the next year, he left China to study at a technical college in Tokyo, where he joined Sun Yatsen's Revolutionary Alliance. When the revolution broke out in 1911, he returned to China and at age twenty-five was made secretary to the president. Disagreeing with Sun's successor, Yuan Shikai, he resigned and went to the United States to study chemistry at Cornell and Columbia (1912–1917), finishing with a master's degree. While there, he became friends with Hu Shi and courted Chen Hengzhe (chuhn heng-juh), who was studying at Vassar. She took the English name Sophia Chen. While still in China, Zen also helped found the Science Society of China, an organization that sponsored scientific monographs and translations, lectures, and exhibitions. He served as its president from 1914 to 1923.

Sophia Chen, from an official family in Jiangsu, had experienced more difficulty getting satisfactory schooling in China, either being tutored at home or studying in mediocre schools. In her teens, she convinced her father to withdraw from a marriage arrangement he had made for her so that she could continue her studies. In 1914 at age twenty-four, she was selected to study in the United States in the examinations held for Boxer Indemnity Fund scholarships. She studied history at Vassar, then went on for a master's degree at the University of Chicago in 1920.

That year she returned to China and became the first woman to be offered a professorship at Peking University. The same year, she and H. C. Zen married.

Since he had returned to China in 1917, Zen had held posts at Peking University and the Ministry of Education. When he became editor of the Commercial Press in 1922, the family moved to Shanghai. Two years later, they moved to Nanjing, where Zen became vice chancellor of Nanjing University and Chen taught Western history. Chen did not continue teaching after 1925, however, deciding to concentrate instead on writing. Her *History of the West* went through many printings. She also edited the *Independent Critic*, a liberal journal that she co-founded and that flourished in the 1930s. Both she and her husband wrote pieces for it. Most of Zen's time, however, was taken up with a series of prominent posts. From 1935 to 1937 he was head of the National Sichuan University.

After the Japanese invasion, the family moved to Kunming, where Zen, as the secretary general of the Academic Sinica and director of its Institute of Chemistry, tried to keep scientific research going under difficult circumstances. After a few years, they moved to Chongqing, where Zen took up other posts.

Both Chen and Zen made return trips to the United States. Chen attended several international conferences and after a meeting in Canada in 1933 traveled in the United States, which she found much changed since the advent of the automobile age. Zen visited the United States after the war in 1946–1947.

After 1949, both Zen and Chen, nearing retirement age, stayed in China, living in Shanghai. Of their three children, two settled in the United States and one stayed in China.

Questions for Analysis
1. How were the lives of Chen and Zen shaped by the period in which they lived?
2. What difference did it make that Chen and Zen had studied abroad?

---

only in major cities but also in county seats and even in market towns. New fortunes were made. For instance, the Rong brothers, from a family of merchants in Wuxi (woo-shee), built a flour mill in 1901 and another in 1913. As opportunities opened

up, they built eight new factories between 1914 and 1920, expanding into textiles.

Industrialization had its predictable costs as well. Conditions in China's factories in the 1910s were as bad as they had been a century earlier in Britain, with twelve-hour days, seven-day weeks, and widespread child labor, especially in textile mills. Labor contractors often recruited in the countryside and kept laborers in conditions of debt slavery, providing the most minimal housing and food. That many of the factories were foreign owned (increasingly Japanese owned) added to management–labor friction.

The May Fourth Incident

In 1914, Japan as an ally of Britain and France seized German territories in China. In 1915, when the European powers were preoccupied with their war, Japan took steps to strengthen its hand in China. It presented Yuan Shikai's government with the Twenty-One Demands, most of which entailed economic privileges in various regions of China. Others confirmed Japan's position in the former German leasehold in Shandong. The fifth group of demands would have made China, in effect, a protectorate of Japan by requiring that Japanese advisers be attached to key organs of the Chinese government, even the police. When a wave of anti-Japanese protests swept China, Japan dropped the last group but gave Yuan an ultimatum to accept the rest. The day he did, May 7, was in later years called National Humiliation Day.

In 1917, the Republic of China joined the allied war effort, and although China sent no combatants, it did send some 140,000 laborers to France, where they unloaded cargo ships, dug trenches, and otherwise provided manpower of direct use to the war effort. China was thus expecting some gain from the Allies' victory, particularly in light of the stress placed on national self-determination by the U.S. president, Woodrow Wilson. Unfortunately for China, Japan had reached secret agreements with Britain, France, and Italy to support Japan's claim to German rights in Shandong. Japanese diplomats had also won the consent of the warlord government that held Beijing in 1918. At Versailles the Chinese representatives were not even admitted, while those from Japan were seated at the table with the Western powers.

On May 4, 1919, when word arrived that the decision had gone in favor of Japan, there was an explosion of popular protest. Some three thousand Beijing students assembled at Tiananmen Square in front of the old palace shouting patriotic slogans and trying to arouse spectators to action. After some students broke through police lines to beat up a pro-Japanese official and set fire to the home

Beixin Book Company, Beijing, 1926/Cultural Relics Press

Cover of Lu Xun's *Hometown*. In addition to writing fiction and essays, Lu Xun promoted new forms of art, particularly woodblock printing. He chose a strikingly modern design for the cover of this 1921 novel.

of a cabinet minister, the governor cracked down on the demonstrators and arrested their leaders. These actions set off a wave of protests around the country in support of the students and their cause. Everyone, it seemed, was on the students' side: teachers, workers, the press, the merchants, Sun Yatsen, and the warlords. Japanese goods were boycotted. Soon strikes closed schools in more than two hundred cities. The Beijing warlord government finally arrested 1,150 student protesters, turning parts of Beijing University into a jail. However, patriotic sympathy strikes, especially in Shanghai, soon forced the government to release them. The cabinet fell, and China refused to sign the Versailles Treaty. The students were ebullient.

The protesters' moral victory set the tone for cultural politics through the 1920s and into the 1930s. The personal and intellectual goals of the New Culture movement were pursued along with, and sometimes in competition with, the national power goals of the May Fourth movement.

Nationalism, patriotism, progress, science, democracy, and freedom were the goals; imperialism, feudalism, warlordism, autocracy, patriarchy, and blind adherence to tradition were the evils to be opposed. Intellectuals struggled with how to be strong and modern but still Chinese. Some concentrated on the creation of a new literature in the vernacular, others on the study of Western science, philosophy, and social and political thought. Among the prominent intellectuals from the West invited to visit China to lecture were Bertrand Russell (in 1920 and 1921), Albert Einstein (in 1922), and Margaret Sanger (in 1922). When the educational reformer John Dewey visited between 1919 and 1921, he was impressed. "There seems to be no country in the world," he commented, "where students are so unanimously and eagerly interested in what is modern and new in thought, especially about social and economic matters, nor where the arguments which can be brought in favor of the established order and the status quo have so little weight—indeed are so unuttered."[*]

Not all intellectuals saw salvation in modern Western culture. Some who for a while had been attracted to things Western came to feel that Western culture was too materialistic. Fear that China was in danger of losing its "national essence" was raised. Liang Qichao, by now a conservative, saw more to admire in China's humanistic culture than in the West's rationalism and hedonism and worried about the threat to China's national character.

The Women's Movement

All the major political and intellectual revolutionaries of the early twentieth century, from Kang Youwei and Liang Qichao to Sun Yatsen, Chen Duxiu, Lu Xun, and Mao Zedong (mow dzuh-dung), spoke out on the need to change the ways of thinking about women and their social roles. Early in the century, the key issues were foot binding and women's education. In a short period of time, women's seclusion and tiny feet went from being a source of pride in Chinese refinement to a source of embarrassment at China's backwardness. Anti–foot binding campaigners depicted the custom as standing in the way of modernization by crippling a large part of the Chinese population. The earliest anti–foot binding societies, founded in the 1890s, were composed of men who would agree both to leave their daughters' feet natural and to marry their sons to women with natural feet. After 1930 it was only in remote areas that young girls still had their feet bound. (Bound feet continued to be seen on the streets into the 1970s or later, as it was difficult and painful to reverse the process once a girl had reached age ten or twelve.)

As women gained access to modern education, first in missionary schools but then also in the new government schools and abroad, they began to participate in politics. Some revolutionaries appeared, most famously Qiu Jin (chyou jin), a woman who became an ardent nationalist after witnessing the Boxer Rebellion and the imperialist occupation of Beijing. Unhappy in her marriage, in 1904 she left her husband and went to Japan, enrolling in a girls' vocational school. Once there, she devoted most of her time to revolutionary politics, even learning to make bombs. She also took up feminist issues. In her speeches and essays she castigated female infanticide, foot binding, arranged marriages, wife beating, and the cult of widow chastity. She told women that they were complicit in their oppression because they were willing to make pleasing men their goal. In 1906 she returned to Shanghai, where she founded the *Chinese Women's Journal* and taught at a nearby girls' school. In 1907 she died a martyr, executed for her role in an abortive uprising.

Schools for women, like the one at which Qiu Jin taught, were becoming more and more common during this period. In 1907 the Qing government mandated the opening of schools for girls. That year 11,936 girls were enrolled in 391 girls' primary schools. By 1919 about twenty times as many primary school students were girls: 215,626 in total. Female students were still greatly outnumbered by male ones. In 1922–1923, some 3,249 girls were attending middle schools, only a tiny fraction of the 100,136 boys in middle schools. Schools offered girls much more than literacy: they offered a respectable way for girls to interact with unrelated people. After 1920, opportunities for higher education also rapidly expanded, leading to a growing number of women working as teachers, nurses, and civil servants in the larger cities. In the countryside, change came much more slowly. A large-scale survey of rural households in the 1930s found that fewer than 2 percent of the women were literate, compared to 30 percent of the men.

---

[*]Cited in Chow Tse-tung, op. cit., p. 183.

Sidney Gamble Photographs, Manuscripts Division, Department of Rare Books and Special Collections, Princeton University Library

Pilgrims at Taishan. Taishan, one of the sacred peaks of China, attracted many pilgrims, like these women photographed in the 1920s. Notice that some have made it up the mountain despite their bound feet.

Young women in middle and high schools read *New Youth* and other periodicals just as avidly as their brothers. Lu Xun wrote essays and short stories that targeted old moral standards that constrained women. In an essay on chastity, he noted how a woman who committed suicide to avoid being ravished won great glory, but no man of letters would write a biography of a woman who committed suicide after being forcibly raped. In his short story "The New Year's Sacrifice," a poor widow who was forced by her parents-in-law to remarry was viewed by herself and others as ill omened after her second husband also died. She ended up surviving by begging, worried that she would have to be split in two after death to serve her two husbands. Foreign literature also had an impact, especially Ibsen's *A Doll's House*, which first appeared in translation in

New Youth and soon was performed on stage many places. Women debated whether, like Ibsen's Nora, they could leave the old system and create their own identities.

In addition to attempting to change people's ways of thinking, activists fought for changes in women's legal status. Efforts to get the vote were generally unsuccessful. However, in the 1920s, both the Nationalist and Communist parties organized women's departments and adopted resolutions calling for equal rights for women and freedom of marriage and divorce. Divorce proved the trickiest issue. As Song Qingling (sung ching-ling), the widow of Sun Yatsen, reported, "If we do not grant the appeals of the women, they lose faith in the union and in the women's freedom we are teaching. But if we grant the divorces, then we have trouble with the peasant's union, since it is very hard for a peasant to get a wife, and he has often paid much for his present unwilling one."[*]

REUNIFICATION BY THE NATIONALISTS

The ease with which Yuan Shikai had pushed the revolutionaries out of power demonstrated to them that they needed their own army. Sun Yatsen in 1917 went to Guangzhou, then controlled by warlords, to try to form a military government there. That year, the Bolshevik Revolution succeeded in Russia, and Sun began to think that Russia might offer a better model for political change than Japan. Russia had been a large, backward, despotic monarchy that had fallen behind the West in technology. Both China and Russia were predominantly peasant societies, with only small educated elites. Why shouldn't the sort of revolution that worked in Russia also work in China? The newly established Soviet Union wanted to help build a revolutionary China. In Marxist–Leninist theory, socialist revolution would occur by stages, and because China had not yet gone through a bourgeois, capitalist stage, a victory by the Nationalist revolutionaries who would overthrow the imperialists appeared to be the next stage for China. Importantly, a weak China might invite the expansion of Japan, the Soviet Union's main worry to the east.

For help in building a stronger revolutionary party and army, in 1920, Sun turned to the Comintern (short for Communist International, the organization Lenin had founded to promote communist revolution throughout the world). The Comintern sent advisers to Sun, most notably Michael Borodin, who drafted a constitution for the Nationalist Party, giving it a more hierarchical chain of command. When some party members thought it resembled the Communist model too closely, Sun countered that "the capitalist countries will never be sympathetic to our Party. Sympathy can only be expected from Russia, the oppressed nations, and the oppressed peoples."[†]

By 1925 there were about one thousand Russian military advisers in China helping the Nationalists build a party army. Chinese officers were also sent to the Soviet Union, including Chiang Kaishek (jyang ky-shek), who was sent there for four months' training in 1923. On Chiang's return, Borodin helped

him set up the Whampoa Military Academy near Guangzhou, and the Soviet Union made a substantial contribution to its costs. The communist Zhou Enlai, recently returned from France, became deputy head of this academy's political education department. The first class was admitted in 1924 with nearly five hundred cadets, ages seventeen to twenty-four. The cadet corps was indoctrinated in Sun's Three Principles of the People and dedicated to the rebuilding of national unity. As they rose within the Nationalist army, the former cadets remained fiercely loyal to Chiang.

At the same time Comintern advisers were aiding the buildup of the Nationalists' power base, they continued to guide the development of a Chinese Communist Party (discussed in Chapter 25). This party grew slowly, and at no time in the 1920s or 1930s did it have nearly as many members or supporters as the Nationalist Party. In 1922, on Comintern urging, the two parties formed a united front, as a consequence of which members of the Communist Party joined the Nationalist Party as individuals but continued separate Communist Party activities on the side. Sun Yatsen endorsed this policy, confident that the Nationalist Party would not be threatened by a small number of Communists and eager to tap all possible resources for building a strong state.

Among those the Comintern sent to Guangzhou was Ho Chi Minh, a Vietnamese who had become a communist in France and had gone to Moscow to work at Comintern headquarters. Ho spent much of the next twenty years in China and Hong Kong organizing a Vietnamese communist movement among Vietnamese patriots in exile in south China.

Nationalism continued to grow during the 1920s as one incident after another served to remind people of China's subjection to the imperialist powers. On May 30, 1925, police in the foreign-run International Settlement of Shanghai fired on unarmed demonstrators, killing eleven. Three weeks later, a sympathy protest in Guangzhou led foreign troops to open fire, killing fifty-two demonstrators. A fifteen-month boycott of British goods and trade with Hong Kong followed. The time seemed ripe to mobilize patriots across the country to fight the twin evils of warlordism and imperialism.

In 1925, before the planned Northern Expedition to reunify the country could be mounted, Sun Yatsen died of cancer. The recently reorganized Nationalist Party soon suffered strain between the leftists, who shared many of the goals of the communists, and the rightists, who thought that Borodin had too much power and the communists were acting like a party within the party. Nevertheless, in July 1926, the two-pronged Northern

---

[*]Cited in Anna Louise Strong, *China's Millions* (New York: Coward-McCann, 1928), p. 125.

[†]Cited in C. Martin Wilbur and Julie Lien-ying How, *Missionaries of Revolution* (Cambridge, Mass.: Harvard University Press, 1989), p. 92.

Expedition was finally launched, with Chiang Kaishek as military commander and Russian advisers helping with strategy. Communists and members of the left wing of the Nationalist Party formed an advanced guard, organizing peasants and workers along the way to support the revolution. Many warlords joined the cause; others were defeated. By the end of 1926, the Nationalist government was moved from Guangzhou to Wuhan (woo-hahn), where the left wing of the party became dominant. By early 1927, the army was ready to attack Shanghai. This would mark the end of the United Front, a topic taken up in Chapter 25.

SUMMARY

At the beginning of the twentieth century, with the Qing Dynasty in disarray, more and more people wanted to find ways to make China strong again. Local elites started new schools; intellectuals studied foreign languages, went abroad to study, and founded new magazines. Some agitated for the overthrow of the Manchus. The Qing government itself announced a series of reforms that included provincial assemblies as a first step toward a constitutional form of government. Before much progress was made, however, a small group of revolutionaries succeeded in overthrowing the Qing and announcing the establishment of a republican government. The most powerful of the Qing generals, Yuan Shikai, was made president. The most prominent of the revolutionaries was Sun Yatsen, the leader of what would become the Nationalist Party.

This alliance did not last long; Yuan soon outlawed the Nationalist Party and abolished the provincial assemblies. In 1915 Yuan even announced that he would become emperor, outraging those who wanted real political change. After Yuan died in 1916, military commanders acted more and more like warlords, with negative consequences of many kinds.

Nevertheless, social and cultural change was occurring at a rapid pace. The magazine *New Youth*, founded in 1915, challenged old Confucian ideas such as filial piety and parental control of marriages and promoted writing in the vernacular language, the way people spoke. It and other new magazines carried articles on Western ideas ranging from anarchy to liberalism, Darwinism, and science. In 1919 the May Fourth Incident got even more young people involved in the fight for political change. What sparked student protest was the decision of the Versailles peace negotiators to grant Japan the leasehold Germany had had in Shandong province, even though China had joined the allied side and sent 140,000 laborers to help in the war effort. After the government in Beijing suppressed spontaneous student protest, strikes closed schools in more than two hundred cities, and China in the end refused to sign the Versailles Treaty. Aroused by the May Fourth movement, all through the 1920s intellectuals agitated to rid China of the evils of the old order and promoted nationalism, democracy, and science. Women's education found wide approval, and girls' schools were built across the country. Some activists advocated equal rights for women and freedom of marriage and divorce.

Change was also occurring at the economic and political level. Foreign companies set up more and more factories in China. Chinese firms also grew in number, in part because war in Europe heightened demand for Chinese goods. Telephone and electric companies brought their services to more and more cities. Politically, Sun Yatsen and other Nationalists worked to build a revolutionary party and army, aiming to rid China of the warlords. After the Bolshevik Party overthrew the Russian monarchy in 1917, many thought Russia might provide a model for China. Because Lenin wanted to promote communist revolutions throughout the world, he instructed the Comintern to offer assistance to Sun. Nationalist officers were invited to the Soviet Union for training, including Chiang Kaishek. In 1922 the Comintern urged a united front between the small Chinese Communist Party and the larger Nationalist Party to defeat the warlords and reunify the country. Before the campaign got underway Sun Yatsen died of cancer and leadership of the Nationalists passed to Chiang Kaishek.

How different was China in 1927 compared to 1900? Two thousand years of monarchical government had come to an end. Nationalism had become a powerful force. Political parties had come into existence. Through the spread of modern schools, the outpouring of new publications, and much more extensive study abroad, a much larger proportion of the population knew something of Western countries and Western ideas. Confucianism was no longer taken to be an obvious good. Radically new ideas such as individualism and democracy were widely discussed and advocated. Young people with modern educations had become important political actors as protesters and agitators. Women had come to play much more public roles in society. An urban proletariat had come into existence with the growth of factories in the major cities. China was changing very rapidly.

World War II

WORLD WAR II WAS CHARACTERIZED by indiscriminate bombing of civilian populations and death tolls in the millions. The aggressors were the Axis: Japan, Germany, and, to a lesser extent, Italy. Allied against them were the British Commonwealth (including India and Australia), the United States, and the Soviet Union, along with the Chinese government under Chiang Kaishek. Japan's part in this larger war began with its invasion of Manchuria in 1931 followed by an all-out war against China launched in 1937. The war in Europe began in 1939 when Hitler provoked a declaration of war from Britain and France by invading Poland. The United States joined when Japan bombed Pearl Harbor on December 7, 1941, and Hitler subsequently declared war on the United States.

Each country had reasons for fighting. Still angry at the punitive terms that included a loss of territory imposed on it by the armistice that ended World War I, Germany insisted that it needed living space for its growing population. Just as Hitler's Nazi Party believed that Aryans were superior to all other races and were destined to rule the world, many people in Japan believed that their country was superior to the rest of Asia. Nazis, Fascists in Italy, and Japan's ultra-nationalists agreed that social dislocations in the early twentieth century had been caused by individualistic liberalism expressed in hedonistic urban culture and the compromises and corruption of politicians. They opposed capitalism and the capitalist powers—England, France, and the United States—that dominated the world economically and militarily. They also feared the universal socialism proclaimed by the Bolshevik revolution in the Soviet Union that threatened the national polity. Germany expanded eastward; Italy conquered Ethiopia; Japan believed that it needed colonies for national security and self-respect. Despite a common ideology, the Axis never coordinated military or diplomatic strategy, especially in comparison with the more ideologically diverse Allies whose leaders met several times during the war.

Timeline: The Asia-Pacific War

1931–1932	Japan's Kwantung army takes over Manchuria
1932	January 28: Japan bombs Shanghai
1933	May 27: Japan withdraws from the League of Nations
1936	December 12–24: United Front against Japan
1937	July 7: Marco Polo Bridge Incident; Japan invades China
	December 13: Rape of Nanjing begins
1939	May through August: Japanese and Soviet troops fight at Nomonhan in Siberia; ceasefire announced in September
1940	Spring: U.S. Pacific Fleet moves to Pearl Harbor in Hawai'i
	September: Japan occupies North Vietnam
	September 27: Japan, Italy, and Germany sign Tripartite Mutual Defense Pact
	October 15: United States embargoes scrap metal and aviation fuel to Japan
1941	April 13: Japan signs neutrality pact with Soviet Union
	July 26: United States freezes Japanese assets, cutting off Japan's access to trade and oil
	December 7: Japan attacks Pearl Harbor, the Philippines, Wake, Guam, Hong Kong, and Malaya

(Continues)

(*Continued*)

1942	February: Japan takes over Rabaul northwest of New Guinea
	February 15: British Army surrenders in Singapore
	February 27–March 1: Battle of the Java Sea
	March 8: Allied forces surrender in Dutch East Indies (Indonesia)
	April 9: U.S. Army on Bataan peninsula in the Philippines surrenders; Bataan death march begins shortly thereafter
	May 6: U.S. forces surrender at Corregidor in the Philippines
	May 7–8: Battle of the Coral Sea
	Late May: Britain withdraws from Burma
	June 4–7: Battle of Midway
	June 5: Japan occupies Attu in Aleutian Islands
	Mid-June: Japan begins construction of airfield on Guadalcanal
	July 21: Japan captures Buna, New Guinea; drives toward Port Moresby
	August 7: U.S. Marines land on Guadalcanal
1943	February 7–8: Japan completes retreat from Guadalcanal
	July 28: United States drives Japan from Aleutian Islands
	November 20: U.S. Marines land on Tarawa in Gilbert Islands
1944	January 31: U.S. invasion of Marshall Islands
	June 15: U.S. Marines land on Saipan
	October 24–25: Battle of Leyte Gulf
1945	January 9: U.S. troops land on Luzon in the Philippines
	February 19–March 26: Battle of Iwo Jima
	March 9–10: Firebombing of Tokyo
	March 20–May 3: British reconquest of Burma
	April 1–June 22: Battle of Okinawa
	July 26: Potsdam Declaration
	August 6: Atomic bomb dropped on Hiroshima
	August 8: Soviet Union declares war on Japan
	August 9: Plutonium bomb dropped on Nagasaki
	August 15: Emperor announces Japan's surrender

WAR IN CHINA

Fear that Soviet expansion threatened Japan's interests in Asia, a perceived need for control over resources, and the belief that Japan's excess population needed room to grow led Japan's army to take over Manchuria where it installed a puppet government in what it called Manchukuo headed by Puyi, the last Qing emperor. Treating Manchukuo as a new frontier, it encouraged settlers from Japan and Korea to farm what became wide-open spaces once the previous farmers had left. By 1945, Manchuria had absorbed approximately 270,000 Japanese immigrants.

Japan's conquest of Manchuria sparked a wave of anti-Japanese demonstrations and a boycott of Japanese goods in China's major cities. The Japanese navy retaliated by bombarding civilian quarters in Shanghai before the eyes of the largest international community in China. An explosion of outrage filled foreign newspapers, but foreign governments did little. The League of Nations sent a fact-finding team to China, and when the League Assembly accepted the team's report condemning Japan's aggression in Manchuria, Japan withdrew from the League.

Japan's attempts to establish a buffer zone in north China fed growing anti-Japanese nationalist sentiment among Chinese people. A national salvation movement led by student demonstrations demanding national unity and resistance to Japan erupted in Beijing and spread to other cities. The rise of calls to resist Japan in China became so strong that even long-term antagonists joined forces in the United Front of 1936 that allied Communists and Nationalists against Japan. When the Japanese army invaded north China in July 1937 to protect its interests in Manchuria, it met fierce opposition.

H.S. Wong/Getty Images

Crying Baby. This photograph of a crying baby, which appeared in *Life* magazine following the Nanjing Massacre, garnered America's sympathy for China in its struggle against Japan.

Atrocities committed against civilian populations marked the war in China. Japan did not expect the fierce resistance offered by Chinese troops in and around Shanghai as its army moved southward. When the Japanese army captured Nanjing in December, spokesmen contended that Chinese troops had taken off their uniforms to mingle with the civilian population, thereby justifying the murder of thousands of Chinese civilians. Frustrated that five months of warfare had not resulted in decisive victory, Japanese officers encouraged their men to loot stores and rape women; the number killed was in the hundreds of thousands. The foreign press dubbed this horror the "Rape of Nanking."

Shocked by the international outcry over Nanjing and disturbed by the troops' behavior, even though they had encouraged it, Japanese officers decided that indiscriminate rape threatened Japan's reputation and military discipline. To provide for what was deemed the soldiers' physical needs and to combat venereal disease, the army further developed the system of "comfort stations," which had already been launched in Shanghai in 1932. Japanese prostitutes were primarily reserved for officers in noncombat areas. To find women for soldiers on the front lines, the military turned to its colonies and

then to territories conquered after 1940. Koreans composed 80 percent of the "comfort women" who serviced troops as far away as Burma, the Dutch East Indies, and the Philippines. In some areas, a woman serviced up to fifty men a day for a modest fee per soldier. Only the end of the war brought release from sexual slavery.

Despite its many successes against Chinese forces, Japan remained unable to fully defeat China. When Chiang moved his government to Chongqing in the mountains of Sichuan, nearly perpetual fog protected the city from Japanese bombers. Because the narrow Yangzi gorges precluded an overland attack, Japanese troops fanned out along the eastern seaboard and along railroad lines in the interior. By the end of 1938, they occupied cities and major towns from Manchuria to Guangdong. The vastness of the territory and the hostility of the local population meant that Japan never gained control of the countryside.

Although Chinese living under Japanese occupation tried to remain inconspicuous, many had to choose between collaboration and resistance. Collaborators set up a provisional government in Beijing in 1937 to administer north China. In 1940, Japan created the Reorganized Government of the

Republic of China under Wang Jingwei, a member of Chiang Kaishek's Nationalist Party who promoted peace with Japan in the name of Greater East Asianism. In 1943, Japan compelled Wang to declare war on the United States and Great Britain. In the countryside, guerrilla warfare led Japanese army units to launch indiscriminate punitive missions against villages thought to be harboring insurgents. These "rural pacification" campaigns proved ineffective. Although 1 million Japanese troops occupied China's richest regions for eight years, they could not subdue the people or find an exit strategy from a war neither side could win.

Japan expected more than collaboration from its Korean subjects in its war with China. It expanded cotton and wool production at the expense of grains; it developed hydroelectric power in the north. In 1936, it declared a new policy of forced assimilation: all Korean were to be taught that as children of the emperor they had to worship at Shinto shrines and pray for the emperor's good health. More than six hundred thousand Korean men were drafted to work in Japanese and Manchurian mines, harbors, and factories. By 1944, upwards of 4 million Koreans worked outside Korea, some as policemen and guards as far away as New Guinea, where they died in battles that made no distinction between combatants and noncombatants.

As was the case with Italy's conquest of Ethiopia in 1936, Japan's aggression in China provoked international outrage but little else. Both the League of Nations and the United States (which had not joined the League) officially deplored Japan's action, but neither tried to stop it, even though Japanese forces destroyed American property, sank an American warship, and killed American civilians.

Fearful of Japan's intentions north of Manchuria, only the Soviet Union provided significant aid to China. It shipped munitions and airplanes to both Communist and Nationalist forces along with military advisers. More than two hundred Soviet pilots died in China's defense. In May 1939, the Japanese army in western Manchuria confronted Soviet forces at Nomonhan. The fight having cost Japan eighteen thousand men and exposed critical weaknesses in the army's tactics and equipment, Japan soon sued for peace. The Germans and the Soviet Union signed a Non-Aggression Pact in August 1939, followed by a neutrality pact between Japan and the Soviet Union in 1941. After Germany invaded the Soviet Union at the end of June, Soviet aid to China came to an end.

THE WAR EXPANDS

The United States relied on sanctions and threats to try to force Japan out of China and check Japan's spread into Vietnam. It placed a series of increasingly stringent embargos on goods to Japan and helped Chiang Kaishek by extending credit with which to buy American arms. When President Roosevelt had the Pacific Fleet move to Pearl Harbor to protect U.S. shipping lanes and intimidate Japan, Japan's navy took it as a threat to its interests in Micronesia and the South Pacific. In September 1940, Japan invaded North Vietnam to secure raw materials for its war machine, cut supply lines running to Chiang Kaishek, and advance on the oil fields in the Dutch East Indies. The response by the United States was to cut off shipments of steel to Japan.

Neither the United States nor Japan understood the other side's motives, and each underestimated the other. Japan claimed to be liberating Asia from colonial powers. In 1940, it promoted the notion of a Greater East Asia Co-Prosperity Sphere, an economic regional power bloc similar to that envisioned in the Western Hemisphere under the Monroe Doctrine. In Japan's eyes, the United States and Soviet Union had everything they needed for an autonomous defense, but without colonies, Japan did not. Japanese soldiers saw themselves as spiritually superior to the materialistic West; they were hard and high-minded, whereas British and Americans were soft.

Whereas Japan saw itself as a liberator pursuing essential economic security, the United States saw Japan as a totalitarian aggressor, with China as the prime victim. Madame Chiang Kaishek gave an impassioned speech before the U.S. Congress in which she contrasted China striving for democracy with Japanese warmongers. Henry Luce, son of missionaries in China and owner of a journalistic empire, flooded his magazines with heart-rending pictures from war-torn China. In later years, editorial cartoons drew on racial stereotypes to mock Japanese for their physical and mental inferiority and portrayed them as vermin to be exterminated.

Japan's desperation to find a solution to its war with China pushed it to open one battlefront after another, many over 3,000 miles from the home islands. Unable to win in China, yet unwilling to withdraw, Japan consumed ever more resources while fearing that it would be denied them. When it moved into south Vietnam and forced an alliance on Thailand, it provoked the very thing it feared: the Americans, British, and Dutch—who, with the Chinese, constituted what Japan called the ABCD encirclement—acted to block Japan's access to oil. To secure the fuel crucial for its China campaign, it struck south and bombed Pearl Harbor in hopes of forcing the United States to negotiate a settlement. Ten hours later, it launched an invasion of the Philippines, a U.S. colony.

Britain had expected attack on Singapore to come from the sea; Japanese troops advanced through jungle to capture the city. (The same month that saw the fall of Singapore also saw President Roosevelt sign Executive Order 9066 to place 110,000 Japanese Americans, more than half of them U.S. citizens, behind the barbed wire of relocation camps.) Within months, Japan captured Indonesia, the Philippines, Guam, Wake, the Gilbert Islands, and the Solomon Islands. The Japanese army chased Britain out of Burma, closed the Burma Road that had carried supplies to Chiang Kaishek's forces, and threatened India and Australia. Combined with the islands taken from Germany in World War I, this gave the Japanese a vast empire, albeit mostly over water. (See Map C7.1.)

Japan's early victories gave it unjustified confidence that it could prevail against the Allies. Six months after its attack on Pearl Harbor, it took aim at capturing Midway, an atoll west of Hawai'i, in part, to solidify its defensive perimeter, in part, to gain a launching pad for future attacks on Fiji or Samoa, and, in part, to force U.S. aircraft carriers (absent from Pearl Harbor on the day it had been attacked) into battle. Little did Japan know that the United States had cracked its military codes, giving it foreknowledge of Japan's plans. Having defeated Japan's navy decisively at Midway, the United States was then free to concentrate its military and industrial might against Germany. The Pacific War became one of attrition that dragged on for another three years.

HOW THE WAR WAS WAGED

Japan's empire lacked administrative coherence. After conquering the Dutch East Indies, Japan divided it among three military commands. In the Philippines, Japan established a republic with a constitution drafted under its supervision, chose the nationalist Jose P. Laurel to be its president, and had

the new republic sign an alliance that put land and resources at Japan's disposal. The French Vichy government, which collaborated with the Nazis, invited Japan to occupy Vietnam, and Japan continued to rely on French administrators until 1945, much to the chagrin of Vietnamese nationalists. In the south, nationalists collaborated with military police and supplied laborers to build boats. When Japan decided to eliminate French rule in March 1945, the nationalists helped, only to suffer betrayal when Japan decided to keep administration in its own hands. Tainted by their association with Japan, noncommunist Vietnamese nationalists lacked credibility in the political strife following the end of the war.

On the Malay Peninsula and in Burma, Japan created patriotic associations ostensibly to resist European colonial powers but in reality to mobilize labor for the Japanese military. In places where Japan ruled through local headmen, the aim was the same: to make each region, each island, self-sufficient and to support Japan's war machine. In some cases, men who were later to lead independence movements against Western imperialism began by collaborating with Japan, as did General Aung San of Burma. When British soldiers retreated to India, units left behind formed the Indian National Army to fight for Indian independence. These instances serve as reminders that South and Southeast Asia welcomed Japan's message of liberation from colonial rule, but not the way it was delivered.

Like Germany, Japan justified its disregard for human life on the basis of racial superiority. Both Ishii Shirō and Joseph Mengele—doctors who tortured individuals in the name of science—believed that their supposedly medical experiments on human test subjects served a larger purpose: ultimate victory for the master race. The same rationale served for labor policies. Japan saw no reason to provide food, clothing, or basic medical care for laborers from the Malay Peninsula, Philippines, and Dutch East Indies who, having been mobilized to work on construction projects from Micronesia to Thailand, died far from home of malaria, cholera, maltreatment, and starvation. After Japan invaded Java, grain production plummeted, in part, because Japan required that fields be planted with textile-related crops.

Across the Japanese empire, the dislocation of individuals and families in the name of the Greater East Asia Co-Prosperity Sphere led to starvation and death. The Indonesian writer Pramoedya Ananta Toer described the conditions he saw

Map C7.1   **World War II in Asia and the Pacific**

during the last days of the war in his novel *The Fugitive*, "Corpses. Wherever you go, unattended corpses."[*] In contrast to such atrocities stand the Nazi and German businessman John Rabe, who saved thousands of Chinese lives during the Rape of Nanjing, and the Japanese diplomat Sugihara Chiune, who also saved thousands of lives by issuing transit visas for Lithuanian Jews fleeing Nazi persecution.

Japan's arrogant sense of racial superiority helped its enemies. Resistance to Japanese occupation from China to Indonesia to the Philippines contributed significantly to the Allies' counterattack. The British led Indian troops to reconquer Burma, Australians helped defeat Japan in New Guinea, the U.S. Army under General Douglas MacArthur advanced through the South Pacific before returning to the Philippines, and the U.S. Navy island-hopped across the Central Pacific.

Much of the fighting in the Pacific and Southeast Asia took place in jungles, which were hated by both sides. After four months on Bataan peninsula

---

[*]Pramoedya Ananta Toer, *The Fugitive*, trans. Willem Samuel (Harmondsworth: Penguin Books, 1990), p. 33.

© Bettmann/Corbis

Signal Corpsmen. Wading through jungle muck, these signal corpsmen in the U.S. army fought in racially segregated units against the Japanese enemy.

in the Philippines, one-third of U.S. troops were in rain-drenched field hospitals suffering from festering wounds, dysentery, and malaria. Although the Japanese army used the jungle to advantage in taking Singapore, its troops too fell victim to disease in Burma and Malaya. Japanese troops tried to cross the spine of New Guinea from Buna to Port Moresby over mountain passes covered with rain forest. Australian forces threw them back, and both sides struggled through knee-deep mud to engage an enemy seen only sporadically. Communications with headquarters broke down, and fighting erupted haphazardly when individual units ran afoul of the enemy.

Fighting on so many fronts meant that Japan lacked the ability to provide its troops with adequate supplies. Troops dispatched to far-flung islands and atolls were expected to live largely off the land. When U.S. submarines sank supply ships, more troops died of starvation than in combat. In 1942, Japan received 40 percent of Indonesia's oil. Owing U.S. submarines and airplanes, it received only 5 percent in 1944 and it received none in 1945. Taxis in Tokyo ran on wood-burning engines, and the air force adulterated scarce fuel with sap from pine roots.

Lacking adequate resources meant that the Japanese army and navy had to rely on men over machines. When Japan built runways on Pacific islands, it used human labor—natives, Koreans, Okinawans, prisoners of war. The Allies used bulldozers. At war's beginning, Japan had well-trained pilots flying the Zero, the most advanced fighter of its day. When those pilots were gone, their barely trained replacements had to fly against planes constantly improved through new technology. Japan lost so many planes trying to defend Saipan in the Marianas that American pilots called the battle "a turkey shoot."

After the Japanese fleet lost its aircraft carriers at the battle of Leyte Gulf, the navy asked its pilots to crash their planes into enemy ships. Designated the Divine Wind Special Attack Corps to recall the typhoon credited with repelling Mongol invaders almost seven hundred years earlier, *kamikaze* pilots struck fear in Allied hearts. Another desperate measure was the human torpedo. Nearly five thousand young men in the air and under the sea sacrificed their lives in a futile effort to stem the Allied tide sweeping toward Japan.

Air power made the decisive difference in battles on sea and land. From the battle of the Coral Sea, to Midway, to Leyte Gulf, although enemy ships saw each other's planes, the ships themselves never fought. At the end of the battle of the Coral Sea, Japan thought it had lost even though it sank more ships than had the Allies. Throughout the war, Japan's admirals sought the decisive sea battle fought with battleships that would turn the tide of war just like Admiral Tōgō's stunning victory over the Russian navy in 1905. Little did they realize that aircraft carriers had made battleships irrelevant.

When Japan destroyed U.S. planes on the ground in the Philippines in 1941, it had left U.S. troops defenseless against aerial assault. Later in the war, Japan's troops, and later its cities, suffered the same experience once its air force had been wiped out. The fall of Saipan in Micronesia—after the navy lost more than four hundred planes and almost every Japanese soldier had died in its defense—put Japan's main islands within range of U.S. heavy bombers. The first raids, carried out at high altitudes, did little but psychological damage. Once General Curtis E. LeMay arrived from Europe, pilots in the Pacific perfected the art of carpet bombing—that is, dropping incendiary bombs at low attitudes, which destroyed Japan's wooden cities in a sea of fire. In the largest air offensive in history, U.S. planes destroyed the remnants of the Japanese navy, shattered Japanese industry, and dropped 40,000 tons of bombs on population centers. Approximately ninety thousand civilians died in the firestorm that engulfed Tokyo. The plane that carried the atomic bomb to Hiroshima took off from Tinian, just south of Saipan. Its flight was virtually unimpeded.

THE END OF THE WAR

Even before the fall of Okinawa, which sacrificed one-quarter of the island's population, cabinet members had begun to call for an end to the war. The army rebuffed them. With its troops relatively unscathed in China and Manchuria, the army demanded that all Japanese prepare to make the ultimate sacrifice: to die like "shattered jewels" in protecting the emperor-centered national polity.

Recalling President Theodore Roosevelt's mediation of an end to the Russo-Japanese War in 1905 and hoping to keep the Soviet Union neutral, the army finally agreed to let the Japanese ambassador to Moscow ask Foreign Minister Molotov for help. Unwilling to commit to an answer before the Soviet Union was ready to enter the war in Asia and busy with preparations for the Potsdam Conference, Molotov put him off. On July 26, Churchill, Truman, and Chiang Kaishek issued the Potsdam Declaration (Stalin did not sign it) demanding that Japan submit to unconditional surrender. Japan was to agree to allow occupation by foreign troops and to renounce all claims to territory on the Asian mainland and Taiwan. Its leaders and soldiers were to be tried for war crimes, and the Japanese people were to choose the form of government they wanted. The alternative was "prompt and utter destruction."

The Potsdam Declaration was both extremely specific and maddeningly vague. Japan's leaders had no way of knowing that destruction was to come via a bomb first tested ten days before. To the distress of the emperor's loyal subjects, the declaration made no mention of him. The cabinet decided to wait and hope for mediation by the Soviet Union. Then, for three days in early August, the atomic bombing of Hiroshima, the Soviet Union's declaration of war, and the plutonium bombing of Nagasaki sent shock waves through the cabinet. At a meeting on August 14, the emperor instructed the cabinet to surrender. Later, he made a recording to tell the Japanese people that they must bear the unbearable. Despite a plot by junior army officers to steal the recording, it was broadcast at noon on August 15. World War II was over, but the debate

© Corbis

Japanese Family on Saipan. This photograph shows one of the remnants of the civilian population caught in the fighting on Saipan and on the verge of starvation when an American soldier found them and tried to coax them out of their cave.

on why Japan surrendered had just begun—was it the bomb, fear of Russians, or exhaustion?

After the war, Japanese military personnel were prosecuted for war crimes. In Indonesia, the Dutch convicted Japanese who had forced European women to service Japanese troops (they ignored cases involving Indonesian women). Other war-crimes trials made no mention of comfort women. Nor did they include men from Unit 731, led by Ishii Shirō, who had given the United States their data on experiments to test biological weapons performed on Chinese in Manchuria. Instead the trials focused on crimes against humanity broadly defined as the decision to wage war; atrocities such as the Bataan death march in which thousands of American and Filipino soldiers died; the indiscriminate bayoneting of British doctors, nurses, and patients in Singapore; the machine-gunning, decapitation, and drowning of civilians in Southeast Asia; and the massacre of Filipinos in Manila at the end of the war. Japan's treatment of prisoners of war merited special condemnation; soldiers who survived surrender were starved, tortured, and forced to labor for the Japanese war machine in contravention of the Geneva Convention. In a display of what was later called "victor's justice," the war crimes tribunals ignored atrocities committed by Allied forces.

Following World War II, the world split into two camps: the free world dominated by the United States and the Communist bloc led by the Soviet Union, with what Winston Churchill called an "iron curtain" between opposing ideologies dividing Europe. Forgetting that Japan's early victories had exposed their weaknesses, Western powers assumed that their former colonies in South and Southeast Asia would welcome them as liberators. While the United States freed the Philippines in 1946, as long promised, Britain was forced to pull out of Burma and India in 1947. Two years later, the Dutch grudgingly granted independence to Indonesia, but France refused to leave Vietnam until defeated in 1954. Civil war in China ended with communist victory in 1949.

Soviet troops began to enter Korea in August 1945. Hoping to prevent the whole country from falling into Russian hands, the United States got the Soviet Union to agree to a dividing line just north of Seoul at the 38th parallel. The two nations then sponsored the creation of two separate states on the Korean peninsula. Japan escaped that fate. Under U.S. occupation, it became a "bulwark against communism."

War and Revolution, China (1927–1949)

During the two decades from 1927 to 1949, China was ruled by the Nationalist Party and its head, Chiang Kaishek. The Nationalist government turned toward the West for help in modernizing the country but in general was distrustful of intellectuals. In its big cities, above all in Shanghai, China took on a more modern look with tall buildings, department stores, and Western dress. The government had to concentrate most of its energies on military matters, first combating the remaining warlords, then the Communist Party bases, then Japan. The Communist Party attracted a small but highly committed following. Because of the Nationalists' pressure, it was on the run much of the time until a base area was established in Yan'an (yen-ahn) in 1935, where Mao Zedong emerged as the paramount leader. During the war with Japan (1937–1945), the Communist Party formed itself into a potent revolutionary force, able to mobilize poor peasants into a well-disciplined fighting force. The Civil War of 1947–1949 resulted in the victory of the Communist Party.

The large questions behind much of the scholarly work on this period revolve around the outcome in 1949. Why did May Fourth liberalism decline in significance? Could the economic policies of the Nationalists have brought prosperity to China if Japan had not invaded? How much of a difference did the Comintern's often misguided instructions make to the development of the Communist Party? How crucial was Mao to the way the policies of the party developed? Why did the Nationalist Party and Chiang Kaishek lose the support of the urban middle class?

THE CHINESE COMMUNIST PARTY

With the success of the Bolshevik Revolution in Russia in 1917, Chinese intellectuals began to take an interest in Marxism–Leninism, which seemed to provide a blueprint for a world of abundance without exploitation. Communism appeared scientific, anti-Western, anti-imperialist, and successful: it had just proved itself capable of bringing revolution to a backward country. For the May 1919 issue of *New Youth*, Li Dazhao (lee dah-jow), the librarian at Beijing University, wrote an introduction to Marxist theory, explaining such concepts as class struggle and capitalist exploitation. Soon intellectuals were also looking into the works of Lenin and Trotsky, who predicted an imminent international revolutionary upheaval that would bring an end to imperialism. Although China did not have much of a proletariat to be the vanguard of its revolution, the nation as a whole, Li Dazhao argued, was exploited by the capitalist imperialist countries. In 1920, Li organized a Marxist study group at Beijing University. At the same time, Chen Duxiu organized one in Shanghai, where he had gone after resigning his university post in Beijing. Another source of knowledge of European Marxism were the thousands of Chinese students, male and female, who had gone to France in 1919 and 1920 to participate in work-study programs. Most worked in factories, where they were introduced to both strikes and Marxism–Leninism.

The early Marxist study groups were offered financial assistance and guidance by the Comintern. In 1920, soon after the Comintern learned of the existence of Marxist study groups in China, agents were sent to help turn the groups into party cells. This entailed teaching "democratic centralism," the secret to party discipline. Each local cell elected delegates to higher levels, up to the national party congress, with its central executive committee and the latter's standing committee. Delegates flowed up, and decisions flowed down. Decisions could be debated within a cell, but once decisions were reached, all were obligated to obey them. This cell structure provided a degree of discipline and centralization beyond anything in the prior repertoire of Chinese organizational behavior.

Following Comintern advice, thirteen delegates met in July 1921 to form the Chinese Communist Party as a secret, exclusive, centralized party. The party broke with the anarchists and guild socialists and asserted the primacy of class struggle. Chen Duxiu was chosen as secretary general. The party agreed to put priority on organizing labor unions and recruiting workers into the party. In Shanghai, the new Communist Party oversaw the establishment of a Russian language school, helped organize labor unions, and formed the Socialist Youth Corps.

At the insistence of the Comintern and against the advice of many of the Chinese members, the decision was made in 1922 to ally with the Nationalists. The United Front between the Nationalist and Communist parties was expedient for both at the time because they could concentrate on their common foe, the warlords. However, it covered over deep differences. The Nationalist military included many staunch anticommunists who were appalled by talk of class warfare. One reason the communists remained in the United Front was that it gave them the opportunity to organize both workers and peasants. Along the route of the Northern Expedition, farmers' associations were established, with membership exceeding 1 million people by the end of 1926.

The United Front ended in the spring of 1927. On March 21, as the Nationalist army neared Shanghai, the Communist-led General Labor Union called for a general strike. More than six hundred thousand workers responded and seized the city. Flush with victory, they began demanding the return of the foreign concessions. On April 11, the head of the union was invited to the home of the leader of the mafia-like Green Gang, where he was murdered. The next day Green Gang members and soldiers loyal to Chiang attacked union headquarters. Soon soldiers were mowing down civilians with machine guns; an estimated five thousand were killed.

The terror quickly spread to other cities. The labor union base of the Communist Party was destroyed. Although the party tried to continue working with the left wing of the Nationalist Party in Wuhan, Chiang's show of force carried the day. By July 1927 the Soviet advisers had withdrawn from the Nationalist army, and the United Front was over.

That fall, the Communist Party tried to organize uprisings in both cities and the countryside, but none met with much success. A failed uprising in Guangzhou led to the execution of three thousand to four thousand worker revolutionaries. From 1927 through 1930, the hunt was on for Communist organizers all over the country; in some areas, the only evidence that troops needed in order to conclude that a young woman was a communist was bobbed hair. The surviving Communist leadership was driven underground and into the countryside. On orders of the Comintern, Chen Duxiu was blamed for these disasters and expelled from the Communist Party. Party membership, which had reached about sixty thousand in April 1927, plummeted to fewer than ten thousand within the year.

Mao Zedong's Emergence as a Party Leader

Through the 1920s, Mao Zedong was just one of hundreds of Communist Party organizers. He ended up playing such an important role in twentieth-century Chinese history that it is useful to begin with his early experiences.

Mao was born in 1893 in a farming village about 30 miles south of Changsha (chahng-shah), the capital of Hunan province. He began helping out on his father's 3-acre farm when he was six. At age eight, in 1901, he entered the local primary school, where he studied for six years. Mao then worked full time on the farm for three years, from ages thirteen to sixteen. When he was fourteen years old, he was betrothed to the eighteen-year-old daughter of a neighbor, but she died in 1910, and Mao left the farm to continue his education. One of his teachers was a returned student from Japan, and from him Mao became fascinated with the writings of Kang Youwei and Liang Qichao. In 1911, at age seventeen, Mao walked the 30 or so miles to Changsha to enter a middle school. Not only was Changsha a large city, but also the new provincial assembly was then meeting, and all sorts of newspapers were in circulation. Mao joined student demonstrations against the Qing government and cut off his queue. Then, in October, revolutionary soldiers seized power in nearby Wuhan, and the fall of the Qing Dynasty soon followed. Mao, wanting to be a part of the action, joined the republican army, but after six months of garrison duty in Changsha, he quit to continue his education.

For a year Mao spent his days at the Changsha public library reading world history and Chinese translations of works by such Western writers as Rousseau, Montesquieu, J. S. Mill, Adam Smith, and Charles Darwin. Only when his father refused to support him any longer unless he enrolled in a school that gave degrees did he enter the Hunan Provincial Fourth Normal School, where he studied for five years (1913–1918). The teacher there who had the greatest impact on him was Yang Changji, a social science teacher deeply interested in philosophy, which he had studied during his decade abroad in Japan, Great Britain, and Germany. Mao came to share Yang's dissatisfaction with the physical fitness of Chinese intellectuals, and he wrote an article on physical education that was published in *New Youth* in 1917.

Mao was twenty-four years old when he graduated. When Yang moved to Beijing to take up an appointment at Beijing University, Mao followed him. Yang helped him get a job as a clerk in the library, which made him a subordinate of Li Dazhao, only four years his senior but already well known in intellectual circles, having studied law for six years in Japan and having been offered a position on the editorial board of *New Youth*. That year Li Dazhao wrote about Marxism and the Russian Revolution for *New Youth*.

Before he had been in Beijing a year, Mao had to return home because his mother was ill, but he stopped to visit Shanghai for a couple of weeks on the way. Mao thus missed the excitement at Beijing University during the May Fourth incident. Back in Changsha, Mao took a teaching job and started his own magazine, producing four issues with articles on topics such as democracy, unions, and fighting oppression. Mao also turned his hand to organizing, forming the Hunan United Students Association and organizing a strike of thirteen thousand middle school students against the local warlord.

After his mother died, Mao returned to Beijing to find Professor Yang desperately ill. At the beginning of 1920, Mao's father and Yang both died. When Mao returned to Hunan a few months later, he was appointed principal of a primary school. That seems to have left him some time; he also organized a cooperative bookstore that proved a commercial success. Professor Yang's daughter Yang Kaihui (yahng ky-hway) also returned to Hunan, and by the end of 1920 she and Mao were living together. Two years later, their first son was born, and they spoke of themselves as married.

It was not until 1920 that Mao showed particular interest in Marxism. Part of this new interest came from letters he received from fellow students who had gone to France. When the first meeting of the Communist Party was held in Shanghai in July 1921, Mao was one of the two delegates from Hunan. He was sent back to Hunan with instructions to build up the party there and develop ties to labor unions. Mao recruited former classmates, his two younger brothers, and others to help him organize unions and strikes. In early 1923, conforming to party policy, Mao joined the Nationalist Party. That June he went to Guangzhou for the third congress of the Chinese Communist Party. In December he sent in a pessimistic report on the situation in Hunan, where peasant organizations had been crushed and many factories had closed.

During much of 1924, Mao was away from home, in Guangzhou or Shanghai, doing United Front work.

In 1925 he did the opposite, returning to his home village to work with peasants out of the reach of party authorities. In October 1925, he returned to Guangzhou and took up work for the Nationalist Party's propaganda department, becoming the director of the Peasant Training Institute in 1926. During the Northern Expedition, Mao and those he had trained organized peasants in advance of the army. In February 1927, Mao submitted a highly positive report to the Communist Party on the revolution among the peasants in Hunan who had seized power from landlords and felt the joy of righting ancient wrongs.

In April 1927, when Chiang Kaishek unleashed the terror in Shanghai, Mao was in Hunan. Following party instructions, he tried to ignite peasant insurrection, but found that the terror had crushed the movement that only recently had looked so promising to him. Mao now wrote a report that emphasized the need to back political ideas with military force, contending, in his oft-quoted phrase, that "political power is obtained from the barrel of the gun." In October 1927 he led his remaining peasant followers into a mountain lair used by secret society members on the border between Hunan and Jiangxi, called Jinggangshan (jing-gahng-shahn). Mao lost contact with Yang Kaihui, who had just given birth to their third son. He also was out of touch with the party hierarchy. He began to draw in other communists, among whom was nineteen-year-old He Zizhen (huh dzih-jun), from a nearby landlord family, who had joined the party during the Northern Expedition. She and Mao, then thirty-four years old, became lovers and had a child in 1929.

In the mountain area that Mao's forces controlled, he pushed through an extreme form of land reform, redistributing all the land of the rich and requiring all the physically able to work. His troops suffered, however, with little in the way of arms or ammunition, clothes, or medicine.

In January 1929, Mao decided to look for a better-supplied base area that would be less vulnerable to Nationalist attacks. His choice was a border region between Jiangxi and Fujian, where he set up what came to be called the Jiangxi (jyahng-shee) Soviet. The party leadership, which could reach him there, quickly condemned him for his views on rural revolution and the role of military force. Mao fell ill and managed to avoid responding to the party's order that he go to Shanghai. In 1929–1930, Mao did, however, conduct an exhaustive study of rural life in one county in the Jiangxi Soviet, Xunwu (shyewn/shyun-woo) County,

to learn more about how a party could be built on a peasant base. In his analysis of landownership, he classified the population into landlords (those who lived off the rents of their lands, subdivided into large, medium, and small landlords), rich peasants (those who rented out some land or made loans but worked the rest themselves), middle peasants (those who worked their own land without borrowing or hiring help), poor peasants (tenants and owners of plots too small to support them), and others, including hired hands, loafers, and those who did such manual labor as boatmen and porters. The vast majority of the population fell into the category of poor peasant or lower. When land was redistributed, many more would receive land than would lose it. In his study of Xunwu, Mao also recorded literacy rates, postal service, shops and services, and even the number of prostitutes.

The Communist Party leadership was still trying to ignite urban uprisings and in October 1930 assaulted Changsha. Not only did the attack fail, but also the Nationalists arrested Yang Kaihui and had her shot. The three young boys were sent by friends to Shanghai. The youngest died, and Mao did not see the other two until 1946.

THE NATIONALIST GOVERNMENT IN NANJING

The decision of the Nationalist Party to purge itself of communists did not delay the military unification of the country, and in 1928 the Nationalists gained the allegiance of three key warlords to reunite the country. It established its capital at Nanjing, not used as a capital since the early Ming Dynasty. International recognition quickly followed, and Western observers were more optimistic about the prospects for China than they had been for decades. Men who had studied in Western countries were appointed to many key government posts, and progressive policies were adopted, such as a new land law limiting rents and a new marriage law outlawing concubinage and allowing women to initiate divorce. (See **Biography: Yuetsim, Servant Girl**.) Over the next several years, most of the foreign powers consented to reductions in their special privileges. Tariff autonomy was recovered, as well as control over the Maritime Customs, Salt Administration, and Post Office. Foreign concessions were reduced from thirty-three to thirteen, and extraterritoriality was eliminated for some minor countries.

BIOGRAPHY   Yuetsim, Servant Girl

Yuetsim, born around 1910, knew nothing about her natal family. All she knew was that she had been kidnapped when she was about three years old and sold, through intermediaries, as a "slave girl." She thought disbanded soldiers then roaming the countryside might have been the ones who kidnapped her.

A Hong Kong family, the Yeos, purchased Yuetsim. Her master's father had been a successful merchant and had three concubines in addition to his wife. Her master, Mr. Yeo, was the son of the first concubine, and he held a modest government position as a clerk. When his wife had no children, he purchased a prostitute as a concubine, and she gave birth to four children. The wife, who had bound feet, rarely left her room. The family bought little Yuetsim to help the concubine with the housework and care of the children. It is difficult to imagine that a three-year-old could be of much use to anyone, but by four or five she could at least fetch and carry. Naturally, she never learned to read or write.

Because Yuetsim knew no other life, she put up with the way she was treated. Her mistress, the concubine, was often harsh and contemptuous. During this period, Hong Kong newspapers were filled with agitation against the custom of selling girls into bondage. Yuetsim, however, never heard anything of the movement or of the 1923 law that took the first steps toward outlawing the selling of girls into service. In December 1929 a further strengthening of the laws against child slavery required owners of slave girls to register them with the government, pay them wages, and free them at age eighteen. Because Mr. Yeo worked for the government and was known to have had a slave girl for years, he had to take some action. He might have married her off, as many masters did, but his concubine was so angry at losing Yuetsim's services that she simply ordered Yuetsim out of the house.

In 1930 one of the officials in charge of the registration of slave girls found a place for Yuetsim in a home for women and girls in need of protection, and she stayed there several years. Finally she went back to the Yeos as a maid, knowing no other place to go. Soon after her return, both the wife and the concubine died. Yuetsim continued to take care of the master and his children.

After the death of his wife and concubine, Mr. Yeo wanted to make Yuetsim his concubine. His children, however, were adamantly opposed and threatened to cut off contact with him if he went through with the marriage. They, after all, had known her all their lives as a humble servant. Although their own mother had been a prostitute before becoming their father's concubine, they thought marriage to a former slave girl would disgrace the family. Mr. Yeo gave in to them.

Yuetsim stayed on anyway. In retirement, Mr. Yeo's fortunes declined, but Yuetsim nursed him in his illnesses and shopped and cooked for him. She was still living with him when she told her story in 1978.

Questions for Analysis
1. How did Yuetsim's experiences shape her personality?
2. From Yuetsim's story, what were the challenges facing those who tried to improve women's situations through legal reform?

Source: Based on Maria Jaschok, *Concubines and Bondservants: The Social History of a Chinese Custom* (London: Zed Books, 1988), pp. 69–77.

From 1928 on, Chiang Kaishek was the leader of the Nationalists. From a landlord–merchant family near Ningbo, Chiang had aspired to take the civil service examinations, but when they were abolished, he went to Japan to study military science, joining the precursor of the Nationalist Party while there. His appointment to head the Whangpoa Academy in 1924 was a crucial one because it allowed him to form strong personal ties to young officers in the party's army. Once Chiang, a skillful politician, became fully enmeshed in party and government matters, he proved able to balance different cliques and build personal ties to key power holders. In 1927 he married Soong Meiling (sung may-ling), the daughter of a wealthy merchant family and the sister of Sun Yatsen's widow.

To modernize his army, Chiang turned to Germany, attracted by the success the Nazis were having in mobilizing and militarizing Germany. Indeed, Chiang once argued, "Can fascism save China? We answer: yes. Fascism is now what China most needs."* German advisers helped Chiang train an elite corps, plan campaigns against the communist base in Jiangxi, and import German arms. Young officers became members of the Blue Shirts, an organization devoted to the nation and against such New Culture ideas as individualism. Chiang entrusted political training in the army and schools to the Blue Shirts, who also took on secret service work.

Chiang was not a political progressive. He made no attempt at elective democracy, as this was to be a period of "political tutelage." The press was heavily censored, and dissenters and suspected communists were arrested and often executed. To combat the intellectual appeal of the communists and build support for his government, Chiang in 1934 launched an ideological indoctrination program, the New Life Movement. Its goal, he claimed, was to "militarize the life of the people of the entire nation" and to nourish in them "a capacity to endure hardship and especially a habit and instinct for unified behavior" to make them "willing to sacrifice for the nation at all times."†

Chiang was a patriot, however, and wanted a strong and modern China. Much progress was made in economic modernization. Life in the major cities took on a more modern look. Conveniences like electricity were gradually changing how all major cities functioned. A professional class, composed of scientists, engineers, architects, economists, physicians, and others with technical expertise, often acquired through study abroad, was gaining influence.

The Nationalists' modernizing programs unfortunately failed to bring improvements to the countryside. Most peasants had seen no improvement in their standard of living since Qing times. The government and private philanthropic organizations sponsored rural reconstruction projects that tried to raise the level of rural education, create facilities for credit, encourage modern enterprises, and form peasant associations, but gains were usually limited to small areas and short periods. Continued population growth to over 500 million by 1930 relentlessly increased the pressure on available

Chiang Kaishek and Soong Meiling. In 1927, Chiang Kaishek married Soong Meiling, the younger sister of Sun Yatsen's widow. Soong came from a wealthy family, had been educated in the United States, and after the Japanese invasion worked hard to gain American support for China.

land. The advantages brought by modernization—cheaper transportation by railroads and cheaper manufactured consumer goods—were yet to have a positive impact on the rural economy. China's exports were struggling, silk and tea having lost ground to Japanese and Indian competition, then all exports facing decreased demand due to the worldwide depression of the 1930s.

Shanghai

During the Nanjing Decade, Shanghai emerged as one of the major cities of the world. Since 1910 it had been China's most populous city, and by the 1930s it had about 4 million residents. It attracted Chinese entrepreneurs, especially those willing to collaborate with foreigners. It had China's largest port and was the commercial center of China. In the 1920s and 1930s it had half of China's modern industry.

---

*Cited in Lloyd Eastman, *Abortive Revolution* (Cambridge, Mass.: Harvard University Press, 1974), p. 40.
†Cited in Jonathan Spence, *The Search for Modern China* (New York: Norton, 1990), p. 415.

Shanghai attracted more foreigners than any of the other treaty ports, a high of more than thirty-six thousand. The British and Japanese were especially numerous because they owned the most foreign companies. Some of Shanghai's foreigners had come in the nineteenth century and stayed; others were there for only a few years. Among the merchant families who amassed huge fortunes were the Sassoons, from a family of Jewish traders active in Baghdad and Bombay. David Sassoon began by trading cotton from Bombay to China in the 1870s; his son Elias Sassoon bought warehouses in Shanghai later in the nineteenth century; and his grandson Victor Sassoon turned to real estate, in the 1930s reportedly owning nineteen hundred buildings in Shanghai, including those that are now the Peace and Cypress hotels. Some of the early employees of the Sassoons also made fortunes, including Silas Hardoon and Elly Kadoorie. Hardoon started as a night watchman in the 1870s. Kadoorie's mansion is now the Shanghai Children's Palace.

Because the international districts admitted anyone, no matter what their passport or visa status, Shanghai became a magnet for international refugees. After the Russian Revolution, many of the Russian bourgeoisie fled east via the trans-Siberian railroad. Later they made their way south through Manchuria, many eventually settling in Shanghai, often to find only menial jobs. In the 1930s, thousands of Jews fleeing the Nazis also found refuge in Shanghai, where they were aided by the wealthy Jewish families already there, such as the Sassoons, Hardoons, and Kadoories.

The foreign presence in Shanghai was visible to all in its Western-style roads and buildings. Along the river an embankment called the bund was built and was made into a park with signs posted that read "No dogs" and "No Chinese."

With its gambling parlors and brothels, Shanghai had a reputation as a sin city. Reportedly about fifty thousand women worked in Shanghai as prostitutes in the 1930s. Young women were also drawn into Shanghai to work in textile mills or as servants. In 1930 more than 170,000 women worked in industry, about half in cotton mills. The typical prostitute or mill hand was a young, unmarried, illiterate woman recruited in the countryside by a labor contractor. The contractor would supply a small advance payment, often to the girl's parents, and would make arrangements in the city for employment, housing, and food. The women were often kept in conditions of debt servitude. Some factory workers joined unions and engaged in strikes; others put their hopes on getting married and returning to the country. Women in Shanghai, from factory girls and prostitutes to office workers and the wealthy, commonly wore dresses called *qipao*, a compromise between Western and Chinese styles. (See **Material Culture: Qipao**.)

Shanghai also attracted Chinese intellectuals, especially as Nationalist censorship became more severe. If they worked from the International District or French Concession, they were usually safe from the Chinese police. Dissidents, radicals, and revolutionaries chose Shanghai for much the same reasons.

Relocating the Communist Revolution

In 1932 the Central Committee of the Communist Party gave up trying to foment urban insurrections and joined Mao in the Jiangxi Soviet. Mao was the chairman of the soviet, but after their arrival, he was on the sidelines, his recommendations often overruled. In the fall of 1934, with the German-planned fifth "extermination campaign" of the Nationalists encircling them with a million-man force, the Communist Party leadership, without consulting Mao, decided to give up the Jiangxi Soviet. In October, about eighty-six thousand Communist soldiers, cadres, porters, and followers broke out of the encirclement, the start of the much mythologized year-long Long March in search of a new place to set up a base. Most wives and children had to be left behind (only thirty-five women joined the march). To protect them and the thousand or so sick or wounded soldiers left behind, about fifteen thousand troops remained in Jiangxi. Mao's wife, He Zizhen, although pregnant, was allowed to come, but they had to leave their two-year-old child behind with Mao's younger brother. When Mao's brother, like many of those left behind, was killed in 1935, Mao lost track of the child.

Month after month the Red Army kept retreating, often just a step or two ahead of the pursuing Nationalist troops. Casualties were enormous. The farther west they went, the more rugged the terrain; as they skirted Tibet, they also had to deal with bitter cold. By the time they found an area in Shaanxi where they could establish a new base, they had marched almost 10,000 kilometers. Only

DOCUMENTS   Wang Shiwei's *Wild Lilies*

Born in 1906, Wang Shiwei was one of eight children of a schoolteacher. During his school years he was strongly affected by the May Fourth Movement. In 1925 he entered Peking University and began to write for publication, both his own articles and translations of European fiction. After joining the Communist Party in 1926, he was sent to the Marxist–Leninist Institute in Moscow for further education. After the war with Japan began in 1937, Wang joined the Communist base camp in Yan'an, where one of his tasks was translating works by Marx and Lenin. In 1942 he published several articles in the Liberation Daily, *which portrayed the Communist Party as less than fully egalitarian. The party responded with a rectification campaign. Wang Shiwei was put on trial and later imprisoned. In 1947, with the civil war raging, he was executed. The excerpt below is one section in a larger essay titled* Wild Lilies, *one of the essays that got him into trouble.*

What is lacking in our lives?

Recently young people here in Yan'an seem to have lost some of their enthusiasm, and to have become inwardly ill at ease.

Why is this? What is lacking in our lives? Some would answer that it is because we are badly nourished and short of vitamins. Others that it is because the ratio of men to women is 18:1 and many young men are unable to find girlfriends. Or because life in Yan'an is very dreary and lacks amusements.

There is an element of truth in all these answers. It is absolutely true that there is a need for better food, for partners of the opposite sex and for more interest in life. That is only natural.

But one must also recognize the fact that all the young people here in Yan'an came with a spirit of sacrifice to make revolution, and certainly did not come to satisfy their desires for food, sex, and an enjoyable life. I cannot readily agree with those who say that their lack of enthusiasm, their inward disquiet even, are a result of our inability to resolve these problems properly.

So what is it that is fundamentally lacking in our lives? Perhaps the following conversation holds some clues for us.

During the New Year holiday I was walking home in the dark one evening from a friend's place. Ahead of me were two girl comrades talking in animated whispers. We were some

about eight thousand of those who began the march made it the whole way, though some new recruits and communists from other base areas had joined en route, to bring the total to nearly twenty thousand. (See Map 25.1.)

To the Nationalists in Nanjing, the Long March must have seemed a huge victory. The Communist Party's urban activists had been crushed in 1927–1928, and now the rural activists had suffered just as devastating a blow, their numbers greatly diminished and the survivors driven into remote and poverty-stricken regions. Those who made the Long March, however, saw it as a victory. That they had overcome such daunting odds reinforced their belief that they were men of destiny with a near-sacred mission to remake China.

It was during the Long March that Mao Zedong reached the top ranks of party leadership. When the marchers reached Zunyi (tsuhn-ee) in Guizhou province in early 1935, they paused to hold an enlarged meeting of the Politburo and assess their strategy. Seventeen veteran party leaders were present, including Mao, the Comintern representative Otto Braun, and thirty-year-old Deng Xiaoping to take notes. Blame was placed on Braun and others who had urged positional warfare to defend against the Nationalist attack. Mao was named to the Standing Committee of the Politburo and given new responsibility for military affairs.

From 1936 to 1946 the Communist Party made its base at Yan'an, a market town in central

way apart so I quietly moved closer to concentrate on what they were saying.

"He keeps on talking about other people's petty-bourgeois egalitarianism; but the truth of the matter is that he thinks he himself is something special. He always looks after his own special interests. As for the comrades underneath him, he doesn't care whether they're sick or whether they're well, he doesn't even care if they die, he hardly gives a damn!"

"Crows are still black, wherever they are. Even our Comrade XXX acts like that."

"You're dead right! All this bullshit about loving your own class. They don't even display ordinary human sympathy. You often see people pretending to smile and be friendly, but it's really all on the surface, it doesn't mean anything. And if you offend them in the slightest, they glare at you, pull their rank and start lecturing you."

"It's not only the big shots who act that way, the smaller fry are just the same. Our section leader XXX crawls when he's talking to his superiors, but he behaves very arrogantly towards us. Many's the time when comrades have been ill and he hasn't even dropped in to see how they are. But when an eagle stole one of his chickens, you should have seen the fuss he made! After that, every time he saw an eagle come flying over he'd start screaming and throwing clods of earth at it—the self-seeking bastard!"

There was a long silence. In one way I admired the comrades' sharp tongue. But I also suddenly felt depressed.

"It's sad that so many comrades are falling ill. As a matter of fact, nobody wants people like that to visit them when they fall ill, they just make you feel worse. Their tone of voice, their manner, their whole attitude—they don't make you feel they care about you."

"How right you are. They don't care about other people, and people don't care about them. If they did mass work, they'd be bound to fail."

They carried on their conversation in animated whispers. At this point our ways parted, and I heard no more of what they had to say. In many ways their views were one-sided and exaggerated. Perhaps the picture they drew does not apply very widely; but there is no denying that it is useful as a mirror....

Questions for Analysis
1. What were Wang Shiwei's main concerns in this piece? Did he make any efforts to blunt his criticisms?
2. Why would party officials have found this article objectionable?

Source: Wang Shiwei's "Wild Lily" from *New Left Review*, Issue 92, July-August 1975. Copyright © New Left Review. Reprinted with permission.

Shaanxi where homes were often built by cutting caves into the loess soil cliffs. When the American journalist Edgar Snow visited Yan'an in 1936, the survivors of the Long March appeared to him to be an earthy group of committed patriots and egalitarian social reformers, full of optimism and purpose. They lived in caves, ate simple food, and showed no disdain for the peasants whom they were mobilizing to fight against the Japanese. During the war, too, outside observers were impressed with the commitment to group goals of the Yan'an forces. All through Mao's lifetime the official media promoted this image of the leaders of the Yan'an Soviet as a cohesive group of idealistic revolutionaries.

Mao's standing in Yan'an was high, but he still had rivals. A group of communists who had gone to Russia for training arrived in late 1935 and provoked debate on the errors that had cost the lives of so many party members. Mao realized that he would have to improve his grasp of Communist dialectic and began systematic study. His new secretary, Chen Boda (chuhn baw-dah), who had studied in Moscow for several years in the late 1920s, began writing of Mao as a theorist. Mao was becoming more set against the claims of the well educated, even if their education was in Marxism. To contrast himself from the urban intellectuals, Mao would act like a peasant, opening his clothes to look for lice with guests present.

MATERIAL CULTURE

Qipao

In the first decades of the twentieth century, as educated young people came to look on the West as the source of everything modern, they turned to Western styles of dress. This was especially true of those who had worn this style while studying abroad. Some people adopted full Western-style dress, but others tried to develop a style that would be both Chinese and modern at the same time. The so-called Mao suit, first popularized in China by Sun Yatsen, is an example of this sort of hybrid style for men. For women in the early twentieth century, the garment that most successfully modernized Chinese dress was the *qipao* (chee-pow).

The *qipao* is a one-piece dress characterized by an upright ("mandarin") collar, an opening from the neck to under the right arm, and a fairly narrow cut, often with a slit, especially if the skirt reached below midcalf. The *qipao* was much more form-fitting than anything worn in the nineteenth century, but reflected traditional styles in its collar, its slanted opening, and sometimes its fastenings. It could be made of silk, cotton, or synthetics for everyday wear or elegant occasions.

Well-Dressed Young Women. These three young women wear *qipao* with short sleeves and high slits. Notice also their high-heeled shoes and curled hair.

Mao was victorious over the Soviet returnees in part because he was the better politician but also because he seems to have become truly confident that he was in the right. He began spending more time lecturing party members. He also started to allow or encourage the beginnings of the cult of Mao: in 1937, a portrait of him appeared in the revolutionary newspaper and a collection of his writings was printed.

It was during this period that Mao took up with Jiang Qing. He Zizhen and Mao's surviving children had gone to the Soviet Union for safety and medical treatment. Jiang Qing (jyang ching), twenty-four years old, had worked as an actress in Shanghai and made her way to Yan'an after the Japanese invasion. Some of the other Communist leaders resented her liaison with Mao, having liked and admired He Zizhen. Mao and Jiang Qing had a daughter in 1940, the last of his four surviving children (six were lost or died).

THE JAPANESE INVASION AND THE RETREAT TO CHONGOING

From the time of the May Fourth protests in 1919, Chinese patriots saw Japan as the gravest threat to China's sovereignty. In 1895, Japan had won Taiwan. In 1905, after an impressive victory over Russia, it gained a dominant position in southern Manchuria. In 1915, by applying pressure on Yuan Shikai, Japan had secured a broad range of economic privileges. The Japanese Army in Manchuria, ostensibly there to protect Japan's railroads and other economic interests, was full of militarists who kept pushing Japanese civil authorities to let the army occupy the entire area. In 1928, Japanese officers assassinated the warlord of Manchuria, Zhang Zuolin (jahng dzaw-lin), hoping for a crisis that would allow Japan to extend its power base.

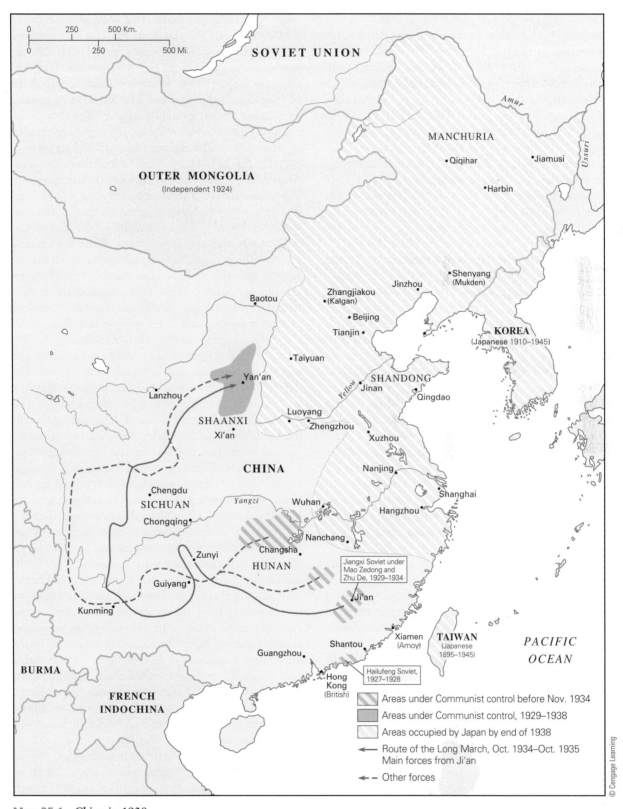

Map 25.1   China in 1938

In 1931, Japanese soldiers set a bomb on the Southern Manchurian Railroad to give themselves an excuse to occupy Shenyang (shuhn-yahng) "in self-defense." China did not attempt to resist militarily but did appeal to the League of Nations, which recognized China as being in the right but imposed no real sanctions on Japan. Then in January 1932, Japan attacked Shanghai to retaliate against anti-Japanese protests. By that point Shanghai was such an international city that the Japanese assault and the bombing of civilian residential areas was widely condemned. After four months, the Japanese withdrew from Shanghai, but in Manchuria they set up a puppet regime, making the last Qing emperor the nominal head of Manchukuo ("Manchu land").

Anger at Japanese aggression heightened Chinese nationalism and led to the formation of national salvation leagues and boycotts of Japanese goods. Still, Chiang, like most other military men of the day, did not see any point in putting up a fight when Japanese firepower was so clearly superior. Chiang was convinced that all Chinese would have to be united under one leader before China could hope to thwart Japan.

In 1936 troops that had been driven out of Manchuria by the Japanese were ordered by Chiang to blockade the Communists in Yan'an. When Chiang came to Xi'an, they kidnapped him and refused to release him until he agreed to form a united front with the communists against Japan. These troops did not want to be fighting other Chinese when the Japanese had occupied their home towns. The Communists played no part in the kidnapping but joined the negotiations when Stalin urged them to keep Chiang alive and create a nationwide united front against Japan.

The next year, Chiang did put up a fight when the Japanese staged another incident as an excuse for taking more territory. Chiang was probably hoping to inflict a quick defeat to convince Japan that the Nanjing government was a power to be reckoned with so Japan would negotiate with him rather than continue to move into China as though it was unoccupied. Japan instead launched a full-scale offensive, sweeping south. Chiang had to abandon Beijing and Tianjin, but he used his best troops to hold off the Japanese at Shanghai for three months. He asked for an all-out stand, and his troops courageously persisted despite heavy shelling and bombing, absorbing 250,000 killed or wounded (compared to 40,000 Japanese casualties). When Shanghai fell, the Nationalist troops streamed toward the Nationalist capital, Nanjing. After the Japanese easily took Nanjing in December 1937, they went on a rampage, massacring somewhere between 40,000 and 300,000 civilians and fugitive soldiers, raping perhaps 20,000 women, and laying the city waste. The seven weeks of mayhem was widely reported in the foreign press, where it was labeled the Rape of Nanking. If this violence was intended to speed a Chinese surrender, it did not achieve its goal.

During the course of 1938, the Japanese secured control of the entire eastern seaboard and set up puppet regimes headed by Chinese collaborators. (See Map 25.1.) Terror tactics continued, including biological and chemical warfare in Zhejiang (juh-jyahng) in 1940, where bubonic plague was spread and poison gas released. Civilian casualties were also inflicted by the Nationalist government. When the Chinese had to retreat from Kaifeng, Chiang ordered his engineers to blow up the dikes on the Yellow River, creating a gigantic flood that engulfed more than four thousand villages, drowned some three hundred thousand people, and left 2 million homeless. It delayed the Japanese for only three months.

Japan had assumed that once it captured the capital at Nanjing and inflicted an overwhelming defeat on the Nationalist army, Chiang Kaishek would come to terms. When he refused and moved inland, the war bogged down. Rather than persuading the Chinese to surrender, Japanese terror tactics instead intensified popular hatred for the Japanese. China's great distances spread Japanese forces. In north China, Japan concentrated on holding rail lines, and Chinese guerrilla forces concentrated on blowing them up. Guerrilla soldiers depended on local peasants to feed them and inform them of enemy concentrations and movements. They acquired weapons and ammunition by capturing them from the Japanese. Many resistance fighters worked in the fields during the day and at night acted as guides or scouts to help blow up bridges, rail lines, and roads. Peasant cooperation with the guerrillas provoked savage Japanese reprisals, including killing everyone in villages suspected of harboring resistance fighters, which the Japanese called their "kill all, burn all, loot all" policy. Chinese resistance forced Japan to keep about 40 percent of its troops in China even after the Pacific War had begun in late 1941 (see **Connections: World War II**).

The Nationalists' capital was moved inland first to Wuhan, then to Chongqing (chung-ching), deep in Sichuan. Free China, as it was called in the Western press, started with the odds heavily against it. The capital, Chongqing, suffered repeated air raids and faced not only shortages of almost everything but runaway inflation as high as 10 percent a month, leading to widespread corruption as government workers' salaries fell to a pittance. The army was in worse shape. The army Chiang had spent a decade training had been destroyed. From 1939 on, the bulk of China's 5 million soldiers were ill-trained peasant conscripts. Press gangs would enter villages and seize the able-bodied. As many as a third of the conscripts died on the forced marches to their bases because they were not given enough to eat or medical care. Desertion, not surprisingly, was a huge problem. Another serious disability for Free China was the lack of an industrial base inland. Chinese engineers made heroic efforts to build a new industrial base, but constant Japanese bombing, the end of Soviet aid in 1939, and the closing of the route through Burma in 1942 frustrated their efforts. From 1942 on, American advisers and American aid flown over the mountains from Burma enabled Chiang to build a number of modern divisions, but not an army able to drive the Japanese out of China.

During World War II, international alignments began to shift. After Britain proved unable to defend Hong Kong, Singapore, or Burma from Japanese invasions in 1941–1942, it lost its standing in Chinese eyes as the preeminent Western power. Its place was taken by the United States, which ended up doing most of the fighting against Japan. The American-educated wife of Chiang, Soong Meiling, was popular with the American press and lobbied effectively for China. President Franklin D. Roosevelt, looking ahead, wished to see China become the dominant power in East Asia after the defeat of Japan, and he convinced his allies to include Chiang in major meetings of the Allies at Cairo and Yalta (though Churchill referred to making China one of the Big Four as an absolute farce). It was as a result of this sort of geopolitics that China, so long scorned as weak and backward, became one of the five permanent members of the United Nations Security Council after the war.

THE CHINESE COMMUNIST PARTY DURING THE WAR

During the first few years of the war, there was some genuine cooperation between the Communists and Nationalists. This largely ended, however, when the Communist divisions of the New Fourth Army were attacked by the Nationalists in January 1941 on the grounds that they had not complied rapidly enough with an order to retreat north of the Yangzi. From this point on, the Nationalists imposed an economic blockade on the Communist base area.

Some one hundred thousand people made their way to Yan'an during the war, about half of them students, teachers, and writers. Party membership swelled from forty thousand in 1937 to about eight hundred thousand in 1940. The fight against Japan helped the Communists build a base of popular support. In areas of north China where the Japanese armies had penetrated, peasants were ready to join forces against the Japanese.

Resistance forces were not exclusively Communist. Patriotic urban students fled to these relatively uncontested rural areas where they helped both Nationalist and Communist resistance forces. The Communists, however, were more successful in gaining control of the social, political, and economic life in villages because they gave peasants what they wanted: an army of friendly troops who not only did not steal their crops but also helped them bring in the harvest and implemented popular economic reforms.

Class struggle was not emphasized during the war against Japan, nor was there much confiscation of land. Still, considerable redistribution was accomplished by imposing graduated taxes that led larger landholders to sell land that was no longer profitable. Landlords were more than welcome to help with forming and supplying militia forces, and educated youth from better-off families were recruited as party members. Party propagandists did their best to stoke patriotic passions, glorify the Soviet Union, and convey the message that the Communist Party could build a better, more egalitarian future. They called so many meetings that rural folk in Hebei quipped, "Under the Nationalists, too many taxes; under the Communists, too many meetings."[*]

The Japanese did not penetrate as far west as Yan'an, and during the war Mao could concentrate on ideological issues. As the party grew rapidly, Mao sought ways to instill a uniform vision. Neither Marx nor Lenin had seen much revolutionary potential in peasants, viewing them as petty capitalist in mentality; in Russia, the party had seized power in an urban setting. Because the communists in China

---

[*]Edward Friedman, Paul G. Pickowics, and Mark Selden, *Chinese Village, Socialist State* (New Haven, Conn.: Yale University Press, 1991), p. 41.

had failed in the cities, Mao reinterpreted Marxist theory in such a way that the peasants could be seen as the vanguard of the revolution. Indeed Mao came more and more to glorify the peasants as the true masses and elaborate the theory of the mass line: party cadres had to go among and learn from the peasant masses before they could become their teachers. Marx was a materialist who rejected idealist interpretations of history. Ideas did not make history; rather, they reflected the economic base, the mode of production, and the relations of production. Mao's vision of revolution, by contrast, was voluntaristic: it emphasized the potential for people, once mobilized, to transform both themselves and the world through the power of their wills.

This "Thought of Mao Zedong" did not win in a free competition of ideas among the survivors of the Long March, but rather in a power struggle in which Mao proved a master tactician, able to eliminate his rivals one after the other and get the Central Committee to label them deviationists of the right or left. To reform the thinking of both old cadres who had deviated from the correct line and new recruits from bourgeois families, in 1942, Mao launched the first of many rectification campaigns. Cadres had to study documents Mao selected in small groups, analyze their own shortcomings in Maoist terms, listen to criticism of themselves at mass struggle sessions, and confess their errors. Everyone watched the dramatic public humiliations of the principal targets, including the party theorist Wang Ming and the writer Wang Shiwei. People learned to interpret any deviation from Mao's line as defects in their thinking due to their subjectivism and liberalism, characteristics of their petty bourgeois background. One man, for instance, who confessed to being bothered by the party elite's special privileges (such as getting to ride on horseback while others walked) was taught that liberal ideas elevating the individual over the collective lay behind his feelings. Those who balked were punished; some even died. Many of those invited to overcome their errors truly developed a new collective consciousness that greatly increased their usefulness to the party. Others simply learned to be more circumspect when they talked.

The Seventh Party Congress, the first since the 1920s, was held at Yan'an in the spring of 1945. The preamble of the new constitution recognized Mao's new role as sage of the party: "The Chinese Communist Party takes Mao Zedong's thought—the thought that unites Marxist–Leninist theory and the

The Communist Leadership. Zhou Enlai, Mao Zedong, and Zhu De (left to right) were photographed in the winter of 1944, by which time the Communist party had gained a foothold behind Japanese lines all across north China.

practices of the Chinese revolution—as the guide for all its work, and opposes all dogmatic or empiricist deviations."[*]

THE CIVIL WAR AND THE COMMUNIST VICTORY

The end of the war with Japan set the stage for the final confrontation between the Nationalists and the Communists. When Japan surrendered in August 1945, there were more than 1 million Japanese troops in China proper and nearly another 1 million in Manchuria, as well as about 1.75 million Japanese civilians. Disarming and repatriating them took months, as the Nationalists, the Communists, the Americans, the Russians, and even some warlords jockeyed for position. The United States airlifted 110,000 Nationalist troops to key coastal cities like Shanghai and Guangzhou, and 53,000 U.S. Marines were sent to help secure Beijing and Tianjin. The Russians had entered Manchuria in early August in fulfillment of their secret

---

[*]Cited in Jonathan Spence, *Mao Zedong* (New York: Viking, 1999), p. 101.

promise to the United States and Britain to join the eastern front three months after victory in Europe. They saw to it that large stores of Japanese weapons got into the hands of the Red Army—some 740,000 rifles, 18,000 machine guns, and 4,000 artillery pieces—giving them about as much Japanese equipment as the Nationalists got.

From August 1945 until January 1947, the United States made efforts to avert civil war by trying to convince Chiang to establish a government in which opposition parties could participate. The American ambassador brought Mao and Chiang together for several weeks of meetings in Chongqing, but the agreements reached on cooperation led nowhere. Full-scale civil war ensued.

The civil war itself lasted only about two years. The Red Army (now called the People's Liberation Army, or PLA) began to isolate the cities, starting in Manchuria and working south. It lost battles but built support through moderate land reform. When Nationalist soldiers defected, they took their equipment with them, and the PLA incorporated them into its armies. Within a year the Nationalist forces in Manchuria were routed, and the PLA was moving into China proper. In 1948 a two-month battle near the railway center of Xuzhou (shyew-joe) pitted six hundred thousand of Chiang's troops against an equal number of Communist ones. Although Chiang had air support, his army was smashed, and he lost almost a half-million men. Thus, although the Nationalists had started with much more in the way of modern armaments and several times the number of troops, they fared poorly on the battlefield. In early 1949, Chiang Kaishek and much of his army and government retreated to Taiwan and reestablished their government there.

The unpopularity of the Nationalists had many roots. Prices in July 1948 were 3 million times higher than they had been in July 1937, and inflation did not let up then. People had to resort to barter, and a tenth of the population became refugees. Nationalist army officers and soldiers were widely seen as seizing whatever they could for themselves rather than working for the common good. Student protests were often put down by violence. When liberals demanded that Chiang widen participation in his government, he had his secret police assassinate them. No amount of American support could make the Chinese want to continue with this government in power.

SUMMARY

The years between 1927 and 1949 were marked by two long and bitter struggles: Chinese against Japanese and Nationalists against Communists.

Marxism did not make much of an impact in China until the success of the Bolshevik Revolution in Russia in 1917. Thinking that Marxism–Leninism might have something to offer China, Marxist study groups were formed both in Beijing and Shanghai. The Comintern, once it learned of them, offered both financial and organizational assistance. In 1921 the Chinese Communist Party was officially formed and began organizing labor unions.

From 1922 to 1927, the Communist Party formed a united front with the Nationalist Party, which broke down after the Nationalist army attacked union members when the Northern Expedition reached Shanghai. For several years, Communists had to work underground. A soviet was established in the hinterlands between Jiangxi and Fujian. After relentless attacks by the Nationalist army, the Communist leadership of the soviet decided to move their base and set out on the "Long March." During this year-long retreat, Mao Zedong emerged as one of the top leaders.

Beginning in 1928, the Nationalist government ruled from Nanjing, with General Chiang Kaishek in charge. He turned to people with Western educations to help modernize the government and the economy. Shanghai became a flashy international city, a magnet for European refugees. In cities across the country living standards improved, but in the countryside little progress was made in alleviating poverty.

Among the most pressing problems the Nationalists faced was Japanese encroachment, which became more and more serious from 1931 on, when Japan seized Manchuria. Chiang wanted to suppress the Communists before dealing with the Japanese, but in 1936 was forced to form a united front with them against Japan. When Japan launched a full-scale offensive in 1937, Jiang used his best troops to defend Shanghai at huge cost. Jiang had to retreat to Nanjing, then later to Chongqing in Sichuan. After the United States declared war on Japan, Chiang received significant American assistance, and after the war the United States unsuccessfully tried to broker a power-sharing agreement between the Nationalists and Communists. The Communists emerged from

World War II stronger than before. During the war they had been able to recruit new members and had gained experience mobilizing peasants. The civil war that broke out in 1947 led to Communist victory in 1949 and the withdrawal of the Nationalists to Taiwan.

What changed between 1927 and the end of 1949? How different was China? More than a half-century of struggle against a Japan intent on imperialist expansion was over: Japan had been thoroughly defeated and had turned against war.

The Nationalist Party had been defeated by the Communist Party and had withdrawn from the mainland. The Communist Party itself had changed dramatically. It had broken free from Comintern control and tied itself intimately to the peasantry. Mao had risen to the top position in the party and established his version of Marxism as the correct ideology. The party had grown enormously and acquired extensive experience in redistributing land, mobilizing peasants, and keeping a tight rein on intellectuals.

War and Aftermath in Japan (1931–1964)

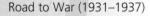
By launching war in Asia and the Pacific in response to domestic problems and what it saw as military imperatives, Japan spurred institutional and economic development while causing devastation and loss of life. After Japan's surrender, the United States occupied Japan and instituted reforms designed to transform it into a demilitarized democracy. Reforms that had lasting impact built on trends apparent during the war; other initiatives, including Japan's diplomatic relations with the United States, sparked controversy. Once the despondency of defeat had turned into a determination to rebuild, high-speed economic growth began in the 1950s. When the economy reached prewar levels of production in 1956, the government declared the postwar period to be officially over. Eight years later, the 1964 Tokyo Olympics marked Japan's return to the world order and restored its self-confidence as a nation.

The further World War II recedes into the past, the more historians emphasize continuities across its divide. Although the impact of the war on individual lives is undeniable, its long-term consequences on the economy and society are debatable. Other questions to consider are: Who was responsible for the war? What impact did the U.S. occupation have on Japan? What enabled Japan's postwar recovery?

ROAD TO WAR (1931–1937)

Military actions and rural crises dominated politics in the 1930s. In 1931, the army demanded support for its takeover of Manchuria in 1931, and the navy criticized the limitations on shipbuilding imposed by the London Naval Treaty. The armed forces transformed Japan into a militaristic state by forcing the Diet to curtail freedom of speech and approve its war budgets. Only a few intellectuals dared criticize imperialist policies. For the majority of citizens, being Japanese meant taking pride in the slogan

"Asia for the Asiatics," which papered over Japan's colonizing project.

Junior Officers and the Citizenry

Radical junior officers drew inspiration from diverse sources. They heard soldiers' stories of sisters being sold into prostitution to save the family farm from moneylenders, read in the newspapers of how the conglomerates profited from currency speculation when Japan went off the gold standard in 1931, and studied Kita Ikki's (KEY-tah E-kkey) *A Plan for the Reorganization of Japan*. Kita proposed that the "people's emperor" suspend the constitution and have the government confiscate surplus wealth, manage the economy, and provide social welfare and "world knowledge based on the Japanese spirit." When these goals had been accomplished, Japan would liberate Asia, and "the Sun Flag of the Land of the Rising Sun will light the darkness of the entire world." [*]

Officers modeled their plans for revolution on the Meiji Restoration. Like the young radicals of that time, they had to act to rid the nation of capitalist conglomerates that sucked the farmers' blood, self-interested and corrupt politicians, and evil advisers who prevented the emperor from making his will known to the people. They credited violence with purifying the state and mistrusted old men who might tarnish their youthful idealism.

Junior officers responded to and intensified factions in the military. Their hero, General Araki Sadao (AH-rah-key SAH-dah-oh), promoted spiritual training to instill devotion to the emperor and martial virtues of loyalty and self-sacrifice. He believed that the Japanese spirit (*Yamatodamashii*, YAH-mah-toe-dah-mah-she-e) sufficed to overcome mere material obstacles. Araki's Imperial Way faction opposed the Control faction's arguments that battles could be won only by rational planning using advanced military technology and sophisticated weaponry. In 1935, an Araki supporter assassinated the Control faction's General Nagata Tetsuzan (NAH-gah-tah TEH-tzu-zahn) and electrified the nation with his rant against military men and their civilian supporters who had corrupted army and *kokutai* (national polity).

---

[*]George M. Wilson, *Radical Nationalist in Japan: Kita Ikki 1883–1937* (Cambridge, Mass.: Harvard University Press, 1969), pp. 75, 81.

On February 26, 1936, junior officers, armed with the slogan "Revere the Emperor, Destroy Traitors," led fourteen hundred troops to seize the Diet building and army headquarters, kill cabinet ministers, and call on the emperor to announce a Shōwa (SHOW-wah) Restoration. Horrified at the threat of revolt, the emperor summoned the army to suppress the rebellion. After a four-day standoff, the junior officers surrendered. They were executed along with their mentor Kita Ikki in a victory for the Control faction.

An interdependent relationship developed between the military and the old middle class of shopkeepers and factory owners as well as teachers, low-ranking officials, and farmers. To promote this relationship, the army founded the Imperial Military Reserve Association in 1910, the Greater Japan Youth Association in 1915, and the Greater Japan National Defense Women's Association in 1932. Organized at the hamlet level, not the amalgamated village level, the Reserve Association took over community functions such as firefighting, police, road and canal repairs, shrine and temple maintenance, emergency relief, and entertainment. It arranged for drill practice, "nation-building" group calisthenics, and bayonet competitions as well as hosting lectures by military-approved speakers, and it corresponded with battalion adjutants regarding the welfare and conduct of conscripts. The Women's Association sank roots in urban as well as rural areas. These associations identified individual with community, community with army, and army with emperor.

Social Reform

In the 1930s, bureaucrats and social reformers focused on the devastated villages resulting from crop failures in northeastern Japan. When students dispatched by Hani Motoko (HAH-knee MOE-toe-co), female journalist and founder of the magazine *Woman's Friend*, reported that farmers knew nothing of modern hygiene and sanitation, spent money foolishly on ceremonies, lazed about, and drank, Hani established settlement houses that taught poor women sewing, cleanliness, etiquette, nutrition, and thrift. The Agriculture Ministry supported similar plans that promoted social education, agricultural cooperatives, economic planning, and moral betterment. The emphasis on thrift and frugality paralleled the nationwide effort by the Home Ministry, social reformers, educators, and women's leaders to

akg-images

Japanese Women Working in an Ordnance Factory. With ablebodied men drafted for the war effort, women had to take their place in industry.

increase Japan's savings rate, both to help individuals plan for emergencies and to fund national projects.

WARTIME MOBILIZATION (1937–1945)

During eight years of war between 1937 and 1945 (see **Connections: World War II**), government ministries were often poorly informed, disorganized, and overextended. Faced with unexpected challenges, they cobbled together ad hoc measures and made mistakes in carrying out the war overseas and on the

home front. Just as the army and navy competed for resources, the former emphasizing the threat from the Soviet Union while the latter focused on the United States, so did civilian ministries duplicate one another's programs and fight for control of domestic policy. Like Germany, Japan at first refused to mobilize women, a policy that limited the war effort.

Civilian commitment to the war varied. Businessmen supported military goals so long as they did not threaten survival of their firms. Under pressure to conform, citizens greeted news of the first victories with exultation, but dwindling food supplies, higher taxes, and a black market led to misery and despair.

Malnutrition increased the incidence of tuberculosis (160,000 deaths in 1942), rickets (bone softening owing to a lack of vitamin D), and eye disease. First children and then adults fled cities for the countryside. When the flower of Japan's youth was summoned to make the supreme sacrifice in the Special Attack Forces (*kamikaze*), many did so gladly; others did not. (See **Documents: Excerpts from the Diary of Hayashi Toshimasa.**)

Unlike other nations fighting in World War II, Japan changed its wartime leadership repeatedly. Seven prime ministers served between outbreak of war with China on July 7, 1937, and surrender on August 15, 1945. Executed as a war criminal for having declared war against the United States, General Tōjō Hideki (TOE-joe HE-deh-key) served concurrently as prime minister (1941–1944), army minister, home minister, and munitions minister and filled other posts as he perceived a need. He never directed naval operations, nor did the navy inform him when it fought. Even the army general staff challenged his authority. Civilian bureaucrats, especially in the Justice Ministry, maintained their constitutional autonomy. Only the Shōwa emperor received complete information on military policy and operations, including plans for surprise attacks on American, Dutch, and British bases in 1941. For fear that he might be replaced, he sanctioned military decisions as his ancestors had done for centuries.

Government planning of the economy began in 1931 when the Diet passed the Major Industries Control Law. It promoted cartels and required industries to tell the government their plans. In 1937 came the New Economic Order to make the Japanese Empire self-sufficient. Bureaucrats allocated funds to critical industries, nationalized electrical plants, supervised banks, and spun a web of regulation. The National Mobilization law of 1938 focused research on chemicals and machine technology. Large companies had to introduce on-the-job training for workers while labor was rationed according to production needs. Military requirements prompted the rise of new industries in fields such as optics, determined techniques used in existing industries such as steel, and stimulated technological innovation. Wartime priorities transformed Japan's industrial structure by forcing a decline in textile industries and an expansion in heavy and chemical industries.

The Home Ministry bent popular culture to the war effort. Foreign words being considered a sign of foreign sympathies, *baseball* became *yakyū*

(YAH-keyu). Martial music replaced jazz. Women had to dress in baggy pants called *monpe* (MOEN-peh) and were discouraged from having their hair permed because hair permanents were Western and wasted resources. The Communications Ministry that already controlled radio broadcasts through NHK, the national public radio station, founded the Dōmei (DOE-meh-e) News Agency in 1936 to channel national and international news to newspapers. To extend its reach, the ministry distributed free radios to rural villages.

The Education Ministry suppressed academic freedom and promoted patriotism. Professors critical of the war in China and military dominance over politics had to resign. Schoolchildren performed physical exercises to build bodies for the emperor; after 1940 they volunteered for community service projects. Starting in 1941, they took paramilitary training to identify enemy aircraft and practiced fighting with bamboo spears. Published in 1937, the textbook *Cardinal Principles of the National Polity* (*Kokutai no hongi*, CO-ku-tah-e no HOHN-gi) taught students that the emperor was the divine head of state and benevolent father to the Japanese people. Japanese were superior because of their racial homogeneity, and they possessed a distinctive culture and history infused by the radiant presence of the imperial house. No sacrifice was too great to protect this unique heritage.

In the name of national unity, the government suppressed all pacifist new religions under the Religious Organizations Law of 1939. Social reformers and feminist activists joined the Greater Japan Women's Society, which sent soldiers to war and promoted frugality. Patriotic associations united tenant farmers and landlords, workers and businessmen. The ideology of "dedicated work" praised labor as a public activity in service to the nation. Neighborhood associations organized air raid drills and kept watch for dangerous thought. In 1944 the Home Ministry folded them all into the Imperial Rule Assistance Association.

A dedicated citizenry and long-range planning could not overcome growing shortages while the government struggled to shore up the collapsing economy. Lacking imported technology, companies developed new techniques that took military needs and scarce resources into account. The Zero Fighter was crafted with extreme precision and used minimal amounts of steel regardless of the pilot's safety. In addition to the lack of fuel because of disruptions to shipping, the

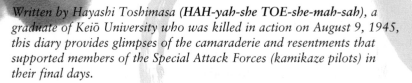

DOCUMENTS

Excerpts from the Diary of Hayashi Toshimasa

*Written by Hayashi Toshimasa (**HAH-yah-she TOE-she-mah-sah**), a graduate of Keiō University who was killed in action on August 9, 1945, this diary provides glimpses of the camaraderie and resentments that supported members of the Special Attack Forces (kamikaze pilots) in their final days.*

April 13, 1945

First Lieutenant Kuniyasu was killed in action, as was Second Sub-lieutenant Tanigawa Takao. Everyone is dying away. The lives of plane pilots are short indeed. I just heard today that Second Sub-lieutenant Yatsunami also died the day before yesterday; he dove straight into the sea while participating in night-training, and his dead body was washed ashore yesterday onto the white beach of Kujuūkuri-hama. Dear Yatsunami! I enjoyed getting together with him again here—the last time was in Mie. Dressed in his nightclothes, he came to my room rather late on the evening of the day before the accident, and we drank beer together. I wonder whether or not it was some kind of premonition. He was very gentle and quiet. When I said, "What a splendid nightwear," he just chuckled and said that it had been made by his wife, whom he just married in January. His wife too suffered the misfortune on this earth of a typical pilot's wife. How is she going to spend the long life that stretches ahead of her?

Tanigawa has a fiancée too, in Kobe. Those who were left behind may be unlucky, but their sacrifice is an offering for Japan's ultimate victory. So I would ask to please continue to live with strength and pride, and in such a way as not to bring shame to the brave men who courageously and willingly died for their country.

April 23

Nighttime flying began. After our flying operation we drank beer at a welcome party for Kamiōseko. I got a little high. Second Sub-lieutenant Kamiōseko and I were enraged at the current situation. It was all about our position as reserve officers in the Imperial Navy. Now I declare! I will not fight, at least not for the Imperial Navy. I live and die for my fatherland, and, I would go so far as to say that it is for my own pride. I have nothing but a strong antipathy for the Imperial Navy—absolutely no positive feelings at all. From now on I can say in and to my heart, "I can die for my own pride, but I would not die—absolutely not—for the Imperial Navy." How terribly we, the 13th class of pilots to come out of the "students mobilized for war" program, have been oppressed by the Imperial Navy! Who exactly is fighting this war now anyway? A full half of my classmates of the 13th class who were bomber pilots on carriers, and my friends, are now already dead.

June 30

It was raining when I woke up this morning, and I was so glad I could sleep some more that I pulled a blanket over me again. I got up a little after seven, took a late breakfast, and at a barracks I went over some slides designed to help us recognize the different types of enemy ships. Now I have finished with the

---

destruction of factories meant fewer manufactured goods such as fertilizer. Food production dropped.

Military conscription created labor shortages in industry and mining. The first to fill the gap were Koreans. Finally, in 1943, the government allowed women to volunteer for work in munitions and aircraft industries. Even before then it had put prisoners of war to work in steel plants and mines. The military ended educational deferments and drafted university students. In 1944, middle school boys started factory work.

The last months of the war brought widespread hardship. Evacuees to the countryside put an extra burden on farm villages that then suffered through a meager harvest in 1944. A few people criticized their leaders in anonymous graffiti and letters to the editor. Worker absenteeism rose, product quality slipped, and work stoppages spread. Although signs

slides. I returned to my own room, and am writing this and playing a record. Next door, on a blanket spread over the floor, Kami ōseko, Yamabe, Tejima, and Nasu are having fun playing bridge. No change outside—the steady rain continues.

I cannot begin to do anything about everything.

Simply because I shall have to leave this world in the very near future.

I should thank the Navy's traditional spirit, or rather their cliquishness, which drove Eguchi to say: "I want to go to the front soon—I want to die soon," and even drove me into that sort of psychological state. It even drove all the rest of us, university students transformed into pilots, into that same state of mind.

July 31

Today is a sortie day. It is the day for the eight planes of our Ryūsei (Falling Star) squad to carry out a special attack. The fog was extremely thick when I got up. It turned into water that dripped from the leaves and treetops on the mountain.

When I arrived at the airport, the items that were to be carried onto our planes were neatly set out in rows.

Last night, I completely changed everything that I was wearing. I also wound tightly around my waist the thousand-stitch cloth my mother sent me. Then there was the brand-new muffler my aunt in Yudate gave me.— In other words, I put on the very best things I had.

I am all alone and, expecting the sortie command to come along at any moment, I am writing this in an air-raid shelter.

Farewell dear Father, Mother, Brothers and Sisters, and other relatives and friends.

Please continue to live on enjoying very good health.

This time I am going right into Hans Christian Andersen's fairyland, and I will become its prince.

And I shall be chatting with little birds, flowers, and trees.

I pray for the eternal prosperity of the great Japanese Empire.

August 9 A clear day

Once again the enemy's mechanized divisions are approaching the home islands.

In one hour and a half I shall leave here for the sortie, as a member of the special attack force. The skies are a breathtakingly deep blue, and there is a sharp touch of autumn.

August 9th!

Today I shall fly one of the very latest in war planes, a Ryūsei, and will slam it into an enemy carrier.

Questions for Analysis
1. What do soldiers think about as they wait to die?
2. How do soldiers occupy their time?
3. Why do soldiers fight?

Source: *Listen to the Voices from the Sea: Writings of the Fallen Japanese Students*, comp. Nihon Senbotsu Gakusei Kinen-Kai, trans. Midori Yamanouchi and Joseph L. Quinn. Copyright © 2000 by University of Scranton Press. Reprinted with permission of the author.

of discontent were slight, they were enough to make politicians and bureaucrats who worried about the threat of social revolution urge an end to the war. By the time most factions in government were willing to admit defeat, approximately 3 million Japanese had died, many in devastating firestorms caused by the bombing of major cities. Despite evidence of destruction, the emperor's announcement of Japan's defeat on August 15 still came as a shock.

OCCUPATION (1945–1952)

Defeat did not bring an end to hardship. The suburban middle class was spared the fate of poor and working-class urban residents who lost everything in firestorms, but everyone was short of food. Farmers were better off, although stunned by defeat that called into question their cherished ideals of loyalty, patriotism, and service to the emperor. The occupation under General Douglas MacArthur that began on August 30, 1945, first considered punishing Japan, perhaps by returning it to an agrarian economy. After the beginning of the Cold War with the Soviet Union and the 1949 communist takeover of China, the emphasis shifted to keeping Japan in the free world.

Despair and Liberation

The war left 6.6 million Japanese soldiers and civilians stranded in enemy territory from Manchuria to Southeast Asia. The Soviet Union sent 575,000 Japanese military personnel and adult male civilians to Siberian labor camps while Soviet soldiers raped and killed women and children. Of Japanese settlers in Manchuria, 50 percent died at the end of the war, many at the hands of Chinese. Japanese settlers in Korea made their way across hostile territory to refugee camps and then onto crowded ships that sailed to Japan. Seventy thousand Japanese in the Philippines had to wait until the end of 1946 before seeing Japan; British and Dutch did not return their prisoners of war until 1947. On Pacific islands, Japanese soldiers resorted to cannibalism or starved before the last soldiers came home in the 1970s.

Returning soldiers and civilians met a cold welcome in war-devastated Japan where war widows, homeless orphans, and maimed veterans had become social rejects. Most shunned were victims from Hiroshima and Nagasaki who were subject to radiation sickness that turned them into outcasts. With the economy at a standstill, there was little work even for the able-bodied, and competition for jobs depressed already low wages. The winter of 1945–1946 was worse than the winters of wartime in that the rationed supplies of coal and food were not enough to stave off freezing and starvation. Urban women traveled to the countryside to trade heirlooms for food and patronized the black market.

For some, defeat meant liberation. If life had no meaning, why not drink, take drugs, and steal? In his 1947 novel *The Setting Sun*, Dazai Osamu (DAH-zah-e OH-sah-mu) mourned the loss of prewar values and presented the only choice left: to live for oneself alone. People who celebrated the end to restrictions on freedom of thought and behavior had an easier time coping with material shortages. Defeat upheld the beliefs of prewar Marxists and socialists who hoped to build a just society out of the rubble of failed capitalist fortunes.

The black market flourished at every train terminal, organized and patrolled by gangsters. Small factory owners made pots instead of helmets, and former soldiers became businessmen. Prostitutes called pan-pan girls who serviced GIs dressed in rayon dresses and nylon hose, permed their hair, and painted their faces in an orgy of self-expression not seen since the 1920s. The dominant themes in popular culture were eroticism and sex; flesh and the body replaced the *kokutai*, the body politic.

Occupation Goals

As Supreme Commander of the Allied Powers (SCAP—also shorthand for the occupation bureaucracy), MacArthur intended to demilitarize Japan and work through existing institutions to install democracy. The United States bought off the Soviet Union by handing over islands north of Hokkaido and kept the Allies out of Japan by putting them on the Far East Commission (FEC) that oversaw SCAP policy, which met in Washington, D.C. Only judges for the Tokyo War Crimes Trials represented countries that had suffered under Japan's war machine. One SCAP faction wanted to restrict Japan's international trade and send what was left of Japan's factories to its victims as war reparations. Another faction consisted of economists and lawyers ready to practice social engineering. By instituting land reform, revising education, promoting labor unions, emancipating women, limiting police powers, and rewriting the constitution, they planned to make Japan fit to rejoin the community of nations.

What was to be done with the Shōwa emperor? He did not sign the document of surrender on September 2, 1945; that humiliation was left to a general and a diplomat. Instead, he, the cabinet, and his staff tried to distance him from responsibility for the war, taking a stance of plausible deniability on all decisions save the last that ended it; at the same time, MacArthur persuaded him against admitting even moral responsibility. Although Britain wanted to try the emperor as a war criminal, MacArthur believed that once the military was gone, he needed the emperor as a bulwark against communism. By refusing to accept responsibility for the war when so many had died in his name, the emperor also alienated far-right militarists. The issue of his responsibility for the war has continued to rankle at home and with Japan's neighbors. On January 1, 1946, he announced that he was a human being, not a manifest god.

Defined by the new constitution as a symbol of the state, he continues to embody a national identity predicated on ethnic homogeneity.

Occupation Reforms

On October 13, 1945, the prime minister appointed a committee at SCAP's urging to consider constitutional revision. At the same time, political parties, progressive and socialist groups, scholars, and think tanks drafted constitutions ignored by the prime minister's committee. Its recommendations were so minor that in February 1946, MacArthur ordered his Government Section to take over the task lest a grassroots movement for a constitutional convention lead to too much democracy and an attack on the emperor. His people hid their work from the U.S. and Japanese governments, the FEC, and other branches of SCAP. After conferences between SCAP officials and cabinet representatives to debate the draft, it was published early in March 1946 and sent to the Diet for ratification. SCAP intervened repeatedly in Diet deliberations to limit discussion and prevent substantial revision. The new constitution replaced the Meiji constitution, to which it was offered as an amendment, upon approval by the Upper House, and the emperor issued it to the people on November 3, 1946.

Articles in the constitution define the rights to life, liberty, and the pursuit of happiness in terms of education, health care, police protection, work, and a minimum standard of living. Women received the right to vote. Freedoms included freedom from arbitrary arrest and unauthorized search and seizure plus freedom of assembly, speech, and religion. The judiciary became separate and independent and people detained by the police had the right to legal counsel. Now that the popular sovereignty was to be exercised through the Diet, the Privy Council was no longer needed. Instead the Diet acquired the sole authority to make laws, and a vote of no confidence sufficed to dissolve the cabinet. Within the Diet, the Lower House of Representatives had more clout than the Upper House of Councilors, which became an elected body, replacing the House of Peers.

The new constitution had clauses that MacArthur would have deplored in the U.S. Constitution. Workers obtained the right to organize unions and bargain collectively, professors had the right of academic freedom, and women were guaranteed equal rights with men. Most controversial was Article 9: "The Japanese people forever renounce war as a sovereign right of the nation....Land, sea, and air forces will never be maintained."[*] This wording was later interpreted to mean that armed forces could be created for self-defense. When FEC insisted on a clause that limited the cabinet to civilians, this too was interpreted as implying the existence of a military. In 1950, SCAP wanted Japan to create an army to fight in Korea, but Prime Minister Yoshida Shigeru (YO-she-dah SHE-geh-rue) refused. Instead he created a Police Reserve, soon transformed into the Self-Defense Force.

Once the constitution had been issued, the Justice Ministry reformed the civil code. The new code emphasized the equality of the sexes and the dignity of the individual, abolished patriarchal authority in the household, repeated the freedom of marriage promised in the constitution, and required that all children share the family estate. This was not a burden for middle-class families whose assets consisted of their children's education. For shopkeepers, restauranteurs, and farmers, an equal division of property plus heavy inheritance taxes all too often meant selling off their heritage.

SCAP quickly imposed additional reforms. The most radical forced landlords to sell their holdings to the government for resale to tenants, a measure met with approval by the Agriculture and Forestry Ministry, which had wanted a class of independent farmers even before the war. Absentee landlords had to relinquish all their land; resident landlords were allowed to keep only land they farmed themselves plus an additional five or so acres depending on the region. Although collecting tenant fees had already proved so burdensome that many landlords welcomed the chance to sell out, they lamented the loss of their ancestral way of life. By 1950, farmer-owners cultivated 90 percent of Japan's agricultural land.

SCAP also intervened in educational reform. With American schools as the model, a new single-track system of primary school, middle school, and high school replaced the specialized higher schools and extended compulsory education to nine years. Teachers embraced the new curriculum that stressed the civic virtues of democracy and individual responsibility. Locally elected school boards selected texts, although in later years they did so from a list vetted by the Education Ministry. Parent-Teacher

---

[*]Dale M. Hellegers, *We, the Japanese People: World War II and the Origins of the Japanese Constitution*, 2 vols. (Stanford: Stanford University Press, 2002), p. 576.

Associations involved mothers in school activities. New junior colleges, colleges, and universities made higher education available to a wider segment of the population than before. None rivaled Tokyo University, and all required students to pass entrance examinations.

SCAP kept itself above the law. Despite the separation of church and state spelled out in the Constitution, MacArthur allowed Christian missionaries to use U.S. government equipment and encouraged the emperor and empress to take instruction in Christianity. Censorship of printed materials and movies continued, with left-wing publications that criticized capitalism facing prepublication scrutiny. In movies, sword fighting and criticism of the emperor were out; romance between men and women was in. The first mouth-to-mouth kiss made headlines.

Economic Developments

Economic reform took many turns. Trustbusters took aim at conglomerates because they had contributed to Japan's war effort (Mitsubishi made the Zero fighter) and because their dominance of the economy appeared inherently undemocratic. SCAP ordered the holding companies for the ten largest conglomerates dissolved, broke up the Mitsui and Mitsubishi trading companies, forced family members to sell their stock and resign from boards, and purged fifteen hundred executives accused of aiding the war machine.

Japanese bureaucrats allowed government assets, including construction materials and machinery, to disappear into the black market or the hands of business cronies. To cover the deficit and the run on savings deposits at war's end, the Finance Ministry printed reams of money. Official prices soared 539 percent in the first year of the occupation, with black market prices ranging from fourteen to thirty-four times higher.

Fearing the destabilizing effects of inflation, at the end of 1948, Washington dispatched a banker from Detroit named Joseph Dodge. At Dodge's command, the government curbed domestic consumption by collecting more in taxes than it paid out, eliminating government subsidies to manufacturers, and cutting public works projects, welfare, and education. To promote exports, Dodge got the United States to agree to an exchange rate of 360 yen to the dollar. Deflation and economic contraction forced small businesses into bankruptcy.

The Korean War rescued Japan from the brink of depression and laid the foundation for future economic development. The industrial sector grew on procurement orders for vehicles, uniforms, sandbags, medicines, electrical goods, construction materials, liquor, paper, and food. Despite the prohibition on the manufacture of war materiel, Japanese companies made munitions while their mechanics repaired tanks and aircraft. Businesses plowed profits into upgrading equipment and buying advanced technology from the United States through licensing agreements and purchase of patent rights. Industries seeking a way to compete in the expanding world economy incorporated the quality control method that the statistician W. Edwards Deming had introduced to Japan in 1949. By the end of the Korean War, the increase in wages and economic expansion had brought food consumption back to pre–World War II levels. Consumers were able to buy household conveniences and still put money into savings accounts.

Labor and the Reverse Course

To promote democracy, SCAP had the Trade Union Law issued in December 1945, and workers seized the opportunity to organize. Now legitimate political parties, the Japan Communist party (JCP) and the Japan Socialist party (JSP) fostered trade unions. By the middle of 1948, unions enrolled more than half of the nonagricultural work force, including white-collar workers, especially in the public sector. Other workers organized production control movements to take over businesses, factories, and mines that owners were accused of deliberately sabotaging in revenge for democratization. Like unionized workers, they wanted to get back to work and make a living wage.

Workers united around issues such as adequate food, support for working mothers, equal pay for equal work, and democratic elections. Before the postwar election of April 10, 1946, in which women voted for the first time, a rally in Tokyo brought together workers, farmers, Koreans, and ordinary citizens to listen to speeches by Communists, Socialists, and liberals demanding a people's constitution and criticizing the cabinet for blocking democratic reform. On May 1, International Workers' Day, cities nationwide witnessed demonstrations in support of worker unity and democracy. On May 19, women joined demonstrations demanding that the emperor force the government to deliver food, and students held demonstrations a week later to demand self-government at their institutions. Socialist- and Communist-led labor unions that had formed in August organized strikes in October.

Labor union activism created a backlash known as "the reverse course." In January 1947, the prime minister warned that striking government workers would be fired. When a coalition of labor unions announced plans for a general strike on February 1, MacArthur called it off. In 1948, SCAP had the Japanese government issue regulations forbidding public employees to strike.

The reverse course took on additional dimensions when the Cold War led the United States to view its former enemy as an ally against communism. SCAP compiled lists of "reds" to purge, first from the public sector and later, during the Korean War, from the private sector. Approximately twenty-two thousand workers lost their jobs, and most of the JCP leaders went underground. Previously purged politicians, bureaucrats, and business leaders were rehabilitated, and the dismantling of the conglomerates came to a halt. When the Diet gave the bureaucracy greater control over trade and investment than it had during the war, the Ministry of International Trade and Industry (MITI) had the Japan Development Bank lend money from the government's postal savings system to private companies, advised the Bank of Japan on its loans to private banks, approved the transfer of foreign technology to industries it deemed worthy, and provided them with administrative guidance. The Finance Ministry regulated currency transactions by restricting funds individuals and corporations could take or send out of the country.

Before ending the occupation, the U.S. Senate had Japan sign a peace treaty with the Nationalist Chinese on Taiwan that prevented recognition of and trade with the People's Republic of China. The peace treaty and security treaty signed with the United States plus associated agreements signed in 1951 continued the occupation under a different name. After SCAP was dismantled in 1952, one hundred thousand American personnel plus dependents stayed on at military bases that dotted the islands. Extraterritoriality protected them from the Japanese judicial system and removed the bases from oversight by the Japanese government. Okinawa remained under U.S. military jurisdiction until 1972.

Under the U.S. security umbrella, Japan was free to pursue economic development, although it had to follow the U.S. lead in international relations. On Bloody May Day 1952, four hundred thousand workers, students, and housewives denounced the security treaty, Japanese rearmament, the status of Okinawa, and government plans to pass an "anti-subversive" bill that threatened academic freedom. In contrast to the left wing that called for neutrality, democratization, and demilitarization, conservatives supported alliance with the United States.

POLITICAL SETTLEMENT AND ECONOMIC RECOVERY (1952–1964)

In the first postwar election of 1946, a host of political parties contended for Diet seats. Yoshida Shigeru pulled together a coalition of conservatives willing to make him prime minister, but he had to resign when elections the following year gave a significant share of the votes to the JSP. Taking advantage of the JSP's inability to deal with economic crises, Yoshida became prime minister again in 1948 and stayed until 1954. He recruited former bureaucrats into his party whose administrative experience and skill at infighting gave them an edge in building factions. Meanwhile the JSP split over whether to support the U.S.–Japan peace treaty; it reunited in October 1955.

At the end of 1955, the two conservative parties formed the Liberal Democratic party (LDP). Except for brief interludes, it dominated the Diet and cabinet into the twenty-first century. During this period of one-party rule, heads of factions within the LDP selected the prime minister, who rewarded his supporters with powerful and lucrative ministerial appointments.

The LDP promoted economic growth as the nation's highest goal, less to enhance state power than to wean workers from socialism by offering them a better life. Starting in the late 1950s, the LDP spread the benefits of a growing economy across all sectors of society through higher wages and a higher standard of living. In 1958, it inaugurated national health insurance.

To help farmers, the LDP encouraged companies to locate factories near the workforce in rural areas. It encouraged farmers to increase productivity by mechanizing production and spreading chemical fertilizers and pesticides; paid villages to reorganize landholdings into fewer, bigger plots with more diversified crops; restricted the import of rice; and subsidized rice production. It built roads and sewer systems. Through these programs and the outright purchase of votes, the LDP acquired a lock on rural electoral districts. The appeal of conservative policies to small businessmen and shopkeepers gave it urban votes as well.

The LDP also maintained power by aligning itself with bureaucrats and businessmen. Advisory groups composed of businessmen, bankers, consumers, and union officials consulted with cabinet ministers on policy and proposed legislation. Former bureaucrats either ran for office or joined corporations whose fortunes they had helped guide. Cash flowed through webs of personal connections from businessmen to politicians to voters.

Political and Social Protest

Opposition parties in the Diet had so little power that citizens with grievances sought other ways to make themselves heard. Demonstrations against American bases and nuclear testing erupted periodically during the 1950s. The Japan Teachers' Union resisted the centralization of educational policy and personnel practices instituted by the Education Ministry in 1955. Sōhyō (SOW-heyo) (the General Council of Japanese Trade Unions) opposed the Japan Productivity Center set up by Japanese businessmen with U.S. assistance because unions feared it would exploit workers.

When the government decided to switch Japan's chief energy source from coal to oil, the Mitsui Mining Company called for the voluntary early retirement of six thousand workers at its Miike mine in Kyushu. The union responded with a strike marked by violence and death that lasted 113 days. In the end, workers learned that radical calls for class struggle undercut job security, and corporate managers learned that it was cheaper to transfer redundant workers to other operations than to fire them.

The largest political demonstrations in Japanese history erupted in late 1959 and extended to June 1960 over revision and extension of the U.S.–Japan security treaty. Negotiations removed the clause that permitted the use of U.S. troops to quell internal disturbances, but bases remained off-limits to Japanese scrutiny. Indicted but never tried

as a war criminal and a former minister in Manchuria, Prime Minister Kishi Nobusuke (KEY-she NO-bu-su-keh) rammed the revised treaty through the lower house with the help of police who evicted the JCP and JSP opposition. Outraged at Kishi's high-handed tactics, masses of demonstrators gathered outside the Diet. Sōhyō coordinated strikes and mobilized workers against the treaty while Zengakuren (ZEHN-gah-ku-rehn) (the All Japan Federation of Student Self-Government Associations) organized weeks of agitation. Some 134 groups and organizations including farmers and housewives joined the protest. Kishi had planned to celebrate the revised security treaty by welcoming U.S. President Dwight D. Eisenhower to Japan, but Eisenhower canceled the trip. On June 18, several hundred thousand people surrounded the Diet, but they could not prevent the treaty's automatic ratification at midnight. Kishi resigned five days later.

The ideological divide between the conservatives in power and progressives on the outside led to political unrest throughout the 1960s. In 1965, Japan signed a peace treaty with South Korea to the outrage of the left wing, which demonstrated against the exclusion of North Korea and the People's Republic of China. Thereafter fears that the United States was bringing nuclear weapons onto its bases in Japan or was using Japan as a staging area for its war on Vietnam sparked repeated demonstrations.

The constitution's guarantee of social equality and the Civil Code's emphasis on human dignity spurred *burakumin* (descendants of hereditary outcast groups) to renew their struggle for equal rights. Founded in 1955, the Buraku Liberation League (BLL) allied itself with the JCP and JSP to publicize unfair treatment by individuals and institutions. It participated in demonstrations against renewal of the U.S.–Japan security treaty that gained it widespread support, and later protest marches focused nationwide attention on the *burakumin*'s plight. After a government commission report in 1965 blamed *burakumin* problems on unwarranted social and economic discrimination, the Diet responded in 1969 by passing the Special Measures Law for Assimilation Projects that denounced discrimination without containing measures to stop it. To repair this defect, the BLL resorted to denunciation campaigns, sometimes escalating to violence and threats that silenced public discussion of *burakumin* problems.

Women's organizations in the 1950s worked to protect children and encourage respect for mothers. Women joined movements to prohibit nuclear testing and to promote world peace, demanded clean elections, and elected women to the Diet who pushed for sexual equality and human rights. Women had campaigned for the abolition of state-sanctioned prostitution before the war; their goal became a reality in 1956 when the Diet passed the Prostitution Prevention Law that took effect two years later. Although it abolished legal protection for prostitutes, it did not eliminate sex work. Women justified political activism on two grounds: their responsibility for their families and their constitutional rights.

Post-Occupation Economic Development

International and domestic factors promoted economic growth. Under the Potsdam Declaration, Japan was guaranteed access to the raw materials it had previously taken from colonies. Exchange rates remained stable until 1971. The world market was relatively open, and economic expansion across the free market world stimulated a growing demand for manufactured goods. Although Japan still had infrastructure developed before and during World War II, the most important prewar legacies were human resources—trained engineers, accountants, and workers—and the commitment to achievement through education. The first postwar generation of workers went into factories on graduation from high school, received on-the-job training, and worked long hours for the sake of their companies. Company-based unions held demonstrations during the yearly spring offensive but interfered as little as possible in production. When management upped basic wages, promised lifetime employment, and distributed raises based on seniority, workers began to live middle-class lives.

The wartime heavy industries and new companies that fashioned products for domestic consumption and export saw the greatest expansion.

Demonstrations Opposing the U.S.–Japan Security Treaty. During demonstrations opposing the U.S.–Japan security treaty, men and women marched on the American embassy demanding cancellation of President Eisenhower's visit, the prime minister's resignation, and dissolution of the Diet.

Steel producers, shipbuilders, synthetic fibers manufacturers, and electronics and household appliance makers invested in technologies imported from the United States and in labor-saving mass-production facilities. The government provided low-cost financing that made Japan the largest shipbuilder in the world in the 1950s. MITI protected car and truck manufacturers by forbidding foreign investment in the auto industry and imposing tariffs of up to 40 percent on imported cars. Companies that enjoyed less help from MITI were Matsushita (MAH-tzu-she-tah), maker of household appliances, and the electronics innovator Sony. (See **Material Culture: The Transistor.**) Supporting corporate growth were subcontractors that produced quality components for finished products. Between 1947 and 1952, the economy grew at an average annual rate of 11.5 percent. From 1954 to 1971, it grew at more than 10 percent a year, to rank second to the United States among free market economies.

Increases in domestic consumption led to high-speed economic growth. During the occupation, SCAP used images of American prosperity in the comic strip *Blondie* and other media to promote American values, while department store exhibitions and magazine advertisements illustrated the material life of the conqueror. Once the quality of food had improved, people wanted fashionable clothes. Every household wanted labor-saving devices such as washing machines, refrigerators, and vacuum cleaners. Television broadcasts began in 1953 because the owner of the *Yomiuri* newspaper and key bureaucrats believed that national pride required Japan to have the latest technology. The wedding of Crown Prince Akihito (AH-key-he-toe) to the industrialist's daughter Shōda Michiko (SHOW-dah ME-che-co) in 1959 swept televisions from retailers' shelves as viewers reveled in the democratic dream of a marriage based on love. Beginning in 1955, a massive exodus from farms to cities fueled a housing boom of high-density apartment buildings in suburbs. In these years, 90 percent of Japan's production went into the domestic market.

Postwar Culture

The consumption of mass culture stimulated growth in entertainment industries, publishing, and film. Commercial television stations demanded an endless supply of programming while the government-owned NHK had two channels, one devoted to news analysis, dramas, and *sumo* wrestling, the other specializing in education. Magazine and book publishers continued prewar trends without fear of the censorship that had kept them from sensitive political topics. Kurosawa Akira (KU-row-sah-wah AH-key-rah) directed *Ikiru* (E-key-ru) (*To Live*), which criticized bureaucratic arrogance. His 1951 film *Rashomon* (Rah-show-mohn), which questioned the possibility of knowing the truth, brought international recognition to Japanese cinema when it won the grand prize at the Venice Film Festival. A series with wider appeal was *Godzilla*, started in 1954, which drew on Japan's sense of victimhood by depicting a monster roused from the deep by nuclear explosion. Misora Hibari's (ME-sew-rah HE-bah-re) heart-wrenching songs of parting and loss spoke to the will to survive that had carried women through the hardships of war and occupation. Public intellectuals and writers such as Maruyama Masao (MAH-ru-yah-mah MAH-sah-oh) and Mishima Yukio (ME-she-mah YU-key-oh) questioned the ingredients of Japan's national identity. What did it mean to be Japanese if the nation's only goal was economic success? Where did responsibility for wartime aggression lie?

New religions provided one answer to these questions. Founded in 1930 and suppressed during the war, Sōka Gakkai (SEW-kah GAH-kkah-e) (value-creating society) was Japan's largest new religion in the 1960s. Its political arm, the Clean Government Party (Kōmeitō, CO-meh-e-toe), founded in 1964, became Japan's third largest political party. Today its leaders serve as town councilors and school board officers. It owns land, businesses, and shops; aids in finding marriage partners, jobs, loans, and higher education; and provides a sense of family and community while its group therapy sessions help followers solve personal problems and gain self-confidence. Sōka Gakkai teaches that the purpose of life is the pursuit of happiness; the three virtues of beauty, gain, and goodness bring happiness; and following the teachings of the thirteenth century Buddhist monk Nichiren and having faith in the *Lotus Sutra* bring virtue. Constitutional guarantees of religious freedom and the population shift from country to town led to an explosion in the numbers of new religions and their membership. Although they criticize the excesses of popular culture and consumerism, part of their appeal lies in their promise of material benefits.

MATERIAL CULTURE

The Transistor

Every electronic product today relies on transistors, a symbol and product of the technological age. Invented by Bell Laboratories in 1948, the early transistors were too unreliable and delicate for consumer products, and they could not handle high frequencies for the human voice. It took Sony researchers months of experimentation to find a usable combination of materials.

Sony introduced a transistor radio in January 1955, only to discover that it melted in summer heat. The second version, placed on the market in August, had poor sound quality, but it sold domestically owing to its battery's long life. Sony could not compete with American transistor radios until 1957, when it started selling a tiny "pocketable" radio. More important than the radio's size was the technological breakthrough based on the high-performance alloy germanium. In 1960 transistor radios became Japan's second biggest earner on the export market after ships. Teenagers loved carrying the radios to parks and beaches to listen to rock 'n' roll.

Sony introduced the world's first all-transistor television in 1960 and successfully miniaturized it two years later. In 1964, Sony displayed a prototype of a transistorized calculator at the New York's World Fair.

The transistors in the early radios, televisions, and calculators were huge compared to today's silicon transistors in integrated circuits that work liquid display calculators and watches. People typically buy electronic goods on impulse, indulging in gadgets that fill purses, pockets, and homes.

Sony Corporation

The TR-63. Sony's first successful transistor radio, the TR-63, could be called "pocketable" only because Sony salesmen wore shirts with extra-large breast pockets.

The Tokyo Olympics of 1964 marked the climax of high-speed economic growth and a turning point in Japan's postwar history. (See **Biography: Daimatsu Hirobumi.**) National and Tokyo metropolitan governments cleaned up and paved city streets; rebuilt stores, schools, and government offices; constructed stadiums at Yoyogi Park; dug new subway lines; laid new roads; and renovated Haneda Airport and connected it to the city by monorail. New hotels became Japan's first postwar high rises. The centerpiece of this vast public works project was the Shinkansen (bullet train), which covered the distance between Tokyo and Osaka in three hours and ten minutes. It was the fastest, most reliable, and safest train in the world.

Japan had been allowed to join the United Nations in 1956, and the Olympics marked the culmination of its reentry into the global community. Worldwide coverage of the games focused attention on Japan as a peaceful modern state. Ichikawa Kon's (E-che-kah-wah COHN) documentary, *Olympiad,* transformed the games into art.

BIOGRAPHY

Daimatsu Hirobumi, Soldier and Volleyball Coach

Soldier, prisoner of war, women's volleyball coach, and Diet member Daimatsu Hirobumi (DAH-e-mah-tzu HE-row-bu-me) (1921–1978) gained worldwide fame for his harsh coaching methods when his team won the gold medal at the 1964 Tokyo Olympics.

Conscripted into the army after the attack on Pearl Harbor, Hirobumi attended an officers' preparatory school in China and fought in China and Southeast Asia. The last months of the war found him in Burma with only raw bamboo shoots for food. Many soldiers died; sheer willpower kept him alive. He ended up a prisoner of war under the British in Rangoon where in revenge for the atrocities that the Japanese army had inflicted on British POWs and the humiliating surrender of Hong Kong and Singapore, British officers subjected Japanese POWs to degrading indignities. Hirobumi later recounted how he cleaned toilets for British and Indian soldiers with his bare hands. Worse, he had to clean female officers' rooms and wash the underwear that they removed before his eyes in a gesture calculated to be emasculating.

Returned to Japan after twenty-two months as a POW, Hirobumi found work coaching a women's volleyball team at a Nichibō textile factory. At that time, volleyball was a popular sport among factory workers because it could be played with just a ball in whatever space was available. In 1954, Nichibō organized a company team with Hirobumi in charge. In 1958 the team won all of Japan's major titles; in 1962 it won the world championship.

Hirobumi's training methods were brutal. He hurled balls at the players until they collapsed from pain and exhaustion and insisted that they play regardless of injuries. He also emphasized the incremental improvement of technique, relying on methods similar to quality control circles. His players once complained to the factory management that he was an enemy of women because he worked them unmercifully. Before the Olympics he allowed them only three-and-one-half hours of sleep a night and had them practice for four hours the day of the final match. He expected them to sacrifice everything for the chance to win, first for the company, then for Japan, just as he had sacrificed himself in wartime.

Eight-five percent of Japan's television sets were tuned to the Olympics the night the Japanese team defeated the Soviet Union in three sets. The women's unprecedented success made volleyball a national obsession. Hirobumi's fame swept him to a seat in the Diet's upper house in 1968, but he lost his bid for a second term.

Questions for Analysis

1. What did Hirobumi remember of his wartime experience?
2. What effect did the war have on the rest of Hirobumi's life?
3. What do Hirobumi's training methods tell you about company culture in postwar Japan?

Source: Yoshikuni Igarashi, *Bodies of Memory: Narratives of War in Postwar Japan* (Princeton, N.J.: Princeton University Press, 2000).

SUMMARY

Historians today argue over whether Japan can be deemed a fascist state in the 1930s, one with an ideology that condemned capitalism and modern individualism, or whether it was militaristic in that the military controlled government policy. The military was divided between technocrats and young men of spirit whose rage at capitalist conglomerates and corrupt politicians led them to advocate the violent overthrow of the state.

During the fifteen-year war that lasted from 1931 to 1945, citizens supported the military; they also participated in self-improvement drives. When the war intensified in 1937, each branch of government defended its turf while extending its reach. Government ministries planned the economy, manipulated popular culture, promoted patriotism, suppressed religious freedom, and tried to make up for growing shortages by demanding greater effort from everyone. In Hiroshima, children were demolishing buildings to make firebreaks when the atomic bomb exploded.

Determined to make Japan a democratic, peace-loving nation, the U.S. occupation protected the emperor from charges of being a war criminal and wrote the military out of existence in Japan's new constitution. It forced landlords to sell their land, instituted an American-style education system, and rewrote the civil code to promote equality. It also intervened in the economy and purged people deemed communist from the public and private sector.

During the occupation, Japanese people went from despair at defeat to a determination to rebuild their shattered lives and nation. Companies made what they could from leftover war materials until the outbreak of the Korean War in 1950 gave them access to capital and supplies provided by the United States. The increase in wages spurred a boom in domestic consumption.

At the end of the 1950s, the government announced an Income Doubling Plan. Even so, the unprecedented prosperity enjoyed by people in both urban and rural areas did not translate into passive acceptance of an increasingly exclusive political system dominated by the Liberal Democratic Party.

What changed between 1931 and 1964? What impact did World War II have on Japan, and what was the war's legacy? In 1931 Japan had an overseas empire, took pride in its strong army, and trained its citizens in patriotism. In 1964 it had lost control of even Okinawa, its Self-Defense Force specialized in domestic humanitarian aid, and academics were free to publicly criticize the emperor and his place in Japan's history. The war destroyed lives, infrastructure, and, for a time, belief in the Japanese spirit. Japan recovered thanks to the changing international climate of the late 1940s and early 1950s, reforms initiated by the U.S. occupation, protection provided by security agreement with the United States, and U.S. recognition that democracy required economic stability. It must not be forgotten that recovery also built on the bureaucratic, educational, and industrial foundation laid before the war. By 1964 Japan's GDP had surpassed its prewar peak, and purchases by Japanese consumers of the latest electronic technology spurred product development in key export industries. Translators had discovered modern Japanese literature, and art house audiences, Japanese film.

China Under Mao (1949–1976)

By the end of 1949, the Communist Party had gained control of almost the entire country, and Mao Zedong had pronounced the establishment of the People's Republic of China (PRC). The party quickly set about restructuring China. People were mobilized to tackle such tasks as redistributing land, promoting heavy industry, reforming marriage practices, and unmasking counterrevolutionaries. Wealth and power were redistributed on a vast scale. Massive modernization projects created new factories, railroads, schools, hospitals, and reservoirs. Ordinary people were subject to increased political control as the central government set policies that determined what farmers would produce, where and how their children would be educated, what they might read in books and newspapers, and where they could live or travel. The most radical phase was the Cultural Revolution, especially 1966 to 1969, when the party itself was attacked by students and workers mobilized to make permanent revolution.

Until the late 1970s, Western scholars had limited access to the PRC and had to rely heavily on analyzing official pronouncements and interviewing refugees. Scholars studied the structure of the government, its policies, its top figures, and their factional struggles. As China has become more open after 1980 and new sources have become available, research has revealed much more complex pictures of how China fared during the Mao years. Not only can the human dramas be examined with more nuance, but variation from one place to another can be assessed. Mao still fascinates. Can the excesses of the Great Leap and the Cultural Revolution be fully blamed on Mao's inadequate grasp of reality? How could one person make such a difference? The party is also a subject of renewed interest. How did policies set at the center play out at the local level? What means did local cadres (party functionaries) use to get compliance with policies? What were the consequences of vilifying intellectuals? How did day-to-day life change for ordinary people in villages and towns?

THE PARTY IN POWER

From 1950 on, the Communist Party, under the leadership of Chairman Mao Zedong (to use the phrase of the time), set about fashioning the New China, one that would empower peasants and workers and limit the influence of landlords, capitalists, intellectuals, and foreigners. New values were heralded: people were taught that struggle, revolution, and change are good; compromise, deference, and tradition are weaknesses. People throughout the country were filled with hope that great things could be achieved.

In terms of formal political organization, the Soviet Union's model was adopted with modifications. Rather than a dictatorship of the proletariat, as the Soviet Union called itself, China was to be a "people's democratic dictatorship," with "the people" including workers, both poor and rich peasants, and the national bourgeoisie, but excluding landlords and certain classes of capitalists. The people so defined were represented by a hierarchy of irregularly scheduled People's Representative Congresses.

Real power, however, lay with the Communist Party. The People's Liberation Army (PLA) was not subordinated to the government but rather to the party through its Military Affairs Commission. By the end of the 1950s, there were more than 1 million branch party committees in villages, factories, schools, army units, and other organizations. Each committee sent delegates to higher units, including county and province committees, leading up to the three top tiers: the Central Committee with a few dozen members, the Politburo with around a dozen members, and its Standing Committee, which in 1949 consisted of Mao Zedong, Liu Shaoqi (lyou shau-chee), Zhou Enlai (joe un-ly), Zhu De (joo duh), and Chen Yun (chuhn yuhn) and later was expanded to include Deng Xiaoping (duhng shyow-ping). Mao Zedong was recognized as the paramount leader and was treated almost as though he was an emperor. In 1953, when he was sixty years old, Mao was chairman of the party, chairman of the Military Affairs Commission, and chairman of the PRC. The central government had dozens of ministries, and Mao needed an array of secretaries to handle all the paperwork he had to process. Expert organizers like Zhou Enlai and Liu Shaoqi, both of whom had been active in the party since the early 1920s, coordinated foreign and economic policy, respectively.

The Communist Party faced enormous challenges. After forty years of fighting in one part of the country or another, the economy was in shambles. Inflation was rampant. Railroad tracks had been torn up and bridges destroyed. Harbors were clogged with sunken ships. People displaced by war numbered in the millions. Many of those manning essential services had been either Japanese collaborators or Nationalist appointees and did not inspire trust. Chiang Kaishek had transferred much of his army to Taiwan and had not given up claim to be the legitimate ruler of China.

In December 1949, Mao went to Moscow to confer with Joseph Stalin. He stayed nine weeks—his first trip abroad—and arranged for Soviet loans and technical assistance. Soon more than twenty thousand Chinese trainees went to the Soviet Union, and some ten thousand Russian technicians came to China to help set up 156 Soviet-designed heavy industrial plants. To pay for these projects, agriculture was heavily taxed, again on the Soviet model. According to the First Five Year Plan put into effect for the years 1953 to 1957, output of steel was to be quadrupled, power and cement doubled. Consumer goods, however, were to be increased by much smaller increments—cotton piece goods by less than half, grain by less than a fifth.

But China could not create everything from scratch. Ways had to be found to maintain the infrastructure of modern urban life, the factories, railroads, universities, newspapers, law courts, and tax-collecting stations, even as the party took them over. When the Red Army entered cities, its peasant soldiers put an end to looting and rounded up beggars, prostitutes, opium addicts, and petty criminals. They set up street committees, which were told to rid the cities of flashy clothes, provocative hairstyles, and other signs of decadence. But illiterate soldiers were not qualified to run all urban enterprises on their own.

The new state took over some enterprises outright. By taking over the banks, the government brought inflation under control within a year. The new government took control of key industries, such as the railroads and foreign trade. In other cases, capitalists and managers were left in place but were forced to follow party directives. A large-scale campaign was launched in 1951–1952 to weed out the least cooperative of the capitalists still controlling private enterprises. City residents were mobilized to accuse merchants and manufacturers of bribery, tax evasion, theft of state assets, cheating in labor or materials, and stealing state economic secrets.

In the single month of April 1952, seventy thousand Shanghai businessmen were investigated and criticized. The targets often felt betrayed when their family members and friends joined in attacking them. Once businessmen confessed, they had to pay restitution, which often meant giving shares of their enterprises to the government, turning them into joint government–private ventures. To keep enterprises running, the former owners were often kept on as government-paid managers, but they had been discredited in the eyes of their former subordinates. Smaller manufacturing plants, stores, and restaurants were gradually dominated by the government through its control of supplies and labor.

As the party took control, it brought the advantages of modern life, such as schools and health care, to wider and wider circles of the urban and rural poor. During the 1950s, rapid progress was made in cutting illiteracy and raising life expectancy. Employment was found for all, and housing of some sort was provided for everyone.

Ideology and Social Control

China's new leaders called their victory in the civil war "the liberation." As they saw it, the Chinese people had been freed from the yoke of the past and now could rebuild China as a socialist, egalitarian, forward-looking nation. China would regain its stature as a great nation and demonstrate to the world the potential of socialism to lift the masses out of poverty. Achieving these goals required adherence to correct ideology, identified as "Mao Zedong Thought." Because Mao's ideas changed over time and put emphasis on practice over theory, even those who had studied Mao's writings could never be totally sure they knew how he would view a particular issue. As long as Mao lived, he was the interpreter of his own ideas, the one to rule on what deviated from ideological correctness.

Spreading these ideas was the mission of propaganda departments and teams, which quickly took over the publishing industry. Schools and colleges were also put under party supervision, with a Soviet-style Ministry of Education issuing directives. Numerous mass organizations were set up, including the Youth League, Women's Federation, and Labor Union Federation. Party workers who organized meetings of these groups were simultaneously to learn from the masses, keep an eye on them, and get them behind new policies. Meeting halls and other buildings were festooned with banners and posters proclaiming party slogans.

The pervasive attack on the old led to the condemnation of many features of traditional culture. Traditional religion was labeled feudal superstition. In 1950 the Marriage Reform Law granted young people the right to choose their marriage partners, wives the right to initiate divorce, and wives and daughters rights to property. The provisions of these laws did not go much farther than the Nationalists' Civil Code of 1930, but they had a considerably greater impact because campaigns were launched to publicize them and to assure women of party support if they refused marriages arranged by their parents or left unbearable husbands or mothers-in-law. During the first five years of the new law, several million marriages were dissolved, most at the request of the wives. Other policies also contributed to the weakening of patriarchal authority. The collectivization of land and appropriation of business assets led to a drastic shrinkage of family property. As more children entered schools and mass organizations like the Youth League, their parents had less authority over them. Women, too, came to see more possibilities beyond the family. The public appearance of women in positions of authority, ranging from street committees to university faculties and the upper echelons of the party, offered women new role models.

Art and architecture were also deployed to spread new ideas. The old city of Beijing was given a new look to match its status as capital of New China. The huge walls around Beijing were torn down as outmoded obstacles to traffic. The area south of the old imperial palace was cleared of buildings to create Tiananmen (tyen-ahn mun) (Gate of Heavenly Peace) Square. (See **Material Culture: The Monument to the People's Heroes.**) On either side of this square, two huge Soviet-style buildings were erected: the Great Hall of the People and the Museum of Chinese History. When huge May Day and National Day rallies were held, China was visually linked to communist countries all around the world.

The Communist Party developed an effective means of social and ideological control through the *danwei* (dahn-way) (work unit). Most people's *danwei* was their place of work; for students it was their school; for the retired or unemployed, their neighborhood. Each *danwei* assigned housing, supplied ration coupons (for grain, other foodstuffs, cloth, and anything else in short supply), managed birth control programs, and organized mass campaigns. Individuals even needed their *danwei*'s permission to get married or divorced.

MATERIAL CULTURE

The Monument to the People's Heroes

With the communist victory, much of China's old visual culture was rejected and new forms put in its place. Although the old palace was retained and transformed into a museum, it also became the backdrop to a huge new square (Tiananmen Square) where mass rallies could be held. Across from the palace, a new monument was erected after years of careful planning. On the front of this ten-story-high obelisk is a quotation from Mao Zedong in his own hand, and on the back is another written out by Zhou Enlai. At the base, ten bas-reliefs depict major moments in the struggles of the people from the Opium War to the final stage of the "War of Liberation." The art was done collaboratively, rather than by individually recognized artists, and the people depicted were not supposed to look like actual historical actors, but to represent the idealized revolutionary. This "international socialist-realist" style was also seen in posters, book illustrations, and paintings.

Sculptural Frieze on Monument to the People's Heroes. The largest of the friezes is on the front of the monument and depicts the final moment in the civil war when the PLA crossed the Yangzi River. Each of the figures shows a similar heroic determination.

The Korean War and the United States as the Chief Enemy

The new government did not have even a year to get its structures and policies in place before it was embroiled in war in Korea. After World War II, with the ensuing Cold War between the United States and the Soviet Union, the Soviet Union was dominant in Korea above the 38th parallel and the United States below it (see Chapter 29). Mao knew that China's development plans hinged on respite from war. Stalin, however, approved North Korea's plan to invade South Korea, and the invasion occurred in June 1950. In October U.S. forces, fighting under the United Nations flag in support of the South, crossed the 38th parallel and headed toward the Yalu River, the border between North Korea and China. Later that month, Chinese "volunteers," under the command of Peng Dehuai (puhng duh-hwy), began to cross the Yalu secretly, using no lights or radios. In late November they surprised the Americans and soon forced them to retreat south of Seoul. In total, more than 2.5 million Chinese troops, as well as all of China's tanks and more than half of its artillery and aircraft, were sent to Korea. A stalemate followed, and peace talks dragged on until 1953, largely because China wanted all prisoners repatriated, but fourteen thousand begged not to be sent back.

This war gave the Communist Party legitimacy in China: China had "stood up" and beaten back the imperialists. But the costs were huge. Not only did China suffer an estimated 360,000 casualties, but the war eliminated many chances for gradual reconciliation, internal and external. The United States, now viewing China as its enemy, sent the Seventh Fleet to patrol the waters between China and Taiwan and increased aid to Chiang Kaishek in Taiwan. China began to vilify the United States as its prime enemy.

With Taiwan occupying the China seat on the UN Security Council, the United States pushed through the UN a total embargo on trade with China and enforced it by a blockade of China's coast. Of necessity, self-reliance became a chief virtue of the revolution in China. When the United States helped supply the French in their war to regain control of Vietnam, China supplied Ho Chi Minh and the Vietminh. China became more afraid of spies and enemy agents and expelled most of the remaining Western missionaries and businessmen. A worse fate awaited those who had served in the Nationalist government or army. A campaign of 1951 against such "counterrevolutionaries" resulted in the execution of tens or hundreds of thousands, with similar numbers sent to harsh labor reform camps. This campaign was also used to disarm the population; more than five hundred thousand rifles were collected in Guangdong alone.

Collectivizing Agriculture

The lives of hundreds of millions of China's farmers were radically altered in the 1950s by the progressive collectivization of land and the creation of a new local elite of rural cadres. Starting in the 1930s, when the Communist Party took control of new areas, it taught peasants a new way to look at the old order: social and economic inequalities were not natural but a perversion caused by the institution of private property. The old literati elite were not exemplars of Confucian virtues but the cruelest of exploiters who pressured their tenants to the point where they had to sell their children. That antiquated "feudal" order needed to be replaced with a communal order where all would work together unselfishly for common goals.

The first step was to redistribute land. Typically, the party would send a small team of cadres and students to a village to cultivate relations with the poor,

organize a peasant association, identify potential leaders from among the poorest peasants, compile lists of grievances, and organize struggles against those most resented. Eventually the team would supervise the classification of the inhabitants as landlords, rich peasants, middle peasants, poor peasants, and hired hands. The analysis of class was supposed to be scientific, but moral judgments tended to intrude. How should one classify elderly widows who rented out their meager holdings because they were incapable of working the holdings themselves? Somewhat better-off families of veterans? Families that had bought land only recently using money earned in urban factories? Or families newly impoverished because the household head was a decadent wastrel or an opium addict?

These uncertainties allowed land reform activists to help friends and get back at enemies. In some villages, there was not much surplus to redistribute. In others, violence flared, especially when villagers tried to get those labeled landlords or rich peasants to reveal where they had buried their gold. Landlords and rich peasants faced not only loss of their land but also punishment for past offenses; a not insignificant number were executed. Another result of the class struggle stage of land reform was the creation of a caste-like system in the countryside. The descendants of those labeled landlords were excluded from leadership positions, while the descendants of former poor and lower-middle peasants gained preference.

Redistribution of land gained peasant support but did not improve productivity. Toward that end, progressive collectivization was promoted. First, farmers were encouraged to join mutual aid teams, sometime later to set up cooperatives. Cooperatives pooled resources but returned compensation based on inputs of land, tools, animals, and labor. In the "old liberated areas" in north China, this was accomplished in the early 1940s; in south China, these measures were extended from 1950 to 1953. From 1954 to 1956 a third stage was pushed: higher-level collectives that amalgamated cooperatives and did away with compensation for anything other than labor. Most of these higher-level cooperatives were old villages or parts of large villages. Once they were in place, economic inequality within villages was all but eliminated.

In 1953 the Chinese state took control of the grain market. After taking 5 to 10 percent of each collective's harvest as a tax, the government allowed the unit to retain a meager subsistence ration per person; then it purchased a share of the "surplus" at prices it set, a hidden form of taxation. Interregional commerce was redefined as criminal speculation, an extreme form of capitalist exploitation. Trade was taken over by the state, and rural markets ceased to function. Many peasants lost crucial sideline income, especially peasants in poorer areas who had previously made ends meet by operating such small enterprises as oil presses, paper mills, or rope factories. Carpenters and craftsmen who used to travel far and wide became chained to the land, unable to practice their trades except in their own localities.

Rural cadres became the new elite in the countryside. How policy shifts were experienced by ordinary people depended on the personal qualities of the lowest level of party functionaries. In some villages, literate middle peasants who knew a lot about farming rose to leadership positions. In other villages, toughs from the poorest families rose because of their zeal in denouncing landlord exploitation. To get ahead, a team leader had to produce a substantial surplus to serve the needs of the revolution without letting too much be taken away and thus losing his team's confidence. As units were urged to consolidate and enlarge, rural cadres had to spend much of their time motivating members and settling squabbles among them. Serving as a rural cadre offered to farmers with the requisite talents the possibilities for social mobility well beyond anything that had existed in imperial China because local team leaders could rise in the party hierarchy.

Much was accomplished during collectivization to improve the lot of farmers in China. Schools were opened in rural areas, and children everywhere enrolled for at least a few years, cutting the illiteracy rate dramatically. Basic health care was brought to the countryside via clinics and "barefoot doctors," peasants with only a few months of training who could at least give vaccinations and provide antibiotics and other medicines. Collectives took on responsibility for the welfare of widows and orphans who had no one to care for them.

Minorities and Autonomous Regions

New China proclaimed itself to be a multinational state. Officially the old view of China as the civilizing center, gradually attracting, acculturating, and absorbing non-Chinese along its frontiers, was replaced by a vision of distinct ethnic groups joined in a collaborative state. "Han" was promoted as the correct term for the most advanced ethnic group; "Chinese" was stretched to encompass all ethnic groups in the People's Republic. The policy of multinationality was copied from that of the Soviet Union, which had devised it as the best way to justify retaining all the lands acquired by the czar in the eighteenth and nineteenth centuries. For China the model similarly provided a way to justify reasserting dominion over Tibet and Xinjiang, both acquired by the Qing but independent after 1911. (Mongolia had fallen away as well; however, under the domination of the Soviet Union, it had established a communist government in the 1920s, so China did not challenge its independence.)

Identifying and labeling China's minority nationalities became a major state project in the 1950s. Stalin had enunciated a nationalities policy with four criteria for establishing a group as a "nationality": common language, common territory, a common economic life, and a common psychological makeup manifested in common cultural traits. Using these criteria, Chinese linguists and social scientists investigated more than four hundred groups. After classifying most as local subbranches of larger ethnic groups, they ended up with fifty-five recognized minority nationalities making up about 7 percent of the population. Some of these nationalities were clear cases, like the Tibetans and Uighurs, who spoke distinct languages and lived in distinct territories. Others seemed matters of degree, like the Hui, Chinese-speaking Muslims scattered throughout the country, and the Zhuang (jwahng) of Guangxi, who had long been quite sinified. In cases where a particular minority dominated a county or province, the unit would be recognized as autonomous, giving it the prerogative to use its own language in schools and government offices. Tibet, Xinjiang, Ningxia (ning-shyah), and Inner Mongolia were all made autonomous provinces, and large parts of Sichuan, Yunnan, and Guizhou were declared autonomous regions of the Zhuang, Miao, Yi, and other minorities. (See Map 27.1.) By 1957, four hundred thousand members of minority groups had been recruited as party members.

Despite the protections given minorities in their autonomous regions, many of them became progressively more Han through migration (see **Biography: Jin Shuyu, Telephone Minder**). Inner Mongolia soon became 90 percent Han Chinese, and the traditional Mongol nomadic culture largely disappeared as ranch-style stock-raising replaced moving the herds with the seasons. In Xinjiang, too, in-migration of Han Chinese changed the ethnic makeup, especially in the cities. Manchuria, now called the Northeast, had for nearly a century been the destination of millions of Han Chinese, a process that continued as the Communists built on the heavy industry base left by the Japanese.

BIOGRAPHY   Jin Shuyu, Telephone Minder

Jin Shuyu was born in 1917 to an ethnic Korean family in southern Manchuria near the border with Korea. Her father was a doctor, but when she finished middle school in the early 1930s, Japan had taken over Manchuria, and Jin, like many of her classmates, ran away into the hills to join the anti-Japanese resistance. The insurrectionaries engaged primarily in guerrilla action, trying to blow up storehouses or convoy trucks and the like. To support themselves, they would kidnap rich people and hold them for ransom. They accepted advice from communist organizers but were not a communist group. Finally, they were hard hit by the Japanese and had to scatter.

Jin's family could not hide her because the Japanese knew she was a "bandit." She therefore decided to try to slip into Korea. She worked first as a servant near the border. After she was able to get forged papers, she went to Seoul, where she got a job teaching middle school. In Seoul she married a Han Chinese eleven years her senior who owned a Chinese restaurant, and the couple soon had children. At the end of the war in 1945, the Japanese ransacked the restaurant. Added to that, the family lost all their savings when the banks failed. Yet they were able to borrow enough money to start another restaurant.

In 1949 when the Communists won in China, Jin was thirty-two and wanted to return to China, but her husband was against it. Then the Korean War started. Their restaurant did well, as Seoul was swollen with foreign soldiers who liked Chinese food, but Jin wanted to return home. Her husband said she could go; he would stay behind until she had sized up the situation. In 1953 she took their children with her across the 38th parallel, then made her way through North Korea back into China. Her husband never followed. They wrote to each other through a cousin in Japan, and in 1983 they were both able to go to Japan to see each other, the first time in thirty years. Her son tried to convince his father to return with them to China, but he said

he still wanted to wait to see how things turned out. Jin thought he kept putting off joining them because he was influenced too much by the anticommunist propaganda of South Korea, or perhaps because he had taken a new wife and never told them.

Jin's life in China was relatively uneventful. In 1958 she was given a job by her street committee to mind the community telephone. Those who wanted to make a call would pay her a fee and she would let them use it. She also would go and get people when calls came in for them. Jin's salary was very low, but she got half the fees people paid to make calls. Moreover, as she told her interviewer in 1958, she enjoyed listening to people talk on the phone, especially young people who often grinned through their calls or bowed and scraped when seeking favors from the people they called.

During the Cultural Revolution, people accused Jin of having a bad class background. She had to locate some of her old comrades to speak up for her, and they said she had distinguished herself in an unofficial anti-Japanese force and should be getting money from the government. After that things were easier because Jin was classified as an "Anti-Japanese Alliance Veteran" and a repatriated overseas Chinese. She also had some minor privileges as an ethnic minority. However, she told her interviewer, "I'm no more Korean than you are. I became Han Chinese long ago."*

Jin's son did well, not only graduating from college but also becoming a college professor. By the early 1980s, Jin lived comfortably. Her only complaint was that her daughter-in-law thought too highly of herself.

Questions for Analysis

1. In what ways was Jin's life shaped by political events?
2. How did Jin understand ethnicity? What role did it play in her life?

---

*Zhang Xinxin and Sang Ye, *Chinese Lives: An Oral History of Contemporary China* (New York: Pantheon Books, 1987), p. 20.

Tibet was a special case. It had not come under rule of any sort from Beijing until the eighteenth century, and the Manchu rulers had interfered relatively little with the power of the Lamaist Buddhist monasteries. From the 1890s on, Tibet fell more under the sway of the British, but Britain left India in 1947, ending its interest in Tibet. In 1950, when Lhasa would not agree to "peaceful liberation," the PLA invaded. On the recommendation of India, the United Nations would not listen to Tibetan appeals.

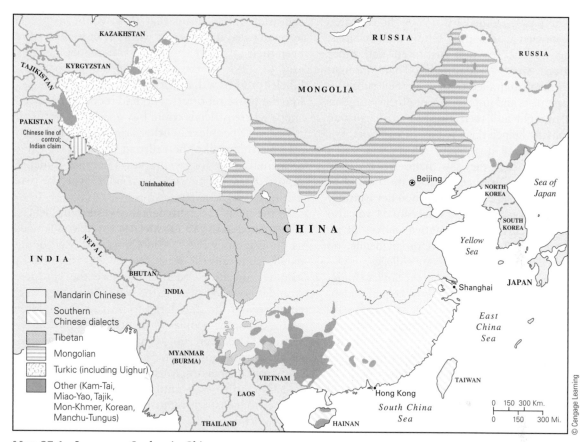

Map 27.1   **Languages Spoken in China**

Tibet had no choice but to negotiate an agreement with the Chinese Communist Party. Tibet recognized China's sovereignty and in exchange was allowed to maintain its traditional political system, including the Dalai Lama. From 1951 to 1959, this system worked fairly well. By 1959, however, ethnic Tibetans from neighboring provinces, unhappy with agricultural collectivization, were streaming into Tibet. When massive protests broke out in Lhasa, the army opened fire. The Dalai Lama and thousands of his followers fled to India. The aftermath included more pressure on Tibet to conform to the rest of the People's Republic and the sense among Tibetans that theirs was an occupied land.

Intellectuals and the Hundred Flowers Campaign

In the 1920s and 1930s some of the most enthusiastic supporters of socialism were members of the educated elite (now usually called intellectuals). Professors like Chen Duxiu and Li Dazhao and writers like Lu Xun and Ding Ling saw socialism as a way to rid China of poverty and injustice. Many intellectuals made their way to Yan'an, where they soon learned that their job was to serve the party, not stand at a critical distance from it (see Chapter 25).

After 1949 the party had to find ways to make use of intellectuals who had not publicly sided with it, but rather had stayed in the eastern cities working as teachers, journalists, engineers, or government officials. Most members of this small, urban, educated elite were ready and eager to serve the new government, happy that China finally had a government able to drive out imperialists, control inflation, banish unemployment, end corruption, and clean up the streets. Thousands who were studying abroad hurried home to see how they could help. China needed expertise for its modernization projects, and most of the educated were kept in their jobs, whatever their class background.

Mao, however, distrusted intellectuals and since Yan'an days had been devising ways to subordinate them to the party. In the early 1950s the educated men and women who staffed schools, universities, publishing houses, research institutes, and other organizations were "reeducated." This "thought reform" generally entailed confessing their subservience to capitalists and imperialists or other bourgeois habits of thought and their gratitude to Chairman Mao for having helped them realize these errors. For some going through it, thought reform was like a conversion experience; they saw themselves in an entirely new way and wanted to dedicate themselves to the socialist cause. For others, it was devastating.

Independence on the part of intellectuals was also undermined by curtailing alternative sources of income. There were no more rents or dividends, no more independent presses or private colleges.

In response to de-Stalinization in the Soviet Union, in 1956 Mao called on intellectuals to help him identify problems within the party, such as party members who had lost touch with the people or behaved like tyrants. "Let a hundred flowers bloom" in the field of culture and a "hundred schools of thought contend" in science. As long as criticism was not "antagonistic" or "counterrevolutionary," it would help strengthen the party, he explained. The first to come forward with criticisms were scientists and engineers who wanted party members to interfere less with their work. To encourage more people to come forward, Mao praised those who spoke up. Soon critics lost their inhibitions. By May 1957 college students were putting up wall posters, sometimes with highly inflammatory charges. One poster at Qinghua University in Beijing even dared attack Mao Zedong by name: "When he wants to kill you, he doesn't have to do it himself. He can mobilize your wife and children to denounce you and then kill you with their own hands! Is this a rational society? This is class struggle, Mao Zedong style!"[*]

Did Mao plan this campaign to ferret out dissidents? Or was he shocked by the outpouring of criticism? Whatever the truth of the matter, in June 1957 the party announced a campaign against rightists orchestrated by the newly appointed secretary general of the party, Deng Xiaoping. In this massive campaign, units were pressed to identify 5 percent of their staff members as rightists. Altogether almost 3 million people were labeled

rightists, which meant that they would no longer have any real influence at work, even if allowed to keep their jobs. A half-million suffered worse fates, sent to labor in the countryside. Some of those labeled rightists had exposed party weaknesses, like the thirty reporters who had reported on secret shops where officials could buy goods not available to ordinary people. But other "rightists" had hardly said anything, like the railroad engineer relegated to menial labor for twenty years because someone reported hearing him say "how bold" when he read a critique of the party.

By the end of the campaign, the Western-influenced elite created in the 1930s was destroyed, condemned as "poisonous weeds." Old China had been dominated, culturally at least, by an elite defined by lengthy education. Mao made sure the educated would know their place in the New China: they were employees of the state hired to instruct the children of the laboring people or to provide technical assistance. They were not to have ideas of their own separate from those of the party or a cultural life distinct from the masses. Most of those labeled rightists in 1957 had to wait until 1979 to be rehabilitated (that is, to have their rightist label removed and their civil rights restored).

DEPARTING FROM THE SOVIET MODEL

By 1957, China had made progress on many fronts. The standard of living was improving, support for the government was strong, and people were optimistic about the future. Still, Mao was not satisfied. Growth was too slow and too dependent on technical experts and capital. As he had found from the Hundred Flowers campaign, people's ways of thinking had not been as quickly transformed as he had hoped. Mao was ready to try more radical measures.

The Great Leap Forward

Why was China unable to find a way to use what it was rich in—labor power—to modernize more rapidly? In 1956, Mao began talking of a Great Leap Forward. Through the coordinated hard work of hundreds of millions of people, China would transform itself from a poor nation into a mighty one. With the latent creative capacity of the Chinese masses unleashed, China would surpass Great Britain in industrial output within fifteen years.

---

[*]Gregor Benton and Alan Hunter, eds., *Wild Lily, Prairie Fire* (Princeton, N.J.: Princeton University Press, 1995), pp. 100–101.

Xinhua News Agency, Beijing/Sovfoto

Producing Steel in Henan Province. During the Great Leap Forward, inexperienced workers labored for long hours to produce steel in makeshift "backyard" furnaces.

These visions of accelerated industrialization were coupled with a higher level of collectivization in the countryside. In 1958, in a matter of months, agricultural collectives all over the country were amalgamated into gigantic communes. Private garden plots were banned. Peasants were organized into quasi-military production brigades and referred to as fighters on the agricultural front. Peasant men were marched in military style to labor on public works projects, while the women took over much of the field work. Those between ages sixteen and thirty were drafted into the militia and spent long hours drilling.

Both party cadres and ordinary working people got caught up in a wave of utopian enthusiasm. During the late summer and fall of 1958, communes, factories, schools, and other units set up "backyard steel furnaces" in order to double steel production. As workers were mobilized to put in long hours

on these projects, they had little time to cook or eat at home. Units were encouraged to set up mess halls where food was free, a measure commentators hailed as a step toward communism. Counties claimed 1,000 and even 10,000 percent increases in agriculture production. The Central Committee announced with great fanfare that production had nearly doubled in a single year.

Some Great Leap projects proved to be of long-term value; bridges, railroads, canals, reservoirs, power stations, mines, and irrigation works were constructed all over the country. All too often, however, projects were undertaken with such haste and with so little technical knowledge that they did more harm than good. With economists and engineers downgraded or removed in the antirightist campaigns of the year before, plans were formulated not by experts but by local cadres eager to show their

Art to Serve the Revolution. Chinese artists were trained in oil-painting techniques and realistic styles and encouraged to create art that would inspire viewers. This oil painting by Sun Zixi, done in 1964, depicts happy visitors to the capital, including minorities and members of the military, posing for a photograph in front of the portrait of Mao at Tiananmen.

political zeal. Fields plowed deep were sometimes ruined because the soil became salinized. The quality of most of the steel made in backyard furnaces was too poor to be used. Instead it filled railroad cars and clogged train yards all over the country, disrupting transportation.

It was not just the legacy of the Hundred Flowers campaign that kept cadres from reporting failures. The minister of defense and hero of the Korean War, Peng Dehuai, tried to bring up problems in a private letter he gave to Mao at a party conference in July 1959. In the letter Peng began by saying that the Great Leap was an indisputable success but pointed to the tendency to exaggerate at all levels, which made it difficult for the leadership to know the real situation. He also noted that people began to think that the food problem was solved and that they could give free meals to all. Peng's language was temperate, but Mao's reaction was not. Mao distributed copies of the letter to the delegates and denounced Peng for "right opportunism." He made the senior cadres choose between him and Peng, and none had the courage to side with Peng, who was soon dismissed from his post. Problems with the Great Leap were now blamed on all those like Peng who lacked faith in its premises.

Mao's faulty economics, coupled with droughts and floods, ended up creating one of the worst famines in world history. The size of the 1958 harvest was wildly exaggerated, and no one attempted to validate reports. Tax grain was removed from the countryside on the basis of the reported harvests, leaving little for local consumption. No one wanted to report what was actually happening in his locality for fear of being labeled a rightist. Grain production dropped from 200 million tons in 1958 to 170 million in 1959 and 144 million in 1960. By 1960 in many places people were left with less than half of what they needed to survive. Rationing was practiced almost everywhere, and soup kitchens serving weak gruel were set up in an attempt to stave off starvation. But peasants in places where grain was exhausted were not allowed to hit the roads, as people had always done during famines in the past. From later census reconstructions, it appears that during the Three Hard Years (1959–1962) there were on the order of 30 million "excess" deaths attributable to the dearth of food. Yet neither Mao nor the Communist Party fell from power.

Deaths in Hard-Hit Provinces, 1957 and 1960			
Province	1957	1960	Change, %
Anhui	c. 250,000	2,200,000	780
Gansu	142,041	538,479	279
Guangxi	261,785	644,700	146
Henan	572,000	1,908,000	233
Hunan	370,059	1,068,118	189

Source: Based on Roderick MacFarquar, *The Origins of the Cultural Revolution, vol. 3: The Coming of the Cataclysm, 1961–1966* (New York: Columbia University Press, 1997), pp. 2–3.

The Great Leap destroyed people's faith in their local cadres, who in the crisis put themselves and their families first. Another blow to peasants were new curbs on their mobility. Beginning in 1955 a system of population registration bound rural people to the villages of their birth or, in the case of married women, to their husbands' villages. When the hasty expansion of the nation's industrial plant was reversed, millions of unemployed workers were sent back to the countryside. To keep them from returning and to keep other peasants from sneaking into the cities, a system of urban household registration was introduced. Only those with permission to reside in a city could get the ration coupons needed to purchase grain there. These residence policies had the unintended effect of locking rural communities with unfavorable man–land ratios into dismal poverty.

It is not surprising that the rural poor would want to move to the cities. Those who got jobs in state-run factories had low-cost housing, pensions, and health care, not to mention a reliable supply of subsidized food. Children in the cities could stay in school through middle school, and the brightest could go farther. In the countryside, only a tiny proportion of exceptionally wealthy communities could come at all close to providing such benefits. In the poorest regions, farmers, forced by the government to concentrate on growing grain, could do little to improve their situations other than invest more labor by weeding more frequently, leveling and terracing fields, expanding irrigation systems, and so on. Such investment often brought little return, and agricultural productivity (the return for each hour of labor) fell across the country.

The Sino-Soviet Split

In the 1920s and 1930s Stalin, through the Comintern, had done as much to hinder the success of the Chinese Communist Party as to aid it. Still, in 1949, Mao viewed the Soviet Union as China's natural ally and went to Moscow to see Stalin. Mao never had the same respect for Stalin's successor, Khrushchev. The Great Leap Forward put further strain on relations between China and the Soviet Union. China intensified its bellicose anti-imperialist rhetoric and began shelling the islands off the coast of Fujian still held by the Nationalists on Taiwan, and the Russians began to fear that China would drag them into a war with the United States. In 1958 and 1959, Khrushchev visited Beijing and concluded that Mao was a romantic deviationist, particularly wrongheaded in his decision to create communes. All the assistance the Soviet Union had given to China's industrialization seemed to have been wasted as Mao put his trust in backyard furnaces.

When Mao made light of nuclear weapons—saying that if using them could destroy capitalism, it would not matter that much if China lost half its population—Khrushchev went back on his earlier promise to give China nuclear weapons. There was also friction over India and its support for the Dalai Lama and other refugees from Tibet. Russia wanted India as an ally and would not side with China in its border disputes with India, infuriating Mao. In April 1960, Chinese leaders celebrated the ninetieth anniversary of Lenin's birth by lambasting Soviet foreign policy. In July 1960, just as famine was hitting China, Khrushchev ordered the Soviet experts to return and to take their blueprints and spare parts with them. By 1963, Mao was publicly denouncing Khrushchev as a revisionist and capitalist roader and challenging the Soviet Union's leadership of the international communist movement. Communist parties throughout the world soon divided into pro-Soviet and pro-China factions. As the rhetoric escalated, both sides increased their troops along their long border, which provoked border clashes. China built air raid shelters on a massive scale and devoted enormous resources to constructing a defense establishment in mountainous inland areas far from both the sea and the Soviet border. As the war in Vietnam escalated after 1963, China stayed on the sidelines, not even helping the Soviet Union supply North Vietnam. Meanwhile, China developed its own atomic weapons program, exploding its first nuclear device in 1964.

THE CULTURAL REVOLUTION

After the failure of the Great Leap Forward, Mao, nearly seventy years old, withdrew from active decision making. Liu Shaoqi replaced Mao as head of state in 1959 and, along with Chen Yun, Zhou Enlai, Deng Xiaoping, and other organization men, set about reviving the economy. Mao grew more and more isolated. Surrounded by bodyguards, he lived in luxurious guest houses far removed from ordinary folk. Senior colleagues had not forgotten the fate of Peng Dehuai, and honest debate of party policy was no longer attempted in front of Mao. Any resistance to his ideas had to be done in secret.

By the early 1960s, Mao was afraid that revisionism was destroying the party—that capitalist methods and ideas were contaminating Marxism. In 1962 he initiated the Socialist Education campaign to try to get rural cadres to focus again on class struggle. When Liu Shaoqi and Deng Xiaoping rewrote the directives to deemphasize class struggle, Mao concluded that the revisionists were taking over the struggle for control of the party. After gathering allies, Mao set out to recapture revolutionary fervor and avoid slipping in the inegalitarian direction of the Soviet Union by initiating a Great Revolution to Create a Proletarian Culture—or Cultural Revolution for short—a movement that came close to destroying the party he had led for three decades.

Phase 1: 1966–1968

The Cultural Revolution began in the spring of 1966 with a denunciation of the mayor of Beijing for allowing the staging of a play that could be construed as critical of Mao. Mao's wife, Jiang Qing, formed a Cultural Revolution Small Group to look into ways to revolutionize culture. Jiang Qing had not played much of a part in politics before and was widely seen as a stand-in for Mao. Soon radical students at Beijing University were agitating against party officials who "took the capitalist road." When Liu Shaoqi tried to control what was going on at Beijing University, Mao intervened, had him demoted by a rump session of the Central Committee, and sanctioned the organization of students into Red Guards.

The Cultural Revolution quickly escalated beyond the control of Mao, Jiang Qing, or anyone else. Young people who had grown up in New China responded enthusiastically to calls to help Mao oust revisionists. In June 1966 high schools and universities throughout the country were closed as students devoted all their time to Red Guard activities. Millions rode free on railroads to carry the message to the countryside or to make the pilgrimage to Beijing, where they might catch a glimpse of Mao, their "Great Helmsman," at the massive Red Guard rallies held in Tiananmen Square. (See **Documents: Big Character Poster.**)

At these rallies, Mao appeared in military uniform and told the students that "to rebel is justified" and that it was good "to bombard the headquarters." The Red Guards in response waved their little red books, *Quotations from Chairman Mao*, compiled a few years earlier by Lin Biao to indoctrinate soldiers. The cult of Mao became more and more dominant, with his pictures displayed in every household, bus, and train, and even in pedicabs, and his sayings broadcast by loudspeaker at every intersection. From early 1967 on, the *People's Daily* regularly printed a boxed statement by Mao on its front page.

In cities large and small, Red Guards roamed the streets in their battle against things foreign or old. They invaded the homes of those with bad class backgrounds, "bourgeois tendencies," or connections to foreigners. Under the slogan of "destroy the four old things" (old customs, habits, culture, and thinking), they ransacked homes, libraries, and museums to find books and artwork to set on fire. The tensions and antagonisms that had been suppressed by nearly two decades of tight social control broke into the open as Red Guards found opportunities to get back at people. At the countless denunciation meetings they organized, cadres, teachers, and writers were forced to stand with their heads down and their arms raised behind them in the "airplane" position and to listen to former friends and colleagues jeer at and curse them. Many victims took their own lives; others died of beatings and mistreatment.

Liu Shaoqi, the head of state but now labeled the "chief capitalist roader," became a victim of the Red Guards. In the summer of 1967, Red Guards stormed the well-guarded quarters where the party hierarchy lived and seized Liu. Then they taunted and beat him before huge crowds. Liu died alone two years later from the abuse he received. His family suffered as well. Liu's wife ended up spending ten years in solitary confinement. Four other members of his family also died either of beatings or of mistreatment in prison where interrogators made every effort to get them to reveal evidence that Liu or his wife was

DOCUMENTS　Big Character Poster

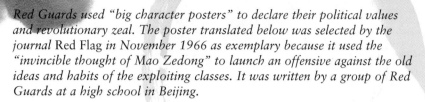

Red Guards used "big character posters" to declare their political values and revolutionary zeal. The poster translated below was selected by the journal Red Flag *in November 1966 as exemplary because it used the "invincible thought of Mao Zedong" to launch an offensive against the old ideas and habits of the exploiting classes. It was written by a group of Red Guards at a high school in Beijing.*

Revolution is rebellion, and rebellion is the soul of Mao Zedong's thought. Daring to think, to speak, to act, to break through, and to make revolution—in a word, daring to rebel—is the most fundamental and most precious quality of proletarian revolutionaries; it is fundamental to the Party spirit of the Party of the proletariat! Not to rebel is revisionism, pure and simple! Revisionism has been in control of our school for seventeen years. If today we do not rise up in rebellion, when will we?

Now some of the people who were boldly opposing our rebellion have suddenly turned shy and coy, and have taken to incessant murmuring and nagging that we are too one-sided, too arrogant, too crude and that we are going too far. All this is utter nonsense! If you are against us, please say so. Why be shy about it? Since we are bent on rebelling, the matter is no longer in your hand! Indeed we shall make the air thick with the pungent smell of gunpowder. All this talk about being "humane" and "all-sided"—let's have an end to it.

You say we are too one-sided? What kind of all-sidedness is it that suits you? It looks to us like a "two combining into one" all-sidedness, or eclecticism. You say we are too arrogant? "Arrogant" is just what we want to be. Chairman Mao says, "And those in high positions we counted as no more than the dust." We are bent on striking down not only the reactionaries in our school, but the reactionaries all over the world. Revolutionaries take it as their task to transform the world. How can we not be "arrogant"?

You say we are too crude? Crude is just what we want to be. How can we be soft and clinging toward revisionism or go in for great moderation? To be moderate toward the enemy is to be cruel to the revolution! You say we are going too far? Frankly, your "don't go too far" is reformism, it is "peaceful transition." And this is what your daydreams are about! Well, we are going to strike you down to the earth and keep you down!

There are some others who are scared to death of revolution, scared to death of rebellion. You sticklers for convention, you toadies are all curled up inside your revisionist shells. At the first whiff of rebellion, you become scared and nervous. A revolutionary is a "monkey king" whose golden rod is might, whose supernatural powers are far-reaching and whose magic is omnipotent precisely because he has the great and invincible thought of Mao Zedong. We are wielding our "golden rods" "displaying our supernatural powers" and using our "magic" in order to turn the old world upside down, smash it to pieces, create chaos, and make a tremendous mess—and the bigger the better! We must do this to the present revisionist middle school attached to Tsinghua University. Create a big rebellion, rebel to the end! We are bent on creating a tremendous proletarian uproar, and on carving out a new proletarian world!

Long live the revolutionary rebel spirit of the proletariat!

Questions for Analysis

1. What do the authors mean by revisionism and reformism?
2. Are the authors trying to attract others to join them? Why or why not?

Source: From Patricia Buckley Ebrey, ed., *Chinese Civilization: A Sourcebook*, rev. ed. (New York: Simon and Schuster, 1993), p. 450.

Big Character Posters. Soldiers of the PLA and peasants of the model commune at Dazhai are shown here putting up big character posters in 1970.

a spy. Deng Xiaoping, another target of Mao, fared better; he was sent off to labor in a factory in Jiangxi after being humiliated at struggle sessions.

By the end of 1966 workers were also being mobilized to participate in the Cultural Revolution. Rebel students went to factories to "learn from the workers" but actually to instigate opposition to party superiors. When party leaders tried to appease discontented workers by raising wages and handing out bonuses, Mao labeled their actions "economism" and instructed students and workers to seize power from such revisionist party leaders. Confusing power struggles ensued. As soon as one group gained the upper hand, another would challenge its takeover as a "sham power seizure" and attempt a "counterpower seizure."

As armed conflict spread, Mao turned to the People's Liberation Army to restore order. Told to ensure that industrial and agricultural production continued, the army tended to support conservative mass organizations and disband the rebel organizations as "counterrevolutionary." Radical Red Guard leaders tried to counterattack, accusing the army of supporting the wrong side. In Wuhan in July 1967, when radicals seized trains loaded with weapons en route to Vietnam, the army supplied their opponents. Then a conservative faction in Wuhan kidnapped two of the radical leaders from Beijing, and the Cultural Revolution Small Group responded by calling on the Red Guards to arm themselves and seize military power from the "capitalist roaders" in the army. Thus began the most violent stage of the

Color Plate 25
Hong Kong After the Opium War. Framed by Chinese junks, a paddle wheel steamship makes its way past hastily built government buildings and merchant storehouses.

Color Plate 26
Boxer Print. The Boxers spread word of their invincibility through woodblock prints like this one, which shows their attack on the treaty port city of Tianjin.

Color Plate 27
People of the Five Nations: A Sunday. This woodblock triptych published in 1861 showed Japan how westerners dressed and entertained themselves in the foreign settlement at Yokohama.

Color Plate 28
Gas Lights. Gas lights illuminating the streets of Tokyo became a favorite subject for modern woodblock print artists.

Color Plate 29
Popular Science.
Magazine covers
for *Kagaku chishiki*
(Scientific Knowledge)
by Sugiura Hisui from
1931–1935 illustrated
the wonders of science
and technology for
young readers.

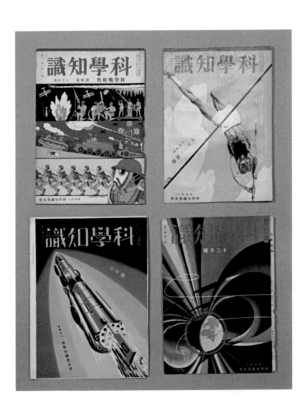

Color Plate 30
Raising Mao Zedong's Thought. This 1967 poster is titled "Revolutionary Proletarian Right to Rebel Troops, Unite!" The books they hold are the selected works of Mao Zedong. The woman's armband reads "Red Guard."

Color Plate 31
Goddess of Democracy. During the 1989 demonstrations in Tiananmen Square, art students provocatively placed a 37-foot tall statue labeled the Goddess of Democracy facing the portrait of Mao Zedong.

Color Plate 32
Earthquake and Tsunami. This photo depicts the wreckage left by the earthquake and tsunami that struck off the northern coast of Japan on March 11, 2011 and left fishing boats piled on top of debris.

Cultural Revolution, during which different factions of Red Guards and worker organizations took up armed struggle against each other and against regional and national military forces. Rebels seized the Foreign Ministry in Beijing for two weeks, and others seized and burned the British diplomatic compound. With communication and transportation at a standstill, consumer goods became scarce in urban areas.

In the first, violent phase of the Cultural Revolution, some 3 million party and government officials were removed from their jobs, and as many as half a million people were killed or committed suicide.

Phase 2: 1968–1976

By the summer of 1968, Mao had no choice but to moderate the Cultural Revolution in order to prevent full-scale civil war. In July he disbanded the Red Guards and sent them off to work in the countryside. Revolutionary committees were set up to take the place of the old party structure. Each committee had representatives from the mass organizations, from revolutionary cadres, and from the army; in most places the army quickly became the dominant force. Culture remained tightly controlled. Foreign music, art, literature, and books (other than works on Marxism, Leninism, and Stalinism) disappeared from stores. Revolutionary works were offered in their place, such as the eight model revolutionary operas Jiang Qing had sponsored. The official line was that it was better to be red than expert, and professionals were hounded out of many fields. High school graduates were sent into the countryside, as the Red Guards had been before them, some 17 million altogether. Although the stated reason for sending them to the countryside was to let them learn from the peasants and give the peasants the advantage of their education, this transfer also saved the government the trouble and expense of putting the graduates on the payroll of urban enterprises or finding them housing when they married.

The dominance of the military declined after the downfall in 1971 of Lin Biao (lin byow). To the public, Lin Biao was Mao's most devoted disciple, regularly photographed standing next to him. Yet according to the official account, Lin became afraid that Mao had turned against him and decided to assassinate him. When Lin's daughter exposed his plot, Lin decided to flee to the Soviet Union. His plane, however, ran out of fuel and crashed over Mongolia. Whatever the truth of this bizarre story, news of his plot was kept out of the press for a year, the leadership apparently unsure how to tell the people that Lin Biao turned out to be another Liu Shaoqi, a secret traitor who had managed to reach the second highest position in the political hierarchy.

By this point Mao's health was in decline, and he played less and less of a role in day-to-day management. The leading contenders for power were the more radical faction led by Jiang Qing and the more moderate faction led by Zhou Enlai. In this rather fluid situation China softened its antagonistic stance toward the outside world and in 1972 welcomed U.S. President Richard Nixon to visit and pursue improving relations. In 1973 many disgraced leaders, including Deng Xiaoping, were reinstated to important posts.

The Cultural Revolution's massive assault on entrenched ideas and the established order left many victims. Nearly 3 million people were officially rehabilitated after 1978. Urban young people who had been exhilarated when Mao called on them to topple those in power soon found themselves at the bottom of the heap, sent down to the countryside where hostile peasants could make life miserable. Their younger siblings received inferior educations, out of school for long periods, then taught a watered-down curriculum. The cadres, teachers, and intellectuals who were the principal targets of the Cultural Revolution lost much of their trust in others. When they had to continue working with people who had beaten, humiliated, or imprisoned them, the wounds were left to fester for years. Even those who agreed that elitist values and bureaucratic habits were pervasive problems in the party hierarchy found little positive in the outcome of the Cultural Revolution.

THE DEATH OF MAO

In 1976 those who still believed in portents from heaven would have sensed that something bad was going to happen. First, Zhou Enlai died in January after a long struggle with cancer. Next, an outpouring of grief for him in April was violently suppressed. Then in July, north China was rocked by a huge earthquake that killed hundreds of thousands. In September Mao Zedong died.

As long as Mao was alive, no one would openly challenge him, but as his health failed, those near the top tried to position themselves for the inevitable. The main struggle, it seems with hindsight, was between the radicals—Jiang Qing and her allies, later labeled the Gang of Four—and the pragmatists—Deng Xiaoping and his allies. In March 1976 a newspaper controlled by the radicals implied that Zhou Enlai was a capitalist roader. In response, on April 4, the traditional day for honoring the dead, an estimated 2 million people flocked to Tiananmen Square to lay wreaths in honor of Zhou. The radicals saw this as an act of opposition to themselves, had it labeled a counterrevolutionary incident, and called the militia out. Yet the pragmatists won out in the end. After a month of national mourning for Mao, Jiang Qing and the rest of the Gang of Four were arrested.

Assessment of Mao's role in modern Chinese history is ongoing. In 1981, when the party rendered its judgment of Mao, it still gave him high marks for his military leadership and his intellectual contributions to Marxist theory, but assigned him much of the blame for everything that went wrong from 1956 on. Since then, Mao's standing has further eroded as doubts are raised about the impact of his leadership style in the 1940s and early 1950s. Some critics go so far as to portray Mao as a megalomaniac, so absorbed in his project of remaking China to match his vision that he was totally indifferent to others' suffering. Some Chinese intellectuals, however, worry that making Mao a monster relieves everyone else of responsibility and undermines the argument that structural changes are needed to prevent comparable tragedies from recurring.

Mao Zedong has often been compared to Zhu Yuanzhang, the founder of the Ming Dynasty. Both grew up in farming households, though Mao never experienced the desperate poverty of Zhu's childhood. Both were formed by the many years of warfare that preceded gaining military supremacy. Both brooked no opposition and had few scruples when it came to executing perceived opponents. Both tended toward the paranoid, suspecting traitorous intentions others did not perceive. But Zhu Yuanzhang cast a shadow over the rest of the Ming Dynasty. As will be seen in the next chapter, within a short period after Mao's death, much of what he had instituted was undone.

SUMMARY

Within a few years of winning the civil war against the Nationalists, the Communist Party had brought striking change to China. The state took control of most large enterprises as well as universities, newspapers, and churches. The Soviet Union provided an example of a way to expand heavy industry using five-year plans. People were told that they had been liberated from the yoke of the past. Mao Zedong was held up as a man of political genius whose writings deserved to be studied carefully.

The first major crisis that the new People's Republic faced was the Korean War. After U.S. forces crossed the 38th parallel in the fall of 1950, China sent troops into Korea, eventually more than 2.5 million. Although the Communists could take pride that China had stood up to the imperialists, the war hardened the enmity between China and the United States. The United States refused to recognize the People's Republic of China, recognizing the Nationalists in Taiwan as the legitimate government of China.

Rural China was radically changed in the 1950s as land reform eliminated the power of landlords and led to the collectivization of most farmland, which was gradually consolidated into huge communes. These communes brought a variety of benefits to farmers, such as schools that reduced illiteracy and clinics that provided vaccinations. Minority ethnic groups received legal recognition and where they dominated a region they were allowed considerable autonomy. However, there were limits to their autonomy, as Tibet discovered when protests against government policies in 1959 led to military suppression and the exodus of thousands of Tibetans into India, including the Dalai Lama.

During the 1950s and 1960s Mao initiated a series of movements aimed to speed China's transition to communism. Three of them took especially large tolls on the people: the Hundred Flowers campaign, the Great Leap Forward, and the Cultural Revolution. After intellectuals were urged to criticize the party in the Hundred Flowers campaign, nearly 3 million people were labeled Rightists, which limited their chances and the chances of their children. A huge famine and the deaths of tens of millions of people were the devastating consequences of the economic policies of the Great Leap Forward. The negative consequences of the Cultural Revolution were felt most heavily on those classed as intellectuals: teachers at the middle school and university levels as well as writers and artists, who were often humiliated and sent to work in the countryside. Young people also suffered because education was first disrupted, then watered down.

In the early 1960s, China split from the Soviet Union and developed its own atomic bomb. Tension with the Soviet Union was so high that air-raid shelters were built on a large scale. In the early 1970s, efforts were made to improve relations with the United States, including a 1972 visit by U.S. President Richard Nixon.

How different was China in 1976 compared to 1949? Although the Cultural Revolution had brought enormous strain and confusion, China was by many measures better off. It was not dominated by any other countries and held itself up as a model to developing nations. The proportion of the population in school more than doubled between 1950 and 1978. Life expectancy reached sixty-seven years for men and sixty-nine years for women, due in large part to better survival of infants and more accessible health care. Unemployment was no longer a problem, and housing was provided for all. Inflation had been banished.

But life was also much more regimented and controlled. There was no longer anything resembling a free press and not many choices people could make about where they would live or what work they would do. Peasants could not leave their villages. Graduates of high schools or universities were given little choice in job assignments. From the experience of repeated campaigns to uncover counterrevolutionaries, people had learned to distrust each other, never sure who might turn on them. Material security, in other words, had been secured at a high cost.

Korea (1945 to the Present)

Liberation from Japanese colonialism resulted in division of the Korean peninsula, with the north and south forming separate states in 1948— the North under the auspices of the Soviet Union and the South under the United States. Following the bloody Korean War between 1950 and 1953 that divided Korea at the demilitarized zone (DMZ), the two states began a race for superiority in military and economic strength, their policies and politics, social change, and culture reflecting their relationships with the dominant powers and their local histories. Each developed in distinctive ways, the North under a cult to the leader of a new dynasty, the South moving from dictatorship to democracy with a pluralistic society and a popular culture that has attracted fans across East Asia. Even today, despite greater contact between the two nations, they continue to follow different paths.

Was the division of Korea in 1945 simply a matter of foreign interference in Korea's affairs, or did it reflect internal differences? Was the Korean War an act of aggression by the North or the continuation of civil conflict? What is responsible for the divergent political, economic, and cultural systems? What are the chances for Korean reunification?

NATIONAL DIVISION AND THE KOREAN WAR (1945–1953)

Rather than divide Japan at the end of World War II, as had been done to Germany, the Allies divided Korea. As soon as Stalin declared war against Japan, Russian forces invaded the Korean peninsula. A week later, after Japan had surrendered, the United States rushed troops to Korea and won Soviet agreement to a division of the peninsula at the 38th parallel. Both Russians and Americans were greeted by the spontaneous organization of People's Committees (PCs) at the local level that spanned the political spectrum. The Soviets used the PCs as a basis for reconstructing civilian rule, but General Hodge, who established a U.S. military government for South Korea, did not. Each side picked a leader who reflected its ideology, the Soviets recruiting the socialist Jo Mansik (JO MAHN-shik) as an interim leader in the North and the Americans bringing Rhee Syngman (RI SING-man) back from the United States to rule the South.

After liberation, millions of Koreans living in Japan and Manchuria flooded back to the peninsula, many radicalized by their experiences during the colonial period. In North Korea, former collaborators were excluded from leadership roles, whereas in South Korea, businessmen and landlords who had prospered under Japanese rule formed the Korean Democratic Party (KDP). Communists jailed by Japan were released, and one of them, Park Heonyeong (PARK HUN-young), formed the Korean Communist Party (KCP) in Seoul, the city that he expected would become the capital of a united Korea.

In North Korea, several communist groups greeted Soviet commanders: the domestic Communists, the Yan'an Communists who had fought with Mao Zedong in the Chinese civil war, Koreans holding Soviet citizenship, and the Manchurian guerrilla fighters who had fought alongside Kim Il Sung (KIM IL-sung). He and his supporters arrived in North Korea from Siberia some weeks later on September 19, 1945. The Soviets established a northern branch bureau of the KCP and introduced Kim at a large public meeting in Pyeongyang, where he praised Stalin and supported Jo Mansik. With Soviet support, Kim then replaced Jo in January 1946 because Jo had opposed Stalin's agreement with the United States to set up a trusteeship for Korea.

The U.S.–Soviet division of Korea between the communist North and the capitalist South soon reflected political and social differences between Koreans. In South Korea, violent protests by workers and peasants began in late 1945. A railroad strike and mass demonstrations broke out in the autumn of 1946 in Busan (BOO-sahn) and Daegu (DAE-goo), followed by farmers' riots against Hodge's grain policies in Jeolla (JEOL-lah) and Gyeongsang (GYONG-sahng), leaving two hundred police and a thousand civilians dead. U.S. authorities blamed the communists, put an end to the PCs, and declared martial law. Pak Heonyeong and other communists fled to North Korea while landlords, businessmen, and Christians from the North moved to the South.

In North Korea, Kim Il Sung became chairman of the Provisional People's Committee (PPC), which carried out land reform in 1946 to eliminate the landlord class and redistribute land to sharecroppers. Kim faced little opposition in nationalizing industries because Japanese factory owners had left the country. He reduced working hours to eight hours per day, banned child labor, created a labor federation, declared equal rights for women, established universal education through the eleventh grade,

and founded Kim Il Sung University. He made his guerrilla allies from Manchuria his chief aides and created the Korean People's Army.

In South Korea, local rivalries, distrust of the central administration, and resentment of outsiders fueled civil conflict. In April 1948, the people of Jeju (JAY-jew) Island rebelled against a repressive right-wing governor and his youth gangs from the northwest who had infiltrated the police. Two regiments of the Korean army assigned to fight the guerrillas on Jeju then rebelled at Yeosu (YUH-sue) on the southern coast and murdered hundreds of police and landlords. U.S. forces helped suppress both rebellions. Forty-five thousand people died on Jeju, forty thousand fled to Japan, and seventy thousand were placed in concentration camps. Fed by tenant anger at high rents, guerrilla war spread throughout the South. The Rhee regime's suppression campaign during the winter of 1949–1950 killed around six thousand people.

The Cold War between the United States and the Soviet Union hardened political divisions. The United States supported Rhee Syngman's plan to hold elections across the peninsula in 1948, but the Soviets refused to allow elections in the North because its population was only half that of the South. Following a separate election in the South, the Republic of Korea (ROK) was proclaimed on August 15, 1948, with a constitution modeled after that of the United States. The elected National Assembly chose Rhee Syngman as its first president. On September 10, 1948, North Korea established the Democratic People's Republic of Korea (DPRK) with Kim Il Sung as chairman of the National People's Assembly. The Soviet Union withdrew its troops in December followed by most of the U.S. forces in 1949.

The Korean War (1949–1953)

Neither North nor South Korea expected the division to be permanent. Both Kim Il Sung and Rhee Syngman began conducting cross-border raids in 1949, hoping to provoke the other into an all-out war. Despite the raids, the United States prevented Rhee from invading the North lest he drag the United States into war with the Soviet Union. When Kim met with Stalin in Moscow to seek backing for invasion of the South, Stalin turned him down. Having sent Korean troops to support the communists in their war for China, Kim Il Sung had a new ally in Mao Zedong, but Mao said that the timing for an invasion was premature.

Korean War Refugees. While armies fought up and down the peninsula, civilians tired to get out of their way. Five million refugees left their homes, many to end up on the opposite side of the DMZ. Hundreds of thousands of families remain divided between North and South to this day.

In 1950, Kim Il Sung gained reluctant acceptance from his big-power supporters for an invasion of the South. Stalin promised to supply weapons, planes, and pilots only because he wanted to avoid a direct challenge to the United States; Mao sent perhaps as many as eighty thousand experienced Korean troops who had fought in the Chinese civil war. On June 25, Kim launched his invasion with seven divisions and 258 Soviet tanks against the four front-line divisions of the ROK Army, which had no tanks. North Korean forces overran the South Korean military and pushed south all the way to Busan.

The United States played a major role in the war that followed. President Truman viewed the invasion as a plot by Stalin to spread communism, and he had already signed a policy document early in 1950, NSC 48, that committed the United States to the containment of communism within its present boundaries in Asia and "where feasible" to reduce communist power in Asia. In addition to dispatching U.S. forces to Korea

as a "police action" rather than declare war, he also used the absence of the Russian delegate from the UN Security Council to win approval of a UN force under the command of U.S. General Douglas MacArthur.

Truman's determination to roll back communism led to China's intervention. The first U.S. forces with remnants of the ROK Army were barely able to defend the Busan perimeter until General MacArthur turned the tide of battle by launching a surprise attack at Incheon, near Seoul. When Kim withdrew his main forces north across the 38th parallel, Truman authorized MacArthur to follow him into North Korea. Oblivious to Chinese warnings passed through India, General MacArthur ordered his troops to the Yalu River with the promise that they would be "home by Christmas." Instead Mao Zedong committed an army of Chinese "volunteers" that overran U.S. positions. The Chinese recaptured Seoul, only to lose it once again. In 1951 the fighting stabilized along a front that eventually became the DMZ. (See Map 28.1.)

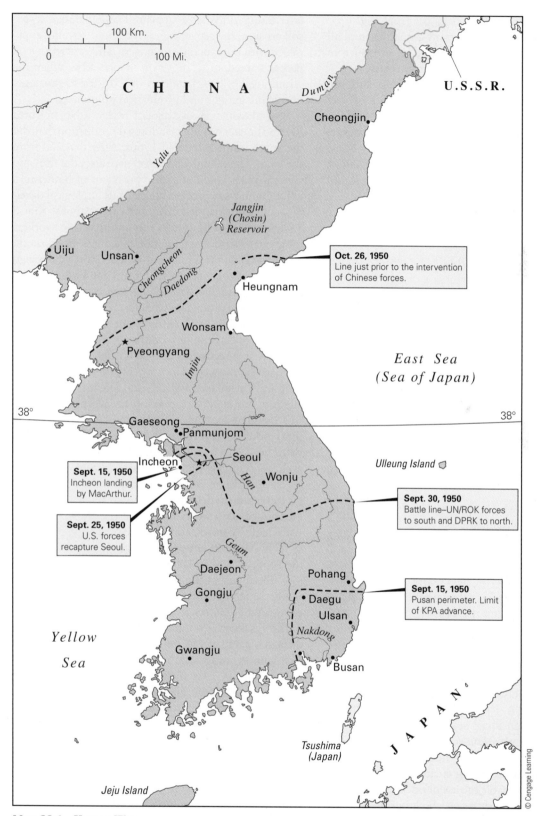

CHINA

U.S.S.R.

Duman

Cheongjin

Yalu

Jangjin (Chosin) Reservoir

Uiju

Unsan

Cheongcheon

Daedong

Heungnam

Oct. 26, 1950
Line just prior to the intervention of Chinese forces.

Wonsam

East Sea (Sea of Japan)

★ Pyeongyang

Imjin

38°   Gaeseong   38°

Panmunjom

Ulleung Island

Incheon   Seoul

Sept. 15, 1950
Incheon landing by MacArthur.

★

Han   Wonju

Sept. 30, 1950
Battle line–UN/ROK forces to south and DPRK to north.

Sept. 25, 1950
U.S. forces recapture Seoul.

Geum

Daejeon

Pohang

Gongju

Daegu

Sept. 15, 1950
Pusan perimeter. Limit of KPA advance.

Ulsan

Yellow Sea

Nakdong

Gwangju

Busan

JAPAN

Tsushima (Japan)

Jeju Island

© Cengage Learning

Map 28.1   Korean War

The battle back and forth across the front raged for two more years at the cost of many casualties until all parties except Rhee Syngman signed an armistice in 1953. To this day there is still no peace treaty.

Each side claimed that the other had suffered the most casualties, claiming total numbers of war dead that range from two to more than five million. Both sides and their big-power supporters committed atrocities against soldiers, POWs, and civilians. North and South suffered such extreme devastation that the industrial capacity built during the colonial period and expanded after 1945 lay in ruins.

THE DEMOCRATIC PEOPLE'S REPUBLIC OF KOREA (1953 TO THE PRESENT)

Kim Il Sung set the basic features of the political system in North Korea even before the Korean War, and they have scarcely changed since. He maximized political power in his own hands as the supreme leader, developed a militarist policy based on arming the entire population, initiated a revolutionary social policy, and launched periodic terrorist acts. His regime experienced a roller-coaster economic ride under a command economy with a downward plunge in 1991 following the withdrawal of Soviet support when communism collapsed in the Soviet Union and Eastern Europe.

Economic Development

After the end of the Korean War in 1953, Kim Il Sung relied on aid from the Soviet Union and China. He invested primarily in heavy and defense industries to create the basis for economic independence and a national arms industry. He postponed the production of consumer goods to the indefinite future, called on the public to accept sacrifice for the greater good of the nation, and compensated by providing cheap housing and food, free education, and free medical treatment.

In the mid-1950s, Kim embarked on a rapid farm collectivization plan aimed at converting all farmers to workers receiving wages on state farms. The plan was never fully implemented and ended with smaller collectives at the village level that created broad fields out of small parcels to enable the use of tractors and chemical fertilizer. In the early years, the program fostered tremendous gains in productivity; not until decades later did its drawbacks appear. These included severe soil erosion, the replacement of age-old farming experience with bureaucratic managers, and restrictions on people's freedom to move or change jobs. When the withdrawal of Soviet support in 1991 led to shortages of fuel oil, agricultural production plummeted.

Blessed with extensive mineral reserves, North Korea enjoyed greater growth in industrial production than did the South through the mid-1960s. After that, aid from the Soviet Union and China declined; also, the five- and six-year plans could not solve problems of bottlenecks in the production process, a lack of technological development, and excessive investment in weapons. Kim Il Sung's solution was to use a moral appeal to workers for greater sacrifice and to undertake mass mobilization efforts such as the Thousand-League Horse campaign of 1958. It was similar to the Great Leap Forward campaign in China, but without the excesses that resulted in massive starvation (see Chapter 27). Instead workers were required to work extra hours, and students were taken out of classrooms to work.

By 1970 the economy needed new technology. It had done well in the second industrial revolution in terms of chemicals, steel, locomotives, and internal combustion engines, but it did not develop the electronics industries based on the transistor that are the hallmark of the third industrial revolution. Kim opened trade relations with the West in 1972 to import advanced machinery and even complete factories from Europe and Japan on credit. Lacking anything to export, he defaulted on his international debt in 1975, and trade with the West evaporated. Despite technological shortfalls, problems with quality control, and wastage of energy, per capita GNP in North Korea probably stayed equal to that in the South at least to 1983.

While much of the rest of the world pursued economic interdependence, North Korea's policy of producing whatever it needed itself led to increasing hardships for the population. One sign of economic difficulty came in 1987 when Kim Il Sung was forced to abandon construction on what was to be the tallest building in East Asia, the 105-story Ryugyeong (RYU-gyong) Hotel. He then decided to shift investment to light industry and consumer products to improve living conditions, opened talks with South Korea on economic and humanitarian cooperation, and sent food aid to flood victims in South Korea. In 1988 he began informal talks with U.S. representatives.

The collapse of the Soviet Union left North Korea without a patron and minus a socialist trading partner. Oil supplies dropped because Russia demanded cash payment, and factories operated at only a fraction of capacity. North Korea opened a free economic trade zone in the northeast in 1991, but no foreign investors responded. The floods of 1995 and 1996 followed by drought in 1997 brought a famine that cost up to 2 million people their lives. Residents of Pyeongyang and the army fared well, while the rest of the civilian population suffered from malnutrition and disease. For the first time, the government allowed people to leave their homes without permission to forage for food, to cultivate small private plots, and to sell the products in farmer's markets.

In the first decade of the twenty-first century the government alternated between interfering with and relaxing controls over the market. In 2005 it cracked down on unofficial markets blamed for creating economic inequality and fueling inflation; in 2009, it revalued its currency, a move that wiped out the value of people's hoarded cash and brought trading to a standstill. At the same time, its strengthened trade ties with China introduced electronic consumer goods for urban residents who could afford them. Many of the most active traders were women.

Declines in industry and agricultural production had a devastating effect on the North Korean population. Illegal emigration into China's northeast province (the former Manchuria) increased, even though China had a policy of returning refugees. Worldwide charitable organizations, South Korea, China, the United States, and Japan supplied perhaps a fifth of North Korea's food in the 1990s and continue to do so in the twenty-first century whenever the political climate allows.

After Kim Il Sung's death in 1994, his son Kim Jong Il (KIM JONG-il) took cautious steps to open the economy. He established the Diamond Mountain tourist center for South Koreans, the Uiju (WI-jew) free trade zone south of the Yalu River, and the Gaeseong industrial park. He permitted construction of rail lines and roads across the DMZ from South Korea to Gaeseong (GAY-song) and the Diamond Mountain and welcomed investment by South Korean companies to build factories that would hire cheap North Korean labor to make products for export. He also counterfeited the currency of other nations and sold ballistic missile technology to enemies of the United States.

State and Society

The new workers' state aimed at remaking economic relationships. It banned collective bargaining, instead allowing only state-sponsored trade and farmers' unions. Kim Il Sung borrowed Mao Zedong's "mass line" strategy in 1960 to force party cadres to consult with workers and farmers in devising production plans. Faced with a lack of industrial workers, he admitted farmers to the Korean Workers' Party (KWP) and tried to make them understand their identity as workers (proletarian class consciousness) through indoctrination and self-criticism. Unlike Mao, he never launched mass mobilization campaigns to purge party cadres and bureaucrats who had lost their revolutionary ideals.

Kim Il Sung divided society into a new status hierarchy. The nuclear masses consisted of KWP members, government officials, military officers, anti-Japanese guerrilla fighters, and martyrs who died in the Korean War. The non-nuclear masses were nonparty workers, farmers, and clerical workers. The lowly mixed masses had tainted backgrounds as descendants of the middle class, landlords, capitalists, and critics. By 1962, Kim had executed all Catholic priests and Protestant ministers and sent Christians who had not fled to the South to reeducation camps. Instead of equal treatment for all, Kim turned the previous status structure upside down, reserving hereditary privilege for the elite and hereditary stigma for the outcasts.

Kim locked all individuals into a variety of state-run mass organizations. Because of labor shortages, he encouraged women to work and had the state provide child-care facilities for working parents. He replaced the home with communal mess halls, gave women the right to divorce, and brought women into the military. Despite these measures, few women had the opportunity to take on political responsibilities.

Expansion of Personal Power

Kim Il Sung's creation of a personality cult defines the North Korean regime. In 1972, Kim introduced a new constitution that created a new office of president, which gave him control of all government agencies. More shocking for ideologically committed communists, he subordinated the KWP to his command and left it out of many of his policy decisions. As signs of his megalomania, he also built gigantic statues of himself and adopted grandiose titles such as "supreme leader," "fatherly leader," "the Great Sun," "the supreme mind of the nation," and "genius of mankind."

Alain Nogues/Corbis

Bronze Statue of Kim Il Sung. North Korea is festooned with murals and statues of Kim Il Sung. This one shows him facing the future with confidence, surrounded by representatives of farmers and workers while his subjects bow to him in respect.

Kim also displaced communism with *juche* (JEW-chae) (self-reliance) as the country's leading ideology. A person who has *juche* has absorbed the correct thought from which will naturally spring correct action in any and all situations: the making of music and steel, getting up in the morning and being a good citizen, being modern and Korean. *Juche* is what makes North Korea proudly independent, self-contained, and the center of the world. In 1973, Kim followed dynastic tradition by grooming his son, Kim Jong Il, to succeed him. Although Kim Jong Il never took over his father's position as president, he raised the personality cult to new heights. He was most commonly known as "dear leader" and enjoyed hearing masses of children sing his praises. Before he died at the end of 2011, he had appointed his youngest son Kim Jong Un (KIM JONG-eun) a four-star general and vice chairman of the Central Military Commission. Backed by his family and the military (his mother had helped promote the generals who now support him), Kim Jong Un has traded on his physical resemblance to his beloved grandfather to win popularity and followed in the East Asian tradition of kingship by

riding a white horse and firing the first shots of the New Year.

The Kim Dynasty owes much to the purges of anyone who might challenge the supreme leader. At first the purges focused on members of the party. After Stalin's death when Khrushchev denounced Stalin for creating a cult of personality in 1956, Kim Il Sung purged members of the Russian and Yan'an factions who accused him of doing the same thing. He also purged three generals after the failure of his military ventures against South Korea and the United States in 1968 (a commando attack on the ROK presidential mansion and the capture of the intelligence-gathering ship USS *Pueblo*) and 1969 (the downing of a U.S. reconnaissance plane). Purges of top leadership continued under his son and more recently under his grandson. In the late 1960s, hundreds of thousands of party members received punishment for violating party rules, and the prison camps received new influxes of political prisoners in the 1970s (see **Biography: Kang Cheol Hwan, Survivor of a North Korean Prison Camp**). Today they often house economic refugees who have had the misfortune to be recaptured and returned to their homeland.

BIOGRAPHY

Kang Cheol Hwan, Survivor of a North Korean Prison Camp

Kang Cheol Hwan (KAHNG CHEOL-hwan) and his family exemplify the potential for mobility in the twentieth century, going from one country to another, from one occupation to another, and from privilege to a concentration camp.

Kang Cheol Hwan's grandmother migrated to Japan from Jeju Island in the 1930s at the age of thirteen. At the age of twenty, she joined the Japanese Communist Party and married a man from Jeju. Their son, Kang's father, was born in the early 1940s. After the end of World War II, Kang's grandfather did what many resident Koreans in Japan did—he opened a pachinko parlor in Kyoto. To stay in what is a somewhat shady business, he made friends with *yakuza* (gangsters). In the 1960s, the grandmother persuaded her reluctant husband to move the whole family, including her brothers, to Pyeongyang. They were treated as celebrities on the ship, received greetings by Kim Il Sung when they arrived, and were provided with a first-class apartment in the capital. The grandmother was elected to the Supreme People's Assembly, and the grandfather was appointed to the Office of Commercial Affairs. Kang's parents married in 1967, and he was born soon after.

One day in 1977, the grandfather disappeared, never to return, shipped off to a concentration camp for treason without a word to his family. Shortly thereafter, at the age of nine, Kang returned home to find that security agents were sending him, his grandmother, his father, and his uncles to a concentration camp because of his grandfather's crime. His mother was left behind with no way to communicate with the rest of the family. When Kang and the others arrived at Yodeok camp, they were placed in a hut with earthen walls and floor where whole families lived together in rags and filth. The camp housed two thousand or three thousand people; every year about a hundred died from hunger and disease. Minor violations were punished by a trip to the sweatbox for as long as three months where the prisoner had to crouch on his knees in darkness without moving or speaking. If he did either, he was beaten. Many failed to survive.

Kang was able to avoid the worst punishments during his ten years in the camp. When he was not working as porter to carry ore from the mines, he hunted rats, frogs, snakes, and insects to supplement the starvation rations of cornmeal and cabbage soup. One of his uncles attempted suicide twice.

Adults worked in the gold mine for thirteen hours a day, and many died from cave-ins. Women caught engaging in sex were humiliated in public or physically abused. Any babies born in the camp were taken away. The entire camp had to turn out for executions. When one prisoner who had tried to escape was dragged to his death behind a car, the other prisoners had to file past and touch his corpse as a warning not to try escaping themselves.

After a decade in the camp, Kang and his family were released by an amnesty, but they were not allowed to return to Pyeongyang. Instead they were sent to the countryside where they were subjected to strict surveillance. Kang finally left his family behind and bribed his way across the border to China. Eventually he made his way to South Korea. Many other refugees have followed him, only to find that starting over is never easy.

Questions for Analysis
1. What was there in Kang Cheol Hwan's family's past that might explain why he ended up as a prisoner?
2. How did Kang Cheol Hwan manage to survive?
3. What does Kang Cheol Hwan's story tell you about the living conditions for people in North Korea?

Source: Chol-hwan Kang and Pierre Rigoulot, *The Aquariums of Pyongyang* (New York: Basic Books, 2001).

International Relations

Until the collapse of the Soviet Union in 1991, Kim Il Sung tried to stay on good terms with both of his giant communist neighbors. He remained neutral during the Sino-Soviet split and signed mutual defense treaties with each. Surprised and alarmed when Mao invited President Nixon to visit Beijing in 1972, he allowed members of families separated by the Korean War to meet for the first time since 1953. He even signed a joint pledge for peaceful reunification with the president of South Korea.

This improvement in relations did not last long. After 1973, Kim Il Sung constructed secret tunnels across the DMZ large enough to launch an invasion while his agents kidnapped Japanese citizens for their passports and language expertise. Possibly in return for the favor of Kim's support for the Soviet Union's invasion of Afghanistan, a Soviet interceptor in August 1983 shot down a South Korean airliner, KAL Flight 007, which had strayed into Russian territory. The next year the Soviet Union shipped more military equipment in return for docking and overfly rights. In 1986 it promised to construct a nuclear power plant in the North.

In 1989 and 1990, North Korean officials indicated a willingness to normalize relations with the United States and Japan, open trade with South Korea, support peaceful coexistence, reduce defense expenditures, and introduce market reforms. They also voiced their objection to U.S. nuclear weapons on South Korean soil, joint ROK–U.S. Team Spirit exercises, and the thirty-seven thousand U.S. troops stationed in South Korea. In 1991, Kim Il Sung signed a denuclearization pact with South Korea. As a return measure to ease tensions, the United States announced withdrawal of all U.S. nuclear weapons from Korean soil and cancelled joint Team Spirit exercises with South Korea.

North Korea's Nuclear Challenge

Between 1964 and 1986, North Korea built several gas-graphite nuclear reactors in the Soviet style at Yongbyon north of Pyeongyang to generate electricity. All produced the by-product plutonium, which could be used to manufacture hydrogen bombs. In 1985, the Soviet Union convinced Kim Il Sung to sign the Nonproliferation Treaty (NPT), which required inspections by the UN International Atomic Energy Agency (IAEA) to prevent military use of nuclear material. The IAEA never followed through on the inspections.

The 1990s saw protracted negotiations over North Korea's nuclear power program. Kim Il Sung offered to replace his gas-graphite reactors with new light-water reactors, which produce less plutonium as a waste product. When the United States ignored the offer and considered taking punitive action, Kim threatened to pull out of the NPT. Sent by President Bill Clinton, former president Jimmy Carter went to Pyeongyang and reached an agreement with Kim to stop processing nuclear waste to extract plutonium in return for light-water reactors. Kim also told Carter he was willing to carry out the North–South denuclearization agreement, pull back forces from the DMZ,

match South Korea in reducing troops by one million men, and accept the presence of U.S. troops in Korea. He died before negotiations could be continued.

His son, Kim Jong Il, signed the Agreed Framework with the United States in 1994. Under this agreement, South Korea and Japan assumed the cost for the light-water reactors, and the United States was to provide 500,000 tons of heavy oil annually to replace energy lost from the inactive reactors. North Korea remained a party to the NPT and promised to allow the IAEA to inspect facilities when the light-water reactors were completed but before the nuclear components were installed.

The Agreed Framework was only partially implemented. The United States delayed delivery of heavy oil, and the economic crash of 1997 rendered the ROK unable to finance construction of a light-water reactor. In 1998, North Korea test-fired an intermediate-range ballistic missile over Japan, an act repeated in 2006, although that missile exploded 40 seconds after takeoff.

The early twenty-first century saw increased tension between North Korea and the United States. After the attacks by the Islamic terrorist al-Qaeda organization on September 11, 2001, President Bush placed North Korea in what he called the "axis of evil," a group of "rogue states." When U.S. intelligence discovered the North's clandestine plan to build atomic weapons from enriched uranium (supplied by Pakistan) in 2002, Bush declared that the North would have to abandon its nuclear weapons program before the United States offered any material aid. North Korea expelled IAEA inspectors, withdrew from the NPT, and tested a plutonium bomb in 2006. Under pressure from China, North Korea rejoined six-nation talks with China, Russia, the United States, South Korea, and Japan. In 2007, Kim Jong Il proposed to shut down his nuclear weapons program in return for a guarantee that other nations would respect North Korea's sovereignty, help in building light-water reactors, and move toward normal diplomatic relations, but negotiations remain deadlocked.

THE REPUBLIC OF KOREA: DICTATORSHIP AND PROTEST (1953–1987)

During the Cold War, dictators ruled South Korea. As in the North, they suppressed civil liberties and tried to promote economic growth through heavy-handed state planning that fostered inefficiency and corruption. Although they never developed personality cults, they killed, jailed, and tortured thousands of their opponents. The only way for protesters to voice opposition and force change was outside the system.

The Dictators

Rhee Syngman constructed a dictatorship based on the police, a new army, and a centralized bureaucracy that appointed district officials. In 1949 he passed a National Security Law that threatened imprisonment for treason of anyone who supported, assisted, or praised an "enemy state" (North Korea), terms so vague that Rhee immediately began to use the law against his political opponents. He railroaded bills through the National Assembly, used officials and police to intimidate voters during elections, distributed favors to politicians, gagged newspapers, jailed critics, and had them tortured. He finally overstepped the bounds with blatant electoral fraud in 1960.

Student protests inadvertently brought South Korea's longest-reigning dictator to power. On April 19, 1960, when police fired on college students opposed to Rhee's attempt to fix his reelection, the students' deaths enflamed public opinion. Having lost the army's support, Rhee retired to Hawai'i. A year later, former Japanese army officer General Park Chung Hee (PARK JUNG-hee) took control. Two years later, under pressure from the United States, Park donned civilian garb, abolished the supreme council, and held elections. By relying on the civil bureaucracy, police, army, and Korean Central Intelligence Agency (KCIA), he won the presidential elections of 1963 and 1967 and majorities for his Democratic Republican Party in the National Assembly.

When Park nearly lost the presidential election of 1971, he took new measures to stay in power. In 1972 he revised the constitution to allow the president to appoint one-third of the members of the National Assembly, guaranteeing him a two-thirds majority and the ability to declare martial law at any time. Decree No. 9 banned any criticism of the president, and he also forbade all labor union activity. To eliminate his strongest political challenger, in 1973 Park authorized the KCIA to kidnap Kim Dae Jung (KIM DAE-jung) from his hotel room in Tokyo and dump him in Tokyo Bay.

Kim Dae Jung (Kim Taejung), Opposition Politician and Later President of South Korea, 1997–2002. Arrested on the phony charge of fomenting the Gwangju uprising of May 1980, he appears here with his head shaved and in a prison uniform following his death sentence.

Protest by the United States then forced Park to bring Kim back to Seoul and put him under house arrest. In 1979 labor protests erupted in Busan and the free export zone of Masan. Park was about to turn the army on the demonstrators when the head of the KCIA shot and killed him.

A second military dictatorship followed. General Chun Doo Hwan (CHEON DO-hwan) declared martial law, closed all universities, banned political activity, suspended the National Assembly, and arrested hundreds of students and opposition politicians. When students in Gwangju in Jeolla province protested en masse on May 18, 1980, and citizens took over the city, elite paratroopers murdered people on the streets. Although the exact number will never be known, it appears that more than two thousand civilians died. Chun Doo Hwan made Kim Dae Jung the scapegoat for the Gwangju massacre and had a kangaroo court sentence Kim to death. (Again, U.S. pressure saved his life.)

Chun's repression of dissent continued. He revised the constitution to establish a seven-year term for the presidency, banned hundreds of politicians from political activity, and won a sham presidential election in February 1981. Four years later Chun lifted the ban against most politicians but dismissed professors, expelled 1,363 university students, forcibly conscripted a third of them into military service where several were murdered on duty, and subjected others to brainwashing in concentration camps. Chun took revenge on his critics in the media by dismissing hundreds of newspaper and broadcast reporters, banning periodicals, closing down hundreds of publishing companies, and taking over the Munhwa Broadcasting Corporation. He required all newspapers to run his picture every day.

The most massive demonstrations in Korean history erupted when Chun Doo Hwan gave signs of reneging on his pledge to retire at the end of his seven-year term. Forced to retreat, he nominated General Roh Tae Woo (NOH TAE-woo), a commander in the Gwangju massacre, to be his party's nominee for president. He authorized Roh to hold direct elections, restore freedom of the press, and allow Kim Dae Jung to run for office. President Reagan had put pressure on Chun to back down, but the main force for democracy came from students who had fought against dictatorship for decades and elements of the urban middle class who joined the democratic struggle at its end.

Building a New Economy

South Korea's economy did not fare well during the Korean War. To compete with the North, Rhee Syngman adopted a land reform policy that created a class of conservative small property owners who voted for Rhee and subsequent dictators. Eleven billion dollars of U.S. civil and military aid kept the economy afloat, with Rhee distributing U.S. dollars to favored businessmen in return for political contributions. His import-substitution policy cut the cost of imported goods, but the country's economic growth rate remained so low that U.S. officials viewed the ROK as incapable of serious development. They proposed turning South Korea into a supplier of agricultural products and raw materials in exchange for Japan's manufactured goods, a policy Rhee opposed.

Military dictators ignored the principles of free market capitalism and adopted a developmentalist strategy. Park Chung Hee controlled the banks to direct foreign exchange and have loans made at preferential low interest rates to labor-intensive export industries, such as textiles, to take advantage of South Korea's low wages. He allowed the most efficient companies to become huge conglomerates, devalued the currency to promote exports, protected companies with tariffs and nontariff barriers, banned the sale of export items on the domestic market, and prevented foreign investors from owning more than 49 percent of businesses. After surprising strikes for higher wages, he created a single national trade union to block labor activism. He maintained a subsistence income for the new class of small-holding farmers by buying their rice crop at high prices and distributing it to low-wage urban factory and white-collar workers below cost, using tax revenues to make up the difference. He also built multistory apartment houses for squatters and the homeless poor.

The South Korean government used foreign policy to raise money for investment. In return for normalizing relations with Japan in 1965, it received $800 million in grants and loans. As a result, the economy grew about 9 percent per year for almost two decades, with most of the investment in industry, not agriculture. During the Vietnam War, South Korean troops fought alongside U.S. forces and the ROK received $1 billion in compensation. Just as Japan had prospered from the Korean War, so did South Korea prosper by sending steel and transport to Vietnam.

In the early decades, workers protested that state-managed economic growth had not benefited them. In the late 1960s, workers in the electronics, chemical, steel, and automobile industries struck against low wages. The nation was particularly shocked in 1970 when Jeon Taeil (JEON TAE-il), a worker in the Peace Market in Seoul (a warren of garment sweatshops), set himself on fire to bring attention to the workers' plight. In 1971, Park established the New Village Movement complete with training camps to mobilize both farmers and workers on behalf of peaceful worker–employer relations.

Despite criticism from foreign advisers, Park decided on a big push: forced industrial development to increase exports and raise per capita income. In 1973 he launched his Heavy and Chemical Industry program to develop steel, ships, automobiles, petrochemicals, and electronics to build capacity in weapons production and increase national power. When the Middle Eastern oil-producing nations raised oil prices in 1973 and 1974, he borrowed from abroad to keep factories going. By the end of the decade, South Korea was exporting machinery, steel, chemicals, freighters, and tankers. In the 1980s, it moved into electronics, following Japan and the United States into the third industrial revolution. Economic growth paid the most handsome dividends to the conglomerates and also put money in the pockets of workers.

Social Change and Official Arts

The Korean War did as much to dissolve the old status system as had Japan's colonization. By dislocating the population, it tore people from their old relations of dependency and control before the development of industry in the 1960s brought a massive migration of the rural population to Seoul and other cities. Although former *yangban* from the southwest still claimed social prestige, they lacked economic clout and political power.

The largest, most cohesive institution became the military. During the decades of military preparedness following the war, male conscripts learned drills, discipline, patriotism, and anticommunism. Large corporations required workers to have completed military service before being considered for employment. They counted military service as work experience that justified higher pay and faster promotion, and veterans received extra points on employment tests. Through universal conscription, men became incorporated into the nation as equal citizens.

By constructing the labor market as masculine, military dictatorships marginalized women in the workplace. Although close to 80 percent of women finished high school and 25 percent attended college by the 1970s, educated women were limited to secretarial or white-collar jobs. They were segregated from men, received less training, and were given lower wages for similar work. With no chance for promotion, they were usually forced to quit once they married or at an earlier age than men. Women also worked in factories. With encouragement by the state, the textile industry hired hundreds of thousands of young women in the early 1970s, but only as temporary and cheap unskilled labor. During the state-sponsored Factory New Village Movement in the mid-1970s and early 1980s, factories set up classes for working women to teach them etiquette, proper behavior, and womanly accomplishments such as flower arranging and embroidery. According to the Ministry of Labor, "Women workers need common sense, civility, thrift, wisdom as well as their duty as workers because they are mothers of future generations."[*]

While training women to be housewives and mothers, military dictatorships also tried to limit their fertility. The state provided financing for women's organizations such as the Korean National Wives' Association and the Korean Federation of Housewives' Clubs to encourage women in rational management of the household. Concerned that unchecked population expansion threatened economic growth, in the 1960s the state promoted family planning by encouraging women to use contraception. In the 1970s, the state promoted female sterilization, with 48 percent of all fertile women being surgically sterilized by 1988. Women had the patriotic duty to have children, but not to have too many.

The dictators used arts and culture to foster a sense of nationhood and promote patriotism. In 1959 each province started to sponsor an annual folk festival to support a sanitized version of traditional arts. Performances of masked dance drama, for example, failed to include lines critical of *yangban*, the old ruling class. In 1962, Park introduced the Cultural Properties Protection Law to designate tangible and intangible cultural assets, folk cultural properties, and monuments. The Ministry of Culture and Information appeared in 1972 with a five-year plan for cultural development that included support for film, translations of Korean literature from Chinese into *Hangul* (HAN-geul), funding for archaeological research, and refurbishment of famous sites. It also subsidized traditional handicrafts (see **Material Culture: Modern Traditional Handicrafts**).

International Relations

Following the Korean War, South Korea grew increasingly frustrated with its reliance on the United States for defense. In 1958, the United States had placed more than two hundred nuclear weapons on South

---

[*]Seungsook Moon, *Militarized Modernity and Gendered Citizenship in South Korea* (Durham, N.C.: Duke University Press, 2005), p. 75.

MATERIAL CULTURE

Modern Traditional Handicrafts

Traditional handicrafts are big business in today's Korea. Stores in Seoul near what was once the main U.S. army base sell massive chests, tables, and other furniture, not just to foreigners but also to Koreans who wish to furnish their homes to look like yangban mansions. There customers can also buy lacquered wood vases inlaid with mother-of-pearl, elaborately carved folding screens, paintings of Korean tigers, and fine Korean silk. Tourists wander through Madong village, a suburb of Gyeongju (GYONG-jew), where families of potters make Korea's famous celadon-glazed ceramics fired in climbing kilns fueled with pinewood, visit the National Folk Museum to see how people lived centuries ago, and visit shops where artisans craft long-stem bamboo pipes.

Given the convenience of mass-produced cigarettes, few people smoke long pipes anymore, except in movies and television dramas set in the Joseon (JOE-son) Dynasty. The pipes vary in the length of the stems made from polished bamboo. The mouthpiece and bowl are made of metal, highly decorated to increase the pipe's quality and hence its price. Collectors cherish a finely made pipe in the old style; tourists enjoy the novelty.

Handicrafts are the opposite of modern mass production. Reflecting the anonymity of the craftsperson rather than the individuality of the artist, they set a diversity of regional styles against the homogenization of globalization. To revive and protect Korea's traditional arts, the government issued the

The Older the Smoker, the Longer the Pipe. Enjoying a well-deserved retirement, these two men, photographed in 1950, display their pipes and their respectable status.

Cultural Properties Protection Law in 1962 and the Culture and Arts Promotion Law of 1972. In this way, it asserted that Korea has a distinctive heritage and a source of national pride.

Korean soil, with missiles aimed at China and the Soviet Union as well as North Korea. The United States refused to retaliate when North Korean commandoes tried to assassinate Park on January 21, 1968; when North Korea captured a U.S. intelligence ship, the USS *Pueblo* two days later and kept its eighty-two crew members captive; or when North Korea shot down a U.S. EC-121 reconnaissance plane in 1969. The "Nixon Doctrine" announced that year shifted responsibility for self-defense to Asian nations, and in February 1970 Nixon removed twenty thousand of the sixty-two thousand U.S. troops in Korea to cut costs. Alarmed, Park had his agents bribe U.S. congressmen to grant more funds to South Korea—the

"Koreagate" scandal. Park perceived Nixon's new policy toward Mao's China in 1971 as capitulation to the communist enemy. He decided to negotiate directly with Kim Il Sung and induced him to sign a joint agreement for peaceful reunification on July 4, 1972. This initiative soon collapsed.

DEMOCRACY IN SOUTH KOREA (1987 TO THE PRESENT)

General Roh Tae Woo deserves great credit for bringing democracy to South Korea. He won the election in 1987 despite gaining only 35.9 percent of the vote because the opposition splintered into regional blocks while in the National Assembly his new Democratic Liberal Party attracted enough opposition members to function. Workers seized the initiative to found a new, independent National Federation of Trade Unions in defiance of the government-controlled Korean Federation of Trade Unions. It did not include schoolteachers because Roh refused to let them unionize. Chun Doo Hwan had founded a private foundation to control Roh after the election, but his hopes were dashed when Roh jailed fourteen of Chun's brothers and relatives for embezzlement and corruption. Chun retired in disgrace to a Buddhist monastery.

Kim Young Sam's (KIM YOUNG-sahm) single-term presidency (1992–1997) removed the curse of military interference in politics. He purged high-ranking military officers who had served dictators and stripped military agencies of the power to investigate domestic politicians. In 1995, he held the first local elections for provincial governors, city mayors, county officials, and local assemblies in Korean history. Even more courageously, he prosecuted former presidents, Chun Doo Hwan and Roh Tae Woo, for treason, mutiny, and corruption. The results of the trial sent Chun to jail for life and Roh for seventeen years. When several cabinet members and his two sons went to jail for evading military service and receiving bribes, his popularity plummeted.

The old regional power bases and patron–client relations could not compete with new political parties. In 1997, the chairman of the Millennium Democratic Party, Kim Dae Jung, won the presidential election with the help of the United Liberal Democratic Party, the first opposition party victory in South Korean history. Kim set up a Human Rights Commission to protect people from the oppression he and others of the dictators' opponents had suffered, and he created a Ministry of Gender Equality. Kim also had to deal with the Asian financial crisis, backlash from his trip to Pyeongyang, and a scandal when his son and many officials were prosecuted for taking bribes.

In the first decade of the twenty-first century, a changing array of political parties contested national and local elections. When liberals were perceived as too conciliatory toward North Korea and inept at economic reform, Lee Myung Bak (YI MYUNG-bahk) of the Grand National Party was voted into office. By the end of his term, he too struggled with declining popularity and corruption scandals implicating his aides. After decades of dictatorship, democracy has become firmly entrenched in South Korea.

Economic Crisis and Recovery

Following decades of central planning under the dictators, President Kim Young Sam's advisers advocated globalization and the adoption of liberal, free market principles. The results were dire. Reduced tariffs and cheap imports undersold home industries. Encouraged to cut costs to increase efficiency, companies laid off workers. Riding on an inflow of foreign capital, the conglomerates glutted the market with autos, semiconductors, and steel and doctored their books to hide debt from banks. By 1996, South Korea's national debt had almost doubled to $109 billion, of which two-thirds was short-term debt.

In 1997, the Asian financial crisis that spread from Thailand to South Korea brought down the economy. By calling in short-term loans, foreign lenders drove six conglomerates and their suppliers into bankruptcy. South Korea was saved from defaulting on its national debt only because the International Monetary Fund (IMF) provided a record bailout package of $55 billion. When the IMF imposed a brutal retrenchment policy by raising interest rates from 12 to 27 percent per annum to stabilize the currency, more companies failed, and thousands of workers were laid off. The unemployment rate rose from less than 2 percent to 7.6 percent in September 1998. Female workers were often the first to be fired. National per capita income dropped from $10,000 to $7,000. The government had to sell off eleven state-owned industries, including the prized Pohang Iron and Steel Company, to raise funds.

Recovery began in the fall of 1998 when the government defied IMF dictates by lowering interest rates to increase business investment. The conglomerates gobbled up the loan money, leaving little for small businesses. Although the conglomerates supported unprofitable subsidiaries, Kim Dae Jung allowed foreign companies majority ownership in failing Korean businesses to save them from bankruptcy. In the twenty-first century the government announced a new initiative to provide every home with broadband access to keep South Korea competitive and allowed former chairmen of conglomerates convicted of tax evasion and bribes to return to their former positions. Although South Korea still suffers from technological gaps and the loss of jobs to low-wage countries like China, it sells electronics, appliances, and cars across the world.

Opening Up International Relations

In addition to reforming South Korea's political process, Roh Tae Woo mended relations with the communist states of the Soviet Union, Eastern Europe, and China. In 1988, when South Korea hosted the Summer Olympics in Seoul, Kim Il Sung sought to ruin the event by having two agents blow up a South Korean plane flying from the Middle East to Seoul. Instead of retaliating, Roh sent officials to Pyeongyang to persuade Kim Il Sung to allow the Hyundai conglomerate to open a park for tourists in the Diamond Mountain area just north of the DMZ. He also punished activists under the National Security Law for traveling to North Korea without his permission to discuss peaceful reunification. In 1991 he gained Soviet and Chinese support to admit South Korea to the United Nations, forcing Kim Il Sung to abandon his previous opposition and accept admission to the United Nations as well.

Upon becoming president of South Korea in 1997, Kim Dae Jung inaugurated a new "sunshine policy" to seek rapprochement with the North that culminated in 2000 in a summit meeting with Kim Jong Il in Pyeongyang. Although Kim Dae Jung won the Nobel Peace Prize, it was later revealed that he had paid a bribe of $500 million to Kim Jong Il to enable the talks. When Kim Jong Il took no further measures to ease tension, Kim Dae Jung's reputation was further damaged. Opposition to the sunshine policy increased following Kim Jong Il's saber rattling. South Koreans support reconciliation with the North, but having observed what reunification did to the West German economy, they are not eager to absorb their poverty-stricken neighbor.

THE KOREAN INFLECTION OF MODERNITY

South Korean society changed dramatically after 1945. Arranged marriages began to decline, with marriage brokers being used for introductions only. College men and women arranged group "meetings" to enable couples to pair off for dates and "love marriages," even though they sought parental approval first. Wives were still subordinated to husbands and mothers-in-law, but middle-class married couples gained some distance from parents who bankrolled large rental deposits for modern apartments. Couples put intense pressure on their

children to gain entry into the best colleges. Virtually abandoned by their overworked white-collar husbands who stayed out drinking until midnight, middle-class wives took to making money in the real estate or stock markets. As women frustrated by unhappy marriages became conscious of gender discrimination, books and movies from the 1990s began to portray (and reflect) married women seeking sexual liberation with lovers.

Modernity brought diversity in employment opportunities; democracy made it possible for workers to unionize and demand reform. Rather than take repetitive factory jobs, young women preferred work in the service industry where they could wear pretty clothes and sell cosmetics to their peers. Educated young men chose white-collar jobs. Their elders had a hard time adjusting to the restructuring caused by the Asian financial crisis and the outsourcing of jobs overseas, and the factories that remain have had to welcome mature women into tasks once reserved for men.

Starting in 1983, when a telephone operator filed suit against company policy that forced her to retire at age forty-three, women have fought one court case after another to gain equal employment rights with men. Passed in the late 1980s, the Equal Employment Law became a target because it did not require equal pay for equal work or require punishment for noncompliant employers. In the 1990s, pressure from women's associations and labor unions forced the government to first pass and then amend equal opportunity laws (see **Documents: Selections from the Sexual Equality Employment Act**). There is now a ministry in charge of gender equality and the family.

A Comparison of Living Standards in North and South Korea, 2010		
	South Korea	North Korea
Population	48.7 million	24.4 million
Life expectancy (at birth)	80	68
Infant mortality rate (per 1,000 live births)	5.0	33.0
Electric power consumption (kWh per capita)	8853	810
Internet users (per 1,000)	809	0
Paved roads (% of total)	79	6.4

Source: World Bank, http://www.worldbank.org.

The growth of income and wealth led to a consumer culture and conspicuous consumption in clothing, appliances, pianos, and luxury apartments. South Koreans today have wide access to goods and technology, while residents of North Korea lag significantly behind. The preceding table compares the two countries in terms of their standards of living and access to technology.

Korean poetry and literature in ordinary language came into its own in the postwar period, with many authors writing about the Korean War, social justice, and the evils of dictatorship. Seonu Hwi's (SUH-nu HWI) *Flowers of Fire* traced the history of the Ko family from the March First demonstrations of 1919 through the Korean War, Chae Mansik's (CHAE MAHN-shik) *Peace Under Heaven* portrayed an evil landlord, and the famous "Five Bandits" poem by Kim Chiha (KIM CHI-ha) condemned bureaucrats and businessmen. Writer and poet Hwang Sunwon (HWANG SOON-won) depicted the lives of the poor in the 1970s, and Hwang Seokyeong (HWANG SUCK-young) wrote about personal problems and Korean soldiers in the Vietnam War in *The Shadow of Arms* (1985). Pak Gyeongni's (PARK GYEONG-li) lengthy *The Land* (1980), a vast saga with hundreds of characters that covered the most turbulent years of Korean history, became so popular that it was adapted for television, film, and opera and brought her international fame. Later short-story writers, women such as Kang Seokgyeong (KAHNG SUCK-gyeong), Kim Jiwon (KIM JI-won), and O Jeonghui (O JUNG-hwi), wrote contemplative stories of anomie under industrialization.

Another response to urban anonymity has been the spread of new religions. Christianity, Buddhism, and Cheondogyo (CHEON-doh-gyo) continue to attract adherents, but many Koreans are attracted to more activist ministries. Korean medical missionaries work in war-torn areas across the world, including Ethiopia and Afghanistan. Reverend Sun Myung Moon (SUN-myung MOON), founder of the Unification Church, has sought to bring happiness to thousands through his mass wedding ceremonies.

In the late 1990s, the "Korean Wave" hit China, Taiwan, Southeast Asia, and Japan. It has since made inroads in the United States, Europe, and South America. Dominated by TV dramas, music, and film, it has popularized Korean fashion, food, cosmetics, and electronic goods. Korean soap operas and their stars are household names in Asia, and Korean films have won awards at international film festivals and hold a larger share of the Korean market than those from Hollywood. Released in 2005, director Yun Jongbin's [YOON JONG-bin] *The Unforgiven* critiques compulsory military service and the harsh military subculture through the eyes of three conscripts. Korea also has a thriving industry in romantic comedies (*Please Teach Me English*, 2003) and animation (*Empress Chung*, 2005). Recorded on DVD, they have even infiltrated North Korea.

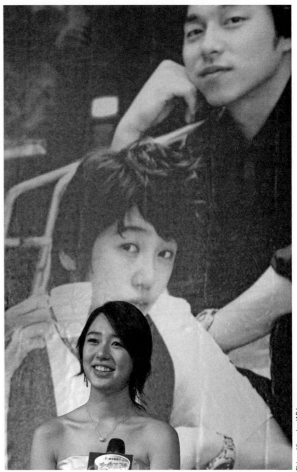

Chiang Ying-ying/AP Images

The Korean Wave in Soap Operas. South Korean actress Yoon Eun-Hye announces the debut of her new soap opera *Coffee Prince* with a poster of her male costars in the background.

DOCUMENTS

South Korean Women Workers and the International Monetary Fund

The 1997 Asian economic crisis hit South Korea so hard that the government was forced to seek help from the International Monetary Fund. In order to get loans, it had to agree to structural adjustment programs (SAPs) designed to reduce demand, decontrol prices, reform trade practices, tighten credit, and privatize government services. When the economy shrank, with the read GDP growth rate falling from 5.0 % to −6.7% in 1998, women were the first to be fired. Interviews with union activists explain what happened.

In the mid-1980s the main activities for community-based women workers' organizations were to assist in forming labor unions and supporting their initiatives. Since then we have focused on women-specific areas such as education and training for women union leaders and raising women-related issues within unions. Although our activities brought fruitful results, the difficulties were overwhelming. For example, in manufacturing areas, the restructuring meant that many industries disappeared and workers lost their jobs in a brief instant. We decided to enlarge our activities to bring more women into our organization by running several programs including a vocational training center, a free job arrangement center, a hotline, and so on. At the same time, we began to think about the possibility of women-only trade unions. In fact here were some initial worries about separating from existing unions, but seeing what happened to women in times of economic crisis, we realized that both the Federation of Korean Trade Unions (FKTU) and the Korean Confederation of Trade Unions (KCTU) totally failed to organize and protect women workers. We had tried to support and assist the KCTU, but it proved unable to organize women workers. So we made our own union (Choi SangRim, president of the Korean Women's Trade Union [KWTU]).

The IMF regime provided a momentum for change in Korean society as a whole. Without any social safety nets, the changes fell heavily on the society's margin—women. The trends for the informalization of women's work were also found in other countries, but there change was gradual or there were safety nets that reduced the total shocks. In the case of South Korea, however, the coercive situation called the IMF forced the margins to absorb the entire shock. Currently (2003) the rate of contingent women workers is over 73% (Choi SangRim).

In the end, the Korea Federation of Small and Medium Business made an agreement

SUMMARY

The political division carried out at the end of World War II divided Korea into two countries with opposing political, economic, and social systems. Neither side expected the division to last, and each expected its vision of Korea's future to prevail. The Korean War that cost so many lives increased the antagonism between the two sides because it ended in an armistice, not a peace treaty.

Supported first by the Soviet Union and later (and more grudgingly) by China, North Korea developed heavy industry and a million-man army with another 4.7 million in the reserves that absorbs one-fifth of the adult male population and costs 31.3 percent of the GDP, making it the most heavily militarized country in the world. Although he preached social equality, Supreme Leader Kim Il Sung founded a new dynasty and created social divisions that preclude social mobility. His philosophy of *juche* explained to his people how to live their lives as patriotic citizens lest they end up in prison camps.

Under the Kim Dynasty, North Korea has alternatively improved relations with the outside world and made them worse. It has fired on ships and territory

(to abolish a general affairs section staffed almost entirely by women) despite the women workers' strong opposition and our persistent advice. That really showed how little influence the Korean Confederation of Trade Unions (KCTU) had on its affiliated unions. In terms of the system, the final decision and agreement are made within each organization between management and union. Unless we steal their seals, we can't do anything. That's the limitation of the KCTU, which is basically based on enterprise level unionism (Lee HyeSoon former staff member of KCTU, General Secretary of KWTU).

I have no expectations for the KCTU. For many activists in South Korea, there has been a strong one-sided love for the KCTU. Studying gender studies caused me to think more critically about male dominated unions. However, I never thought that they would betray us until experiencing the IMF regime. That is when I felt a deep sense of betrayal (Park JinYoung, Director of Research Department at the Korean Women Workers Association United (KWWAU).

When we found that female janitors' average wages were below the minimum wage, we decided to raise this issue through a big campaign. The minimum wage committee consisted of representatives from labor, management, and the public interest. There was never any agreement between them. For members of the two major unions, none receive below minimum wage. However for us there are lots of cases. We began to intervene in the minimum wage committee through demanding that the representatives of labor not withdraw and persuading them to raise the minimum wage. Outside the building we held demonstrations. Ours was the first rally since the committee was formed. Finally the minimum wage increased (Park JinYoung).

The situation confronting women workers at the gateway to the twenty-first century can be summed up in the following facts: 64% are employed in workplaces with less than four workers; 70% are employed on an irregular basis. They are the primary targets for dismissal and pressured to resign upon marriage or pregnancy. The rate of organized women is only 5.6% (Choi SangRim).

Questions for Analysis

1. What kinds of difficulties did women (and also men) face as a result of the 1997 Asian economic crisis?
2. Why did women decide that they needed their own trade union?
3. What is particular to the Korean case (what do Korean workers have in common with workers elsewhere?)

Source: Seo Youngju, "Industrialization, Globalization and Women Workers in South Korea, 1960–2003" MA thesis, University of Massachusetts, Lowell, 2004, pp. 87, 101, 102, 103, 104. Reprinted with permission of the author.

claimed by South Korea, detonated a plutonium bomb, and threatened to turn Seoul into a sea of fire. Some analysts believe that these threats occur when the Kim family needs to overawe potential opponents within ruling class circles; others point to paranoia regarding the intentions of its foreign enemies, as when the Bush administration declared North Korea to be part of the "axis of evil."

South Korea too suffered under dictatorships until 1987, although as a client state of the United States, it had to bow to U.S. pressure on human rights issues. The dictators kept a number of industries under state control, encouraged the growth of conglomerates such as Hyundai, and paid little attention to the workers' quality of life or the needs of women. To foster a Korean national identity, the dictators promoted Korea's heritage.

South Korea's turn to democracy gave its citizens freedom from arbitrary arrest, new opportunities, a new urban society of capitalists and white- and blue-collar workers, and better relations with the outside world. Koreans have learned to speak out against government corruption; they use video recordings of lawbreakers to earn rewards from the police. Although nearly every household has Internet access, young urbanites depend on their cellphones for all their daily needs, from measuring biorhythms to paying for train tickets or buying groceries.

How has Korea changed in the last sixty years? Although repressive regimes once dominated both the communist North and the bureaucratic capitalist South, North Korea has become a nationalistic hereditary monarchy, while military dictatorship in South Korea was transformed into democracy. Society in both North and South has changed through social leveling and the partial liberation of women, although in different ways. Religion was replaced by hero worship and patriotism in the North, while in the pluralistic South people follow varied practices. Both North and South Korea have gained new standing on the world stage—the North through the threat posed by its nuclear program, the South through its economic dynamism and popular culture.

In today's South Korea, there are an estimated three hundred thousand shamans who placate the gods, comfort the spirits of the dead, intimidate evil spirits by walking barefoot on knife blades, and help politicians decide whether relocating their ancestors' tomb will win elections. They maintain websites offering online fortunetelling while young shamans keep blogs.

Although there are probably not as many shamans in the other East Asian countries, the popular religious traditions of China, Japan, and Korea share a wide range of ideas and practices. Mediators between the visible and invisible worlds have long histories in China and Japan as well as in Korea. Much of our knowledge of Shang China comes from the bones cracked by diviners trying to communicate with ancestors and gods. In the northern kingdom of Goguryeo (GO-goo-ryeo), shamans exorcized the vengeful spirits of people executed by the king and performed divination by reading cracks on turtle shells. The gold crowns worn by Silla kings and queens resemble headdresses worn by shamans in Siberia and Manchuria. The earliest ruler in Japan described in Chinese records from the third century relayed messages from the gods. Her tradition continues in the founders of new religions who by channeling gods have gained the power to speak in public and in mediums who communicate with spirits. Some of Japan's mountain priests have the power to leave their bodies to roam through the invisible world, a power also granted Chinese shamans. Today in Taiwan, shamans carry bribes to the king of the underworld on behalf of the recently deceased.

Local deities populate the landscapes of popular religion. Over time the Chinese spirit world came to be organized like the visible world, with a king of hell, local rulers, bureaucrats, and police officials. Demons plague the living. There are gods for specific problems such as illness, various Daoist immortals, and gods who were once historical human beings. Others were once ghosts or the spirits of mountains and rivers. If the protective deities for cities do not do their job, they can be dismissed and new city gods brought in to take their place. Some temples are dedicated to the goddess of mercy and overseer of families and children; others focus on the goddess of waters; and then there is Guandi, the red-faced god of war and patron of business.

Koreans saw gods in mountains, waters, trees, tigers, bears, and founding kings. In the third century C.E., rulers inveighed against blood sacrifices to local gods, a prohibition repeated in the twelfth century. Japanese too worshipped nature spirits. From the sixteenth century on, men who strove for self-perfection or power worshipped the god in themselves. When commercial development in the eighteenth century brought surprising prosperity to entrepreneurs, those not so favored assumed that the newly rich had control of fox spirits who stole the wealth of others.

Another characteristic of popular religion is the need to appease the dead. Regardless of whether Confucian ancestral rites carry religious significance, ordinary Chinese families might come close to bankruptcy to pay for elaborate funerals that sent a father and mother to the afterlife in a style far above their standing in the visible world. They assumed that parents who cared about the family before they died would continue to be so after death; they also believed that life after death replicates this life on another plane. To keep ancestral spirits from turning into unhappy ghosts, they had to be provided with paper furnishing, paper money, and food.

In Korea and Japan, one reason for funerary rites was to eliminate the dead person's dangerous influence. Buddhism spread during the Goryeo Dynasty in part because Buddhist funerals removed the fear that the dead might cause havoc for the living. Travelers, infants, and single men and women were likely to hold grievances, and women who had been mistreated by their communities might return as vengeful spirits. Because ghosts troubled only those who had known them in life, it was particularly important to treat dead relatives with respect.

Fear is not the only reason to placate the spirits; they also bring this-worldly benefits. Rulers summoned shamans in Goryeo Korea and diviners in Heian Japan to bring about the release of water-giving dragons during droughts. Across East Asia, women pray for safe childbirth; men and women pray for prosperity, good health, and long life. The object of their prayers may be a god; it may also be a Buddha, or in China a Daoist immortal or deified hero. Because no one knows which will work, better to ask them all.

Xunzi in China's Warring States period questioned whether praying to gods for rain or other benefits had any value, and ever since his time skeptics have associated popular religion with ignorance. In China under Mao, popular religion was seen as a useless "feudal superstition," and most temples were converted to other uses. Old people were allowed to continue making offerings or praying to gods, but the young were educated to view such behavior as silly and wasteful. Since the death of Mao, popular religion has been revived. It is especially strong in Fujian and Guangdong, undoubtedly because those provinces have strong connections to Chinese outside the PRC, where religious traditions have been maintained.

Contemporary Japan (1965 to the Present)

The protests of the 1960s provoked by public policy decisions and industrial pollution signaled that the consequences of Liberal Democratic Party (LDP) domination and high-speed economic growth could no longer be ignored. The 1970s saw political scandals, diplomatic crises, economic setbacks, and economic adjustments that positioned Japanese companies to expand in export markets while minorities and working women demanded political initiatives to overcome discrimination. In the 1980s, Japan had the world's second largest economy, and the euphoria of seemingly unstoppable growth led to a bubble in overpriced investments. When the bubble burst in 1990, the economy deflated with the latest in a series of economic rallies foundering in the aftermath of the 2011 earthquake and tsunami. Despite political, economic, and social problems, most Japanese people have enjoyed low crime rates, clean cities, superb public transportation, and unprecedented prosperity.

Why did the Japanese economy rise so far and fall so fast? Did protests and demonstrations have any impact, given the power of the LDP and bureaucrats? Which social trends will prove enduring, and which will prove beneficial?

POLITICAL PROTEST AND ENVIRONMENTAL POLLUTION

The 1960s saw student movements worldwide, and Japan was no exception. Students protested Japan's support for the American war in Vietnam under the U.S.–Japan Security Treaty at the same time that they attacked educational policies and assembly-line–style courses. At Tokyo University, medical students opposed a top-down reorganization of the program that ignored their concerns, finally going on strike in January 1968. When university administrators refused to hear their grievances and expelled their leaders, students in other departments struck in sympathy. They wanted curriculum control, amnesty for students arrested in confrontations, and exclusion of riot police from campus. To make their point, they barricaded the central building, forcing the administration to cancel entrance examinations for 1969. On campuses across Tokyo, students launched sympathy strikes.

That January, eighty-five hundred riot police retook the campus in a two-day battle broadcast live on TV. When the Diet passed a University Control Bill giving the Education Ministry enhanced authority to punish students, radical student groups went underground.

The increase in air travel and a desire to position Japan more prominently in world affairs led the LDP and Transportation Ministry to decide on a new international airport for Tokyo in 1965. Farmers who owned land at the proposed site outside Narita protested because taking their land destroyed their livelihood, secrecy surrounding the decision demonstrated that popular opinion had been ignored, and the airport might be used to support the American war effort in Vietnam. Farmers petitioned prefectural and national ministries; they rallied support in the Diet among the opposition parties. When these measures failed, they built barricades and fortresses; they dug ditches to trap bulldozers; they chained themselves to fences. The radical student union Zengakuren helped with agricultural work and publicity. Peace, antinuclear, and environmental activists joined them because they were fighting against government indifference to the social costs of economic growth.

Plans called for the airport to be built in six years; it took twelve. The government reduced the number of runways from three to one; a proposal in 1998 to add a second also faced opposition. Having learned its lesson, the government later built Osaka International Airport on an artificial island in the bay.

At the end of the 1960s, the left and right wings attacked capitalism and materialism. The world famous author Mishima Yukio created his own militia and received permission to join Self Defense Force (SDF) military maneuvers. In 1970, he called on the soldiers at SDF headquarters to remember the sacrifices made in World War II and rally behind nationalist goals by overthrowing the government. When they laughed at him, he committed samurai-style suicide by cutting open his belly. Between 1970 and 1972, students in the Red Army robbed banks and post offices, hijacked a plane to North Korea, and machine-gunned travelers in Tel Aviv's Lod airport in support of Maoist revolution and Palestinian rights.

Less dramatic but longer lasting, citizens' movements arose in response to industrial pollution. In the 1950s, local governments encouraged industrial development that spread pollution from cities to towns and made Japan the most polluted nation on earth. By the early 1970s, about half the population complained of suffering from pollution. Citizens' movements mobilized hundreds of thousands of ordinarily apolitical residents to sign petitions, visit industrial sites, display posters, and launch education drives to rally support in stopping polluters from building in their neighborhood. They warned against trusting promises by industry and local government that a proposed factory would not pollute, and they rejected charges that fighting to protect the individual's quality of life is egotistical.

Between 1932 and 1968 at Minamata in southern Kyushu, a Chisso factory produced acetaldehyde, a key ingredient in making plastics through a process that released methyl mercury as a by-product. Dumped into the water, mercury concentrated in marine life and then attacked brain cells in domestic animals and humans. Victims became increasingly feeble until they reached a vegetative state and death.

In 1959, a Kumamoto University research team traced the cause to the Chisso factory. The team lost its government funding. With support from the Ministry of International Trade and Industry, Chisso hired researchers who proved mercury was not at fault while workers at the plant and community leaders blamed the victims' poor diet and unsanitary living conditions. In 1965, another outbreak of the disease in Niigata on the Japan Sea was traced to mercury discharged by a chemical factory. Despite efforts by company officials and government bureaucrats to undermine the investigators' credibility, the Niigata outbreak lent weight to the Minamata case.

The victims launched petitions, demonstrations, and sit-ins. They attracted enough support from doctors, lawyers, filmmakers, journalists, and academics that in 1971, they sued Chisso. The verdict against the company in 1973 brought it to the verge of bankruptcy. The victims then sued the government, but the Environmental Agency refused to comply with the court's recommendation to settle. In 1995, the cabinet accepted an out-of-court settlement that denied government responsibility for either the disease or delay in acknowledging the problem. In 2004, the Supreme Court placed responsibility for having failed to prevent the disease on the central government and Kumamoto prefecture, but local officials still urge victims not to apply for compensation.

Diseases caused by pollution in Minamata and elsewhere exposed the costs of high-speed economic growth and the way politicians and bureaucrats had insulated themselves from citizens. Owing to protest by pollution victims launched outside normal political channels, the government instituted strict pollution controls in the 1970s and began spending

A Victim of Mercury Poisoning. Held by her mother, this sufferer has a malformed hand along with other physical deformities characteristic of the Minamata disease.

a larger portion of the gross national product (GNP) on antipollution measures than any other developed nation. By 1978, air and water pollution had declined, and manufacturers had learned how to profit from measures to keep the environment clean.

STRAINS OF THE 1970s

To retain its dominance in the Diet and cabinet, the LDP catered to its supporters, sometimes to the point of scandal. Prime Minister Tanaka Kakuei (TAH-nah-kah KAH-ku-eh-e) had Japan National Railroad (JNR) build a bullet train line through the mountains to his district in Niigata, at the cost of $60 million a mile. It provided government contracts for his cronies in the construction business and fattened the purses of real estate developers. Tanaka's excesses were so blatant that public outcry drove him from office in 1974. Despite the stench of corruption, LDP politicians held on to power because voters believed that the opposition parties were too ideologically driven and too fragmented to be trusted with national policy.

Having enjoyed the economic benefits of supporting the United States during the Cold War, Japan was unprepared for the international crises that punctuated the 1970s. When President Richard Nixon announced in 1971 that the United States would no longer accept fixed exchange rates that overvalued the dollar, the yen rose 14 percent. Nixon intended to make Japanese exports to the United States more expensive and less competitive. Japanese companies survived by taking advantage of lower costs for imported raw materials.

The second shock came in 1972 when Nixon recognized the People's Republic of China without notifying Japan in advance. Prime Minister Tanaka followed Nixon to China, but seven months later. In 1978, China and Japan signed a peace and friendship treaty.

The first oil shock came when the Organization of Petroleum Exporting Countries (OPEC) embargoed oil to countries that had supported Israel in the 1973 war. Dependent on oil for 80 percent of its energy, Japan had to pay premium prices on the world market. Inflation rose, companies reduced energy use by cutting production, and consumers stopped spending. During the remainder of the

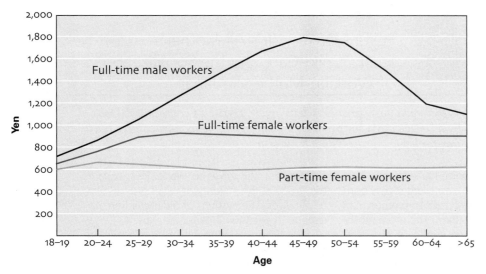

Figure 29.1 Hourly Wages for Japanese Workers, by Age, 1989 *(*Mary C. Brinton, *Women and the Economic Miracle: Gender and Work in Postwar Japan*, Berkeley: University of California Press, 1992, p. 47)

decade, Japan focused on building nuclear power plants. Japanese companies so rationalized energy use that when OPEC raised prices again in 1978–1980, they had a competitive advantage over less efficient firms in their primary export markets.

Industry too faced new problems in the 1970s. A 1979 report to the European Economic Community Executive Committee called the Japanese "work maniacs who live in houses little better than rabbit hutches."[*] Nixon demanded that Japan reduce its textile imports through voluntary restraints. The increase in oil prices hurt petrochemical and energy-intensive industries and pushed down the market for tankers, which hurt steel.

The shipbuilding industry survived through consolidation and moving into new fields such as ocean drilling platforms. The government helped workers with wage subsidies, retraining programs, and relocation expenses. To compete with low-labor-cost countries, the steel industry developed specialty high-value-added products helped by growth in automobile and electrical manufacturing. In 1980, Japan produced more cars than any other country. Big electrical companies made generating plants and electric motors for trains; small firms made office equipment, household appliances, and entertainment stations.

[*]"Europe Toughens Stand Against Japan's Exports," *New York Times*, April 2, 1979, D:1, 5.

Although lifetime employment became a watchword, it covered less than half the work force. Toyota, for example, had permanent workers who received regular salary increases based on seniority and fringe benefits; during good times, it hired temporary workers who could easily be fired. More than two hundred independent contractors made parts and components for cars in accordance with guidelines and timetables established by Toyota. Their workers enjoyed no job security.

A white-collar worker joined a firm straight out of college and expected to stay with the firm for life. To learn company culture, first-year recruits lived in dormitories where they maintained constant contact with their coworkers by working together and drinking together after work. Because only family men were deemed suitable for promotion, most workers soon married, perhaps to an "office lady" (OL) who understood that the company came first. Introduced in 1969, a popular movie series, *It's Tough Being a Man* (*Otoko wa tsurai yo*), commented on the conformity engineered by the straitjacket of company life through the eyes of a wandering peddler who rejected job security for the byways of modern Japan.

Husbands and wives lived in separate worlds. Only 2 to 5 percent of rural men farmed full time, with most leaving farming to parents, wives, and children while they worked in factories. For the urban middle class, a wife's job was to provide a stress-free environment for her husband. She managed the household,

DOCUMENTS

Fujita Mariko, "'It's All Mother's Fault': Child-Care and the Socialization of Working Mothers in Japan"

Various sectors in postwar society have made a fetish of conformity. This essay by a college professor provides a glimpse of how women enforce the standards for being a professional housewife.

A woman should recognize herself as the best educator of her child. An excellent race is born from excellent mothers....Only women can bear children and raise them. Therefore mothers should be proud and confident in raising their children. It is also a fundamental right of children to be raised by their own mothers.

—*1970 Family Charter by the Committee on Family Life Problems*

I live in a small-scale *danchi* (apartment block) built for national governmental employees in the southeastern part of Nara City. The complex consists of three four-story buildings, which house about 70 families. The occupants are mostly young and early middle-aged couples, though some are tanshin-funinsha (husbands who reside away from their families due to the relocation of their jobs). The ages of the children in this complex range from babies to junior-high-school students. There are only a handful of high school students. Therefore, the mothers' ages range roughly between 25 and 45.

Because the rent is substantially lower than in private housing, there is not much economic pressure for the wives to work. This explains the fact that the majority of wives are full-time housewives. The mothers of older children may engage in occasional part-time jobs. As far as I know, those women who work full-time are without children. If a couple has preschool children, the wives most certainly stay at home to raise them.

As soon as my neighbors found out that I had a toddler, they assumed that I was a full-time housewife and mother. They never thought to ask whether I worked outside the home. Because I did have a job, they often found me walking alone without my son and they would always ask, "Where is Hosaki today?" indicating their expectation that I would always be with my child. The situation was complicated because at the time I was a part-time lecturer at a university and I did most of my work at home. My neighbors found this kind of work pattern very difficult to understand because to them work means regular employment between 8:00 AM and 5:00 PM. Telling them that my son was at day care was tricky because they would wonder what I was doing at home during the day instead of being

raised the children (preferably two), and did household repairs. The husband handed her his paycheck; she gave him an allowance, allocated money for food and other expenses, and saved the rest.

Mothers devoted themselves to their children's education, earning the title of *kyōiku mama* (education mothers, implying an obsession with their children's educational success). Mothers consulted with teachers, attended Parent-Teacher Association meetings, volunteered at school, and supervised their children's nutrition, health, and homework. When children needed extra help, mothers sent them to afterschool private schools. For the professional housewife, her child was her most important product.

(See **Documents: Fujita Mariko, "'It's All Mother's Fault': Child-Care and the Socialization of Working Mothers in Japan."**)

Continuing Social Issues

Women's career choices were limited. They typically worked after graduating from high school or junior college; to the mid-1980s almost 90 percent of companies rejected female graduates of four-year colleges because they had to be placed on a management track. Instead, women were hired as clerical or assembly line workers with the understanding they would retire at marriage or when they turned thirty. In the late

at work. Only after I took a full-time teaching position, which keeps me away from home most of the time, were my neighbors convinced that I was actually working.

The fact that working mothers and nonworking mothers do not belong to the same circle of friends became clear to me when I spent a day with my son instead of sending him to day care. I took him to the neighborhood playground where he played in the sand box by the other children. Since he did not have toys of his own (I did not know the children were supposed to bring their own toys), a mother told her son to let my son use his toys. Several mothers were present; they talked among themselves and politely ignored me. I said a few words to them and they replied, but that was the end of our conversation. I basically watched my son, and later played with him when he wanted to play ball. After half an hour, one of the mothers finally asked me whether I lived in the same apartment complex. The question astonished me because I had frequently seen them in the neighborhood. But, as far as they were concerned, I was a total stranger.

Our son frequently became ill his first year in Japan, perhaps due to lack of immunity to the viruses he was exposed to at day care. Soon after enrolling our son at Sakura Day Care, we asked the director if she had a list of baby-sitters, or if she would introduce us to people who would be willing, with pay, to take care of our son when he became sick. Her answer made us realize how unusual our request was in Japan: she was truly astonished by our question and replied that she had never heard of such people.

Our neighbors frequently offered the folk belief that "boys are more susceptible to all sorts of illness than girls when they are young" to explain my son's frequent sicknesses. But as soon as they found out that my work required me to spend two nights a week away from home, they started to use my absence to explain my son's illness. They thought Hosaki was lonely and thus became ill. No one openly criticized me for working until they found out about my absence. Then, they were quick to criticize the mother, making her absence the cause of illness, although the times of Hosaki's illness and my absence did not coincide and although his father was with him and took care of him. They sympathized with the father, who was, from their point of view, unduly burdened while the "selfish" mother was neglecting her duty of childcare.

Questions for Analysis

1. What are the conflicts between working and being a mother?
2. How do women interact across the work divide?
3. What roles are fathers expected to play in child rearing?

Source: *Journal of Japanese Studies* 15:1 (Winter 1989): 70–71, 72–73, 80, 86, 87, 89, modified. Reprinted with permission.

1960s women got the courts to agree that this practice constituted sex discrimination. In the early 1970s the courts forbade mandatory retirement because of pregnancy or childbirth or at a younger age than men. Women objected to being kept from managerial positions and to well-meaning restrictions on the hours they could work and the kinds of work they were allowed to do. In response, the Diet passed the Equal Employment Opportunity Act of 1985. Although it urged employers to treat women the same as men, it made no provisions for sanctions if they did not.

In 1976, women's earnings stood at 56 percent of men's; in 1988, they declined to 50 percent. Companies still refuse to promote women at the same rate as men. Rather than pay women equal wages, some companies do not hire women at all. Full responsibility for home and children makes it hard for women to work past childbirth. Only once the children are in school can mothers take part-time or temporary jobs in small, often marginally profitable companies. Although the working woman in Japan is imagined to be single, most are married women over age thirty-five.

Despite decades of denunciation tactics, *burakumin* (descendants of hereditary outcast groups) still faced economic hardship and discrimination. Under the Special Measures and Enterprise Law concerning Assimilation of 1969, national and local governments put sewage systems, paved streets, better housing, schools, hospitals, and fire stations in *burakumin* communities. In 1976, the Justice Ministry agreed to restrict access to family registers that could be used to trace individuals back to the "new commoners" category established in 1871. Private detective agencies then published lists giving *burakumin* addresses. Their customers were companies, especially the largest and most prestigious, individuals, and colleges.

In 1977, the overall unemployment rate was around 3 percent, but 28.5 percent of Osaka *burakumin* were unemployed. Those with jobs worked in small enterprises for low wages. Although most *burakumin* lived next to factories, they never received more than temporary or part-time work.

Ainu and Okinawans launched movements in the 1970s to assert pride in their ethnic identities. Ainu protested that the 1968 celebration for the hundredth anniversary of Hokkaido's colonization ignored them and their suffering. Kayano Shigeru (KAH-yah-no SHE-geh-ru) opened an ethnographic museum in 1972 and wrote on Ainu language, folktales, and practices of daily life. In 1994, he became the first Ainu elected to the Diet. He and other cultural activists sought to restore seasonal ceremonies and protested plans to turn Hokkaido into an energy source for the rest of Japan with an oil-generated power station.

The United States returned Okinawa to Japan in 1972, but left its bases on the islands. The local economy depended on servicing them and catering to Japanese tourists in search of a tropical experience at home. Okinawan music, dance, and crafts attracted fans on the mainland because they were seen as both a variant on primitive Japanese folk arts and an exotic island culture, while Okinawa's most famous export is karate.

Although the national government has spent lavishly on construction projects, it hires minorities only in low-level jobs. *Burakumin*, Ainu, and Okinawan poverty rates and school dropout rates have been higher than the national average. Negative stereotypes abound, with the usual consequences for marriage and employment.

Koreans resident in Japan (637,000 in 1999) faced special challenges in fighting discrimination. As long as Korea was part of Japan's empire, Koreans were Japanese citizens. The postwar constitution defined Japanese citizens as those born of Japanese fathers, and Koreans became permanent resident aliens. Although celebrities and spouses of diplomats found the naturalization process easy, working-class Koreans did not. They also suffered a division between supporters of North Korea, who followed a separatist path, and supporters of the South, who tried to preserve traces of Korean identity while sending their children to Japanese schools. Children and grandchildren of Korean residents who grew up in Japan and spoke only Japanese paid taxes, but they could not vote. They had to be fingerprinted for their alien registration cards. After years of protest, that requirement changed in 1991, and resident Koreans were allowed to vote in local elections. Still, Japanese refused to marry Koreans, employers to hire them, and landlords to rent to them. Resident Koreans who protested were told they should go back to Korea.

Japanese nationalists ignored all evidence to the contrary in praising the virtues of their uniquely homogeneous race. The debate on *Nihonjinron* (KNEE-hohn-gene-rohn) (Japaneseness) arose in response to the protest movements of the late 1960s, universalizing social science theories that pigeonholed Japan solely in terms of economic development, and foreign criticism of Japan's economic policies. The more Japanese people ate, dressed, and lived like people throughout the developed world, the more they had to be reminded that they possessed an exceptional culture. According to *Nihonjinron*, "we Japanese" speak a language fundamentally incomprehensible to outsiders, think with both sides of the brain, and have intestines too short to digest Australian beef. "We Japanese" innately prefer consensus and harmony, and we put the interests of the group above the individual.

Despite social problems, by the mid-1970s most Japanese people enjoyed unprecedented levels of prosperity. Income disparities remained relatively narrow, and 90 percent of the population considered itself to be middle class. The proportion of total income spent on food declined, while quantity, quality, and variety increased. The older generation ate rice, vegetables, and fish. Young people ate meat, dairy products, and spaghetti. Although Japan maintained the highest savings rate in the industrialized world, people had enough money to eat out, go to movies, and take vacations.

THE ROARING 1980s

Japan's recovery from the shocks of the 1970s put it on a collision course with its major trading partner, the United States. Japan adjusted to oil and pollution crises by building fuel-efficient, less-polluting cars.

Koichi Kamoshida/Getty Images

Japanese Automobile Export. Although Honda and other Japanese automobile manufacturers worry that a strong yen will price them out of the U.S. market, they continue to export cars to the United States. This photograph from 2003 shows 3,000 Honda Accords waiting to be loaded onto ships bound for North America.

When stricter pollution emission requirements, consumers' demand for higher quality, and increased gasoline prices caught Detroit by surprise, Japan's automobile makers seized the American market. To make Japanese goods less competitive, President Ronald Reagan devalued the dollar in 1985, making Japan twice as rich as before. The yen bought twice as much oil, and because Japanese manufacturers had already streamlined production techniques, they needed half as much to make their products as their American competitors did. When Honda raised the price of the Accord by a thousand dollars, American manufacturers raised their prices as well.

American negotiators demanded that Japan import more foreign products. Japan had lower tariffs on manufactured goods than other industrialized countries, but it protected farmers by restricting food imports. It also had non-tariff structural barriers to trade—regulations to ensure quality and safety, a multilayered distribution system, and zoning that favored shops over supermarkets and discount stores. Despite reluctance to disturb a system that provided employment and political support, the LDP and the bureaucracy gradually reduced restrictions. Australian cheese appeared in supermarkets; McDonald's, Kentucky Fried Chicken, and family-style restaurants invaded Japan; and Seven-Eleven spawned a boom in convenience stores. In 1983, Disneyland opened its first international venue near Tokyo, welcoming 16.5 million visitors in 2000, the largest number for any theme park in the world.

Trade surpluses and a strong currency generated more capital than Japan could absorb domestically. With unemployment rates at about 3 percent and labor costs rising, companies built labor-intensive factories in low-wage countries on the Asian mainland. To get around protective tariffs and quotas, they built high-technology factories in developed countries, and Toyota became a multinational corporation. Japanese capital serviced the U.S. debt, Japan became the world's largest supplier of loans to developing countries and the chief donor of foreign aid, and it supplied 50 percent of lendable capital to the World Bank.

The electronics industry had two modes of expanding overseas. In setting up production facilities, first in Southeast Asia in the mid- to late 1970s and then in developed countries in the 1980s, parent companies retained complete control of local subsidiaries. The managerial staff was Japanese; the workers were local. The U.S. Semiconductor Industry Association accused Japan of dumping (selling products for less than they cost) in 1985. In an agreement a year later, Japan agreed to voluntary quotas. Corporations then sought partners in the United States and Europe to develop new technology or combine specialties. Automobile manufacturers followed suit: Toyota and General Motors, Nissan, Honda, and Ford operate joint ventures and exchange components at factories from Australia to Brazil to Europe and the United States.

Japanese capital investment deepened ties with Asian neighbors, while nationalist sentiment strained diplomatic relations. Japan dominated China's Special Economic Zones and invested heavily in Korea and the Pacific Rim, leading critics to claim that it had succeeded in creating a Greater East Asia Co-Prosperity Sphere. In 1982 the Education Ministry approved a textbook for middle school and high school students that minimized Japanese aggression in China. This led China, North and South Korea, and other Asian nations to denounce renewed Japanese nationalism. Japan's aggression and its refusal to acknowledge the suffering it inflicted on Korean women were still issues in the textbooks prepared for 2005. Asians and some Japanese criticized visits by prime ministers to Yasukuni Shrine, where war criminals are enshrined. The content of textbooks and Japan's refusal to apologize for waging war inflamed popular opinion even as government leaders drew closer together. When the president of South Korea visited Japan for the first time in 1984, demonstrations erupted in Seoul.

The government faced domestic problems as well. The LDP did not want to raise taxes to cover deficit spending that started in 1973. Among the culprits were subsidies for farmers, public corporations—Japan National Railroad (JNR) and Nihon Telephone and Telegraph (NTT)—and national health insurance, which initiated free care for the elderly in 1972. Following the lead of Prime Minister Margaret Thatcher in Britain, a commission set up in 1981 suggested privatizing public corporations to rid the government of drains on its resources and undermine the strength of the railroad workers' union. Although allowed to bargain collectively, unions in the public service sector did not have the right to strike, nor did they have incentive to boost productivity. In 1975 railroad workers had shut down JNR for eight days in a strike to win the right to strike.

The conservative leadership of the free market world consisted of Margaret Thatcher, Ronald Reagan, and Nakasone Yasuhiro (NAH-kah-so-neh YAH-su-he-row), Japan's prime minister from 1982 to 1987. Nakasone privatized JNR and NTT and took the government out of the business of selling tobacco and cigarettes. Beginning in 1982 the elderly had to contribute payments for health services. Nakasone urged a return to family values, especially the obligation of the younger generation to care for elders, attributed Japan's economic success to its ethnic homogeneity, and funded research into Japan's distinctive identity. He also called for internationalization so that government leaders would learn how to reduce trade friction and businessmen would feel comfortable with foreigners. His promotion of corporate capitalism made Japan a major player at the Group of 7 conferences of industrialized nations, while he attributed social and economic problems in the United States to racial diversity and the lack of a work ethic.

The Good Life

For many people, old and young, the good life meant material possessions. It meant automated bread-making machines, three-dimensional TV, and self-heating canned saké. It meant laughing at Itami Jūzō's (E-TAH-me JU-zo) movies about funeral practices, food, tax evasion, new religions, and gangsters. The good life made it easy to buy books and magazines (1.45 billion and 4.01 billion, respectively, in 1987). (See **Material Culture: Manga.**)

Whether a meaning for life could be found in a late capitalist society divided Japanese writers. Murakami Haruki (MU-rah-kah-me HAH-ru-key) captured the absurdity of modernity in his novels *A Wild Sheep Chase, Hardboiled Wonderland*, and *Sputnik Sweetheart*. His most recent work, *1Q84*, became an international bestseller in 2011. *Yoshimoto Banana*'s (YO-she-moe-toe BAH-nah-nah) *Kitchen*, a novella popular with college students, depicted a dysfunctional family and individuals alone in a postmodern world. Nostalgia for simpler times under the occupation sold 4 million copies of *Totto-chan, The Little Girl at the Window* by the fast-talking television celebrity Kuroyanagi Tetsuko (KU-ro-yah-nah-gy TEH-tzu-co).

Rejecting materialism by seeking the roots of Japanese identity, a self-styled Kyoto philosopher creatively interpreted the prehistoric Jōmon era as a time when Japanese lived in harmony with nature

MATERIAL CULTURE

Manga

Japanese comics called manga (MAHN-gah) attained their present form in 1959 when they became a source of entertainment and information for all ages. Early manga were printed on cheap paper and sold at a price working poor could afford. The first generation born after World War II grew up reading them and continued the habit through college and into their working lives. Manga gave them a chance to laugh at the restrictive conditions that enforced conformity while warning them that failing to work hard and toe the corporate line would cause them shame. Manga and their close cousins, animated films, became the domain of Japan's most creative minds.

From the 1960s to the mid-1990s, manga offered escapist fantasies, often violently pornographic, for white-collar workers on their daily commute; science-fiction manga appealed to children and teenagers. Manga taught history to students studying for entrance exams with *Barefoot Gen* graphically illustrating the horrors of the atomic bomb dropped over Hiroshima. Cookbooks and biographies could be found in the form of manga. Manga explained energy policy, the value-added tax, investment strategies, and the principles of superconductors. *Japan Inc.: An Introduction to Japanese Economics in Manga* (1986; in English 1988) sold more than 1 million copies in hardcover.

Manga reached their peak sales in 1994 when publishing houses devoted one-third of their total output to manga and sold 5.33 million copies a year. Shibuya, the crossroads for youth culture in Tokyo, contained manga superstores where the clerks dressed as manga characters. Today manga and the Japanese publishing industry are in decline. Former readers thumb cell phones with Internet connections or play handheld computer games.

U.S.-Japan Trade Tensions. Starting in the 1980s, manufacturers in Japan and the U.S. gave different reasons for why Japan sold more goods to the U.S. than it bought. Translated from Japanese into English, the manga Japan Inc. tried to convey Japan's perspective to an American audience. *(JAPAN, INC.: Introduction to Japanese Economics [The Comic Book] by Ishinomori Shotaro, University of California Press Books, Copyright © 1988, The Regents of the University of California. Reprinted with permission.)*

and each other in a community of man and gods. Mystically transmitted through the emperor system and buried deep within every Japanese, the national essence could be recovered by a visit to the *furusato* (FU-ru-sah-toe) (home village). JNR's "Discover Japan" and "Exotic Japan" advertising campaigns promoted visits to thatched roof farmhouses foreign to urban residents. Villages struggling with depopulation revived agricultural festivals to attract tourists; castle towns put on daimyo processions. On Yaeyama in the Ryukyu Islands, a new tradition of weaving sashes for betrothal gifts became a way to create a folk identity and sell souvenirs to tourists.

The search for origins scarcely concealed new and, to conservative eyes, troubling trends among Japanese youth. In 1978 the "bamboo shoot tribe" of middle and high school students dressed in outlandish and expensive costumes started appearing every Sunday near trendy Harajuku in Tokyo. Late at night, gangs of motorcycle riders roared through residential neighborhoods, disrupting the sleep of salary men. In 1985 newspapers started reporting

Gyaru. Following constantly evolving fashions, gyaru (gals) can be divided into various subcultures depending on whether their faces are darkly tanned with white makeup or white with black makeup, their hairstyles, the mix of Japanese and western apparel, and their shoes.

Peter M. Wilson Photography

an increase in incidents of bullying, some leading to murder or suicide, in elementary through high schools. The "new breed of human beings" rejected the work ethic, harmony, and consensus of their elders, taking part-time jobs that did not require the commitment of a regular position. Because many of them lived with their parents, their income allowed them to splurge on designer clothes, meals and entertainment, and trips abroad. Married couples demanded bigger living spaces and better plumbing, a shorter work week, and longer vacations. Rather than put up with low initial salaries and long hours of after-work socializing, a few workers switched jobs and some husbands went home to their wives.

Despite these problems, Japan's economy appeared unstoppable. In 1988, its per capita GNP surpassed that of the United States. The next year, Morita Akio (MOE-re-tah AH-key-oh), chairman of Sony, and Ishihara

Shintarō (E-she-hah-rah SHEEN-tah-row), mayor of Tokyo in the twenty-first century, published *The Japan That Can Say No*. It criticized U.S. business practices and claimed that Japan bashing was the result of racial prejudice, but it also criticized the Japanese government for fearing reform and Japanese people for being soft.

Banks awash with yen urged capital on borrowers. Japanese art purchases led to an outcry that the cream of Western heritage was being shipped to Asia, Mitsubishi bought Rockefeller Center in New York City, and Sony bought Columbia Pictures. Real estate costs rose so high that land in Tokyo was valued at three times the entire United States. The tripling of the stock market inflated a speculative bubble.

TWENTY YEARS WITHOUT PROGRESS

In the last twenty years, Japan has faced international criticism of its role in world affairs. The United States grumbled when Japan refused to commit troops to the Gulf War in 1991, even though Japan's military spending ranked third, below the United States and Russia. Six months after the war, Japan sent minesweepers to the Persian Gulf amid debate over whether their dispatch violated constitutional restrictions. Japan also paid $10 billion toward the cost of the war and permitted its troops to participate in peacekeeping missions in Cambodia and East Timor. After terrorist attacks in the United States on September 11, 2001, the Diet passed an antiterrorism law that allowed Japanese troops to provide rear-echelon support for the war in Iraq in 2004.

For the LDP, political problems began in 1989. The Shōwa emperor died at the beginning of the year, and the new emperor took Heisei (HEH-e-seh-e) (translatable as "achieving peace" or "maintaining equilibrium") for his era name. Prime Minister Takeshita Noboru (TAH-keh-she-tah NO-bo-ru) inaugurated a value-added tax of 3 percent that infuriated consumers before resigning two months later because of publicity surrounding 150 million yen he had received from Recruit Cosmo, an employment information firm with investments in real estate and publishing. LDP faction bosses had difficulty identifying an untainted successor, with one prime minister lasting barely six weeks before demands for financial support by his mistress brought him down. In the election that summer, the JSP under the female leadership of Doi Takako (DOE-e TAH-kah-co) ran an unprecedented number of women candidates and gained control of the upper house.

Frustrated by elderly faction bosses in the LDP who monopolized the prime ministership, younger politicians split the party. In 1993, the Japan New Party chose the prime minister when the LDP suffered defeat in elections for the lower house. Farmers were outraged when the worst rice harvest in two hundred years forced the prime minister to allow rice imports from Asia for the first time since World War II. Like so many others, he too was caught in a financial scandal. Two more non-LDP prime ministers followed him, neither capable of dealing with Japan's economic woes or the Kobe earthquake on January 17, 1995, which killed more than 520,000 people and left more than 300,000 homeless. In 1996 a chastened LDP returned to power, and faction bosses picked the next prime minister. In 2001 they chose a third-generation Diet member, Koizumi Jun'ichirō (CO-e-zu-me JUNE-e-che-row), who promised liberals he would make structural reforms needed to bolster the economy and pleased conservatives by his call to revise the pacifist constitution.

Koizumi inherited a stagnant economy. The speculative bubble of the late 1980s collapsed when a recession in the developed world sent sales tumbling, and competition from low-labor-cost countries eroded corporations' market share. The stock market lost nearly 40 percent of its peak value in 1990 and 65 percent by August 1992. Corporations that had borrowed billions of yen to buy land or expand their businesses discovered that their debts exceeded their assets. The Asian economic turmoil of 1997 caused by speculators who dumped Asian currencies caused another recession in Japan. Two brokerage houses and a bank went bankrupt, leading to fears of depression. Economic growth, which had limped along at barely 1 percent per annum between 1992 and 1995, went negative in 1997. Except for an occasional quarter of slight expansion, deflation has stalked Japan.

The LDP scrambled to stimulate the economy. In the 1980s it tried to revitalize rural communities by building culture halls and art museums and encouraging production of traditional handicrafts as souvenirs. In the 1990s it poured money into dams, roads, and postmodern public buildings. Koizumi halted a project to turn a saltwater swamp into farmland, while the government paid farmers not to plant rice. His decision to privatize the post office threatened the Finance Ministry's control over the $3 trillion in postal savings accounts kept outside government budgets that it used to finance public works projects, prime the stock market, and buy government bonds.

Proposals to streamline the bureaucracy, reduce regulatory oversight, and eliminate positions failed in the face of bureaucratic inertia while near-zero interest rates and government support for nonperforming loans failed to stimulate business investment. The Education Ministry made universities more responsive to the interests of industry, eliminated irrelevant fields in the humanities and social sciences, and turned national universities into independent entities.

No prime minister since Koizumi has managed to put Japan back on a path of sustained economic growth. After nearly two decades of spending on stimulus projects, in 2009 Japan had a gross public debt twice the size of its $5 trillion economy, giving it the highest debt levels of the industrialized world. Fed up with a series of weak leaders, voters rejected the LDP for the new Democratic Party that promised to rein in spending by curtailing public works projects and forcing the bureaucracy to accept steep cuts in ministry budgets.

The March 11, 2011, earthquake off the coast of northeastern Japan that killed nearly 20,000 people and destroyed more than 125,000 buildings, leaving thousands homeless, once again exposed the weakness of government leadership. The earthquake's worst effects came from the gigantic tsunami that swept up to six miles inland and caused a nuclear power plant meltdown in Fukushima (see **Color Plate 32**). Although workers moved quickly to restore power and transportation systems, enormous problems remain. Many villages that suffered the worst damage had aging populations. Does it make sense for them to be rebuilt given that young people are the least likely to return? The power plant released so much radiation that nearly ninety thousand people had to be evacuated from a twelve-mile zone around the plant. Japan's leaders argue that because Japan has so little habitable land, the area must be cleaned up rather than abandoned, as the Russians did with Chernobyl, the only nuclear disaster larger than Fukushima. Doing so will revitalize the nation by showcasing Japan's technological prowess and determination to succeed. Critics reply that the cleanup may not prove successful, and it will cost billions that Japan does not have.

Social Problems for the Twenty-First Century

Japan's social problems also defied easy solution. In the 1980s, American social scientists praised Japan's educational system for producing literate students who scored higher on mathematics tests than did

Americans. Japanese critics feared that schools were turning out soulless automatons with weak characters and no sense of national identity, unable to think for themselves and lacking the creativity to put Japan in the lead of technological innovation.

Labor shortages in the 1980s in the sex trade and the dangerous, dirty, and low-paid work of construction and stevedoring brought women and men from Taiwan, the Philippines, Iran, and other countries to work as prostitutes and day laborers. About half entered illegally because the Labor and Justice ministries refused to acknowledge the need for their services. Immigration by Latin Americans of Japanese ancestry was encouraged because it was thought that they would assimilate to the dominant culture. In 1999, 1.56 million foreigners lived legally in Japan out of a total population of 126.6 million. Tokyo became a more cosmopolitan city, but mainstream Japanese were quick to accuse foreigners of robbery, rape, and drug trafficking.

Economic stagnation and rising unemployment had social consequences. To keep middle-aged men employed, corporations stopped competing to hire college graduates, even though "pay for performance" started to replace the seniority system of merit raises. Unemployment rose to an historic high of 5.6 percent in 2009. This figure excluded part-time workers who had lost their jobs, most of them women. Realizing that college no longer provided the escalator to permanent employment, some young people now care little about school and find no identity in work. Although they are criticized as "parasite singles," structural changes in the economy have left them with few options for finding satisfaction in the workplace.

Tokyo, Yokohama, and Osaka had long had a floating population of farm men from the north who spent the winter working as day laborers and congregated in flophouses. In the late 1980s, permanent dropouts started to swell their numbers and added to the homeless population. Once in the public eye, sleeping on benches and in pedestrian tunnels near train terminals, they and their blue tarp camps have been moved to less conspicuous locations.

The search for meaning in a materialistic world took new paths. Right-wing militants who rode sound trucks blaring martial music and decorated with posters calling for return of the northern territories held by Russia attacked offices of the Asahi publishing company because of articles showing disrespect for the emperor. Adherents of new religions such as the Unification Church and Mahikarikyō (MAH-he-kah-re-keyo) sought a sense of community and a merging of the individual ego in a larger entity. Aum Shinrikyō (AH-um SHEEN-re-keyo) attracted students from Japan's elite universities, lawyers, and businessmen. In March 1995, feeling persecuted by the Justice Ministry, its followers released a poison gas in the Tokyo subway system adjacent to National Police headquarters, killing twelve people and injuring thousands. The LDP tried to revise the 1951 Religious Corporations Law to bring government oversight to the fundraising, educational activities, and business-related income of the 183,970 registered religious organizations. Opposition by Sōka Gakkai's political arm and other religious organizations kept the 1951 law intact.

Starting in the late 1960s, LDP politicians urged women to have more children; thereafter they lamented the selfishness of young women who put consumerism ahead of maternal responsibilities. National health insurance, a 99 percent literacy rate, sanitary housing, and nutritious diets contributed to one of the lowest infant mortality rates in the world at 5 per 1,000 in 1989. By 2011 the longevity rate for men was nearly 79 and for women, 86. Women had 1.3 children apiece, well below the 2.2 necessary to maintain a population that started to decline in 2005. Couples who wanted a higher standard of living or were worried about the costs of their children's education limited their family size regardless of political propaganda.

In 2010, 23 percent of the population was age sixty-five or older, giving Japan the oldest population in the industrialized world. It is projected to grow to 25 percent by 2015, when 25 percent of the national budget will have to be spent on social welfare. Through the 1990s, corporations had plentiful sources of investment capital at low interest rates because Japan had the highest rate of personal savings in the world. With more retired people, the savings rate will drop.

The government wants to limit its costs for hospitals and nursing homes by having children care for parents. Elder sons with the traditional responsibility for parental care have trouble finding marriage partners because women increasingly prefer to take care of their own parents. Some farmers now marry brides from the Philippines.

Although marriage is still the norm, it too has changed. The mean age of marriage for women crept from twenty-two in 1950 to over twenty-nine in 2011.

So many women opt for four years of higher education that the former junior colleges have become universities, even though the decline in the college age population means that some have trouble meeting their enrollment targets. In hopes of better futures than they perceive possible in Japan, some women seek academic degrees and employment abroad. Women want careers, and they have become increasingly choosy about whom they will marry and under what conditions. Older women have been known to divorce their retired husbands because they cannot stand having "that oversized garbage" underfoot every day.

SUMMARY

Even though Japan's economy stagnated along with its population in the last twenty years, its remarkable rise after World War II meant that it became rich before it became old. Demonstrations against an unfeeling bureaucracy and even citizens' movements against pollution are largely a thing of the past. After the political and oil shocks of the 1970s, Japan mended relations with China, adjusted to having a strong currency, and learned to live with volatility in oil supplies and prices in part by reducing energy consumption and in part by building nuclear power plants, at least until the Fukushima meltdown.

Although Japan's businesses have adjusted so well to a changing international and domestic environment that Japan has the world's third largest economy, social problems have persisted. Discrimination against women, *burakumin*, the Ainu, Okinawans, and resident Koreans continues despite laws against it. Young people apparently reject the work ethic of their elders, some indulging in conspicuous consumption, others delighting in breaking the law, some even retreating into their rooms as "shut-ins." The population of day laborers and the homeless has increased beyond the reach of the government's social services.

From the 1970s to the twenty-first century social critics have argued that economic prosperity alone should not define what it means to be Japanese. They worry about what children are learning in schools, they try to define "we Japanese" as uniquely different from everyone else, and they deplore the postwar constitution that has kept Japan from becoming a normal nation with a publicly recognized military. Most of all they worry that unless women start having more babies, the Japanese race will disappear.

How has Japan changed since the 1960s? It has become a mature industrial society with a functioning democracy. Its cities are among the world's cleanest and safest. It has become a major player on the international stage with Japanese foods eaten in Europe and the United States and Japanese fashions and popular music followed in Asia. Introduced in 1980, karaoke is performed around the world. The diplomatic road has been rougher, with Japanese politicians infuriating their Asian neighbors by calling the emperor a living god and Japan a divine nation while participating in Asian economic conferences. Lingering memories of the war and Japan's wariness of China's growing economic and military strength have not prevented Japan from trading more with China than with the United States, even as it offers support for the global war on terrorism.

China Since Mao (1976 to the Present)

After the death of Mao in 1976, the Chinese Communist Party turned away from class struggle and made economic growth a top priority. The resulting transformation of China is little short of amazing. For most of the three decades 1980–2010, China had the fastest-growing economy in the world, growing by about ten percent per year. It has also witnessed the greatest migration in world history, as a hundred million Chinese migrated from remote rural areas to the booming cities. Much as China's standing in the world plummeted in the nineteenth century, during the three and a half decades after Mao's death, China's standing soared.

Although millions of Chinese were lifted out of poverty during this period, not everyone has benefited equally. In broad terms, people in cities have gained more than those in the countryside, those in the coastal provinces more than those in the interior, and those entering the job market during these decades more than their parents and grandparents.

Every facet of China's rapid changes since 1976 has intrigued scholars and journalists who have been able to live in China and observe development first-hand. With the collapse of communism in Russia and eastern Europe, many have speculated on the hold of the Communist Party in China. Can the party maintain tight control over political expression when communications with the rest of the world have become so much more open? Can it dampen the unrest that results from unemployment, unpaid pensions, and political corruption? Will the disparities between the rich and the poor in China continue to widen? Can the damage to the environment be checked? Is China becoming, as it claims, a country that follows the rule of law? Will China accept the pressure to conform to international standards that comes with its increased participation in international organizations? Is a return to Maoist policies still possible?

POLITICAL TRANSFORMATION

In the first decade after Mao's death much of what had been instituted in the 1950s was abolished outright or slowly transformed. The Communist Party, however, maintained its large membership and its political power.

In the immediate aftermath of Mao's death, Hua Guofeng (hwa gwaw-fung) took over as head of the Communist Party. He was a relatively obscure party veteran singled out by Mao only months before his death. Soon after Mao's funeral, Hua sided with the pragmatists and arranged for the arrest of Mao's wife, Jiang Qing, and three of her closest associates. This "Gang of Four" was blamed for all the excesses of the Cultural Revolution. In 1977, Deng Xiaoping was reappointed to his old posts, and in December 1978 he supplanted Hua as the top official.

Like Mao, Deng had an impressive revolutionary pedigree, going back to the early 1920s when he was active with Zhou Enlai in France and continuing through the Shanghai underground, the Long March, and guerrilla warfare against Japan. In 1956, at age fifty-two, he became a member of the Standing Committee of the Politburo and secretary general of the party. Twice ousted from power during the Cultural Revolution, he labeled absurd the Cultural Revolution slogan that it was "better to be poor under socialism than rich under capitalism," insisting that "poverty is not socialism."

A pragmatist, Deng Xiaoping took as his catchphrase "the Four Modernizations" (of agriculture, industry, science and technology, and defense). He openly admitted that China was poor and backward, and he saw no reason not to adopt foreign technology if it would improve the lives of the masses. Thousands of people who had been sent to the countryside were allowed to go home. People everywhere were eager to make up for what they saw as the "wasted years."

Party membership stood at 39 million when Mao died. Deng quickly set about weeding out the leftists recruited during the Cultural Revolution and rehabilitating those who had been persecuted. Deng knew that party members qualified to manage and direct the modernization projects were in short supply. Only 14 percent of party members had finished the equivalent of high school, and only 4 percent had college educations. Moreover, many of those who had gone to high school or college did so during the 1970s when admission was based on political fervor

and the curriculum was watered down to conform to the anti-elitist and anti-intellectual ideology of the period. About 15 million party members were sent back to school to learn to read and write. Retirement ages were imposed to reduce the number of elderly party members. Party recruitment was stepped up to bring in younger people with better educations.

Asserting that the influence of the Gang of Four had created "an entire generation of mental cripples," Deng pushed for reform of universities. Intellectuals responded to the more open atmosphere with a spate of new magazines and a new frankness in literature. In 1978, the Democracy Wall in Beijing attracted a wide variety of self-expression until it was shut down the following spring.

In 1980, with Deng Xiaoping's sponsorship, the first Special Economic Zone was created at Shenzhen, just across the border from Hong Kong. By the early 1980s China was crowded with foreign visitors. Thousands of Western teachers were brought to China to teach English and other foreign languages. Christian churches reopened, as did Buddhist and Daoist temples. People began wearing more varied colors, giving the streets a very different look from China in the 1960s.

Economic restructuring placed many party cadres in positions where corruption was easy and tempting; they were the ones to supervise distribution or sale of state and collective assets. Between 1983 and 1986 some 40,000 party members were expelled for corruption, and in 1987 the number reached 109,000. Prosecution has not removed the temptation, and corruption remains the most serious problem for the party (see **Documents: Bloggers on Corruption**).

Older party members were often unhappy with the speed of change and with the new interest of young people in the West. In 1983 the party launched a campaign against "spiritual pollution" to warn against overenthusiasm for things Western. After political unrest at several universities in 1986, the party revived a campaign from the early 1960s to "learn from Lei Feng," a model of the selfless party member devoted to advancing China's development. Still, an even bigger political protest movement occurred in 1989, with huge demonstrations at Beijing's Tiananmen Square (see Color Plate 31). After its bloody suppression, the 48 million party members had to submit self-evaluations in order to weed out sympathizers. About 1 million were sent to the countryside to learn from the masses.

By the early 1990s, the collapse of communism in eastern Europe and the Soviet Union added to Deng Xiaoping's determination to persist in economic

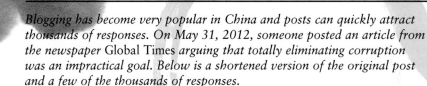

DOCUMENTS   Bloggers on Corruption

Blogging has become very popular in China and posts can quickly attract thousands of responses. On May 31, 2012, someone posted an article from the newspaper Global Times *arguing that totally eliminating corruption was an impractical goal. Below is a shortened version of the original post and a few of the thousands of responses.*

Global Times: People Should Permit a Moderate Amount of Corruption in China

It was announced yesterday that former Railway Minister and Party Secretary Liu Zhijun was fired, the issues of his suspected crimes to be dealt with by judicial authorities in accordance with the law. This piece of news once again touched the public's most sensitive nerve, that dealing with corruption. . . .

China obviously has a high incidence of corruption, but the conditions for completely eliminating corruption do not exist at present. Some people say, as long as we have "democracy," the problem of corruption can be easily solved. However, this kind of view is naive. Asia has many "democratic countries," such as Indonesia, the Philippines, India, etc., all of which have worse corruption than China. . . .

Singapore and China's Hong Kong have a policy of high pay to discourage corruption. Many American political candidates are wealthy, and normally when someone becomes a government official there, they accumulate renown and connections. After leaving office, they can then use various "revolving doors" to trade what they have accumulated for financial gain. However, these options would not work in China. Giving government officials large salaries is something Chinese public opinion cannot accept. Allowing government officials to step down and use their influence and connections to make big money is illegal. Allowing the wealthy to become government officials is something that people find even more unpalatable.

The legal salaries of China's government officials are very low, and officials' compensation is often realized through "unwritten rules." . . . What are the boundaries for "unwritten rules"? This isn't clear. This is also one of the reasons there are so many corruption cases now and talk of a culture of corruption. Among the people, there is the popular saying that "what is commonplace among the people cannot be punished by the law." The moment a government official believes this saying and that "others are the same as me," then he is in danger [of becoming corrupt]. . . .

The people must resolutely increase supervision through public opinion, pushing the government to fight corruption. However, the people must also understand the objective fact that China is unable at its present stage to thoroughly suppress corruption, and not sink the entire country into despair. Writing this definitely does not mean fighting corruption is not important or should be put off. Quite the opposite; we believe fighting corruption indeed is the number one problem that must be solved for the reform of China's political system. . . . The problem lies with the individual corrupt official and the system, but also China's overall level of development.

reform. In Deng's view, the Soviet Union broke up because central planning had not produced prosperity. To show his support for market reforms in 1992, Deng went south to visit the Special Economic Zones. He told people not to worry if policies were capitalist or socialist, only whether they would make China more prosperous. Soon the party constitution was rewritten to describe China as a "socialist market economy" and to declare "the essential nature of socialism" to be "to liberate and develop productive forces." Joint ventures grew more and more common in the 1990s, with businessmen from Hong Kong, Taiwan, and South Korea especially active. Local elections that allowed people to elect some of their leaders were changing the nature of political participation.

By the year 2010, there were some 80 million party members, about 77 percent of whom were male, about 6 percent members of minorities, and about 4 percent migrant workers.

Fighting corruption is a difficult battle in the development of Chinese society, but its victory hinges upon the clearing of various obstacles on other battlefields. China can never be a country where other aspects are very backward and only its government officials are clean....Eliminating corruption would be a breakthrough for China, but it requires overall development.

A few of the thousands of responses posted on NetEase by the next day:

a. There are no less than eight types of Chinese corrupt officials, and everyone should know these classic types:
   1. Doesn't have a high salary but has no shortage of money in the bank;
   2. Doesn't understand a foreign language but has no shortage of trips abroad;
   3. Doesn't look handsome but has no shortage of mistresses;
   4. Doesn't go to work much but has no shortage of social events;
   5. Doesn't speak well but has no shortage of applause;
   6. Doesn't write essays but has no shortage of opinions;
   7. Doesn't have any skill but has no shortage of prize money;
   8. Doesn't handle things fairly but has no shortage of collecting money.

b. After seeing the news of a Philippine Chief Justice being impeached for concealing millions in assets, I now know the reason for why the imperialist Philippines is a strong country.

c. Actually, without corruption, some things may not be able to be done or would take longer, so we can't just look at the superficial corruption but should look at the essence of the matter. When officials have expended their efforts, suitable compensation for them is appropriate. We can't demand that only we can have money and government officials be incorrupt.

d. Global Times: People should permit a moderate amount of corruption in China======Can poor people with low wages moderately go rob a bank?

e. Moderate, moderate, what great wording! However, can one talk about moderation in corruption? As long as it is corruption, it is excessive.

d. This discussion is very intense, but even if you criticize [corruption], so what? Nothing will change.

e. This isn't the first time the *Global Times* has been slandered by NetEase, nor does the *Global Times* always sing praises [of China]. Under *Global Times* is a periodical called *Satire and Humor*, which has been needling social ills for decades now. It has even attacked some unpopular government policies. Social problems that netizens are concerned about, they have that too. Internet netizens even often forward and repost their political cartoons.

Questions for Analysis

1. What are the merits of the original argument that ridding China of corruption would require a higher level of development?
2. What can you learn from the bloggers' responses about the mood in China?

Source: Copyright © 2012 chinaSMACK, www.chinasmack.com. Reprinted with permission.

THE ECONOMIC MIRACLE

Deng Xiaoping's economic policies set in motion an economic boom. In a manner reminiscent of Japan in 1947–1971, the economy grew rapidly every year, often at more than 10 percent. Overall poverty declined sharply. According to the World Bank's statistics, the population below the poverty line fell from 250 million in 1978 to 80 million in 1993 and then to 27 million in 2001. Life expectancy has risen steadily (to seventy-three for men and seventy-seven for women in 2010), as has the average height of Chinese, both reflecting improvements in nutrition.

Encouraging Capitalist Tendencies

In the countryside the most important reform was the dismantling of collective agriculture. In the early 1980s, Deng Xiaoping instituted a "responsibility

Shenzhen. In the three decades since the fishing village of Shenzhen was made a "special economic zone," its population has grown to about 9 million, and its skyline has been transformed by the rapid construction of high rise buildings and factories.

system" under which rural households bid for land and other assets that they could treat as their own (though the land was legally held on leases of up to fifty years). In turn they agreed to provide specified crops; whatever the household produced above what it owed was theirs to keep or sell. Sideline enterprises like growing vegetables and raising pigs or chickens were encouraged, as were small businesses of all sorts, ranging from fish farming and equipment repair to small factories producing consumer goods for export. Rural industry boomed. By 2004, there were 22 million township and village enterprises employing 139 million workers. Especially in the coastal provinces, where commercial opportunities were greatest, the income of farmers rapidly increased.

Deng Xiaoping abandoned Mao's insistence on self-sufficiency and began courting foreign investors. Special Economic Zones were created; the best known were Shenzhen on the border with Hong Kong and Pudong across the Huangpu River from Shanghai. These zones offered incentives to foreign firms, including low taxes, new plants, and a well-trained but cheap labor force. China had to bring its legal system more into line with international standards to

court these foreign investors, but the payoff was substantial because joint ventures pumped a lot of capital into the Chinese economy and brought in up-to-date technology.

Foreign manufacturers were attracted to the low labor costs in China. They both set up factories to produce goods for the Chinese market (such as vehicles) and contracted with Chinese manufacturers to produce consumer goods for Western markets (such as clothing, toys, watches, and computers). Guangdong, with the best access to the financial giant Hong Kong, did especially well in the new environment. Between 1982 and 1992, 97 percent of Hong Kong's thirty-two hundred toy factories relocated to Guangdong. By 1996, China was the world's largest garment maker, accounting for 16.7 percent of world garment exports. In 1997 it manufactured 1.55 billion shirts. The market for shoes, too, came to be dominated by China, which in 1998 made 6.3 billion pairs of leather shoes and about 1 billion pairs of sports shoes. By 2004 China had become the world's top exporter of computer and related equipment and components. By 2006 it was the world's leading supplier of seafood.

Shrinking the State Sector

During the 1980s and 1990s, people who worked for the state found that reform meant that they could lose their jobs. Between 1990 and 2000 some 30 to 35 million workers were shed by state-owned enterprises under pressure to become profitable. Still, few state enterprises could compete with private or collective enterprises. The mines run by the Ministry of Coal could not produce coal as cheaply as the eighty thousand small mines operated by local governments and private individuals. By 1992 the ministry had a debt of 6 billion yuan and needed to lay off 1 million miners. More jobs had probably been created at the small mines, but those jobs lacked the benefits and pensions of the state jobs.

The province of Liaoning in northeast China can be taken as an example. In the 1990s about half of the 10 million people who worked in state-owned enterprises there lost their jobs. The mayor of Shenyang tried to find buyers for the city's bankrupt factories, but no one wanted to take on their obligations to retirees. The situation was even worse farther north. In the cities of Heilongjiang at the end of the 1990s, up to 60 percent

of the urban population was either unemployed or not being paid. Bankrupt companies paid neither salaries nor pensions, but they were not dissolved because the government did not want to take over their obligations.

The military is another part of the state sector that has shrunk considerably. The PLA peaked at 4.75 million troops in 1981. Many were later moved to the People's Armed Police, a domestic force. By 2010 soldiers on active duty were thought to number about 2.3 million. The PLA also divested itself of many of the factories it owned and operated, even many military ones. Some factories that once produced tanks have been converted to produce buses or trucks; others have been abandoned.

Regional Disparities and Internal Migration

Deng Xiaoping announced early on that he was willing to tolerate growing inequalities, saying it was acceptable that "some get rich first." Because most of the industrial growth was in the coastal provinces, regional inequalities increased. (See Map 30.1.) Some regions of the country, especially regions far from good roads, remain extremely poor. In Shanxi

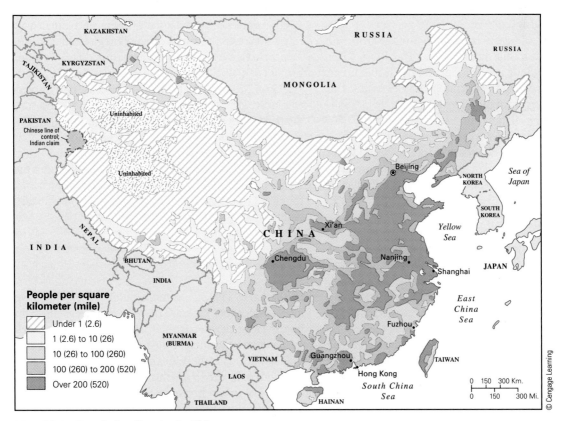

People per square kilometer (mile)

- Under 1 (2.6)
- 1 (2.6) to 10 (26)
- 10 (26) to 100 (260)
- 100 (260) to 200 (520)
- Over 200 (520)

© Cengage Learning

Map 30.1   Population Density in China

province, the uplands are occupied by about 9 million people, a third of whom fall below the poverty line. In the late 1990s, half the boys and most of the girls in this area did not attend school. About 80 percent of the adult women were illiterate.

When internal controls on migration collapsed in the early 1980s, the coastal regions were flooded with job seekers willing to live in shantytowns or a dozen to a room to get a chance to share in the wealth that the market economy was bringing to the fortunate regions (see **Biography: Cheng Junyu, Migrant Worker**). In the 1980s about 10 million migrated to the dozen largest cities. In 1992 city authorities estimated that 100 million migrant laborers were working away from home or roaming China in search of work. Crime in cities grew, much of it blamed on migrants. In Guangdong internal migrants, especially those who could not speak Cantonese, became an exploited class, hired for the worst work, kept on the job for ten or twelve hours a day, seven days a week, and unable to protest without losing their jobs. In the 1990s, as newly unemployed workers from state factories took jobs migrants had previously taken, cities began to deport larger numbers of migrants back to the countryside. Still, in 2010 there were a reported 230 million migrants. Between 2001 and 2010, the percent of the population living in rural areas fell from 64 percent to 50 percent.

There has been some trickle-down effect from the booming areas to the poorer ones. The Pearl River Delta in Guangdong imports pigs and rice from Hunan and Sichuan, helping their economies. The millions of migrant laborers from those provinces also help, sending home whatever they can spare from their wages. Yet it is often the poorer areas that are most pressed by cadres. All through the 2000s peasants protested when local cadres seized their land for development projects; only rarely were they able to block the action, however.

Environmental Degradation

Under Mao, Chinese were encouraged to harness nature to increase production. Little thought was given to the ecological consequences of terracing mountains, plowing grasslands, reclaiming wetlands, damming rivers, or killing all the sparrows. Soil erosion, desertification, and massive flooding were among the results. With the rapid expansion of industry since 1978, air and water pollution have been added to China's environmental woes. A 1998 World Health Organization study concluded that seven of the ten most polluted cities in the world were in China. Air quality in cities will not improve soon because China depends on coal for 75 percent of its energy, and cars are rapidly replacing bicycles. Air pollution contributes significantly to death rates from respiratory diseases. The water supply in much of the country is unfit to drink. Water pollution comes from untreated sewage as well as industrial effluent and agricultural runoff. Paper mills, chemical plants, and tanneries dump their wastes in rivers, making the water not only unsafe to drink but also often ruining it as a source for irrigation.

Not only is the quality of water at issue but the supply as well. In the north, so much water has been diverted from the Yellow River that it runs dry for longer and longer periods each year. So much water gets brought up from underground that the water table is dropping steadily in many places. To cope with the water shortage, the government has initiated a controversial water diversion project to move water from the Yangzi River to the north China plain.

In the Yangzi region, floods have gotten worse because of tree cutting and soil erosion coupled with dams that have reduced floodplains. Development projects of all sorts have led to the paving over of more and more arable land, leading to questions about how China will be able to feed its growing population in the decades to come.

Environmental activism is growing in China, with more than two thousand officially registered environmental nongovernmental organizations. These groups protest dam construction, file lawsuits against polluters, promote conservation, and publicize new threats to biodiversity. In June 2007 about ten thousand residents of Xiamen, alerted by cell phone calls, took to the streets to protest a huge new chemical plant that they considered too dangerous for an urban area. The national government increasingly recognizes the seriousness of environmental issues and implements tougher laws, but enforcement lags at the local level, where officials face competing demands for jobs and development.

Consumer Culture

In the early 1980s, although people began to have more disposable income, there was not yet much to buy, even in city department stores, which were well stocked with thermos bottles and inflatable children's toys but not with the TVs and tape recorders customers wanted. By the 1990s this had changed. Disposable incomes of urban households steadily increased, and more and more factories were turning out consumer

BIOGRAPHY

Cheng Junyu, Migrant Worker

Cheng Junyu (Chuhng jyewn-yew) was born in 1986, a decade after Mao died, in a small hamlet in Sichuan province to a family of farmers who raised pigs and grew crops. When she was three, a younger brother was born. Two years later her father took a job in a nearby coal mine because it paid better than farming. When she was nine, her mother left the family, and Junyu began skipping school two or three days a week to tend the fields. When she was thirteen, her father, suffering from black lung, had to quit the mine, and Junyu became the family's main provider. An aunt said she would take Junyu to the city to find work.

Their first stop was Chongqing, the largest city in their province. Her aunt arranged a series of jobs for Junyu as a maid, a waitress, a cook in a mining camp, and a cashier. The aunt took a cut of her wages and also sent money home to her father. After Junyu and her aunt relocated to booming Guangdong province, Junyu got a job as a cook for a foreign factory owner and within weeks talked him into letting her work at the factory, which made small generators. At that point she broke with her aunt and became independent.

Even though Junyu had little formal education, the factory owner quickly recognized that she was intelligent and gave her other jobs to do. She helped him with shippers and suppliers and kept track of parts, inventory, and costs on a computer. Junyu was able to bring her younger brother to town, and the factory owner agreed to pay for him to attend a three-year technical school.

Junyu went back to visit her father and other relatives once or twice a year—the 600-mile trip taking her thirty-six hours on a train and eleven hours on a bus. Although she earned only US$206 per month in 2006, she was able to send $50 to $100 to her family every month. This was enough money for her father to build a new five-room house with concrete floors but no plumbing; the only heat came from a small charcoal burner kept in the living room. Still, it was the most impressive house in the village. Junyu's money was also used to buy a color television, but it still stayed in its box, as television broadcasts had not yet reached the region.

Most of the young people in Junyu's village had, like her, left to find better-paying work elsewhere, though few with so much success. Many factory jobs paid only

Chien-min Chung/Getty Images

Cheng Junyu. Young people like Cheng Junyu adjust quickly to life in big cities.

$100 per month, leaving much less to send home. For the village, however, the money sent back by the young people was a lifesaver. Junyu's father's younger brother wanted to give up working in the mine, where he earned about $65 a month, but his seven- and nine-year-old children were too young to send out to work. So it was his wife who would go, leaving the boys with him and joining Junyu at the generator factory. Keeping the family financially afloat required breaking it up.

Once her brother finishes school and can become the family wage-earner, Junyu would like to go back to school to get a high school diploma.

Questions for Analysis
1. Did Cheng Junyu have much choice about becoming a migrant worker?
2. From the examples in this article, what sort of impact do job opportunities have on families?

Based on Alwyn Scott, "Bridging Two Worlds: A New Life for Susie Cheng," *Seattle Times*, July 9, 2006.

goods. Like people elsewhere in the world, Chinese bought TVs, stereos, clothes, furniture, air conditioners, and washing machines. Shopping streets of major cities abounded in stores well stocked with imported as well as domestically produced goods. Between 1986 and 1995, the number of refrigerators per hundred households went from 62 to 98 in Beijing, 47 to 98 in Shanghai, and 14 to 83 in Xi'an. Acquisition of washing machines made similar gains. Telephone service lagged, but Chinese responded eagerly when pagers and cellular phones became available. By 2000 there were already 26 million cellular phones in China, but the numbers kept rising rapidly; by 2011 there were 907 million cellular phones in use. That year there were 389 million Internet users, up from 8 million in 2000. Within five days of a deadly collision on China's new high-speed rail line in 2011, 26 million messages about it had been posted on China's two main microblogs.

In the 1990s many grew rich enough to buy imported cars, build lavish houses, and make generous gifts to all the officials they dealt with. In 1978 there had not been a single privately owned car in China; by 1993 there were more than 1 million, and by 2007 the number had reached 13 million, with 4 million new cars being produced every year. In 2010, almost 14 million passenger cars were manufactured.

Consumer culture also came to the countryside, though there it is limited by the much lower level of disposable income. In the 1980s, as farm incomes grew, farmers began building new homes, buying better food, and purchasing consumer goods such as TVs, furniture, and clothing. Villages without electricity built small local generators. With migrant workers bringing home knowledge of city life and with television bringing everyone images of modern living, families in the countryside steadily added to the list of goods they considered essential. Chinese, like people in more developed countries, were identifying more with the goods they consumed than with politics.

SOCIAL AND CULTURAL CHANGES

Education

Education at all levels had deteriorated during the Cultural Revolution, when it was considered more important to be Red than to be expert. An important symbolic reversal of these policies occurred in 1977 with the reinstitution of college entrance examinations. Soon those graduating from college could also apply to study abroad, which led to a craze for studying foreign languages. In 2009, more than 600,000 Chinese were in the United States on student visas.

Educational opportunities had always been better in the cities than in the countryside, and in the 1990s the disparity seemed to grow. During the Cultural Revolution, when the educated were ousted from their jobs, teaching positions were filled by peasant teachers paid like other workers on the commune through work points (redeemable largely in shares of the commune's grain). With the dismantling of the communes in the early 1980s, other ways had to be found to pay teachers, most commonly by charging parents fees, often too high for peasants. Sometimes rural schools tried to make ends meet by having the students work, peddling apples on the streets or assembling firecrackers in their classrooms. After a blistering analysis of the disadvantages faced by rural children in Hunan province published in *China Youth Daily* in 2005, the government announced that rural school fees would be eliminated by 2007. By the end of the 1990s, universities were also charging fees, generally about 10,000 yuan per year. Bitter complaints about how these fees kept out children from rural areas led to the introduction of scholarship programs.

The Arts

During the decade of the Cultural Revolution, intellectuals learned to keep quiet, and ordinary people were fed a dull and repetitive diet of highly politicized stories, plays, and films. With the downfall of the Gang of Four, people's pent-up desire for more varied and lively cultural expression quickly became apparent. A literature of the "wounded" appeared at the end of the 1970s, when those who had suffered during the Cultural Revolution found it politically possible to write of their experiences. Greater tolerance on the part of the government quickly resulted in much livelier media, with everything from investigative reporters exposing corruption of cadres, to philosophers who tried to reexamine the premises of Marxism, to novelists, poets, and filmmakers who experimented with previously taboo treatments of sexuality.

During the Mao period, feature films were produced by state-run studios under the Ministry of Culture. Particularly during the Cultural Revolution, most movies had predictable plots and stereotyped characterizations. Even within China, these films would not have had much of an audience except for the lack of other forms of entertainment and distribution of free tickets. After the graduation of a new generation of directors from

Gilles Sabrie/The New York Times/Redux Pictures

Reality Show. Chinese audiences have responded favorably to reality TV shows, such as "If You Are the One," a dating show in which 24 attractive young women question possible romantic partners. When too many of the women rejected men because they were not rich enough, government censors decreed that there be no mention of income.

the Beijing Film Academy beginning in 1982, highly artistic films began to be made. By the 1990s, Chinese films were regularly screened at international film festivals. Notable recent films include *Not One Less* (2000), which had children from a remote area as its main characters; *Blind Shaft* (2003), about itinerant miners and illegal privately run mines; and *City of Life and Death* (2009), about the Nanjing Massacre in 1937. The 2010 historical drama, *Let the Bullets Fly,* became the highest grossing film in China's cinematic history.

Television programming has made similar strides, and today's shows often reflect the issues on people's minds. One of the most popular television shows in 2009 was a 33-part serial called "Snail House," or "Dwelling Narrowness," about the tribulations of young people trying to buy a home in the midst of a property bubble. At the center of the story are two sisters, Haiping and Haizao. Haiping gets into a big city university and wants to stay there after graduating and getting married. To save for a down payment, she and her husband live very frugally, sending their daughter to be raised by her grandparents and making do in a small, shabby room and a diet of instant noodles. But they cannot save as fast as property prices rise. Meanwhile, the younger sister Haizao graduates from college and moves in with them. She finds a job with a real estate developer, who introduces her to a corrupt government official whose favor the developer needs. She becomes the official's mistress and takes money

from him to give to her sister for the down payment. Haizao's relationship with the corrupt official goes through many twists and turns, until he kills himself on the eve of being arrested. But Haiping finally gets her home and brings her daughter back to live with them. From the lively online discussion of the show it is apparent that many viewers identified with the young people, seeing themselves as "house slaves."

Gender Roles

The Communist Party, from its beginnings in the 1920s, had espoused equality for women, and women were eligible to join the party on the same terms as men. Moreover, the party pushed for reforms in marriage practice that were generally seen as improving women's situations, such as giving them the right to initiate divorce. The reality never came up to the level of the rhetoric, but women did play more active roles in the revolution than they had in earlier eras of Chinese history.

After 1949 official rhetoric encouraged people to think of men and women as equal. With collectivization, women were mobilized to participate in farm work, and efforts were made to get girls enrolled in schools. Images of tough women who could do jobs traditionally done by men were part of everyday propaganda. Women did increase their presence in many jobs; the proportion of elementary school teachers who were women increased from 18 percent in 1951 to 36 percent

MATERIAL CULTURE

High-Speed Railways

China has been upgrading its transportation infrastructure at a rapid rate. Subway systems have been built in many cities; expressways have been built across the country; 400 airports are now serviced by nine airlines. After 2000, the most dramatic of the changes has been the creation of a high-speed railroad system, defined as trains going 200 or more km per hour (124 miles per hour). Between 2005 and 2010, China went from having no high-speed rail to having more than all of Europe. By 2012 China is expected to have more miles of high-speed rail tracks than the rest of the world put together.

The new trains have drastically cut the time it takes to get from one city to another. Beijing to Tianjin, which had been a two-hour trip in 1980, now is only 30 minutes. Shanghai to Hangzhou had been a four-hour trip but now takes just over an hour. Beijing to Shanghai had been an overnight trip, usually of twelve or more hours, but can now be done in less than five hours going at 300 km/hour.

For the design of the trains, China opened bidding to foreign countries but wanted the cars to be built in China and the technology to be shared. Although critics have charged that safety was being sacrificed for the sake of speed (especially after a major accident in July 2011 led to 40 deaths) and many complain of the high cost of tickets, the high-speed rail lines are tying China together as never before.

Michael Christopher Brown for Time

High-Speed Train. The speed of the new trains mean that they can compete with planes for passengers.

in 1975 and continued to increase in the reform era to 49 percent in 1998.

In the reform era women still had complaints. With fees charged by elementary schools, poorer families did not send their daughters to school for as long as their sons. New opportunities opened up by the expanding economy favored males. Young men could join construction companies and do relatively well-paid work far from home; young women could work in textile, electronic, and toy factories for lower wages. For those who did not want to leave their hometowns, employment patterns were also skewed by gender. The women often did the field work, while the men got the better-paid skilled work.

In the cities girls were more likely to stay in school as long as boys did, but once the state withdrew from the hiring process, their degrees were not worth as much. New female graduates of high schools or colleges tended not to get jobs that were as good as the ones their male classmates got, something that happened less frequently when state bureaus made job assignments. The decline in the state-owned factories has hurt both men and women, but women complain that they are the first to be laid off.

Population Control and the One-Child Family

From 1957 to 1970, China's population grew from about 630 million to 880 million. Public health measures promoted in the 1950s deserve much of the credit for reducing the death rate and thus improving life expectancy, which increased dramatically from forty years in 1953 to sixty in 1968, sixty-five in 1984, and seventy-five in 2010. As a consequence, even the horrible famine of 1959–1962 made only a temporary dent in the upward course of China's population. Mao had opposed the idea that China could have too many people, but by the time Mao died, China's population was approaching 1 billion, and his successors recognized that China could not afford to postpone bringing it under control.

Beginning in the late 1970s, the government has worked hard to promote the one-child family in the cities and the one- or two-child family in the countryside. Targets were set for the total numbers of births in each place and quotas then assigned to smaller units. Young people needed permission from their work units to get married, then permission to have a child. In the early 1980s, women who got pregnant outside the plan faced often unrelenting pressure from birth control workers and local cadres to have abortions. In the 1990s, the campaign was relaxed a little, making it easier for families with only daughters to try again for a son. By 2011 government officials were talking of ending the one-child policy in the near future so that the working age population does not start to shrink.

The preference for boys remains so strong that China faces a shortage of young women in coming decades as female fetuses are more likely to be aborted (after being identified by ultrasound) and girl babies are more likely to be made available for adoption. In the mid-1990s, China quietly began to allow unwanted children, primarily baby girls, to be adopted by foreigners, and by the end of the century, more orphans were adopted from China into the United States than from any other country.

Population control policies have had some unintended consequences. By the 1990s, with increased prosperity, people talked about the pampered only children in the cities whose parents would take them to Western fast-food restaurants and pay for all sorts of enrichment experiences. Not only will this generation grow up without siblings, but their children will have no aunts and uncles. Planners are already worrying about how they will take care of their aging parents because one young couple could well have four elderly parents to support.

Family Life

Both changing gender roles and population control policies have had an impact on family organization and family dynamics. So too have many other policies put into effect by the government since 1949. Ancestor worship, lineages, and solidarity with patrilineal kin were all discouraged as feudal practices. The authority of family heads declined as collectives took over property and allocated labor. As both women and children spent much more time away from the home, the family became less central in their lives. Coerced marriages became less common, and in the cities at least, people did in fact choose their own spouses much of the time.

The reform era has not turned the clock back on these changes in family structure and authority. Scholars who have studied families in rural areas have shown that although patrilineal stem families are still quite common—the newly married couple living with or very near the husband's family—the older couple has much less power over the younger one. Even in the countryside, young people are likely to have decided to marry on their own and seek a companionate marriage. They may extract a hefty bride price from the husband's family, but they use it to purchase things they want for their home. If

Nir Elias/Reuters /Landov

Factory Workers. Plush and stuffed toys are among the many goods now made predominately in China.

a new house is built or an extension added, they will work hard to give themselves more privacy. Although the man's parents may push for grandsons, younger couples often are quite comfortable with birth control policies and are happy with only one or two children, even if they are daughters. They are more concerned with the happiness of their nuclear family than with family continuity. Although divorce is still very rare in the countryside, women believe that the ability to threaten divorce gives them more voice in family decision making.

CRITICAL VOICES

From early in the reform period, people found ways to express political criticism. The first big character posters were pasted on Democracy Wall in Beijing in the fall of 1978. Many of those who participated were blue-collar workers with high school educations, and Deng gave them his blessing. Soon a twenty-eight-year-old electrician named Wei Jingshen (way jing-shuhn) courageously pasted up a call for the "fifth modernization":

What is true democracy? Only when the people themselves choose representatives to manage affairs in accordance with their will and interests can we speak of democracy. Furthermore, the people must have the power to replace these representatives at any time in order to prevent them from abusing their powers to oppress the people. Is this possible? The citizens of Europe and the United States enjoy just this kind of democracy and could run people like Nixon, de Gaulle, and Tanaka out of office when they wished and can even reinstate them if they want to, for no one can interfere with their democratic rights. In China, however, if a person so much as comments on the now-deceased "Great Helmsman" or "Great Man peerless in history" Mao Zedong, the mighty prison gates and all kinds of unimaginable misfortunes await him. If we compare the socialist system of "democratic centralism" with the "exploiting class democracy" of capitalism, the difference is as clear as night and day.*

---

*From *Sources of Chinese Tradition: From 1600 Through the Twentieth Century*, by Wm. Theodore de Bary and Irene Bloom, eds. Copyright © 2000 by Columbia University Press, reprinted with permission of the publisher.

Wei was soon to know those prison gates himself. By April 1979 he had been arrested and Democracy Wall shut down. Wei spent most of his time from then on in prison, with long stretches in solitary confinement, until he was exiled to the United States in 1997.

Intellectuals also spoke up. In 1986 the physicist Fang Lizhi (fahng lee-jih) told students that the socialist movement "from Marx and Lenin to Stalin and Mao Zedong, has been a failure" and advocated adopting the Western political system.* That year students at 150 campuses demanded greater freedom, less corruption, and better living conditions in their dormitories. After the protests were suppressed, Deng had party secretary general Hu Yaobang (hoo yow-bahng) dismissed from his post because he had been too conciliatory toward the students.

In the spring of 1989, huge student protests erupted in Beijing. The protests began modestly in April with a parade honoring the memory of recently deceased Hu Yaobang, viewed as the strongest voice in the government for political reform. Buoyed by the positive reaction of the Beijing citizenry, student leaders gradually escalated their activities and their rallying cries. They called for more democratic government: Make officials disclose their income and assets! Renounce the use of mass political campaigns! Abolish prohibitions against street protests! Permit journalists to report protest activities! End corruption! Many evoked the ideas of the May Fourth movement, claiming that the goals of science and democracy were still unfulfilled. When Deng Xiaoping called the students' actions "counterrevolutionary turmoil," they did not tone down their rhetoric. When the momentum seemed to be flagging, a couple of thousand students staged a hunger strike to testify to their sincerity and determination.

On May 17, 1989, with the international press present to cover the visit of the Soviet Premier Gorbachev, Tiananmen Square was filled not merely with students from every university in Beijing but also with people from other organizations, even government units like the Foreign Ministry, the Central Television Station, and the Public Security Bureau Academy. Workers in their work clothes held banners inscribed with the names of their factories. The students themselves had no experience with democracy, and the leaders who emerged often disagreed on the best tactics. The public's support for the students was a humiliation to Deng and the other leaders, who declared martial law as soon as Gorbachev left and dismissed the more conciliatory Zhao Ziyang (jow dzih-yahng) from his post as secretary general of the Communist Party. On June 3–4, seasoned troops were brought into central Beijing through underground tunnels, and tanks and artillery soon followed. Many unarmed citizens still tried to halt their advance, but the armored vehicles got through the blockades after bloody clashes and successfully ended both the protest and the occupation of the square. Several hundred people lost their lives that night, many of them ordinary citizens trying to stop the soldiers from entering central Beijing.

Suppression of this movement, coupled with compulsory political study classes at universities, kept political discussion subdued within China for the next several years. In the 1990s no single issue united critics of the government. Some activists tried to organize workers who were facing unsafe conditions or were not being paid. Farmers often protested the arbitrary addition of taxes.

The government was more alarmed by the political potential of a school of Qigong (chee-gung) teachings. Until then, the government had pointed with pride to the elderly who early each morning could be seen in parks practicing the stretching and balancing exercises called Qigong, believed to nurture the practitioners' *qi* (vital energy). Masters of Qigong often attributed all sorts of powers to their techniques. In the 1990s one such teacher, Li Hongzhi (lee hung-jih), developed Falun Gong (fah-lun gung), a form of Qigong that drew on both Buddhist and Daoist ideas and promised practitioners good health and other benefits. Many from the party and PLA, as well as their wives and mothers, were attracted to this system of knowledge beyond the understanding of Western science. When in 1999 Li organized fifteen thousand followers to assemble outside the party leaders' residential complex in Beijing to ask for recognition of his teachings, the top leadership became alarmed and not only outlawed the sect but also arrested thousands of members and sent them for reeducation. The potential of Falun Gong to reach the masses and offer an alternative to the party was seen as particularly threatening.

---

*Richard Baum, *Burying Mao: Chinese Politics in the Age of Deng Xiaoping* (Princeton, N.J.: Princeton University Press, 1994), p. 201.

TAIWAN

In 1949, when the victory of the Communist Party in the civil war seemed imminent, Chiang Kaishek and large parts of the Nationalist government and army evacuated to the island of Taiwan, less than a hundred miles off the coast of Fujian province. Taiwan had been under Japanese colonial rule from 1895 to 1945 and had only recently been returned to Chinese rule. The initial encounter between the local population and the Nationalist government had been hostile: in 1947, the government responded to protests against the corruption of its politicians by shooting at protesters and pursuing suspected leaders, killing, it is estimated, eight thousand to ten thousand people, including many local leaders. In part because of the support the United States gave Chiang and his government as the Cold War in Asia intensified, the Nationalists soon stabilized their government and were able to concentrate on economic development. After Chiang Kaishek died in 1975, he was succeeded by his son Chiang Chingkuo (Jiang Jingguo, jyang jing-gwaw). During his presidency in the late 1980s, Taiwan succeeded in making the transition from one-party rule to parliamentary democracy.

During the 1950s and 1960s, the United States treated Chiang's Republic of China as the legitimate government of China and insisted that it occupy China's seat at the United Nations. When relations between the United States and the PRC were normalized in the 1970s, Taiwan's position became anomalous. The United States and the PRC agreed that there was only one China and that Taiwan was a part of China. The United States maintained that any unification of China should come by peaceful means and continued its military aid to Taiwan. China insisted that countries that wanted embassies in Beijing had to eliminate their embassies in Taiwan. As China joined more and more international organizations, Taiwan was frequently forced out.

This loss of political standing has not prevented Taiwan from becoming an economic power. In 2010, Taiwan's per capita income for its 23 million citizens was about $35,700, up with Japan and South Korea and way beyond China. Several factors contributed to this extraordinary economic growth. The Nationalists started with the advantage of Japanese land reform and industrial development. They also benefited from considerable foreign investment over the next couple of decades, especially from the United States and Japan. But hard work and thoughtful planning also deserve credit for Taiwan's growth. The government of Taiwan gave real authority to those with technical training. Economists and engineers, including many trained abroad, became heads of ministries. Through the 1950s, emphasis was placed on import substitution, especially by building up light industry to produce consumer goods. The 1960s saw a shift toward export-oriented industries, especially electronics, as Taiwan began to try to follow along behind Japan, moving into stereos and televisions as Japan moved into cars. In

Country	GDP per Capita (in U.S. dollars)	Life Expectancy (years)	Literacy Rate (%)	Fertility Rate	Population (millions)
United States	47,200	78.4	99	2.1	313
Taiwan	35,700	78.3	96	1.2	23
Japan	34,000	82.3	99	1.2	126
South Korea	30,000	79.1	98	1.2	49
China	7,600	74.7	92	1.5	1,337
India	3,500	66.8	61	2.6	1,189
Vietnam	3,100	72.2	94	1.9	91
North Korea	1,800	68.9	99	2.0	24

Comparisons of China, Taiwan, and Other Countries

Source: World Factbook, 2011.

1966 the first tax-free export processing zone was set up, attracting foreign capital and technology. By the 1980s, there was adequate wealth in Taiwan to develop capital-intensive industries such as steel and petrochemicals.

Over the past twenty-five years, there has been increasing contact between Chinese in Taiwan and the PRC. In 1987, when Taiwan lifted restrictions on travel, thousands of people from Taiwan visited the mainland. The scale of Taiwan's investment in its giant neighbor has been a staggering $100 billion since 1987. Taiwan's semiconductor and personal computer manufacturing plants have been relocated to the mainland, where wages are much lower. Trying to adjust to this exodus of manufacturing jobs, Taiwan's own economy has been strained. In 1996, Taiwan held its first open elections for the presidency and the National Assembly. In 2000, the Nationalist Party lost the general election for the first time, losing to the Democratic Progressive Party, long associated with Taiwan independence. In 2008, however, the Nationalist Party was returned to power after promising improved ties to the mainland.

CHINA IN THE WORLD

After China split with the Soviet Union in the early 1960s, it severely limited its contacts with the rest of the world. It provided some assistance to African countries and to Maoist revolutionary groups, but had too great a fear of spies to encourage people to maintain ties with relatives abroad. Mao's death changed this. China sought entry into international organizations, invited overseas Chinese to visit and participate in China's development, and began sending its officials on trips around the world.

In the 1980s, China worked to improve its relationship with Western countries, partly to reduce the threat from the Soviet Union. In 1984, the British government agreed to return Hong Kong to China when the ninety-nine–year lease on the New Territories expired in 1997. China promised to let Hong Kong maintain its own political and economic system for fifty years.

In the 1990s, to help expand its economy, China joined the World Bank, the International Monetary Fund, and the Asian Development Bank, which offered both low-interest loans and various types of technical and economic advice but also required that China

report its economic situation more openly. In 2001, China was admitted to the World Trade Organization. China used the 2008 Olympics in Beijing to showcase how it has been transformed in the last three decades. In 2010 China overtook Japan as the world's second largest economy, and in 2011 China overtook the United States as the world's largest manufacturer.

SUMMARY

After the death of Mao, much of China's socialist system was dismantled step by step. Mao's wife was imprisoned after she and the other members of the "Gang of Four" were blamed for the excesses of the Cultural Revolution. People who had been labeled as Rightist or Counterrevolutionaries were allowed to return to normal life. Entrance to college again required doing well on nation-wide examinations. Collectivization of agriculture was largely reversed. Sideline enterprises and small businesses of all sorts were encouraged. Foreign companies were encouraged to invest in China.

In the 1990s the pace of change picked up. The state began closing many state-owned enterprises, and working in a state factory no longer meant secure life-time income. Regional disparities widened, as the coastal regions were better placed to attract factories making goods for export. Young people left rural areas in large numbers to work as migrant labor in the coastal cities. As factories proliferated, so did environmental degradation.

How different is China in 2012 than it was at the time of Mao's death in 1976? In the more modernized coastal provinces, the standard of living has improved enormously. Everywhere knowledge of the outside world is much more extensive. Inequalities are also more extreme: some Chinese have grown fabulously wealthy, while others have not been able to find work or cannot afford to send their children to school or to pay for medical care. The party is no longer as dominated by a single person as forms of collective leadership have been developed, and leaders now can rise as much because of their technical expertise as their political fervor. Nevertheless, the Communist Party still dominates the government and has its hands in much of what goes on in the country. The Chinese state does not interfere in everyday affairs to the extent it used to but it still has tremendous coercive force.

East Asia in the Twenty-First Century

IT SHOULD COME AS NO SURPRISE IN OUR increasingly global world that the countries of East Asia are now more connected than ever before. Hundreds of thousands of Korean, Taiwanese, and Japanese businesspeople live in China to work in the manufacturing operations they have located there, and they regularly fly back and forth to their home countries. Thousands of Chinese live in Japan, often illegally, some as students or businesspeople, others as laborers. Cheap international phone service, as well as access to e-mail and the Internet, make it easy for travelers to keep in contact with friends and relatives back home, creating diasporas different from the immigrant communities of earlier times.

For two decades, Japanese, Korean, and Taiwanese tourists have been visiting China, often on package tours, and today Chinese who have prospered during the reform period are reciprocating by visiting nearby countries in increasing numbers. Popular and classical music no longer respect national boundaries. Singers and instrumentalists often have large followings throughout East Asia, adding to the huge popularity of karaoke in the region. Popular TV serials are often dubbed so that they can be shown in other East Asian countries.

Japan, Korea, Taiwan, and China all participate in contemporary global culture. The Korea wave that inundated Japan, Taiwan, and China made a soap opera, *Winter Sonata*, and its star, Bae Yong Jun, so popular that when he visited Japan, middle-age women threw themselves in front of his car and swarmed his hotel. It was also the rage in Uzbekistan and Egypt. In China, "Korea" stands for fashionable or stylish. To Chinese ears, even American hip-hop sounds better in Korean. Episodes of *The Marrying Type*, a sitcom about three single professional women in Seoul, were so popular that they were sold on pirated DVDs.

East Asian countries cooperate and compete in the production of popular culture. One movie project calls for a Japanese company to produce the script and direction, a South Korean company to handle three-dimensional graphics, and the animation to be done in Shanghai. A Japanese wedding company exports Japanese-style weddings to Shanghai. Young people in Japan study Korean and Chinese; Chinese is as popular in Korea today as English is in China. Japanese too is studied in the rest of East Asia, although given Japan's wartime legacy, not with the same enthusiasm.

East Asia has leaped to the forefront of electronic technology. In China cell phones and fiber optics have lowered the costs of telephones and electrical transmission. Computers have given Internet access to about 384 million people (29 percent of the Chinese population) as of 2009, and the number is rising. Microsoft opened a research laboratory in the Haidian District of Beijing, where some 810,000 Chinese research scientists and engineers live. Oracle, Motorola, Siemens, IBM, Intel, General Electric, and Nokia (which produces mobile phones) run research facilities in China to develop new products as well, opening the door to innovative and independent research for young scientists. When Shanghai hosted a World Expo in 2010, visitors were rocketed from the airport to the exhibition by magnetic levitation trains traveling at speeds of up to 270 mph.

Aware that unlimited contact with the outside world poses a political threat to the regime, the Chinese leadership has ordered operators of Internet sites to monitor government bans against rumors, libel, subversion, sabotage of national security, the promotion of cults and feudal superstition, pornography, violence, and gambling. In the meantime, foreign movies, popular songs, and chain stores from Japan, South Korea, and the United States have penetrated the country. Whether the leadership is right to fear their liberalizing effect remains to be seen.

Modern communications have impacted both Koreas. In the South, it seems that everyone

Walmart in China. Sales clerks at a Beijing Sam's Club operated by Walmart sell Western-style dairy products along with soy milk, fresh pork along with dried deer tendons to China's consumers. At the end of 2011, Walmart operated more than 350 stores in China.

(especially teenagers) has a cell phone, computer, and Internet access. The movie industry has produced an internationally renowned generation of directors, producers, and actors. Thousands of young students travel to the United States to get an education, and interest in China is growing rapidly. North Korea has tried to insulate itself from the communications revolution and the cultural effects of globalization, but access to the Internet has already proved subversive to the closed society by cracking open the window of information from the world outside.

Contemporary Japanese culture in the form of Japanese comic books (manga), computer cartoon and video games, animation (anime), designer clothing, pop music, new dance steps, and accessories has become a major export industry. In Japan, more than 99 million people (78 percent of the population) are connected to the Internet, and cell phones are everywhere. Japan leads the world in new and innovative products and designs in electronics that aim at the young and create new job opportunities outside the rigid hierarchies of big business, opening possibilities for individual creativity and entrepreneurship.

Signs of American culture abound in East Asia. Fast-food restaurants—McDonald's, Burger King, Kentucky Fried Chicken, and Starbucks—are found in cities of any size. Designer boutiques from the United States and Europe have taken over floors in major department stores, and Walmart has set up big box stores across China. American teenage clothing and music styles are everywhere. Baseball and basketball are played in East Asia, with Japanese and Korean ballplayers having joined several American major-league teams. The seven-foot-six-inch-tall Yao Ming played basketball for the Houston Rockets until repeated bone fractures forced his retirement in 2011. In 2002, South Korea and Japan jointly hosted the World Cup soccer tournament, and in 2008, Beijing hosted the summer Olympics. No matter what the political differences, cultural convergence (albeit with national variations) has gone too far to be stopped.

Japan, South Korea, and Taiwan are all democratic countries with freely elected governments, but that has not saved them from political problems. Chief among these is corruption caused by businessmen who offer bribes and kickbacks to further their companies' interests. Despite the highly publicized executions of party officials for corruption, it is a growing problem in China and North Korea as well. The Kim family is notorious for living off the fat of the land, and grandchildren of China's revolutionary elite have won notoriety for breaking the law.

Although both the Chinese Communist Party and the Korean Communist Party govern in the name of the people, their officials are often as unresponsive to people's needs as are Japanese bureaucrats who created the issue of most pressing concern to the middle class—scandals surrounding the pension system. South Korean political parties have shown no lasting power because they consist of leader–follower groups that shift allegiance from one party to another. Even the most liberal government has refused to repeal the national security law put in place under the dictators. In Taiwan an independence movement backed by native Taiwanese had its candidate elected president in 2000, but after 2008, voters supported politicians who promised economic benefits from close ties with the mainland.

Although the 1990s were a difficult period for East Asian economies, double-digit growth in China has raised South Korean, Taiwanese, and Japanese economic boats. China is South Korea's biggest export market, and since 2004, Japan has traded more with China than with any other country, including the United States. The booming Chinese economy had lifted Japan out of a fifteen-year recession before the 2011 earthquake struck and also helped South Korea recover from the Asian financial crisis.

Korean and Japanese companies are eager for access to Chinese consumers and labor, while China welcomes all the foreign investment it can get. Taiwan has invested heavily in China, in terms of both hard cash and human capital, with 1 to 1.5 million Taiwanese, including many managers, working there. More than 100 million Chinese men and women toil in China's factories, and the Pearl River Delta of Guangdong has become the world's manufacturing center. New Japanese prime ministers make their first overseas visits to China, not to the United States. At an economic summit in 2012, the presidents of China, South Korea, and Japan called for strengthened economic ties and a free trade zone. "The future trend in East Asia is economic integration," said Huang Dahui, professor of international affairs at People's University in Beijing. "Without Sino-Japanese cooperation, real integration is impossible."[*]

In this growing economic interdependence, the balance is tilting in China's favor. For the United States this means that its purchase of Chinese products is not only the largest contributor to its trade deficit

but also that China is also the largest purchaser of U.S. national debt. Someday China will decide that it would be better off investing its surplus cash in infrastructure—roads, railways, education.

China has begun to show many of the problems that Japan and South Korea have experienced: bad loans that the state forced banks to grant insolvent companies, collusive and corrupt agreements between bureaucrats and businessmen, a huge housing bubble, and inefficient state owned enterprises that substitute for welfare payments to workers. China is notorious for ignoring international copyright laws by stealing trade and manufacturing secrets from its competitors; recently private Chinese companies have complained that state owned enterprises steal their technology.

In China, the gap between rich and poor, between flourishing coastal urban regions and backward rural areas in the interior, and between skilled and unskilled workers is growing. Millions of underemployed and homeless migrant workers from the countryside fill urban slums. Strikes by workers have increased, only to be met by government repression. Owners of coal mines ignore safety measures that could save thousands of lives annually; owners of brick factories kidnap children for slave labor; and the lack of quality control has become an international scandal. Industrial pollution may be killing as many as 750,000 Chinese every year, and China now produces more greenhouse gases than the United States. China's leaders are trying to address these problems with the help of Japanese technology and foreign pressure.

The possibility of creating a regional free trade bloc in East Asia, such as that in the European community, faces serious obstacles. The Chinese economy has by far the highest growth rate based on a huge population and low wages and stands to gain the most from unrestrained trade until its wage rates rise. North Korea needs economic assistance from China so long as its economy remains stagnant, but its intense nationalism resists the idea of domination by any foreign economy. South Korean business is shipping its factories to China, but the public fears the loss of industry and the resulting economic decline. Japan has much to gain from exports of high-tech products and investment in factories in China, but lingering Chinese resentment of Japanese atrocities in World War II, Japan's military alliance with the United States, and suspicion of Japanese rearmament could put a brake on further integration.

---

[*]Bruce Wallace and Mark Magnier, "China, Japan Patching Up Diplomacy," *Los Angeles Times*, Saturday, February 17, 2007, p. A5.

All East Asian nations except North Korea continue to benefit from exports to the United States and, although on a smaller scale, to Europe. Trade with Southeast Asia and Latin America is growing. The potential for exports to Russia and surrounding states in return for oil and gas could be enormous if political and bureaucratic obstacles to free trade in those countries were to be removed.

One obstacle to continued economic growth may be demographic, now that education for women, urbanization, and industrialization have brought about a collapse in birth rates. Japan's birth rate has been stuck at approximately 1.3 births per woman for so long that it now has the world's oldest population. In 2005 the population officially started to decline, and politicians worry that Japan will lose half its population by 2100. At 0.9 births per woman, Hong Kong has the world's lowest fertility rate. Taiwan and South Korea both have fertility rates lower than Japan's, with Korea's falling to 1.1 in 2009.

Owing to the official "one child" policy in China, the fertility rate there is 1.6. China's working age population will peak in 2015 before starting a steep decline, leading to fears that as the population ages, China will grow old before it gets rich. Because so much of China's large population still resides in the countryside, where sons are the chief form of old-age insurance, there is a serious sex imbalance. By 2020 the number of twenty- to forty-five-year-old men will exceed women by 30 million. Given that young, unattached males are the most likely to cause trouble, the sex imbalance could have political consequences.

The declining birth rates in Japan and South Korea have also led to labor shortages and aging bachelors. To some extent, sex selection techniques are to blame, but women are also more choosey in whom they marry and whether they marry. In both countries, the myth of ethnic purity has made it difficult to welcome immigrants in any number with the exception of guest workers. To find brides for farmers, Japan turns to the nearby Philippines; Korea turns to Vietnam because the two countries share a common Confucian tradition. Of the farmers in South Jeolla province who married in 2009, 44 percent took a foreign bride.

South Korea and Japan also share high rates of suicide. Both countries have extremely competitive economies where the pressure to succeed in school and business is intense. The number of people committing suicide in Japan has topped thirty thousand a year for more than ten years. Young people blame the school problems of bullying and poor grades; the middle-aged cite employment issues; and the elderly blame health concerns. In South Korea, the number of suicides has more than doubled in the past decade, and its rate of 31.0 per 100,000 people was higher than Japan's (24.4) in 2009. Although it is not responsible for the majority of suicide deaths, the most disturbing trend in both countries is the increase in the number of group suicides. The culprit is the Internet, where people contemplating suicide can meet and then use e-mail and cell phones to plan their deaths. On the other hand, homicide is relatively rare throughout East Asia.

Despite economic and cultural convergence, memories of World War II continue to trouble international relations in East Asia, where suspicions about Japanese attitudes and policies remain strong. Japan refuses to correct lies in school textbooks about its conduct in China and mistreatment of Koreans during the colonial period, to apologize publicly and pay reparations to the comfort women, and to share advanced technology in some industries. Not only do Japanese revisionist historians deny the Nanjing massacre, but some have also put the blame for starting the war on China. Although Japanese businessmen would prefer that prime ministers not pay homage to the war dead at Yasukuni shrine because of its effect on trade, nationalists insist that respect is owed the men who sacrificed themselves for a sacred cause.

As China's economic clout increases, it is becoming increasingly dominant politically, not just in East Asia but in world affairs as well. Its relations with Tibet remain troubled because of ongoing nationalistic resistance to the Chinese and Chinese migration that has overwhelmed the smaller Tibetan population. China has taken advantage of the "war on terror" to suppress what it says are Uighur Muslim separatists in the northwest. Despite international disapproval, China's voracious appetite for raw materials has led to support for African dictators.

Throughout the developing world, China has put on a "charm offensive," building government buildings for the new East Timor government and an aqueduct and major highways in the Philippines. As it moves aggressively to buy raw materials from South America and Africa, infrastructure projects promote the idea that China is a friendly partner. At the same time, China undercuts this effort by claiming islands also claimed by other nations, sending its fishing fleet close to foreign shores, and threatening to build dams across the rivers that water Southeast Asia.

The biggest concern for the United States is China's growing military strength. China has a large army capable of defending against invasion, and it is building up a navy and air force to enforce its claims to offshore islands. As one response, the United States has repeated its commitment to the defense of Japan and Taiwan and strengthened its ties with China's neighbors.

The U.S. military presence in East Asia has had a strong stabilizing effect. It has prevented Japan's formal rearmament and has stemmed both the growing Taiwanese desire for independence and China's ability to take Taiwan by force. It has blocked a North Korean invasion of the South and a southern invasion of the North. The major challenge it faces is to find a way to reach a negotiated solution to the problem of North Korea's nuclear arms, but in an increasingly interconnected world, it shares this challenge with Russia, China, South Korea, and Japan.

South Korea, Taiwan, and Japan are at a crossroads. In terms of security, they face east, allied militarily with the United States and Australia. In terms of prosperity, they now face west as they strengthen economic cooperation with China.

INDEX

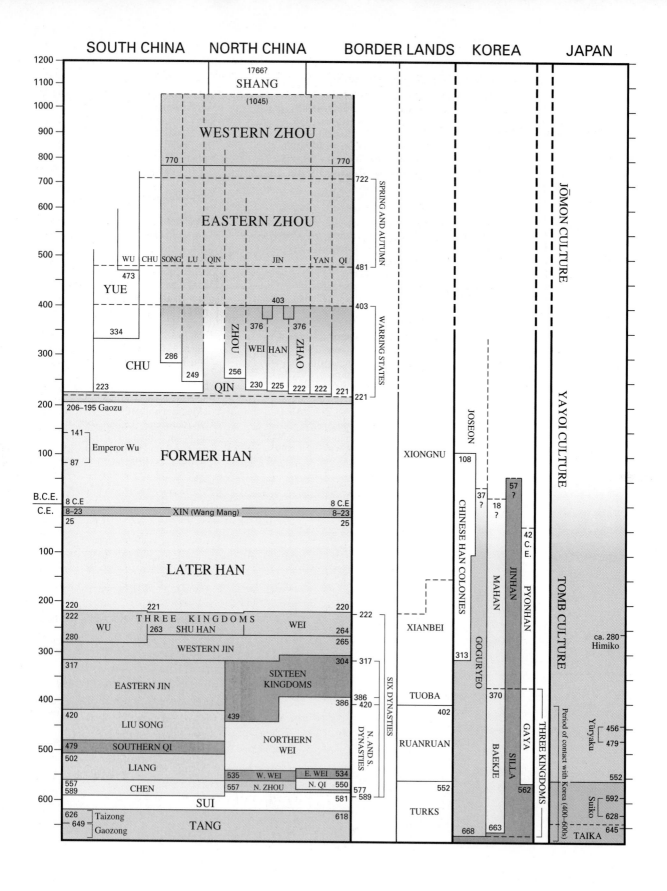